Statistics for the Social Sciences
A General Linear Model Approach

Written by a quantitative psychologist, this textbook   le
language to undergraduates in all branches of the social   -
work of the general linear model (GLM), *Statistics for*   /
different statistical methods are interrelated to one another   students with
varying levels of background are better equipped to inter   and learn more advanced
methods in their later courses. Dr. Warne makes statistics relevant to students' varying majors by
using fascinating real-life examples from the social sciences. Students who use this book will benefit
from clear explanations, warnings against common erroneous beliefs about statistics, and the latest
developments in the philosophy, reporting, and practice of statistics in the social sciences. The
textbook is packed with helpful pedagogical features including learning goals, guided practice, and
reflection questions.

Dr. Russell T. Warne is a quantitative psychologist in the Department of Behavioral Science at
Utah Valley University who earned his PhD from Texas A&M University in 2011. Since 2009 he
has taught introductory statistics to undergraduates majoring in psychology, sociology, education,
anthropology, communications, family science, exercise science, and biology. At Utah Valley
University his statistics course is one of his department's highest rated classes, with an average
student rating of 4.7 out of 5.

Dr. Warne doesn't just teach statistics. He uses statistics in his research, too. He has published over
40 articles in professional journals in psychology, education, methodology, medicine, sociology,
health, business, and the arts. For many of these articles his coauthors were students. Dr. Warne has
earned awards for his research from the National Association for Gifted Children, the Southwest
Educational Research Association, Texas A&M University, and Utah Valley University. He also
uses his statistical training to serve on the editorial board of three scientific journals – *Journal of
Psychoeducational Assessment*, *Gifted Child Quarterly*, and *Journal of School Psychology*.

Statistics for the Social Sciences

A General Linear Model Approach

RUSSELL T. WARNE

Utah Valley University

CAMBRIDGE
UNIVERSITY PRESS

CAMBRIDGE
UNIVERSITY PRESS

University Printing House, Cambridge CB2 8BS, United Kingdom

One Liberty Plaza, 20th Floor, New York, NY 10006, USA

477 Williamstown Road, Port Melbourne, VIC 3207, Australia

314–321, 3rd Floor, Plot 3, Splendor Forum, Jasola District Centre, New Delhi – 110025, India

79 Anson Road, #06–04/06, Singapore 079906

Cambridge University Press is part of the University of Cambridge.

It furthers the University's mission by disseminating knowledge in the pursuit of
education, learning, and research at the highest international levels of excellence.

www.cambridge.org
Information on this title: www.cambridge.org/9781107576971

First published 2018

Printed in the United States of America by Sheridan Books, Inc.

A catalogue record for this publication is available from the British Library.

Library of Congress Cataloging-in-Publication Data
Names: Warne, Russell T., 1983- author.
Title: Statistics for the social sciences : a general linear model approach / Russell T. Warne.
Description: New York : Cambridge University Press, 2018. | Includes bibliographical references and index.
Identifiers: LCCN 2017023186 | ISBN 9781107576971 (paperback)
Subjects: LCSH: Statistics–Textbooks. | Social sciences–Statistical methods–Textbooks.
Classification: LCC QA276 .W367 2017 | DDC 519.5–dc23 LC record available at
https://lccn.loc.gov/2017023186

ISBN 978-1-107-57697-1 Paperback

For Katie.

The likelihood of finding a woman as wonderful as her is $P = .000001$.

Contents

Preface

If you had told me 15 years ago that I would write a statistics textbook, I would have laughed. Sitting in that first statistics course a decade and a half ago as an undergraduate psychology major, I struggled with the concepts that my professor was teaching. I didn't understand why statistical methods were relevant to my major or my career goals. The terminology was difficult, and the explanations that I received were confusing. I tried my hardest, and I passed the course – but not with an impressive grade. My goal in writing this textbook is to help students in the social sciences avoid the unpleasant experience I had in my first statistics course. I've had 15 years to think about what went wrong in the course, and I have designed this textbook to help students have the best possible introduction to statistics.

Decades of research in educational and cognitive psychology have shown that students learn more material when they have a way to organize what they are expected to learn. I have therefore given students and instructors a way to think about statistical methods called the general linear model (GLM). The GLM underlies most of the statistical analyses that are used in applied and social science research, and having this general framework of understanding statistics will avoid the tendency of students to see statistics as a disconnected set of procedures. My hope is that the GLM can help students understand statistical methods so that their commonalities and differences make sense.

Another common finding in the research on learning is that students retain more knowledge when the material is relevant to them. Whenever possible, I have used examples of real data from across the social sciences to illustrate statistical concepts. Empirical research suggests that using real data to teach statistical concepts increases student learning (e.g., Allen & Baughman, 2016). I also believe that using real data shows students how the equations and theory of statistics have been used to create real knowledge in their fields. Additionally, the examples from the actual work in the social sciences are far more likely to be interesting and relevant to students than the made-up examples that my professor gave me when I was an undergraduate.

My final goal with this textbook is to reduce anxiety for students. When I took my first statistics course (and the second and the third), I was overwhelmed. Statistics was intimidating, and my anxiety made it more difficult to learn what I was supposed to. To avoid this, I have made several efforts to make statistics accessible and manageable for students. First, I have made explanations simple and straightforward. Technical terminology is defined clearly, and a glossary in the back of the book provides easy reference for students. Second, because formulas can be intimidating for some students, every formula is labeled, and the various symbols are explained. I also have shown why the formulas are set up in the way that they are and how they are linked with their interpretation. Finally, I have included detailed examples of statistical problems that are worked out step-by-step. By following these examples, students will better understand the steps and interpretation of statistical analyses, and solve problems and complete homework assignments more efficiently.

What Makes this Textbook Different

- **A foundation in the research on student learning**. Although I consider myself a quantitative psychologist, my doctoral program was housed in a college of education, and my PhD is in educational psychology. That means that I am familiar with the research on how people learn, and I have applied this research to the structure and writing of every chapter. Although I rarely make my debt to cognitive and educational psychology explicit, readers can be assured that every decision behind this book was made from an evidence-based perspective.

- **Teaching statistical concepts the way that experts think about them**. Statistical novices see statistics as an unrelated hodgepodge of analysis methods. On the other hand, statistical experts see statistics as all being united by general concepts, such as their correlational nature or the universality of effect sizes. Yet, no other author of a textbook for social science undergraduates teaches about these general concepts – most of which are united in the GLM. I think that students will master and retain more material by learning about the GLM in their first statistics course. Moreover, learning the GLM makes future statistical procedures (e.g., nonparametric statistics, multivariate statistics) easier to learn because they are also members of the GLM – albeit more complex ones.

- **Practical application**. The use of examples from real studies in the social sciences was done with an eye on showing students how statistics can lead to practical knowledge in the social sciences. Browsing through the book will show that I have included examples from psychology, sociology, family studies, anthropology, education, social work, and more. This is the result of my effort to make statistics relevant to students from a broad cross-section of majors.

- **Discussion of controversies**. For the sake of simplicity, most authors of undergraduate textbooks try to avoid controversies in statistics. I can sympathize with this viewpoint, but I think that it is not beneficial to students. Social science statistics is a field that has been punctuated by periodic controversies for the last 120 years. I believe that avoiding these controversies encourages simplistic thinking and a naive view of statistics. Instead, I feel that undergraduate students can be more nuanced thinkers and more professional in their interpretations if they are aware of some of the disagreements and arguments among professionals. Therefore, I have included discussions of the shortcomings of null hypothesis testing, the interpretation of effect sizes, questionable research practices, and more. I believe that this enlivens the textbook and prepares students for joining the social science community.

For Students

If you are a student using this textbook, there are a few things you can do to improve your performance in your statistics course.

First, make this course a priority. Devote the time and attention necessary to do well in your statistics course. Although I have tried to make this textbook accessible, some concepts are simply counterintuitive or strange, and very few people can grasp the logic and mathematics of statistics without effort. Read the text carefully and with full attention. Cognitive psychologists have shown that human beings can only effectively focus attention on one thing at a time, and it is going to be difficult to learn statistics with any distractions, including the TV, your phone, or social media. Make sure you can devote all of your attention to what you are reading.

Second, study carefully. As you read, highlight important sentences. Take notes in the margins, and jot down questions that come to your mind as you read. Coming to class prepared with questions and notes will make you more able to excel in the course. I also recommend that you practice the concepts you read about by working out the questions at the end of each chapter – even if they are not assigned as homework. My students have found these questions to be particularly useful in cementing their understanding of statistical concepts.

Third, participate in class. Ask those questions you prepared in advance. My experience in teaching statistics is that when a student asks a question, there are almost always classmates who have the same question. Also, don't hesitate to ask your instructor to repeat a concept or to restate it in other words. You won't look stupid – it's just part of learning statistics. When I learn a new statistical concept, I have to hear it stated a few different ways before it "clicks" and makes sense to me. Most of my students are the same.

Fourth, pay close attention to the Guided Examples throughout this textbook and make sure you clearly understand every step of a procedure. Get out a piece of scratch paper and have a go at the Guided Examples first, to ensure you know how to find the correct answer and aren't just reading passively. This will make homework and tests go more smoothly.

Fifth, if your instructor does not require you to do so, take advantage of the software guides so that you can learn how to perform statistical procedures with a computer. Learning about the mathematics of statistics is valuable. But the reality of the twenty-first century is that almost all statistical work is done by computer. Using the Software Guides to learn how to perform and interpret statistical procedures will give you a valuable skill. More employers and graduate schools are seeking people who can analyze data, and mastering a software program can give you an advantage when you apply for jobs or graduate school.

Finally, if it has been a long time since you have had to do math or if you have forgotten your algebra, then a basic review may be helpful. I wrote this book expecting that students would have already mastered decimals, fractions, percentages, graphs, linear equations, and basic algebra. If you do not remember these concepts or you need a review, I recommend getting an algebra refresher from Khan Academy (www.khanacademy.org/math/algebra) or from Udacity (www.udacity.com/course/intro-algebra-review–ma004). Your university's tutoring center or your instructor may also be useful resources.

For Instructors

When using this textbook, instructors should be aware of a few things. First, it may be difficult to teach every concept in this textbook during a single semester. So, most instructors will have to select the concepts they teach. A route I recommend is to skip Chapter 10 (dependent samples t-tests), Chapter 14 (nonparametric and advanced methods), and Chapter 15 (which serves as a reference guide for students who wish to encounter more complex statistical methods as they read published articles or hope to execute their first research project). Some instructors may also find that their students are sufficiently prepared that they can skip – or cover very quickly – Chapter 3 (visual models) and Chapter 4 (central tendency and variability). Additionally, parts of some chapters can be skipped, such as the trimmed mean (in Chapter 4), the arbitrary nature of axes (at the end of Chapter 5), null hypothesis testing of correlation coefficients (in Chapter 12), or the last half of Chapter 11, which covers the logic and assumptions of ANOVA and *post hoc* tests. It is not essential for students to master the minutia of every chapter to have a basic understanding of statistical thinking and methods.

Second, even though the chapters are generally arranged in ascending order of complexity of the statistical procedures, some chapters can be taught out of order. Sometimes I prefer to teach

Chapter 12 (correlation and regression) before Chapter 7 (null hypothesis testing and z-tests) because one of the basic themes of the GLM is that all statistical procedures examine the relationship between variables. This is easiest to see in a correlation, so I sometimes teach about correlations first in order to show how other procedures are themselves correlational. Other instructors may prefer to teach Chapter 13 (χ^2 tests) before Chapter 12 (ANOVA) and save the complex hand calculations of ANOVA for the end of the semester. I also sometimes teach unpaired-samples t-tests (Chapter 10) before paired-samples t-tests (Chapter 9) because it makes the concept of paired data easier for students to understand. The point is to be flexible and teach concepts in the order that works best for you and your students.

I have placed boxed texts throughout the book. These contain ideas that are relevant, but that may not be essential to understanding a concept. They range from handy tips (like mnemonic devices and restatements of important material) to discussions of controversies and statistical practices related to the main ideas of the chapter or the book. Instructors may find these boxes useful in generating classroom discussions. Be creative and flexible in how you use these features to increase students' understanding.

Finally, this textbook includes step-by-step guides for conducting statistical analyses using the Statistical Package for the Social Sciences (SPSS) and Microsoft Excel. Although some instructors will prefer to use other programs, I chose these because (1) Microsoft Excel – or very similar spreadsheet programs – will often be available to students after they graduate, and (2) in the social sciences SPSS is one of the most frequent statistical analysis packages students use in graduate school. I hope that these software guides will make the textbook a useful reference guide for students after they finish their statistics course. Some instructors believe that using statistical software is an important component of an introductory class; this textbook is designed to handle that need, and instructors who wish to emphasize software use will likely concentrate on the software guides and skip the step-by-step calculation found in many chapters. On the other hand, some people believe that it is important to understand the mathematics and theory of statistics in order to properly interpret computer program output. Instructors with this viewpoint will see value in hand calculation while recognizing that computers dominate modern statistical process. Additionally, some instructors are forced to emphasize hand calculation for various reasons, such as a lack of computer resources at their institution or an assessment requirement that emphasizes calculation. In my opinion, there are valid reasons to spend time on hand calculation or on software use. This book is designed to handle both methods of learning statistics.

Last Words

This textbook is the textbook that I wish I had had 15 years ago. I remember what it was like for statistics to be non-intuitive and confusing. The struggle was not fun, but in an odd way I'm grateful for my negative experience in my first statistics class because it has made me a better teacher today. Hopefully, this book will help students leave the course with a positive view of statistics. If there is anything I can do to improve the book, please contact me at rwarne@uvu.edu or via Twitter, where my handle is @Russwarne. I would love to hear from my readers.

Have a great semester!

Acknowledgements

Left to my own devices, I could never have produced a textbook of this quality without the input and help of many people. At Cambridge University Press, the acquisitions editor David Repetto convinced me to write this textbook and had faith in a young, untried psychologist. His confidence never wavered, and his belief in my competence was a great source of encouragement when problems arose or when the writing became a challenge. His associates, Claudia Bona-Cohen, Elisa Adams, and Claire Eudall, all provided help and input in drafts of the chapters. Their responses to my drafts and their efficient coordination of the peer reviews of my chapters were immensely helpful in removing inaccuracies. Indeed, I hold a special appreciation for the anonymous peer reviewers – all of whom (even the ones who passionately hated the drafts they read) made suggestions that improved the book greatly. These reviewers saved me from several foolish errors, and my thanks for them know no bounds.

As with any piece of writing, this book is a product of the time in which it was written. The months when I drafted the chapters (March 2014–September 2016) were a particularly fierce time in the "replication crisis" in psychology, a time in which many long-respected findings were brought into question after these studies could not be replicated. Many readers will notice the concern for replicable findings and stable results, which is a result of the current debate about replication. I appreciate the social and biomedical scientists who have worked tirelessly to make their fields aware of the seriousness of these replication problems. I have tried to incorporate their suggestions into the textbook so that the next generation of students can avoid the mistakes of the past (including some that I made in my career).

I am also indebted to several colleagues whose ideas have shaped my thinking about statistical issues. Ross Larsen gave me insight into important issues related to the central limit theorem and has been a valued friend and coauthor since my graduate school days. The statistical thinking of my former professors and mentors, including Bruce Thompson and Oi-mon Kwok, is also apparent in most chapters. One unanticipated influence on the content of the book was Twitter. Ulrich Schimmack, Victoria Savalei, Daniël Lakens, Jelte Wicherts, Uri Simonsohn, Rickard Carlsson, and others provided inspiration and clarification for chapters – often without knowing that they were doing so. I have said it many times, and now I want to say it in print: "Science Twitter is the best Twitter."

The hundreds of students I have taught statistics to over the years were another source of help and inspiration for this book. I am very grateful for the students enrolled in my classes as I wrote this book. These students were my "guinea pigs" as I tried out different ways of explaining statistical concepts. Many students helped me see which examples were effective (or not) and worked out the problems in my explanations and datasets.

A few students were particularly helpful as I worked on this book. Kimberlee Waite graciously allowed me to use her data from her study on sibling relationships among people with and without autism. Zachary Rawlings assembled the key for the end-of-chapter problems, many of which were tested as homework assignments for the students in my classes. However, three students were "all-stars" and deserve unending praise for their help: Kathy L. Youngkin, Becky Bytheway, and Liliana López Lemus. These three students read the drafts of every chapter and met with me to give feedback. They ensured that every chapter of the book was student-centered, comprehensible, and used as little jargon as possible. These three students were phenomenal in ferreting out the weaknesses in my writing and teaching. If this book is accessible to students, it is largely because of their efforts.

On a more personal note, it is essential to acknowledge the help and support of my amazing wife, Katie. She was the one who talked me into committing myself to write this book. Every time I had a "writing day," she let me work undisturbed, even though it was difficult for her sometimes. It was often very challenging to meet every single deadline (especially with seven family trips to the hospital during the 18 months I was writing), but with my wife's unwavering support, it happened. I do not deserve a woman as wonderful as she is.

I used to think it was a cliché for authors to state that the credit for the strengths of their book belongs to many people, but that the faults belong to the author alone. Now that I have finished my first book, I understand why so many authors say this. Every person listed in these acknowledgements made the book better; their influence was always positive. As a result, I must frankly admit that the book's shortcomings are solely my responsibility. This isn't magnanimity. Rather, it is reality.

Examples

Chapter(s)	Example	Field
1	Baby naming	Sociology
1	Birth dates and hockey teams	Sports
1	Freud's theories were not scientific	Psychology/philosophy of science
1	Working memory theory is falsifiable	Psychology
1	Personality and job performance	Psychology/business
1, 3, 4, 9	Sibling relationships and autism	Psychology/family studies
1	Parental spending on children	Psychology/sociology/family studies
1	Why do people commit crimes?	Sociology/criminology
1	Changing schools and dropout rates	Education
1	Mate selection (matching hypothesis)	Psychology/sociology/family science
1	Darwin's theory of evolution	Biology
1	Newton's laws of motion	Physics
2	Affection	Psychology/family science
2	Perception of stimuli and actual stimuli intensity	Psychology
2	Levels of data examples (temperature, weight, gender, etc.)	Social sciences
2	Educational and psychological test scores and rating scales	Education/psychology
3	Murder rate in Canadian provinces	Sociology/criminology
3	Deceptive truck ad	Business/marketing
3	Deceptive political poll	Political science/journalism
3	Advanced placement tests (interactive map link)	Education
3	Baby Name Voyager (interactive chart link)	Sociology
4	Outliers in math ability	Education/psychology
4	Resilient children in poverty	Psychology/sociology
4	65% of households have below-average income	Economics/sociology
5	Quetelet's data	Biology
5	Normally distributed variables	Biology/psychology/education

Chapter(s)	Example	Field
11, 14	Aspirin's impact on surviving a heart attack	Medicine
12	Video games and intelligence	Psychology
12	National corruption and legislature functioning	Sociology
12	Talking speed and schizophrenia	Psychology
12	Test anxiety	Psychology
12	Depression and job satisfaction	Psychology
13	Air temperature	Earth science
12	ADHD and creativity	Psychology
12	Sugar consumption and behavioral changes	Psychology/medicine
12	Husbands' and wives' personality traits	Psychology/family science
12	High-school grades and first-year college grades	Education/psychology
12	Height at birth and in adulthood	Medicine/physical anthropology
12	Height and weight	Medicine/physical anthropology
12	Lifelong stability of intelligence	Psychology
12	Stability of extraversion	Psychology
12	Husband and wives' religiousness	Family science/psychology
13	Intergenerational height increases	Biology/physical anthropology
13	Test score increases and decreases in children	Psychology/education
13	Regression to the mean in patients with high blood pressure	Medicine
13	Movie sequels are not very good	Entertainment
13	The Sports Illustrated curse	Sports
12	Company earnings over time	Economics
13	High-school size and math achievement scores	Education
13	Football players and restriction of range	Sports
12, 13	Job testing	Psychology/sociology
13	Test validity for different groups	Psychology
12	Vocabulary size differences in children from different income groups	Psychology/sociology
14	The Titanic	History/sociology
14	Therapy outcomes	Psychology

1 Statistics and Models

"Why do I need to take statistics?"

Every semester that I teach statistics I have students asking this question. It's a fair question to ask. Most of my students want to work as therapists, social workers, psychologists, anthropologists, sociologists, teachers, or in other jobs that seem far removed from formulas and numbers. As students majoring in the social sciences, almost all of them are more interested in people than they are in numbers. For many students (including me, a long time ago), statistics is something to get out of the way so that they can devote their attention to the stuff they *really* want to do (Rajecki, Appleby, Williams, Johnson, & Jeschke, 2005).

The purpose of this chapter is to show you why students majoring in the social sciences have to take statistics. This chapter will also explore some introductory concepts and terminology that are necessary to understand the book. The most important concept introduced in this chapter is models, which many experts use to understand their statistical results. Because my goal is to help you think about statistics like a professional, I will use that perspective throughout the book.

Learning Goals

- Explain why students in the behavioral sciences need statistics to be successful in their majors.

- Outline the general process for designing and executing a research study.

- Describe the benefits of using models to understand reality.

- Demonstrate why using a model – even if it is not completely accurate – is useful for people working in the social sciences.

- Identify the three types of models and describe their characteristics.

Why Statistics Matters

Although many students would not choose to take a statistics course, nearly every social science department requires its students to take a statistics course (e.g., Norcross et al., 2016; Stoloff et al., 2010). Why? Apparently, the professors in these departments think that statistics is essential to their students' education, despite what their students may think.

The main reason that many students must take statistics is that research in the social sciences is dominated by methodologies that are statistics-based; this family of methods is called **quantitative research**. Researchers who use quantitative research convert their data into numbers for the purpose of analysis, and the numbers are then analyzed by **statistical methods**. Numerical data are so important that one social scientist even argued that "progress in science is impossible without numbers and measurement as words and rhetoric are not enough" (Bouchard, 2014, p. 569).

Quantitative methods – and therefore statistics – dominate most of the behavioral sciences: psychology, sociology, education, criminal justice, economics, political science, and more. Most researchers working in these fields use statistics to test new theories, evaluate the effectiveness of therapies, and learn about the concepts they study. Even workers who do not conduct research must understand statistics in order to understand how (and whether) to apply scientific knowledge in their daily work. Without statistics a practitioner risks wasting time and money by using ineffective products, therapies, or procedures. In some cases this could lead to violations of ethics codes, accusations of malpractice, lawsuits, and harm to clients or customers. Even students who do not become scientists may need statistics to verify whether an anecdotal observation (e.g., that their company sells more products after a local sports team wins a game than after a losing one) is true. Thus, a mastery of statistics is important to many people, not just researchers and social scientists.

There are four main ways that practitioners use statistics in their work in the social sciences:

1. Separating good research from bad
2. Evaluating the conclusions of researchers
3. Communicating findings to others
4. Interpreting research to create practical, real-world results.

There is some overlap among these four points, so some job tasks will fall into more than one category. Nevertheless, this is still a useful list of ways that professionals use statistics.

Separating good research from bad is important for any practitioner. The quality of the research published in scientific journals varies greatly. Some articles become classics and spark new avenues of research; others report shoddy research. Thus, the fact that a study was published in a scientific journal is not, by itself, evidence of good-quality scientific work. A knowledge of statistics is one of the most important tools that a person can have in distinguishing good research from bad. Having the ability to independently judge research prevents practitioners from being susceptible to fads in their field or from wasting resources on practices that provide few benefits.

The benefits of separating good research from bad research are important for the general public, too (not just practitioners). Most people rely on reports from the news media and the Internet to learn about scientific findings. However, most journalists are not trained scientists and do not have the skills needed to distinguish between a high-quality study and a low-quality one (Yettick, 2015). Readers with statistical training will be able to make these judgments themselves, instead of relying on the judgment of a journalist or social media contacts.

Statistical savviness can also help people in *evaluating researchers' conclusions*. Ideally, the conclusions in a scientific article are supported by the data that the researchers collected. However, this is not always the case. Sometimes researchers misinterpret their data because they either used the wrong statistical procedures or did not understand their results. Having statistical competence can prevent research consumers from being at the mercy of the authors and serve as an independent check on researchers.

Another way that people employed in the social sciences use statistics is in *communicating findings and results to others*, such as their clients and colleagues. Increased global competition now means that stakeholders are demanding evidence that the services they receive are effective. Government entities, insurance companies, school districts, and customers are now more likely than ever to demand that people working in the social sciences use "evidence-based practices," meaning that practitioners are expected to use techniques and tools that are supported by scientific evidence (Capraro & Thompson, 2008). Workers who can understand statistics are at an advantage in this type of environment because they will be able to collect and analyze the data that show that their work is effective. But without statistical data, even the best therapist, teacher, or sociologist could appear to be ineffective – perhaps even incompetent.

Finally, people working in the social sciences must be able to use statistics in *translating research into day-to-day practice*. Because most social science research is quantitative, this means understanding statistical analyses and interpreting them in a way that is relevant to their work. Without statistics, practitioners will not be able to understand or implement new therapies, interventions, or techniques. In time these practitioners' work could become outdated or obsolete.

The Quantitative Research Process. The quantitative research process may take many forms, but generally it requires the researcher to follow these steps:

1. Form a research question or research hypothesis
2. Define the population of interest
3. Select a sample of population members
4. Choose variables to measure and operationalize them
5. Select independent and dependent variables
6. Collect data on the variables
7. Analyze the data with statistics and test the hypothesis to determine whether it is supported by the data.

This is a simplified outline, but it is really all that we need to know to understand statistics. Most students take a research methods course after their statistics course that will explain the research process in detail (Norcross et al., 2016; Stoloff et al., 2010). (And if your department doesn't require a research methods course, you should definitely sign up for one anyway!)

The first step in the scientific research process is to form a **research question** or **research hypothesis**. A **research question** is the question that a research study is designed to answer. For example, in a fascinating sociological study, Lieberson and Mikelson (1995) were interested in the ways that some parents invent original names for their children. They had a central research question: "Do parents who create names do so in such a way that the names still convey their child's gender?" (Lieberson & Mikelson, 1995, p. 933). The researchers understood that – from a sociological perspective – new parents do not randomly create names. Rather, a child's name often communicates information, and one of the most fundamental pieces of information that a name can convey is the child's gender. Therefore, they wanted to learn if invented names communicate information, so they posed their research question and designed their study to answer it. (The results indicated that strangers can indeed usually guess the gender of a child with an original, unique name.)

A **hypothesis** is similar to a research question; but rather than a question, a research hypothesis is a testable belief that researchers have about the outcome of their scientific study. For example, one Canadian research team (Barnsley & Thompson, 1988) studied the impact that a child's birth date had on the likelihood that they would play hockey on an elite youth team. In Canada many youth hockey leagues require students to reach a certain age by January 1, meaning that players with birthdays early in the year would be larger and taller than players with later birthdays. A previous study (Barnsley, Thompson, & Barnsley, 1985) had shown that there were more than about four times more professional hockey players born in January, February, and March than were born in October, November, and December. Therefore, the researchers hypothesized that this trend towards hockey players having birthdays in the beginning of the year would also be apparent in elite youth teams. (Their hypothesis was supported by the research.)

These two examples show an important distinction between research questions and research hypotheses. Research questions tend to be more exploratory, and researchers usually ask research questions when they have little or no basis on which to make an educated guess about the results of their study. On the other hand, research hypotheses are expected results that a researcher has, and this expectation is often formed on the basis of previous research or theory.

A research hypothesis is more than just a belief about the world. To be scientific, a hypothesis must be falsifiable, or possible to disprove. If it is impossible to design a study that would produce results that would disprove the hypothesis, then the hypothesis is not scientific (Popper, 1935/2002). For example, one of the reasons that Freud's theory of psychoanalysis is unscientific was that it is impossible to devise an experiment that would produce results that would show the theory to be untrue. Instead, Freud (and, in later years, his followers) always had some sort of explanation for behaviors that seemed – at first glance – to contradict his theory (Cioffi, 1998). They built up an entire body of ideas that could explain away any apparent evidence that disproved the theory. For example, Freud claimed that male clients who said they did not have a desire to murder their father and marry their mother were using a "defense mechanism" called denial, and the very use of this defense mechanism supported Freud's theory. But not using the defense mechanism would also support psychoanalytic theory. Therefore, there was no way to disprove the theory, making it unscientific.

In contrast, a falsifiable theory could be found to be untrue. If the theory were untrue, then evidence could emerge that would disprove it – forcing scientists to suggest other interpretations of the data. On the other hand, when a falsifiable theory withstands attempts to disprove it, the theory is strengthened and becomes more believable. For example, in one famous article, Miller (1956) proposed that people's working memory had a limited capacity, which was "seven, plus or minus two" (p. 81) and that people would have a great deal of difficulty remembering a longer list of items without a memory aid (e.g., writing things down, using a mnemonic device). This theory is quite easy to test: all it requires is finding the limits of what a person can remember in a short period of time and seeing if they do more poorly when a list exceeds 5–9 items. Despite efforts to disprove this theory, it has held up well and led to an increased understanding of human memory (e.g., Baddeley, 2003) and improved educational practices (e.g., Paas, Renkl, & Sweller, 2003). Likewise, Barnsley and Thompson's (1988) hypothesis that elite youth hockey players would be born earlier in the calendar year is easily falsifiable. For example, if these elite hockey players had birthdays evenly distributed throughout the year, or if most birthdays were at the end of the year, then it would falsify the hypothesis. Thus, the hypothesis that better hockey players are born earlier in the year is a scientific hypothesis.

The second step in this process is to define the **population** of interest. A population consists of every person, event, or object that a researcher could wish to study. The choice of a population is completely at a researcher's discretion. For example, criminal justice researchers could define their population as all crimes committed in Australia in a year. Family science researchers may define their population as all children whose biological parents are divorced or had never married. Psychologists may define their population as every person who suffers from anorexia nervosa. In the social sciences, populations usually consist of people, although they do not have to.

The third step in the quantitative research process is to select a sample from the population. Many populations have millions of people in them, and the constraints of money and time may make it unfeasible to gather data from every person in the population. Moreover, studying people means that often we don't have data on every person in a population because those people may refuse to participate in a study, and it is not ethical to force them to participate. Because of these limitations,

Sidebar 1.1 **Example of a research design**

Here is an example that should clarify the nature of quantitative research. Many psychologists are interested in personality because they believe it consists of a set of stable traits that influence how a person acts in different circumstances. In one study (Barrick, Stewart, & Piotrowski, 2002), psychologists chose to measure extraversion – which is the degree that a person is outgoing – and job performance. They wanted to test their belief – i.e., their research hypothesis – that more-extraverted people would also be better at their jobs. The operational definitions of these two variables were rather straightforward: an extraversion score obtained from a pencil-and-paper test and a supervisor's rating (on a scale from 1 to 7) of the person's job performance. Psychologists believe that personality is a stable trait through the life span, so it seems unlikely that people's job performance would affect or change their personality. It is much more likely that differences in people's personalities would lead to differences in job performance. Therefore, in this example, extraversion (a personality trait) is an independent variable, and job performance is a dependent variable.

After operationalizing their variables and deciding which variable would be the independent variable and which would be the dependent variable, the researchers collected their data. They found that their belief about extraverted people being better at their jobs was supported by the results of their statistical analyses. This is an oversimplified description of the study. The authors were interested in more than two variables, and some of their statistical analyses were more sophisticated than anything in this book. But this summary serves as a good explanation of the quantitative research process.

quantitative researchers in the social sciences almost always select a **sample** of population members to study. A sample is a subset of the population that the researcher collects data from. Ideally, a researcher has a sample that is representative of the population at large so that the data gathered from the sample can teach the researcher about the entire population.

In the fourth step of the process, after selecting a sample, a researcher collects data on specific variables. A **variable** is a characteristic that sample or population members can differ on. For example, in Sidebar 1.1 (see box), the researchers were interested in extraversion and job performance. These are both variables because some sample members in the study were more extraverted (i.e., outgoing) than others, and some sample members were better at their jobs than others. Because there is variation among the sample members, both of these characteristics are variables. On the other hand, a characteristic that is the same for all sample or population members is called a **constant**. In the example a constant may be the species that the sample members belonged to. Because all of them were human and there is no variability among sample members on this trait, this is a constant.

The fifth step of the research process is to choose independent and dependent variables. The **dependent variable** is the outcome variable in the study. The **independent variable** is the variable that is believed to cause changes in the dependent variable. Often social scientists create a design that permits them to have total control over the independent variable, but this is not always possible. After the variables are chosen, it is necessary to operationalize the variable. An **operationalization** is a researcher's definition of a variable that permits a researcher to collect quantitative data on it. Operationalization is very common in the social sciences because many of the things that social scientists are interested in – personality, anger, political opinions, attitudes, racism, and more – are not inherently expressed as numbers. Therefore, it is necessary for researchers to create a definition of the variable that can allow them to collect numerical data. An example of an operationalization is counting the number of times a teacher reprimands a child as a measure of how disruptive the child is in class. Other common operationalizations in the social sciences include scores on a test (as in Sidebar 1.1), ratings of the subject's behavior, and measuring the time a person takes to complete a task.

The majority of quantitative research in the social sciences can be classified as experimental research or correlational research (Cronbach, 1957). These are not the only two types of research designs in the social sciences, but they make up the bulk of research. In **experimental research** a researcher creates controlled changes in an independent variable in order to learn how those changes affect the dependent variable. On the other hand, in **correlational research** the researcher does not manipulate or control the independent variable; rather, the researcher measures people's existing levels of the independent variable. The study in Sidebar 1.1 (Barrick et al., 2002) is a correlational study because the authors did not change or manipulate people's levels of extraversion.

Both kinds of research designs have their benefits and drawbacks. Experimental research designs give scientists more control over their subjects and data, and often experimental research permits more conclusions about cause-and-effect relationships (see Sidebar 12.4). However, because it is frequently laboratory-based, experimental research is often criticized for being too artificial. On the other hand, correlational research is often very applicable to real-life situations, but because of the poor control over the data, researchers usually cannot draw strong conclusions about the nature of the relationships between variables (Cronbach, 1957).

This classification and the discussion of experimental and correlational research is simplified. Other common designs include descriptive research and quasi-experimental research. Descriptive research describes variables and often does not attempt to investigate relationships among variables. Opinion polls are a common example of this type of research. Quasi-experimental methods are a hybrid between experimental and correlational designs, where researchers attempt to manipulate a variable, but may not have complete control over it (as when subjects choose whether to participate in an intervention or control group). In a research methods class, you will learn more about these four research designs and perhaps additional important ones, such as single-case designs and qualitative research.

The sixth step in the quantitative research process is to collect data. The mechanics of data collection is beyond the scope of this book, but it is necessary to mention that it is one of the steps of quantitative research. Finally, the seventh and last step is to analyze data with statistics. Most of this book will be concerned with this last step in the quantitative research process.

Qualitative Research. Although quantitative research is the predominant methodology in the social sciences, it is important to mention the principal alternative to quantitative research: a methodology called **qualitative research**. Researchers who specialize in qualitative research believe that it is not beneficial to convert aspects of their sample members into numbers, because most people do not experience their world through numbers. For example, in response to the Barrick et al. (2002) study (see Sidebar 1.1), a qualitative researcher would say that it is nonsensical and too simplistic to convert a person's job performance into a number ranging from 1 to 7. Instead, a qualitative researcher might interview the subject's supervisor to learn which aspects of the job the person excels at and how the person views the work experience, and would then analyze the text of the interview transcript to learn about the nuances of the person's experience. Qualitative methods are popular in anthropology, family science, and some branches of education, psychology, and political science. However, because qualitative research is a methodology that intrinsically rejects numerical data, we will not discuss it further in this book. Nevertheless, you should be aware that qualitative methodologies are valuable in answering questions that quantitative methods cannot.

Check Yourself!

- What are the four reasons a student majoring in the social sciences needs to take a statistics course?

- What are some of the possible consequences for a practitioner who does not understand statistics?

- Explain the difference between an independent variable and a dependent variable.

- What is the difference between qualitative and quantitative research?

- Why is operationalization necessary in the quantitative research process?

- What is the relationship between a sample and a population?

Two Branches of Statistics

As the science of quantitative data analysis, statistics is a broad field, and it would be impossible for any textbook to cover every branch of statistics while still being of manageable length. In this book we will discuss two branches of statistics: descriptive statistics and inferential statistics. **Descriptive statistics** is concerned with merely describing the data that a researcher has on hand. Table 1.1 shows an excerpt from a real collection of data from a study (Waite, Cardon, & Warne, 2015) about the sibling relationships in families where a child has an autism spectrum disorder. (We will discuss this study and its data in much more detail in Chapters 3 and 10.) Each row in the dataset represents a person and each column in the dataset represents a variable. Therefore, Table 1.1 has 13 people and 6 variables in it. Each piece of information is a **datum** (plural: **data**), and because every person in the table has a value for every variable, there are 84 data in the table (13 people multiplied by 6 variables = 78 data). A compilation of data is called a **dataset**.

Sidebar 1.2 **Terminology**

Remember that the term "statistics" has two major meanings. The first meaning of "statistics" is the science of data analysis. The second meaning of "statistics" is the procedures of an analysis, which are often used to estimate population parameters (Urbina, 2014).

Even though the dataset in Table 1.1 is small, it is still difficult to interpret. It takes a moment to ascertain, for example, that there are more females than males in the dataset, or that most people are satisfied with their relationship with their sibling with autism. Table 1.1 shows just an excerpt of the data. In the study as a whole, there were 45 variables for 13 subjects, which totals to 585 data. No person – no matter how persistent and motivated they are – could understand the entire dataset without some simplification. This is actually a rather small dataset. Most studies in the social sciences have much larger sample sizes. The purpose of descriptive statistics is to describe the

Table 1.1 Example of quantitative dataset (from **Waite, Cardon, & Warne**, 2015)

Gender	Are satisfied with sibling relationship	Believe that the sibling understands the respondent well	Believe that the sibling understands respondent's interests	Subject worries about their sibling with autism	Believe that parents treated the sibling with autism differently
Female	5	4	3	5	1
Female	5	4	4	1	3
Female	5	5	5	4	5
Female	5	4	2	5	3
Male	3	4	3	5	4
Female	3	1	1	4	5
Male	4	2	2	5	4
Female	4	4	3	4	4
Male	2	2	2	5	5
Female	4	3	3	4	3
Female	5	3	4	5	4
Male	3	2	2	4	5
Female	5	3	4	1	4

Note. In this table, 1 = strongly disagree, 2 = disagree, 3 = neutral, 4 = agree, 5 = strongly agree.

dataset so that it is easier to understand. For example, we could use descriptive statistics to say that in the range of scores on the variable that measures people's satisfaction with their sibling relationship, the average score is 4.1, while the average score on the variable measuring whether the sibling with autism understands the respondent's interests is 2.9. Chapters 2–5 are concerned with descriptive statistics.

On the other hand, if a researcher only has sample data on hand, descriptive statistics tell the researcher little about the population. A separate branch of statistics, termed **inferential statistics**, was created to help researchers use their sample data to draw conclusions (i.e., inferences) about the population. Inferential statistics is a more complicated field than descriptive statistics, but it is also far more useful. Few social scientists are interested just in the members of their sample. Instead, most are interested in their entire population, and so many social scientists use inferential statistics to learn more about their population – even though they don't have data from every population member. In fact, they usually only have data from a tiny portion of population members. Inferential statistics spans Chapters 6–15 of this book.

An example of a use of inferential statistics can be found in a study by Kornrich (2016). This researcher used survey data to examine the amount of money that parents spend on their children. He divided his sample into five groups, ranked from the highest income to the lowest income. He then found the average amount of money that the parents in each group spent on their children and used inferential statistics to estimate the amount of money each group in the population would spend on their children. Unsurprisingly, richer parents spent more money on their children, but Kornrich (2016) also found that the gap in spending on children between the richest 20% and poorest 20% of families had widened between 1972 and 2010. Because Kornrich used inferential statistics, he could draw conclusions about the general population of parents – not just the parents in his sample.

Check Yourself!

- What is the purpose of descriptive statistics?

- What is the purpose of inferential statistics?

- How are inferential statistics different from descriptive statistics?

Models

This book is not organized like most other textbooks. As the title states, it is built around a **general linear model (GLM)** approach. The GLM is a family of statistical procedures that help researchers ascertain the relationships between variables. Chapter 7 explains the GLM in depth. Until then, it is important to understand the concept of a model.

When you hear the word "model," what do you think of? Some people imagine a fashion model. Others think of a miniature airplane model. Still others think of a prototype or a blueprint. These are all things that are called "models" in the English language. In science, **models** are "simplifications of a complex reality" (Rodgers, 2010, p. 1). Reality is messy and complicated. It is hard to understand. In fact, reality is so complex – especially in the social sciences – that in order for people to comprehend it, researchers create models.

An example from criminology can illustrate the complexity of reality and the need for models. One of the most pressing questions in criminology is understanding who will commit crimes and why. In reality, it is impossible to comprehend every influence that leads to a person's decision to commit a crime (or not). This would mean understanding the person's entire personal history, culture, thoughts, neighborhood, genetic makeup, and more. Andrews and Bonta (2010) have developed the risk-need-responsivity (RNR) model of criminal conduct. Although not its only purpose, the RNR model can help users establish the risk that someone will commit a crime. Andrews and Bonta do not do this by attempting to understand every aspect of a person. Rather, they have chosen a limited number of variables to measure and use those to predict criminal activity. Some of these variables include a history of drug abuse, previous criminal behavior, whether the person is employed, the behavior of their friends, and the presence of certain psychological diagnoses (all of which affect the probability that someone will commit a crime). By limiting the number of variables they measure and use, Andrews and Bonta have created a model of criminal behavior that has been successful in identifying risk of criminal behavior and reducing offenders' risk of future reoffending after treatment (Andrews, Bonta, & Wormith, 2011). This model – because it does not contain every possible influence on a person's criminal behavior – is simplified compared to reality.

This example illustrates an important consequence of creating a model. Because models are simplified, every model is – in some way – wrong. Andrews and Bonta (2010) recognize that their model does not make perfect predictions of criminal behavior every time. Moreover, there are likely some influences not included in the RNR model that may affect the risk of criminal behavior, such as a cultural influence to prevent family shame or the dying request of a beloved relative. Therefore, one can think of a trade-off between model simplicity and model accuracy: simpler models are easier to understand than reality, but this simplification comes at a cost because simplicity makes the model wrong. In a sense, this is true of the types of models most people usually think about. A miniature airplane model is "wrong" because it often does not include many of the parts that a real airplane has. In fact, many model airplanes don't have any engines – a characteristic that definitely is *not* true of real airplanes!

Because every model is wrong, it is not realistic to expect models to be perfectly accurate. Instead, models are judged on the basis of how *useful* they are. A miniature model airplane may be useless in understanding how a full-sized airplane works, but it may be very helpful in understanding the aerodynamic properties of the plane's body. However, a different model – a blueprint of the engine – may be helpful in understanding how the airplane obtains enough thrust and lift to leave the ground. As this example shows, the usefulness of the model may depend on the goals of the researcher. The engineer interested in aerodynamics may have little use for the engine blueprint, even though a different engineer would argue that the engine blueprint is a vital aspect of understanding the airplane's function.

This example also shows one last important characteristic of models: often multiple models can fit reality equally well. In other words, it is possible for different models to fit the same reality, such as the miniature airplane model and the plane engine blueprint (Meehl, 1990). As a result, even if a model explains a phenomenon under investigation very well, it may not be the only model that could fit reality well. In fact, there is no guarantee that the model is even the best possible model. Indeed, many researchers in the social sciences are interested in improving their models because that would lead to an improved understanding of the things they investigate. This improvement can happen by combining two models together, finding improved operationalizations of variables, or eliminating unnecessary parts from a model.

Three Types of Models. There are three kinds of models: (1) statistical models, (2) visual models, and (3) theoretical models. **Statistical models** are models that use a limited number of specific variables and are expressed as mathematical equations. These models are often the result of quantitative research, and they are very common in the social sciences. For example, in a study on the consequences of changing high schools, Gasper, DeLuca, and Estacion (2012) found that the dropout rate was 2.36 times higher for students who attended two high schools between grades 9 and 12 than for those who attended just one high school during those same grades (19.1% compared to 8.1%; see p. 502). This is a simple mathematical model, but it basically tells users that the probability that students will drop out of high school more than doubles if they have changed schools.

This example also illustrates some of the characteristics of models in general: this model is simpler than the real world, and therefore this statistical model is wrong to an extent. The decision to drop out of high school is probably the result of many influences. This statistical model does not take into account a student's history, such as academic difficulties, discipline problems, family environment, extracurricular activities, and more. It's unlikely that most high-school dropouts decide to stop their education solely because they changed schools.

Notwithstanding these limitations, the statistical model is still useful. In their study Gasper et al. (2012) found that over one-fourth of all students changed schools in their 4-year high-school career. For school personnel this can be an indicator that they should be aware of the student's risk of

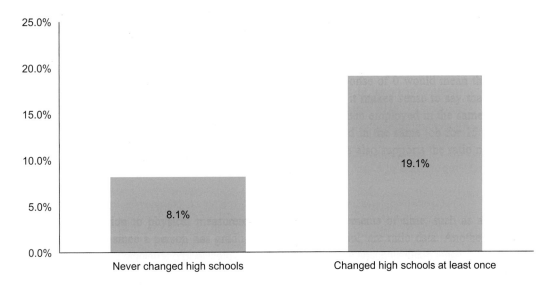

Figure 1.1 A bar graph showing the different rates of dropping out of high school for students who either never changed high schools (*left*) or changed high schools at least once (*right*). This bar graph is an example of a simple visual model. Data from Gaspar et al. (2012, p. 502).

dropping out. Knowing whether a student has changed schools is an easy piece of information to obtain. If it makes teachers and administrators aware of the academic challenges a student faces, it may help them target specific students for extra help or support in an effort to keep them in school.

A **visual model** – which is the second type of model – is a visual representation of data. By creating a picture of the data, a researcher or reader can understand the data at a glance and often without much effort. Thus, visual models simplify data and create a simplified version of the data. An example of a visual model (i.e., a bar graph) is Figure 1.1, which shows the differences in dropout rate between students who stay at the same school and those who change schools. Most readers have experience of visual models, such as line graphs, bar graphs, pie charts, and more. However, in Chapter 3, we will discuss these models and other common visual models in statistics, such as histograms, stem-and-leaf plots, and scatterplots.

The final type of model, the **theoretical model**, is not described in terms of numbers or mathematical equations. Rather, a theoretical model is a causal explanation of reality, usually in verbal terms. An example of a theoretical model in the social sciences is the "matching hypothesis," which states that when selecting a mate people tend to find a person who is about as socially desirable as themselves. This occurs because people self-assess their own desirability and then maximize their chances of finding a desirable mate by (1) avoiding people who would have a high probability of rejecting them, and (2) avoiding potential mates who are much less desirable than themselves because they can likely find someone more desirable (Shaw Taylor, Fiore, Mendelsohn, & Cheshire, 2011). The matching hypothesis explains, for example, why romantic partners tend to have similar levels of physical attractiveness (Feingold, 1988).

But this theoretical model is – like the statistical model example – simplified, and that makes it wrong to an extent because people may become romantically involved with one another for reasons other than "social desirability." The main differences between this theoretical model and a statistical model are that (1) the theoretical model suggests a causal explanation for phenomena, and (2) the theoretical model does not use numbers or equations in its expression.

A theoretical model differs from a scientific **theory**, however, because a theory has the ability to explain causes of phenomena in many different contexts. A theory is a logically consistent system of principles that posits causal explanations for a wide range of phenomena in many different contexts. Theories also tend to be unified around a coherent set of principles that govern the way the theory is manifest in the world. On the other hand, theoretical models are much more limited in their scope, and most only explain a small number of phenomena in limited contexts. Many theoretical models have no governing principles that apply outside the immediate situation that they were designed for.

Sidebar 1.3 **Importance of exact language**

This textbook defines a theory as a logically consistent set of principles that explain many aspects of reality in many different contexts. Some people define a theory as a working idea or a hunch, as when they say, "I have a theory about why he acted that way." This may be an acceptable use of the word in everyday speech. But language in science is much more precise. The terminology in this chapter has several terms (like "theory," "model," and "population") that have scientific meanings which differ from their meanings in everyday speech. I strongly suggest that in class you never use technical vocabulary to have meanings other than the precise definitions that these words have in science. Using scientific terminology in its everyday sense can cause confusion (Lilienfeld et al., 2015; Warne, Yoon, & Price, 2014). Communication in science should always be precise, clear, and unambiguous. This not only aids in communication but also improves the quality of thinking of both the speaker and the listener.

The difference between theories and theoretical models can be seen by re-examining the matching hypothesis example. The matching hypothesis is a theoretical model because it only explains one specific aspect of human behavior – mate selection. A much broader theory related to mate selection would be Darwin's theory of evolution. From an evolutionary perspective, the matching hypothesis makes sense because it would ensure that as many members of the species as possible would be able to pass on their genes. As a result, the next generation would be maximized in both number of individuals and in genetic diversity. Both of these traits improve the ability of a species to survive and reproduce. Thus, the matching hypothesis fits perfectly with the much broader theory of evolution. Indeed, evolutionary theory's scope extends far beyond human behavior: it also explains patterns in the fossil record, the similarities in anatomical structure across many different species, the differences in DNA structure across individuals and across species, and much more.

This example also shows how theoretical models may provide evidence for the theory. In this case, the theoretical model supports the notion that the principles of evolutionary theory also apply to humans, just as they do to all other species on Earth. On the other hand, if the theoretical model did not reflect reality well, it would be evidence that the theoretical model is flawed or that the theory does not apply to the specific variables or situations examined in the theoretical model. If this happens, then it is best for scientists either to modify or discard either the theory or the theoretical model (or both). Many of the advancements in the physical, biological, and social sciences that have occurred in the past 300 years have been the result of scientists modifying their theories or forming new ones when old ones cannot generate theoretical or statistical models that accurately reflect reality (Kuhn, 1996).

The interrelationships among theories, theoretical models, statistical models, and visual models are shown in Figure 1.2. To sum up, theories are broad in scope (as shown in the figure, where "Theories" has the largest oval and is at the top of the diagram) and are formulated to attempt to

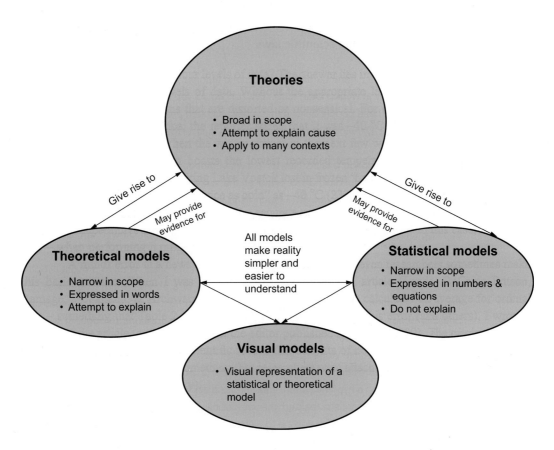

Figure 1.2 The relationship among theories, theoretical models, statistical models, and visual models.

explain many aspects of the world that scientists study. These theories give rise to theoretical models as scientists apply their theories to specific situations (which are smaller, lower ovals in the diagram). If scientists choose to use statistics or mathematics to illustrate how the theory operates in a specific situation, then they are building a statistical model. Statistical and theoretical models are much more narrow in scope and often do not try to create cause-and-effect explanation. Both statistical and theoretical models are simplifications of reality, and often one can convert a statistical model into a theoretical model (by describing it verbally) or vice versa (by building an equation that describes the data collected on the phenomenon). Finally, a person can build a visual model to represent the data in a statistical model or the organization of a theoretical model to make the models easy to understand.

Check Yourself!

- In the world of science, what is a model?

- What are the three types of models? How is each different from the others?

- If every model is wrong in some way, why would scientists want to use models?

- What is the difference between a model and a theory?

Scientific theories and scientific laws

Some people see a difference between scientific theories and scientific laws. This is because in everyday language a theory is weaker than a law. (Which would *you* rather be caught disobeying when the police are watching?) These people believe that a law has been proven, but that a theory has not. They may say, for example, that Darwin's theory of evolution is "just a theory," but that Newton's laws of motion are "scientific laws."

This distinction is false. Newton's laws of motion have been disproven for over a century, as they fail to account for phenomena observed at the astronomical level (such as the motion of the planet Mercury) and at the subatomic level (such as in the behavior of photons and other subatomic particles). On the other hand, Darwin's theory of evolution has been widely supported by data from geology, anatomy, ecology, and even genetics – a field which didn't even exist when Darwin formulated his theory.

In reality, no scientific hypothesis can be proven true once and for all. That is because it only takes one observation to disprove the scientific law. On the other hand, to prove a hypothesis true would require a scientist to make *every* possible observation of a phenomenon – otherwise, it is possible that there is a situation where the hypothesis does not function. But it is simply unfeasible to make every possible observation because it would require making observations throughout the universe from the beginning of time (Popper, 1935/2002). We will discuss this point more in Chapter 7 (see Sidebar 7.1).

So why are Newton's discoveries called "laws" and Darwin's are merely "theories"? Because a massive amount of evidence in support of Newton's work accrued before philosophers and scientists realized that proving a hypothesis true was impossible. Evolutionary theory, however, is much younger, and philosophers and scientists realized the impossibility of establishing "laws of nature" before enough evidence had accumulated for anyone to call evolution a "law." Basically, Isaac Newton discovered "laws" and Charles Darwin developed a "theory" because of an accident of history and language.

Summary

Although few students majoring in the social sciences would choose to take statistics, it is a necessary part of their education. Most of the social sciences are dominated by quantitative research, which means that many researchers use statistics to analyze their data and communicate their results. A practitioner in the social sciences who does not understand statistics is incapable of understanding most research in their field and applying it to real-life situations.

This chapter also covered some of the basic principles of research design, including the nature of research hypotheses and research questions, the difference between experimental and correlational research, and how descriptive statistics and inferential statistics serve different purposes. These foundational concepts are necessary to understand the rest of the textbook.

This book is organized around the principle of models. A model is a simplified version of reality that is designed to help people understand the real world better. There are three kinds of models that we will discuss in this textbook: statistical models, visual models, and theoretical models. Statistical models are expressed as numbers or equations, while theoretical models are expressed verbally. Theoretical models tend to have a causal component, while statistical models usually do not. Both theoretical and statistical models differ from theories because models are narrower in scope and usually involve specific variables. Visual models are visual representations of either a theoretical model or a statistical model, and visual models are designed to foster easy understanding of the data or idea under consideration. Theories, on the other hand, are attempts to explain many aspects of the natural or social world and have applications that span many contexts. Theories often spur researchers to create models, and models are frequently used to test the applicability of theories to specific situations.

Reflection Questions: Comprehension

1. Why do researchers in the social sciences rarely have data from the entire population of subjects that they are interested in?
2. Why is it important to have the ability to independently evaluate researchers' interpretation of their data?
3. What trait do theoretical models, statistical models, and visual models all have in common?
4. Most undergraduate students in the social sciences will not become professional researchers in their careers. So why is it necessary that they take a statistics course?
5. What is a model? How does the scientific usage of the word "model" differ from the everyday definition of a model? How is it similar?
6. Explain:
   a. Why every model is wrong in some way.
   b. Why practitioners and researchers in the social sciences should use models if they are all wrong.
   c. How researchers and practitioners judge whether they should use a particular model.
7. What are the four main ways that social science practitioners use statistics in their work?

Reflection Questions: Application

8. Carl believes in the power of magnets in relieving physical pain, and he wears magnets on his body for this purpose. However, his magnetic bracelet doesn't help with his arthritis pain. He consulted a website about healing magnets, and found that he needs to periodically change the location of the magnet on his body until his pain is relieved. Why is Carl's hypothesis about the healing properties of magnets unscientific?
9. What would be an example of a theory in your major? Can you give an example of how that theory has given rise to a theoretical model? What would be a possible situation that would disprove the theory?
10. A researcher wishes to study stress, and so she records the heart rate of each of her subjects as they are exposed to a distressful situation. Is "heart rate" an independent or dependent variable? Justify your response.
11. A social worker wants to study the impact of the instability of a child's home life on the child's academic performance. She defines "instability" as the number of homes that the child lives in during a year and "academic performance" as the child's grades that the teacher assigns on a scale from 0 to 100. Which step of the quantitative research process is this?
12. Teresa wants to know if people who post more messages about themselves on social media are more selfish than people who do not.

a. She decides to count the number of Facebook status updates that her subjects post in a week that include the word "I." She also administers a psychological test that her professor told her measures selfishness. By using these methods of measuring her variables, what step of the research is she engaging in?

b. Teresa believes that selfishness also causes people to post more self-centered messages on social media. Which variable is the independent variable in her study? Which variable is the dependent variable? Why?

c. Is this a correlational design or an experimental design?

13. Some cultural anthropologists study "rites of passage," which are certain rituals where people transition from one stage of their life to another. The idea of "rites of passage" is very broad and can be applied to rituals in many cultures and in all stages of life from birth to death. An anthropologist decides to use the rite of passage framework to understand how adolescents in a specific tribal culture become recognized as adults.

a. In this context, is the idea of "rites of passage" a theory, a theoretical model, a statistical model, or a visual model?

b. When the anthropologist applies this idea to a specific culture and explains the stages of that culture's rites of passage, is this a theory, a theoretical model, a statistical model, or a visual model?

14. A political science student is interested in the votes that legislators in different countries cast when considering different bills. The student decides that it is impractical to study every vote by every politician in every country. So, he decides to study only a selection of votes.

a. What is the population in this example?

b. What is the sample in this example?

15. A family science professor wants to study the impact of frequent quizzes on her students' study habits. In one of her classes she does not offer quizzes. In another class, she offers a quiz once per week. In her last class she offers a quiz in every class session. In each class she asks her students how many hours per week they studied.

a. What is the independent variable in this example?

b. What is the dependent variable in this example?

c. How did the professor operationalize "study habits"?

d. Is this an experimental design or a correlation design?

Software Guide

At the end of every chapter, I will provide a brief guide to using statistical software so that you can take advantages of modern computing power to conduct statistics. These guides will cover two programs: Microsoft Excel and the Statistical Package for the Social Sciences (SPSS). Excel is a widely available spreadsheet program that comes as part of the Microsoft Office package of software, and there are several similar programs that operate similarly. SPSS is produced by the IBM Corporation and is one of the most common statistical analysis programs in use in the social and behavioral sciences. Many instructors require their statistics students to learn how to use one or both programs.

These end-of-chapter guides will help you understand how the mathematical and theoretical principles of statistics are implemented with modern technology. Because this chapter is mostly theoretical, the current guide will serve as a general introduction to both programs.

Excel

After opening Excel, you should see a screen similar to the one below, which shows a blank grid. Each of the boxes in the grid is called a cell. Selecting a cell permits you to enter a datum into it. In Excel it doesn't matter whether each row represents a variable or whether each column represents a variable, though many users find it easier to treat columns as variables. (This also makes it easier to import a file from Excel into another data analysis program, like SPSS.) Most people use the first row or column to label their variables so that they can easily remember what the data mean.

There are a few features that you can see in Figure 1.3. First, the bottom left has three tabs labeled "Sheet1," "Sheet2," and "Sheet3." A sheet is the grid that you see taking up the majority of the screen. Each Excel file can store multiple sheets, which is convenient for storing multiple datasets in the same file. The top bar displays several tools useful for formatting, permitting the user to make cosmetic changes to the data, such as select a font, color-code cells, and select the number of decimal places in a cell. If your instructor or an employer requires you to use software for data analysis, I suggest that you invest some time into exploring these and other features in the program.

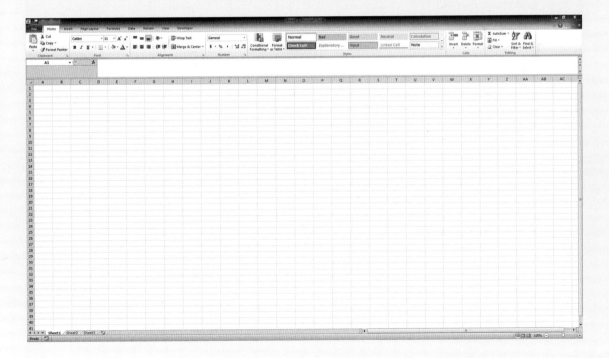

Figure 1.3 The default opening screen in Microsoft Excel.

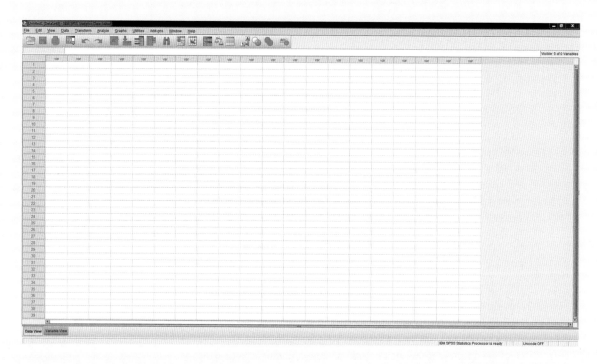

Figure 1.4 The default opening screen in SPSS. This is the data view.

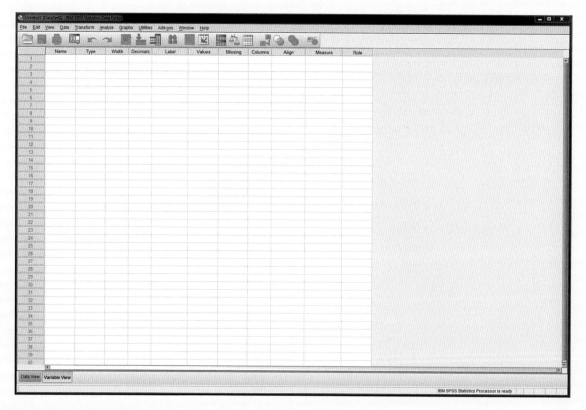

Figure 1.5 Variable view in SPSS.

SPSS

The opening screen for SPSS looks similar to Excel's opening screen, as is apparent when comparing Figures 1.3 and 1.4. Both programs feature a grid made of cells that permit users to enter data directly into the program. In SPSS this is called the "data view." In the data window the columns are variables and the rows are called "cases" (which are usually individual sample members, though not always).

On the bottom left of the screen in SPSS are two tabs. One highlighted in Figure 1.4 is the data view; the other is the variable view. Clicking "Variable View" will change the screen to resemble Figure 1.5. Variable view allows users to enter information about variables, including the name, the type of variable, the number of decimal places, and more. We will discuss variable view more in Chapter 2. Until then, I recommend that you experiment with entering data into SPSS and naming variables.

Further Reading

- Cronbach, L. J. (1957). The two disciplines of scientific psychology. *American Psychologist*, *12*, 671–684. doi:10.1037/h0043943

    * This article is a classic in psychology. In the article Cronbach discusses the experimental and correlational approaches to researching human behavior and the strengths and shortcomings of each method.

- DiCicco-Bloom, B., & Crabtree, B. F. (2006). The qualitative research interview. *Medical Education*, *40*, 314–321. doi:10.1111/j.1365–2929.2006.02418.x

    * For readers interested in qualitative research, this article serves as an introduction to that family of research methods. Many (perhaps most) qualitative researchers conduct interviews in their research, and this article's authors focus on different types of interviews in the qualitative approach and how qualitative researchers collect and analyze qualitative interview data.

- Rodgers, J. L. (2010). The epistemology of mathematical and statistical modeling: A quiet methodological revolution. *American Psychologist*, *65*, 1–12. doi:10.1037/a0018326

    * An excellent explanation of models, with special focus on statistical models. Rodgers explains the strength of building models while also understanding that models are simplified versions of reality and will never explain every nuance of human behavior.

2 Levels of Data

In Chapter 1, we saw that most of the social sciences are dominated by quantitative research, which is a form of research in which researchers convert their data into numbers so that they can be analyzed with statistics. This chapter is about the process of converting data into numbers – a process called measurement.

For researchers in the physical sciences, the process of measuring data numerically is often relatively straightforward. Physicists, chemists, and biologists all know how to measure the weight, speed, or length of an object, and there are few disagreements in these fields about how to gather numerical data. For social scientists the process of recording data in numbers can be a particularly difficult problem. For example, let's imagine a researcher who wants to determine whether parents who are more affectionate to one another are also more attentive to their children. How should the researcher measure "affection" and "attentiveness"? Unlike height or weight, there is no obvious way that these variables should be measured. Indeed, it is possible that researchers – especially from different branches of the social sciences – could disagree vigorously about how to measure these variables. This chapter explains the basic principles of measurement and the main framework for thinking about the measurement of variables.

Learning Goals

- Explain what an operationalization is and why it is necessary to create operationalizations to conduct research.

- Distinguish among the four levels of data in the organization system created by Stevens (1946).

- Demonstrate the benefits of collecting data at the highest level possible.

- Explain the differences between continuous and discrete data.

Defining What to Measure

The first step in measuring quantitative variables is to create an operationalization for them. In Chapter 1, an operationalization was defined as a description of a variable that permits a researcher to collect quantitative data on that variable. For example, an operationalization of "affection" may be the percentage of time that a couple holds hands while sitting next to each other. Strictly speaking, "time holding hands" is not the same as "affection." But "time holding hands" can be objectively observed and measured; two people measuring "time holding hands" for the same couple would likely produce similar data. However, "affection" is abstract, ambiguous, and unlikely to produce consistent results. Likewise, a researcher could define "attentiveness" as the number of times a parent makes eye contact with a child or the number of times he or she says the child's name. Again, these operationalizations are not the same thing as "attentiveness," but they are less ambiguous. More important, they produce numbers that we can then use in statistical analysis.

Sidebar 2.1 **Operationalizations and reductionism**

You may have a problem with operationalizations because using operationalizations means that researchers are not *really* studying what interests them, such as "affection" or "attentiveness." Rather, they are studying the operationalizations, which are shallow approximations for the ideas that really interest them. It is understandable why operationalizations are dissatisfying to some: no student declares a major in the social sciences by saying, "I am so excited to learn about the percentage of time that parents hold hands!"

Critics of operationalizations say that – as a result – quantitative research is *reductionist*, meaning that it reduces phenomena to a shadow of themselves, and that researchers are not really studying the phenomena that interest them. These critics have a point. In a literal sense, one could say that no social scientist has *ever* studied "affection," "racism," "personality," "marital satisfaction," or many other important phenomena. This shortcoming is not unique to the social sciences. Students and researchers in the physical and biological sciences operationalize concepts like "gravity," "animal packs," and "physical health" in order to find quantifiable ways of measuring them.

There are two responses to these criticisms. First, it is important to keep in mind that quantitative research is all about creating models, which are simplified versions of reality – not reality itself (see Chapter 1). Part of that simplification is creating an operationalization that makes model building possible in the first place. As long as we remember the difference between the model and reality, the simplified, shallow version of reality is not concerning.

My second response is pragmatic (i.e., practical) in nature: operationalizations (and, in turn, models) are simply necessary for quantitative research to happen. In other words, quantitative research "gets the job done," and operationalizations and models are just necessary parts of the quantitative research process. Scientists in many fields break down the phenomena they study into manageable, measurable parts – which requires operationalization. A philosopher of science may not think that the "because it works" response is satisfactory, but in the day-to-day world of scientific research, it is good enough.

If you are still dissatisfied with my two responses and you see reductionism as an unacceptable aspect of quantitative science, then you should check out qualitative methods, which are much less reductionist than quantitative methods because they focus on the experiences of subjects and the meaning of social science phenomena. Indeed, some social scientists combine qualitative and quantitative research methods in the same study, a methodology called "mixed methods" (see Dellinger & Leech, 2007). For a deeper discussion of reductionism and other philosophical issues that underlie the social sciences, I suggest the excellent book by Slife and Williams (1995).

Levels of Data

Operationalizations are essential for quantitative research, but it is necessary to understand the characteristics of the numerical data that operationalizations produce. To organize these data, most social scientists use a system of organizing data created by Stevens (1946). As a psychophysicist, Stevens was uniquely qualified to create a system that organizes the different types of numerical data that scientists gather. This is because a psychophysicist studies the way people perceive physical stimuli, such as light, sound, and pressure. In his work Stevens often was in contact with people who worked in the physical sciences – where measurement and data collection are uncomplicated – and the social sciences – where data collection and operationalizations are often confusing and haphazard (Miller, 1975). Stevens and other psychophysicists had noticed that the differences in perceptions that people had of physical stimuli often did not match the physical differences in those stimuli as measured through objective instruments. For example, Stevens (1936) knew that when a person had to judge how much louder one sound was than another, their subjective reports often did not agree with the actual differences in the volume of the two sounds, as measured physically in decibels. As a result, some researchers in the physical sciences claimed that the data that psychologists gathered about their subjects' perceptions or experiences were invalid. Stevens had difficulty accepting this position because psychologists had a record of success in collecting useful data, especially in studies of sensation, memory, and intelligence.

The argument between researchers in the physical sciences and the social sciences was at an impasse for years. Stevens's breakthrough insight was in realizing that psychologists and physicists were both collecting data, but that these were different **levels of data** (also called levels of measurement). In Stevens's (1946) system, **measurement** – or data collection – is merely "the assignment of numerals to objects or events according to rules" (p. 677). Stevens also realized that using different "rules" of measurement resulted in different types (or levels) of data. He explained that there were four levels of data, which, when arranged from simplest to most complex, are nominal, ordinal, interval, and ratio data (Stevens, 1946). We will explore definitions and examples of each of these levels of data.

Nominal Data. To create **nominal data**, it is necessary to classify objects into categories that are mutually exclusive and exhaustive. "Mutually exclusive" means that the categories do not overlap and that each object being measured can belong to only one category. "Exhaustive" means that every object belongs to a category – and there are no leftover objects. Once mutually exclusive and exhaustive categories are created, the researcher assigns a number to each category. Every object in the category receives the same number.

There is no minimum number of the objects that a category must have for nominal data, although it is needlessly complicated to create categories that don't have any objects in them. On the other hand, sometimes to avoid having a large number of categories containing only one or two objects, some researchers create an "other" or "miscellaneous" category and assign a number to it. This is acceptable as long as the "miscellaneous" category does not overlap with any other category, and all categories together are exhaustive.

The word *nominal* means "in name only." In fact, the word "nominal" comes from the Latin word for "name," *nomen*. Thus, it makes sense that the numbers in nominal data are merely labels. They do not actually have a mathematical function; rather, they serve as a label. Because the numbers do not have any mathematical purpose, the choice of which numbers to use is completely arbitrary. If a researcher has two groups of subjects, such as people diagnosed with a mental disorder and people not diagnosed with a mental disorder, then after classifying people into one group or another, the researcher would assign a number to each group. In this example, perhaps everyone without a disorder would be given the value of 0 and everyone with a disorder would be given a value of 1. Because these numbers are arbitrary, there is nothing special about the numbers 0 and 1. It would make just as much sense to use the numbers –25 and 13. Or 1 and 1.52. Or ½ and ¾. Due to the arbitrary nature of these numbers, the values do not indicate that one group is greater than another or possesses more of the quality being measured. For example, if we assign the value of 1 to males and the value of 2 to females, it does not mean that we think men are no. 1 in a ranking sense

Table 2.1 Acceptable mathematical operations for each level of data

Mathematical function	Nominal data	Ordinal data	Interval data	Ratio data
Classification	Yes	Yes	Yes	Yes
Counting	Yes	Yes	Yes	Yes
Proportions and percentages	Yes	Yes	Yes	Yes
Rank ordering	No	Yes	Yes	Yes
Addition	No	No	Yes	Yes
Subtraction	No	No	Yes	Yes
Dividing to form averages	No	No	Yes	Yes
Dividing to form ratios	No	No	No	Yes

or that women have more gender than men. This is merely a way of labeling categories that differ in type – not amount.

Because of the arbitrary nature of the numbers in nominal data, there are limits to the type of data analysis we can do with nominal data. If a researcher has nominal data, it only makes sense to classify objects into categories, count the number of objects within each category, and express the number of group members as a percentage or a proportion. This is because classifying, counting, and calculating percentages and proportions only requires mutually exclusive and exhaustive categories; these mathematical functions don't even use the "name" (i.e., numerical value) of the categories. As a result, the numbers that a researcher assigns to each category do not interfere with these mathematical functions. As a reference, Table 2.1 shows which mathematical functions can be performed with nominal data, and any other level of data.

Nominal variables are frequently used in data analysis. For example, subjects' race or ethnicity is a common variable in analysis. In one study I did (Warne, Anderson, & Johnson, 2013), I labeled White subjects as Group 0, African-American subjects as Group 1, Asian-American subjects as Group 2, Hispanic subjects as Group 3, multiracial subjects and subjects belonging to other races as Group 4, Native American subjects as Group 5, and Pacific Islander subjects as Group 6. The order of these groups and the numbers assigned to them are completely arbitrary – as is the fact that Group 4 consists of a combination of multiracial subjects and those who belong to other racial groups. Some other examples of nominal variables include the group that subjects are assigned to in an experiment (e.g., experimental group or control group), the marital status of a couple (e.g., married, engaged, cohabitating, divorced), and a subject's dominant hand (e.g., left-handed, right-handed, or ambidextrous).

Ordinal Data. An important feature of Stevens's (1946) system is that each level of data has all of the characteristics of the lower levels of data, plus additional characteristics that distinguish it from lower levels. Therefore, ordinal data also consist of mutually exclusive and exhaustive categories. However, the numbers for the categories in ordinal data indicate some sort of rank, meaning larger numbers indicate more of the quality being measured and smaller numbers indicate that category members possess less of the quality being measured (or vice versa). For example, if a researcher assigns the number 0 to short people, 1 to people of medium height, and 2 to tall people, then the researcher has created ordinal data because higher numbers in this example are assigned to taller people. If the numbers are reversed, this is still ordinal data, but now lower numbers would indicate taller people. However, it is not possible to calculate averages or to perform addition or subtraction with ordinal data. In fact, Stevens (1946, p. 679) said that this was an "illegal" statistical operation.

Because ordinal data have all the characteristics of nominal data, it is also possible to categorize, count, and express ordinal data as proportions or percentages – as shown in Table 2.1. However, it is also possible to rank objects with ordinal data. Additionally, due to the mutually exclusive and exhaustive categories of ordinal data, it is also possible to convert ordinal data to nominal data. All that this conversion requires is mixing up the numbers applied to each group. For example, if we assign the number 0 to short people, 1 to tall people, and 2 to people of medium height, then the order of the numbers is lost, because higher numbers no longer indicate taller people. Thus, the meaning that the numbers had in their previous order (i.e., 0 = short people, 1 = medium people, 2 = tall people) is lost, because the numbers assigned to each category have been rearranged. The result is that the numbers now are nominal data. The lesson from this example is that *it is always possible to convert data to a lower level of data. However, it is never possible to convert data to a higher level.*

Ordinal variables are also very common in data analysis in the social sciences. Some examples of these variables include income levels (e.g., low income, middle income, high income), age groups (e.g., infants, children, adolescents, adults), education levels, and military ranks. What all of these variables have in common is that the categories – in addition to being mutually exclusive and exhausting – have a distinct order to them. For example, the age groups categories are arranged from the youngest group to the oldest.

Interval Data. Interval data also consist of (1) mutually exclusive and exhaustive categories, and (2) numbers that indicate rank or magnitude. Additionally, the scale of interval data has an equal distance between all adjacent points (or "intervals") along the entire range of the scale. In other words, the distance between any pair of adjacent numbers will be equal, no matter which pair of numbers one chooses to examine.

One example of interval data from Stevens (1946) is the Celsius temperature scale, which defines $0°$ as the freezing point of water and $100°$ as the boiling point of water. The difference in heat between $0°$ and $1°$ is the same as the difference in heat between $99°$ and $100°$. In fact, this constancy does not just apply from $0°$ to $100°$, but rather to any possible temperature on the scale. This regularity in the difference in numbers is what makes this an example of interval-level data.

The equal intervals between adjacent numbers in interval data are what make it possible to add, subtract, and compute averages with interval data. This is why, for example, it makes sense to say that today is $3°$ hotter than yesterday, or to compute the average temperature in a location. Moreover, because interval data have the qualities of nominal and ordinal data, it is also possible to count, classify, compute proportions and averages, and find ranks. Hence, it also makes sense to record the hottest day of the year in a location (a ranking) or to count the number of days above 25 °C in a year (counting). Table 2.1 shows the new mathematical functions that can be performed with interval data: counting, classifying, finding proportions and percentages (like nominal data), producing rank data (like ordinal data), adding, subtracting, and dividing to form averages.

Ratio Data. The highest level of data in the Stevens (1946) system is ratio-level data. Ratio data possess all of the characteristics of lower levels of data: mutually exclusive and exhaustive categories, numbers that indicate rank or order, and equal intervals between adjacent numbers on the scale. Additionally, ratio data have the property of an absolute zero, which indicates the complete absence of the variable being measured. For example, most weight scales are ratio-level scales because zero indicates that the object has no weight. This absolute zero is what distinguishes ratio data from interval data.

The absolute zero on a ratio scale permits researchers to form ratios between two measurements of ratio data. For example, if Person A weighs 45 kilograms (99 lbs.) and Person B weighs

90 kilograms (198 lbs.), then it makes sense to say that Person A weighs half as much as B (Marcus-Roberts & Roberts, 1987). The phrase "half as much" is a way of expressing a 1:2 ratio of the two people's weights. Also, notice how the 1:2 ratio is observed whether weight is measured in kilograms or pounds; that is because both measures of weight produce ratio data. Both kilograms and pounds have an absolute zero, a consistent difference between adjacent numbers across the entire length of the scale, rank order to the numbers, and mutually exclusive and exhaustive categories.

However, the Celsius and Fahrenheit temperature scales are not ratio-level data. Instead, they are interval-level, and ratios between two measures do not make sense. For example, if location A has a temperature of 15 °C (59 °F) and location B has a temperature of 30 °C (86 °F), then the ratio using the Celsius scale is 1:2, but the ratio using the Fahrenheit scale is 1:1.46. These differing ratios don't make sense. It would mean that location B is simultaneously twice as hot as location A and also 46% hotter. This is because the zero points on the Fahrenheit and Celsius scales do not represent the total absence of heat. However, there is a temperature scale where zero signifies the complete absence of heat: the Kelvin scale. When we measure temperatures on the Kelvin scale, it *does* make sense to talk about one location being twice as hot as another.

Sometimes it can be difficult to grasp the concept of "absolute zero" because it may be an impossible score in a sample. For example, no one in a sample of people will weigh 0 kg. That may be true, but the fact that a zero may not be obtainable in a study is irrelevant. Rather, the important issue is whether zero would indicate the absence of the characteristic that the researcher is measuring. The fact that nobody in a sample would have a weight of 0 kg does not matter (nor does the fact that no recorded temperature on Earth has ever been 0 °K).

Guided Practice 2.1

While preparing this textbook chapter, I received a survey from my bank that has examples of questions that collect data at different levels. For each of these examples, I will explain the level of data that the question generates.

- "Do you currently own or rent your home?"
  - This question produces nominal data because it produces answers that can be classified into two mutually exclusive and exhaustive categories. Any number assigned to either category (i.e., owners and renters) would be arbitrary.
- "Do you find your cell phone plan to be unsatisfactory, somewhat satisfactory, or very satisfactory?"
  - The three categories in this survey question can easily be ordered from least satisfactory to most satisfactory, which would produce ordinal data. But this question won't produce interval data because it is not clear that the distance between adjacent categories is the same.
- "On a scale from 1 to 7, please indicate how likely you are to buy a new car in the next year."
  - This type of rating scale – like test scores – is somewhat ambiguous (see Sidebar 2.3). The seven scale points and the possibility that we could add scores from this variable with scores from another variable indicates that this is probably an item

that produces interval-level data. But, Sidebar 2.3 shows that rating scales like these can be ambiguous.

- "How many years have you had your job?"
  - This question produces ratio data because a response of 0 would mean that the person had just acquired their job. Additionally, it makes sense to say that someone who has had their job for 3 years has been employed in the same job for one-fifth of the time as someone who has worked in the same job for 15 years. This sort of ratio (e.g., 1:5) makes sense, and this also supports the ratio nature of this question's data.

In addition to physical measurements, most measurements of time, such as age or the number of years since a person has graduated from high school, are ratio data. Another frequent form of ratio data in the social sciences occurs when researchers count the number of a particular object that a person possesses. For example, if a researcher visits participants' homes and counts the number of books that each person owns, then the researcher is producing ratio data. After all, it makes sense to say that one person is twice as old as another, or that one person owns three times as many books as another person. Likewise, a person with an age of zero years was just born, and a person who owns zero books has a total absence of books.

Table 2.1 shows that every mathematical function that can be performed with a lower level of data can be performed with ratio-level data. Additionally, ratio-level data can be divided to form ratios, such as the 2:1 ratio of ages in the previous paragraph.

Check Yourself!

- As defined by Stevens (1946), what is measurement?
- What are the four levels of data, in order from most basic to most advanced?
- For nominal data, why does the choice of numbers assigned to each category not matter?
- What is the property that interval data have that ordinal data do not?
- What is the meaning of absolute zero in the context of ratio data?

Sidebar 2.2 **Memory aid**

Some people have difficulty remembering the order of the levels of data. My students like a simple memory aid: NOIR, which stands for *nominal, ordinal, interval,* and *ratio* – the order of the levels of data from simplest to most complex. "Noir" is the French word for "night." The word also makes some people think of old movies from the *film noir* genre (like *Sunset Boulevard*). Some of my female students have told me that "noir" is also the name of a perfume. Hopefully, one of these tips will help you remember the order of Stevens's (1946) four levels of data.

Test scores and rating scales

Most types of data can be easily classified into one of Stevens's (1946) four levels of data. However, it can be difficult to classify them as one particular level of data. For example, consider a spelling test for kindergarteners that consists of four words:

- cat
- bag
- tan
- Brobdingnagian

The total test score for a child can be ordinal, interval, or ratio-level data, depending on how the researcher conceptualizes the data. If the researcher counts the number of words spelled correctly, then he or she is collecting ratio-level data. However, if the researcher believes that zero does not represent a complete absence of spelling ability – perhaps because a child could spell other words correctly – then the data would be considered interval-level data. Finally, one could make the argument that the "distances" between points on this scale are not equal. A researcher making this argument would say that the difference in spelling ability between spelling one word correctly and spelling two words correctly is not the same as the difference in ability between three and four words. If this argument is correct, then the data would be ordinal.

Stevens (1946) himself recognized that test scores are ambiguous and difficult to classify in his system. In the three generations since he published his article, the debate about the level of data of test scores has not been fully resolved. Some social scientists claim that scores from tests and surveys are always ordinal data (e.g., S. Jamieson, 2004; van der Eijk & Rose, 2015), while others (e.g., Borgatta & Bohrnstedt, 1980; Norman, 2010) have argued that many test scores function so similarly to interval data that any distortions from treating test scores as interval data are minimal (and sometimes non-existent). Usually, whether a given set of scores is ordinal, interval, or ratio depends on how the test was scored and how the numbers are interpreted. Most researchers, though, treat their test scores and survey data as if they were interval-level unless they have reason to suspect otherwise. It is an argument that has been going on for over 70 years, and it shows no sign of being resolved completely.

Rating scales have the same problem. For example, the old rating scale on Netflix has five labels: "Hated It" (1 star), "Didn't Like It" (2 stars), "Liked It" (3 stars), "Really Liked It" (4 stars), and "Loved It" (5 stars). It's not completely clear whether these are categories in ordinal data or in interval data. It all depends on whether people using the rating scale consider there to be an equal distance between categories. In other words, is it as easy for a film to move from 3 stars to 4 stars as it is to move from 1 star to 2 stars? If so, then the scale may be interval. If not, then it's ordinal. But it is extremely difficult to know for sure, and it is possible that some of Netflix's customers gave equal distances between numbers and other customers did not. Just like test scores, there is no clear-cut solution to this question, and it is a controversy that is unlikely to be fully resolved soon. As a result, there is disagreement about which statistical methods are appropriate for rating scales (and test scores). Experts who say that rating scales are ordinal data claim quite forcefully that data from these scales cannot be averaged; those who think that rating-scale data are interval-level disagree and often average their rating-scale data.

So What?

Why should we care about the four levels of data? The answer lies in Table 2.1: certain mathematical operations require certain levels of data. Without the appropriate level of data, a researcher will produce results or conclusions that are distorted or nonsensical. For example, in one news article about researchers in Antarctica, the reporter stated that it was –40 °C at Lake Vostok (the coldest place on Earth), but that, "When the winter arrives in the next few weeks, the temperature can get twice as cold. Vostok Station boasts the lowest recorded temperature on Earth: –89.4 degrees Celsius" ("Russian scientists seeking Lake Vostok lost in frozen 'Land of the Lost'?", 2012, para. 7). In reality, –80 °C (193 °K) is not "twice as cold" as –40 °C (233 °K); it is actually just 17.2% colder (233 – 193 = 40, and 40 ÷ 233 = 17.2%). An accurate understanding of the true differences between these two temperatures is only possible when using the correct level of data – in this case, ratio-level data – when performing a mathematical calculation.

A minor error in a news report is bothersome. However, even researchers sometimes make this basic mistake. When I was in graduate school I read an article (Lewis, DeCamp-Fritson, Ramage, McFarland, & Archwamety, 2007) in which the authors calculated an average for ordinal data – something that Table 2.1 shows is not permitted. Noticing this error (and others), I wrote a critique of the article to the journal, and the editor published it (Warne, 2009). The original authors now have another article in the scientific record that consists of nothing but a discussion about the flaws in their work. This is not something that researchers want attached to their work (see Reynolds, 2010, pp. 2–3, for a similar story).

Other Ways to Classify Data

The Stevens (1946) system is – by far – the most common way to organize quantitative data, but it is not the only possible scheme. Some social scientists also attempt to ascertain whether their data are continuous or discrete. **Continuous data** are data that permit a wide range of scores that form a constant scale with no gaps at any point along the scale and also have many possible values. Many types of data in the social sciences are continuous, such as intelligence test scores, which in a normal human population range from about 55 to 145 on most tests, with every whole number in between being a possible value for a person.

Continuous data often permit scores that are expressed as fractions or decimals. All three temperature scales that I have discussed in this chapter (i.e., Fahrenheit, Celsius, and Kelvin) are continuous data, and with a sensitive enough thermometer it would be easy to gather temperature data measured at the half-degree or tenth-degree.

The opposite of continuous data are **discrete data**, which are scores that have a limited range of possible values and do not form a constant, uninterrupted scale of scores. All nominal data are discrete, as are ordinal data that have a limited number of categories or large gaps between groups. A movie rating system where a critic gives every film a 1-, 2-, 3-, or 4-star rating would be discrete data because it only has four possible values. Most interval or ratio data, however, are continuous – not discrete – data. The point at which a variable has "too many" values to be discrete and is therefore continuous is often not entirely clear, and whether a particular variable consists of discrete or continuous data is sometimes a subjective judgment. To continue with the movie rating system example, the website Internet Movie Database (IMDb) asks users to rate films on a scale from 1 to 10. Whether ten categories are enough for the data to be continuous is a matter of argument, and opinions may vary from researcher to researcher.

Check Yourself!

- Why is it important to understand the four levels of data?
- Why is there controversy about the level of data that rating scales produce?
- What is the difference between discrete and continuous data?

Summary

Before conducting any statistical analyses, researchers must decide how to measure their variables. There is no obvious method of measuring many of the variables that interest social scientists. Therefore, researchers must give each variable an operationalization that permits them to collect numerical data.

The most common system for conceptualizing quantitative data was developed by Stevens (1946), who defined four levels of data, which are (in ascending order of complexity) nominal, ordinal, interval, and ratio-level data. Nominal data consist of mutually exclusive and exhaustive categories, which are then given an arbitrary number. Ordinal data have all of the qualities of nominal data, but the numbers in ordinal data also indicate rank order. Interval data are characterized by all the traits of nominal and ordinal data, but the spacing between numbers is equal across the entire length of the scale. Finally, ratio data are characterized by the presence of an absolute zero. This does not mean that a zero has been obtained in the data; it merely means that zero would indicate the total lack of whatever is being measured. Higher levels of data contain more information, although it is always possible to convert from one level of data to a lower level. It is not possible to convert data to a higher level than it was collected at.

It is important for us to recognize the level of data because, as Table 2.1 indicates, there are certain mathematical procedures that require certain levels of data. For example, calculating an average requires interval or ratio data; but classifying sample members is possible for all four levels of data. Social scientists who ignore the level of their data risk producing meaningless results (like the mean gender in a sample) or distorted statistics. Using the wrong statistical methods for a level of data is considered an elementary error and a sign of flawed research.

Some researchers also classify their data as being continuous or discrete. Continuous data are data that have many possible values that span the entire length of a scale with no large gaps in possible scores. Discrete data can only have a limited number of possible values.

Reflection Questions: Comprehension

1. Explain why scores on many tests and surveys can be ordinal, interval, or ratio data.
2. Explain why most researchers do not actually measure the phenomena they are interested in, but rather choose variables that they believe are related to the phenomena of interest.

3. A researcher wishes to add together the scores from different subjects. Which level(s) of data should the researcher collect in order to perform this mathematical function?

4. A different researcher wants to count the number of subjects who obtain each score on a variable. What is the lowest level of data that the researcher should collect in order to perform this mathematical function?

5. Knowing that it is only possible to convert data down to simpler levels, what would you suggest to researchers who want their data to be as flexible as possible?

Reflection Questions: Application

6. Classify the following variables into the correct level of data (nominal, ordinal, interval, or ratio):
   a. Number of Facebook friends
   b. Height, measured in centimeters
   c. Reaction time
   d. Kelvin temperature scale
   e. Race/ethnicity
   f. Native language
   g. Military rank
   h. Celsius temperature scale
   i. College major
   j. Movie content ratings (e.g., G, PG, PG-13, R, NC-17)
   k. Personality type
   l. Hours spent watching TV per week
   m. Percentage of games an athlete plays without receiving a penalty
   n. Marital status (i.e., single, married, divorced, widowed)
   o. Fahrenheit temperature scale

7. Label each of the examples in question 6 (*a–o*) as continuous or discrete data.

8. Kevin has collected data about the weight of people in his study. He couldn't obtain their exact weight, and so he merely asked people to indicate whether they were "skinny" (labeled group 1) "average" (group 2), or "heavy" (group 3).
   a. What level of data has Kevin collected?
   b. Could Kevin convert his data to nominal level? Why or why not? If he can, how would he make this conversion?
   c. Could Kevin convert his data to ratio level? Why or why not? If he can, how would he make this conversion?

9. At most universities the faculty are – in ascending seniority – adjunct (i.e., part-time) faculty, lecturers, assistant professors, associate professors, and full professors.
   a. What level of data would this information be?
   b. If a researcher instead collected the number of years that a faculty member has been teaching at the college level, what level of data would that be instead?
   c. Of the answers to the two previous questions (9a and 9b), which level of data is more detailed?

10. What is the *minimal* level of data students must collect if they want to
   a. classify subjects?
   b. add scores together?

    c.   create proportions?

    d.   create ratios?

    e.   subtract scores?

    f.   form averages?

Software Guide

This chapter only discusses how to conduct measurement and to classify data into the appropriate level of measurement. Excel does not have any functionality that allows you to categorize variables

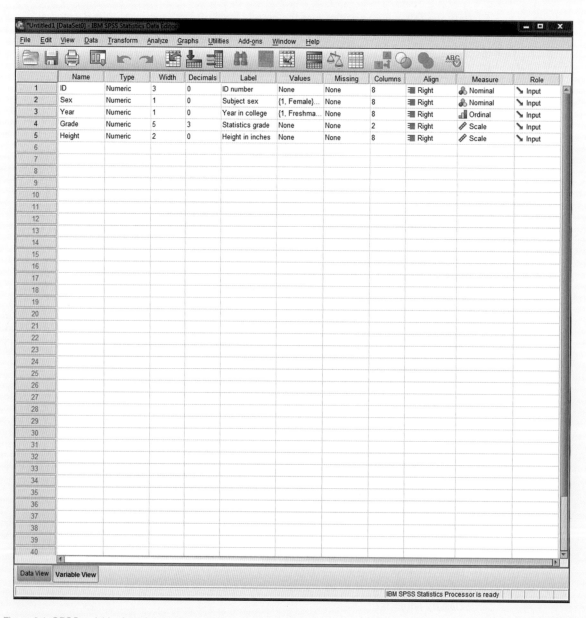

Figure 2.1 SPSS variable view showing five variables and their characteristics.

into nominal, ordinal, interval, or ratio data. It is the responsibility of the Excel user to keep track of what level of data they are working with in each variable.

SPSS

SPSS permits users to specify the level of data in the variable view. (See the Software Guide for Chapter 1 for information about variable view.) Figure 2.1 shows five variables that have been entered into SPSS. Entering the name merely requires clicking a cell in the column labeled "Name" and typing in the variable name. In the column labeled "Type," the default option is "Numeric," which is used for data that are numbers. (Other options include "String" for text; dates; and time measurements.) The next two columns, "Width" and "Decimals" refer to the length of a variable (in terms of the number of digits). "Width" must be at least 1 digit, and "Decimals" must be a smaller number than the number entered into "Width." In this example, the "Grade" variable has 5 digits, of which 3 are decimals and 1 (automatically) is the decimal point in the number. The "Label" column is a more detailed name that you can give a label. This is helpful if the variable name itself is too short or if the limits of SPSS's "Name" column (e.g., no variables beginning with numbers, no spaces) are too constraining.

The "Values" column is very convenient for nominal and ordinal data. By clicking the cell, the user can tell SPSS what numbers correspond to the different category labels. An example of this appears in Figure 2.2. This window allows users to specify which numbers refer to the various groups within a variable. In Figure 2.2, Group 1 is for female subjects, and Group 2 is for male subjects. Clicking on "Missing" is similar, but it permits users to specify which numbers correspond to missing data. This tells SPSS to not include those numbers when performing statistical analyses so that the results are not distorted. The next two columns (labeled "Columns" and "Align") are cosmetic; changing values in these columns will make the numbers in the data view appear differently, but will not change the data or how the computer uses them.

To change the level of data for a variable, you should use the column labeled "Measure." Clicking a cell in this column generates a small drop-down menu with three

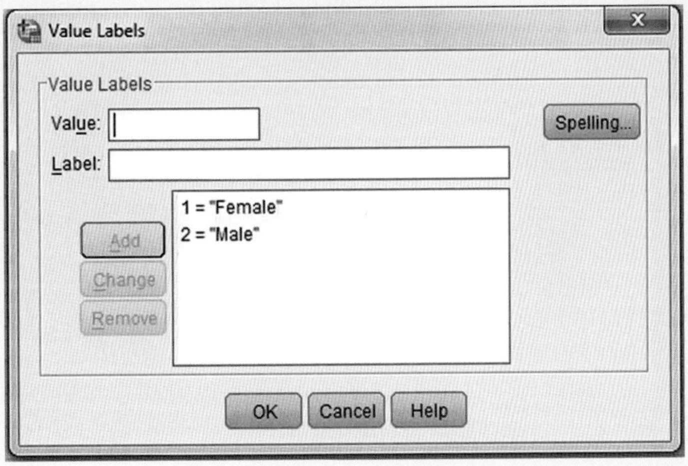

Figure 2.2 The SPSS Value Labels window, which permits a user to specify the numbers in a nominal or ordinal variable that correspond to each group.

options, "Nominal" (for nominal data), "Ordinal" (for ordinal data), and "Scale" (for interval and ratio data). Assigning a variable to the proper level of data requires selecting the appropriate option from the menu.

Further Reading

- Jamieson, S. (2004). Likert scales: How to (ab)use them. *Medical Education, 38,* 1217–1218. doi:10.1111/j.1365–2929.2004.02012.x

    * Jamieson argues strongly that it is inappropriate to treat scores from rating scales as being interval-level data. Although I do not agree with her, Jamieson's article is very readable, and she makes arguments that many people who share her perspective treat seriously.

- Slife, B. D., & Williams, R. N. (1995). *What's behind the research? Discovering hidden assumptions in the behavioral sciences.* Thousand Oaks, CA: Sage.

    * Much more accessible than most books about the philosophy of science, this book describes and then critiques the philosophical assumptions behind social science research. Chapter 5 of this book covers reductionism, but other important topics that the authors discuss in their book include determinism, the nature of theory, causality, and whether the traditional quantitative research approach is even appropriate for studying human beings.

- Stevens, S. S. (1946). On the theory of scales of measurement. *Science, 103,* 677–680. doi:10.1126/science.103.2684.677

    * Although I have tried to make Stevens's ideas clear, there is still value in reading his original article. In fact, there is always value in reading articles and books where prominent ideas were first discussed. I recommend Stevens's article to anyone who wants to see an important idea being discussed publicly for the first time.

3 Visual Models

Biology has equipped humans to process a great deal of information through their senses, especially vision. For many people one of the easiest ways to remember that information is through pictures and other visual aids. A well-designed image can often help others understand complex and abstract ideas (Robinson & Kiewra, 1995). The benefits of a picture even extend into the world of statistics, though we will use the term *visual models* to refer to these images.

In Chapter 1, a model was defined as a simplified version of reality. This chapter focuses on visual models, which are pictures that people create so that they can understand their data better. Like all models, visual models are simplified, which means that they are inaccurate to some extent. Nevertheless, visual models can help data analysts understand their data before any analysis actually happens.

Learning Goals

- Create a frequency table and histogram from raw data.

- Describe histograms in terms of their skewness, kurtosis, and number of peaks.

- Correctly choose an appropriate visual model for a dataset.

- Identify the similarities and differences that exist among histograms, bar graphs, frequency polygons, line graphs, and pie charts.

- Read a scatterplot and understand how each person in a dataset is represented in a scatterplot.

Sample Data

To illustrate the most common visual models, we will use data from the same study that we first saw in Chapter 1. This is a study that one of my students conducted on the relationships that people have with their sibling diagnosed with an autism spectrum disorder (Waite et al., 2015). Some of the data in the study are displayed in Table 3.1.

The table shows six variables: ID, sex, age, sibling age, the level of agreement that the subject has with the statement "I feel that my sibling understands me well," and the level of language development in the sibling with autism. The table also shows how to interpret each number in the table. For example, for the sex variable, male respondents are labeled as "1," and female respondents are "2."

ID	Sex[a]	Age[b]	Sibling age[b]	"Sibling understands me"[c]	Language development[d]
			Table 3.1 Example data from a study on relationships with siblings with autism		
1	2	24	18	4	4
2	2	23	21	4	4
3	2	33	37	5	4
4	2	19	18	4	3
5	1	38	30	4	4
6	2	21	19	1	1
7	1	24	18	2	2
8	2	20	13	4	4
9	1	23	10	2	4
10	2	31	38	3	2
11	2	18	11	3	3
12	1	25	21	2	4
13	2	35	37	3	3

[a] 1 = male; 2 = female.
[b] Measured in years.
[c] 1 = strongly disagree; 2 = disagree; 3 = neutral; 4 = agree; 5 = strongly agree.
[d] 1 = simple, one word; 2 = 1–3 word sentences; 3 = emerging; 4 = typical.

Frequency Tables

One of the simplest ways to display data is in a **frequency table**. To create a frequency table for a variable, you need to list every value for the variable in the dataset and then list the **frequency**, which is the count of how many times each value occurs. Table 3.2a shows an example from Waite et al.'s (2015) study. When asked how much the subjects agree with the statement "I feel that my sibling understands me well," one person strongly disagreed, three people disagreed, three felt neutral about the statement, five agreed, and one strongly agreed. A frequency table just compiles this information in an easy to use format, as shown below. The first column of a frequency table consists of the response label (labeled "Response") and the second column is the number of each response (labeled "Frequency").

Frequency tables can only show data for one variable at a time, but they are helpful for discerning general patterns within a variable. Table 3.2a, for example, shows that few people in the Waite et al. (2015) study felt strongly about whether their sibling with autism understood them well. Most responses clustered towards the middle of the scale.

Table 3.2a also shows an important characteristic of frequency tables: the number of responses adds up to the number of participants in the study. This will be true if there are responses from everyone in the study (as is the case in Waite et al.'s study).

Frequency tables can include additional information about subjects' scores in new columns. The first new column is labeled "**Cumulative frequency**," which is determined by counting the number of people in a row and adding it to the number of people in higher rows in the frequency table. For example, in Table 3.2b, the cumulative frequency for the second row (labeled "Disagree") is 4 – which was calculated by summing the frequency from that row, which was 3, and the

Table 3.2a Frequency table example: "I feel that my sibling understands me well"

Response (score)	Frequency
Strongly disagree (1)	1
Disagree (2)	3
Neutral (3)	3
Agree (4)	5
Strongly agree (5)	1
Total	13

Table 3.2b Frequency table example: "I feel that my sibling understands me well"

Response	Frequency	Cumulative frequency
Strongly disagree	1	1
Disagree	3	4
Neutral	3	7
Agree	5	12
Strongly agree	1	13
Total	13	13

frequency of the higher row, which was 1 (3 + 1 = 4). As another example, the cumulative frequency column shows that, for example, 7 of the 13 respondents responded "strongly disagree," "disagree," or "neutral" when asked about whether their sibling with autism understood them well.

It is also possible to use a frequency table to identify the **proportion** of people giving each response. In a frequency table, a proportion is a number expressed as a decimal or a fraction that shows how many subjects in the dataset have the same value for a variable. To calculate the proportion of people who gave each response, use the following formula:

$$Proportion = \frac{f}{n} \qquad \text{(Formula 3.1)}$$

In Formula 3.1, f is the frequency of a response, and n is the sample size. Therefore, calculating the proportion merely requires finding the frequency of a response and dividing it by the number of people in the sample. Proportions will always be between the values of 0 to 1.

Table 3.3 shows the frequency table for the Waite et al. (2015) study, with new columns showing the proportions for the frequencies and the cumulative frequencies. The table nicely provides examples of the properties of proportions. For example, it is apparent that all of the values in both the "Frequency proportion" and "Cumulative proportion" columns are between 0 and 1.0. Additionally, those columns show how the frequency proportions were calculated – by taking the number in the frequency column and dividing by n (which is 13 in this small study). A similar process was used to calculate the cumulative proportions in the far right column.

Table 3.3 is helpful in visualizing data because it shows quickly which variable responses were most common and which responses were rare. It is obvious, for example, that "Agree" was the most common response to the question of whether the subjects' sibling with autism understood them well,

Table 3.3 Frequency table example: "I feel that my sibling understands me well"

Response	Frequency	Frequency proportion	Cumulative frequency	Cumulative proportion
Strongly disagree	1	1/13 = .077	1	1/13 = .077
Disagree	3	3/13 = .231	4	4/13 = .308
Neutral	3	3/13 = .231	7	7/13 = .538
Agree	5	5/13 = .385	12	12/13 = .923
Strongly agree	1	1/13 = .077	13	13/13 = 1.000
Total	13	13/13 = 1.000	13	13/13 = 1.000

which is apparent because that response had the highest frequency (5) and the highest frequency proportion (.385). Likewise, "strongly disagree" and "strongly agree" were unusual responses because they tied for having the lowest frequency (1) and lowest frequency proportion (.077). Combined together, this information reveals that even though autism is characterized by pervasive difficulties in social situations and interpersonal relationships, many people with autism can still have a relationship with their sibling without a disability (Waite et al., 2015). This is important information for professionals who work with families that include a person with a diagnosis of autism.

Sidebar 3.1   Proportions and percentages

Proportions and percentages have a direct mathematical relationship. To convert a proportion to a percentage, multiply the proportion by 100. Converting a percentage to a proportion requires dividing the percentage by 100. For example, in Table 3.3, the proportion of responses that were neutral was .231. Multiplying this proportion by 100 results in a value of 23.1%. In other words, slightly under one-quarter (25%) of respondents felt neutral about agreeing with the statement that their sibling with autism understands them well.

Check Yourself!

- How do frequency tables make data easier to understand?
- How can you convert frequencies to proportions?
- Why do frequencies always add up to the sample size?
- What is the difference between a frequency and a cumulative frequency?

Histograms

Frequency tables are very helpful, but they have a major drawback: they are just a summary of the data, and they are not very visual. For people who prefer a picture to a table, there is the option of creating a histogram, an example of which is shown below in Figure 3.1.

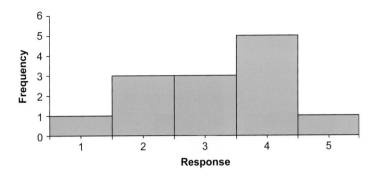

Figure 3.1 A histogram for the data shown in Table 3.1. The height of each bar is the frequency of that response. For the responses, 1 = strongly disagree, 2 = disagree, 3 = neutral, 4 = agree, and 5 = strongly agree.

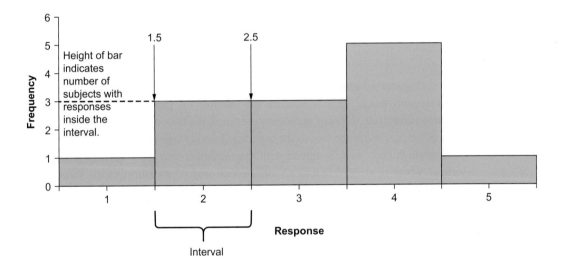

Figure 3.2 Explanation of some characteristics of a histogram. This figure shows that intervals span a range of continuous values − in this example the range is from 1.5 to 2.5 − and that the height of the histogram represents the number of subjects in the dataset that gave a response that was within the range of the interval. Data taken from Waite et al. (2015); see Table 3.1.

A histogram converts the data in a frequency table into visual format. Each bar in a histogram (called an **interval**) represents a range of possible values for a variable. The height of the bar represents the frequency of responses within the range of the interval. In Figure 3.1 it is clear that, for the second bar, which represents the "disagree" response, three people gave this response (because the bar is 3 units high).

Notice how the variable scores (i.e., 1, 2, 3, 4, or 5) are in the middle of the interval for each bar. Technically, this means that the interval includes more than just whole number values. This is illustrated in Figure 3.2, which shows that each interval has a width of 1 unit. The figure also annotates how, for the second bar, the interval ranges between 1.5 and 2.5. In Waite et al.'s study (2015), all of the responses were whole numbers, but this is not always true of social science data, especially for variables that can be measured very precisely, such as reaction time (often measured in milliseconds) or grade-point average (often calculated to two or three decimal places).

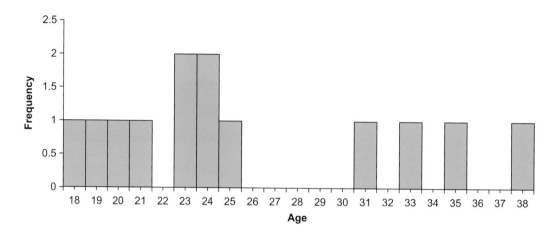

Figure 3.3 Histogram representing the subjects' ages in the Waite et al. (2015) study. The gaps between these bars represent ages that were not reported in the study. See Table 3.1.

Figures 3.1 and 3.2 also show another important characteristic of histograms: the bars in the histogram touch. This is because the variable on this histogram is assumed to measure a continuous trait (i.e., level of agreement), even if Waite et al. (2015) only permitted their subjects to give five possible responses to the question. In other words, there are probably subtle differences in how much each subject agreed with the statement that their sibling with autism knows them well. If Waite et al. (2015) had a more precise way of measuring their subjects' responses, it is possible that the data would include responses that were not whole numbers, such as 1.8, 2.1, and 2.3. However, if only whole numbers were permitted in their data, these responses would be rounded to 2. Yet, it is still possible that there are differences in the subjects' actual levels of agreement. Having the histogram bars touch shows that, theoretically, the respondents' opinions are on a continuum.

The only gaps in a histogram should occur in intervals where there are no values for a variable within the interval. An example of the types of gaps that are appropriate for a histogram is Figure 3.3, which is a histogram of the subjects' ages.

The gaps in Figure 3.3 are acceptable because they represent intervals where there were no subjects. For example, there were no subjects in the study who were 32 years old. (This can be verified by checking Table 3.1, which shows the subjects' ages in the third column.) Therefore, there is a gap at this place on the histogram in Figure 3.3.

Some people do not like having a large number of intervals in their histograms, so they will combine intervals as they build their histogram. For example, having intervals that span 3 years instead of 1 year will change Figure 3.3 into Figure 3.4.

Combining intervals simplifies the visual model even more, but this simplification may be needed. In some studies with precisely measured variables or large sample sizes, having an interval for every single value of a variable may result in complex histograms that are difficult to understand. By simplifying the visual model, the data become more intelligible. There are no firm guidelines for choosing the number of intervals in a histogram, but I recommend having no fewer than five. Regardless of the number of intervals you choose for a histogram, you should always ensure that the intervals are all the same width.

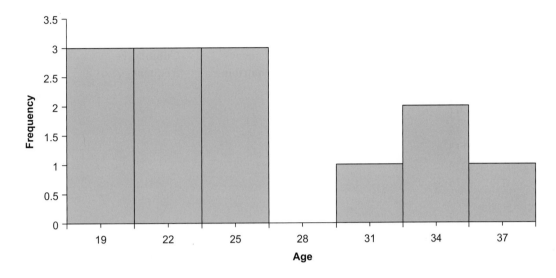

Figure 3.4 Histogram representing subjects' ages in the Waite et al. (2015) study. The data used in creating this histogram are the same data as for Figure 3.3; the intervals now span 3 years instead of 1 year.

Check Yourself!

- How do you determine the height of a bar in a histogram?
- Why is it important that the bars on a histogram touch?
- What are the advantages and disadvantages of combining intervals in a histogram?

Guided Practice 3.1

This guided practice will show you how to create a frequency table and histogram. For this example we will use the variable of the age of the sibling with autism in the Waite et al. (2015) study. As Table 3.1 shows, the ages were as follows:

18   21   37   18   30   19   18   13   10   38   11   21   37

The first step is to create the rows and columns you need for the frequency table, which should look like Table 3.4.

(In Table 3.4 the scores are in ascending order. In their histograms, some people like to order the scores from highest to lowest, which is also acceptable.) The next step is to count the number of times each age appears in the dataset. This information is used to fill in the "Frequency" column. After filling in that column, add up the numbers in it and ensure that they sum to n (which is 13 in this example; see Table 3.5).

The next step is to calculate a proportion for each frequency. This is done by dividing the frequency in each row by n (which is 13). In the table below, I have deleted all of the rows that had

Table 3.4				
Sibling age	Frequency	Frequency proportion	Cumulative frequency	Cumulative proportion
10				
11				
12				
13				
14				
15				
16				
17				
18				
19				
20				
21				
22				
23				
24				
25				
26				
27				
28				
29				
30				
31				
32				
33				
34				
35				
36				
37				
38				
Total				

a frequency of 0. Some people prefer to do this in their frequency tables because it saves space. Others prefer to keep rows with a frequency of 0 so that they know where to put the gaps in the histograms later (Figure 3.6). Consult your instructor about this issue.

The next column to fill in is the cumulative frequency column. This is done by adding the frequency for each row with the frequencies of all higher rows. For how this is done in each column, see Table 3.7.

The final step in completing a frequency table is to find the proportion for each cumulative frequency. This is done by dividing the cumulative frequency in each row by n, as shown in Table 3.8.

Table 3.5				
Sibling age	Frequency	Frequency proportion	Cumulative frequency	Cumulative proportion
10	1			
11	1			
12	0			
13	1			
14	0			
15	0			
16	0			
17	0			
18	3			
19	1			
20	0			
21	2			
22	0			
23	0			
24	0			
25	0			
26	0			
27	0			
28	0			
29	0			
30	1			
31	0			
32	0			
33	0			
34	0			
35	0			
36	0			
37	2			
38	1			
Total	13			

With the frequency table completed, we now have all the information needed to create a histogram. For all histograms, the vertical axis (i.e., the y-axis) is the frequency and the horizontal axis (i.e., the x-axis) is the values of the variable. So the blank histogram will appear as shown in Figure 3.5.

Now you should add bars. To make things easy, I have set up this example so that each row in the frequency table is its own bar. Therefore, the height of each bar is just the frequency for that row. For example, there is only one sibling who was 10 years old in the sample. Therefore, the bar at the value of 10 should be 1 unit high. When you are done making your bars, the histogram should appear as shown in Figure 3.6.

Table 3.6

Sibling age	Frequency	Frequency proportion	Cumulative frequency	Cumulative proportion
10	1	1 / 13 = .077		
11	1	1 / 13 = .077		
13	1	1 / 13 = .077		
18	3	3 / 13 = .231		
19	1	1 / 13 = .077		
21	2	2 / 13 = .154		
30	1	1 / 13 = .077		
37	2	2 / 13 = .154		
38	1	1 / 13 = .077		
Total	13	13 / 13 = 1.000		

Table 3.7

Sibling age	Frequency	Frequency proportion	Cumulative frequency	Cumulative proportion
10	1	1 / 13 = .077	1 (top row frequency, no higher rows to add)	
11	1	1 / 13 = .077	1 + 1 = 2 (this row's frequency added to the top row's frequency)	
13	1	1 / 13 = .077	1 + 1 + 1 = 3 (this row's frequency added to the previous rows' frequencies)	
18	3	3 / 13 = .231	1 + 1 + 1 + 3 = 6 (same method)	
19	1	1 / 13 = .077	1 + 1 + 1 + 3 + 1 = 7 (same method)	
21	2	2 / 13 = .154	1 + 1 + 1 + 3 +1 + 2 = 9 (same method)	
30	1	1 / 13 = .077	1 + 1 + 1 + 3 +1 + 2 +1 = 10 (same method)	
37	2	2 / 13 = .154	1 + 1 + 1 + 3 +1 + 2 +1 + 2 = 12 (same method)	
38	1	1 / 13 = .077	1 + 1 + 1 + 3 +1 + 2 +1 + 2 + 1 = 13 (same method)	
Total	13	13 / 13 = 1.000	13 (this number will always be equal to n)	

Figure 3.6 has a lot of empty spaces (representing the large number of rows with a frequency of 0) and may be too complex to be a useful model. Therefore, we are going to create another histogram in which some of the intervals are combined. Instead of intervals that are 1 unit wide, we are going to create intervals that are 5 units wide. This will make the blank histogram appear as shown in Figure 3.7.

Now, because the interval width has changed, it is necessary to recount how many subjects have an age between each new interval's boundaries. The first interval ranges from 9.5 to 14.5

Table 3.8

Sibling age	Frequency	Frequency proportion	Cumulative frequency	Cumulative proportion
10	1	1 / 13 = .077	1	1 / 13 = .077
11	1	1 / 13 = .077	1 + 1 = 2	2 / 13 = .154
13	1	1 / 13 = .077	1 + 1 + 1 = 3	3 / 13 = .231
18	3	3 / 13 = .231	1 + 1 + 1 + 3 = 6	6 / 13 = .462
19	1	1 / 13 = .077	1 + 1 + 1 + 3 + 1 = 7	7 / 13 = .538
21	2	2 / 13 = .154	1 + 1 + 1 + 3 + 1 + 2 = 9	9 / 13 = .692
30	1	1 / 13 = .077	1 + 1 + 1 + 3 + 1 + 2 + 1 = 10	10 / 13 = .769
37	2	2 / 13 = .154	1 + 1 + 1 + 3 + 1 + 2 + 1 + 2 = 12	12 / 13 = .923
38	1	1 / 13 = .077	1 + 1 + 1 + 3 + 1 + 2 + 1 + 2 + 1 = 13	13 / 13 = 1.000
Total	13	13 / 13 = 1.000	13 (this number will always be equal to *n*)	13 / 13 = 1.000

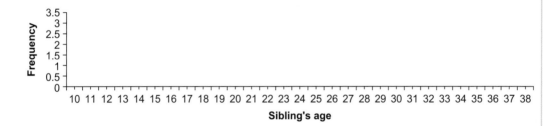

Figure 3.5 Blank example histogram.

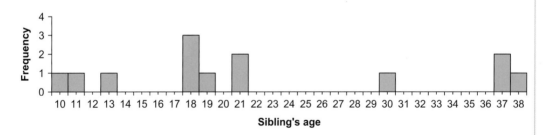

Figure 3.6 Histogram representing siblings' ages from the Waite et al. (2005) study.

(because this was the range of the interval boundaries for the first five intervals of Figure 3.6, when each interval was 1 unit wide). According to the frequency table, there were three siblings with ages in this range. The next interval (from 14.5 to 19.5) had four siblings in it. Counting the frequencies within each interval and drawing the results produces the histogram shown in Figure 3.8.

Figure 3.8 has fewer intervals, making it a simpler visual model than what was shown in Figure 3.6. This makes it easier to understand, even though it sacrifices some detail. Whether it is appropriate to reduce the number of bars in a histogram is a subjective decision. There is no right or wrong answer necessarily, although too few bars will make a histogram provide little useful information, while too many bars may make it too complex to be useful.

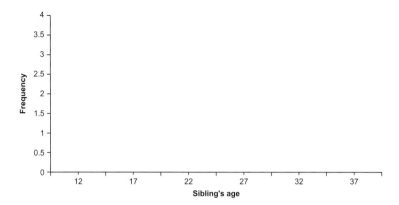

Figure 3.7 Blank histogram with interval size of 5.

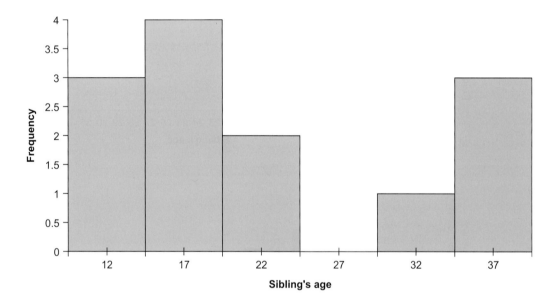

Figure 3.8 Histogram of sibling's ages from the Waite et al. (2015) study with intervals that are 5 units wide.

Describing Shapes of Histograms

Histograms can take on many shapes, and a special terminology has been developed to describe them. One way to describe distributions is in terms of how symmetrical they are; another is in terms of the height of parts of the distribution. Both ways of describing distributions require a standard to compare against. That standard is the normal distribution.

The Normal Distribution. The normal distribution is a special distribution, as shown in Figure 3.9. The normal distribution has several characteristics, all of which are apparent in Figure 3.9:

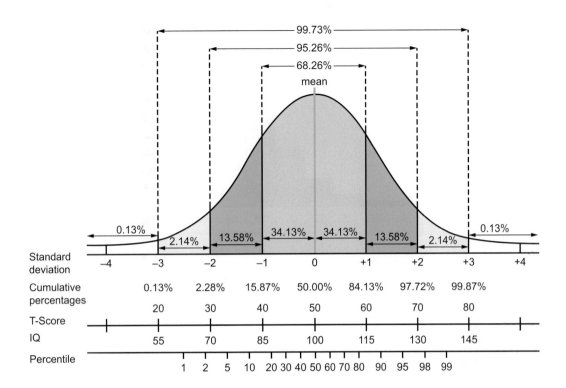

Figure 3.9 The normal distribution. Notice how (1) the distribution is symmetrical; (2) the peak is in the exact middle of the distribution; (3) the mean, median, and mode are equal; and (4) the tails of the curve never touch the horizontal axis.

- The normal distribution is a symmetrical histogram. In other words, the left and right halves of the distribution are mirror images of one another.
- The peak is in the exact middle of the distribution.
- Mean = median = mode.
- The tails of the distribution never touch the *x*-axis. This means that the normal distribution theoretically extends from $-\infty$ to $+\infty$.

Figure 3.9 is a histogram. However, it differs from other histograms (e.g., Figures 3.3 and 3.8) in that it appears to consist of a smooth curve, instead of boxy intervals. This is because the normal distribution is idealized; instead of a limited number of intervals, the normal distribution theoretically has an infinite number of intervals, all of which are extremely narrow. When viewed together, the intervals lose their boxiness and instead appear as a smooth curve. (A computer screen has much the same effect, where square pixels can combine to form smooth curves when viewed from a distance.)

The normal distribution was originally observed in data from the physical sciences, especially astronomy. But in the nineteenth century scientists noticed that measurements of human beings were often normally distributed (Patel & Read, 1996). One of the first people to realize this was the Belgian mathematician Lambert Adolphe Jacques Quetelet (1796–1874), who was one of the world's first social scientists. Quetelet collected measurements of soldiers' chest circumferences and found that they resembled the normal distribution (Stigler, 1986). Quetelet's data are displayed

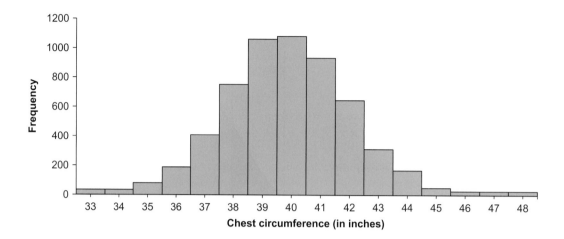

Figure 3.10 Chest circumference of nineteenth-century Scottish soldiers, a dataset that Quetelet used to demonstrate that some human characteristics are normally distributed. Quetelet took the data from a Scottish medical journal. This figure is based on data reported by Stigler (1986, p. 208), who corrected some arithmetic errors in Quetelet's original report.

as a histogram in Figure 3.10. Since Quetelet's day, scientists have realized that other human characteristics form histograms that resemble a normal distribution (see Sidebar 5.1).

Sidebar 3.2 Normally and non-normally distributed variables

Many variables that scientists examine are normally distributed – or very closely normal. Some normally distributed variables include the length of pregnancies (Baskett & Nagele, 2000), height, weight, body mass index, and head circumference (Cole, Freeman, & Preece, 1998). Generally, normally distributed variables tend to be either (1) randomly determined, or (2) determined by a large number of small influences that combine together (such as characteristics that are created by many genes). Chapter 6 will show how random variables become normally distributed.

The examples of normally distributed variables listed above are all biological or physical measurements. Since Quetelet's time, scientists have made measurements of large samples of people in order to build histograms like the one in Figure 3.10. These histograms showed that some physical variables are normally distributed. But in the social sciences we often work with variables that are harder to measure. This can make it more difficult to say that the distribution of a personality trait like extraversion is normal than it is to conclude that the distribution of heights is normal. After all, it is easy to measure height; there is more disagreement about how to measure personality. So, most social scientists often assume that their variables are normally distributed (or somewhat normally distributed) unless there is reason to believe otherwise. However, some experts (e.g., Micceri, 1989) strongly disagree with this practice and believe that researchers should assume their data are non-normal unless they can show that the data are normally distributed. After sufficient advances in data collection techniques and debate, some social science variables seem to be normally distributed when measured well in a healthy sample representative of the population, such as intelligence (Jensen, 1998) or mathematical knowledge (Warne, Godwin, & Smith, 2013).

But it is still important to keep in mind that not every variable is normally distributed. Income (Department for Work and Pensions, 2015), the number of children in a household (US Census

Bureau, 2013), and reaction time (Der & Deary, 2006) are examples of variables that are almost always severely non-normal. The easiest way to determine whether a variable resembles the normal distribution or not is to build a histogram and see whether the result is similar to Figure 3.9.

The normal distribution is also important because it is the standard that we compare other distributions to. There are two ways to compare distributions to the normal distribution: skewness and kurtosis. In the rest of this section we will discuss how to make these comparisons.

Sidebar 3.3 Deriving the normal distribution

The normal distribution can be graphed as an equation:

$$f(x) = \frac{e^{\frac{-(x-\mu)^2}{2}}}{\sqrt{2\pi\sigma^2}}$$

Selecting any value for the population mean (μ) and standard deviation (σ) will produce a bell-shaped normal distribution centered on μ. If the mean of the population is 0 and the standard deviation is 1, then the equation simplifies to:

$$f(x) = \frac{e^{\frac{-x^2}{2}}}{\sqrt{2\pi}}$$

These equations can be used to estimate the frequency of any value of a score x that is plugged into the equations. Most students in the social sciences will not need to work with these equations. But these equations are still useful to know. I present them solely to help readers understand where the normal distribution comes from and how it is mathematically defined.

Skewness. The first way to describe distributions is in terms of their **skewness**, which is the degree to which a histogram or distribution is non-symmetrical. A symmetrical distribution is a distribution that can be divided into two halves that are mirror images of one another. The normal distribution in Figure 3.9 is symmetrical, with the left and right halves being mirror images of each other.

Skewness is calculated through the following formula:

$$Skewness = \frac{\sum(x_i - \overline{X})^3}{(n-1)s^3} \qquad \text{(Formula 3.2)}$$

This formula is included for reference purposes only (see Chapter 4 for explanations of the symbols Σ, x_i, $\overline{X}$, n, and s). If the skewness value is equal to 0, then the distribution is symmetrical. Figure 3.9, which shows the normal distribution, is an example of a symmetrical distribution. Figure 3.11 is another example of a symmetrical distribution (the specific type of distribution in Figure 3.11 is called a **uniform distribution** because all its bars are of uniform, or the same, height). Another term for a symmetrical distribution is an *unskewed* distribution. Unskewed distributions can take many shapes, so long as they are symmetrical.

If the skewness value is less than zero, then the distribution is **negatively skewed**. A negatively skewed distribution has a longer tail on the left side and the peak is closer to the right side. An example of a negatively skewed distribution is Figure 3.12, which shows the college grade-point averages (GPAs) of undergraduates who were hoping to go to medical school. The skewness value for this distribution is –1.04. Another term for a negatively skewed distribution is *skewed left*.

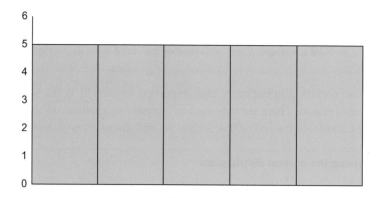

Figure 3.11 An example of an unskewed distribution. The third bar is the median of the data that divides the histogram into left and right halves of the distribution. The left half and the right half are mirror images of each other, which means that skewness = 0 for these data. Some experts call a distribution like this a uniform distribution because the bars for each interval all have a uniform (i.e., equal) height.

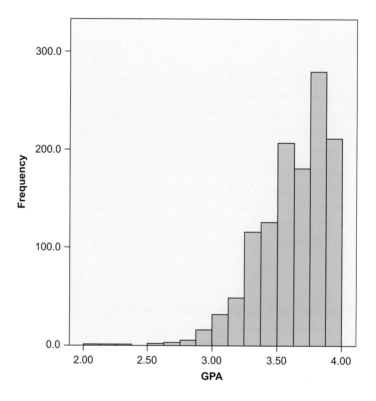

Figure 3.12 A negatively skewed histogram of the college grade-point averages (GPAs) of 1,323 undergraduate pre-medical students. The range of possible GPAs is 0 to 4, but all the students scored at least 2.0. Because most of these students were hard-working and bright, high GPAs were common – as demonstrated by the peak on the right side of the distribution. The long tail on the left side of the distribution is one of the reasons why this distribution is negatively skewed. For these data, skewness = −1.04, and kurtosis = 1.70. Data from Warne, Nagaishi, Slade, Hermesmeyer, and Peck (2014).

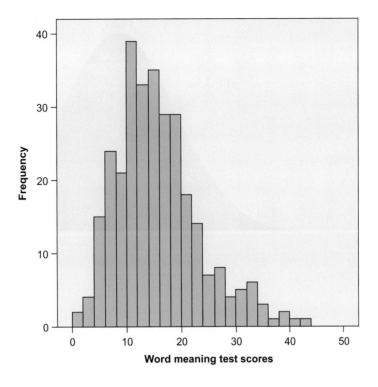

Figure 3.13 A positively skewed histogram of 301 children's scores on a test of word knowledge. Most scores cluster around the median (near the peak on the left side), but a small number of subjects know the meaning of many more words than the typical subject (as shown by the longer tail on the right side of the distribution). For these data, skewness = 0.87, and kurtosis = 0.88. Data from Holzinger and Swineford (1939).

If the skewness value for a distribution is greater than 0, then the distribution is **positively skewed**. A positively skewed distribution has a longer tail on the right side and the peak on the left side. An example of a positively skewed distribution is Figure 3.13, which shows a histogram of scores on a test of knowledge of word meanings. The skewness value for this distribution is 0.87. Another term for a positively skewed distribution is *skewed right*.

Check Yourself!

- Why are normal distributions useful?

- Normal distributions are unskewed. But are there distributions that are unskewed *and* non-normal?

- What type of distribution has a peak on the right side of the distribution and a longer tail on the left side?

- What is the term for a distribution that has a peak on the left side of the distribution and a longer tail on the right side?

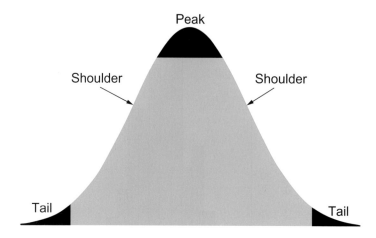

Figure 3.14 Schematic showing the location of the peak, shoulders, and tails of a distribution. This is a normal distribution.

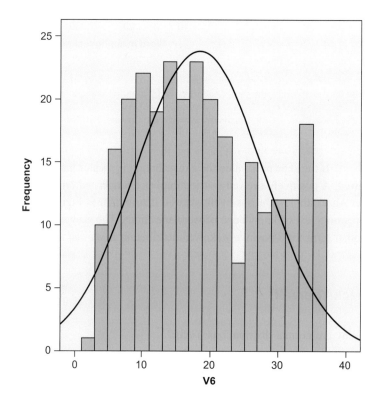

Figure 3.15 A platykurtic distribution of sentence completion scores in children. Notice how the peak is about the same height as in the normal distribution, but the shoulders are taller than in the normal distribution. It also has tails that are shorter than what would be expected in a normal distribution. Because several of the bars are roughly the same height, the name "platykurtic" (from the Greek word for "flat," see Sidebar 3.5) is appropriate for this distribution. For these data, skewness = 0.292, kurtosis = −1.022. Data adapted from Holzinger and Swineford (1939).

Kurtosis. Another way a distribution can be described is in terms of its **kurtosis**, which compares the height of three parts of the distribution to the corresponding parts of a normal distribution with the same mean and standard deviation. Those three parts are the peak, the shoulders, and the tails. Figure 3.14 shows the location of each of these parts on a normal distribution. The peak is the tallest part of a distribution; the tails are the ends of the distribution; and the shoulders are the parts of a distribution that are between the peak and the tails.

There are three terms that describe the kurtosis of a distribution: platykurtic, leptokurtic, and mesokurtic. Kurtosis values are calculated as:

$$Kurtosis = \frac{\sum (x_i - \overline{X})^4}{(n-1)s^4} - 3 \qquad \text{(Formula 3.3)}$$

Like the skewness formula (Formula 3.2), Formula 3.3 is included for reference purposes only (see Chapter 4 for explanations of the symbols Σ, x_i, $\overline{X}$, n, and s). If the kurtosis value is less than 0, then the distribution is platykurtic. A **platykurtic** distribution has a peak and tails that are shorter than in a normal distribution and "shoulders" that are taller than in a normal distribution (DeCarlo, 1997). Figure 3.14 shows an example of a platykurtic distribution with the peak, tails, and shoulders labeled. As a reference, the normal distribution has been placed on top of the histogram. It is clear in Figure 3.15 that the peak and tails are shorter than in the normal distribution, while the histogram intervals in the shoulders are taller than in the normal distribution.

When kurtosis is equal to 0, the distribution is mesokurtic. A mesokurtic distribution has a peak, shoulders, and tails that are as tall as in normal distribution. An example of a mesokurtic distribution is Quetelet's data in Figure 3.10, which have a kurtosis value of 0.03 – close enough to 0 to be considered mesokurtic.

Sidebar 3.4   **How close is "close enough" to 0 for skewness and kurtosis?**

Skewness values of 0 represent unskewed distributions, and kurtosis values of 0 represent mesokurtic distributions. But, as Quetelet's data show, real-world data are rarely perfectly normal (Micceri, 1989), with skewness or kurtosis values equal to exactly 0. There is no universally accepted range of skewness and kurtosis values that are "close enough" to 0 for a distribution to be considered unskewed or mesokurtic. In an examination of nearly 700 datasets, one team of researchers decided that values of ±0.25 were close enough to 0 for a distribution to be considered unskewed and mesokurtic, though they also recognized that ±0.75 was a justifiable cutoff, too (Blanca, Arnau, López-Montiel, Bono, & Bendayan, 2013). Research shows that these guidelines are realistic in many cases, though they may not be appropriate for all samples (Jones, 1969).

If the kurtosis value is greater than 0, then the distribution is leptokurtic. A **leptokurtic** distribution is the opposite of a platykurtic distribution. In other words, it has a peak and tails that are taller than a normal distribution's and shoulders that are shorter. Figure 3.16 shows an example of a leptokurtic distribution. As a reference, the normal distribution has been placed on top of the histogram. The figure shows how the tails and peak are taller than the normal distribution's tails and peak, while the shoulders are shorter than the normal distribution's shoulders. Figure 3.12 is another example of a leptokurtic distribution because its kurtosis is equal to 1.70.

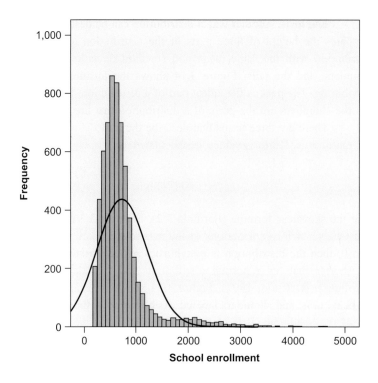

Figure 3.16 A highly leptokurtic distribution. Notice how the peak of the histogram and the right tail are taller than the peak of the normal distribution. (The distribution is too skewed for it to have a left tail.) The shoulders are shorter than the shoulders of the normal distribution. The distribution shows the number of students enrolled at public schools in Texas. For these data, skewness = 2.86, and kurtosis = 10.86. Data from Warne and Price (2016).

Sidebar 3.5 **Memory aid**

It can be hard to remember all of the terms to describe the shape of distributions. The purpose of this sidebar is to give you a few tips to memorize the technical terms discussed in this chapter.

For skewness terms (i.e., negatively skewed and positively skewed), the important aspect is which side the *tail* is on. For negatively skewed distributions, the tail of the distribution is on the left, and for positively skewed distributions the tail of the distribution is on the right. If you remember that on a number line negative numbers are on the *left* of zero, and positive numbers are on the *right* of zero, then the names "negatively skewed" and "positively skewed" are easier to remember.

For kurtosis, the origin of the terms "platykurtic," "mesokurtic," and "leptokurtic" hold keys to memorizing their meanings:

- The term "platykurtic" comes from an ancient Greek word meaning "flat." Other English words that come from the same ancient Greek word include "plateau" (a relatively flat piece of land that is more elevated than the surrounding land), "plate" (a flat serving dish), and "platypus" (an Australian mammal with a flat bill). Therefore, platykurtic distributions tend to be short and flat.
- The term "mesokurtic" comes from an ancient Greek word meaning "middle." Other English words that come from the same ancient Greek word include "Mesoamerica" (another term for Central America), "Mesopotamia" (an area of the Middle East that is between the Tigris and Euphrates rivers), and "Mesozoic" (the middle of the three eras in the Earth's Phanerozoic eon).

Therefore, mesokurtic distributions tend to be middle height – taller than platykurtic distributions but shorter than leptokurtic distributions.

- "Leptokurtic" comes from an ancient Greek word meaning "thin." There are no common words in English that use the "lepto-" prefix, but several scientific terms in biology are derived from this term. All of these words refer to some thin or skinny aspect of an organism. Leptokurtic distributions, therefore, are tall and have peaks that are thin. If you still want a way to remember that leptokurtic distributions, you can think of the histogram as being like a tall hurdle that someone must *leap* over.

The terms for the number of peaks can also be remembered through understanding the origins of the words "unimodal" and "bimodal." A unimodal distribution has one peak, which is appropriate because "uni-" means "one" (as in "unicycle," "unicorn," and "unity"). Likewise, a bimodal distribution has two peaks, which makes sense because "bi-" means "two" (as in "bicycle," "bifocals," and "biweekly").

Number of Peaks

Another way to describe distributions is to describe the number of peaks that the histogram has. A distribution with a single peak is called a **unimodal** distribution. All of the distributions in the chapter so far (including the normal distribution in Figure 3.9 and Quetelet's data in Figure 3.10) are unimodal distributions because they have one peak. The term "-modal" refers to the most common score in a distribution, a concept explained in further detail in Chapter 4.

Sometimes distributions have two peaks, as in Figure 3.17. When a distribution has two peaks, it is called a **bimodal** distribution. In the social sciences most distributions have only one peak, but bimodal distributions like the one in Figure 3.17 occur occasionally, as in Lacritz et al.'s (2004) study that found that people's test scores on a test of visual short-term memory were bimodal. In that case the peaks of the histograms were at the two extreme ends of the distribution – meaning people tended to have very poor or very good recognition of pictures they had seen earlier. Bimodal distributions can occur when a sample consists of two different groups (as when some members of a sample have had a treatment and the other sample members have not).

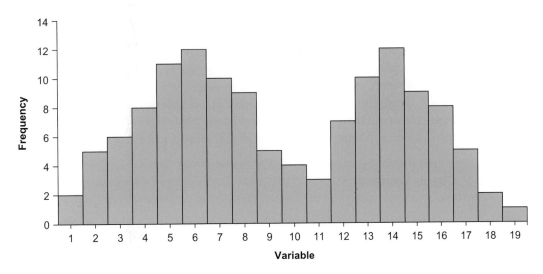

Figure 3.17 A bimodal distribution of theoretical data. Notice how the two peaks (at 6 and 14) are the same height. In these hypothetical data, the distribution has a skewness value of 0.07, and a kurtosis value of −1.27.

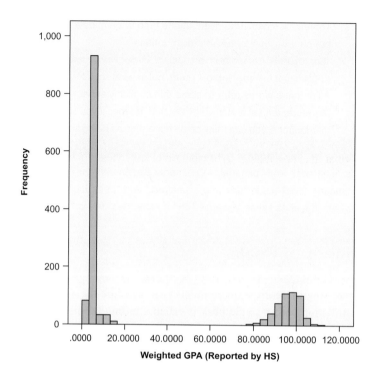

Figure 3.18 An example of real data with a bimodal distribution where the two peaks are not the same height. The left peak is clearly much higher than the right peak. But many social scientists would still consider this histogram bimodal because there is a clear gap between the two peaks. In fact, there were no people in this dataset with a score between 15 and 70. Scores were students' GPAs reported by their high schools – each of which had its own unique method of calculating GPAs. Data from Warne, Nagaishi et al. (2014).

In the strictest definition of the word, "bimodal" indicates that the two peaks of the histogram should be the exact same height, as they are in the idealized example of Figure 3.17. However, most people use the word "bimodal" for any distribution that has two peaks, even if those peaks are not equally tall (e.g., Micceri, 1989). Indeed, bimodal distributions of real data do not usually have peaks that are precisely the same height. Figure 3.18 is an example of a distribution where one peak is clearly not as tall as the other. But because of the distinct gap between the two groups of scores, many people would still consider this a bimodal distribution.

Finally, it is theoretically possible that a distribution could have more than three or more peaks (perhaps called a "trimodal" or "multimodal" distribution), but this is extremely unusual in the social sciences. Almost all distributions of real social science data are unimodal or bimodal.

Check Yourself!

- Describe the type of distribution shape that you can expect from a positive kurtosis value.

- What word is used to describe a distribution with a generally flat shape and negative kurtosis?

- What is the difference between a unimodal and a bimodal distribution?

Describing Distribution Shapes: A Caveat

Skewness, kurtosis, and the number of peaks can all be used to describe the shape of a distribution. As stated above, a normal distribution has a skewness value of 0 and a kurtosis value of 0, and it is unimodal. However, it is important to remember that there are other requirements that make a distribution normal, such as having an equal mean, median, and mode. Therefore, if a distribution has a skewness value of 0, a kurtosis value of 0, and a single peak, that is *not* proof that the distribution is normal. It is possible for a distribution to have these characteristics and still be non-normal.

Frequency Polygons

A visual model very similar to a histogram is the **frequency polygon**. Like the histogram, a frequency polygon is a visual model that has the frequency on the vertical axis (i.e., *y*-axis) and the variable scores on the horizontal axis (i.e., the *x*-axis). However, instead of using vertical bars to show the frequency of each value of the variable, a person making a frequency polygon plots a dot in the middle of each interval and then connects the dots with straight lines. An example of a frequency polygon is shown in Figure 3.19, which uses the same data from the Waite et al. (2015) study as Figure 3.1.

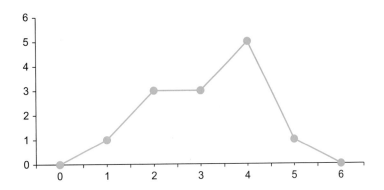

Figure 3.19 A frequency polygon for the data shown in Table 3.1. The height of each bar is the frequency of that response. For the responses, 1 = strongly disagree, 2 = disagree, 3 = neutral, 4 = agree, and 5 = strongly agree. Responses 0 and 6 were not available for subjects to select, so the frequencies for those responses are 0.

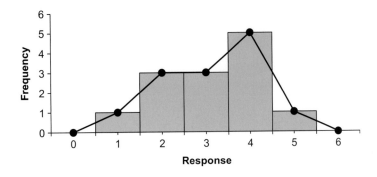

Figure 3.20 A frequency polygon displayed on top of a histogram. Both visual models display the data from Table 3.1.

Because Figures 3.1 and 3.19 were created with the same data and use the same axes, they have some similarities. First, the highest dot on the frequency polygon is for response 4 – which also has the highest bar on the histogram. In fact, the pattern of high and low dots on the frequency polygon will be the same as the pattern of high and low bars on the histogram. This is apparent in Figure 3.20, which shows the histogram (i.e., Figure 3.1) and the frequency polygon (i.e., Figure 3.19) on the same axis. This shows how similar both visual models are.

The only characteristic of a frequency polygon that does not apply to a histogram is that a frequency polygon should begin and end with an interval that has a frequency of zero. This is to ensure that the frequency polygon touches the *x*-axis and makes a polygon that is fully enclosed.

Frequency polygons are not as common as histograms, but frequency polygons have one distinct advantage: multiple frequency polygons can be displayed in the same picture. This requires putting the different frequency polygons on top of each other. Placing multiple frequency polygons in the same visual model facilitates comparisons across variables.

Box Plot

Another alternative to the histogram is a box plot (also called a box-and-whisker plot), which is a visual model that shows how spread out or compact the scores in a dataset are. An example of a box plot is shown in Figure 3.21, which represents the age of the subjects in the Waite et al. (2015) study. In a box plot, there are two components: the box (which is the rectangle at the center of the figure) and the fences (which are the vertical lines extending from the box). The middle 50% of scores are represented by the box. For the subject age data from the Waite et al. (2015) dataset, the middle 50% of scores range from 21 to 31, so the box shown in Figure 3.21 extends from 21 to 31. Inside the box is a horizontal line, which represents the score that is in the exact middle, which is 24. The lower

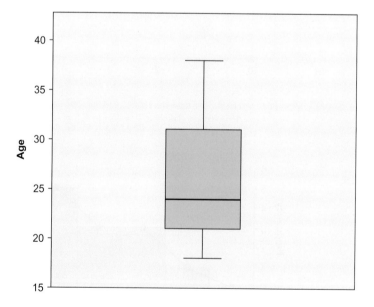

Figure 3.21 A box plot showing the distribution of the subjects' ages in the Waite et al. (2015) study. The thick horizontal line in the middle of the box is the middle score. The box encompasses the middle 50% of scores. The fences (i.e., the lines protruding above and below the box) extend to the lowest score and to the highest score.

fence extends from the bottom of the box to the minimum score (which is 18). The upper fence extends from the top of the box to the maximum score (which is 38).

The example in Figure 3.21 shows some useful characteristics of box plots that are not always apparent in histograms. First, the box plot shows the exact middle of the scores. Second, the box plot shows how far the minimum and maximum scores are from the middle of the data. Finally, it is easy to see how spread out the compact the scores in a dataset are. Figure 3.21 shows that the oldest subjects in the Waite et al. (2015) study are further from the middle of the dataset than the youngest subjects are. This is apparent because the upper fence is much longer than the lower fence – indicating that the maximum score is much further from the middle 50% of scores than the minimum score is.

Like frequency polygons, box plots have the advantage of being useful for displaying multiple variables in the same picture. This is done by displaying box plots side by side. Formatting multiple box plots in the same figure makes it easy to determine which variable(s) have higher means and wider ranges of scores.

Check Yourself!

- How are frequency polygons similar to histograms?

- What does the horizontal line in a box plot represent?

- In a box plot, what percentage of scores is inside the box?

- In a box plot, what do the fences represent?

- What percentage of scores are inside each fence?

Bar Graphs

Another visual model that is similar to a histogram is a bar graph. Figure 3.22 shows a bar graph for the variable of subject sex in the Waite et al. (2015) study. The major visual difference between

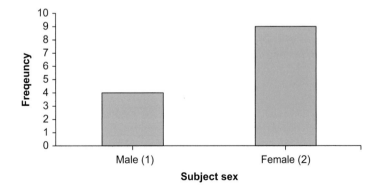

Figure 3.22 Bar graph showing the frequency that subjects in the Waite et al. (2015) study reported they were male (left bar) or female (right bar). Raw data are displayed in Table 3.1. Notice that the bars do not touch because the variable is not continuous.

a histogram and a bar graph is that in a bar graph the bars do not touch. This is because a bar graph is used to display discrete data. In other words, because biological sex is a nominal variable, it doesn't make sense to think of a bar as spanning a range of variable values or that the variable is continuous.

Bar graphs are best for displaying discrete data, which include nominal variables and some ordinal variables. For continuous data (i.e., ratio and interval variables, and some ordinal variables), a histogram is best.

Stem-and-Leaf Plots

Another visual model that some people use to display their data is the **stem-and-leaf plot**, an example of which is shown on the right side of Figure 3.23. This figure shows the age of the subjects from Table 3.1. The left column is the tens place (e.g., the 2 in the number 20), and the other columns represent the ones place (e.g., the 0 in the number 20) of each person's age. Each digit on the right side of the visual model represents a single person. To read an individual's score, you take the number in the left column and combine it with a number on the other side of the graph. For example, the youngest person in this sample was 18 years old, as shown by the 1 in the left column and the 8 on the right side of the model. The next youngest person was 19 years old (as represented by the 1 in the left column and the 9 in the same row on the right side of the visual model). The stem-and-leaf also shows that seven people were between 20 and 25 years old and that the oldest person was 38 years old. In a way, this stem-and-leaf plot resembles a histogram that has been turned on its side, with each interval 10 years wide.

Stem-and-leaf plots can be convenient, but, compared to histograms, they have limitations. Large datasets can result in stem-and-leaf plots that are cumbersome and hard to read. They can also be problematic if scores for a variable span a wide range of values (e.g., some scores in single digits and other scores in double or triple digits) or precisely measured variables where a large number of subjects have scores that are decimals or fractions.

Before personal computers were widespread, stem-and-leaf plots were more common because they were easy to create on a typewriter. As computer software was created that was capable of generating histograms, frequency polygons, and box plots automatically, stem-and-leaf plots gradually lost popularity. Still, they occasionally show up in modern social science research articles (e.g., Acar, Sen, & Cayirdag, 2016, p. 89; Linn, Graue, & Sanders, 1990, p. 9; Paek, Abdulla, & Cramond, 2016, p. 125).

Original data	Stem-and-leaf plot
18 19	1 89
20 21 23 23 24 24 25	2 0133445
31 33 35 38	3 1358

Figure 3.23 Stem-and-leaf plot for the age of the subjects in the Waite et al. (2015) study. Data taken from Table 3.1.

Guided Practice 3.2

The subjects in Waite et al.'s (2015) study also reported the age of their sibling with autism. The ages they reported (from Table 3.1) were as follows:

| 10 | 11 | 13 | 18 | 18 | 18 | 19 | 21 | 21 | 30 | 37 | 37 | 38 |

      Just as in Figure 3.23, we are going to make the stem of the plot the "tens" digit of each score and the leaves will be made up of the "ones" digit of each score. The first step is to identify all of the first digits for the scores. Because the ages range from 10 to 38, all of the scores begin with 1, 2, or 3. These numbers will serve as the stem of the visual model:

1
2
3

For the sake of convenience, I am going to put the numbers that begin with each digit in parentheses to the right of the stem:

1	(10)	(11)	(13)	(18)	(18)	(18)	(19)
2	(21)	(21)
3	(30)	(37)	(37)	(38)

To build the leaves, we need to eliminate the first digit from the scores in each row:

1	(0)	(1)	(3)	(8)	(8)	(8)	(9)
2	(1)	(1)
3	(0)	(7)	(7)	(8)

The remaining digits will serve as the leaves. To create the leaves we need to eliminate the parentheses and squish the remaining digits together:

1   0138889
2   11
3   0778

What remains is our stem-and-leaf plot. The plot shows that most respondents in this study had a sibling who was between the ages of 10 and 19. But a few respondents had a sibling with autism who was in their twenties or thirties.

Check Yourself!

- What is the major visual difference between a bar graph and a histogram?

- What level of data is most appropriate to use with a bar graph?

- Which other visual model is most like a stem-and-leaf graph?

Line Graphs

Another common visual model for quantitative data is the **line graph**. Like a frequency polygon, line graphs are created by using straight-line segments to connect data points to one another. However, a line graph does not have to represent continuous values of a single variable (as in a frequency polygon and histogram) or begin and end with a frequency of zero. Line graphs can also be used to show trends and differences across time or across nominal or ordinal categories.

Since their invention over 200 years ago, line graphs have been recognized as being extremely useful for showing trends over time (Friendly & Denis, 2005). When using it for this purpose, the creator of the line graph should use the horizontal axis to indicate time and the vertical axis to indicate the value of the variable being graphed. An example of this type of line graph is shown in Figure 3.24, which shows the murder rates in the five most populous Canadian provinces over the course of 5 years. Line graphs are also occasionally used to illustrate differences among categories or to display several variables at once. The latter purpose is common for line graphs because bar graphs and histograms can get too messy and complex when displaying more than one variable.

Pie Charts

A **pie chart** is useful for showing percentages and proportions. An example of a pie chart using data from the Waite et al. (2015) study is displayed in Figure 3.25. It shows that 31% of subjects in the study were male, and 69% of subjects were female. With this visual model, it is very easy to see that females were a majority of participants in the study.

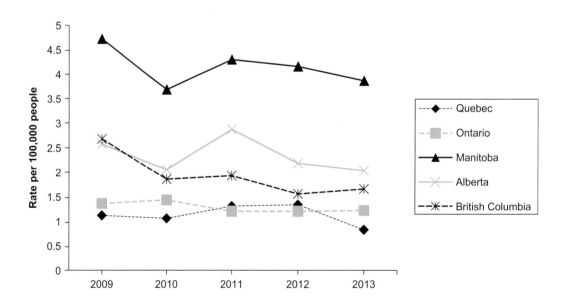

Figure 3.24 Example of a line graph. *Statistics Canada.* Table 253-0001 - Homicide survey, number and rates (per 100,000 population) of homicide victims, Canada, provinces and territories, annual, CANSIM (database). (accessed: 2015-08-17)

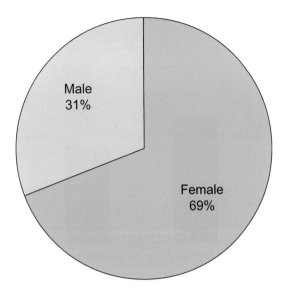

Figure 3.25 Pie chart showing the percentage of subjects in each sex. Data from the Waite et al. (2015) study. See Table 3.1.

Sidebar 3.6 **Misleading charts and graphs**

Visual models are very useful for helping people understand their data, but sometimes they can be misleading. This sidebar shows a few ways in which people can create charts and graphs that are misleading. The purpose of this section is not to teach you how to make a deceptive chart, but rather to show you the ways that people sometimes create charts that mislead their audience. By being aware of how charts can be deceptive, you can avoid being fooled by a poorly designed visual model.

Distorted Axis. One common way to make a distorted visual model is to either squish or stretch an axis. This can either exaggerate or minimize apparent differences between groups. One example of this is shown below, which is adapted from an American motor vehicle company's advertisement in 1992 boasting that more of its trucks were operational after 10 years than those of its competitor. The company supported its claim with a bar graph similar to the one in Figure 3.26a.

A more accurate representation of this same information is shown in Figure 3.26b. This visual model better represents the data because the vertical axis starts at 0%. In its version of the graph, the company started its y-axis at 95%, and the slight differences between the companies were exaggerated. Figure 3.26b shows why Company A created a misleading graph: the more accurate version is a much less compelling advertisement.

Incorrect Graph Type. Distorted axes are one way to create a misleading visual model. Using the incorrect graph type is another. One news organization created a pie chart similar to the one in Figure 3.27 where poll respondents were permitted to support more than one candidate in an upcoming election. This pie chart is misleading because it implies that if these three candidates were to face off in an election the outcome would be very close (as demonstrated by the similar size of each candidate's slice of the pie). However, it is obvious that these percentages add up to more than 100%. (Such an evident error indicates that this misleading pie chart was not created with the intention of deceiving the public.) A better visual model would have been a bar graph.

(a)

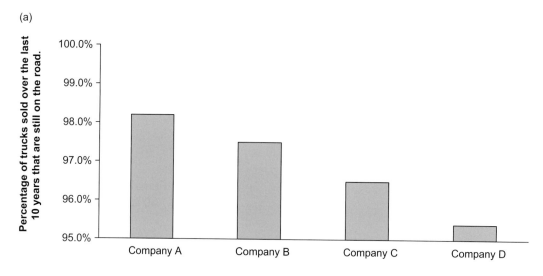

Figure 3.26a Example of a misleading bar graph. This graph is based on an actual advertisement produced by Company A.

(b)

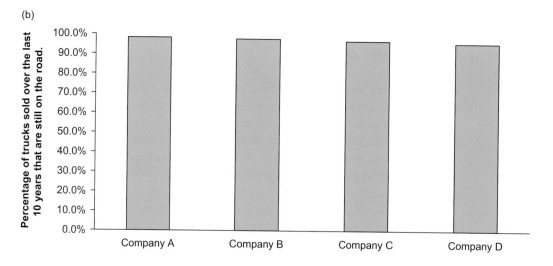

Figure 3.26b A more accurate visual model for the same data from Figure 3.26a. This graph is based on an actual advertisement produced by Company A.

Scatterplots

Every visual model in this chapter so far has shown how to display data from one variable at a time. However, many social science students are interested in more than one variable at a time. The most common way to display data from two variables at once is the **scatterplot** (also called a *scattergram*). In a scatterplot, each variable is represented by an axis, with the independent variable on the horizontal axis and the dependent variable on the vertical axis. Each person in the sample is

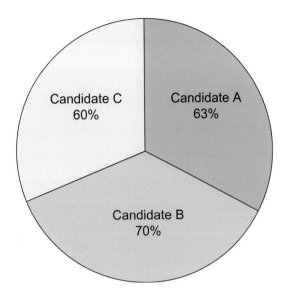

Figure 3.27 A misleading pie chart. This chart – based on a real poll about a national American election – is incorrect because the percentages add up to 193%. A more appropriate visual model would be a bar graph.

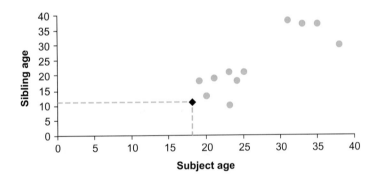

Figure 3.28 Example scatterplot showing data from Table 3.1. In this visual model each dot represents a person. The diamond represents the subject with ID no. 11. The dashed lines show how that subject's dot is at the location where their age (18) and their sibling's age (11) meet. There are 13 people in the study, but the scatterplot has 12 dots because two people (ID nos 1 and 7) have the same age and same sibling's age, meaning that one dot is on top of the other. This makes their data appear as one dot.

represented by a dot, and the dots are plotted at the coordinates that correspond to each person's score on the two variables.

An example of a scatterplot is shown in Figure 3.28, which shows data from the Waite et al. (2015) study. The youngest subject in the study was 18 and her sibling was 11, so this person is represented by a point at the coordinates (18, 11) in the scatterplot. This person is represented as a diamond in the scatterplot, along with two dashed lines that show how that person's point is at the location where a vertical line at 18 (the subject's age) and a horizontal line at 11 (the sibling's age) meet.

The scatterplot is useful for understanding data because it may show general relationships between variables (something that will be discussed at length in Chapter 12). For example, in Figure 3.28 it is apparent that people in the study tend to be close to the age of their sibling with autism. Scatterplots can also show groupings of individuals. Figure 3.28 shows that the majority of subjects in the study are in their late teens or early twenties, while a second, smaller group is in their thirties.

Check Yourself!

- What type of information is best to display with a line graph?
- What is the visual difference between a line graph and a frequency polygon?
- What type of information is best to display in a pie chart?
- What is the advantage that scatterplots have over other visual models described in this chapter?

Selecting the Proper Visual Model

In Chapter 2 we learned that certain statistical methods are only appropriate for particular levels of data. The same is true for visual models. Table 3.9 shows which level or levels of data are appropriate for each visual model. The table also shows other considerations that might be relevant when choosing a visual model.

Other Visual Models

With advances in technology since the 1990s, the number of visual models available to data analysts has exploded. One exciting development is the use of geographic information, which has

Table 3.9 Appropriate levels of data for visual models

Visual model	Appropriate level(s) of data	Other considerations
Frequency table	Nominal, ordinal, interval, and ratio	More detailed than a histogram, but may become unwieldy.
Histogram	Ordinal, interval, and ratio	
Frequency polygon	Ordinal, interval, and ratio	Provides same information as a histogram.
Stem-and-leaf plot	Interval and ratio	More detailed than a histogram, but may become unwieldy.
Line graphs	Trend data (and sometimes other types of data)	
Pie charts	Nominal, ordinal, interval, and ratio	Percentages must add up to 100%. Counts must add up to the total sample size.
Scatterplot	Interval and ratio	Shows sample members' scores for two variables at once.

resulted in cartograms, interactive maps, and other interesting developments. For example, one of my students created an interactive map (at http://bit.ly/APtestmap) that permits users to examine the popularity of different Advanced Placement tests in different US states. Another great example of interactivity is the Baby Name Voyager (www.babynamewizard.com/voyager), which shows how baby names have changed in the United States since the late 1800s. The Baby Name Voyager permits users to explore broad trends (like how the number of girls' names has expanded much faster than the number of boys' names) or trends in individual names. These examples show how visual models can now be interactive and adapt to the viewer's interests and needs. The website Flowing Data (http://flowingdata.com/) is a blog that collects examples of visual models, many of which are interactive and combine many sources of data that help users see patterns and other interesting information.

Summary

Like all models, visual models are a simplified version of reality. Visual models are useful in helping people understand their data.

The frequency table is one of the most important visual models. A frequency table shows the number of subjects in a dataset who have each score for a variable. Frequency tables can also show the proportion or percentage of subjects who have each score for a variable.

Another important visual model is the histogram, which shows the frequency of scores by the height of bars. We can classify histograms in three ways: skewness, kurtosis, and the number of peaks in the histogram. Skewness and kurtosis require comparing the histogram to the normal distribution. Skewness is a measure of how symmetrical a histogram is around the mean. A histogram with a skewness of 0 is perfectly symmetrical. A histogram with negative skewness has a longer tail on the left side of the histogram and the peak on the right, while a histogram with positive skewness is reversed, with the longer tail on the right and the peak to the left of the mean. Kurtosis is a measure of the height of the peak, shoulders, and tails of a distribution. A kurtosis value of 0 means that these parts of a histogram are the same height as they would be for a normal distribution with the same mean and standard deviation. A histogram with a negative kurtosis value is called platykurtic, and it has a shorter peak, shorter tails, and taller shoulders than in a normal distribution. This results in a flattened shape. A histogram with a positive kurtosis is called leptokurtic and has a taller peak, taller tails, and shorter shoulders than in a normal distribution. This results in a tall, skinny shape. If the peak, shoulders, and tails of a histogram are the same height as a normal distribution's peak, shoulders, and tails, then the histogram is mesokurtic. In terms of the number of peaks, a unimodal distribution has one peak; a bimodal distribution has two peaks.

Other visual models in the social sciences include histograms, frequency polygons, bar graphs, stem-and-leaf plots, line graphs, pie charts, and scatterplots. All of these visual models help researchers understand their data in different ways, though none is perfect for all situations. Modern technology has resulted in the creation of new ways to visualize data. These methods are more complex, but they provide data analysts with new insights into their data. Table 3.9 can help you choose the right visual model for your data. The incorporation of geographic data and interactive tools give people more options than ever existed in previous eras.

Reflection Questions: Comprehension

1. Explain the similarities and differences between a histogram and a bar graph. When is it appropriate to use each one?
2. Is the normal distribution unimodal or bimodal?
3. Skewness is a measurement of what aspect of a shape of a distribution?
4. Explain the difference between a platykurtic distribution and a leptokurtic distribution.
5. What are the skewness and kurtosis values of the normal distribution?
6. What is an advantage of scatterplots over other visual models described in this chapter?
7. In Figure 3.2, why do the intervals span from 0.5 to 1.5, from 1.5 to 2.5, etc., when all of the numbers in the dataset are whole numbers?
8. When comparing the frequency tables in this chapter (Table 3.3 and the frequency table in the guided practice section), Myeongsun noticed that the proportions in the bottom row of each table (labeled "Total") were exactly 1.000.
    a. Why did both of these tables – which were built from different sets of data – have the same proportions in their bottom rows?
    b. Why were the proportions equal to 1.000?
    c. Will all frequency tables have this proportion in their "Total" row? Why or why not?

Reflection Questions: Application

9. Using the data in Table 3.1, make a frequency table and a histogram for the language development variable data in the Waite et al. (2015) study.
10. A distribution has skewness of –2.5 and a kurtosis of +1.8.
    a. Draw approximately what this distribution should look like.
    b. What terms would you use to describe this distribution?
11. A distribution has a skewness of +4.1 and a kurtosis of –1.1.
    a. Draw approximately what this distribution should look like.
    b. What terms would you use to describe this distribution?
12. A distribution has a skewness of –0.14 and a kurtosis of +0.09.
    a. Draw approximately what this distribution should look like.
    b. What terms would you use to describe this distribution?
13. Build a stem-and-leaf plot for the sibling age data in Table 3.1.
14. Create a pie chart showing the percentage of subjects in Table 3.1 who gave each response for the language development data in the Waite et al. (2015) study.
15. The following data represent the height of 26 statistics students as measured in inches:

62	63	62	72	56	64	62	63	68	73	60	61
68	70	59	62	62	67	63	67	62	76	64	69
63	67

a. Create a frequency table for these data.
b. Create a histogram for these data with an interval width of 1 unit.
c. Create a frequency polygon for these data with an interval width of 1 unit.
d. Create a histogram for these data with an interval width of 3 units.

e. Create a frequency polygon for these data with an interval width of 3 units.
f. Create a stem-and-leaf plot for these data.

16. Create a scatterplot for the last two variables in Table 3.1 (i.e., "Sibling understands me" and "Language development"). Note that some subjects' dots will be on top of each other in this scatterplot.
    a. What does this scatterplot tell you about your subjects?
    b. What does this scatterplot tell you about the two variables in the dataset?

17. Karen is examining data from her company's website. In a random sample of 300 visitors to the website, 114 left the website immediately (within 1 minute), 120 left the website later but did not buy anything, and 66 bought an item on the website.
    a. Create a bar graph using this information.
    b. Create a pie chart using this information.
    c. Why is a histogram not appropriate for Karen's data?

18. What are two ways that people can create misleading visual models?

19. The data below show the average price of a US movie ticket for the past several years (data from Box Office Mojo).

2006: $6.55   2007: $6.88   2008: $7.18   2009: $7.50   2010: $7.89   2011: $7.93
2012: $7.96   2013: $8.13   2014: $8.17   2015: $8.34   2016: $8.65

    a. Create a line graph using the trend data.
    b. What can you learn about ticket prices over time from the visual model?

20. The skewness value for a distribution is 0.10, and the kurtosis value is –0.60. How would you describe this distribution?

21. Find some data online and use them to create a visual model. I recommend using the Statistics Canada, US Census Bureau, or the UK Office for National Statistics websites, all of which provide high-quality, accurate data for free.

Software Guide

Both Excel and SPSS are adept at creating visual models. This Software Guide will show you how to create a histogram in these computer programs. Although this guide does not include step-by-step instructions for all visual models discussed in this chapter, it will show the icons in each program that allow users to create some of these visual models. For detailed instructions on creating a scatterplot, see the Software Guide in Chapter 12.

Excel

Histograms and bar graphs. To create a histogram or bar graph, it is first necessary to enter a frequency table into the Excel sheet. All visual models are created in Excel through the "Insert" ribbon at the top of the screen. You should then highlight the frequencies and select the "Column" button. A bar graph will appear that will resemble Figure 3.29.

The figure also shows a series of "Chart Layout" option icons, which permit different options for displaying the axes, the legend of the visual model, and the title of the graph. One of these options (the second icon in the "Chart Layout" section in Figure 3.30) converts the bar graph into a histogram.

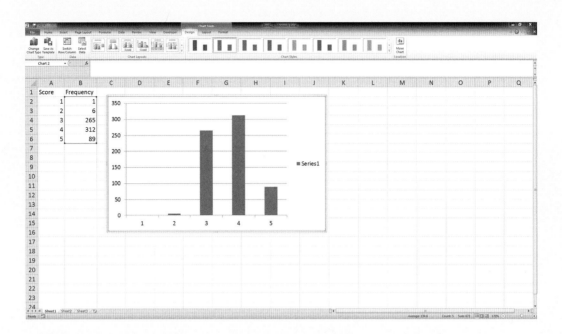

Figure 3.29 Screenshot of a bar graph (at right) created from the frequency table data (at top left).

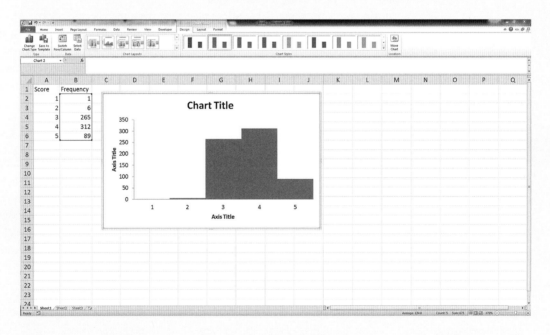

Figure 3.30 The same data in Figure 3.29 displayed as a histogram. The second icon in the "Chart Layouts" row automatically created this histogram, and added the axis titles and the chart title.

The icon looks like a small histogram, so it is easy to find. Excel calls this option "Layout 8." The result is shown in Figure 3.30.

Double-clicking the axis and chart titles will allow the user to edit them. I like to make other cosmetic changes to my histograms by right-clicking the blue intervals and selecting "Format

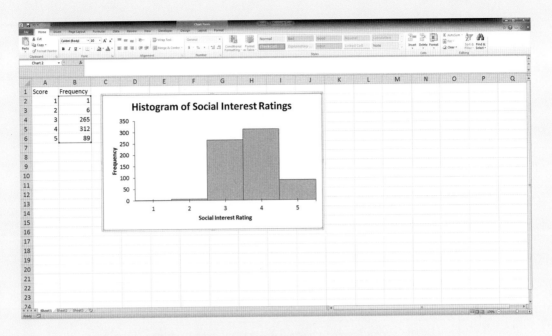

Figure 3.31 Finished histogram. Data from Warne and Liu (2017).

Data Series." This allows users to add or remove gaps between bars (converting the visual data from a histogram back to a bar graph), change the color, and add an outline around each bar. Right-clicking each axis and selecting "Format Axis" also gives users the option of making changes to the axis, such as adding marks to the axis or changing its color. After making these sorts of changes, I created Figure 3.31.

One final note is about scales of histograms and bar graphs. By default, Excel assumes that the bars in a histogram or bar graph should be numbered in ascending order, starting with the number 1. For a rating scale like Figure 3.31, this default option works well. But if you would like to change the numbering of the x-axis, then you should right-click the axis and choose "Select Data." A new window will appear. Beneath the text "Horizontal (Category) Axis Labels," you should select the "Edit" button. You can then select the cells in the Excel sheet which have the names or numbers you want for the axis.

Other Visual Models. Other visual models can be easily selected by choosing a different chart type from the "Insert" ribbon. Options include "Line" (suitable for line graphs and frequency polygons), "Pie" (for pie charts), "Bar" (another option for bar graphs), "Scatter" (for scatterplots), and more. Users can select the appropriate graph, add axis labels, change colors, and make other changes to the appearance of the visual model, using the same procedures as making these changes with a bar graph or histogram. However, Excel cannot create box plots or stem-and-leaf plots. Excel can create frequency tables, but these must be done manually.

SPSS

Creating visual models is easy in the SPSS point-and-click interface. From the menu at the top of the page, you should select "Graphs" ➔ "Chart Builder." A new window, called the Chart Builder

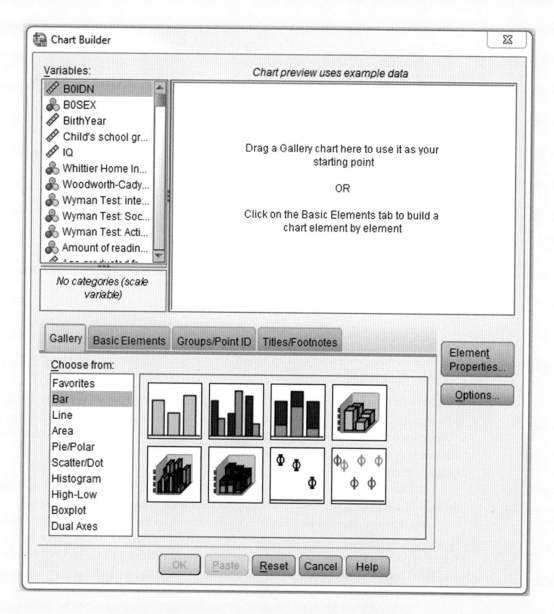

Figure 3.32 The Chart Builder window in SPSS.

window, should appear (shown in Figure 3.32). From the bottom half of the Chart Builder window, you should select the type of visual model you wish to build.

After selecting a type of chart from the list at the lower left, several icons will appear to the right that broadly resemble the different visual models that SPSS can create. You should select one of these icons and drag it into the white space at the upper right. The next step is to drag the variable(s) that you want to include in the visual model from the top-left list into the chart preview area on the upper right. Please note that the preview in the upper-right area may not resemble the final histogram. This is apparent in Figures 3.33a (which shows the preview in the Chart Builder window) and 3.33b (which shows a histogram built with the same data as the Excel-built histogram in Figure 3.31).

(a)

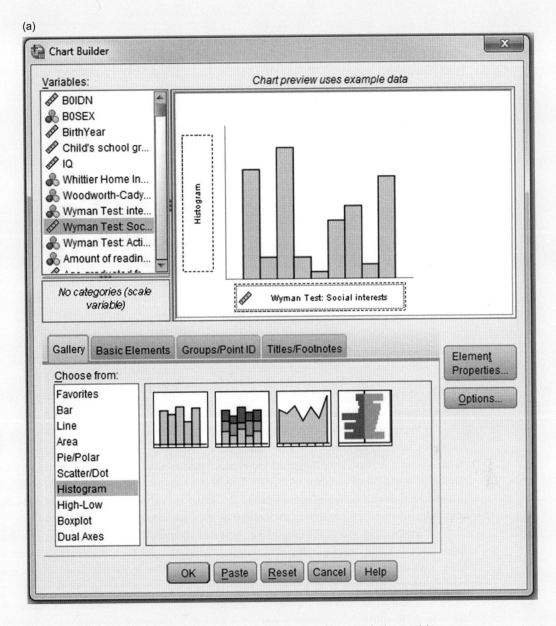

Figure 3.33a The SPSS Chart Builder window with a preview for a histogram in the top-right area.

In SPSS, finished histograms and other visual models appear in a new window called the output window. This is also where the results of statistical analysis will appear. For most of the rest of these Software Guides, we will discuss how to interpret the results that SPSS produces in the output window.

Creating other visual models is just a matter of choosing the appropriate option from the bottom-left menu in the Chart Builder window and then dragging the variables you want to examine into the preview area. SPSS permits customization of colors, axes, and other cosmetic aspects of the visual model by right-clicking the visual model in the output window and then

(b)

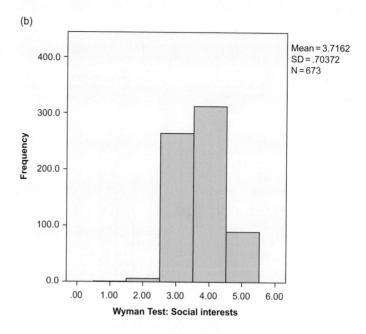

Figure 3.33b A histogram produced by SPSS. Data from Warne and Liu (2017).

adjusting the defaults appropriately. SPSS can create all the visual models discussed in this chapter, except stem-and-leaf plots.

Frequency Tables. Creating a frequency table, though, is different in SPSS. To create a frequency table, in the data view you should select "Analyze" → "Descriptive statistics" → "Frequencies." A small window called the Frequencies window will open, as shown in Figure 3.34. On the left is the list of variables in the file. To select which variable(s) to build a frequency table for, just choose the variable(s) and move them to the white box on the right. Once all of the variables are selected, click the "OK" button at the bottom of the Frequencies window.

Figure 3.35 shows the output. The first table is a summary of the number of subjects with data (labeled "Valid") and missing data (labeled "Missing") for the variable. In this example, there are 1,528 subjects in the data file; 673 of them have data for the social interests variable, and 855 are missing data.

The next table is the frequency table itself. The first column shows the scores that are in the dataset. Because this variable is a scale from 1 to 5, those are the only values for the variable in the dataset. The next column is the frequency column, which shows the number of individuals with each score. After the first five rows, the computer automatically adds the frequency together. You should notice that this total (673) is equal to the number of people with data in the previous table. After that total, SPSS lists the number of sample members missing data (in this case, 855). The bottom row is the total number of individuals in the dataset (1,528). The third column lists the percentage of individuals in the dataset who have each score. It also lists the percentage of people with data (44.0% in Figure 3.35) and of those who are missing data (56.0%). The next column also lists percentages, but it calculates these on the basis of only people who have data for that variable. The last column is a cumulative percentage calculated only with people who have data for a variable.

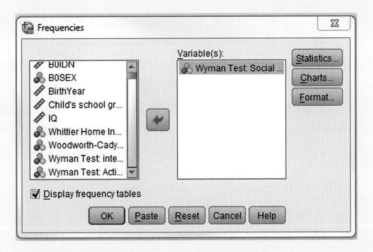

Figure 3.34 The Frequencies window in SPSS.

Statistics

Wyman Test: Social interests

N	Valid	673
	Missing	855

Wyman Test: Social interests

		Frequency	Percent	Valid Percent	Cumulative Percent
Valid	1.00	1	.1	.1	.1
	2.00	6	.4	.9	1.0
	3.00	265	17.3	39.4	40.4
	4.00	312	20.4	46.4	86.8
	5.00	89	5.8	13.2	100.0
	Total	673	44.0	100.0	
Missing	System	855	56.0		
Total		1528	100.0		

Figure 3.35 The output for the Frequencies function in SPSS.

Further Reading

- Blanca, M. J., Arnau, J., López-Montiel, D., Bono, R., & Bendayan, R. (2013). Skewness and kurtosis in real data samples. *Methodology: European Journal of Research Methods for the Behavioral and Social Sciences*, *9*, 78–84. doi:10.1027/1614–2241/a000057

  * Blanca and her colleagues calculated skewness and kurtosis statistics for almost 700 datasets. The result shows typical skewness and kurtosis values for real data.

- DeCarlo, L. T. (1997). On the meaning and use of kurtosis. *Psychological Methods*, *2*, 292–307. doi:10.1037/1082–989x.2.3.292

  * This article is the best source of information about kurtosis. DeCarlo explains kurtosis and clarifies common misconceptions.

- Friendly, M., & Denis, D. (2005). The early origins and development of the scatterplot. *Journal of the History of the Behavioral Sciences*, *41*, 103–130. doi:10.1002/jhbs.20078

  * This article explains the history of the scatterplot with its roots in physics and biology. The authors also show how scatterplots have helped scientists make major discoveries in astronomy, chemistry, and economics.

- Tufte, E. R. (2001). *The visual display of quantitative information* (2nd ed.). Cheshire, CT: Graphics Press.

  * This book is comprehensive in its discussion of the most common visual models. Tufte gives a lot of practical advice about how to make visual models that are both informative and aesthetically pleasing.

4 Models of Central Tendency and Variability

The last chapter showed the most common ways to create visual representations of data, the histogram being the most popular model. Visual models are helpful for understanding data, but they have their limitations. In a large dataset, for example, it can be cumbersome – even with the aid of a computer – to create a histogram for every single variable. For this reason statisticians have created two families of statistical models that describe the characteristics of a dataset. These are statistical models of central tendency and models of variability – both of which are types of descriptive statistics.

Learning Goals

- Calculate the four major models of central tendency: the mode, median, mean, and trimmed mean.

- Calculate the four major models of variability: the range, interquartile range, standard deviation, and variance.

- Explain the complementary nature of models of central tendency and variability.

Models of Central Tendency

Models of central tendency are statistical models that are used to describe where the middle of the histogram lies. For many distributions, the model of central tendency is at or near the tallest bar in the histogram. (We will discuss exceptions to this general rule in the next chapter.) These statistical models are valuable in helping people understand their data because they show where most scores tend to cluster together. Models of central tendency are also important because they can help us understand the characteristics of the "typical" sample member.

Mode. The most basic (and easiest to calculate) statistical model of central tendency is the **mode**. The mode of a variable is the most frequently occurring score in the data. For example, in the Waite et al. (2015) study that was used as an example in Chapter 3, there were four males (labeled as Group 1) and nine females (labeled as Group 2). Therefore, the mode for this variable is 2, or you could alternatively say that the mode sex of the sample is female. Modes are especially easy to find if the data are already in a frequency table because the mode will be the score that has the highest frequency value.

Calculating the mode requires at least nominal-level data. Remember from Chapter 2 that nominal data can be counted and classified (see Table 2.1). Because finding the mode merely requires counting the number of sample members who belong to each category, it makes sense that a mode can be calculated with nominal data. Additionally, any mathematical function that can be performed with nominal data can be performed with all other levels of data, so a mode can also be calculated for ordinal, interval, and ratio data. This makes the mode the only model of central tendency that can be calculated for all levels of data, making the mode a useful and versatile statistical model.

One advantage of the mode is that it is not influenced by outliers. An **outlier** (also called an extreme value) is a member of a dataset that is unusual because its score is much higher or much lower than the other scores in the dataset (Cortina, 2002). Outliers can distort some statistical models, but not the mode because the mode is the most frequent score in the dataset. For an outlier to change the mode, there would have to be so many people with the same extreme score that it becomes the most common score in the dataset. If that were to happen, then these "outliers" would not be unusual.

The major disadvantage of the mode is that it cannot be used in later, more complex calculations in statistics. In other words, the mode is useful in its own right, but it cannot be used to create other statistical models that can provide additional information about the data.

Sidebar 4.1   **Outliers aren't bad people!**

We will see later in this chapter how outliers can distort some statistical models. If you encounter an outlier in a dataset, the first thing to do is ensure that there has not been an error in entering the data into the computer or your calculator (e.g., typing "55" instead of "5"). If that happens, fixing the typo will get rid of any distortion that the outlier may cause (Barnett, 1978). If the data entry was accurate, then you should ensure that the outlier belongs to the population of interest. Occasionally, people who don't belong to the population accidentally get selected to participate in social science studies, and they may show up in the dataset as outliers. Their scores should be removed from the dataset.

But often outliers are not the result of an error. When this happens, some researchers get frustrated because the outliers are distorting their results. Although this distortion is sometimes unavoidable, it is important to remember that outliers are not trying to mess up a research study. In other words, outliers aren't bad people. In fact, everyone is an outlier on some variable. Perhaps you are an outlier because you have an extremely high knowledge of rap lyrics, or you are a much better football player than the average person, or you are much shorter than average. With a little brainstorming you can probably list several variables for which you are an outlier.

Also, outliers are sometimes inherently interesting. For example, Olympians are outliers because they are capable of extraordinary athletic feats, and these are fascinating to watch in competition. People pay a lot of money to watch outliers in athletics, music, and more.

Outliers can be entertaining, but they are also interesting from a scientific perspective. An example of this can be seen in one important educational study where researchers identified teenagers who were in the top 1% to the top 0.01% of math ability and gathered data many years later when these people were adults. The researchers found that the frequency of adult accomplishments (e.g., earning a PhD, earning a patent) increased as the subject's math ability increased. This study demolished the belief that there is a point where additional cognitive ability stops being beneficial to people (Lubinski & Benbow, 2006; Lubinski, Webb, Morelock, & Benbow, 2001). Scientific interest in outliers is not limited to individual studies. Some entire fields of knowledge in the social science are concerned with the study of outliers, such as criminology and special education.

Outliers can also provide hints on how social scientists can help typical people. For example, Buckner, Mezzacappa, and Beardslee (2003) studied resilient children in poverty with the hopes of learning which behavioral skills these children had that helped them overcome the negative aspects of poverty. Learning about how a small proportion of children grew up to escape many of the negative consequences of poverty may show counselors, teachers, and social workers how to help other children in poverty. This can help more children have a brighter future.

In conclusion, outliers can distort results of a study, but there are still reasons to appreciate outliers – including yourself!

Median. Another model of central tendency is the **median**, which is the middle score for a variable when those scores are ordered from smallest to largest (or from largest to smallest). If there is an even number of scores in a dataset, then there is no single middle score. In this case calculating a median requires finding the two middle scores and using the following formula:

$$Mdn = \frac{C_1 + C_2}{2}$$
(Formula 4.1)

In Formula 4.1, C_1 and C_2 are the two most central scores in the dataset. Therefore, to find the median when there are an even number of scores, you should add the two most central scores together and then divide by 2.

At a minimum, calculating a median requires ordinal data because one of the steps of finding the median is to order the scores. Table 2.1 showed that rank ordering scores requires at least ordinal data (though interval and ratio data can also be ordered). Therefore, it is not sensible to calculate a median for nominal data.

Despite this drawback, the median is still highly useful. First, it truly is a statistical model of central tendency because no number can possibly be more central than the middle number in a dataset. Second, the influence of outliers on the median is slight because adding an outlier to a dataset will only adjust the median trivially.

Check Yourself!

- What is the lowest possible level of data that can be used to calculate a mode?
- What is the lowest possible level of data that can be used to calculate a median?
- What are the strengths and weaknesses of the mode and the median?

Mean. Another frequent model of central tendency is the **mean** (also called the average). The mean (abbreviated $\overline{X}$ for a variable x) is calculated with the following formula:

$$\overline{X} = \left(\sum_{i=1}^{n} x_i \right) \div n$$
(Formula 4.2)

Formula 4.2 looks complicated, but once you understand what the different symbols mean, the formula is more manageable. The first step (in parentheses) says to add up every score for variable x.

The subscript i is notation that is used to assign an identification number to each score. The first score in a dataset has $i = 1$. The second score in a dataset has $i = 2$, and so forth. There is no mathematical value in these subscripts; they are in the formula because the capital sigma (Σ) tells us to add up the x values starting with the first one – as shown in the $i = 1$ below the sigma – and ending with the last one – as demonstrated by the n above the sigma. (The last score will have the same number as n because n is the sample size, and the numbering of i will stop when the last score has been numbered.) After adding all the scores together, the second step is to divide by n (i.e., the sample size or number of total scores). Therefore, all of the mathematical notation in Formula 4.2 exists to tell you to add up all the scores for variable x and divide by the number of scores (which is n).

One advantage of the mean is that it is easy to interpret. Most people learn how to calculate a mean in their high-school math classes. Additionally, the mean is used frequently in everyday language. For example, college students are often concerned with their grade-point average, which is a composite calculated by averaging their grades. News reports are full of information about means (or averages), and this frequent use means that non-scientists understand that the mean is the "typical" value for a dataset. If the purpose of a model is to understand data better, then the mean is an ideal model of central tendency.

Another advantage of the mean is that it provides the foundation for many statistics in this textbook. The mean will be a component in many formulas; as a result, the mean is often the first step in building and understanding complex statistical models.

One final advantage of the mean is that a sample mean ($\overline{X}$) is the best estimate for the population mean (μ). Mathematically, this is expressed as:

$$\overline{X} = \hat{\mu} \hspace{4cm} \text{(Formula 4.3)}$$

With only sample data it is impossible to know the exact value of the population mean (i.e., μ). To show that the sample mean is the estimate of population mean (and not necessary equal to the *exact* value of μ), we put a carat ($\wedge$) over μ. The carat simply means "estimate." Therefore, the sample mean is not only a model of central tendency for the sample; it is also a statistical model of central tendency for the population – a model that is often interesting to social scientists. Neither the median nor the mode is a good model of population central tendency.

The mean has some unfortunate downsides, though. One is that it requires interval- or ratio-level data. In fact, Stevens himself called the mean an "illegal statistic" for ordinal data (1946, p. 679). Some variables (such as whether a person has a mental diagnosis or not) are simply nominal- or ordinal-level data, so for these variables it is impossible to calculate a mean. Other variables (such as income, or the number of sexual partners they have had) may be difficult to collect at interval or ratio levels without invading subjects' privacy or running the risk that the subject will leave the study. Another drawback of the mean is that it is highly sensitive to the influence of outliers, and this sensitivity is greatest in (1) small samples and (2) samples with vastly extreme outliers.

This is clearly seen in a variable that has many scores above the mean: household income. In the UK in 2013, 65% of households had an income that was below the mean (Department for Work and Pensions, 2015). Given the fact that exactly 50% of household incomes should be below the median, a percentage of 65% of households being below the mean seems alarmingly high. Yet, this is merely the result of a number of outliers (i.e., extremely rich people) who pull the mean closer to their scores.

An example like this leads some students to wonder how the mean can still be a model of central tendency if outliers can distort the mean so much. The answer is shown in Figure 4.1, which conceptualizes the mean as being like a seesaw (or teeter-totter) on a playground. In real life, a

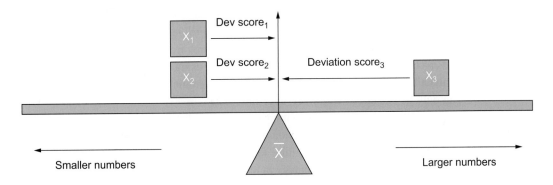

Figure 4.1 Visual representation of the mean as a balance point in a sample. The difference between each score (labeled as x_1, x_2, and x_3) and the mean (labeled as $\overline{X}$) is called the **deviation score**. Because x_1 and x_2 are both smaller than the mean, their deviation scores are negative (see Formula 4.4), while x_3 has a positive deviation score because it is larger than $\overline{X}$. Adding x_3's large positive deviation score and the smaller negative deviation scores for x_1 and x_2 produces a value of 0.

fulcrum is placed underneath the bar of a seesaw at a certain point where the weights balance out. If you imagine that a histogram is like a set of weights placed on a seesaw, then the mean is the location that you would need to place the fulcrum to balance the histogram, or seesaw, perfectly.

From a mathematical perspective, Figure 4.1 shows that the mean is always a central balance point where the difference between each score and the mean cancel out (Kline, 2013). This difference between a score and the mean is called a deviation score, and it is calculated as:

$$Deviation\ Score_i = x_i - \overline{X} \qquad \text{(Formula 4.4)}$$

The subscript i signifies that each score in the dataset has its own deviation score. (Again, the i subscript is just notation without any mathematical value.) All of these deviation scores are calculated by taking each score (x_i) and subtracting the mean ($\overline{X}$). In a dataset some of the deviation scores will be negative (if x_i is smaller than $\overline{X}$), and some deviation scores will be positive (if x_i is larger than $\overline{X}$). But the mean will always be the point where deviation scores cancel out. Mathematically, this means:

$$\sum_{i=0}^{n} \left(x_i - \overline{X}\right) = 0 \qquad \text{(Formula 4.5)}$$

In other words, the sum of all deviations scores will *always* equal 0. This is why the mean is the point in Figure 4.1 where the dataset is "balanced out" and why the mean is a measure of central tendency, even if outliers have distorted it.

Check Yourself!

- What level of data is required to calculate a mean?

- In statistical notation, what does a carat (^) symbolize?

- What is a deviation score?

- Why do deviation scores sum to 0?

- What is the impact of an outlier on the mean?

Trimmed Mean. The **trimmed mean** is a method devised to overcome some of the drawbacks of the mean – especially its sensitivity to outliers (Tukey, 1962). The trimmed mean is calculated by eliminating the same number of scores from the top and the bottom of a distribution and calculating the mean for the remaining scores, using Formula 4.2. After throwing out scores, the formula for the trimmed mean is the same as the formula for the mean. Therefore, the trimmed mean can only be calculated with interval or ratio data.

How many scores to eliminate from the distribution is arbitrary, and if you choose to calculate a trimmed mean, you should always specify how many scores were eliminated from the distribution. This is done by stating that you have calculated the "1% trimmed mean," the "5% trimmed mean," etc. The percentage in the name specifies the percentage of scores eliminated from each side of the distribution. In other words, a 1% trimmed mean was calculated after eliminating the highest 1% of scores *and* the lowest 1% of scores before calculating a mean with the remaining scores. Likewise, the 5% trimmed mean is calculated by eliminating 5% of scores from the top and bottom of their distribution. Therefore, the 1% trimmed mean is calculated with 98% of the data (not 99%!), and the 5% trimmed mean is calculated with 90% of the data (Bickel, 1965). There is no widespread agreement about how much to trim from a dataset, though Wilcox (1998) recommends trimming 10% from each end of the distribution.

The trimmed mean is resistant to the influence of outliers for an obvious reason: the researcher eliminates the outliers from the dataset before calculating a trimmed mean. As a result, the trimmed mean is an accurate statistical model of central tendency when there are outliers in a distribution – especially when those outliers are mostly concentrated on one side of the distribution, such as the household income example.

Like the other statistical models of central tendency, the trimmed mean has some drawbacks. One of the most serious is that some experts (e.g., Cortina, 2002) disagree with the practice of regularly eliminating outliers from a dataset. Researchers themselves can be hesitant about throwing out data, especially because data collection is often the most time-consuming step of the research process. Therefore, throwing away 20% of the data gives the impression that 20% of that time was wasted. Yet, if used as a foundation in creating more complex statistical models, the trimmed mean may give more accurate results than the mean (Wilcox, 1998).

Guided Practice 4.1

As shown in Table 3.1 (in the previous chapter) the 13 people in the Waite et al. (2015) study had the following ages:

| 18 | 19 | 20 | 21 | 23 | 23 | 24 | 24 | 25 | 31 | 33 | 35 | 38 |

This guided practice will walk you through the calculation process of the mode, the median, the mean, and the trimmed mean.

Mode. The mode is the most common score in a dataset. Only two scores appear in this dataset more than once: 23 appears twice, and 24 appears twice. Therefore, both 23 and 24 are modes in this dataset. It is acceptable to have multiple modes in a dataset as long as each score appears in the dataset the exact same number of times.

Median. For your convenience these scores are already arranged into ascending order. Because there are 13 scores, the middle score will be the 7th score, which is 24.

Mean. To calculate the mean, we must use Formula 4.2. This formula requires us to add the scores together and then divide by the number of scores in the dataset:

$$\overline{X} = \frac{18 + 19 + 20 + 21 + 23 + 23 + 24 + 24 + 25 + 31 + 33 + 35 + 38}{13}$$

Adding the numbers in the numerator together produces the following result:

$$\overline{X} = \frac{334}{13}$$

The final step is to divide by 13, which produces the final answer:

$$\overline{X} = 25.69$$

Trimmed Mean. Trimming the lowest and the highest scores produces the 7.7% trimmed mean (because 1 out of 13 scores is 7.7%). The equation below is the same as the equation for the mean, but the highest and lowest numbers have been eliminated and the denominator has been reduced by two (which reflects the elimination of two scores):

$$7.7\% trimmed\ mean = \frac{\cancel{18} + 19 + 20 + 21 + 23 + 23 + 24 + 24 + 25 + 31 + 33 + 35 + \cancel{38}}{\cancel{13}11}$$

Cleaning this formula up produces:

$$7.7\% trimmed\ mean = \frac{19 + 20 + 21 + 23 + 23 + 24 + 24 + 25 + 31 + 33 + 35}{11}$$

Summing the numbers in the numerators simplifies the formula to:

$$7.7\% trimmed\ mean = \frac{278}{11}$$

This produces a final answer of:

$$7.7\% trimmed\ mean = 25.27$$

All four of these models of central tendency are similar to one another (ranging from 23 to 25.69), indicating that we can have a great deal of confidence that the middle of the distribution is in the low twenties.

Differing Models of Central Tendency. Although there are other models of central tendency, the mode, median, mean, and trimmed mean are – by far – the most commonly used models of central tendency in the social sciences. For many datasets these four models will produce similar results. When this happens, you can have greater confidence that you understand where the center of the distribution lies.

It is possible that one or more models of central tendency will produce results that are very different from the other models. When this occurs, you should choose the statistical models that make the most sense to you and explain why you are using them. When choosing a model you should remember that all of the models of central tendency fit the data equally well. In other words, there is no single "right model." You should consider the level of data you have, and the purpose of the model. You may also consider whether the model is being distorted by outliers. Creating a histogram is helpful in making this last determination (see Chapter 3). Some researchers report multiple models of central tendency in their data so that people reading their research can determine which model(s) is/are most appropriate.

Check Yourself!

- How is a trimmed mean calculated?

- Why would someone want to calculate a trimmed mean instead of a mean?

- What is a drawback of a trimmed mean?

- What should you do if your models of central tendency are very different from one another?

Sidebar 4.2 **Statistical assumptions**

Each statistical model has certain requirements that the data have to meet before that model can be calculated. For example, a mode requires nominal-level data or higher, while a median requires at least ordinal-level data. The mean and the trimmed mean cannot be calculated without interval- or ratio-level data. A statistical model of central tendency requiring a certain level of data is an example of a statistical **assumption**. In statistics, assumptions are requirements that data must meet in order for a statistical procedure to be used without producing distorted or inaccurate results.

Many statistics have multiple assumptions that the data must meet before that statistic can be used. However, not all assumptions are created equal. Some assumptions are extremely strict, and violating them will result in nonsensical or highly inaccurate results. An example of this is the assumption that a mean is calculated with interval- or ratio-level data. As stated in this chapter and Chapter 2, there are no situations where it would be appropriate to calculate a mean with nominal or ordinal data. Other assumptions are more flexible, such as the assumption that the outliers are not distorting a mean. For some datasets the high and low outliers may balance out each other, or the number of non-outliers may be large enough to dilute the influence of any outliers.

Statistical assumptions are like driving laws. Some driving laws are extremely strict: anyone who is found driving while intoxicated will be pulled over immediately by the police and arrested. This example is like a strict statistical assumption, which cannot be violated under any circumstances without serious consequences for the statistical results. Other driving laws are less strict, and people often break these laws slightly, such as speed limits. On the highway near my university many people drive about 5 miles per hour (8 km per hour) over the speed limit without getting arrested. Breaking this law slightly seems to have few negative consequences. Likewise, weaker assumptions can be violated a little and still produce accurate and useful statistical models that suffer from little or no distortion. Throughout this book I will communicate the assumptions of the various statistical methods, along with the level of strictness of each assumption.

Models of Variability

Statistical models of central tendency are useful, but they only communicate information about one characteristic of a variable: the location of the histogram's center. Models of central tendency say nothing about another important characteristic of distributions – their variability. In statistics **variability** refers to the degree to which scores in a dataset vary from one another. Distributions with high variability tend to be spread out, while distributions with low variability tend to be compact. In this chapter we will discuss four models of variability: the range, the interquartile range, the standard deviation, and the variance.

Range. The **range** for a variable is the difference between the highest and the lowest scores in the dataset. Mathematically, this is:

$$Range = Highest\ Score - Lowest\ Score \qquad \text{(Formula 4.6)}$$

The advantage of the range is that it is simple to calculate. But the disadvantages should also be apparent in the formula. First, only two scores (the highest score and the lowest score) determine the range. Although this does provide insight into the span of scores within a dataset, it does not say much (if anything) about the variability seen among the typical scores in the dataset. This is especially true if either the highest score or the lowest score is an outlier (or if both are outliers).

The second disadvantage of the range as a statistical model of variability is that outliers have more influence on the range than on any other statistical model discussed in this chapter. If either the highest score or the lowest score (or both) is an outlier, then the range can be greatly inflated and the data may appear to be more variable than they really are. Nevertheless, the range is still a useful statistical model of variability, especially in studies of growth or change, where it may show effectively whether sample members become more alike or grow in their differences over time.

A statistical assumption of the range is that the data are interval- or ratio-level data. This is because the formula for the range requires subtracting one score from another – a mathematical operation that requires interval data at a minimum.

Interquartile Range. Because the mean is extremely susceptible to the influence of outliers, a similar model of variability was developed in an attempt to overcome these shortfalls: the **interquartile range**, which is the range of the middle 50% of scores. There are three **quartiles** in any dataset, and these three scores divide the dataset into four equal-sized groups. These quartiles are (as numbered from the lowest score to the highest score) the first quartile, second quartile, and third quartile.[1] There are four steps to finding the interquartile range:

1. Calculate the median for a dataset. This is the second quartile.
2. Find the score that is halfway between the median and the lowest score. This is the first quartile.
3. Find the score that is halfway between the median and the highest score. This is the third quartile.
4. Subtract the score in the first quartile from the third quartile to produce the interquartile range.

[1] One common misconception is that the term "quartile" refers to one-quarter of the scores in a dataset. This is not true. Quartiles are the scores that divide a dataset into four groups – not the actual groups of scores themselves. This is why there are only three quartiles, a fact that seems counterintuitive at first. Likewise, there are only nine deciles (even though dec = 10) because these nine scores divide the data into ten equal-sized groups. It is also worthy to note that there are 99 percentiles – not 100 – even though the percentiles divide a dataset into 100 equal-sized groups. As a result, it is incorrect to say that someone's score is "in the top quartile," though someone can be "at the top quartile." The same is true for deciles and percentiles.

We have already encountered the interquartile range in this textbook. In the previous chapter Figure 3.11 showed a box plot, which had a box and two whiskers. The box spanned the range of the middle 50% of the scores. In other words, the box part of the box plot was a visual model of the interquartile range. Like all models of variability, high numbers for the interquartile range represent more spread out scores, and smaller numbers represent scores that tend to be more tightly packed together.

Like the range, the interquartile range requires subtracting scores from one another as part of the calculation process. Therefore, the interquartile range requires interval- or ratio-level data (which are levels of data that permit subtraction of scores from one another; see Table 2.1).

Check Yourself!

- How do you calculate a range?

- How do you calculate an interquartile range?

- What level of data is required to calculate a range or the interquartile range?

- What are the advantages and disadvantages of the range and the interquartile range?

Standard Deviation. By far, the most common model of variability used in the social sciences is the **standard deviation**. The formula for the standard deviation of a sample is:

$$s_x = \sqrt{\frac{\sum (x_i - \overline{X})^2}{n}}$$ (Formula 4.7)

In Formula 4.7, s_x is the standard deviation for variable x, $(x_i - \overline{X})$ is the deviation score for each individual in the sample, and n is the sample size. Therefore, the standard deviation of a sample is defined as the square root of the sum of the squared deviation scores that have been divided by the sample size. The standard deviation is interpreted as the typical difference between the mean and the scores in the dataset.

The abbreviation s_x shows that Formula 4.7 is used to calculate the standard deviation of a sample. However, if you have data from every population member, then the appropriate formula is:

$$\sigma_x = \sqrt{\frac{\sum (x_i - \overline{X})^2}{N}}$$ (Formula 4.8)

The steps of Formulas 4.7 and 4.8 are the exact same. Their differences are in two minor changes of notation: the s_x (sample standard deviation) has been replaced by σ_x (population standard deviation). Additionally, the sample size (n) has been replaced by the population size (N). But – again – none of this changes the calculation of Formula 4.8.

There is an important terminology difference, though, between Formulas 4.7 and 4.8. Because Formula 4.7 describes one of the properties of a sample, we refer to this model as a **statistic**. A model that describes the characteristics of a population, just as Formula 4.8 does, is a **parameter**.

Sidebar 4.3 **Sample and population abbreviations**

Formula 4.3 shows an important aspect of mathematical notation: the type of abbreviations that are used. In general, sample statistics are abbreviated with letters from the Latin alphabet. These are the letters that are used in the English language. (Almost all of the letters in our alphabet were developed by the ancient Romans, which is why it is said that we use the Latin alphabet.) Population parameters are usually abbreviated with letters from the Greek alphabet. This can be seen in this chapter, where $\overline{X}$ is used to represent the sample mean and s is used to represent the sample standard deviation. Both of these are Latin letters. On the other hand, μ and σ are both Greek letters, which are used to represent population parameters – the population mean and standard deviation, respectively.

The only exception to this rule is the population size. Sample size is abbreviated as n (in accordance with the rule), but the population size is abbreviated as N.

You should not let the similarities between Formulas 4.7 and 4.8 deceive you. Even though they have the same steps and are nearly identical, they are not interchangeable. In other words, calculating the sample standard deviation (s) does not mean you have correctly calculated the population standard deviation (σ). This is because a sample – by definition – does not have all of the data in the population, and this usually makes samples smaller and less variable than populations. Therefore, a sample standard deviation is consistently smaller than the population standard deviation, and it is not an accurate statistical model of the variability in the population. To correct for this, we use Formula 4.9:

$$\hat{\sigma}_x = \sqrt{\frac{\sum (x_i - \overline{X})^2}{n - 1}} \qquad \text{(Formula 4.9)}$$

There are two differences between Formulas 4.8 and 4.9. The first is the change in notation on the left side of the equal sign. As stated above, the carat (^) shows that this formula produces an estimate of the population parameter. This is just a handy reminder that the result of this formula is not the exact population standard deviation (that would require population data, in which case Formula 4.8 would be appropriate).

The other change is in the denominator on the right side of the equation, which is $n - 1$, instead of n. This adjustment in the denominator makes the overall value of the fraction (and therefore of the estimate of the population standard deviation) slightly larger, correcting for the underestimation that would result if we used Formula 4.7 to estimate the population standard deviation from sample data. This adjustment is called **Bessel's correction**. As n gets larger, the sample standard deviation (in Formula 4.6) and the estimate of the population standard deviation (in Formula 4.8) get closer together, and Bessel's correction becomes very small (Kline, 2013). But for small sample sizes (as in the guided practice examples in the textbook), the underestimation of Formula 4.6 is severe, and Bessel's correction makes the result from Formula 4.8 much larger.

So, how do you know which formula to use for the standard deviation? The answer lies in the type of data and the purposes that the data will be used for:

- If you have data from every member of the population, you should always use Formula 4.8.
- If you have sample data, but you do not wish to estimate the population standard deviation, you should always use Formula 4.7.
- If you have sample data, and you want to estimate the population standard deviation, you should always use Formula 4.9.

Like the mean, the standard deviation has the advantage of being a statistic that can be used in other, more complex statistical methods. It also has the benefit of not being as sensitive to outliers as the range (though it is more sensitive to outliers than the interquartile range).

However, the biggest disadvantage of the standard deviation is that it cannot be calculated with ordinal or nominal data. This is because the sample mean is part of the standard deviation equation, and, at a minimum, interval-level data are required for calculating a mean (Stevens, 1946). Another drawback of the standard deviation is that its formula is complicated, as is shown in the Guided Practice 4.2.

Sidebar 4.4   **Why the standard deviation?**

The standard deviation formula may seem needlessly complicated. Some of my students notice that one step in the standard deviation formula is to square the deviation scores, and the final step in the formula is to take the square root. These two steps seem unnecessary to some students. After all, $\sqrt{x^2} = x$, so it seems the last step in the formula reverses an earlier step.

The purpose of squaring the deviation scores is to eliminate the negative numbers in the deviation scores. Without eliminating those negative values, summing the deviation scores will always produce 0 as a result (see Formula 4.5). It is necessary to square root the final result so that the standard deviation is in the same scale as the original data.

If the purpose of squaring the deviation scores is to eliminate negative values, some students wonder why they cannot just take the absolute value of the deviation scores before summing them. This formula would be:

$$MD = \frac{\sum |(x_i - \overline{X})|}{n - 1}$$ (Formula 4.10)

This statistic is called the **mean deviation**, and it has two advantages over the standard deviation. First, it is easier to calculate. Second, the mean deviation is a true average difference between the mean and the scores in the data.

However, the mean deviation has two major drawbacks which prevent its widespread usage. First, when a variable is normally distributed (we will discuss this in Chapter 5), the mean deviation produces less stable results than the standard deviation. Second, the standard deviation is necessary for most of the statistical procedures that we will discuss in later chapters in this book (for example, Chapter 11).

This is not to say that the mean deviation is useless. It is used in business research to measure the volatility of some financial indexes and the accuracy of business projections. Moreover, some behavioral scientists (e.g., Gorard, 2005) have advocated the use of the mean deviation, believing that its advantages have been underappreciated. The biggest hurdle to adopting the mean deviation, though, is that five generations of statisticians have used the standard deviation as a foundation for building more complex statistical models. These statistical procedures work well, so throwing out the standard deviation means throwing out more than a century of work – most of which has no replacements yet.

Variance. The final model of variability we will discuss in this chapter is the **variance**. Calculating the variance is easy to learn because the variance is the square of the standard deviation. Therefore, the formula for the sample variance is:

$$s_x^2 = \frac{\sum (x_i - \overline{X})^2}{n} \qquad \text{(Formula 4.11)}$$

Formula 4.11 very closely resembles Formula 4.7. However, because the variance is the square of the standard deviation, both sides of the equation have been squared. On the left side of the equation, the s_x (which was the symbol for the sample standard deviation in Formula 4.7) has become s_x^2 – the symbol for the sample variance. The right side of the equation is identical to what we saw in Formula 4.7, except the square root in Formula 4.7 has been eliminated (because squaring cancels out a square root).

Calculating the variance based on population data is similar, requiring squaring the population standard deviation, which was in Formula 4.8. The result is:

$$\sigma_x^2 = \frac{\sum (x_i - \overline{X})^2}{N} \qquad \text{(Formula 4.12)}$$

Squaring both sides of Formula 4.8 produced this equation. Like Formula 4.11, this means the square root on the right side of the equation has been eliminated, and the left side of the equation has been squared. As a result, σ_x^2 is the symbol for the population variance.

Finally, if a researcher has sample data and wishes to estimate the population variance, the formula is:

$$\hat{\sigma}_x^2 = \frac{\sum (x_i - \overline{X})^2}{n - 1} \qquad \text{(Formula 4.13)}$$

Like the other variance formulas, 4.13 is the result of squaring both sides of one of the standard deviation formulas (in this case Formula 4.9). The $n - 1$ in the denominator shows that Bessel's correction is also needed when estimating the population variance using sample data.

Deciding which formula to use when calculating the variance is the same as choosing an appropriate standard deviation formula. If you have data from all members of the population, you should use the formula with N in the denominator (i.e., Formula 4.12). Likewise, if you have only sample data and you do not wish to estimate the population variance, you should use the formula with n in the denominator (i.e., Formula 4.11). Finally, if you wish to estimate the population variance ($\hat{\sigma}$) with sample data, you should use the formula with $n - 1$ in the denominator (i.e., Formula 4.13).

Guided Practice 4.2

To practice calculating models of variability, we are going to use the same scores from Waite et al. (2015) that we used to calculate the models of central tendency. As a reminder, those scores are:

| 18 | 19 | 20 | 21 | 23 | 23 | 24 | 24 | 25 | 31 | 33 | 35 | 38 |

Range. To calculate the range, we need to subtract the lowest score from the highest score:

$$Range = 38 - 18$$

The result of this calculation is 20, indicating that the difference between the oldest and the youngest subjects in the study was 20 years.

Interquartile Range. Calculating the interquartile range requires finding the scores that are halfway between the median and the minimum and the maximum. As we saw in Guided Practice 4.1, the median for these data was the seventh score (24). The score halfway between the maximum and the seventh score is the tenth score, which is 31. The score halfway between the minimum and the median is the fourth score, which is 21. The final step is to subtract the lower of these two scores from the higher score:

$$Interquartile\ range = 31 - 21$$

The result of this calculation is 10, indicating that the middle 50% of people in this dataset are between the ages of 21 and 31.

Standard Deviation. For the purposes of this example, we are going to use Formula 4.7, which is the formula for the sample standard deviation that is used when we do not wish to generalize to the population. The formula is:

$$s_x = \sqrt{\frac{\sum (x_i - \overline{X})^2}{n}}$$

This formula requires first calculating a deviation score, which is calculated by subtracting the mean (which was 25.69):

$18 - 25.69 = -7.69$ $19 - 25.69 = -6.69$ $20 - 25.69 = -5.69$ $21 - 25.69 = -4.69$
$23 - 25.69 = -2.69$ $23 - 25.69 = -2.69$ $24 - 25.69 = -1.69$ $24 - 25.69 = -1.69$
$25 - 25.69 = -0.69$ $31 - 25.69 = 5.31$ $33 - 25.69 = 7.31$ $35 - 25.69 = 9.31$
$38 - 25.69 = 12.31$

The next step is to square each of these deviation scores:

$(-7.69)^2 = 59.17$ $(-6.69)^2 = 44.79$ $(-5.69)^2 = 32.40$ $(-4.69)^2 = 22.02$
$(-2.69)^2 = 7.25$ $(-2.69)^2 = 7.25$ $(-1.69)^2 = 2.86$ $(-1.69)^2 = 2.86$
$(-0.69)^2 = 0.48$ $(5.31)^2 = 28.17$ $(7.31)^2 = 53.40$ $(9.31)^2 = 86.63$
$(12.31)^2 = 151.48$

The next step is to add the squared deviation scores together:

$59.17 + 44.79 + 32.40 + 22.02 + 7.25 + 7.25 + 2.86 + 2.86 + 0.48 + 28.17 + 53.40 + 86.63 + 151.48$
$= 498.77$

(You may get slightly different results from what is shown here because these results are calculated with no rounding at any step throughout this example.) Then you should divide this sum by the number of scores in the dataset:

$$\frac{498.77}{13} = 38.37$$

The final step in calculating the standard deviation is to take the square root of this number:

$$s_x = \sqrt{38.37} = 6.19$$

Variance. The variance is defined as the square of the standard deviation. With a standard deviation of 6.19, the variance is:

$$s_x^2 = 6.19^2 = 38.37$$

This number, 38.37, probably seems familiar. That's because it was the result of the second-to-last step in the standard deviation formula. In fact, the variance will *always* be the second-to-last number that you obtain from the standard deviation formula.

Bessel's Correction. For the purposes of learning about models of variability, it is valuable to see the impact of Bessel's correction on the standard deviation and variance calculations. For the standard deviation, all of the steps are the same until the sum of the squared deviation scores is divided by $n - 1$.

$$\hat{\sigma}_x = \sqrt{\frac{498.77}{n-1}} = \sqrt{\frac{498.77}{13-1}} = \sqrt{\frac{498.77}{12}}$$

This produces:

$$\hat{\sigma}_x = \sqrt{\frac{498.77}{12}} = \sqrt{41.56} = 6.45$$

And the variance ($\hat{\sigma}_x^2$) is 41.56. Comparing these results with the previous standard deviation and variance calculations shows that Bessel's correction produces higher results. This is to be expected because Bessel's correction compensates for the fact that the results with n in the denominator are underestimates of the population standard deviation and variance.

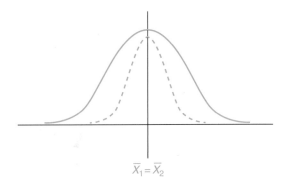

$$\overline{X}_1 = \overline{X}_2$$

Figure 4.2 An example of two data distributions that have the same mean and different standard deviations. Judged solely on their means, these distributions appear equal. However, their differing standard deviations show that the distributions are quite different.

Using Models of Central Tendency and Variance Together

Models of central tendency and models of variance provide different, but complementary information. Neither type of model can tell you everything you need to know about a distribution. However, when combined, these models can provide researchers with a thorough understanding of their data. For example, Figure 4.2 shows two samples with the same mean, but one has a standard deviation that is twice as large as the other. Using just the mean to understand the two distributions would mask the important differences between the histograms. Indeed, when reporting a model of central tendency, it is recommended that you report an accompanying model of variability (Warne et al., 2012; Zientek,

Capraro, & Capraro, 2008). It is impossible to fully understand a distribution of scores without a knowledge of the variable's central tendency and variability, and even slight differences in these values across distributions can be important (Voracek, Mohr, & Hagmann, 2013).

Check Yourself!

- How do you calculate a standard deviation if you have population data?

- What is the relationship between the standard deviation and the variance?

- There are three formulas for the standard deviation. How do you determine which formula to use?

- Why is Bessel's correction necessary when using sample data to estimate the population standard deviation or variance?

- How should models of variability be used with models of central tendency?

Summary

This chapter discussed two types of descriptive statistics: models of central tendency and models of variability. Models of central tendency describe the location of the middle of the distribution, and models of variability describe the degree that scores are spread out from one another.

There were four models of central tendency in this chapter. Listed in ascending order of the complexity of their calculations, these are the mode, median, mean, and trimmed mean. The mode is calculated by finding the most frequent score in a dataset. The median is the center score when the data are arranged from the smallest score to the highest score (or vice versa). The mean is calculated by adding all the scores for a particular variable together and dividing by the number of scores. To find the trimmed mean, you should eliminate the same number of scores from the top and bottom of the distribution (usually 1%, 5%, or 10%) and then calculate the mean of the remaining data.

There were also four principal models of variability discussed in this chapter. The first was the range, which is found by subtracting the lowest score for a variable from the highest score for that same variable. The interquartile range requires finding the median and then finding the scores that are halfway between (a) the median and the lowest score in the dataset, and (b) the median and the highest score in the dataset. Score (a) is then subtracted from score (b). The standard deviation is defined as the square root of the average of the squared deviation scores of each individual in the dataset. Finally, the variance is defined as the square of the standard deviation (as a result, the variance is the mean of the squared deviation scores). There are three formulas for the standard deviation and three formulas for the variance in this chapter. Selecting the appropriate formula depends on (1) whether you have sample or population data, and (2) whether you wish to estimate the population standard deviation or variance.

No statistical model of central tendency or variability tells you everything you may need to know about your data. Only by using multiple models in conjunction with each other can you have a thorough understanding of your data.

Reflection Questions: Comprehension

1. Identify which model of variability will *always* be larger and explain why:
    a.   The range and the interquartile range
    b.   The range and the standard deviation
    c. s_x and $\hat{\sigma}_x$.
2. Explain why deviation scores always add up to 0.
3. Answer the following questions about Bessel's correction:
    a.   What is Bessel's correction?
    b.   Which statistics can Bessel's correction be applied to?
    c.   When is it appropriate to use Bessel's correction?
4. Which two models of central tendency are not susceptible to the influence of outliers?
5. Which two models of central tendency are susceptible to the influence of outliers?
6. Why is it important to examine models of central tendency and models of variability when trying to understand your data?

Reflection Questions: Application

7. In the Waite et al. (2015) dataset, the ages of the subjects' siblings with autism were as follows:

10	11	13	18	18	18	19	21	21	30	37	37	38

    a.   Calculate the mode of the scores.
    b.   Calculate the median of the scores.
    c.   Calculate the mean of the scores.
    d.   Calculate the 7.7% trimmed mean of the scores.
    e.   Compare your models of central tendency. Are they close to one another, or is there a model that differs from the others? What does that mean when trying to ascertain the middle of the distribution?
    f.   Calculate the range of the scores.
    g.   Calculate the standard deviation of the scores. Assume that you want to use the data in this sample to estimate the population standard deviation.
    h.   Calculate the variance of the scores. Assume that you want to use the data in this sample to estimate the population variance.
    i.   In Guided Practices 4.1 and 4.2, we learned that the age of the subjects had a mean of 25.69 and a standard deviation of 6.45. How do these descriptive statistics compare to the mean and standard deviation of the siblings' ages?
8. Twelve students were comparing test scores in their statistics course. Their scores were as follows:

45	76	82	82	85	85	85	89	91	94
80	99								

    a.   Calculate the mode of the scores.
    b.   Calculate the median of the scores.
    c.   Calculate the mean of the scores.
    d.   Calculate the 8.3% trimmed mean of the scores.

e. Compare your models of central tendency. Why does one model differ from the others? What does that mean when trying to ascertain the middle of the distribution?

f. Calculate the range of the scores.

g. Calculate the interquartile range of the scores.

h. Calculate the standard deviation of the scores. Assume that you want to use the data in this sample to estimate the population standard deviation.

i. Calculate the variance of the scores. Assume that you want to use the data in this sample to estimate the population variance.

9. Jill counted how many pages of reading she must do for her anthropology class each day, which produced the following data:

14	16	18	18	22	25	27	29	30	31
18	21								

a. Calculate the mode of the scores.

b. Calculate the median of the scores.

c. Calculate the mean of the scores.

d. Calculate the 8.3% trimmed mean of the scores.

e. Calculate the range of the scores.

f. Calculate the interquartile range of the scores.

g. Calculate the standard deviation of the scores. Assume that you want to use the data in this sample to estimate the population standard deviation.

h. Calculate the variance of the scores. Assume that you want to use the data in this sample to estimate the population variance.

10. Create your own dataset where $n = 20$, $s_x > 2.5$, and $\overline{X} = 35$.

a. What is the mean, median, mode, trimmed mean, range, interquartile range, standard deviation, and variance of your data?

b. What is the average of the deviation scores for the scores? Why?

11. Justin works for a company that sells clothes online. He finds that 30% of website visitors view his company's site for less than 30 seconds. His boss doesn't think that these people are viewing the merchandise, or are likely customers.

a. Why would the median probably be a better measure of central tendency for Justin's company than the mean of the time people view the company's website?

b. Even though the people who visit the website for very brief periods of time are not outliers, what would be the advantage of using the trimmed mean?

Software Guide

Excel

Calculating central tendency and variability is easy, thanks to pre-programmed mathematical functions in Excel. To use these functions, you must have already entered data into your sheet. Each function is typed into an empty cell and begins with an equal sign. The functions all have a set of parentheses which you type into the cells that contain the data you are interested in. This Software Guide will show you the different Excel functions that can be used to calculate models of central tendency and variability. Figure 4.3 shows an example.

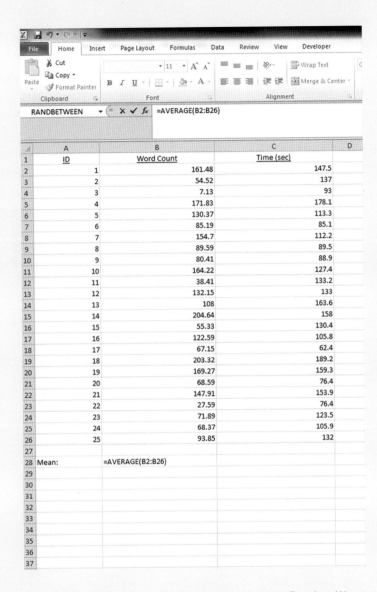

Figure 4.3 Screenshot from Microsoft Excel showing the calculation of a mean. Data from Warne et al. (2016).

To calculate a mean, you should type =AVERAGE(XX:XX), where the XX's are replaced by the coordinates for the cells containing your data. In Figure 4.3 the Excel function is =AVERAGE(B2:B26) because the cells that contain that Word Count variable's data are B2–B26. A colon between cells means that Excel should include all data between the two cells you type in the function. The function for the mean from the Time variable would be =AVERAGE (C2:C26).

Calculating other descriptive statistics is similar, requiring the following computer commands:

- Median: =MEDIAN(XX:XX)
- Mode: =MODE(XX:XX)
- Range: =MIN(XX:XX)-MAX(XX:XX)

- Population standard deviation estimate: =STDEV.S(XX:XX)
- Sample standard deviation: =STDEV.P(XX:XX)
- Population variance estimate: =VAR.S(XX:XX)
- Sample variance: =VAR.P(XX:XX)
- Skewness: =SKEW(XX:XX)
- Kurtosis: =KURT(XX:XX)

Unfortunately, Excel is not equipped to calculate trimmed means or interquartile ranges. This means that the user has to eliminate the highest and lowest cases manually before using the AVERAGE

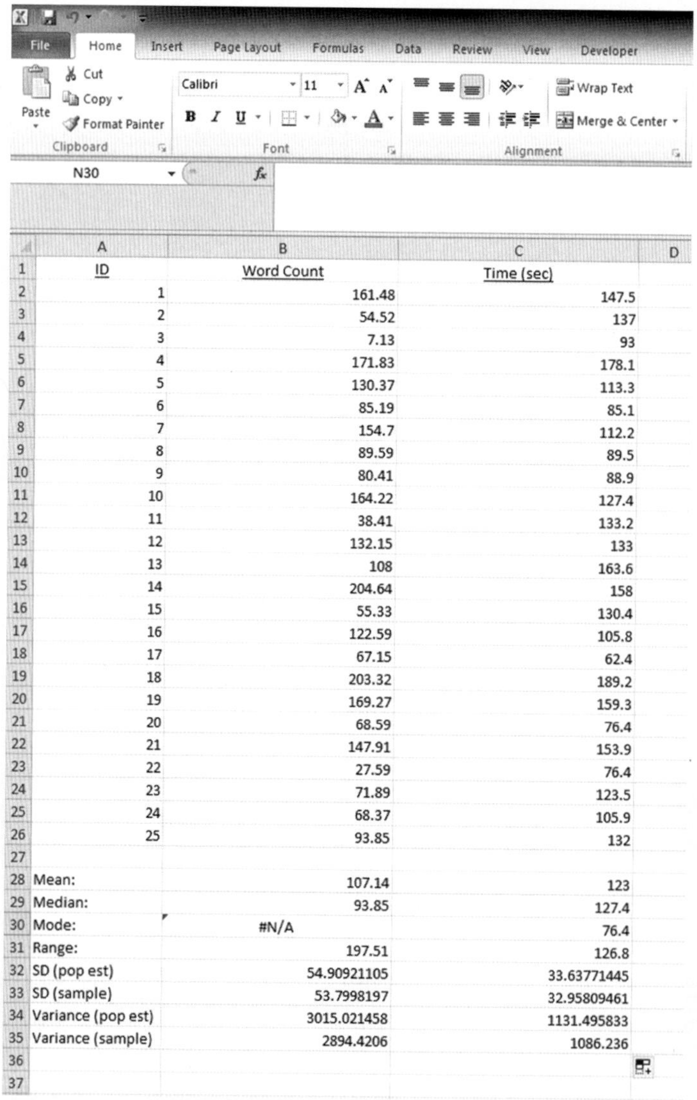

	A	B	C	D
1	ID	Word Count	Time (sec)	
2	1	161.48	147.5	
3	2	54.52	137	
4	3	7.13	93	
5	4	171.83	178.1	
6	5	130.37	113.3	
7	6	85.19	85.1	
8	7	154.7	112.2	
9	8	89.59	89.5	
10	9	80.41	88.9	
11	10	164.22	127.4	
12	11	38.41	133.2	
13	12	132.15	133	
14	13	108	163.6	
15	14	204.64	158	
16	15	55.33	130.4	
17	16	122.59	105.8	
18	17	67.15	62.4	
19	18	203.32	189.2	
20	19	169.27	159.3	
21	20	68.59	76.4	
22	21	147.91	153.9	
23	22	27.59	76.4	
24	23	71.89	123.5	
25	24	68.37	105.9	
26	25	93.85	132	
27				
28	Mean:	107.14	123	
29	Median:	93.85	127.4	
30	Mode:	#N/A	76.4	
31	Range:	197.51	126.8	
32	SD (pop est)	54.90921105	33.63771445	
33	SD (sample)	53.7998197	32.95809461	
34	Variance (pop est)	3015.021458	1131.495833	
35	Variance (sample)	2894.4206	1086.236	
36				
37				

Figure 4.4 Results of descriptive statistics calculations in Microsoft Excel. For the first mode the result is #N/A because there is no score that appears twice in the dataset.

function to find the trimmed mean. Figure 4.4 shows the results of using these functions for both variables in the Excel spreadsheet.

SPSS

In SPSS there are two ways to produce descriptive statistics. The first method requires selecting "Analyze" → "Descriptive statistics" → "Descriptives." This makes a small window labeled "Descriptives" appear on the screen. It is shown in Figure 4.5a. On the left side is a list of variables in the dataset. You should move each variable you want to calculate statistics for from the left side to the right side by either clicking and dragging the variable(s) or by using the mouse to select a

(a)

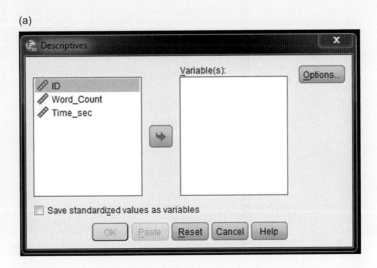

Figure 4.5a The Descriptives window in SPSS.

(b)

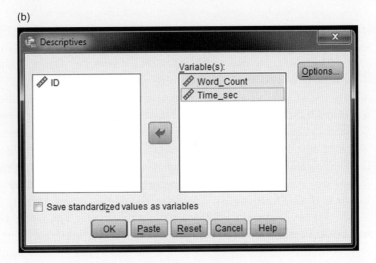

Figure 4.5b The Descriptives window in SPSS with two variables selected.

Figure 4.6 Window showing options for calculating descriptive statistics.

variable and then clicking the arrow in the middle to move the selected variable to the right side of the window. In Figure 4.5b, I have selected the two variables Word_Count and Time_sec.

After selecting the variables, you should push the "Options" button in the top-right corner of the Descriptives window. Another small window appears, as shown in Figure 4.6. The square boxes in the window are all the statistics that can be calculated automatically in SPSS. The window in Figure 4.6 shows the SPSS defaults. For this example, I am selecting "Mean," "Std. deviation," "Variance," "Range," "Skewness," and "Kurtosis." The circles at the bottom of the window (labeled "Display Order") are options for choosing the order in which the variables will appear in the output. The SPSS default (Figure 4.6) is to display variables in the order that the user selected them (in Figure 4.5b). After choosing the appropriate options, you choose "Continue." This makes the menu disappear. In the Descriptives window, you should then select "OK."

Figure 4.7 shows the SPSS output for these steps. You should be aware that SPSS assumes that standard deviations and variances are population estimates, and automatically applies Bessel's correction. Also, these steps do not permit the user to calculate the median or mode.

The other method of calculating models of central tendency and variability is to select "Analyze" → "Descriptive Statistics" → "Frequencies." This produces the Frequencies window shown in Figure 3.34. At the top right of the window is a button labeled "Statistics." Clicking that

Descriptive Statistics

	N	Range	Mean	Std. Deviation	Variance	Skewness		Kurtosis	
	Statistic	Statistic	Statistic	Statistic	Statistic	Statistic	Std. Error	Statistic	Std. Error
Word_Count	25	197.51	107.1400	54.90921	3015.021	.139	.464	-.924	.902
Time_sec	25	126.80	123.0000	33.63771	1131.496	.083	.464	-.726	.902
Valid N (listwise)	25								

Figure 4.7 SPSS output showing descriptive statistics.

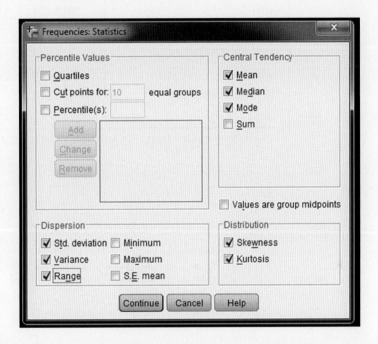

Figure 4.8 SPSS menu permitting the user to select statistics to calculate.

produces a new window shown in Figure 4.8. The default of this menu is for all of the boxes to be unchecked. After checking all desired boxes, the user should select "Continue." The remaining window that is open is the Frequencies window. The default in this window is for the option directing the computer to create histograms (as shown in Chapter 3's Software Guide). Keeping this box checked will ensure that the computer will produce a histogram for every variable selected.

Figure 4.9 shows the descriptive statistics for this example. Users should be aware that in SPSS, when there are multiple modes, the smallest mode is displayed. Also, SPSS cannot calculate interquartile ranges automatically, but telling the computer to display quartile values will produce the numbers needed to make this calculation. They will be labeled as "Percentiles 25" and "75." The interquartile range is calculated by subtracting the smaller number from the larger one.

Statistics

		Word_Count	Time_sec
N	Valid	25	25
	Missing	0	0
Mean		107.1400	123.0000
Median		93.8500	127.4000
Mode		7.13[a]	76.40
Std. Deviation		54.90921	33.63771
Variance		3015.021	1131.496
Skewness		.139	.083
Std. Error of Skewness		.464	.464
Kurtosis		-.924	-.726
Std. Error of Kurtosis		.902	.902
Range		197.51	126.80

a. Multiple modes exist. The smallest value is shown

Figure 4.9 SPSS output from the Frequencies command.

Further Reading

- Barnett, V. (1978). The study of outliers: Purpose and model. *Journal of the Royal Statistical Society. Series C (Applied Statistics)*, *27*, 242–250. doi:10.2307/2347159

  * This article is an excellent introduction to outliers. Barnett gives real-life examples of outliers in meteorology, legal cases, agriculture, biology, and more. The author discusses why outliers occur, how they affect data analysis, and whether the appearance of outliers can be explained with statistical models.

- Gorard, S. (2005). Revisiting a 90-year-old debate: The advantages of the mean deviation. *British Journal of Educational Studies*, *53*, 417–430. doi:10.1111/ j.1467–8527.2005.00304.x

  * Gorard explains in this article why statisticians and social scientists use the standard deviation instead of the mean deviation. He also advocates more widespread use of the mean deviation and shows that it may be more appropriate for many types of real-life data. Gorard's ideas are not mainstream, but they are well reasoned, and I think that they deserve a fair hearing.

- Leys, C., Ley, C., Klein, O., Bernard, P., & Licata, L. (2013). Detecting outliers: Do not use standard deviation around the mean, use absolute deviation around the median. *Journal of Experimental Social Psychology*, *49*, 764–766. doi:10.1016/j.jesp.2013.03.013

* This article gives an excellent summary of the absolute deviation around the median, which is conceptually similar to the mean deviation explained in Sidebar 4.4. The authors also explain how using the absolute deviation around the median is a more accurate method of detecting outliers.

- Wilcox, R. R. (1998). How many discoveries have been lost by ignoring modern statistical methods? *American Psychologist, 53*, 300–314. doi:10.1037/0003–066X.53.3.300

  * In this article Wilcox explains robust statistics, which are statistics that are resistant to violations of their assumptions. He also makes a strong argument for more widespread use of the trimmed mean and similar statistics. Wilcox also shows the shortcomings of more traditional models of central tendency.

5 Linear Transformations and *z*-Scores

Visitors from other nations sometimes have trouble adapting to American measurement units. For people who have lived their whole life with the metric system, adjusting to the use of pounds, feet, inches, and Fahrenheit degrees can be a challenge. Converting some of these units into their metric equivalents is not always easy, but it may be needed to avoid misunderstandings or problems. Converting measurements from one unit to another is a common example of what statisticians call a linear transformation. In this chapter, I will explain linear transformations, show how they are performed, and talk about a special linear transformation: the conversion of data into *z*-scores.

Learning Goals

- Conduct a linear transformation.
- Accurately predict the impact of a linear transformation on the mean and standard deviations of a dataset.
- Calculate and interpret a *z*-score for a member of a dataset.
- Explain why *z*-scores are useful.

Linear Transformations

To perform a **linear transformation**, you need to take a dataset and either add, subtract, multiply, or divide every score by the same constant. (You may remember from Chapter 1 that a constant is a score that is the same for every member of a sample or population.) Performing a linear transformation is common in statistics. Linear transformations change the data, and that means they can have an impact on models derived from the data – including visual models and descriptive statistics.

Linear transformations allow us to convert data from one scale to a more preferable scale. For example, converting measurements recorded in inches into centimeters requires a linear transformation (multiplying by 2.54). Another common linear transformation is to convert Fahrenheit temperatures to Celsius temperatures (which requires subtracting 32 and then dividing by 1.8) or vice versa (which requires multiplying by 1.8 and then adding 32). Sometimes performing a linear transformation is done to make calculations easier, as by eliminating negative numbers (by adding a constant so that all scores are positive) or eliminating decimals or fractions (by multiplying by a constant). As you will see in this chapter, making these changes in the scale of the data does not fundamentally alter the relative pattern of the scores or the results of many statistical analyses.

Linear transformations are common in statistics, so it is important to understand how linear transformations change statistics and data.

Impact of linear transformations on means. Chapter 4 showed how to calculate the mean (Formula 4.2) and standard deviation (Formulas 4.7–4.9). An interesting thing happens to these sample statistics when a constant is added to the data. If we use the Waite et al. (2015) data and add a constant of 4 to every person's age, then the results will be as follows:

18 + 4 = 22   19 + 4 = 23   20 + 4 = 24   21 + 4 = 25   23 + 4 = 27   23 + 4 = 27   24 + 4 = 28
24 + 4 = 28   25 + 4 = 29   31 + 4 = 35   33 + 4 = 37   35 + 4 = 39   38 + 4 = 42

Finding the mean of these scores is as follows:

$$\overline{X}_{new} = \frac{22 + 23 + 24 + 25 + 27 + 27 + 28 + 28 + 29 + 35 + 37 + 39 + 42}{13}$$

$$\overline{X}_{new} = \frac{386}{13} = 29.69$$

The original mean (which we will abbreviate as $\overline{X}_{orig}$) was 25.69, as shown in Guided Example 4.1. The difference between the original mean and the new mean is 4 (29.69 – 25.69 = 4), which is the same value as the constant that was added to all of the original data. This is true for any constant that is added to every score in a dataset:

$$\overline{X}_{orig} + constant = \overline{X}_{new} \tag{Formula 5.1}$$

Another example shows that something similar happens when a constant is subtracted from every score. We may want to subtract 18 from every age score, which would produce a new score that represents how long the subject has been an adult:

18 – 18 = 0   19 – 18 = 1   20 – 18 = 2   21 – 18 = 3   23 – 18 = 5   23 – 18 = 5   24 – 18 = 6
24 – 18 = 6   25 – 18 = 7   31 – 18 = 13   33 – 18 = 15   35 – 18 = 17   38 – 18 = 20

Calculating a mean for these new scores is:

$$\overline{X}_{new} = \frac{0 + 1 + 2 + 3 + 5 + 5 + 6 + 6 + 7 + 13 + 15 + 17 + 20}{13} = 7$$

$$\overline{X}_{new} = \frac{100}{13} = 7.69$$

Notice that the new mean of 7.69 is 18 points lower than the original mean (25.69 – 7.69 = 18). In fact, this is true of any constant that is subtracted from every score. This can be expressed as a new equation:

$$\overline{X}_{orig} - constant = \overline{X}_{new} \tag{Formula 5.2}$$

Thus, whenever a constant is added to or subtracted from a dataset, it is not necessary to add that constant to every score and calculate the new data's mean. Instead, all you have to do to find the new mean is add or subtract the constant from the original mean. Formulas 5.1 and 5.2 show that we can select our data's mean to be any value we wish by just adding or subtracting a constant.

Something similar happens when scores are multiplied by a constant. Here's an example where the ages from the Waite et al. (2015) study have been multiplied by 12, which would convert the variable from the number of years in someone's age to the number of months:

18 × 12 = 216 19 × 12 = 228 20 × 12 = 240 21 × 12 = 252 23 × 12 = 276 23 × 12 = 276 24 × 12 = 288
24 × 12 = 288 25 × 12 = 300 31 × 12 = 372 33 × 12 = 396 35 × 12 = 420 38 × 12 = 456

Calculating a new mean for these scores is:

$$\overline{X}_{new} = \frac{216 + 228 + 240 + 252 + 276 + 276 + 288 + 288 + 300 + 372 + 396 + 420 + 456}{13}$$

$$\overline{X}_{new} = \frac{4008}{13} = 308.31$$

The $\overline{X}_{orig}$ value was 25.69. Notice that the $\overline{X}_{new}$ is exactly 12 times larger than the value of the original mean ($25.69 \times 12 = 308.3$). Therefore, when multiplying by a constant, the new mean is calculated by multiplying the original mean by the constant:

$$\overline{X}_{orig} \times constant = \overline{X}_{new} \qquad \text{(Formula 5.3)}$$

Dividing the scores by a constant has a similar impact on means. For example, we can divide every score by a constant of 4:

$18 \div 4 = 4.5$ $19 \div 4 = 4.75$ $20 \div 4 = 5$ $21 \div 4 = 5.25$ $23 \div 4 = 5.75$ $23 \div 4 = 5.75$ $24 \div 4 = 6$
$24 \div 4 = 6$ $25 \div 4 = 6.25$ $31 \div 4 = 7.75$ $33 \div 4 = 8.25$ $35 \div 4 = 8.75$ $38 \div 4 = 9.5$

Calculating a mean from these scores is:

$$\overline{X}_{new} = \frac{4.5 + 4.75 + 5 + 5.25 + 5.75 + 5.75 + 6 + 6 + 6.25 + 7.75 + 8.25 + 8.75 + 9.5}{13}$$

$$\overline{X}_{new} = \frac{83.5}{13} = 6.42$$

Again, comparing this new mean with the original mean shows that the constant has a similar impact on the new mean. The new mean is now one-quarter of the original mean value ($25.69 \div 4 = 6.42$). Therefore,

$$\overline{X}_{orig} \div constant = \overline{X}_{new} \qquad \text{(Formula 5.4)}$$

Impact of Linear Transformation on Standard Deviations. Adding a constant to a set of scores does not have the same impact on a standard deviation that it has on the mean. Using the same numbers as above (when a constant of 4 was added to the scores, which produced a $\overline{X}_{new}$ of 29.69), we can see what happens to a standard deviation after adding a constant to the scores. The deviation scores would be as follows:

$22 - 29.69 = -7.69$ $23 - 29.69 = -6.69$ $24 - 29.69 = -5.69$ $25 - 29.69 = -4.69$
$27 - 29.69 = -2.69$ $27 - 29.69 = -2.69$ $28 - 29.69 = -1.69$ $28 - 29.69 = -1.69$
$29 - 29.69 = -0.69$ $35 - 29.69 = 5.31$ $37 - 29.69 = 7.31$ $39 - 29.69 = 9.31$
$42 - 29.69 = 12.31$

Squaring these produces the following numbers:

$(-7.69)^2 = 59.17$ $(-6.69)^2 = 44.79$ $(-5.69)^2 = 32.40$ $(-4.69)^2 = 22.02$
$(-2.69)^2 = 7.25$ $(-2.69)^2 = 7.25$ $(-1.69)^2 = 2.86$ $(-1.69)^2 = 2.86$
$(-0.69)^2 = 0.48$ $(5.31)^2 = 28.17$ $(7.31)^2 = 53.40$ $(9.31)^2 = 86.63$
$(12.31)^2 = 151.48$

The next step in calculating the standard deviation is to add these squared deviation scores together:

$59.17 + 44.79 + 32.40 + 22.02 + 7.25 + 7.25 + 2.86 + 2.86 + 0.48 + 28.17 + 53.40 + 86.63 + 151.48$
$= 498.77$

The last steps are to divide the sum by n (which is 13) and then square root the result.

$$s_x = \sqrt{\frac{498.77}{13}} = 6.19$$

This new standard deviation is precisely equal to the original data's standard deviation in Guided Practice 4.2. This example shows that *adding a constant to a set of data has no impact on the standard deviation.*

Calculating the standard deviation for the scores that have had a constant subtracted from them illustrates a similar point. We can show this with the data above that had a constant of 2 subtracted from every score. The deviation scores for these data are as follows:

$16 - 23.69 = -7.69$ $17 - 23.69 = -6.69$ $18 - 23.69 = -5.69$ $19 - 23.69 = -4.69$
$21 - 23.69 = -2.69$ $21 - 23.69 = -2.69$ $22 - 23.69 = -1.69$ $22 - 23.69 = -1.69$
$23 - 23.69 = -0.69$ $29 - 23.69 = 5.31$ $31 - 23.69 = 7.31$ $33 - 23.69 = 9.31$
$36 - 23.69 = 12.31$

Squaring these produces the following numbers:

$(-7.69)^2 = 59.17$ $(-6.69)^2 = 44.79$ $(-5.69)^2 = 32.40$ $(-4.69)^2 = 22.02$
$(-2.69)^2 = 7.25$ $(-2.69)^2 = 7.25$ $(-1.69)^2 = 2.86$ $(-1.69)^2 = 2.86$
$(-0.69)^2 = 0.48$ $(5.31)^2 = 28.17$ $(7.31)^2 = 53.40$ $(9.31)^2 = 86.63$
$(12.31)^2 = 151.48$

The next step in calculating the standard deviation is to add these squared deviation scores together:

$59.17 + 44.79 + 32.40 + 22.02 + 7.25 + 7.25 + 2.86 + 2.86 + 0.48 + 28.17 + 53.40 + 86.63 + 151.48 = 498.77$

The last steps are to divide the sum by n (which is 13) and then square root the result.

$$s_x = \sqrt{\frac{498.77}{13}} = 6.19$$

This standard deviation is precisely equal to the original standard deviation and the standard deviation that we calculated after adding a constant of 4 to every score. This shows that – just like adding a constant – *subtracting a constant from a set of scores does not change the standard deviation.*

Multiplying the scores in a dataset by a constant does change the standard deviation, though. This is shown by calculating the standard deviation in the example data above (which were all multiplied by 12). The deviation scores for the scores that have been multiplied by 2 (which had a mean of 308.3) are as follows:

$216 - 308.31 = -92.31$ $228 - 308.31 = -80.31$ $240 - 308.31 = -68.31$ $252 - 308.31 = -56.31$
$276 - 308.31 = -32.31$ $276 - 308.31 = -32.31$ $288 - 308.31 = -20.31$ $288 - 308.31 = -20.31$
$300 - 308.31 = -8.31$ $372 - 308.31 = 63.69$ $396 - 308.31 = 87.69$ $420 - 308.31 = 111.69$
$456 - 308.31 = 147.69$

Squaring these deviation scores produces the following numbers:

$(-92.31)^2 = 8520.71$ $(-80.31)^2 = 6449.33$ $(-68.31)^2 = 4665.94$ $(-56.31)^2 = 3170.56$
$(-32.31)^2 = 1043.79$ $(-32.31)^2 = 1043.79$ $(-20.31)^2 = 412.40$ $(-20.31)^2 = 412.40$
$(-8.31)^2 = 69.02$ $(63.69)^2 = 4056.71$ $(87.69)^2 = 7689.94$ $(111.69)^2 = 12475.17$
$(147.69)^2 = 21813.02$

Summing these squared deviation scores is as follows:

$8520.71 + 6449.33 + 4665.94 + 3170.56 + 1043.79 + 1043.79 + 412.40 + 412.40$
$+69.02 + 4056.71 + 7689.94 + 12475.17 + 21813.02 = 71,822.8$

Finally, we divide the sum by n (which is 13) and then square root the result.

$$s_x = \sqrt{\frac{71,822.8}{13}} = 74.33$$

The original standard deviation was 6.19. This new standard deviation is 74.33, which is exactly 12 times larger than the original standard deviation. Therefore, multiplying the scores in a dataset by a constant also multiplies the standard deviation by the same constant. This can be expressed mathematically as Formula 5.5:

$$s_{orig} \times constant = s_{new} \qquad \text{(Formula 5.5)}$$

An example can also show us the impact of dividing every score in a dataset by a constant. Using the scores from above (where every score had been divided by 4), we can calculate the deviation scores:

$4.5 - 6.42 = -1.92 \quad 4.75 - 6.42 = -1.67 \quad 5 - 6.42 = -1.42 \quad 5.25 - 6.42 = -1.17$
$5.75 - 6.42 = -0.67 \quad 5.75 - 6.42 = -0.67 \quad 6 - 6.42 = -0.42 \quad 6 - 6.42 = -0.42$
$6.25 - 6.42 = -0.17 \quad 7.75 - 6.42 = 1.33 \quad 8.25 - 6.42 = 1.83 \quad 8.75 - 6.42 = 2.33$
$9.5 - 6.42 = 3.08$

The next step is to square these values:

$(-1.92)^2 = 3.70 \quad (-1.67)^2 = 2.80 \quad (-1.42)^2 = 2.03 \quad (-1.17)^2 = 1.38$
$(-0.67)^2 = 0.45 \quad (-0.67)^2 = 0.45 \quad (-0.42)^2 = 0.18 \quad (-0.42)^2 = 0.18$
$(-0.17)^2 = 0.03 \quad (1.33)^2 = 1.76 \quad (1.83)^2 = 3.34 \quad (2.33)^2 = 5.41$
$(3.08)^2 = 9.47$

Again, the next step is to add these squared deviation scores together.

$3.70 + 2.80 + 2.03 + 1.38 + 0.45 + 0.45 + 0.18 + 0.18 + 0.03 + 1.76 + 3.34 + 5.41 + 9.47$
$= 31.17$

The last steps are to divide by n (which is 13) and to square root the result.

$$s_{new} = \sqrt{\frac{31.17}{13}} = 1.55$$

Comparing this new standard deviation (1.55) to the original standard deviation (6.19) shows that the new standard deviation is one-fourth the size of the original standard deviation. This means that dividing every score in a dataset by a constant will change the standard deviation by the same amount. This is expressed in Formula 5.6:

$$s_{orig} \div constant = s_{new} \qquad \text{(Formula 5.6)}$$

Table 5.1 shows how linear transformations change other descriptive statistics.

Impact of Linear Transformations on Histogram Shapes. In addition to the impact of linear transformations on descriptive statistics, it is also important to recognize how linear transformations affect the shape of histograms. Figure 5.1a shows the histogram for the age data that we used to illustrate linear transformations. Figure 5.1b shows the histogram for the same scores after a

Table 5.1 Impact of different types of linear transformations on descriptive statistics

Statistic	Adding	Subtracting	Multiplying	Dividing
Mode	Mode + constant	Mode – constant	Mode × constant	Mode ÷ constant
Median	Median + constant	Median – constant	Median × constant	Median ÷ constant
Mean	Mean + constant	Mean – constant	Mean × constant	Mean ÷ constant
Trimmed mean	Trimmed mean + constant	Trimmed mean – constant	Trimmed mean × constant	Trimmed mean ÷ constant
Range	No change	No change	Range × constant	Range ÷ constant
Interquartile range	No change	No change	Interquartile range × constant	Interquartile range ÷ constant
Standard deviation	No change	No change	Standard deviation ×constant	Standard deviation ÷ constant
Variance	No change	No change	(Standard deviation × constant)^2	(Standard deviation ÷ constant)^2

(a)

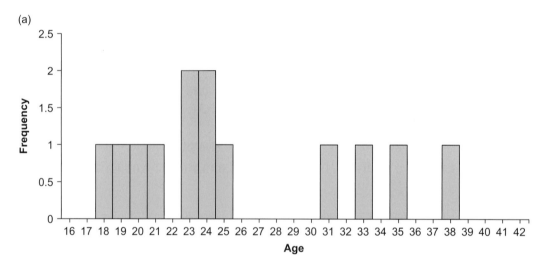

Figure 5.1a Histogram of the original data. Notice how the shape of the distribution and the pattern of the histogram's bars are the same as the data that had a constant added to the scores (Figure 5.1b) and the data that had a constant subtracted from the scores (Figure 5.1c). Only the scale of the horizontal axis (i.e., x-axis) has changed.

constant (of 4) was added to every score. Likewise, Figure 5.1c illustrates a histogram of the same scores after a constant (of 2) was subtracted from every score. A quick glance shows that Figures 5.1a–5.1c look similar. In fact, the shape of the histograms is completely identical in every way. These figures show that adding and subtracting a constant from a series of scores does not change the shape of the distribution. The only thing that changes when a constant is added or subtracted from a dataset is that the distribution shifts to the right (when a positive constant is added) or to the left (when a positive constant is subtracted). The amount of shift is equal to the constant. The pattern and height of the bars of a histogram do not change.

(b)

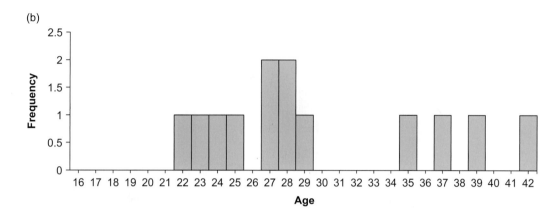

Figure 5.1b Histogram of the same data after a linear transformation in which a constant of 4 was added to every score. Notice how the shape of the distribution and the pattern of the histogram's bars are the same as the original data (Figure 5.1a) and the data that had a constant subtracted from the scores (Figure 5.1c). The histogram has merely shifted to the right by 4 units.

(c)

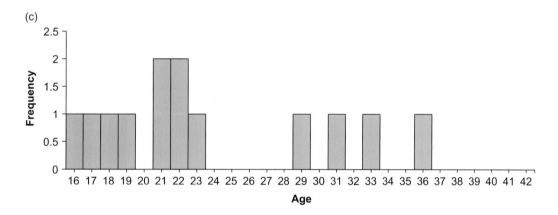

Figure 5.1c Histogram of the same data after a linear transformation in which a constant of 2 has been subtracted from every score. Notice how the shape of the distribution and the pattern of the histogram's bars are the same as the original data (Figure 5.1a) and the data that had a constant added to the scores (Figure 5.1b). The histogram has merely shifted to the left by 2 units.

Figure 5.1d shows the impact of multiplying every score in a dataset by a constant. The first difference between Figure 5.1d and the other figures is that this histogram is more spread out than the histograms in Figures 5.1a–5.1c. In fact, its range is twice as wide as the range of the data in Figures 5.1a–5.1c. Additionally, the gaps between histogram intervals are now twice as large. In effect, multiplying all the data by 12 has stretched out the histogram to be twice as wide as it was before. To save space, the intervals in the histogram have a width of 12 units, which is why the histogram looks much like the original histogram in Figure 5.1a. But the height of the bars and the pattern in which they appear in the histogram have not changed.

Figure 5.1e shows the impact of dividing scores by a constant. At first glance, the figure looks nearly identical to Figures 5.1a–5.1c. But close inspection shows that the x-axis has a much narrower range than the other figures. Indeed, the range of data is only one-fourth of the range of the original data, and the reason that the histograms look similar is that now the

(a)

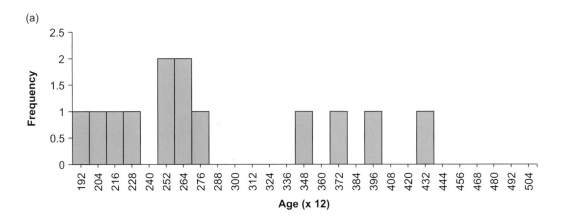

Figure 5.1d Histogram of the same data after a linear transformation in which every score has been multiplied by a constant of 12. Notice that each interval has a width of 12 units (instead of 1). Therefore, the histogram has been stretched out to cover a range of scores that is 12 times as wide as the range of the original data (in Figure 5.1a). The pattern of bars in the histogram is still the same.

(e)

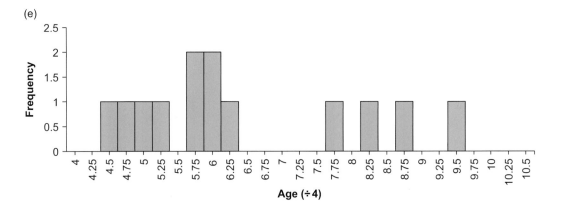

Figure 5.1e Histogram of the same data after a linear transformation in which every score has been divided by a constant of 4. The histogram now covers a range of scores that is only one-fourth as wide as the original data. Now each bar represents a .25-unit interval instead of a 1-unit interval (as in Figures 5.1a–5.1d). Compared to the other figures, these data are more compressed. The pattern of bars in the histogram is still the same.

intervals of each bar in the histogram only span one-fourth of a unit. In essence, dividing by a constant has squished the data together.

In summary, Figures 5.1a–5.1e show the possible impacts of linear transformations on histograms. First, adding and subtracting a constant merely shifts the distribution along the *x*-axis (i.e., the horizontal axis) while maintaining the distances between scores and without changing the shape of the distribution at all. In other words, you can think of adding and subtracting a constant as moving the location of the distribution. Second, multiplying and dividing by a constant stretches the distribution or squishes it together – thereby increasing or decreasing variability. Scores may get closer together or further apart after multiplying or dividing by a constant, but the rank order of scores or the relative pattern of scores does *not* change, nor does the overall shape of the distribution, or its skewness or kurtosis.

z-Scores: A Special Linear Transformation

One common linear transformation in the social sciences is to convert the data to *z*-**scores**. A *z*-score is a type of data that has a mean of 0 and a standard deviation of 1. Converting a set of scores to *z*-scores requires a formula:

$$z_i = \frac{x_i - \overline{X}}{s_x}$$ (Formula 5.7)

In Formula 5.7 the x_i refers to each individual score for variable x, $\overline{X}$ is the sample mean for variable x, and s_x is the standard deviation for the same variable. The i subscript in z_i indicates that each individual score in a dataset has its own *z*-score.

There are two steps in calculating *z*-scores. The first step is in the numerator where the sample mean is subtracted from each score. (You may recognize this as the deviation score, which was discussed in Chapter 4.) This step moves the mean of the data to 0. The second step is to divide by the standard deviation of the data. Dividing by the standard deviation changes the scale of the data until the deviation is precisely equal to 1. Guided Practice 5.1 shows how to calculate *z*-scores for real data.

The example *z*-score calculation in Guided Practice 5.1 illustrates several principles of *z*-scores. First, notice how every individual whose original score was below the original mean (i.e., $\overline{X} = 25.69$) has a negative *z*-score, and every individual whose original score was above the original mean has a positive *z*-score. Additionally, when comparing the original scores to the *z*-scores, it is apparent that the subjects whose scores are closest to the original mean also have *z*-scores closest to 0 – which is the mean of the *z*-scores. Another principle is that the unit of *z*-scores is the standard deviation, meaning that the difference between each whole number is one standard deviation. Finally, in this example the person with the lowest score in the original data also has the lowest *z*-score – and the person with the highest score in the original data also has the highest *z*-score. In fact, the rank order of subjects' scores is the same for both the original data and the set of *z*-scores because linear transformations (including converting raw scores to *z*-scores) do not change the shape of data or the ranking of individuals' scores. These principles also apply to *every* dataset that is converted to *z*-scores.

There are two benefits of *z*-scores. The first is that they permit comparisons of scores across different scales. Unlike researchers working in the physical sciences who have clear-cut units of

Guided Practice 5.1

This guided practice will show you how to calculate z-scores. Like the other examples of linear transformations in this chapter, we will use the age data from the Waite et al. (2015) study to practice with. As a reminder, the raw scores of these data are as follows:

| 18 | 19 | 20 | 21 | 23 | 23 | 24 | 24 | 25 | 31 | 33 | 35 | 38 |

The descriptive statistics for these data are $\overline{X} = 25.69$ and $s_x = 6.19$. Therefore, the first step is to subtract 25.69 from each score:

$18 - 25.69 = -7.69$ $19 - 25.69 = -6.69$ $20 - 25.69 = -5.69$ $21 - 25.69 = -4.69$
$23 - 25.69 = -2.69$ $23 - 25.69 = -2.69$ $24 - 25.69 = -1.69$ $24 - 25.69 = -1.69$
$25 - 25.69 = -0.69$ $31 - 25.69 = 5.31$ $33 - 25.69 = 7.31$ $35 - 25.69 = 9.31$
$38 - 25.69 = 12.31$

The second step in Formula 5.7 is to divide each deviation score by the standard deviation:

$-7.69 \div 6.19 = -1.24$ $-6.69 \div 6.19 = -1.08$ $-5.69 \div 6.19 = -0.92$ $-4.69 \div 6.19 = -0.76$
$-2.69 \div 6.19 = -0.43$ $-2.69 \div 6.19 = -0.43$ $-1.69 \div 6.19 = -0.27$ $-1.69 \div 6.19 = -0.27$
$-0.69 \div 6.19 = -0.11$ $5.31 \div 6.19 = 0.86$ $7.31 \div 6.19 = 1.18$ $9.31 \div 6.19 = 1.50$
$12.31 \div 6.19 = 1.99$

These are the z-scores for each individual in the sample. Notice that the mean of the z-scores is 0:

$$\frac{-1.24 - 1.08 - 0.92 - 0.76 - 0.43 - 0.43 - 0.27 - 0.27 - 0.11 + 0.86 + 1.18 + 1.50 + 1.99}{13}$$
$$= \frac{0}{13} = 0$$

Likewise, the standard deviation is 1. This can be seen by calculating the standard deviation. The first step is to find a deviation score for each z-score:

$-1.24 - 0 = -1.24$ $-1.08 - 0 = -1.08$ $-0.92 - 0 = -0.92$ $-0.76 - 0 = -0.76$
$-0.43 - 0 = -0.43$ $-0.43 - 0 = -0.43$ $-0.27 - 0 = -0.27$ $-0.27 - 0 = -0.27$
$-0.11 - 0 = -0.11$ $0.86 - 0 = 0.86$ $1.18 - 0 = 1.18$ $1.50 - 0 = 1.50$
$1.99 - 0 = 1.99$

Squaring these values produces:

$(-1.24)^2 = 1.54$ $(-1.08)^2 = 1.17$ $(-0.92)^2 = 0.84$ $(-0.76)^2 = 0.57$
$(-0.43)^2 = 0.19$ $(-0.43)^2 = 0.19$ $(-0.27)^2 = 0.07$ $(-0.27)^2 = 0.07$
$(-0.11)^2 = 0.01$ $(0.86)^2 = 0.73$ $(1.18)^2 = 1.39$ $(1.50)^2 = 2.26$
$(1.99)^2 = 3.95$

The next step is to add these values together:

$1.54 + 1.17 + 0.84 + 0.57 + 0.19 + 0.19 + 0.07 + 0.07 + 0.01 + 0.73 + 1.39 + 2.26 + 3.95$
$= 13.00$

Dividing by *n* produces a variance of 1 (13 ÷ 13 = 1), the square root of which is also 1. This is the standard deviation. This proves that the linear transformation that produced these *z*-scores via Formula 5.7 produced a set of scores that have a mean of 0 and a standard deviation of 1. All *z*-score transformations will produce this mean and standard deviation.

measurement (e.g., meters, grams, pounds), researchers and students in the social sciences frequently study variables that are difficult to measure (e.g., tension, quality of communication in a marriage). For example, a sociologist interested in gender roles may use a test called the Bem Sex Roles Inventory (Bem, 1974) to measure how strongly the subjects in a study identify with traditional masculine or feminine gender roles. This test has a masculinity subscale and a femininity subscale, each of which has scores ranging from 0 to 25, with higher numbers indicating stronger identification with either masculine or feminine sex roles. A psychologist, though, may decide to use the Minnesota Multiphasic Personality Inventory's masculinity and femininity subscales (Butcher, Dahlstrom, Graham, Tellegen, & Kaemmer, 1989) to measure gender roles. Scores on these subscales typically range from 20 to 80. Even though both researchers are measuring the same traits, their scores would not be comparable because the scales are so different. But if they convert their data to *z*-scores, then the scores from both studies are comparable.

Another benefit is that *z*-scores permit us to make comparisons across different variables. For example, an anthropologist can find that one of her subjects has a *z*-score of +1.20 in individualism and a *z*-score of –0.43 in level of cultural traditionalism. In this case she can say that the person is higher in their level of individualism than in their level of traditionalism. This example shows that comparing scores only requires that the scores be on the same scale. Because *z*-scores can be compared across scales and across variables, they function like a "universal language" for data of different scales and variables. For this reason *z*-scores are sometimes called **standardized scores**.

Sidebar 5.1   ***z*-Scores and the normal distribution**

Figure 5.2 shows a **normal distribution**, and the first line under the distribution (labeled "standard deviation") displays the scale of a normal distribution in *z*-score units. The diagram shows the percentage of subjects who have a score between different *z*-score values. For example, 34.13% of people have a *z*-score between −1 and 0. On the other hand, 99.73% of people have a *z*-score between −3 and +3.

Another important feature is the row of numbers labeled "cumulative percentages." These percentages show the percentage of subjects who have a *z*-score equal to or lower than a particular point on the scale. For example, 84.13% of subjects will have a *z*-score lower than or equal to +1, while only 2.28% of people have a *z*-score lower than or equal to −2. It is important to remember, though, that the percentages in Figure 5.2 only apply when a variable is normally distributed. Histograms with other shapes will have other percentages.

If the whole-number values for *z*-scores do not provide enough detail for you, the *z*-table in Appendix A1 in this book can provide more information. The proportion of individuals with a *z*-score between 0 and any given value is listed in column B of the table. Multiplying this number by 100 will

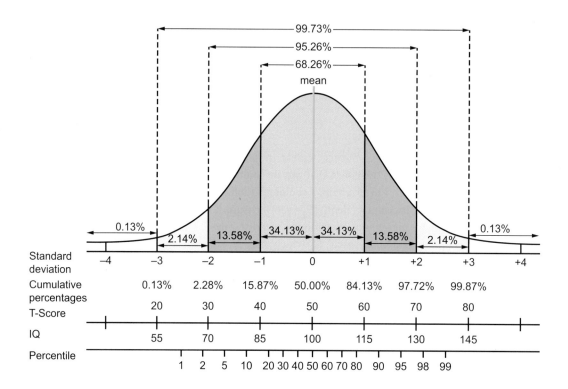

Figure 5.2 The normal distribution. The z-score scale is the first one below the distribution, labeled "Standard Deviation."

convert it to a percentage. For example, 27.34% of people will have a z-score between 0 and −0.75 (because .2734 is the number in column B for the row that has +0.75 in column A). Because half (i.e., 50%, or a proportion of .5000) of people must have a z-score below 0, we can determine that 22.66% of people will have a z-score below −0.75. This is because .5000 − .2734 = .2266. Similarly, adding .5000 to .2734 shows us that 77.34% of individuals have a z-score equal to or higher than −0.75 (because .5000 + .2734 = .7734). As in Figure 5.2, the values in Appendix A1 only apply to normally distributed variables.

Converting z-Scores to Another Scale. Converting scores to a z-score requires another linear transformation. Therefore, it makes sense that converting z-scores to another scale requires another linear transformation. This linear transformation is

$$z_i(s_x) + \overline{X} = x_i \qquad \text{(Formula 5.8)}$$

The notation in Formula 5.8 is almost the same as in Formula 5.7. Here, z_i is the z-score for a particular sample member. The s_x represents the standard deviation of the new scale, and $\overline{X}$ is the mean of the new scale. This formula produces x_i, which is the score for the individual on the new scale. Guided Practice 5.2 shows an example of how to convert z-scores to another scale.

Guided Practice 5.2

For this example, we are going to convert 5 depression z-scores to a new scale. They are:

–2.0   –1.4   0   +0.3   +3.2

We are going to convert this example to a scale that has a mean of 50 and a standard deviation of 10. This is the mean and standard deviation of a depression subscale on the Minnesota Multiphasic Personality Inventory. If we use Formula 5.8, each of these scores must first be multiplied by the standard deviation of the new scale:

$(-2.0)(10) = -20$ $(-1.4)(10) = -14$ $(0)(10) = 0$ $(0.3)(10) = 3$ $(3.2)(10) = 32$

The next step is to add the new scale's mean to each of these numbers:

$-20 + 50 = 30$ $-14 + 50 = 36$ $0 + 50 = 50$ $3 + 50 = 53$ $32 + 50 = 82$

Like any other linear transformation, Formula 5.8 does not change the rank order of the scores. Also, notice how the individual with a z-score of 0 (which was the mean of the z-scores) now has a score equal to the mean of the new data. This is always the case when converting z-scores to another scale.

Linear Transformations and Scales

In this chapter we have seen how linear transformations can be used to change the scale of the data. A common transformation is from the original data to z-scores, which have a mean of 0 and a standard deviation of 1. We can change the scale into any form through applying linear transformations. Adding and subtracting a constant shifts data over to the desired mean, and multiplying and dividing by a constant condenses or expands the scale. This shows that all scales and axes in statistics are arbitrary (Warne, 2014a). This will be an important issue in later chapters. Regardless of how we change the scale, a linear transformation will never change the shape of the histogram of a dataset (and, consequently, its skewness and kurtosis).

Check Yourself!

- What are the mean and standard deviation of a set of z-scores?

- What are the benefits of z-scores?

- How can you judge if a person's z-score is close to or far from the mean?

- What does converting the data to z-scores do to the shape of a distribution?

Summary

We can change the scale of a distribution by performing a linear transformation, which is the process of adding, subtracting, multiplying, or dividing the data by a constant. Adding and subtracting a constant will change the mean of a variable, but not its standard deviation or variance. Multiplying and dividing by a constant will change the mean, the standard deviation, and the variance of a dataset. Table 5.1 shows how linear transformations change the values of models of central tendency and variability.

One special linear transformation is the z-score, the formula for which is Formula 5.7. All z-score values have a mean of 0 and a standard deviation of 1. Putting datasets on a common scale permits comparisons across different units. Linear transformations, like the z-score, force the data to have the mean and standard deviation that we want. Yet, they do not change the shape of the distribution – only its scale. In fact, all scales are arbitrary, and we can use linear transformations to give our data any mean and standard deviation we choose. We can also convert data from z-scores to any other scale using the linear transformation equation in Formula 5.8.

Reflection Questions: Comprehension

1. How are linear transformations performed?
2. Why would someone want to perform a linear transformation?
3. What are the mean and standard deviation of a set of z-scores?
4. What does it mean when an individual's z-score is negative?
5. What are the mean and standard deviation of a set of standardized scores?

Reflection Questions: Application

6. A social worker finds that his clients require a mean of 65.1 days to find employment (standard deviation = 12.6 days). Because he meets with the clients weekly, he thinks it makes more sense to convert the data from days to weeks. Doing this would require dividing every person's datum by 7.
    a. What would the new mean for the data be?
    b. What would the new standard deviation for the data be?
    c. The original data was positively skewed and mesokurtic. What would the shape of the data be after converting the variable's unit from days to weeks?
    d. How would you convert the original scores (measured in days) for this dataset to z-scores?
7. A sample of 171 men and 198 women had a mean reaction time of 260.9 milliseconds and standard deviation of 35.3 milliseconds (Reed, Vernon, & Johnson, 2004, p. 1711). Converting these values to seconds requires dividing by 1,000.
    a. What would the mean for the data be if it were converted to seconds? Express your answer to four decimal places.
    b. What would the standard deviation for the data be if it were converted to seconds? Express your answer to four decimal places.

    c.   The original data were positively skewed and leptokurtic. What would the shape of the data be after converting the variable's unit from days to weeks?

8.   A small dataset has 10 numbers: 10, 12, 13, 13, 14, 15, 15, 17, 18, and 19.

    a.   Find the mean and standard deviation for this dataset. When calculating the standard deviation, use $n - 1$ in the formula.

    b.   Convert all the score to z-scores.

    c.   Does the rank order of the subjects change when you convert their scores to z-scores?

    d.   The skewness value for the original data is 0.10, and the kurtosis value is –0.60. What would the skewness value and kurtosis value be for the z-scores?

9.   In a normal distribution, what percentage of individuals have a z-score:

    a.   Below 0?

    b.   Above 0?

    c.   Below –1?

    d.   Above +2?

    e.   Above +3?

    f.   Between –1 and 0?

    g.   Between –1 and +1?

    h.   Between –2 and +1?

    i.   Between –2 and +2?

    j.   Above –3?

    k.   Between 0 and –1.3? (Hint: use Appendix A1.)

10. Four people were randomly selected from a population. Mark's z-score was –0.04, Tammy's was +1.21, Maren's was –0.68, and Phillip's was +3.52.

    a.   Which person's original score will be closest to the original mean?

    b.   Which two people had a score in the original data that was greater than the mean of the original dataset?

    c.   Which two people had a score in the original data that was less than the mean of the original dataset?

    d.   Which person is most likely to be an outlier?

11. A small dataset has 12 values: 4.5, 5.2, 5.3, 5.4, 5.5, 5.7, 5.7, 5.8, 5.9, 6.1, 6.2, and 12.4.

    a.   Find the mean and standard deviation for this dataset. When calculating the standard deviation, use $n - 1$ in the formula.

    b.   Convert all the scores to z-scores.

    c.   What is the mean and standard deviation of the new z-scores?

    d.   Does the rank order of the subjects change when you convert their scores to z-scores?

    e.   Based on the z-scores, which score from the original data is probably an outlier?

    f.   Why are so many z-scores in this dataset negative?

12. If Ann has a z-score of –0.30, what is the z-score of someone who scored one standard deviation higher on the original scale?

13. A student wants to convert a set of six z-scores (–4.2, –1.6, +0.1, +0.6, +1.4, +2.1) to a scale that has a mean of 80 and a standard deviation of 20.

    a.   What is the new score for each of these six individuals?

    b.   What would the new score be for an individual with a z-score of 0? Why?

   c.   What would the new scores be if the *z*-scores were converted to a scale that had a mean of 10 and a standard deviation of 1?

   d.   What would the new scores be if the *z*-scores were converted to a scale that had a mean of 0 and a standard deviation of 5?

14. A small dataset has 10 numbers: –4, –2, –1, 0, 0, 5, 6, 7, 7, and 8.

   a.   Find the mean and standard deviation for this dataset. When calculating the standard deviation, use $n - 1$ in the formula.

   b.   Convert all the scores to *z*-scores.

   c.   Does the rank order of the subjects change when you convert their scores to *z*-scores?

   d.   The skewness value for the original data is –0.11 and the kurtosis value is 1.40. What would the skewness value and kurtosis value be for the *z*-scores?

15. For a dataset, $\overline{X} = 6.8$ and $s_x = 1.2$. What is the impact on the mean of a dataset of the following linear transformations:

   a.   Adding 1 to every score?

   b.   Dividing every score by 10?

   c.   Subtracting 3 from every score?

   d.   Adding 10 to every score?

   e.   Subtracting 1.5 from every score?

   f.   Multiplying every score by 4?

   g.   Multiplying every score by 3.2?

   h.   Dividing every score by 0.2?

   i.   Adding 4 and then dividing by 2?

   j.   Subtracting 1 and then multiplying by 2?

   k.   Adding 1.3 and then multiplying by 4?

   l.   Adding 1.3 and then subtracting 0.8?

Software Guide

Like other concepts explained in this book, modern software has made performing linear transformations simple. In this Software Guide, I will show how to perform a linear transformation and to calculate *z*-scores in both Excel and SPSS.

Excel

Linear Transformations. Performing linear transformations requires using a function – just like calculating descriptive statistics did in Chapter 4's Software Guide. One of the variables in that Software Guide was time measured in seconds. But it may be more convenient to convert that variable to minutes. Because there are 60 seconds in a minute, this means dividing the scores by 60. To do this, you should find an empty cell and type "=XX/60," replacing XX with the cell number. This is shown in Figure 5.3a. The final result of applying the linear transformation to every score in Column C is shown in Figure 5.3b.

(a)

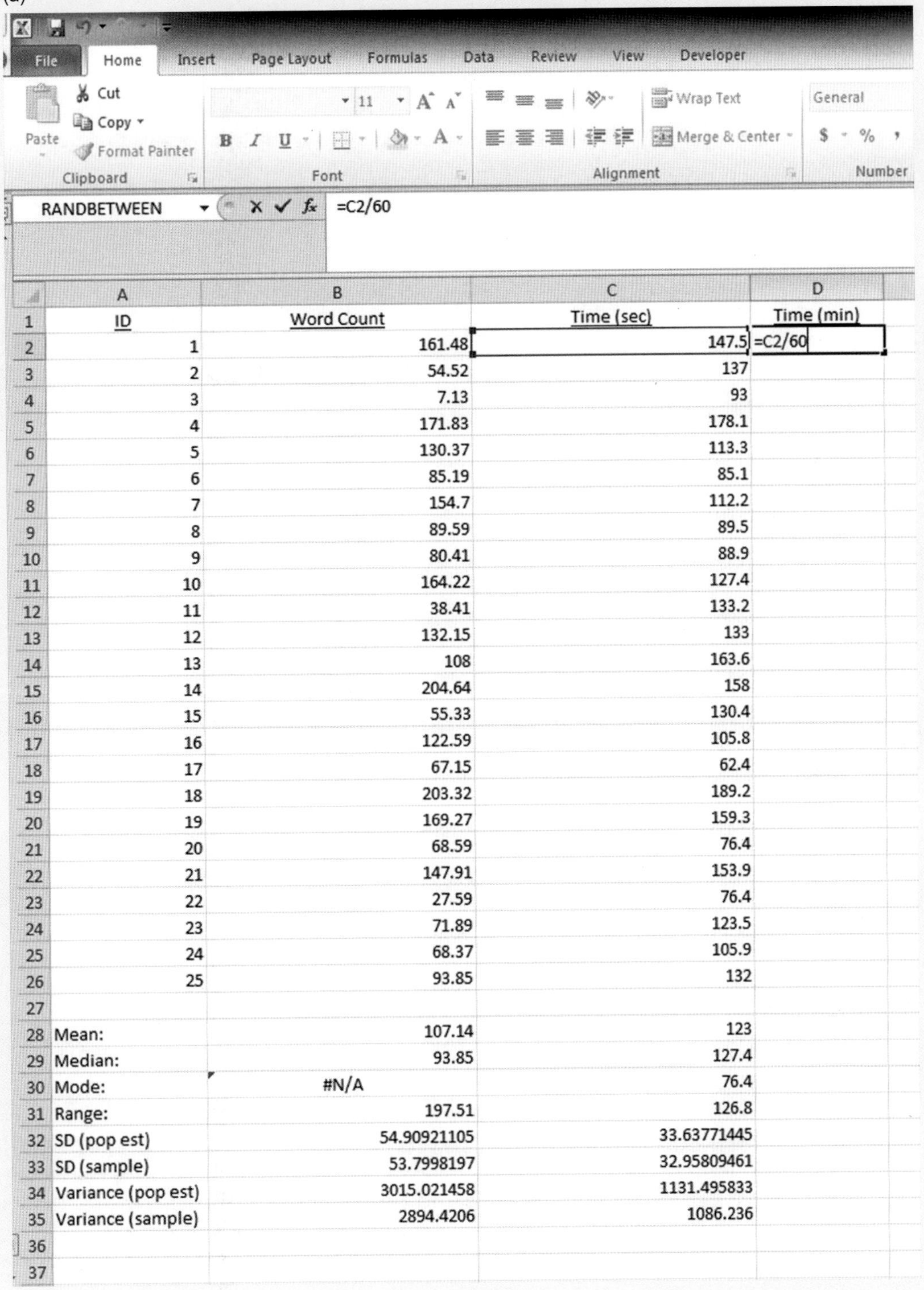

	A	B	C	D
	ID	Word Count	Time (sec)	Time (min)
1				
2	1	161.48	147.5	=C2/60
3	2	54.52	137	
4	3	7.13	93	
5	4	171.83	178.1	
6	5	130.37	113.3	
7	6	85.19	85.1	
8	7	154.7	112.2	
9	8	89.59	89.5	
10	9	80.41	88.9	
11	10	164.22	127.4	
12	11	38.41	133.2	
13	12	132.15	133	
14	13	108	163.6	
15	14	204.64	158	
16	15	55.33	130.4	
17	16	122.59	105.8	
18	17	67.15	62.4	
19	18	203.32	189.2	
20	19	169.27	159.3	
21	20	68.59	76.4	
22	21	147.91	153.9	
23	22	27.59	76.4	
24	23	71.89	123.5	
25	24	68.37	105.9	
26	25	93.85	132	
27				
28	Mean:	107.14	123	
29	Median:	93.85	127.4	
30	Mode:	#N/A	76.4	
31	Range:	197.51	126.8	
32	SD (pop est)	54.90921105	33.63771445	
33	SD (sample)	53.7998197	32.95809461	
34	Variance (pop est)	3015.021458	1131.495833	
35	Variance (sample)	2894.4206	1086.236	
36				
37				

Formula bar: RANDBETWEEN ▼ X ✓ f_x =C2/60

Figure 5.3a Screenshot from Microsoft Excel showing how to perform a linear transformation in which every score will be divided by 60. Data taken from Warne et al. (2016).

(b)

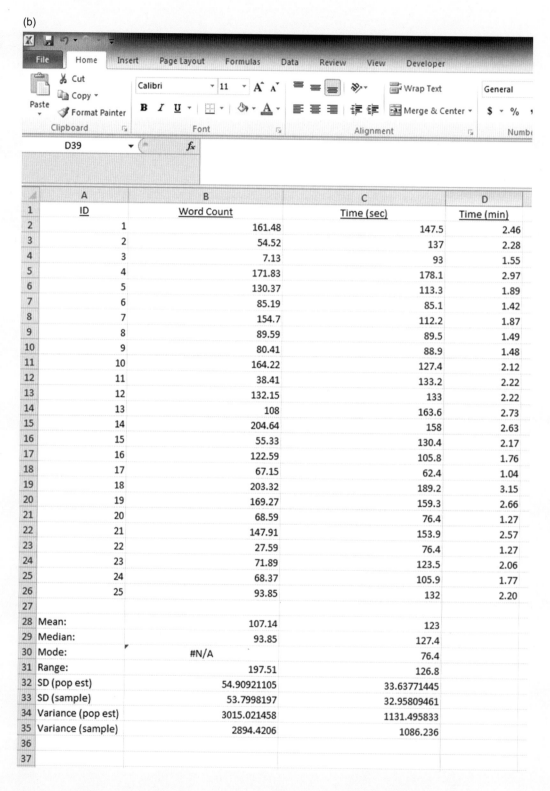

🔺	A	B	C	D
1	ID	Word Count	Time (sec)	Time (min)
2	1	161.48	147.5	2.46
3	2	54.52	137	2.28
4	3	7.13	93	1.55
5	4	171.83	178.1	2.97
6	5	130.37	113.3	1.89
7	6	85.19	85.1	1.42
8	7	154.7	112.2	1.87
9	8	89.59	89.5	1.49
10	9	80.41	88.9	1.48
11	10	164.22	127.4	2.12
12	11	38.41	133.2	2.22
13	12	132.15	133	2.22
14	13	108	163.6	2.73
15	14	204.64	158	2.63
16	15	55.33	130.4	2.17
17	16	122.59	105.8	1.76
18	17	67.15	62.4	1.04
19	18	203.32	189.2	3.15
20	19	169.27	159.3	2.66
21	20	68.59	76.4	1.27
22	21	147.91	153.9	2.57
23	22	27.59	76.4	1.27
24	23	71.89	123.5	2.06
25	24	68.37	105.9	1.77
26	25	93.85	132	2.20
27				
28	Mean:		107.14	123
29	Median:		93.85	127.4
30	Mode:	#N/A		76.4
31	Range:		197.51	126.8
32	SD (pop est)	54.90921105		33.63771445
33	SD (sample)	53.7998197		32.95809461
34	Variance (pop est)	3015.021458		1131.495833
35	Variance (sample)	2894.4206		1086.236
36				
37				

Figure 5.3b Excel data showing results of the linear transformation converting the time variable (Column C) from seconds to minutes (Column D).

Other linear transformations are relatively easy. The symbol / is used for division in this example, but the + symbol is used for addition, the – symbol for subtraction, and the * symbol is appropriate for multiplication. Changing the "60" in this number changes the constant that is applied to the linear transformation.

z-Scores. Converting data to *z*-scores means using the function "=STANDARDIZE(XX,YY, ZZ)." XX should be replaced with the original score that you want converted to a *z*-score. YY should be replaced with the mean of the dataset, and ZZ should be replaced with the standard deviation of the dataset. XX, YY, and ZZ can be either numbers that are manually typed in or cells that already contain

(a)

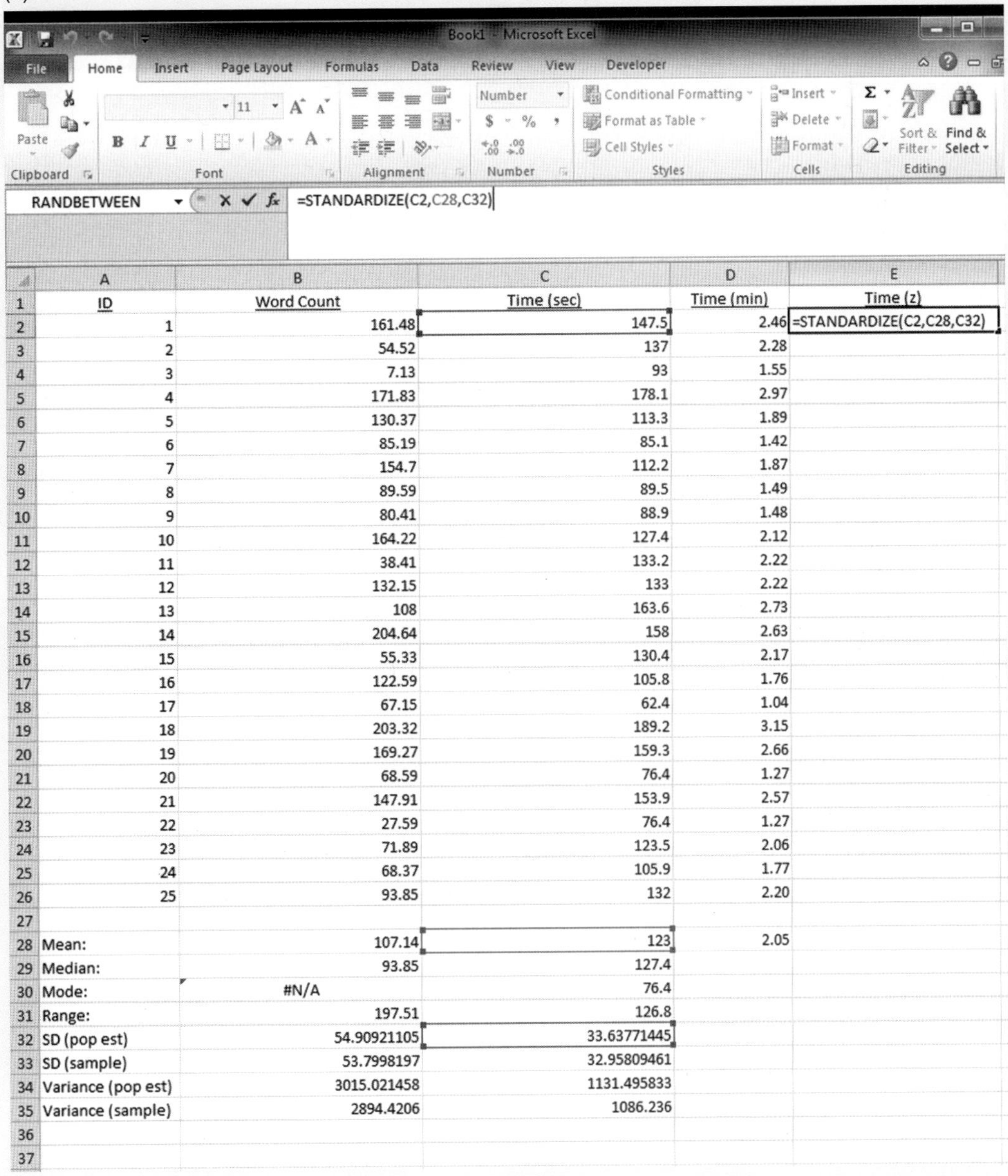

Formula bar: =STANDARDIZE(C2,C28,C32)

	A	B	C	D	E
1	ID	Word Count	Time (sec)	Time (min)	Time (z)
2	1	161.48	147.5	2.46	=STANDARDIZE(C2,C28,C32)
3	2	54.52	137	2.28	
4	3	7.13	93	1.55	
5	4	171.83	178.1	2.97	
6	5	130.37	113.3	1.89	
7	6	85.19	85.1	1.42	
8	7	154.7	112.2	1.87	
9	8	89.59	89.5	1.49	
10	9	80.41	88.9	1.48	
11	10	164.22	127.4	2.12	
12	11	38.41	133.2	2.22	
13	12	132.15	133	2.22	
14	13	108	163.6	2.73	
15	14	204.64	158	2.63	
16	15	55.33	130.4	2.17	
17	16	122.59	105.8	1.76	
18	17	67.15	62.4	1.04	
19	18	203.32	189.2	3.15	
20	19	169.27	159.3	2.66	
21	20	68.59	76.4	1.27	
22	21	147.91	153.9	2.57	
23	22	27.59	76.4	1.27	
24	23	71.89	123.5	2.06	
25	24	68.37	105.9	1.77	
26	25	93.85	132	2.20	
27					
28	Mean:		107.14	123	2.05
29	Median:		93.85	127.4	
30	Mode:	#N/A		76.4	
31	Range:		197.51	126.8	
32	SD (pop est)		54.90921105	33.63771445	
33	SD (sample)		53.7998197	32.95809461	
34	Variance (pop est)		3015.021458	1131.495833	
35	Variance (sample)		2894.4206	1086.236	
36					
37					

Figure 5.4a Screenshot from Microsoft Excel showing the use of the STANDARDIZE function to calculate *z*-scores.

(b)

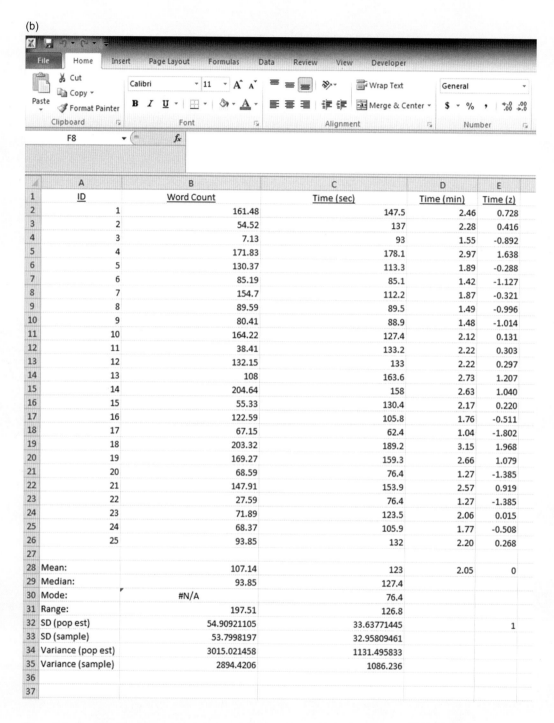

Figure 5.4b Results of the time variable being converted to *z*-scores. Notice how the mean of the *z*-scores is 0 and the standard deviation is 1.

the original score, mean, and standard deviation. Figure 5.4a shows an example of this function being used. Figure 5.4b shows the results of an entire variable being converted to *z*-scores.

SPSS

Linear Transformations. Performing a linear transformation in SPSS requires clicking "Transform" → "Compute Variable." A window appears which looks like a calculator, as shown in Figure 5.5a. Type the new variable name in the top-left corner (in the area labeled "Target Variable"). In the top-right area, you should type in the linear transformation you want to perform. In this example dividing every score in the "Time_sec" variable by 60 means typing in "Time_sec / 60." You can see this example in Figure 5.5a (where the new variable will be named "Time_min"). The variable list and arrow can also let you select a variable instead of typing it in. Like Excel, changing the number (from 60 in this example to something else) will change the constant used in the linear transformation. Changing the sign (from / for division to + for addition, – for subtraction, or * for multiplication) will change the mathematical operation that the computer performs. Figure 5.5b shows the results of this linear transformation. Notice how the new variable is named "Time_min."

(a)

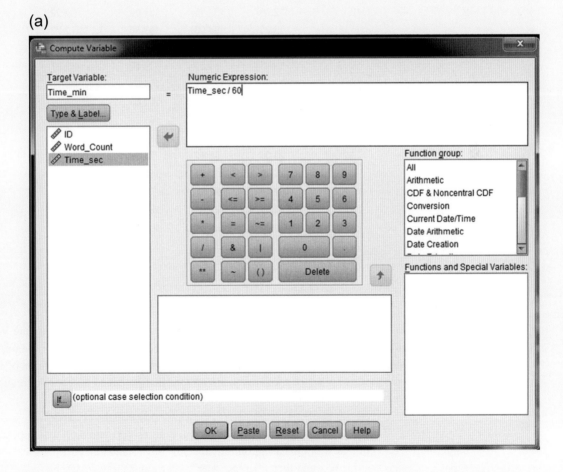

Figure 5.5a The SPSS window used to perform linear transformations.

(b)

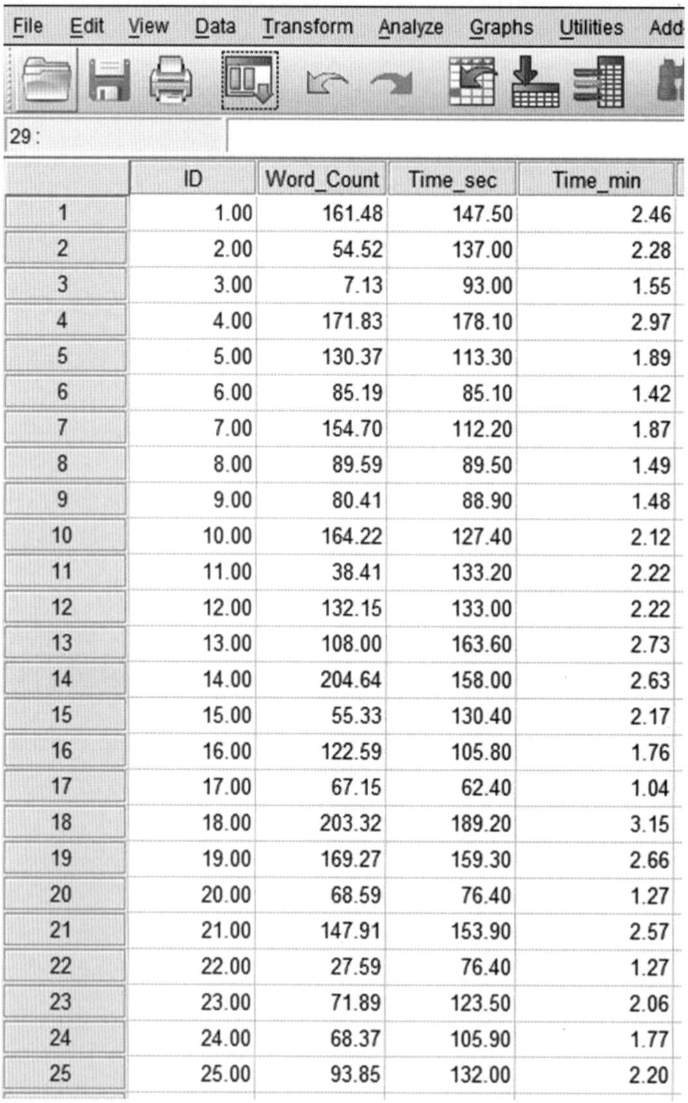

	ID	Word_Count	Time_sec	Time_min
1	1.00	161.48	147.50	2.46
2	2.00	54.52	137.00	2.28
3	3.00	7.13	93.00	1.55
4	4.00	171.83	178.10	2.97
5	5.00	130.37	113.30	1.89
6	6.00	85.19	85.10	1.42
7	7.00	154.70	112.20	1.87
8	8.00	89.59	89.50	1.49
9	9.00	80.41	88.90	1.48
10	10.00	164.22	127.40	2.12
11	11.00	38.41	133.20	2.22
12	12.00	132.15	133.00	2.22
13	13.00	108.00	163.60	2.73
14	14.00	204.64	158.00	2.63
15	15.00	55.33	130.40	2.17
16	16.00	122.59	105.80	1.76
17	17.00	67.15	62.40	1.04
18	18.00	203.32	189.20	3.15
19	19.00	169.27	159.30	2.66
20	20.00	68.59	76.40	1.27
21	21.00	147.91	153.90	2.57
22	22.00	27.59	76.40	1.27
23	23.00	71.89	123.50	2.06
24	24.00	68.37	105.90	1.77
25	25.00	93.85	132.00	2.20

Figure 5.5b SPSS data window showing the results of the linear transformation in Figure 5.5a.

z-Scores. There are two methods of calculating z-scores. The first is to use the "Compute Variable" method shown above (because the z-score conversion is just a special linear transformation). But an easier – and more precise – method is to use a feature that permits automatic calculation of z-scores. This method requires using one of the same menu options that produced descriptive frequencies, which we learned about in last Software Guide.

To calculate z-scores in SPSS, click "Analyze" → "Descriptive Statistics" and then "Descriptives." The Descriptives window that we saw in Figures 4.5a and 4.5b will appear. The bottom-left section of that window has an option labeled, "Save standardized values as variables." Checking this box and then clicking "OK" will produce a new variable in the data file.

You can see this in Figure 5.6. SPSS has labeled this variable "ZTime_sec." By default, when SPSS creates *z*-scores, it gives the *z*-score variable a name that starts with "Z" and ends with the name of the original variable.

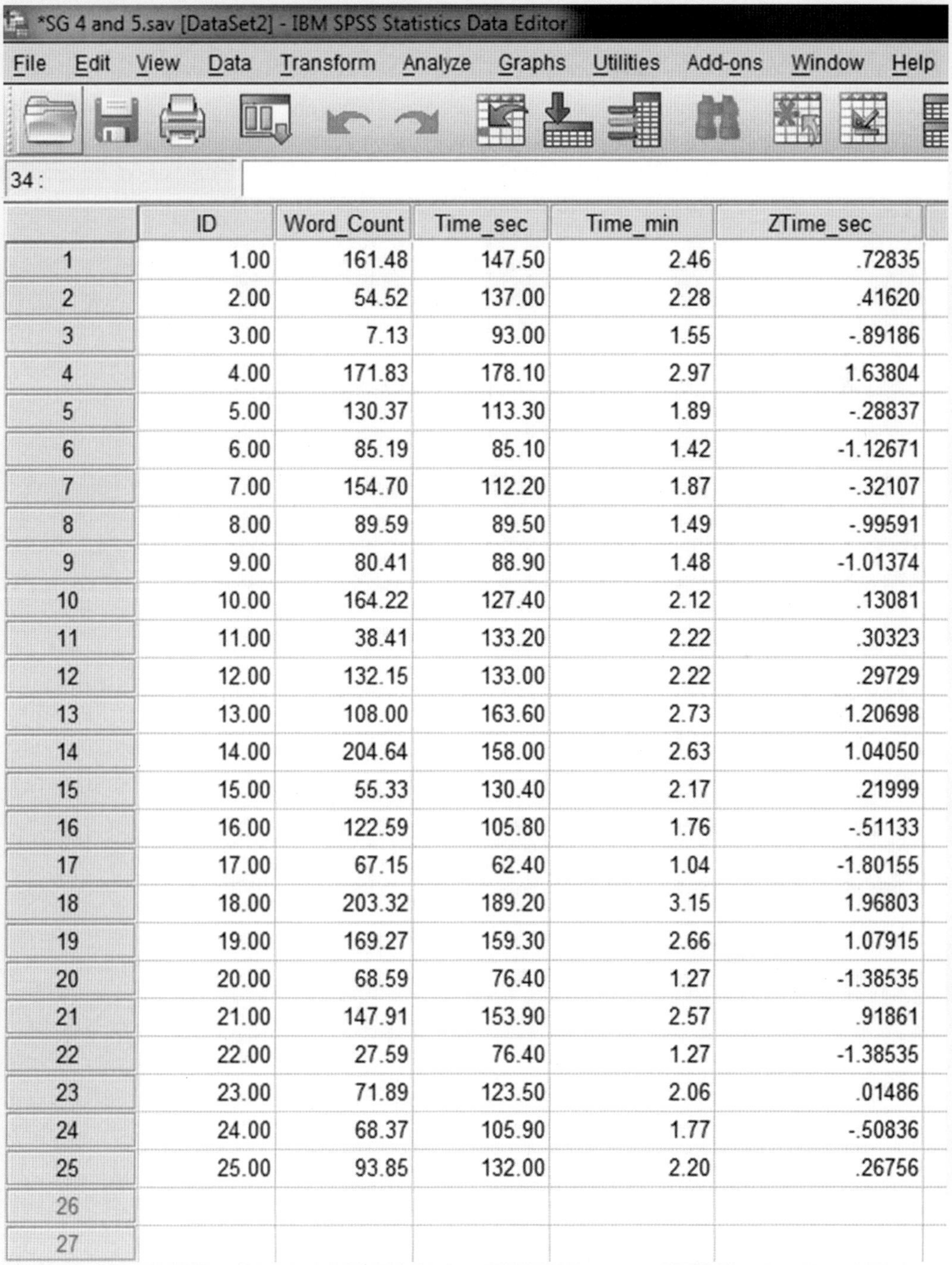

	ID	Word_Count	Time_sec	Time_min	ZTime_sec
1	1.00	161.48	147.50	2.46	.72835
2	2.00	54.52	137.00	2.28	.41620
3	3.00	7.13	93.00	1.55	-.89186
4	4.00	171.83	178.10	2.97	1.63804
5	5.00	130.37	113.30	1.89	-.28837
6	6.00	85.19	85.10	1.42	-1.12671
7	7.00	154.70	112.20	1.87	-.32107
8	8.00	89.59	89.50	1.49	-.99591
9	9.00	80.41	88.90	1.48	-1.01374
10	10.00	164.22	127.40	2.12	.13081
11	11.00	38.41	133.20	2.22	.30323
12	12.00	132.15	133.00	2.22	.29729
13	13.00	108.00	163.60	2.73	1.20698
14	14.00	204.64	158.00	2.63	1.04050
15	15.00	55.33	130.40	2.17	.21999
16	16.00	122.59	105.80	1.76	-.51133
17	17.00	67.15	62.40	1.04	-1.80155
18	18.00	203.32	189.20	3.15	1.96803
19	19.00	169.27	159.30	2.66	1.07915
20	20.00	68.59	76.40	1.27	-1.38535
21	21.00	147.91	153.90	2.57	.91861
22	22.00	27.59	76.40	1.27	-1.38535
23	23.00	71.89	123.50	2.06	.01486
24	24.00	68.37	105.90	1.77	-.50836
25	25.00	93.85	132.00	2.20	.26756

Figure 5.6 SPSS window showing the newly created *z*-scores for the "Time_sec" variable. The *z*-score of the time variable is labeled "ZTime_sec."

Further Reading

- Hoover, H. D. (1984). The most appropriate scores for measuring educational development in the elementary schools: GE's. *Educational Measurement: Issues and Practice*, *3*(4), 8–14. doi:10.1111/j.1745-3992.1984.tb00768.x

  * This article gives an example, using educational test scores, of how linear transformations can convert scores from one scale. As an example, Hoover explains grade equivalent scores, which are a common score in educational testing where the child's performance is compared to the typical performance on the same test of different grade levels of examinees.

6 Probability and the Central Limit Theorem

Everything in the preceding chapters of this book has been about using models to describe or represent data that have been collected from a sample – which we learned is a branch of statistics called descriptive statistics. Describing data is an important task. (It would be difficult to learn about data without describing it!) But it is often of limited usefulness because almost all datasets are collected from samples – and most researchers and practitioners in the social sciences are interested in the population as a whole. After all, if a psychologist says, "I have discovered that 35 out of 50 people in my sample got better after therapy," that isn't very interesting to anyone who isn't a friend or family member of the people in the sample.

The vast majority of social science researchers are interested in how their data from their sample applies to a population. But drawing conclusions about an entire population (which may consist of millions of people) based on a sample that consists of a tiny fraction of the population is a difficult logical leap to make. Yet, that leap is not impossible. In fact, the process of how to draw conclusions about a population from sample data was worked out in the early twentieth century, and it is now common in the social sciences to draw these conclusions about populations. This chapter provides the necessary theory of this process. The rest of the chapters in this textbook will discuss the nuts and bolts of actually performing the calculations needed to learn valuable information about a population with just sample data.

Learning Goals

- Calculate the probability that a particular outcome will occur in a set of events.

- Construct a probability distribution based on theoretical probabilities or empirical probabilities and describe why the differences between the two distribution types occur.

- Explain the process of generalizing a conclusion based on sample data to the entire population.

- Differentiate between a sample histogram, a sampling distribution, and a probability distribution.

- Explain the Central Limit Theorem (CLT) and why it permits estimation of the population mean and standard deviation.

- Estimate a population mean and standard deviation by taking multiple samples from the population.

Basic Probability

Statistics is based entirely on a branch of mathematics called **probability**, which is concerned with the likelihood of outcomes for an event. In probability theory, mathematicians use information about all possible outcomes for an event in order to determine the likelihood of any given outcome. The first section of this chapter will explain the basics of probability before advancing to the foundational issues of the rest of the textbook.

Imagine an event repeated 100 times. Each of these repetitions – called a **trial** – would be recorded. Mathematically, the formula for probability (abbreviated p) is:

$$p = \frac{\text{Number of trials with the same outcome}}{\text{Total number of trials}} \qquad \text{(Formula 6.1)}$$

To calculate the probability of any given outcome, it is necessary to count the number of trials that resulted in that particular outcome and divide it by the total number of trials. Thus, if the 100 trials consisted of coin flips – which have two outcomes, heads and tails – and 50 trials resulted in "heads" and 50 trials resulted in "tails," the probability of the coin landing heads side up would then be $\frac{50}{100}$. To simplify this notation, it is standard to reduce the fraction to its simplest form or to convert it to a decimal: ½ or .50 in this example.

This is called the **empirical probability** because it is based on empirical data collected from actual trials. Some readers will notice that this is the same method and formula for calculating the relative frequency in a frequency table (see Chapter 3). Therefore, empirical probabilities have the same mathematical properties as relative frequencies. That is, probability values always range from 0 to 1. A probability of zero indicates that the outcome never occurred, and a probability value of 1 indicates that the outcome occurred for every trial (and that no other outcome occurred). Also, all probabilities for a trial must add up to 1 – just as all relative frequencies in a dataset must add up to 1.

Interpreting probability statistics only requires an understanding of percentages, fractions, and decimals. In the coin-flipping example, a probability of .50 indicates that we can expect that half of those trials would result in an outcome of "heads." Similarly, the chances that any particular trial will result in an outcome of "heads" is 50%. Mathematically, it really doesn't matter whether probability values are expressed as percentages (e.g., 50%), fractions (e.g., ½), or decimals (e.g., .50). Statisticians, though, prefer to express probabilities as decimals, and this textbook will stick to that convention.

Guided Practice 6.1

Below is a dataset showing the outcomes of 30 random trials that had three possible outcomes, A, B, and C. Use Formula 6.1 to calculate the empirical probability of each outcome. Because there are three outcomes, there will be three empirical probabilities (and, therefore, three fractions) that we will calculate in this example.

C	B	C	A	A	A
B	A	B	A	A	C
B	A	B	A	C	B
B	B	A	C	A	B
A	A	B	A	C	B

The first step in calculating an empirical probability of each outcome is to count the number of times that each outcome occurred. Outcome A occurred 13 times, outcome B occurred

11 times, and outcome C occurred 6 times. Each of these numbers will go into the numerator of the fraction in Formula 6.1.

The denominator of each fraction is the total number of trials, which in this example is 30. Therefore, the empirical probability for the outcome A is $p_A = \frac{13}{30} = .433$. The empirical probability for outcome B is $p_B = \frac{11}{30} = .367$. The empirical probability for outcome C is $p_C = \frac{6}{30} = .200$. Notice that these three values add up to 1 (.433 + .367 + .200 = 1.0).

Sidebar 6.1   **Terminology**

Don't forget that the term *probability* can refer to both the branch of mathematics dealing with likelihood of outcomes and the calculated likelihood that a particular outcome will occur.

Conducting a large number of trials is an accurate way of measuring the probability of various outcomes, but it is often not feasible. There is a simpler way to estimate probability if two assumptions are met: (1) the trials are all independent, and (2) the outcomes are equally likely. Independent trials are trials that do not influence or relate to the outcome of any other trial. For example, having a coin land on tails does not influence the outcome of future coin tosses. With equally likely outcomes and independent trials, the probability of an outcome is equal to 1 divided by the total possible number of outcomes. Consider a coin toss with two possible outcomes (heads and tails) – the probability of having a coin land with the tails side up is 1 divided by the number of outcomes (i.e., 2). This produces a probability value of ½ or .50. This produces a value called the **theoretical probability**. As the name implies, theoretical probabilities are estimated from the theoretical principles of probability – number of possible outcomes, whether the outcomes are equally likely, etc.

Probability of Multiple Outcomes. Calculating the empirical or theoretical probability of coin tosses is simple (and not very interesting). More complex situations require extensions of probability theory and a more complex example than a simple coin toss. One common desire that researchers have is to calculate the probability that a trial will result in one of two mutually exclusive outcomes. To do this, it is merely necessary to add up the probabilities of each individual outcome:

$$p_{mult\ outcomes} = p_{outcome\ 1} + p_{outcome\ 2} + \ldots + p_{last\ outcome} \qquad \text{(Formula 6.2)}$$

For example, a person playing a board game may wish to know the theoretical probability of rolling a die and obtaining an outcome of either a 5 *or* a 6. There are six possible outcomes (values of 1, 2, 3, 4, 5, and 6), and each of these outcomes is equally likely. These outcomes are also mutually exclusive because having one outcome occur automatically means that other outcomes cannot occur. The theoretical probability of rolling a 5 is 1/6 (or .167), and the probability of rolling a 6 is 1/6 (or .167). To calculate the theoretical probability of rolling either a 5 *or* a 6 in one roll, the player should use Formula 6.2 to add the theoretical probability of rolling a 5 with the theoretical probability of rolling a 6. This would be 1/3 because 1/6 + 1/6 = 2/6 = 1/3 = .333.

Joint Probabilities. On the other hand, sometimes someone wishes to calculate the probability of an outcome across multiple trials – a situation that requires **joint probability**. These trials can occur either at the same time or in succession. For example, the probability that two dice thrown at the same time would *both* be a 5 or a 6 would be an application of joint probability.

To calculate a joint probability, it is necessary to (1) find the probability of each event, and then (2) multiply the two probabilities by one another. Thus, the formula is:

$$p_{joint} = (p_{outcome\ 1})(p_{outcome\ 2}) \cdots (p_{last\ outcome})$$ (Formula 6.3)

Therefore, since the probability that rolling one die will produce an outcome of a 5 or a 6 is .333 and since there are two dice, the joint probability that both dice will produce either a 5 or 6 at the same time is (.333)(.333) = .111. Please be aware that this formula relies on the assumption that the two events are independent of one another (i.e., the outcome of one die does not influence the outcome of the other).

Check Yourself!

- How do you calculate the probability of an outcome?

- Describe the difference between theoretical probability and empirical probability.

- When is it appropriate to use Formula 6.2, and when is it appropriate to use Formula 6.3?

Guided Practice 6.2

A real-life example of the application of joint probabilities occurs when women give birth. The theoretical probability of giving birth to a boy is .50, because there are two possible outcomes (boy and girl), and there is an equal probability of either one occurring in a single pregnancy.

However, there are two scenarios where joint probabilities are an issue in pregnancy. The first is with fraternal twins – which are twins produced from two independently fertilized eggs. Using Formula 6.3, let us calculate the joint probability that a woman pregnant with fraternal twins will give birth to two boys. The theoretical probability that the first baby will be a boy is .50. Likewise, the theoretical probability that the second baby is a boy is .50. Multiplying their probabilities together to produce the joint probability that both will be boys is:

$$(.50)(.50) = .25$$

We can also calculate the probability that both babies will be girls. The theoretical probability that the first baby will be a girl is .50, and the theoretical probability that the second baby will be a girl is .50. Plugging these numbers into Formula 6.3 shows that the probability that both babies will be girls is:

$$(.50)(.50) = .25$$

Lastly, we can calculate the joint probability that one baby will be a boy and the other baby will be a girl. In this scenario, it doesn't matter what the first baby's sex is because regardless of this baby's sex what matters is that the other baby's sex is the opposite. Therefore, we must use Formula 6.2 to find the probability that the first baby will be either a boy or a girl:

$$(.50) + (.50) = 1.00$$

Given the first baby's sex, it is only necessary that the other child be the opposite sex. That probability is .50 whether the first child is a boy or a girl.[2] To find the joint probability that the two babies will be the opposite sex, it is necessary to multiply their probabilities together, using Formula 6.3:

$$(1.00)(.50) = .50$$

Therefore, if a woman is pregnant with fraternal twins, there is a .25 probability that both will be boys, a .25 probability that both will be girls, and a .50 probability that they will be of opposite sex. Notice that these probabilities add up to 1.00.

The other birth scenario where joint probabilities matter is sequential births (i.e., births that occur one at a time in separate pregnancies). If a set of parents intends to have two children, then the probability that both will be boys is .25, the probability that both will be girls is .25, and the probability that both will be of different sex is .50. These probabilities are the same as for fraternal twins because the characteristics of two sequential births and two fraternal twins are the same (two independent outcomes, each of which has a probability of .50 of occurring).

It is possible to expand Formula 6.3 to consider more than two outcomes. I grew up in a family of five brothers and no sisters. The joint probability that the mother of five children will give birth to all boys is

$$(.50)(.50)(.50)(.50)(.50) = .03125$$

Therefore, the probability of a family of five children having all boys is 3.125%, even though the probability of *each* pregnancy *individually* resulting in a boy is .50. This example from my family shows the difference between theoretical probabilities of individual trials (e.g., each pregnancy) and the joint probability of a set of trials (e.g., all five pregnancies combined).

Sidebar 6.2 **Independent outcomes**

This entire chapter is based on the assumption that the trials of the trials are independent of one another. In other words, the outcome of one trial does not affect the outcomes of any other trials. We use the examples of a coin toss or a roll of a die because these are trials that are unquestionably independent of one another.

But what is a non-independent (also called a "dependent trial")? An example would be drawing multiple cards from the same pack sequentially. This is non-independent because drawing cards from a pack sequentially (1) reduces the number of possible outcomes of later card draws, and (2) eliminates a card from being drawn more than once. There are two important consequences to having non-independent

---

[2] Because if the first child is a boy, the probability that the other child is the opposite sex – that is, a girl – is .50. This same probability applies if the first child is a girl: the probability that the other child is a boy is .50.

trials. First, non-independent trials mean that the probability of a particular outcome can change from trial to trial. For example, if the first card drawn from a pack is the four of diamonds, then the probability of drawing a four from the remaining cards decreases (from .077 to .059), and the probability of drawing a card that is not a four increases (from .922 to .941). This is because the number of possible outcomes has decreased (from 52 to 51) because the four of diamonds is now an impossible outcome. These changes alter the probability of the remaining outcomes.

The second consequence of non-independent trials is that they make the estimation of probability values more complex, but not impossible. It is not necessary to understand how to estimate the likelihood of non-independent probabilities for the purposes of this class. But as you read this textbook, you should be aware that – unless stated otherwise – trials like separate experiments or different sampling events are independent of one another.

Probability Distributions. After calculating the probability of every possible outcome of an event, it is possible to build a histogram of these probabilities. This histogram of probabilities is called a **probability distribution**. Figure 6.1 shows a probability distribution based on the theoretical probabilities for many throws of a standard 6-sided die. Each bar in the histogram represents a possible outcome, and the height of each bar represents the probability of that particular outcome. Because all outcomes have the exact same probability, the bars are all exactly the same height.

Figure 6.1 is hypothetical, meaning that it is based on probability theory and the equations that have been discussed in this chapter so far. In real life, it is unusual to have the exact same number of trials resulting in each outcome – even if each outcome is theoretically equally likely. An example of this is shown in Figure 6.2a, which shows data from 600 independent throws of a die. The bars in the histogram are not precisely the same height, with the bar for 6 being the lowest (a frequency count of 88), and the bar for 2 being the highest (frequency count of 107).

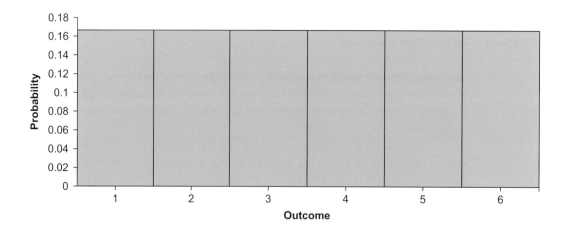

Figure 6.1 A hypothetical probability distribution for tossing a 6-sided die. The only difference between a probability distribution and a histogram is in the y-axis. The y-axis for a histogram is the frequency of the values within each bar's interval. On a probability distribution, the y-axis is the probability of the outcome represented by a bar.

The gambler's fallacy and the hot-hand fallacy

As I was collecting the data for Figure 6.2a and 6.2b, there was a series of 32 consecutive die throws where the outcome was *not* a 5. This is an extremely improbable series of outcomes; the joint probability would be $p = (5/6)^{32} = .0029$. Therefore, it seems likely that rolling a 5 was "due." Right?

Wrong. The belief that a drought of a particular outcome means that the outcome will probably occur soon is what statisticians call the "gambler's fallacy." In reality, dice rolls, lottery numbers, roulette wheel spins, and wins on a slot machine are all independent random events. Because the outcomes are independent, each one has no influence on other outcomes. The roulette wheel does not remember what the last outcome was – and therefore that outcome cannot influence what happens when the wheel is spun again. Mathematically, a way to think about this is that the joint probability of a sequence of trials is not relevant to the actual probability of any particular trial. Therefore, the fact that 31 trials in a row did not produce a die roll of 5 was irrelevant to the 32nd trial. The 32nd trial still had a 1/6 probability of producing a 5 – regardless of the outcomes of previous trials.

Do people actually believe in the gambler's fallacy? Anecdotal evidence suggests they do. A *Wall Street Journal* article (Copeland, 2014) mentioned a slot machine at the MGM Grand casino in Las Vegas, Nevada, that had not paid out its major jackpot in 20 years. As a result, the machine was – by far – the casino's most popular slot machine. Scientific research also provides evidence that people truly do believe the gambler's fallacy. Clotfelter and Cook (1993) studied a state-run lottery in Maryland that people could win by buying a ticket that matched three randomly selected one-digit numbers in the same order. The joint probability of winning this game is 1 in 1,000 because $p = (.10)(.10)(.10) = .001$. The researchers found that after a three-digit combination was selected, bets on that three-digit combination dropped by approximately one-third and did not fully recover for nearly three months. Apparently, lottery players believe that after a combination of numbers has won that it is time for some other combination of numbers to win – behavior consistent with the gambler's fallacy.

An idea related to the gambler's fallacy is the "hot-hand fallacy," which suggests that the occurrence of an outcome makes the outcome more likely in the future. In other words, people who believe in the hot-hand fallacy believe that "streaks" are more likely to continue than to be broken. In the data used to create Figures 6.2a and 6.2b, there were five die rolls that were all 1's. Again, this is an extremely unlikely event, with a joint probability of $p = (.167)(.167)(.167)(.167)(.167) = .00013$. To some people, such an unlikely streak seems lucky, and it appears that the dice rolls are not really random.

Again, this is incorrect reasoning for the same reason that the gambler's fallacy is faulty: random events do not "remember" what occurred before and earlier events have no impact on later ones. As with the gambler's fallacy, people really do believe in "hot streaks," as research on roulette players' behavior has shown (Sundali & Croson, 2006).

To convert the histogram in Figure 6.2a into a probability distribution, it is necessary to divide each frequency count by the total number of trials – in this case, 600. This produces the probability estimates for each outcome. These are diagrammed in Figure 6.2b.

Notice how Figure 6.2b looks very similar to Figure 6.2a. This is because dividing every frequency by the total number of trials is a linear transformation, which, as Chapter 3 showed, does not change the overall pattern of results in a visual model. Linear transformations only change the axis of a visual model (in this case, the *y*-axis). Therefore, the most common outcome in the 600 trials (a die roll of 2, which was the outcome of 107 trials) also has the highest empirical

(a)

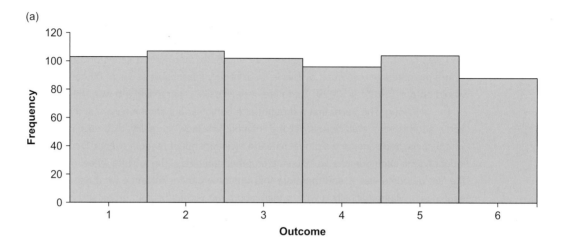

Figure 6.2a A histogram of outcomes of 600 tosses of a 6-sided die. In these trials, 103 resulted in a 1, 107 resulted in a 2, 102 resulted in a 3, 96 resulted in a 4, 104 resulted in a 5, and 88 resulted in a 6.

(b)

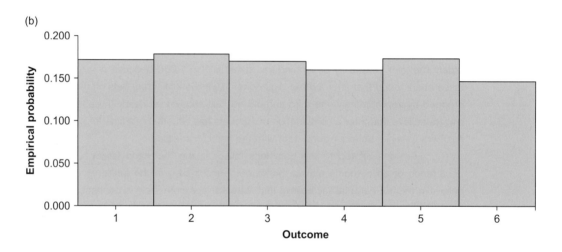

Figure 6.2b An empirical probability distribution based on the outcomes of the same 600 tosses of a 6-sided die shown in Figure 6.2a. In these trials, the empirical probability was calculated by dividing the numbers in Figure 6.2a's caption by 600, which was the total number of trials (see Formula 6.1).

probability: .178. This was calculated using Formula 6.1: 107 / 600 = .178. The least common outcome in Figure 6.2a – a die roll of 6 – also has the smallest empirical probability.

A more complex probability distribution would be the result of tossing two dice and adding their numbers together. Table 6.1 shows the outcomes of 600 trials of this sort. The data from Table 6.1 were then used to create the empirical probability distribution shown in Figure 6.3a.

Table 6.1 and Figure 6.3a show two interesting facts about probability. First, when an outcome has multiple independent causes (in this case, two dice), the probability is *not* equal to the joint probability of those two causes. In this example with two dice, the most common outcome was two numbers that added up to 8 (which had an empirical probability of .148). But the theoretical joint probability of rolling a pair of 4's is .028. (This is because the probability of rolling

Table 6.1 Frequency count of outcomes from 600 trials of tossing two 6-sided dice		
Outcome	**Frequency**	**Empirical probability**
1	0	0 / 600 = .000
2	19	19 / 600 = .032
3	41	41 / 600 = .068
4	48	48 / 600 = .080
5	54	54 / 600 = .090
6	79	79 / 600 = .132
7	86	86 / 600 = .143
8	89	89 / 600 = .148
9	76	76 / 600 = .127
10	50	50 / 600 = .083
11	35	35 / 600 = .058
12	17	17 / 600 = .028
13	0	0 / 600 = .000

(a)

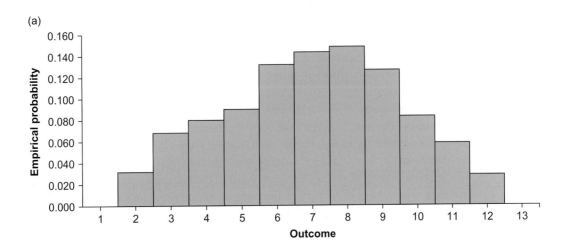

Figure 6.3a An empirical probability distribution based on the outcomes of the same 600 tosses of two 6-sided dice shown in Table 6.1.

a 4 is 1/6 = .167. Therefore, the probability of rolling two 4's is .167 multiplied by .167, which is .028.) So why is the probability of rolling 8 so high? It is because there are multiple ways of obtaining an 8 from two dice: a 2 and a 6, a 3 and a 5, etc. The probability of obtaining an 8 should be the sum of the joint probabilities of every possible combination that produces an 8. The empirical probabilities in Figure 6.2a show that rolling a 2 or a 12 is an unlikely outcome. This is because there is only one possible combination of dice that can produce a 2 (a pair of 1's) or a 12 (a pair of 6's), whereas all other outcomes have multiple combinations of dice that can produce them, resulting in higher probabilities for those outcomes.

   Comparing Theoretical and Empirical Probabilities. Figure 6.3a shows the empirical probability distribution for 600 outcomes of tossing two standard 6-sided dice. The theoretical

(b)

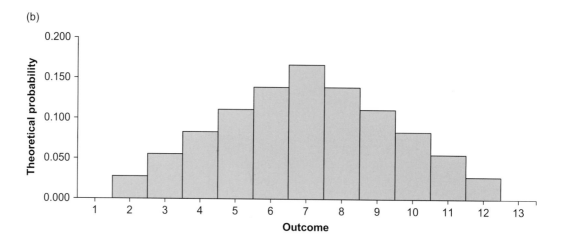

probabilities for the same outcomes are shown in Figure 6.3b. Like the last comparison between theoretical and empirical probability distributions (i.e., Figures 6.2a and 6.2b), there are differences between the two figures. First, the theoretical distribution in Figure 6.2b is symmetrical and more regular than the empirical distribution. Second, according to the empirical distribution, the most probable outcome is rolling an 8 (empirical probability of .148), whereas in the theoretical probability distribution the most probable outcome is rolling a 7 (theoretical probability of .167).

These sorts of discrepancies are typical when comparing empirical and theoretical probabilities. However, as the number of outcomes increases, the empirical and theoretical probability values for each outcome *converge*, or grow closer to one another. The two probability distributions also converge towards one another. This is illustrated in Figures 6.4a–6.4d, which show empirical probability distributions for increasing numbers of outcomes of rolling two dice. The figures show that, as the number of outcomes increases, the empirical probability distributions more closely resemble the theoretical probability distribution. Figure 6.4a (100 trials) does not resemble the theoretical probability distribution (in Figure 6.3b) very much. For example, the empirical probability of 9 is less than the empirical probability of 10, whereas in the theoretical distribution, 9 is clearly a more likely outcome than 10. Also, the empirical theoretical probability distribution is symmetrical, but the empirical probability distribution in Figure 6.4a is not.

But as the number of trials increases, the empirical probability distribution becomes more and more like the theoretical probability distribution. With 1,000 trials (Figure 6.4b), the distribution is appearing more symmetrical, but there are still some anomalies – such as the fact that 9 and 10 appear to be equally likely outcomes. However, with 10,000 trials (Figure 6.5c), the differences between the empirical probability distribution and theoretical probability distribution are extremely subtle. After 100,000 trials (Figure 6.4d), the empirical and theoretical probability distributions are indistinguishable to the naked eye, and all the probabilities are equal (to the second decimal place) to their corresponding values in the theoretical probability distribution.

The convergence shown in Figures 6.4a–6.4d between theoretical and empirical probabilities and probability distributions continues as long as the number of trials in the empirical

(a)

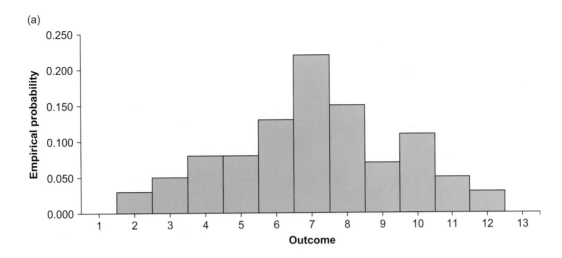

Figure 6.4a An empirical probability distribution for the outcomes of 100 trials of tossing two 6-sided dice.

(b)

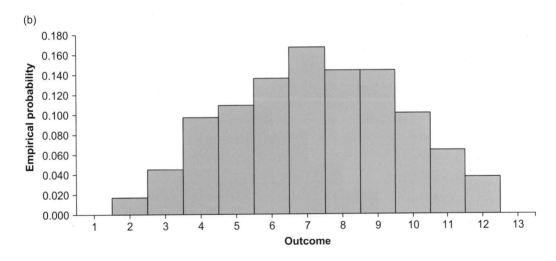

Figure 6.4b An empirical probability distribution for the outcomes of 1,000 trials of tossing two 6-sided dice.

probability distribution increases. If there were an infinite number of dice rolls, the empirical probability distribution and theoretical probability distribution would be exactly equal to one another. Because of this, most researchers just use theoretical probabilities and theoretical probability distributions for two reasons. First, they are easier to calculate. After all, it is much easier to use Formula 6.1 than to roll a pair of dice thousands of times. Second, theoretical probabilities and probability distributions are accurate "in the long run." In other words, even if a set of trials does not produce results that resemble the theoretical probabilities, additional trials will eventually converge to the theoretical probabilities with enough trials.

Readers may feel there is something familiar about the shape of Figure 6.4c. It appears to resemble the normal distribution, which was discussed in Chapters 3 and 5. This is because,

(c)

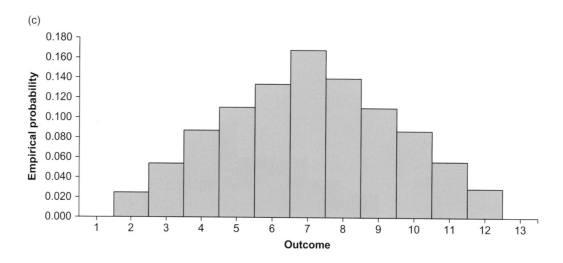

Figure 6.4c An empirical probability distribution for the outcomes of 10,000 trials of tossing two 6-sided dice.

(d)

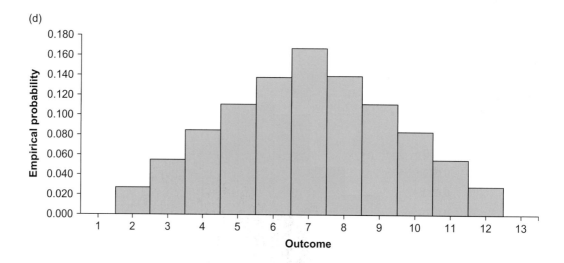

Figure 6.4d An empirical probability distribution for the outcomes of 100,000 trials of tossing two 6-sided dice.

as the number of trials increases, the shape of a histogram *or* a probability distribution that consists of sums of random variables will converge to the shape of the normal distribution. In fact, the more random variables that are added together to produce the probability distribution, the smoother the probability distribution will be. This is easily apparent in Figures 6.5a and 6.5b, which show the probability distributions of 10,000 trials consisting of five dice and ten dice, respectively.

It is clear in these two examples that the distribution created from ten dice (Figure 6.5b) more closely resembles the smooth curve of the normal distribution than the distribution created from five dice (Figure 6.5a). Remember from Chapter 3 that the normal distribution is theorized to consist of an infinite number of intervals that are so packed together that they appear to form a

(a)

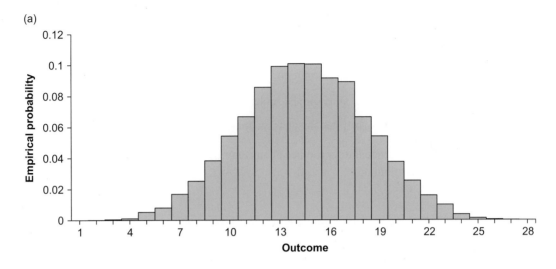

Figure 6.5a An empirical probability distribution for the outcomes of 10,000 trials of tossing five 6-sided dice.

(b)

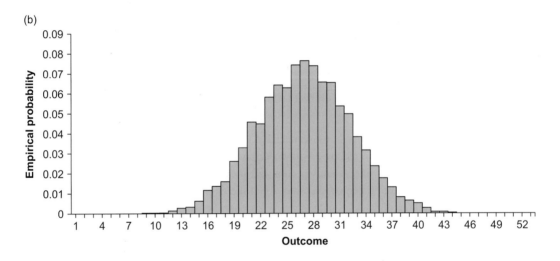

Figure 6.5b An empirical probability distribution for the outcomes of 10,000 trials of tossing ten 6-sided dice. Notice that because more outcomes are possible (because of a larger number of dice) outcomes are generally less probable in this figure than in Figure 6.5a.

smooth curve. This is why Figure 6.5b, with its larger number of intervals, looks more similar to the gentle curve of a normal distribution than Figure 6.5a, which has fewer intervals. This is true, even though both consist of 10,000 trials.

This convergence of the shape of a probability distribution of a random variable to a normal distribution is a regular outcome of any large set of random trials. It is also the main principle of the **central limit theorem** (CLT) – the foundation of the rest of this textbook and the topic of discussion for the rest of this chapter.

Check Yourself!

- What is a probability distribution?

- How do you create an empirical probability distribution?

- How do you create a theoretical probability distribution?

- What happens to the appearance of an empirical probability distribution as more trials are added to the distribution?

Sidebar 6.4 **Remember!**

In this section the discussion is solely on probability distributions. However, remember that the same principles can also apply to the histogram of outcomes in a series of trials. That is because the linear transformation that converts frequency counts of outcomes to empirical probabilities does not change the shape or other properties of the distribution (see Figures 6.2a and 6.2b).

The Logic of Inferential Statistics and the CLT

The beginning of this book, especially Chapter 4, discussed descriptive statistics, which is the branch of statistics concerned with describing data that have been collected. Descriptive statistics are indispensable for understanding data, but they are often of limited usefulness because most social scientists wish to make conclusions about the entire population of interest – not just the subjects in the sample that provided data to the researcher. For example, in a study of bipolar mood disorders, Kupka et al. (2007) collected data from 507 patients to examine how frequently they were in manic, hypomanic, and depressed mood states. The descriptive statistics that Kupka et al. provided are interesting – but they are of limited use if they only apply to the 507 people in the study. The authors of this study – and the vast majority of researchers – want to apply their conclusions to the entire population of people they are studying, even people who are not in the sample. The process of drawing conclusions about the entire population based on data from a sample is called **generalization**, and it requires inferential statistics in order to be possible. **Inferential statistics** is the branch of statistics that builds on the foundation of probability in order to make generalizations.

The logic of inferential statistics is diagrammed in Figure 6.6. It starts with a population, which, for a continuous, interval- or ratio-level variable, has an unknown mean and unknown standard deviation (represented as the circle in the top left of Figure 6.6). A researcher then draws a random sample from the population and uses the techniques discussed in previous chapters to calculate a sample mean and create a sample histogram. The problem with using a single sample to learn about the population is that there is no way of knowing whether that sample is typical – or *representative* – of the population from which it is drawn. It is possible (although not likely if the

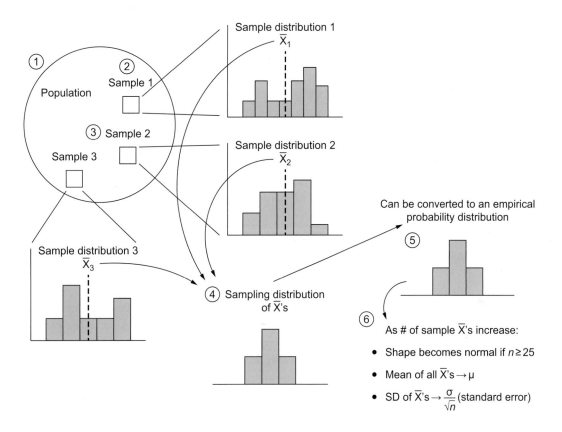

Figure 6.6 The logic of inferential statistics starts with a population (pop) (marked as no. 1) that has an unknown mean, standard deviation, and distribution. A researcher then draws repeated samples with the same n (marked as no. 2 and no. 3) and creates sample distributions and calculates a mean for each sample. The means from each sample are then used to create a sampling distribution of means (marked no. 4), which can easily be converted to an empirical probability distribution by dividing by the total number of trials (marked no. 5). With an infinitely large number of samples, the probability distribution will take on three characteristics (marked no. 6). First, the shape of the sampling distribution of means will become normal as long as the size of each sample is at least 25. Second, the mean of all the sample means will be equal to the population mean (μ). Third, the standard deviation of the sample distribution of means (called the "standard error") will be equal to $\frac{\sigma}{\sqrt{n}}$. The researcher can then solve for the population standard deviation (σ) because n and the standard error are known in an empirical sampling distribution of means.

sampling method was truly random) that the sample consists of several outliers that distort the sample mean and standard deviation.

The solution to this conundrum is to take multiple random samples with the same n from the population. Because of natural random variation in which population members are selected for a sample, we expect some slight variation in mean values from sample to sample. This natural variation across samples is called **sampling error**. With several samples that all have the same sample size, it becomes easier to judge whether any particular sample is typical or unusual because we can see which samples differ from the others (and therefore probably have more sampling error). However, this still does not tell the researcher anything about the population. Further steps are needed to make inferences about the population from sample data.

After finding a mean for each sample, it is necessary to create a separate histogram (in the middle of Figure 6.6) that consists solely of sample means. The histogram of means from a series of samples is called a **sampling distribution** of means. Sampling distributions can be created from other sample statistics (e.g., standard deviations, medians, ranges), but for the purposes of this chapter it is only necessary to talk about a sampling distribution of means.

Because a sampling distribution of means is produced by a purely random process, its properties are governed by the same principles of probability that govern other random outcomes, such as dice throws and coin tosses. Therefore, there are some regular predictions that can be made about the properties of the sampling distribution as the number of contributing samples increases. First, with a large sample size within each sample, the shape of the sampling distribution of means is a normal distribution. Given the convergence to a normal distribution, as shown in Figures 6.4a–6.4d, this should not be surprising. What is surprising to some people is that *this convergence towards a normal distribution occurs regardless of the shape of the population, as long as the* n *for each sample is at least 25 and all samples have the same sample size.* This is the main principle of the CLT.

Sidebar 6.5 Avoid this common misunderstanding of the CLT

Remember that the CLT is a property of sampling distributions – not of distributions of histograms or raw data. Some statistical novices mistakenly believe that the CLT means that their distributions of raw sample data will become normally distributed as the sample size grows. This is a mistaken interpretation. There is no guarantee that histograms of raw sample data will ever be normally distributed. In fact, for populations with very non-normal shapes, a normally distributed sample may be highly unusual. The CLT only states that a *sampling distribution of means* will eventually be normally distributed, as long as each sample is large enough (and of equal size) and as the number of sample means approaches infinity. The CLT says nothing about the shape of individual sample histograms (Kline, 2013).

CLT Implication No. 1: Estimating the Population Mean. A normally distributed sampling distribution is convenient, but it does not tell a researcher much about the population – especially because highly skewed or non-normal population distributions will always produce this normally distributed sampling distribution (as long as each sample has the same sample size, which is at least 25). After all, the whole purpose of inferential statistics is to learn about the entire population on the basis of sample data.

One of the essential population parameters that researchers want to know is the population mean. To make an estimate of the population mean from a group of means from random samples, use the following formula:

$$\hat{\mu} = \frac{\sum \overline{X}}{n \; of \; \overline{X}'s} \qquad \text{(Formula 6.4)}$$

In Formula 6.4, the estimate of the population mean μ is equal to the mean of all sample means. Please note that in this equation *the denominator is the number of sample means* – not the sample size of each sample. Formula 6.4 works because the sampling process that generated each sample mean was random. As such, roughly half of samples will produce $\overline{X}$ values above μ, and half of samples will produce $\overline{X}$ values below μ. Therefore, the best estimate of the population mean ($\hat{\mu}$) will be the average of all the sample means. Across many samples, the sample means that are too high and the sample means that are too low will cancel each other out. This may seem surprising, but it is shown clearly in the theoretical probability distribution in Figure 6.3b. That figure shows that when rolling two 6-sided dice and adding their numbers together, the most common outcome is 7, and that outcomes become less likely as the numbers get further from 7. The least likely outcomes are 2 and 12, both with a probability of .028. Both of these outcomes are equally distant from 7 (–5 and +5), and due to their equal probabilities, all the 2's and all the 12's will cancel each other out. The same is true for other pairs of numbers in Figure 6.3b (i.e., 3's and 11's, 4's and 10's, 5's and 9's, and 6's and 8's). This shows an important implication of the CLT: *as the number of samples in a sampling distribution increases, the mean of the sample means will converge to the population mean.*

CLT Implication No. 2: Estimating the Population Standard Deviation. Another implication of the CLT concerns σ – the population standard deviation. Unfortunately, estimating σ is not as easy as estimating μ. The standard deviation of the sampling distribution of means is too small – especially for sampling distributions made up of means from large samples.[3] As a result, a set of means will be less variable than the original population data. Thus, the standard deviation of means of a set of samples will be smaller than the original population's standard deviation.

To solve this problem, statisticians created the following formula:

$$SE = \frac{\sigma}{\sqrt{n}}$$
(Formula 6.5)

In Formula 6.5, SE is the **standard error**, which is the standard deviation of the sampling distribution of means. The standard error is a measure of sampling error; when the standard error is large, there is a lot of sampling error in the data, and the sampling distribution of means will be very spread out. Conversely, when the standard error is small, the sample means are consistent, and the sampling distribution is narrow – indicating very little sampling error across samples.

To estimate the population standard deviation, it is necessary to plug in values for the standard error (found by calculating the standard deviation of the sample means) and n (the size of each sample that produced a mean in the sampling distribution). The researcher should then solve for σ. It is important to realize, though, that the result is an estimate of the population standard deviation ($\hat{\sigma}$) unless it is calculated from an infinite number of means in the sampling distribution. This shows another important implication of the CLT: *as the number of sample means in the sampling distribution increases, the standard deviation of the means converges to $\frac{\sigma}{\sqrt{n}}$.*

Be Cautions When Estimating Population Parameters. It is important to remember that $\hat{\mu}$ and $\hat{\sigma}$ are merely estimates of the population parameters. These estimates may not be accurate. Fortunately, there are two ways that researchers can increase the accuracy of their estimates. The first is to increase the number of samples that the researcher takes. This increases accuracy because the discrepancies that occur with small numbers of samples get canceled out when there are a large number of samples (just as the differences in empirical and theoretical probability distributions get smaller as the number of samples increases). The second method of making the estimates of population parameters more accurate is to increase the sample size for each sample that is taken from the population. This reduces sampling error because the differences in statistics among samples are smaller with large samples. This is easiest to see in Formula 6.5: as the n of each sample increases, the overall value of the fraction $\frac{\sigma}{\sqrt{n}}$ decreases and there is less variation from sample to sample. Therefore, the estimates of the population mean and standard deviation will be more accurate because the data producing them will be more consistent. On the

---

[3] The standard deviation of the sampling distribution is too small because in the process of averaging each sample to produce a sample mean, the outliers within each sample are canceled out and their influence lessened. This makes the distribution of means less variable than the original population distribution.

other hand, Formula 6.5 shows that, as σ increases, the standard error also increases. This means that in populations that have high variability there is more variation from sample to sample than in populations with low variability.

Guided Practice 6.3

Below are a series of sample means ($n = 35$) taken from the same population. These means can be used to estimate the population mean and standard deviation.

3.8	4.2	4.0	4.6
3.2	3.7	4.2	4.3
4.1	3.9	4.8	3.8
4.2	4.1	3.9	4.0

Formula 6.4 states that to calculate $\hat{\mu}$, it is necessary to find the mean of all of these sample means. The 16 means sum to 64.8. There are 16 means, so, using Formula 6.4, we can estimate the population mean as $\hat{\mu} = 64.8 / 16 = 4.05$.

To obtain a value for $\hat{\sigma}$, it is first necessary to find the standard deviation of these means, which is the standard error. This requires using Formula 6.5 (the standard deviation of a sample). First, find a deviation score for each mean:

$3.8 - 4.05 = -0.25$	$4.2 - 4.05 = 0.15$	$4.0 - 4.05 = -0.05$	$4.6 - 4.05 = 0.55$
$3.2 - 4.05 = -0.85$	$3.7 - 4.05 = -0.35$	$4.2 - 4.05 = 0.15$	$4.3 - 4.05 = 0.25$
$4.1 - 4.05 = 0.05$	$3.9 - 4.05 = -0.15$	$4.8 - 4.05 = 0.75$	$3.8 - 4.05 = -0.25$
$4.2 - 4.05 = 0.15$	$4.1 - 4.05 = 0.05$	$3.9 - 4.05 = -0.15$	$4.0 - 4.05 = -0.05$

The next step is to square each of these deviations scores:

$(-0.25)^2 = 0.0625$	$(0.15)^2 = 0.0225$	$(-0.05)^2 = 0.0025$	$(0.55)^2 = 0.3025$
$(-0.85)^2 = 0.7225$	$(-0.35)^2 = 0.1225$	$(0.15)^2 = 0.0225$	$(0.25)^2 = 0.0625$
$(0.05)^2 = 0.0025$	$(-0.15)^2 = 0.0225$	$(0.75)^2 = 0.5625$	$(-0.25)^2 = 0.0625$
$(0.15)^2 = 0.0225$	$(0.05)^2 = 0.0025$	$(-0.15)^2 = 0.0225$	$(-0.05)^2 = 0.0025$

Then these squared deviation scores should be added:

$$0.0625 + 0.7225 + 0.0025 + 0.0225 + 0.0225 + 0.1225 + 0.0225 + 0.0025$$
$$+0.0025 + 0.0225 + 0.5625 + 0.0225 + 0.3025 + 0.0625 + 0.0625+$$
$$0.0025 = 2.02$$

The next step is to divide by the number of means minus 1. (Do not divide by the size of each mean's sample minus 1!)

$$2.02/(16 - 1/) = 2.02/15 = 0.13467$$

It is now necessary to find the square root of this value:

$$\sqrt{0.13467} = 0.367 \leftarrow \textbf{This value is the standard error.}$$

Now that we have calculated the standard error, it should be plugged into Formula 6.5 along with the n of each sample (which was 35):

$$0.367 = \frac{\sigma}{\sqrt{35}}$$

Solving for σ,

$$0.367 = \frac{\sigma}{5.916}$$

$$5.916(0.367) = \left(\frac{\sigma}{5.916}\right)5.916$$

$$2.171 = \sigma$$

If we calculated this value from an infinite number of sample means, this would be a precise, correct value for σ. However, with just 16 samples, this value is actually an estimate of σ. Therefore, it is proper to put a carat over σ to demonstrate that this is an estimate:

$$\hat{\sigma} = 2.171$$

Therefore, these 16 sample means likely came from a population with an estimated mean ($\hat{\mu}$) of 4.05 and an estimated standard deviation ($\hat{\sigma}$) of 2.171. (These results were produced without any rounding – if you rounded as you worked out this problem, then you may have a slightly different answer.)

Importance of the CLT. Some people have difficulty perceiving the importance of the CLT when they first learn it. However, it is almost impossible to overstate the importance of the CLT to the science of statistics. This is because the rest of the procedures in this textbook – and many more advanced statistical procedures – are based on probability and sampling distributions. In every remaining chapter, we will be using probability distributions in sample data to make inferences about the population. If we know that a large number of samples will always produce a sampling distribution that is normal (as long as the n of each sample is ≥ 25), we can compare results from different studies to one another, compare sample data to a population (even without all the population data!), and estimate the degree to which sampling error contributes to observed differences among samples or between a sample and its parent population. Making these judgments and inferences is the topic of inferential statistics – and the rest of this textbook.

Caveat. In this chapter, I have shown how an empirical sampling distribution of means will gradually form a normal distribution after a large number of samples. I also showed that the mean of those sample means will converge to μ, and the standard deviation will converge to $\frac{\sigma}{\sqrt{n}}$. However, readers should be aware that real social science researchers do not build sampling distributions in this fashion. One reason is that they already know that the sampling distribution will be normally distributed if there are enough sample means in it, and there is no reason to verify this eventual normal distribution of a sampling distribution by "checking" the CLT.

Another reason that scientists do not build sampling distributions in the way I described in this chapter is that theoretical sampling distributions are easier to work with than building an empirical sampling distribution. Creating a high-quality sampling distribution of a variable would require taking hundreds – perhaps thousands – of samples and calculating a mean for each one in order to build a histogram of means. Few researchers have access to the necessary resources to gather so many samples. Instead, it is far easier to use a theoretical sampling distribution based on an equation. Although the procedure of building a sampling distribution is not an actual research practice, it is still useful to illustrate for teaching purposes how the CLT functions. Just remember that in real life, social scientists use a theoretical sampling distribution – which will have the same shape, mean, and standard deviation that an empirical distribution would have if it consisted of an infinite number of samples.

Check Yourself!

- What is the purpose of inferential statistics?
- What does the CLT state about the shape of a sampling distribution of means?
- What is the name of the standard deviation of a sampling distribution?
- How can a researcher use the CLT to calculate the mean and standard deviation of a population?

Summary

The basics of probability form the foundation of inferential statistics. Probability is the branch of mathematics concerned with estimating the likelihood of outcomes of trials. There are two types of probabilities that can be estimated. The first is the empirical probability, which is calculated by conducting a large number of trials and finding the proportion of trials that resulted in each outcome, using Formula 6.1. The second type of probability is the theoretical probability, which is calculated by dividing the number of methods of obtaining an outcome by the total number of possible outcomes. Adding together the probabilities of two different events will produce the probability that either one will occur. Multiplying the probabilities of two events together will produce the joint probability, which is the likelihood that the two events will occur at the same time or in succession.

With a small or moderate number of trials, there may be discrepancies between the empirical and theoretical probabilities. However, as the number of trials increases, the empirical probability converges to the value of the theoretical probability. Additionally, it is possible to build a histogram of outcomes of trials from multiple events; dividing the number of trials that resulted in each outcome by the total number of trials produces an empirical probability distribution. As the number of trials increases, this empirical probability distribution gradually converges to the theoretical probability distribution, which is a histogram of the theoretical probabilities.

If an outcome is produced by adding together the results of multiple independent events, the theoretical probability distribution will be normally distributed. Additionally, with a large number of trials, the empirical probability distribution will also be normally distributed. This is a result of the CLT.

The CLT states that a sampling distribution of means will be normally distributed if the size of each sample is at least 25. As a result of the CLT, it is possible to make inferences about the population based on sample data – a process called generalization. Additionally, the mean of the sample means converges to the population mean as the number of samples in a sampling distribution increases. Likewise, the standard deviation of means in the sampling distribution (called the standard error) converges on the value of $\frac{\sigma}{\sqrt{n}}$.

Reflection Questions: Comprehension

1. Explain the difference between how theoretical probability distributions and empirical probability distributions are created.
2. What is the interpretation of a probability value of
    a. .00?
    b. .20?
    c. .50?
    d. .75?
    e. 1.00?
3. Explain the purpose of generalization and why it is so important for researchers in the social sciences.
4. Define the standard error and explain its importance in the CLT.
5. Based on the principle of the CLT, what are the two things that researchers can do to make their estimate of the population mean or standard deviation more exact?

Reflection Questions: Application

6. A standard pack of playing cards (without the jokers) has 52 cards. There are four suits: clubs, hearts, spades, and diamonds. Each suit consists of 13 cards, with values from 2 to 10, plus an ace, a jack, a queen, and a king. As each card value appears the same number of times (4) and each suit has the same number of cards, what is the probability that a person would draw a card that is:
    a. A king?
    b. An ace?
    c. A heart?
    d. A spade or a club?
    e. A card with a value of 2, 3, 4, or 5?
    f. Any face card (i.e., jack, queen, or king)?
    g. An odd number (not including the ace)?
    h. A single card with a value of 16?
7. A person has two standard packs of playing cards and draws one card from each pack. (Having two separate packs ensures that the draws are independent events.) What is the joint probability of drawing the following combination of cards?
    a. A heart and a spade?
    b. A three and an ace?
    c. A jack and a queen?
    d. Two kings?
8. Using the data in Guided Practice 6.1, answer the following questions:
    a. What is the probability of an outcome of either A *or* C?
    b. What is the probability of an outcome of either B *or* C?
    c. What is the probability of an outcome of either A *or* B?
    d. What is the probability that the outcome of two independent trials will be B *and* C?

    e.   What is the probability that the outcome of two independent trials will be A *and* C?

    f.   What is the probability that the outcome of two independent trials will be C for both trials?

    g.   Why are the probability values in 3a–3c smaller than the values in 3d–3f?

9.   A student is taking a standardized test to apply to college. The test is multiple choice with four options (A, B, C, and D) for each question.

    a.   The student notices that he hasn't selected option D for the past eight questions. What is the probability of this sequence of independent random events?

    b.   If there has been no D option for the past eight questions, what is the probability that the next answer will be D?

    c.   The student is sure that because there hasn't been a D option for the past eight questions the next answer is probably going to be a D. What is the name of the fallacy he believes in? Why is his reasoning incorrect? How would you explain to him that he is wrong?

10. Every month a street with 10 houses on it has a neighborhood party. The host is drawn randomly each month, and each house has an equal chance of being selected.

    a.   What is the probability that any family will be selected twice in a row?

    b.   In February and March two different families were hosts for the neighborhood party. In April what is the probability that March's host family *or* February's host family will be selected?

    c.   What is the probability that a particular family will be selected twice in a row?

    d.   The Steinman family was selected five times in the past two years – more than any other family. They believe that this proves that the selection process isn't random. Why is their reasoning wrong? Theoretically, would the Steinman family be selected more than any other family if the selection process continued an infinite number of times?

11. Claudia found a quarter (US coin) on the ground three days in a row. She feels that she has been lucky and will therefore find a quarter on the ground tomorrow. Which fallacy is she engaging in?

12. Camryn has five cards, numbered 1–5. She repeatedly draws two of them randomly from a hat, adds the numbers together, and uses the information to build a histogram. After 50 draws, her histogram doesn't resemble a normal distribution. Why not? What would she need to do in order for her data to produce a histogram that is normally distributed?

13. Below are the means of 12 samples ($n = 40$ for each sample) drawn at random from a population.

25.4	26.0	22.8	23.9	24.7	25.3
24.9	23.6	22.7	25.8	25.3	24.6

    a.   Based on these sample means, calculate the best estimate for the population mean.

    b.   Calculate the standard error for the sampling distribution made from the 12 sample means above.

    c.   Calculate the best estimate for the population standard deviation.

    d.   If there were an infinite number of sample means, what would the shape of the *sampling distribution of means* be?

14. Below are the means of 15 samples ($n = 55$ for each sample) drawn at random from a population.

4.2	4.9	3.8	3.7	4.0
5.2	4.6	5.2	3.5	4.4
3.8	5.0	4.1	4.8	5.1

a.   Based on these sample means, calculate the best estimate for the population mean.

b.   Calculate the standard error for the sampling distribution made from the 15 sample means above.

c.   Calculate the best estimate for the population standard deviation.

d.   Can a researcher learn about the distribution of the population from these sample means? Why or why not?

e.   If the n of each sample were 30 instead of 55, what impact would it have on the estimate of the population mean?

f.   If the n of each sample were 30 instead of 55, what impact would it have on the standard error?

15. A group of friends are about to play a game of basketball. To choose teams, two team captains take turns choosing players one at a time until the last person is chosen. As Carlos waits to be chosen, he realizes that each selection that a team captain makes is a trial. Carlos also realizes that the probability that he will be selected changes as each person is selected before him. Why does his probability of being selected keep changing?

16. Calculate the standard error when:

a. $\sigma = 9.8$ and $n = 12$.

b. $\sigma = 9.8$ and $n = 25$.

c. $\sigma = 9.8$ and $n = 180$.

d. $\sigma = 4.2$ and $n = 12$.

e. $\sigma = 12.9$ and $n = 25$.

f. $\sigma = 1.3$ and $n = 180$.

g.   Compare the standard errors in 16a–16f. What happens to the standard error as σ increases?

h.   Compare the standard errors in 16a–16f. What happens to the standard error as n increases?

Further Reading

- Dunn, P. K. (2005). We can still learn about probability by rolling dice and tossing coins. *Teaching Statistics*, *27*(2), 37–41. doi:10.1111/j.1467–9639.2005.00205.x

  * Instructors have been using coins and dice to teach about probability for over a century. For instructors who want to create a more elaborate lesson on probability than what I have provided, Dunn gives several ideas that would be useful and entertaining in the classroom.

- Matz, D. C., & Hause, E. L. (2008). "Dealing" with the central limit theorem. *Teaching of Psychology*, *35*, 198–200. doi:10.1080/00986280802186201

  * In this article Matz and Hause describe a hands-on activity that you can do in a class or a study group to see that means from a series of random samples will produce a normally distributed sampling distribution – regardless of the shape of the population distribution. D. E. Johnson (1986) has a similar activity that is simpler and faster to do.

- Rice Virtual Lab in Statistics sampling distribution simulation: http://onlinestatbook.com/stat_sim/sampling_dist/index.html

  * This website has a Java applet that I use in my classes to demonstrate how the central limit theorem operates. The applet allows users to customize the shape of a population distribution and the size of each sample. This allows students to explore how the CLT functions under diverse conditions to produce normally distributed sampling distributions.

7 Null Hypothesis Statistical Significance Testing and *z*-Tests

In the previous chapter, we learned about the theory of statistical inference. This theory provides statisticians, researchers, and students with the background information they need to make inferences about a population based on sample data. This chapter builds upon that theoretical foundation by teaching about the simplest possible inferential statistics procedure: the *z*-test. Although *z*-tests are not common in social science research, learning the *z*-test is still important. Mastering a *z*-test will make the more complicated procedures discussed in later chapters easier to learn because those procedures are variations of a *z*-test that have been adapted to other types of data and research situations.

Learning Goals

- Execute the eight steps of null hypothesis statistical significance testing (NHST).

- Conduct a *z*-test and explain how it fits into the general linear model (GLM).

- Recognize how effect sizes can compensate for some of the weaknesses of the decision to reject or retain a null hypothesis.

- Calculate and interpret Cohen's *d* for a *z*-test.

- Define Type I and Type II errors and explain why it is always possible to commit one or the other when conducting a null hypothesis statistical significance test.

Null Hypothesis Statistical Significance Testing

The main purpose of this chapter is to transition from the theory of inferential statistics to the application of inferential statistics. The fundamental process of inferential statistics is called **null hypothesis statistical significance testing (NHST)**. All procedures in the rest of this textbook are a form of NHST, so it is best to think of NHSTs as statistical procedures used to draw conclusions about a population based on sample data.

There are eight steps to NHST procedures:

1. Form groups in the data.
2. Define the null hypothesis (H_0). The null hypothesis is always that there is no difference between groups or that there is no relationship between independent and dependent variables.
3. Set alpha (α). The default alpha = .05.
4. Choose a one-tailed or a two-tailed test. This determines the alternative hypothesis (H_1).
5. Find the *critical* value, which is used to define the rejection region.

6. Calculate the *observed* value.
7. Compare the observed value and the critical value. If the observed value is more extreme than the critical value, then the null hypothesis should be rejected. Otherwise, it should be retained.
8. Calculate an *effect size*.

Readers who have had no previous exposure to statistics will find these steps confusing and abstract right now. But the rest of this chapter will define the terminology and show how to put these steps into practice. To reduce confusion, this book starts with the simplest possible NHST: the z-test.

z-Test

Recall from the previous chapter that social scientists are often selecting samples from a population that they wish to study. However, it is usually impossible to know how representative a single sample is of the population. One possible solution is to follow the process shown at the end of Chapter 6 where a researcher selects many samples from the same population in order to build a probability distribution. Although this method works, it is not used in the real world because it is too expensive and time-consuming. (Moreover, nobody wants to spend their life gathering data from an infinite number of populations in order to build a sampling distribution.) The alternative is to conduct a **z-test**. A z-test is an NHST that scientists use to determine whether their sample is typical or representative of the population it was drawn from.

In Chapter 6 we learned that a sample mean often is not precisely equal to the mean of its parent population. This is due to sampling error, which is also apparent in the variation in mean values from sample to sample. If several samples are taken from the parent population, the means from each sample could be used to create a sampling distribution of means. Because of the principles of the central limit theorem (CLT), statisticians know that with an infinite number of sample means, the distribution will be normally distributed (if the *n* of each sample is ≥ 25) and the mean of means will *always* be equal to the population mean.

Additionally, remember that in Chapter 5 we saw that the normal distribution theoretically continues on from $-\infty$ to $+\infty$. This means that any $\overline{X}$ value is possible. However, because the sampling distribution of means is tallest at the population mean and shortest at the tails, the sample means close to the population mean are far more likely to occur than sample means that are very far from μ.

Therefore, the question of inferential statistics is not whether a sample mean is possible but whether it is *likely* that the sample mean came from the population of interest. That requires a researcher to decide the point at which a sample mean is so different from the population mean that obtaining that sample mean would be highly unlikely (and, therefore, a more plausible explanation is that the sample really does differ from the population). If a sample mean ($\overline{X}$) is very similar to a population mean (μ), then the null hypothesis ($\overline{X} = \mu$) is a good model for the data. Conversely, if the sample mean and population mean are very different, then the null hypothesis does not fit the data well, and it is reasonable to believe that the two means are different.

This can be seen in Figure 7.1, which shows a standard normal distribution of sampling means. As expected, the population mean (μ) is in the middle of the distribution, which is also the peak of the sampling distribution. The shaded regions in the tails are called the **rejection region**. If, when we graph the sample mean, it falls within the rejection region, the sample is so different from the mean that it is unlikely that sampling error alone could account for the differences between $\overline{X}$

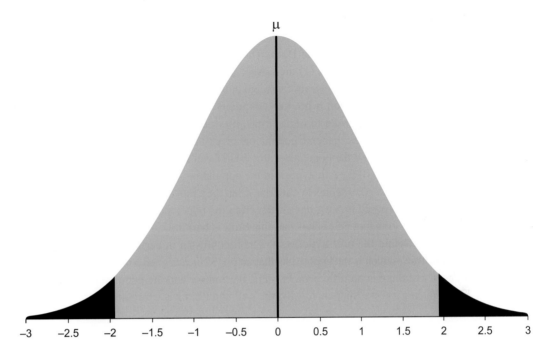

Figure 7.1 A standard normal sampling distribution of means. Theoretically, the distribution ranges from −∞ to +∞, but this figure shows only the range from −3 to +3. As a sample mean ($\overline{X}$) is further from the population mean (μ), it becomes less and less likely that the sample is representative or typical of the population. In NHST, the shaded region in the tails − called the rejection region − is an arbitrarily chosen region. If the sample mean falls into the rejection region, it is highly unlikely that the sample mean is typical of the population and the null hypothesis ($\overline{X} = \mu$) is rejected. If the sample mean falls outside the rejection region, the sample may be typical of the population and the null hypothesis is retained. This figure shows a two-tailed z-test, which has an alternative hypothesis of $H_1 : \overline{X} \neq \mu$.

and μ – and it is more likely that there is an actual difference between $\overline{X}$ and μ. If the sample mean is outside the rejection region, then $\overline{X}$ and μ are similar enough that it can be concluded that $\overline{X}$ is typical of the population (and sampling error alone could possibly account for all of the differences between $\overline{X}$ and μ).

Judging whether differences between $\overline{X}$ and μ are "close enough" or not due to just sampling error requires following the eight steps of NHST. To show how this happens in real life, we will use an example from a UK study by Vinten et al. (2009).

In this study, the researchers examined a sample of children whose mothers had taken an anti-seizure medication while pregnant. Vinten et al. (2009) had previously researched the anti-seizure medication and found that children exposed in the womb to the medication had lower intelligence test scores (Vinten et al., 2005). For a follow-up study, the researchers wanted to examine whether the children functioned more poorly in their environment. This is a valuable research question because intelligence tests are administered under very controlled circumstances, and it is possible that lower scores on these tests did not reflect an impairment in the children's functioning in daily life. Vinten et al.'s (2009) operational definition of "functioning" was a score on the Vineland Adaptive Behavior Scales (VABS), a psychological test that measures how well a person functions in three domains: communication, daily living, and socialization. The VABS is designed to have a population mean (μ) of 100 and standard deviation (σ) of 15. Because their previous study (Vinten et al., 2005) showed evidence that the anti-seizure medication was harmful, the authors had the research hypothesis that the children in their sample would also have lower VABS scores than average.

Form Groups in the Data. The first step of NHST is to form groups in the data. For a *z*-test the groups are always (1) the sample and (2) the population. Vinten et al. (2009) studied 242 children, ages 6 to 16, whose mothers had epilepsy. The sample that we will use in this example is a subgroup of 41 children who were exposed to sodium valproate (VPA) while in the womb. (The others were exposed to other drugs, no drugs, or a combination of VPA and another drug.) The population is the general population of children. By comparing this sample of 41 children exposed to VPA and the population, this NHST can show whether this sample of children is typical of the population. If they are typical of the population, then it is reasonable to conclude that the drug does not lower VABS scores in children when their mothers take it while pregnant. But if the sample of children exposed to VPA does differ from the population of all children, that would be evidence supporting Vinten et al.'s belief that this drug is harmful.

Define the null hypothesis. The second step in performing a NHST is to define the **null hypothesis**, which is the hypothesis that an NHST is designed to test. The null hypothesis in a *z*-test states that there is no difference between the sample and the population (which are always the two groups in a *z*-test). Mathematically, the null hypothesis is expressed as:

$$H_0 : \overline{X} = \mu$$ (Formula 7.1)

H_0 is the abbreviation for the null hypothesis, while $\overline{X}$ is the sample mean and μ is the population mean. If we remember that the null hypothesis is always that there is no difference between group means, then Formula 7.1 makes sense because if two numbers are equal, there is no difference between them. The sample mean and the population mean are used in Formula 7.1 because they are excellent measures of central tendency, and the sample mean is an unbiased estimate of the population mean (see Chapter 4). Formula 7.1 is *always* the null hypothesis for a *z*-test. The null hypothesis is important because it is this belief – that the two groups do not differ in their means – that is tested.

Sidebar 7.1   **Why test the null hypothesis?**

In the *z*-test example in this chapter, it may not seem logical to test the null hypothesis that the sample children have a mean VABS score that is equal to the mean VABS score in the general population mean ($H_0 : \overline{X} = \mu$). After all, Vinten et al.'s (2009) research hypothesis is that the VPA *harms* children *in utero* and therefore should have lower mean VABS scores than the population. So, why should Vinten et al. (2009) test a hypothesis that they don't really believe?

As this example shows, testing the null hypothesis seems nonsensical at first glance because the null hypothesis is often the exact opposite of the research hypothesis that a social scientist is interested in (Greenwald, 1975). But it is the most logical hypothesis to test. Remember from Chapter 1 that it is impossible to prove a hypothesis true, but that it *is* possible to disprove a hypothesis. Therefore, disproving the null hypothesis often provides evidence in support of the research hypothesis. In the example in this chapter, disproving the null hypothesis that the sample children's mean VABS score is equal to the population mean VABS score would provide evidence that the sample is different from the general population. (However, note that disproving the null hypothesis does *not* prove the research hypothesis true.)

A silly, extreme example may illustrate this point better. One of my students could come to class claiming that he had brought his invisible dog with him. I'll call this the "invisible dog research hypothesis."

In an effort to prove his research hypothesis true, he may say test this hypothesis by looking at the location where he believes his dog is sitting. "I don't see anything," the student says, "Therefore, my invisible dog must be there."

The flaw in his logic is obvious: the fact that he sees nothing may be consistent with the invisible dog research hypothesis, but it does not prove the research hypothesis true. There could be nothing there at all. Or there could be an invisible cat or an invisible rabbit. These hypotheses are also consistent with the data (of seeing nothing). Therefore, the data do not prove the research hypothesis true because there are other models (i.e., explanations) that fit the data just as well.

But we can test and *disprove* the null hypothesis, which would be that the student does *not* have an invisible dog. There are several ways to disprove this null hypothesis. We could accidentally kick the invisible dog and hear it yelp. Or we could pet its fur. Or we could step in its feces. Any of these would disprove the null hypothesis that there is no invisible dog and at the same time provide support (*but not proof*) of the invisible dog research hypothesis.

This absurd example is also useful for showing one more characteristic of the null hypothesis: it is the default belief in science. In the physical and social sciences, researchers start with the assumption that a phenomenon (like an invisible dog, or a difference between means) does *not* exist, and then seek to disprove this assumption. This default belief also extends to differences in groups (like the sample and population in the Vinten et al., (2009) study) and to relationships between independent and dependent variables. Generally, scientists are a skeptical lot.

Set Alpha. The third step in a NHST is to set alpha (α). Alpha is the size of the rejection region. Alpha is the proportion of the area in the normal distribution that is inside the rejection region. Because α is a proportion, it can only range from 0 to 1.0. In Figure 7.1 α is .05, indicating that 5% of the normal distribution is shaded in black. The choice of a value for α is completely arbitrary, meaning that the size of the rejection region is the researcher's decision (Murray & Dosser, 1987). In the social sciences the default value of α is .05 (Cohen, 1992). Therefore, the value of α for the *z*-test example using the Vinten et al. (2009) data will be .05.

Choose a One-Tailed or a Two-Tailed Test. This is the fourth step. Alpha determines the size of the rejection region, but it does not show where the rejection region should be in the sampling distribution of means. It is logical that the rejection region should be in the tails because that is where sample means will be most different from the population mean. But a researcher still has the option of either dividing the rejection region in half and putting each half in a tail (as in Figure 7.1) or putting the entire rejection region in either the left tail or the right tail (as in Figures 7.2a and 7.2b). If the entire rejection region is on one side of the distribution, the researcher is conducting a **one-tailed test**. If half of the rejection region is on each side of the distribution, the researcher is conducting a **two-tailed test**.

The decision of whether to conduct a one- or a two-tailed test is determined by whether the researcher has any previous research or theory about what results they can expect from the NHST. If a researcher has no theory or prior research about their topic, then a two-tailed test is most appropriate. This is because a researcher wants to ensure that they can reject the null hypothesis, whether $\overline{X}$ is greater or less than μ.

On the other hand, if there is prior research or theory about the topic, then a researcher should choose a one-tailed test. In the Vinten et al. (2009) example, the researchers had a previous study (Vinten et al., 2005) showing that the children exposed to VPA in the womb had lower

(a)

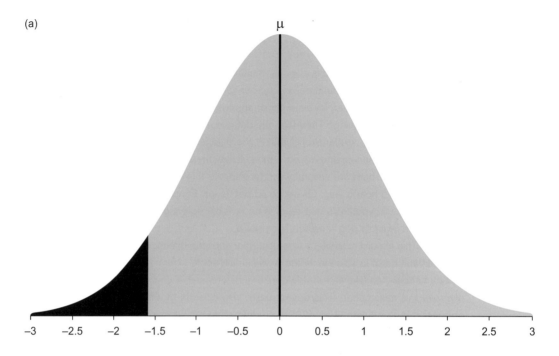

Figure 7.2a A standard normal sampling distribution of means with a one-tailed rejection region in the left tail. Putting the entire rejection on the left side of the distribution is appropriate if the researcher believes that the sample mean ($\overline{X}$) will be *lower* than the population mean (μ). The alternative hypothesis for this scenario is $H_1 : \overline{X} < \mu$, which is Formula 7.2.

(b)

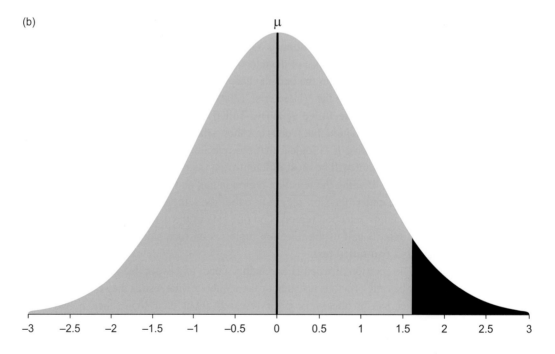

Figure 7.2b A standard normal sampling distribution of means with a one-tailed rejection region in the right tail. Putting the entire rejection on the right side of the distribution is appropriate if the researcher believes that the sample mean ($\overline{X}$) will be *greater* than the population mean (μ). The alternative hypothesis for this scenario is $H_1 : \overline{X} > \mu$, which is Formula 7.3.

intelligence test scores. Therefore, a one-tailed test is appropriate for this example. It is also logical to put the entire rejection region on the left side of the sampling distribution of means, as is shown in Figure 7.2a, because that would indicate that the researchers expect the VABS scores for the sample to be lower than the VABS scores for the population. (Putting the rejection region on the right side would not make sense in this example because that would mean that Vinten et al. think that VPA makes people function *better* in their environment than the average person. That is not a logical belief in light of the earlier findings indicating that the medication may *lower* intelligence test scores.)

The advantage of a one-tailed test is that it makes it easier to reject the null hypothesis – but only if the researcher puts the rejection region in the correct tail of the sampling distribution. On the other hand, the risk of this is that if the researcher chooses to put the rejection region on the wrong side of the sampling distribution, it is impossible to reject the null hypothesis, no matter how large the difference is between $\overline{X}$ and μ (Ryan, 1959). This is not too much of a concern, though, because most researchers seem to choose the correct side of the sampling distribution to put their rejection region. However, it is important to recognize that one-tailed tests in general are controversial for some experts precisely for the reason that these tests make it easier to reject the null hypothesis (which is what the researcher typically wants to do; see Sidebar 7.1). They view one-tail tests as a way to "cheat" to get the desired results. I take the view that one-tailed tests are justifiable, but students should recognize that there is a disagreement among statisticians and researchers on this point, and both sides have good reasons for their opinions. If your instructor says that a one-tailed test is never appropriate, they have a valid reason for this belief, and I suggest you follow their guidance.

The determination of a one- or two-tailed test also helps researchers decide their alternative hypothesis. The **alternative hypothesis** is the hypothesis that the data support if the null hypothesis is rejected. If researchers reject the null hypothesis, then the alternative hypothesis is what they will believe instead. This is important because if the null hypothesis – the default belief (see Sidebar 7.1) – is rejected, then the researchers must believe *something*. That "something" is the alternative hypothesis.

In a z-test, there are only three possible alternative hypotheses. Two of these alternative hypotheses correspond to a one-tailed z-test, while one of them corresponds to a two-tailed z-test. If the researcher is conducting a one-tailed test and the rejection region is all on the left side of the distribution (as in Figure 7.2a), then the formula for the alternative hypothesis is:

$$H_1 : \overline{X} < \mu \qquad \text{(Formula 7.2)}$$

This alternative hypothesis makes sense because if the rejection region is all on the left side of the sampling distribution and the null hypothesis is rejected, it must be because that the sample mean ($\overline{X}$) is *less than* the population mean (μ). In fact, Figure 7.2a shows that when the entire rejection region is at the left side of the sampling distribution, *any* $\overline{X}$ greater than μ could never reject the null hypothesis. So, if the null hypothesis is rejected, it must be because $\overline{X}$ is less than μ – which is what the alternative hypothesis in Formula 7.2 states.

However, if a researcher places all of the rejection region on the right side of the distribution – as in Figure 7.2b – then the alternative hypothesis is:

$$H_1 : \overline{X} > \mu \qquad \text{(Formula 7.3)}$$

Formula 7.3 closely resembles Formula 7.2 because they are both alternative hypotheses for one-tailed z-tests. In fact, their only difference is that in Formula 7.3 $\overline{X}$ is greater than μ, and in

Formula 7.2, the reverse is true. This is because the rejection region is at the opposite side of the sampling distribution, and that is why Figures 7.2a and 7.2b look like mirror images of each other.

Finally, for a two-tailed z-test, the alternative hypothesis is:

$$H_1 : \overline{X} \neq \mu \qquad \text{(Formula 7.4)}$$

Because a two-tailed z-test – like what is shown in Figure 7.1 – has the rejection region divided, it is possible that when the null hypothesis is rejected, $\overline{X}$ is greater or less than μ. To avoid having two alternative hypotheses, statisticians simply state that the two means are not equal. We can think of a two-tailed hypothesis as a way for researchers to "hedge their bets" and still reject the null hypothesis, whether the sample mean turns out to be higher or lower than the population mean.

Find the Critical Value. The fifth step is to find the critical value. The **critical value** is the point in the sampling distribution at which the rejection region starts. Everything within the tail that is beyond the critical value is in the rejection region, and everything between the mean and the critical value is outside the rejection region.

To find the critical value (called z-critical in a z-test and abbreviated z_{crit}), you should use Appendix A1. Finding the critical value requires finding the number in column C that corresponds to the value for α (for a one-tailed test). The number in that same row in column A is the z-critical value. If the rejection region is on the left – as in Figure 7.2a – the z-critical value should be negative because it must be less than 0. If the rejection region is on the right, the z-critical value should be positive.

For the example data from Vinten et al. (2009), the α value is .05, and we are conducting a one-tailed test with the rejection region on the left side of the distribution. In Appendix A1, there is no value in column C that is equal to exactly .05. There are two values that are close, however: .0495 and .0505. Whenever the exact α value is not in Appendix A1, you should choose the highest value that is less than α. I call this the *Price Is Right* rule, named for an American game show in which contestants can win prizes by being the closest to guessing the price of an item without having their guess exceed the item's actual value. Applying the *Price Is Right* rule to the Vinten et al. (2009) data means that we should choose the value in column C that is closest to .05 without exceeding it, and that is .0495 in this case.

After finding the correct value in column C, the z-critical value is the number in the same row under column A, which is ±1.65. But because the rejection region is on the left side of the distribution, the critical value should be negative. Therefore, the z-critical value for this example is −1.65. If the rejection region were all on the right side of the sampling distribution, then the critical value would be +1.65.

For a two-tailed test, the value of α must be divided in half before finding the value in column C. If $\alpha = .05$ (as it often is), then $\alpha / 2 = .025$. After we find this number in column C, it is apparent that the number in the same row in column A is ±1.96. Because two-tailed tests have half of the rejection region on each side of the sampling distribution (as in Figure 7.1), two-tailed tests have two critical values. So, the z-critical values in a two-tailed z-test where $\alpha = .05$ are −1.96 *and* +1.96.

Calculate the Observed Value. The sixth step in all NHST procedures – and the first to require any calculation – is to find the observed value. For a z-test, the formula for the observed value (called z-observed and abbreviated z_{obs}) is:

$$z_{obs} = \frac{\overline{X} - \mu}{\left(\frac{\sigma}{\sqrt{n}}\right)} \qquad \text{(Formula 7.5)}$$

This formula produces a value that can be positive or negative, with positive numbers indicating that the sample mean ($\overline{X}$) is greater than the population mean (μ), and negative numbers indicating that $\overline{X}$ is less than μ. (Remember from previous chapters that σ is the population standard deviation and n is the sample size.)

With the data from Vinten et al.'s (2009) study, calculating the z-observed is relatively easy. In their study, $\mu = 100$, $\sigma = 15$, $\overline{X} = 76.7$, and $n = 41$. Plugging these numbers into Formula 7.5 produces the following:

$$z_{obs} = \frac{76.7 - 100}{\left(\frac{15}{\sqrt{41}}\right)}$$

Solving for the z-observed value follows the steps below:

$$z_{obs} = \frac{-23.3}{\left(\frac{15}{\sqrt{41}}\right)}$$

$$z_{obs} = \frac{-23.3}{\left(\frac{15}{6.403}\right)}$$

$$z_{obs} = \frac{-23.3}{2.343}$$

$$z_{obs} = -9.95$$

Formula 7.5 should look vaguely familiar to readers because the formula bears a striking resemblance to the formula for calculating a z-score (see Formula 5.1). These similarities are illustrated in Figure 7.3:

- Both formulas consist of a fraction, where the numerator is the mean of the distribution being subtracted from another number.
- The denominator of both formulas is the standard deviation of the distribution. In the z-score formula it is the standard deviation of the scores in a sample distribution; for the z-observed formula the denominator is the standard error (SE), which, according to the CLT (as explained in Chapter 6), is the standard deviation of a sampling distribution of means.

Therefore, the z-observed value is a z-score for one particular sample mean when compared to other sample means in a sampling distribution – just as a z-score compares one particular score to other scores in a distribution of raw scores. (If you need a reminder of how to interpret z-scores, please see Chapter 5.)

Sidebar 7.2 Dividing the rejection region

When I teach about two-tailed tests and dividing α in half, some students ask me whether they can divide the rejection region in other ways (such as putting .04 on the left side and .01 on the right side). Although there are no statistics police that would stop a student from doing this, it would not make sense. Two-tailed tests are designed for situations where researchers have no prior research or theory which can provide them with clues of their expected results. If researchers have enough knowledge about their study to have a logical reason to create lop-sided regions, then they have too much information for a two-tailed test. Whenever a researcher has enough prior research or theory to expect that a particular result is likely, then a one-tailed test is appropriate.

- *The z-score formula uses the distribution of raw scores in a sample.*
- *The z-observed formula uses the sampling distribution of means.*

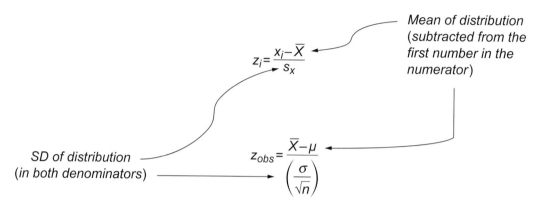

Mean of distribution (*subtracted from the first number in the numerator*)

SD of distribution (*in both denominators*)

$$z_i = \frac{x_i - \overline{X}}{s_x}$$

$$z_{obs} = \frac{\overline{X} - \mu}{\left(\frac{\sigma}{\sqrt{n}}\right)}$$

- *These similarities show that a z-observed value is just a z-score for a mean compared to the sampling distribution of all other means.*

Figure 7.3 Similarities between the z-score and the z-observed formulas. These similarities show that, conceptually, a z-observed value is a z-score for a sample mean when compared to the other sample means in a sampling distribution.

Compare the Observed Value and the Critical Value. Step 7 in conducting a NHST is to compare the observed and critical values. If the observed value is inside the rejection region, the researcher should reject the null hypothesis. If the observed value is outside the rejection region, the researcher should retain the null hypothesis.

Figure 7.4 shows in visual form how to make this comparison with the Vinten et al. (2009) data. Remember that in this example, the z-observed value was –9.95 and the z-critical value was –1.96. The one-tailed rejection region (shaded in black on the left side of the distribution) starts at the critical value of –1.65 and includes all values lower than that. Because the sampling distribution ranges from –∞ to +∞, the rejection region includes values from –∞ to –1.65. The observed value of –9.95 is between –∞ and –1.65, meaning that the z-observed value is in the rejection region. Therefore, we should reject the null hypothesis of $H_0 : \overline{X} = \mu$.

The null hypothesis was that there was no difference in mean VABS scores between children whose mothers had taken VPA while pregnant and the general population. Because the null hypothesis has been rejected, it is not reasonable to believe that it is supported by the data. Therefore, these results are evidence (though not proof – see Sidebar 7.1) that there may be a difference in VABS scores between the groups. Because the $\overline{X}$ value was lower than μ, we can conclude that children who were exposed to VPA may have poorer functioning in the environment than the average child in the general population.

Calculate an Effect Size. This is the eighth and final step. The previous seven steps of NHST are useful for producing a yes or no answer on whether the null hypothesis is a good statistical model for the data. In the Vinten et al. (2009) example, the null hypothesis was not a good model of the data, as shown by the extreme z-observed value. However, researchers are rarely interested in whether or not the null hypothesis is a good model (Fidler & Cumming, 2007). (Remember that – as in this example – the null hypothesis is often not the same as the research hypothesis, which is what the researcher is actually interested in.) It would be far more useful to

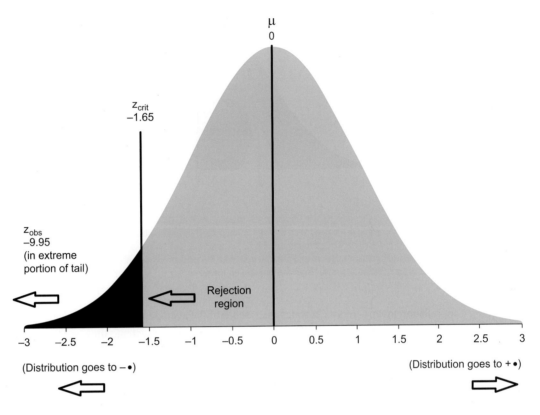

Figure 7.4 Schematic showing the logic of rejecting the null hypothesis with the Vinten et al. (2009) data. Because the rejection region starts at −1.65 and includes everything lower than that number, the z-observed value of −9.95 is inside the rejection region. The exact location of the observed value is not shown because the x-axis of the graphic only shows values in the sampling distribution between −3 and +3.

learn how different the sample is from the population. To get this information, it is necessary to calculate an effect size.

An **effect size** is a statistic that quantifies the degree to which the null hypothesis is wrong. There are many effect sizes (Kirk, 1996),[4] the first of which is called Cohen's d. It is defined (Cohen, 1962, p. 147) as

$$d = \frac{\overline{X} - \mu}{\sigma} \qquad \text{(Formula 7.6)}$$

As the numerator in Formula 7.6 shows, Cohen's d is a measure of the difference between the sample mean ($\overline{X}$) and population mean (μ). (In fact, it may be helpful to think that the d stands for "distance," as in the "distance between two means.") Dividing the numerator by the standard deviation performs the same function as it did in Formula 5.7, which was the z-score formula. It changes the scale so that it is standardized (i.e., converted to z-scores). Cohen's d thus has two interpretations. It (1) quantifies the number of standard deviations that are between the sample and

---

[4] The other effect sizes in this textbook are Glass's Δ ("delta," Chapter 9), η^2 ("eta-squared," Chapter 11), r^2 (Chapter 12), the odds ratio (Chapter 14), relative risk (Chapter 14), ϕ ("phi," Chapter 14), Cramér's V (Chapter 14), R^2 (Chapter 15), and AUC (Chapter 15). See Kirk (1996) for a listing of even more effect sizes.

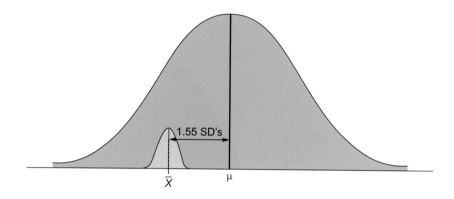

Figure 7.5 A diagram showing the effect size in the Vinten et al. (2009) example. Notice that the smaller distribution – consisting of the sample – has a mean that is 1.55 standard deviations below the mean of the larger distribution (which is the population). Cohen's *d* is a measure of how far apart the two means are. The negative value in Cohen's *d* example (*d* = −1.55) indicates that the sample mean is less than the population mean. A positive Cohen's *d* value would indicate that the sample mean is greater than the population mean.

population means, and it (2) states the *z*-score of the average person in the sample when compared to the population as a whole. These interpretations are equivalent; they are just different ways of thinking about the same result.

These two interpretations can be applied to Cohen's *d* calculated from the Vinten et al. (2009) data, where $\overline{X} = 76.70$, $\mu = 100$, and $\sigma = 15$. Plugging these values into Formula 7.6 produces:

$$d = \frac{76.70 - 100}{15}$$

Solving for this equation produces Cohen's *d* value of −1.55. According to the first interpretation of Cohen's *d*, this means that the sample mean is 1.55 standard deviations below the population mean. If you prefer the second interpretation, you would understand this Cohen's *d* value to indicate that the average child in the sample has a VABS score that is 1.55 standard deviations below the mean of the general population.

Theoretically, Cohen's *d* has no limits, and it can take on any value from $-\infty$ to $+\infty$. However, values outside the range of ± 2.0 are rare in the social sciences. A Cohen's *d* of 0 would indicate that there is no difference between the sample and the population means because $\overline{X}$ and μ would be equal. Therefore, when $d = 0$, the null hypothesis ($H_0 : \overline{X} = \mu$) is a perfect statistical model for the data because the null hypothesis was that these two means are equal (Thompson, 2007). Therefore, the larger the Cohen's *d* value, the more likely that the null hypothesis will be rejected in an NHST.

Check Yourself!

- What are the eight steps of NHST?

- What is the null hypothesis in a *z*-test?

- When is a one-tailed test appropriate for a researcher to use? When is a two-tailed hypothesis appropriate to use?

- How is the *z*-observed formula similar to the *z*-score formula (discussed in Chapter 5)?

- How do you know when to reject a null hypothesis in a *z*-test? How do you know when to retain the null hypothesis?

- What is the effect size for a *z*-test and how do you interpret it?

Guided Practice 7.1

To comply with a national law, a professional social work organization collects data about job satisfaction from all employed social workers every year. Because it is mandatory for all employed social workers to respond, the organization has population data, so parameters for this population are $\mu = 6.1$ and $\sigma = 2.4$ on a scale from 1 to 10, with higher numbers signifying higher job satisfaction. A researcher – knowing that social work is a field where burnout and job turnover are sometimes major problems (Kim & Stoner, 2008) – wondered if a sample of social workers who work with children have a different level of job satisfaction than the population average. She found that the sample ($n = 104$) had $\overline{X} = 6.5$. This example will walk you through the process of conducting a *z*-test.

Step 1: Form Groups

As in all *z*-tests, the two groups in this example are the population and the sample.

Step 2: Define the Null Hypothesis

The null hypothesis (abbreviated H_0) is that the sample mean and population mean are equal. Mathematically, this is written as $H_0 : \overline{X} = \mu$. This is always the null hypothesis for a *z*-test.

Step 3: Set Alpha

The default α value in the social and medical sciences is .05, and there is no reason to change alpha in this example.

Step 4: Choose a One- or Two-Tailed Test, Which Determines the Alternative Hypothesis

In the description above there is no prior research or theory that would help the researcher create an educated guess about the results of this *z*-test. Therefore, a two-tailed test is appropriate, and the alternative hypothesis is $H_1 : \overline{X} \neq \mu$.

Step 5: Find the Critical Value

This requires Appendix A1. But before using it, you should remember that because this is a two-tailed z-test, half of the rejection region is in each tail of the sampling distribution. Therefore, it is necessary to divide alpha in half before looking up a z-critical value. The $\alpha = .05$, so $\frac{.05}{2} = .025$. Find this number in column C in Appendix A1. The number in column A that is in the same row is ± 1.96. Because this is a two-tailed test, we need both critical values, so z-critical values are $+1.96$ *and* -1.96.

Step 6: Calculate the Observed Value

The formula for the z-observed value is $z_{obs} = \frac{\overline{X} - \mu}{\left(\frac{\sigma}{\sqrt{n}}\right)}$. All of the numbers needed in this formula are in the description above ($\mu = 6.1$, $\sigma = 2.4$, $\overline{X} = 6.5$, $n = 104$). Plugging these numbers into the z-observed formula produces

$$z_{obs} = \frac{6.5 - 6.1}{\left(\frac{2.4}{\sqrt{104}}\right)}$$

Solving for the z-observed value produces a value of 1.70. The $\pm$ is necessary because this is a two-tailed test.

Step 7: Compare the Observed and Critical Values and Find p

The easiest way to perform this step is to draw the sampling distribution and plot the rejection region and the critical and observed values. (The unofficial motto in my classroom for NHSTs is, "When in doubt, draw it out.") Because $z_{obs} = 1.70$ and $z_{crit} = \pm 1.96$, the sampling distribution in this example would look like Figure 7.6.

Because the z-observed value is outside the rejection region, we should not retain the null hypothesis. In other words, social workers who work with children do not have a level of job satisfaction that differs from the population mean. The null hypothesis is a statistical model that fits these data well, and maybe it is not necessary to consider the alternative hypothesis to understand these data. Because we did not reject the null hypothesis, we do not need to worry about Type I error, but we do need to worry about Type II error. This means that even though we retained the null hypothesis, it is possible that there really is a difference between our $\overline{X}$ and μ – but we just didn't detect that difference.

The p-value is also represented in Figure 7.6. As is apparent (by the striped area in the figure), p represents the area in the sampling distribution from the observed value to the end of the tail. To find p, you should use Appendix A1. In that table find observed value (1.70) in column A. The number in column C in the same row is .0446. But this value only applies to one tail in the sampling distribution. Because we performed a two-tailed test, we need to double the number in column C to produce the real p-value. In this example $2(.0446) = .0892$. Therefore, $p = .0892$.

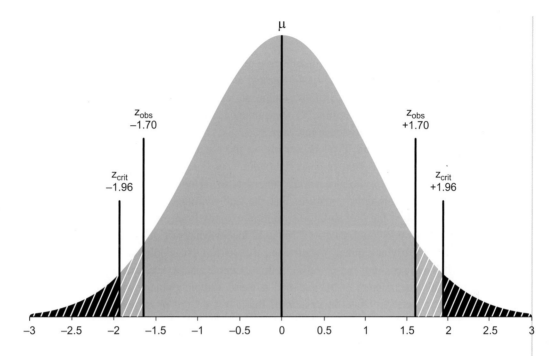

Figure 7.6 A schematic showing the relationship between the z-observed (z-obs) and z-critical (z-crit) values on the sampling distribution in the guided practice example. The striped area is the portion of the distribution represented by p.

Step 8: Calculate an Effect Size

The formula for Cohen's d, which is the appropriate effect size for a z-test is $d = \frac{\overline{X} - \mu}{\sigma}$. Plugging the values from this example into this equation produces:

$$d = \frac{6.4 - 6.1}{2.4}$$

Solving for d produces a value of 0.125. This can be interpreted as meaning either (1) sample members have a job satisfaction that is just .125 standard deviation higher than the population average, or (2) the average sample member has a job satisfaction that is only .125 standard deviation higher than the average population member's job satisfaction.

Although the effect size is positive and the sample mean slightly higher than the population mean, retaining the null hypothesis shows that this difference could possibly be due to sampling error. Additionally, the effect size is very small, so it makes sense that the null hypothesis was retained. An effect size of 0 would fit the null hypothesis perfectly; the small effect size means that the data are not very different from what we would expect with the null hypothesis. In short, there is no strong evidence in this example that social workers who work with children have levels of job satisfaction that are different from the population of social workers.

Cautions for Using NHSTs

NHST procedures dominate quantitative research in the behavioral sciences (Cumming et al., 2007; Fidler et al., 2005; Warne, Lazo, Ramos, & Ritter, 2012). But it is not a flawless procedure, and NHST is open to abuse. In this section, we will explore three of the main problems with NHST: (1) the possibility of errors, (2) the subjective decisions involved in conducting an NHST, and (3) NHST's sensitivity to sample size.

Type I and Type II Errors. In the Vinten et al. (2009) example, we rejected the null hypothesis because the *z*-observed value was inside the rejection region, as is apparent in Figure 7.4 (where the *z*-observed value was so far below zero that it could not be shown on the figure). But this does not mean that the null hypothesis is definitely wrong. Remember that – theoretically – the probability distribution extends from $-\infty$ to $+\infty$. Therefore, it is possible that a random sample could have an $\overline{X}$ value as low as what was observed in Vinten et al.'s (2009) study. This is clearly an unlikely event – but, theoretically, it is possible. So even though we rejected the null hypothesis and the $\overline{X}$ value in this example had a very extreme *z*-observed value, it is still possible that Vinten et al. just had a weird sample (which would produce a large amount of sampling error). Thus, the results of this *z*-test do not prove that the anti-seizure medication is harmful to children in the womb.

Scientists never know for sure whether their null hypothesis is true or not – even if that null is strongly rejected, as in this chapter's example (Open Science Collaboration, 2015; Tukey, 1991). There is always the possibility (no matter how small) that the results are just a product of sampling error. When researchers reject the null hypothesis and it is true, they have made a **Type I error**. We can use the *z*-observed value and Appendix A1 to calculate the probability of Type I error if the null hypothesis were perfectly true and the researcher chose to reject the null hypothesis (regardless of the α level). This probability is called a ***p*-value** (abbreviated as *p*). Visually, it can be represented, as in Figure 7.6, as the region of the sampling distribution that starts at the observed value and includes everything beyond it in the tail.

To calculate *p*, you should first find the *z*-observed value in column A. (If the *z*-observed value is not in Appendix A1, then the *Price Is Right* rule applies, and you should select the number in column A that is closest to the *z*-observed value without going over it.) The number in column C in the same row will be the *p*-value. For example, in a one-tailed test, if *z*-observed were equal to +2.10, then the *p*-value (i.e., the number in column C in the same row) would be .0179. This *p*-value means that in this example the probability that these results could occur through purely random sampling error is .0179 (or 1.79%). In other words, if we selected an infinite number of samples from the population, then 1.79% of $\overline{X}$ values would be as different as or more different than μ. *But remember that this probability only applies if the null hypothesis is perfectly true* (see Sidebar 10.3).

In the Vinten et al. (2009) example, the *z*-observed value was –9.95. However, because Appendix A1 does not have values that high, we will select the last row (because of the *Price Is Right* rule), which has the number ±5.00 in column A. The number in column C in the same row is .0000003, which is the closest value available for the *p*-value. In reality, *p* will be smaller than this tiny number. (Notice how the numbers in column C get smaller as the numbers in column A get bigger. Therefore, a *z*-observed value that is outside the ±5.00 range will have smaller *p*-values than the values in the table.) Thus, the chance that – if the null hypothesis were true – Vinten et al. (2009) would obtain a random sample of 41 children with such low VABS scores is less than .0000003 – or less than 3 in 10 million. Given this tiny probability of making a Type I error if the null hypothesis were true, it seems more plausible that these results are due to an actual difference between the sample and the population – and not merely to sampling error.

Sidebar 7.3 A *p*-value cannot be zero

It is important to realize that although *p* can be very tiny, it can never be equal to 0. In a *z*-test, that would indicate that it is impossible to randomly select the sample from the population. But if the sample could never come from the population, why would researchers bother comparing their sample to a population? Yet, in a minority of quantitative articles (including 12.2% in five educational psychology journals that my colleagues and I examined; see Warne et al., 2012, p. 143), the authors stated that their *p*-value was equal to or less than 0. Researchers who make this mistake are probably misinterpreting their computer program's results, which often round the *p*-value to the third or fourth decimal place. In this case a very tiny *p*-value will often be displayed as .000 or .0000. Reporting that *p* is less than or equal to zero is always a very basic error of statistical reporting, and I urge readers to avoid this mistake when they report their NHST results.

On the other hand, when researchers retain a null hypothesis that is actually untrue, they are making a **Type II error**. Calculating the probability of Type II error is complicated and beyond the scope of this textbook. However, students should be aware that whenever the null hypothesis is not rejected a Type II error is a possibility. This is shown in Table 7.1.

Table 7.1 also shows that whatever the decision at the end of a NHST, a researcher *always* needs to worry about either Type I error or Type II error. But it is only necessary, with a given NHST result, to worry about one of them – never both at once because it is impossible to both reject and retain the null hypothesis at the same time. In the Vinten et al. (2009) example, we rejected the null hypothesis. Therefore, we need to worry about Type I error (although the probability of making a Type I error if the null hypothesis is true would be less than .0000003, so it is not much of a worry).

Subjective Decisions. Despite its outward appearance as an objective data analysis procedure, NHST requires researchers to make a few subjective decisions. The most obvious is that the researcher gets to choose the value of α. Nefarious researchers could manipulate their α level to make it easier to reject the null hypothesis by making α – and therefore the rejection region – larger. Conversely, a person could make it difficult to reject the null hypothesis by making α – and, again, the rejection region – smaller. This is why in the social sciences the default α is .05, and any changes in the α value should be explicitly justified (e.g., Warne, 2014b).

Table 7.1 Relationship between Types I and II errors and correct decisions in NHST

Decision	Reality	
	H_0 is true	H_0 is false
Reject H_0 →	Type I error	Correct decision
Retain H_0 →	Correct decision	Type II error

Sensitivity to Sample Size. Manipulating α is a well-known potential flaw in NHST procedures, and it is relatively easy for other scientists to detect. A lesser known flaw in NHST is its susceptibility to sample size. For *all* NHST procedures, it is easier to reject the null hypothesis for larger sample sizes than for small sample sizes (Ferguson, 2009; Murray & Dosser, 1987). In fact, with a large enough sample size, it is possible to reject almost any null hypothesis. Likewise, a small enough sample size can make it extremely difficult to reject almost any null hypothesis (Cohen, 1994; Rodgers, 2010; Sedlmeier & Gigerenzer, 1989; Thompson, 1992). This can be seen in Formula 7.5:

$$z_{obs} = \frac{\overline{X} - \mu}{\left(\frac{\sigma}{\sqrt{n}}\right)}$$

If all other values are held constant, then increasing the sample size will make the standard error (in parentheses) smaller as a whole. A smaller standard error makes the z-observed value as a whole larger, because the small denominator will result in a fraction that, overall, has a higher value. Thus, *increasing the sample size will make it easier to reject the null hypothesis in a z-test (and any other NHST) unless the null hypothesis is a perfect statistical model for the data.*

This sensitivity to sample size is another reason why it is so important to report effect sizes. Cohen's *d* is not affected by sample size. This is apparent in the formula for Cohen's *d* (Formula 7.6), which does not include sample size. Therefore, sample size cannot have an impact on the effect size.

Guided Practice 7.2

We are going to conduct another z-test using data taken from the US Centers for Disease Control, which collect information about every recorded birth and death in the country. (Because of practical limitations and how the data are reported publicly, this example does not include unrecorded deaths or deaths that occurred at age 100 or older. The population size was $N = 2,571,872$.) The population mean age of death (μ) in 2013 was 72.96, and the standard deviation (σ) was 18.18. In that same year there were 156,089 deaths from lung cancer, which had a mean age of death ($\overline{X}$) of 71.22. In this example we will test the null hypothesis that the age in the sample of lung cancer deaths is equal to the population mean age of death.

Step 1: Form Groups

As in all z-tests, the two groups in this example are the population and the sample.

Step 2: Define the Null Hypothesis

All z-tests have the same null hypothesis, which is that the population and sample means are equal. Mathematically, this is Formula 7.1, which was $H_0 : \overline{X} = \mu$.

Step 3: Set Alpha

The default value for α is .05.

Step 4: Choose a One- or Two-Tailed Test, Which Determines the Alternative Hypothesis

As social scientists, we do not know enough about the age when lung cancer usually ends someone's life, so we are going to perform a two-tailed test. Therefore, the alternative hypothesis is $H_1 : \overline{X} \neq \mu$, which is Formula 7.4.

Step 5: Find the Critical Values

(Appendix A1 shows that the critical values are ± 1.96. If this number seems familiar, it is because they are the same critical values as in the last Guided Practice (2009) example. This is because both examples are two-tailed tests and both have the same α value.

Step 6: Calculate the Observed Value

The formula for the observed value is $z_{obs} = \dfrac{\overline{X} - \mu}{\left(\frac{\sigma}{\sqrt{n}}\right)}$. Plugging the numbers from above into this formula produces:

$$z_{obs} = \frac{71.22 - 72.96}{\left(\dfrac{18.18}{\sqrt{156,089}}\right)}$$

Solving for this produces a z-observed value of 37.81. Again, remember that the $\pm$ is necessary for two-tailed z-tests.

Step 7: Compare the Observed and Critical Values and Find p

With a critical value of ± 1.96 and an observed value of 37.81, it is clear that the z-observed value is much more extreme (and therefore much further in the tail) than the z-critical value. Therefore, the observed value must be in the rejection region. (If you draw the sampling distribution, you will get a picture that looks like Figure 7.1, and the critical value would be so extreme that it would be off the chart on the left side.)

Finding the exact p-value using Appendix A1 involves finding the z-critical value first in column A, and the number in column C in the same row will be p. Unfortunately, Appendix A1 does not have enough rows to display ± 37.81, so we will have to take the highest number in column A without exceeding ± 37.81. This is ± 5.00 (the last row in the table). The corresponding p-value (in column C) is .0000003. But because this is a two-tailed z-test, we must double this value to .0000006. Therefore, the p-value in this test is less than .0000006.

Step 8: Calculate an Effect Size

According to Formula 7.6, Cohen's d is calculated as $d = \frac{\overline{X} - \mu}{\sigma}$. Plugging these numbers into the formula produces:

$$d = \frac{71.22 - 72.96}{18.18}$$

Solving for this produces a Cohen's *d* value of –0.096. In other words, people who die of lung cancer die an average of 1.74 years younger than the average death (72.96 – 71.22 = 1.74), which is the equivalent of 0.096 standard deviations lower than μ. This small effect size may seem surprising, given the fact that the *z*-observed value was so extreme and that the decision to reject the null hypothesis was so clear. However, we should remember that as the sample size in a NHST grows, it becomes easier and easier to reject the null hypothesis (unless the null hypothesis is a model that perfectly fits the data). In fact, with a sample size of 156,089, the null hypothesis would have been rejected, even if the Cohen's *d* were as small as $\pm$ .011, which is the equivalent of 0.20 years (18.18 × .011 = .020), or 72 days.

Check Yourself!

- Define Type I and Type II errors.

- Why can *p* never equal 0?

- What are the three weaknesses of NHST procedures?

Sidebar 7.4 **The importance of effect sizes**

How important are effect sizes? Individual scientists and professional organizations are reaching a consensus that effect sizes are vital information to provide when reporting research. Here are some examples:

- Two official groups of scientists commissioned by the American Psychological Association (APA) stated that reporting effect sizes should be required (APA Publications and Communications Board Working Group on Journal Article Reporting Standards, 2008; Wilkinson & the Task Force on Statistical Inference, 1999).
- The American Educational Research Association (2006, p. 37) states that it is "critical" to report effect sizes.
- The APA publication manual – which sets standards for over 1,000 journals in the social sciences in the English-speaking world – stated that "it is almost always necessary to include some measure of effect size" (APA, 2010, p. 34) when reporting research.
- The British Psychological Society requires researchers who wish to publish in their journals to report effect sizes (P. E. Morris & Fritz, 2013).
- Many journal editors in the social sciences now will not publish a quantitative study unless the authors report an effect size (Thompson, 2007; see, for example, McCoach & Siegle, 2009).

Why do these authorities value effect sizes so much? Because effect sizes compensate for some of the shortcomings of NHSTs. Effect sizes are not sensitive to the influences of sample size, for example. Additionally, effect sizes and NHSTs provide complementary information. An NHST merely states whether the null hypothesis is a statistical model that fits the data or not. (In a z-test, this would be whether the difference between μ and $\overline{X}$ is large enough that the null hypothesis is rejected.) Instead, Cohen's d quantifies the size of the difference between the means and answers the question, "*How large* is the difference between the means?" This is information that NHSTs cannot provide. These reasons are why many social science authorities value effect size reporting.

Researchers seem to be getting the message. Progress is sometimes slow, but since the 1990s effect size reporting has increased (Fidler et al., 2005; Warne et al., 2012), although some branches of the social sciences are better at reporting effect sizes than others (Kirk, 1996; P. E. Morris & Fritz, 2013). As these examples and the cited articles show, psychologists seem to be leading the way in this effort, and a growing number of researchers in psychology agree that effect sizes should almost always be reported in statistical analysis (Fidler et al., 2005; Finch, Cumming, & Thomason, 2001). Yet, experts in education, sociology, and other social sciences are also making valuable contributions to ensuring that researchers, practitioners, and students in all the social sciences understand the importance of effect sizes.

General Linear Model

Characteristics of the General Linear Model (GLM). The z-test is the most basic NHST and also the most basic member of the GLM, which is a family of statistical procedures that have three characteristics, as explained by Vacha-Haase and Thompson (2004):

1. All GLM procedures examine the relationships between independent and dependent variables. Another way of stating this point is that all GLM procedures are correlational in nature. (See Chapter 12 for an explanation of correlation.)
2. All GLM procedures apply weights to data during the analysis process.
3. All GLM procedures can produce an effect size.

Not all of these characteristics are immediately apparent to students learning NHST procedures. In fact, in a z-test only the third characteristic is obvious (with Cohen's d). Yet, the first two points are true about z-tests. For details, see the box "General Linear Moment 7.1."

The GLM seems to complicate a z-test needlessly, but learning it now will make learning future statistical procedures easier. This is because GLM procedures are organized in a hierarchy, where simpler procedures are special cases of more complicated procedures (Zientek & Thompson, 2009). In statistics, a **special case** is a simplification of a more complicated procedure that occurs in certain circumstances. This means that all members of the GLM are basically the same procedure (which is concerned with finding relationships between independent and dependent variables), which simplifies to its most basic possible form in a z-test. Therefore, as you approach each new chapter in this book, you should remember that the new NHST method is really just a z-test that has been adapted to fit more complicated circumstances. All procedures you learn in the rest of this textbook will follow the eight steps listed at the beginning of this chapter.

There are two ways in which the GLM is a model. First, it is a statistical model because of the way that all statistical procedures are special cases of more complex procedures. Recall from

General Linear Moment 7.1

This is the first General Linear Moment text box in the textbook. The purpose of General Linear Moments is to show how the different methods taught in the textbook are interrelated and are all members of the GLM. You should expect to see at least one General Linear Moment box in most of the remaining chapters. For this first General Linear Moment, I will use an example from Vinten et al. (2009) to explain how a *z*-test has all of the characteristics of the GLM that Vacha-Haase and Thompson (2004) described.

Independent and Dependent Variables. In a *z*-test the independent variable is *always* a nominal variable of whether the person was in the sample (which we will arbitrarily label as Group 1) or the population (labeled as Group 0). The dependent variable is the variable that is used to calculate $\overline{X}$, μ, and σ. In the Vinten et al. (2009) example, the dependent variable was VABS scores. As we conducted a *z*-test of the data from Vinten et al.'s study, we were determining whether there was a relationship between the group that the children belonged to (i.e., the sample or the population) and their VABS scores. The null hypothesis was that there was no relationship between these two variables. Because the null hypothesis was rejected, we can conclude that there *is* likely a relationship between group membership and VABS scores; sample members (exposed to VPA in the womb) had lower VABS scores on average than population members.

Another way to think of this point is in terms of correlation – a topic that we will discuss in depth in Chapter 12. For now, it is only necessary to understand correlation as a relationship between variables. When a relationship between variables is strong, the correlation between the variables is high. Likewise, when the correlation is weak, the relationship between variables is also weak. In the context of a *z*-test, a strong relationship between the independent variable (of membership in the sample or the population) and the dependent variable would indicate that there is a large degree of separation between the two groups. This is most easily indicated by a large Cohen's *d* value. When the correlation between variables is weak in a *z*-test, there is a lot of overlap between the groups' distributions, indicating a smaller Cohen's *d* statistic. This point will become more clear after you learn more about correlation.

Weighting Data. **Statistical weights** are numbers that are multiplied by the raw data to create statistical models. In a *z*-test, Cohen's *d* is a statistical weight. If we multiply the person's score on the independent variable (0 = population member, 1 = sample member) by Cohen's *d*, the result is the predicted VABS *z*-score for that person. For the Vinten et al. (2009) example, this would mean that a child who is in the general population would be expected to have a *z*-score of 0 on the VABS (because $0 \times -1.55 = 0$). A person in the sample who had been exposed to VPA before birth would be expected to have a VABS *z*-score of -1.55 (because $1 \times -1.55 = -1.55$). Notice how this matches one of the interpretations of Cohen's *d*. Statistical weights will become more important in later chapters in this textbook.

Effect Sizes. In this chapter we have already learned about Cohen's *d* and how to interpret it, so it is not necessary to discuss it again here. What is important to recognize is that all GLM methods will produce an effect size. For some procedures this is Cohen's *d*, but there are other effect sizes that we will discuss in later chapters.

Chapter 1 that statistical models use a limited number of specific variables and are expressed as mathematical equations. Because more complex statistical methods can simplify to any other GLM member, we have the option of always building one complex statistical model that then simplifies to an appropriate, more basic method. (This would not usually be practical, but it is theoretically possible.) This is why the GLM is really just one big statistical model – and why it is "general."

Second, the GLM is a theoretical model because it is a way of verbally understanding how statistical methods relate to one another. Even if you don't understand every aspect of the GLM, the theoretical model of the GLM can still provide you with a mental framework that will help you understand new statistical procedures. Research in cognitive and educational psychology shows that people learn better when they have a way to organize new information (Bransford, Vye, & Bateman, 2002; Kintsch, 1998). Without the GLM, statistical procedures seem disconnected from each other and are much harder to learn.

The rest of this textbook is designed to use the GLM to help you see similarities and differences across procedures and learn new procedures more quickly. Here are a few tips to help you as you read future chapters:

- Remind yourself when you start a new chapter that the method you just learned is a special case of the method in the new chapter. That means that the two procedures will be the same, but the newer one will have some modifications so that it can be applied to more complicated situations.
- Remember that all NHST procedures are members of the GLM and that they are all testing the null hypothesis (Cohen, 1968). The null hypothesis is always that there is no relationship or correlation between the independent and dependent variable; often (e.g., in a z-test) this means the null hypothesis will be that there is no difference between group means.
- Be aware that every statistical procedure in this book is a member of the GLM, which means that it investigates whether an independent variable and a dependent variable have a relationship or correlation.
- Don't forget about effect sizes. Every member of the GLM has at least one effect size that accompanies it. The NHST procedure merely tells a researcher whether or not the null hypothesis is a good model for the data. But the effect size quantifies the degree to which the data fit the null hypothesis (or not). Rather than a simple yes-or-no answer (as in NHST), effect sizes allow more nuance in interpretation (Durlak, 2009; Ferguson, 2009).

Check Yourself!

- What is the GLM? Why is it important?
- What are the three main points of the GLM?
- How does a z-test fit into the GLM?
- How can understanding the GLM help you understand other statistical methods you will learn in this textbook?

Summary

All null hypothesis statistical significance testing procedures follow eight steps. These steps are:

1. Form groups in the data.
2. Define the null hypothesis (H_0). The null hypothesis is always that there is no difference between groups or that there is no relationship between independent and dependent variables.
3. Set alpha (α). The default alpha $= .05$.
4. Choose a one-tailed or a two-tailed test. This determines the alternative hypothesis (H_1).
5. Calculate the *observed* value.
6. Find the *critical* value, which is used to define the rejection region.
7. Compare the observed value and the critical value. If the observed value is more extreme than the critical value, then the null hypothesis should be rejected.
8. Calculate an *effect size*.

A *z*-test is the simplest type of NHST, and it is used to test the null hypothesis that a sample mean and a population mean are equal. If this null hypothesis is retained, then the difference between means is no greater than what would be expected from sampling error, and the data support the idea that the sample and population means are equal. If the null hypothesis is rejected, it is unlikely (though still possible) that the null hypothesis serves as a good statistical model for the data.

Although NHST procedures are useful, it is possible to make the wrong decision about the null hypothesis. A Type I error occurs when a person rejects a null hypothesis that is actually true. A Type II error occurs when a person retains a null hypothesis that is actually false. When conducting a *z*-test or any other NHST procedure, it is impossible to know whether a correct decision has been made or not. It is just something that researchers need to consider as they interpret their data. A related idea is the *p*-value, which is the size of the region in the tail that starts at the observed value (see Figure 7.6). The *p*-value is the probability that a sample mean could be randomly selected from the population *if the null hypothesis were true*.

Because NHST results and *p*-values can be manipulated and are sensitive to sample size, it is always appropriate to calculate an effect size to accompany the NHST results. For a *z*-test the appropriate effect size is Cohen's *d*. Positive Cohen's *d* values indicate that the sample mean is greater than the population mean; negative Cohen's *d* values indicate the reverse. Cohen's *d* can be interpreted as either (1) the number of standard deviations between the two means, or (2) the *z*-score of the average person in the sample when compared to the entire population. The closer the Cohen's *d* is to 0, the more similar the two means are. A set of data with a Cohen's *d* exactly equal to 0 will fit the null hypothesis perfectly because there will be no difference between the two means.

Reflection Questions: Comprehension

1. What are the three possible alternative hypotheses in a *z*-test? When is it appropriate to use each alternative hypothesis?
2. What are the two methods that a researcher could use to make it easier to reject the null hypothesis? What could a researcher do to make it harder to reject the null hypothesis?
3. Why is it impossible to obtain a *p*-value of 0?
4. Explain why there are two *z*-critical values in the guided practice examples in this chapter.
5. List the similarities between the *z*-score formula and the *z*-observed formula.

Reflection Questions: Application

6. A student using Appendix A1 is looking for the z-observed value (3.02) in column A in order to find the p-value. Unfortunately, the exact z-observed value is not available in the table. What should the student do?

7. Kevin thinks that his sample of patients who have experienced therapy have fewer symptoms of depression ($\overline{X}$) than the average person with depression (μ). He conducts a z-test and rejects the null hypothesis. He states that this is proof that his patients get better after experiencing his therapy. What is the flaw in Kevin's logic?

8. Conduct a z-test for a dataset where $\mu = 4.1$, $\sigma = 0.8$, $\overline{X} = 3.7$, $n = 20$.
    a. What are the groups for this z-test?
    b. What is the null hypothesis for this z-test?
    c. What is the value of α?
    d. Should the researcher conduct a one- or two-tailed test?
    e. What is the alternative hypothesis?
    f. What is the z-observed value?
    g. What is(are) the z-critical value(s)?
    h. Based on the critical and observed values, should the researcher reject or retain the null hypothesis?
    i. What is the p-value for this example?
    j. What is the Cohen's d value for this example?
    k. If the α value were dropped to .01, would the researcher reject or retain the null hypothesis?

9. In a study of social media habits, a company finds that their population of users write $\mu = 9.2$ messages per week ($\sigma = 4.4$). A researcher finds that a sample of teenagers ($n = 55$) send $\overline{X} = 10.3$ messages per week. Because this social media company markets itself to young people, the researcher thinks that teenagers may be more likely to send more messages than the average user. Conduct a z-test on these data.
    a. What are the groups for this z-test?
    b. What is the null hypothesis for this z-test?
    c. What is the value of α?
    d. Should the researcher conduct a one- or a two-tailed test?
    e. What is the alternative hypothesis?
    f. What is the z-observed value?
    g. What is(are) the z-critical value(s)?
    h. Based on the critical and observed values, should the researcher reject or retain the null hypothesis? Does this mean that teenagers send more messages, fewer messages, or approximately the same number of messages as the population of social media users?
    i. What is the p-value for this example?
    j. What is the Cohen's d value for this example?
    k. If the α value were dropped to .01, would the researcher reject or retain the null hypothesis?
    l. If α were .05 and the sample size were increased to 75, would the researcher reject or retain the null hypothesis?

10. A small dataset consists of the following values, which come from a population with $\mu = 7$ and $\sigma = 3.5$. Conduct a z-test on these data to answer the questions below.

3	13	7	7	4
11	9	6	0	2
8	7	10	5	12

a.   What are the groups for this *z*-test?

b.   What is the null hypothesis for this *z*-test?

c.   What is the value of α?

d.   Is a one-tailed test or a two-tailed test more appropriate for this situation?

e.   What is the alternative hypothesis?

f.   What is the *z*-observed value?

g.   What is(are) the *z*-critical value(s)?

h.   Based on the critical and observed values, should the researcher reject or retain the null hypothesis?

i.   What is the *p*-value for this example?

j.   What is the Cohen's *d* value for this example?

k.   If the α value were raised to .08, would the researcher reject or retain the null hypothesis?

l.   If the α value were raised to .10, would the researcher reject or retain the null hypothesis?

m.   If α were .05 and the sample size were increased to 125, would the researcher reject or retain the null hypothesis?

n.   If α were .05 and the sample size were increased to 11,000, would the researcher reject or retain the null hypothesis?

11. Two researchers each conduct their own study. Researcher no. 1 has a Cohen's *d* of .25, and researcher no. 2 has a Cohen's *d* of .40. If both researchers have the same sample size, which researcher is more likely to reject the null hypothesis? Why?

12. Stephanie and Rosie are classmates who each conduct their own study on the same topic. Stephanie has a sample size of 150. Rosie has a sample size of 285. Which student is more likely to retain the null hypothesis? Why?

13. A student conducting a *z*-test rejects the null hypothesis because his *z*-observed is 2.02 and his *z*-critical is ± 1.96.

a.   What is his *p*-value?

b.   The student interprets this small *p*-value to be the probability that he was wrong to reject the null hypothesis. What is wrong with this interpretation?

c.   What is the correct interpretation of his *p*-value?

14. Conduct a z-test for a dataset where $\mu = 114.6$, $\sigma = 13.2$, $\overline{X} = 109.4$, and $n = 88$.

a.   What are the groups for this *z*-test?

b.   What is the null hypothesis for this *z*-test?

c.   What is the value of α?

d.   Is a one-tailed test or a two-tailed test appropriate for this situation?

e.   What is the alternative hypothesis?

f.   What is the *z*-observed value?

g.   What is(are) the *z*-critical value(s)?

h.   Based on the critical and observed values, should the null hypothesis be rejected or retained?

i.   What is the *p*-value for this example?

j.   What is the Cohen's *d* value for this example?

k.   If the α value were dropped to .01, would the researcher reject or retain the null hypothesis?

    l.   If the α value were raised to .10, would the researcher reject or retain the null hypothesis?

    m. If α were .05 and the sample size were increased to 140, would the researcher reject or retain the null hypothesis?

    n.   If α were .05 and the sample size were decreased to 45, would the researcher reject or retain the null hypothesis?

    o.   If α were .05 and the sample size were decreased to 15, would the researcher reject or retain the null hypothesis?

15. If z-observed is equal to 0, will the researcher reject or retain the null hypothesis?

16. If z-observed is equal to 0, what will the Cohen's d value be?

17. Malisa calculates her Cohen's d as +.40. How should she interpret this effect size?

18. Austin and Charlotte are classmates who each conduct their own study on the same topic. Austin has a sample size of 350. Charlotte has a sample size of 210. Which student is more likely to reject the null hypothesis? Why?

19. Conduct a z-test for a dataset where $\mu = 104.2$, $\sigma = 18.2$, $\overline{X} = 106.4$, and $n = 102$.

    a.   What are the groups for this z-test?

    b.   What is the null hypothesis for this z-test?

    c.   What is the value of α?

    d.   Is a one-tailed test or a two-tailed test appropriate for this situation?

    e.   What is the alternative hypothesis?

    f.   What is the z-observed value?

    g.   What is(are) the z-critical value(s)?

    h.   Based on the critical and observed values, should the null hypothesis be rejected or retained?

    i.   What is the p-value for this example?

    j.   What is the Cohen's d value for this example?

    k.   If the α value were dropped to .01, would the researcher reject or retain the null hypothesis?

    l.   If the α value were raised to .10, would the researcher reject or retain the null hypothesis?

    m. If α were .05 and the sample size were increased to 1,000, would the researcher reject or retain the null hypothesis?

    n.   If α were .05 and the sample size were decreased to 22, would the researcher reject or retain the null hypothesis?

    o.   If α were .05 and the sample size were decreased to 6, would the researcher reject or retain the null hypothesis?

Software Guide

As stated in the chapter, the z-test is the most basic member of the GLM. However, z-tests are rare in real-world situations because researchers rarely know the population mean and standard deviation. To perform a z-test, Microsoft Excel uses a function called ZTEST. However, SPSS cannot conduct z-tests through the point-and-click program interface, so this Software Guide will only show how to use Microsoft Excel. Readers who are interested in using SPSS to conduct a z-test can program SPSS to do so. See, for example, www.how2stats.net/2014/03/one-sample-z-test.html for details including downloadable computer code.

(a)

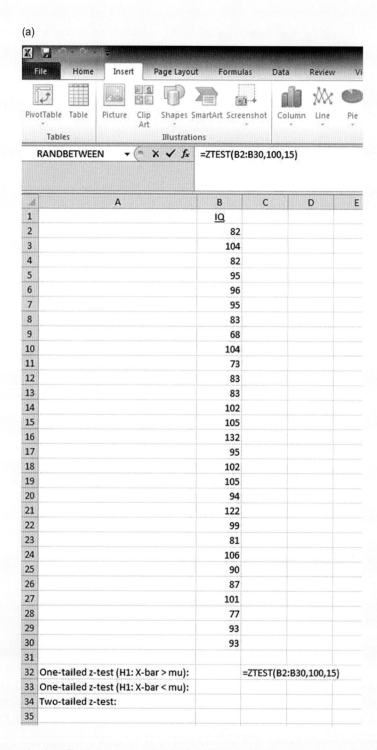

Figure 7.7a Screenshot from Excel showing how to use the ZTEST function to conduct a z-test.

(b)

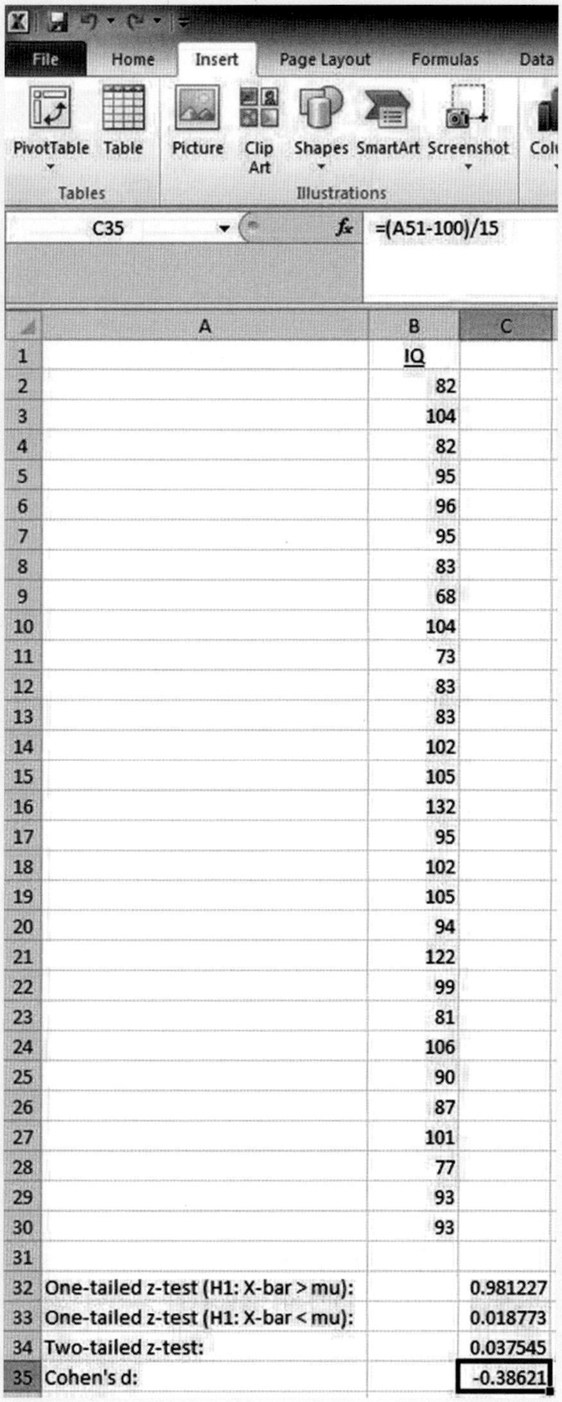

Figure 7.7b Screenshot from Excel showing the results of the ZTEST function and Cohen's *d*. The results for the *z*-tests (in cells C32, C33, and C34) are *p*-values.

Excel

To conduct a z-test, the ZTEST function has three formats:

- For a one-tailed z-test where H_1: $\overline{X} > \mu$: "=ZTEST(XX:XX,YY,ZZ)"
- For a one-tailed z-test where H_1: $\overline{X} < \mu$: "=1-ZTEST(XX:XX,YY,ZZ)"
- For a two-tailed z-test: "=2*ZTEST(XX:XX,YY,ZZ)"

In each of these formats, the "XX:XX" should be replaced with cells for the sample. The YY should be replaced with the mean of the population, and the ZZ should be replaced with the standard deviation of the population. Figure 7.7a shows how to use the function, and Figure 7.7b shows the results. The results in Excel are the p-values – not the z-observed values. If the p-value is less than alpha, the user should reject the null hypothesis. If the p-value is greater than alpha, the user should retain the null hypothesis.

Excel does not calculate Cohen's d as part of the z-test. Calculating Cohen's d requires a new function: "=(XX-YY)/ZZ." In this function YY and ZZ are the same as before (i.e., population mean and standard deviation, respectively). But XX should now be the sample mean. Figure 7.7b shows that the Cohen's d value in this example is $-.386$.

Further Reading

- Abelson, R. P. (1997a). On the surprising longevity of flogged horses: Why there is a case for the significance test. *Psychological Science*, *8*, 12–15. doi:10.1111/j.1467–9280.1997.tb00536.x

  * This is an insightful article written at the height of the controversy over NHST. Abelson here gives a reasonable argument why NHST procedures should still be used. Yet, Abelson is realistic about the pitfalls and potential for abuse of NHST.

- Cohen, J. (1994). The earth is round ($p < .05$). *American Psychologist*, *49*, 997–1003. doi:10.1037/0003–066x.49.12.997

  * This article is a classic in the debate about NHST. Because of the shortcomings of NHST results, Cohen cautions against relying solely on NHST results when interpreting statistical results.

- Ferguson, C. J. (2009). An effect size primer: A guide for clinicians and researchers. *Professional Psychology: Research and Practice*, *40*, 532–538. doi:10.1037/a0015808

  * In this article Ferguson explains the value of effect sizes, provides formulas for many effect sizes (including all the ones discussed in this book), and explains how to know when an effect size is appropriate.

8 One-Sample *t*-Tests

One of my favorite stories from ancient mythology is the tale of Hercules fighting the Hydra – a monster with several heads. During the fight Hercules cut off several of its heads. But every time he did, two heads grew in the place of each severed head.

I like this story because learning statistics is like fighting the Hydra; learning a statistical method gives me a feeling of accomplishment (not unlike Hercules may have felt after cutting off a head of the ferocious Hydra), but after mastering a statistical method, it becomes clear that the method has limitations. Overcoming those limitations requires learning more statistical methods – much like conquering one head of the Hydra means defeating two more.

The *z*-test was the first head of our statistical Hydra. However, it often cannot be used because our data frequently do not meet the assumptions required to use it. In this chapter we will discuss the limitations of the *z*-test and learn a new method to replace it, much like a new head on the Hydra. This new method is called the one-sample *t*-test.

Learning Goals

- Explain the differences between a *z*-test and a one-sample *t*-test and how the two methods are related.

- Recognize the situations in which it is more appropriate to use a one-sample *t*-test than a *z*-test.

- Conduct a one-sample *t*-test.

- Describe the purpose of a confidence interval (CI).

- Calculate the CI of a mean.

Shortcomings of the *z*-Test – and a Solution

The *z*-test is the simplest type of NHST, which makes it a suitable starting point for learning other NHST procedures. In Chapter 7 we learned that a *z*-test has three assumptions. They are (1) the variable consists of interval- or ratio-level data, (2) μ is known, and (3) σ is known. The first assumption is rather easy to meet because often the level of the data that are collected is under the researcher's control. The second assumption is sometimes difficult to meet, but often reasonable approximations of μ are known. The last assumption – having a known σ – can be difficult to meet. Therefore, it was necessary to invent an NHST procedure that could be used when σ was unknown. That procedure is the **one-sample *t*-test**.

If you search the last chapter, you will find that the first time that σ is used in a *z*-test is when calculating the *z*-observed value. That was in formula 7.5, which was

$$z_{obs} = \frac{\overline{X} - \mu}{\left(\dfrac{\sigma}{\sqrt{n}}\right)}$$ (Formula 7.5)

If σ is unknown, it is impossible to use Formula 7.5; some other formula is necessary. But the solution is logical. Because σ is the population standard deviation, s_x (i.e., the sample standard deviation) can be a substitute for σ in Formula 7.5. The new formula would be:

$$t_{obs} = \frac{\overline{X} - \mu}{\left(\dfrac{s_x}{\sqrt{n}}\right)}$$ (Formula 8.1)

Just as in Formula 7.5, $\overline{X}$ is the sample mean, μ is the population mean, and n is the sample size. For the parts in Formula 8.1 that are different from Formula 7.5, s_x is the sample standard deviation, and the result is now called the *t*-observed value, abbreviated t_{obs} (whereas the result of Formula 7.5 was *z*-observed, abbreviated z_{obs}). Replacing σ with s_x requires a few other changes to the NHST procedures, which further distinguishes the *z*-test from the one-sample *t*-test. The best way to learn about and discuss these differences is to perform a one-sample *t*-test, looking for the new characteristics of a one-sample *t*-test along the way.

Steps of a One-Sample *t*-Test

Because it is a member of the GLM and is a null hypothesis statistical significance test (NHST), *a one-sample t-test has the exact same steps as a z-test*. Replacing σ with s_x does not change the steps or their sequence at all, though it does change what we do to execute some of those steps. As a reminder, the steps of NHST procedures are as follows:

1. Form groups in the data.
2. Define the null hypothesis (H_0). The null hypothesis is always that there is no difference between groups or that there is no relationship between independent and dependent variables.
3. Set alpha (α). The default alpha = .05.
4. Choose a one-tailed or a two-tailed test. This determines the alternative hypothesis (H_1).
5. Find the *critical* value, which is used to define the rejection region.
6. Calculate the *observed* value.
7. Compare the observed value and the critical value. If the observed value is more extreme than the critical value, then the null hypothesis should be rejected. Otherwise, it should be retained.
8. Calculate an *effect size*.

To show how these steps are executed, we will use data from two sources: the Centers for Disease Control (CDC), which is a government agency that collects health data in the United States, and an article by Komlos, Hau, and Bourguinat (2003). According to the CDC (2012, p. 15), the average height of a representative sample of adult men in the United States was $\overline{X}$ = 175.9 centimeters (SD = 15.03 cm, n = 5,647). Komlos et al. (2003) reported population means of the height of French men born between 1666 and 1760,[5] some of the oldest surviving quantitative data on a large group of individuals. In this section of the chapter, we will conduct a one-sample *t*-test to test the null hypothesis that a modern sample of American men ($\overline{X}$) and the population of French men born between 1725 and 1740 ($\mu = 167.8$ cm) have equal means.

Form Groups in the Data. The first step of any NHST procedure is to form groups with the data. Just as with a *z*-test, the groups in a one-sample *t*-test are always the population and the sample. As the previous paragraph stated, the population is French men born between 1725 and 1740; the sample is a group of 5,647 modern American men.

Define the Null Hypothesis. The second step in an NHST is to define a null hypothesis, which is abbreviated H_0. In a *z*-test, the null hypothesis is $H_0 : \overline{X} = \mu$. (This was Formula 7.1.) A one-sample *t*-test always has the exact same null hypothesis as a *z*-test because both NHST procedures test whether a sample mean ($\overline{X}$) and a population mean (μ) are equal. As in a *z*-test, in a one-sample *t*-test we will retain the null hypothesis if the two means are highly similar, and we will reject the null hypothesis if they are different.

Set Alpha. The third step in any NHST is to set alpha (α). In a one-sample *t*-test (and any other NHST, including a *z*-test), the default α value is .05, indicating that the rejection region is 5% of the area in the sampling distribution. Again, the choice of α is completely arbitrary (just as it was in a *z*-test), and you should have a reason for altering α from its default value. In this case, our sample size is large ($n = 5,647$), and as we saw in Chapter 7, NHST procedures are sensitive to sample size, with larger sample sizes making it easy to reject the null hypothesis. So, to prevent us from rejecting the null hypothesis solely because of a large sample size, we are going to make it harder to reject the null hypothesis and change our α value to .01. This is a legitimate reason to change α.

Choose a One-Tailed or a Two-Tailed Test. The fourth step in NHST procedures is to choose a one- or two-tailed test. In a *z*-test, this was decided on the basis of whether there was prior research and/or theory (which would result in a one-tailed test) or not (which would result in a two-tailed test). The exact same rules apply to a one-sample *t*-test.

The choice of a one- or a two-tailed test also determines the alternative hypothesis in a one-sample *t*-test. For a two-tailed test (in which there is no prior research or theory guiding a researcher's expectations of their findings), the alternative hypothesis is $H_1 : \overline{X} \neq \mu$. However, there are two possible alternative hypotheses for a one-tailed, one-sample *t*-test. They are $H_1 : \overline{X} < \mu$ (if you expect $\overline{X}$ to be smaller than μ) and $H_1 : \overline{X} > \mu$ (if you expect $\overline{X}$ to be larger than μ). If these alternative hypotheses look familiar, it is because they are the exact same alternative hypotheses that were available for a *z*-test, and they were displayed in the last chapter as Formulas 7.2–7.4.

The alternative hypotheses in a one-sample *t*-test also correspond to the same visual models as they did for a *z*-test. In other words, when the alternative hypothesis is $H_1 : \overline{X} \neq \mu$, the rejection region is divided in half, with each half of the rejection region being in each tail (see Figure 8.1a for an example). For a one-tailed test where $H_1 : \overline{X} < \mu$, all of the rejection region is in the left tail below μ, which is in the middle of the sampling distribution (see Figure 8.1b). Finally, for a one-tailed test where $H_1 : \overline{X} > \mu$, all of the rejection region is in the right tail above μ (see Figure 8.1c).

---

[5] Technically, the population means in Komlos et al.'s (2003) article are not exact population means taken from every French adult male. Rather, they are estimated population means ($\hat{\mu}$ values) extrapolated from the measurements of French soldiers from the time period. However, these means are likely very close to the actual means for the population at the time.

(a)

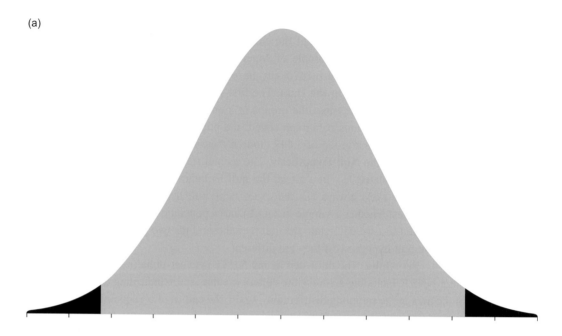

Figure 8.1a A visual model showing a sampling distribution in a two-tailed, one-sample *t*-test where $H_1 : \overline{X} \neq \mu$ and $\alpha = .01$.

(b)

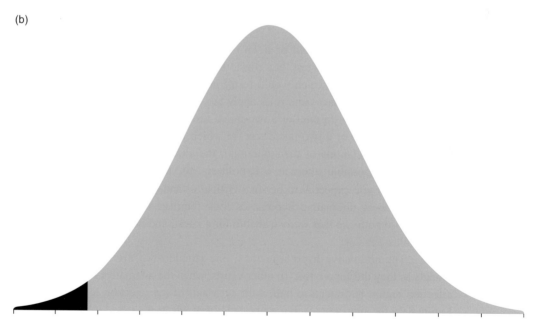

Figure 8.1b A visual model showing a sampling distribution in a one-tailed, one-sample *t*-test where $H_1 : \overline{X} < \mu$ and $\alpha = .01$.

For this chapter's example, there is research from health, nutrition, economics, psychology, and sociology showing that people today in many countries are taller than they were in the early and mid twentieth century. Moreover, increases in other variables – including weight, body mass index, and intelligence test scores – have been recorded across the twentieth century in many countries

(c)

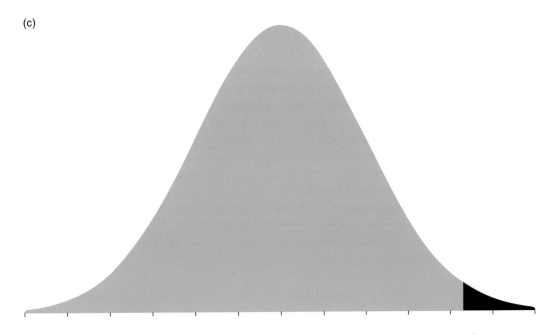

Figure 8.1c A visual model showing a sampling distribution in a one-tailed, one-sample *t*-test where $H_1 : \overline{X} > \mu$ and $\alpha = .01$.

(e.g., Flynn, 1984, 1987; Ho et al., 2008; Komlos & Lauderdale, 2007; Kryst, Kowal, Woronko-wicz, Sobiecki, & Cichocka, 2012). Therefore, it seems likely that because people today are taller than their grandparents' generation was 50 years ago, they are also probably taller than people born in the 1700s. As a result, we will use the alternative hypothesis of $H_1 : \overline{X} > \mu$.

Sidebar 8.1   **HARKing – a questionable research practice**

Researchers conduct NHSTs after they have collected data. This can lead to the temptation to **HARK**, which is an acronym that stands for *h*ypothesizing *a*fter the *r*esults are *k*nown. The term, coined by Kerr (1998), is defined as generating or altering a research hypothesis after examining data and then presenting results as if the hypothesis was created before the researcher collected the data.

HARKing is one of many **questionable research practices**, which are behaviors that social scientists can engage in, but which are inappropriate and may distort the scientific literature (Bouter, Tijdink, Axelsen, Martinson, & ter Riet, 2016; Greenwald, 1975; Kerr, 1998; Makel, 2014). An example of HARKing in a one-sample *t*-test would be to collect the data first, find that the sample mean is greater than the population mean, and then decide to conduct a one-tailed, one-sample *t*-test with the entire rejection on the right side of the sampling distribution. When this decision is made on the basis of prior knowledge or theory (as in the example in this chapter and the Vinten et al., 2009, example in Chapter 7), this decision is appropriate. But if this decision is made in order to make it more likely to reject the null hypothesis or to ensure that the researcher presents a research hypothesis that ends up being supported, then HARKing has occurred.

This caution against HARKing should not be interpreted as a prohibition against changing one's beliefs after analyzing the data. Indeed, if a scientist finds that the data do not support his or her research hypothesis, then it is acceptable to discard or alter a hypothesis or theory. When faced with unexpected results, it is also acceptable to search for explanations for the results of a study (Kerr, 1998). These are not examples of HARKing. However, if researchers do these things and then present their results as if they were always expected, then HARKing has occurred.

To avoid HARKing, you should be clear about the research hypotheses or questions that you had at the beginning of the study. If you find that the results contradicted your prior beliefs, then say so explicitly. There is no shame or stigma in doing this. In fact, it makes me respect and trust researchers when they admit that their research hypotheses were wrong (e.g., Moffitt, Caspi, Harkness, & Silva, 1993). I have admitted being wrong in my research articles (e.g., Warne, Anderson, & Johnson, 2013), and it does not make a study unpublishable, nor does it make readers think that the researchers did something wrong.

If you are doing exploratory research, which, by definition, does not begin with any sort of theory or research hypothesis, then there are two ways to avoid HARKing. The first way is to admit to your audience that your research is not based on any prior theory. Second, in exploratory research you should avoid using statistical procedures (like one-tailed tests) that require prior research or theory for their use. Instead, use a statistical procedure (like a two-tailed test) that does not require prior theory.

Find the Critical Value. The fifth step in performing a one-sample *t*-test is to find the critical value. Just as in a *z*-test, the critical value is the point at which the rejection region begins; everything within the tail beyond the critical value is in the rejection region.

Because we have replaced σ with s_x in the *t*-critical equation, we cannot compare the observed values in a one-sample *t*-test to the *z*-critical values of a *z*-test. Doing so will sometimes produce distorted results – especially when sample sizes are small. (See General Linear Moment 8.1.) Therefore, we need to use a different table to find *t*-critical values: Appendix A2.

The table in this appendix has two sets of columns, the three columns on the left are for a one-tailed test, and the three columns on the right are for a two-tailed test. If you are conducting a one-tailed test, you should use only the left three columns. If you are conducting a two-tailed test, it is appropriate to use the right three columns.

The first column in each half of the table is labeled "df," which stands for degrees of freedom. In a one-sample *t*-test, the formula for calculating the degrees of freedom is

$$df = n - 1 \qquad \text{(Formula 8.2)}$$

In this formula, *n* is equal to the sample size. After calculating df, find the row with the number in the first column that is equal to your degrees of freedom. If there is no row that corresponds to the exact number of degrees of freedom you have in your data, use the *Price Is Right* rule that we learned in Chapter 7. In other words, you should select the row in Appendix A2 that has the highest degrees of freedom *without* exceeding the number of degrees of freedom in your data.

After finding the correct row, your *t*-critical value is either the number immediately to the right of your degrees of freedom (when α = .05), or the number that is two columns to the right of the number of your degrees of freedom (when α = .01). Notice that in Appendix A2 the one-tailed test *t*-critical values have the symbols +/− in front of them. This indicates that you will have a *t*-critical value that is either positive (if your rejection region is on the right side of the sampling distribution) or negative (if your rejection region is on the left side of the sampling distribution). Similarly, the two-tailed test *t*-critical values have the symbol ± in front of them. This indicates that your *t*-critical values will be both the positive and negative values because a two-tailed test has the rejection region in both tails, meaning that each tail needs its own critical value where its half of the rejection region starts.

In our example, because we are performing a one-tailed test, we will be using the left three columns of Appendix A2 (which are labeled "One-Tailed Test"). With a sample size of 5,647, there are 5,646 degrees of freedom (because df $= n - 1$ in Formula 8.2). Appendix A2 does not have a row for 5,646 degrees of freedom. Instead, we will use the row with the highest degrees of freedom that does not exceed 5,646. This is the row labeled 1,000 degrees of freedom. Finally, $\alpha = .01$ in our example, so we will use the *t*-critical value that is two columns to the right of our degrees of freedom. This is labeled "+/–2.330." That means we need to choose a *t*-critical value of either –2.330 or +2.330. When we chose our alternative hypothesis, we did so because we thought the sample mean would be greater than the population mean ($H_1 : \overline{X} > \mu$). Therefore, our *t*-critical value is +2.330 – because in the sampling distribution μ will be in the middle, where 0 is (see Figure 8.2).

Sidebar 8.2 Degrees of freedom

The one-sample *t*-test is the first NHST procedure that will use degrees of freedom. But what are **degrees of freedom**? A simple way to describe degrees of freedom is the number of data points that can vary, given the statistical results for the dataset.

An example makes this definition more clear. Imagine a dataset where $n = 5$ and $\overline{X} = 12$. There are many possible sets of five numbers that could have a mean of 12. For example, these numbers could be 2, 6, 14, 18, and 20. Or they could be 12, 12, 12, 12, and 12. Or −2, 0, 13, 20, 29, and 60. In fact, there are an infinite possible set of five numbers that have a mean of 12.

But if we know what the first four numbers are, there is only one possible value for the last number. In other words, that last number cannot vary. Continuing the example above, if we know that $n = 5$ and $\overline{X} = 12$ and that the first four numbers are 6, 9, 11, and 14, then the last number must be 20. (This is because $\sum X$ must equal 60, and the first four numbers add to 40. There, the last number must be equal to $60 - 40$, which is equal to 20.) This value of the last number is predetermined by the first four numbers, meaning that it doesn't have the ability to vary. Therefore, only the first four numbers have the "freedom" to vary − hence, the name "degrees of freedom" and why there are four degrees of freedom when $n = 5$ (remember that df $= n - 1$).

Don't worry if this concept seems confusing. It is not necessary to internalize the definition of degrees of freedom in order to successfully perform an NHST. However, it is important to use the correct formula. These formulas may change from one NHST procedure to another, so always make sure that you are calculating degrees of freedom correctly.

So, why do we need a different table? Because with a different equation for the observed value in a one-sample *t*-test, we cannot use the *z*-table (i.e., Appendix A1) because the sampling distribution is no longer normally distributed. With s_x replacing σ, the sampling distribution for a one-sample *t*-test is more platykurtic than a normal distribution. As the number of degrees of freedom increases, the distribution becomes more normal (DeCarlo, 1997). With an infinite number of degrees of freedom, the sampling distribution is normally distributed (see General Linear Moment 8.1).

Calculate the Observed Value. Step 6 of conducting a one-sample *t*-test is to calculate the observed value. As stated in the beginning of the chapter, the formula for this calculation is:

$$t_{obs} = \frac{\overline{X} - \mu}{\left(\frac{s_x}{\sqrt{n}}\right)}$$

Plugging in the values from the example (i.e., $\overline{X} = 175.9$, $s_x = 15.03$, $n = 5{,}647$, $\mu = 167.8$), we get the following result:

$$t_{obs} = \frac{175.9 - 167.8}{\left(\frac{15.03}{\sqrt{5{,}647}}\right)}$$

which leads to a *t*-critical value of 40.50.

Compare the Observed Value and the Critical Value. The seventh step in a one-sample *t*-test is to compare the *t*-observed and *t*-critical values. If the *t*-observed value is more extreme than the *t*-critical value, then the *t*-observed value is inside the rejection region – which indicates that the null hypothesis should be rejected. If the *t*-observed value is less extreme (i.e., closer to the center of the sampling distribution) than the *t*-critical value, then the *t*-observed value is outside the rejection region – meaning that the null hypothesis should be retained. But, as in a *z*-test, the easiest way to make this comparison is to draw the sampling distribution with the rejection region and to plot the *t*-observed value. (Remember from Guided Practice 7.1: "When it doubt, draw it out.") This sort of diagram is shown in Figure 8.2.

With the example comparing the heights of modern American men and eighteenth-century French men, the t_{obs} value is +40.50, and the *t*-critical value is +2.330. This means that the

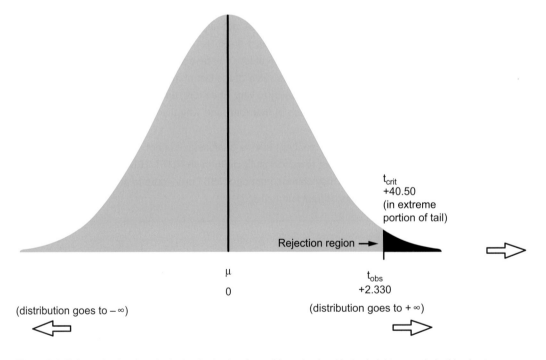

Figure 8.2 Schematic showing the logic of rejecting the null hypothesis with the height example in this chapter. Because the rejection region starts at +2.330 and includes all *t*-observed values higher than that number, the *t*-observed value of +40.50 is inside the rejection region. The exact location of the observed value is not shown because the *x*-axis of the graphic only shows values in the sampling distribution between −3 and +3.

t-observed value is more extreme than the *t*-critical value. Therefore, we should reject the null hypothesis that the sample mean and the population mean are equal (i.e., $H_0 : \overline{X} = \mu$) because the null hypothesis does not fit the data very well. Thus, we can say that there is likely a difference between the two groups' average heights and that the alternative hypothesis ($H_1 : \overline{X} > \mu$) is a better model for the data.

Calculate an Effect Size. This is the eighth and final step. Rejecting the null hypothesis in a one-sample *t*-test (or any other NHST, including a *z*-test) merely tells us that there is a difference between the two means. But it does not state how large the difference is between the two means. Only effect sizes can describe the magnitude of the differences between the population and sample means, and that is why they are so important in social science research (see Sidebar 7.4). Therefore, it is also necessary in a one-sample *t*-test to calculate an effect size. For a *z*-test, the effect size was called Cohen's *d*, and it was calculated with Formula 7.6:

$$d = \frac{\overline{X} - \mu}{\sigma}$$

However, we cannot use this same formula for a one-sample *t*-test because we do not know σ. When we didn't know σ in the *z*-observed formula, we replaced σ with s_x to create the *t*-observed formula. We can do the same thing to calculate Cohen's *d* in a one-sample *t*-test. Therefore, the formula for calculating an effect size for a one-sample *t*-test is:

$$d = \frac{\overline{X} - \mu}{s_x} \qquad \text{(Formula 8.3)}$$

In Formula 8.3, $\overline{X}$ symbolizes the sample mean, μ symbolizes the population mean, and s_x symbolizes the sample standard deviation (just as in Formula 8.1).

For our example in this chapter, plugging the values for the sample mean, population mean, and sample standard deviation into Formula 8.3 produces the following equation:

$$d = \frac{175.9 - 167.8}{15.03}$$

This produces a Cohen's *d* value of .539. Cohen's *d* value for a one-sample *t*-test has the exact interpretations it had for a *z*-test. One interpretation is to say that Cohen's *d* is the number of standard deviations between the population mean and the sample mean. Another valid interpretation is to say that Cohen's *d* is the average *z*-score for a sample member when compared to the population. In this example, we would use the first interpretation to say that the two means are 0.539 standard deviation apart. For the second interpretation, we could say that the average American man today is 0.539 standard deviations taller than the average French man in the eighteenth century. Both interpretations of Cohen's *d* are equally correct.

Interpreting Cohen's *d* values can be challenging at first, mostly because few non-scientists deal with *z*-scores on a regular basis. I believe that the best way for beginners to understand Cohen's *d* values is to see examples of Cohen's *d* values in the literature. Table 8.1 displays a collection of Cohen's *d* values from clinical psychology, educational psychology, and physical anthropology. As is apparent, most Cohen's *d* values in these fields are less than 0.50, indicating a one-half (or less) standard deviation difference in means between two groups.

I suggest you examine Table 8.1 and ponder whether these effect sizes reflect your everyday experience. My personal guideline is that Cohen's *d* values of 0.20 are just barely

Table 8.1 Examples of Cohen's *d* values from clinical psychology, educational psychology, and physical anthropology

Groups	Dependent Variables	d	References
Extraverted and **introverted students**	Academic achievement (e.g., school grades)	0.02	Poropot (2009)
Bright students enrolled in advanced courses during high school and bright students not enrolled in advanced courses	Self-esteem	0.07	Rogers (2007)
Child abuse survivors before play therapy and **the same individuals after play therapy**	Mental health measures	0.10	Slade & Warne (2016)
Males and **females**	Verbal ability	0.14	Calvin, Fernandes, Smith, Visscher, & Deary (2010)
Child abuse survivors before cognitive-behavioral therapy (CBT) and **the same individuals after CBT**	Mental health measures	0.21	Slade & Warne (2016)
Gifted students enrolled in regular classes and **gifted students enrolled in advanced classes**	Academic achievement (e.g., school grades)	0.29	Rogers (2007)
African-American students whose parents are involved with their education and African-American students with less involved parents	School grades	0.32	Jeynes (2003)
Males and **females**	Language arts grades	0.33	Calvin et al. (2010)
People without attention deficit/hyperactivity disorder (ADHD) and people with ADHD	Creativity test scores	0.35	Paek et al. (2016)
Mental health patients receiving psychological assessment information about themselves and a control group	Mental health measures	0.37	Poston & Hanson (2010)
Students in mixed-ability classrooms and **students in classrooms homogeneously grouped by academic abilities**	Attitude towards school	0.37	Kulik & Kulik (1982)
Adult American males and adult American females	Weight	0.44	Centers for Disease Control (2012)
People with schizophrenia and **people without schizophrenia**	Intelligence test scores	0.54	Woodberry, Giuliano, & Seidman (2008)
Gifted children who have skipped a grade and gifted children who have not skipped a grade	Academic achievement (e.g., school grades)	1.00	Rogers (2007)

Table 8.1 (*cont.*)

Groups	Dependent Variables	*d*	References
Applicants for a medium-skill job (cashiers) and **applicants for a high-skill job** (chemists)	Intelligence test scores	1.00	Gottfredson (1997)
Adult American males and adult American females	Height	1.06	Centers for Disease Control (2012)

Note. Groups in boldface have higher mean values.
Note. All values are taken from meta-analyses (see Sidebar 14.4) or from large samples representative of the general population.

noticeable to the attentive observer in daily life. For example, the smallest effect size is only 0.02, indicating almost no differences in academic achievement across introverted and extraverted students. This probably reflects your personal experience; you likely know many introverted and extraverted students who do well in school, and it would be hard to pick out which group excels more academically. On the other hand, notice that females have higher language arts grades than males ($d = 0.33$). This effect size is large enough for most people to notice in their daily lives. For example, at most universities there are more females majoring in language arts and the humanities – both of which are very heavily verbal – and most people notice that women disproportionately choose those majors. This could be one manifestation of the higher language arts grades among women. Even more noticeable is the difference in average height among men and women. This $d = 1.06$ difference is so large that it would be nearly impossible to ignore in daily life.

Table 8.1 can also give students an idea of how interpretation of effect sizes can happen in context. For example, the Slade and Warne (2016) study shows that child survivors of abuse have better outcomes after experiencing cognitive-behavioral therapy ($d = 0.21$) than after receiving play therapy ($d = .10$), indicating that the former therapy may be a better choice for treating children for the psychological aftermath of abuse. (For a similar comparison of interventions, compare also the effect size for having gifted children enrolled in advanced classes to the effect size for having gifted children skip a full grade.) On the other hand, notice how the difference in verbal ability favors females slightly ($d = 0.14$) and difference in language arts grades favors females even more ($d = 0.33$). This may indicate that the sex difference in language arts grades may partially be a consequence of sex differences in verbal ability, but that ability differences do not explain the entire gap in grades between groups.

As you gain more experience in reading the scientific literature in your field, you will learn how to better interpret effect sizes. In addition to being able to compare effect sizes across studies, you may find that your field typically has stronger or weaker effect sizes than those in Table 8.1. For example, memory research tends to have stronger effect sizes than what is often seen in the rest of psychology (P. E. Morris & Fritz, 2013). This textbook also has additional resources to help you interpret effect sizes in a savvy manner (e.g., Sidebar 11.4 and discussions about specific effect sizes in Chapters 11–15). Although interpreting Cohen's *d* and other effect sizes is not always intuitive at first, you will probably find that experience in dealing with real effect sizes in scientific studies will make you better at understanding these statistics.

Check Yourself!

- Why is it necessary to make changes to the *z*-test steps in order to conduct a one-sample *t*-test?

- Which two formulas change when making the transition from a *z*-test to a one-sample *t*-test?

- When is a one-tailed test appropriate for a researcher to use? When is a two-tailed hypothesis appropriate to use?

- How do you know when to reject the null hypothesis in a *z*-test? How do you know when to retain the null hypothesis?

- What is the effect size for a one-sample *t*-test and how do you interpret it?

General Linear Moment 8.1

As you read through this chapter you may notice that I make comparisons between the one-sample *t*-test and the *z*-test. Already in this chapter, I have used phrases like, "just as with a *z*-test," and "as in a *z*-test." I have used this language to emphasize the similarities between the *z*-test and the one-sample *t*-test. These two NHST procedures share so many similarities because they are both members of the GLM. In fact, not only are a *z*-test and a one-sample *t*-test similar, but also this General Linear Moment will show that – under certain circumstances – the two procedures are the same and produce the exact same results.

If you examine Appendix A2, you will notice that as the number of degrees of freedom increases, the *t*-critical values decrease. In the bottom row the number of degrees of freedom is infinity (∞), and the critical values in that row are the *t*-critical values that we would expect if we had an infinitely large sample size. If you look at the critical values in the bottom row, you may notice that some of the numbers look familiar. For example, in a two-tailed test when $\alpha = .01$ and with ∞ degrees of freedom, the critical value is ± 1.960. This is the exact same critical value in Appendix A1 (i.e., the *z*-table) for a two-tailed *z*-test when $\alpha = .01$. Likewise, when $\alpha = .05$ for a one-tailed test with ∞ degrees of freedom, the *t*-critical value is $+/-1.645$, which is the exact *t*-critical value for a one-tailed *z*-test when $\alpha = .05$.

Through these similarities we can see that in a one-sample *t*-test, as the number of degrees of freedom (and therefore sample size) increases, the critical values for a *t*-test get closer to the critical values for a *z*-test. This is because *a z-test is merely a one-sample t-test with an infinite number of degrees of freedom*. If you perform a one-sample *t*-test with an infinite sample size – which would have an infinite degrees of freedom – then you will get the exact same results as a *z*-test every time. Therefore, a *z*-test is just a specific type of one-sample *t*-test. In statistics language, we say that a *z*-test is a special case of a one-sample *t*-test. We learned in Chapter 7 that a special case is a statistical procedure that is a simplification of a more complicated procedure that occurs under special circumstances. The opposite of a special case is a **generalization**, which is a statistical procedure that includes the special case, but can be used in other situations. Therefore, the one-sample *t*-test is a generalization of a *z*-test.

For a one-sample *t*-test, the special circumstances that reduce it to a *z*-test are an infinitely large sample size. Although we never have a sample size of ∞ with real data, this relationship between the one-sample *t*-test and the *z*-test still applies in theory. It is that relationship that makes conducting a *z*-test and conducing a one-sample *t*-test so similar. After all, they really are the same procedure!

The concepts of special cases and generalizations are the links between the different procedures of the GLM. In General Linear Moment sections in other chapters, we will explore these sorts of linkages across methods because *every* NHST procedure in this textbook is either a special case or a generalization of one or more other GLM methods.

The *p*-Value in a One-Sample *t*-Test

Finding *p* in a One-Sample *t*-Test. As is also true with a *z*-test, it is possible to derive a *p*-value from NHST results. Remember from the previous chapter that *p* is the region in the sampling distribution that begins at the observed value and includes all areas of the distribution that are more extreme than the observed value (see Figure 7.5 for a visual representation). With Appendix A2, it is not possible to calculate an exact *p*-value. However, we can determine broad ranges for *p* based on whether we rejected or retained the null hypothesis. We can use this information to state whether (1) *p* is greater than .05, (2) *p* is less than .05 but greater than .01, or (3) *p* is less than .01.

To determine which of the three options is appropriate for *p*, you should use a simple rule that is true for *all* NHST procedures: if $p < \alpha$, you will *always* reject the null hypothesis. Conversely, if $p > \alpha$, you will *always* retain the null hypothesis. In other words, if you reject the null hypothesis, then *p* must be less than α. Likewise, if you retain the null hypothesis, *p* must be greater than α. Therefore, it is easy to determine *p*, using three rules:

- If the null hypothesis is retained when $\alpha = .05$, then $p > .05$.
- If the null hypothesis is rejected when $\alpha = .05$, but retained when $\alpha = .01$, then $.01 < p < .05$.
- If the null hypothesis is rejected when $\alpha = .01$, then $p < .01$.

These rules apply to all NHSTs in the GLM.

In the example comparing height of modern American men and eighteenth-century French men, we rejected the null hypothesis when $\alpha = .01$. Therefore, $p < .01$. Calculating more precise values requires more detailed tables (e.g., Lindley & Scott, 1995) or the use of a computer. The latter option is far more common in modern times. The Software Guides at the end of each chapter show how to calculate exact *p*-values using a computer.

Statistical Significance. A related concept to the *p*-value is **statistical significance**. When a null hypothesis has been rejected (i.e., when $p < \alpha$), the results are called statistically significant. On the other hand, if the null hypothesis was retained, the results are "statistically insignificant." The term "statistical significance" *only* refers to whether the null hypothesis was rejected. Although the word "significant" may mean "important" in everyday language, the term "significant" has nothing to do with importance in statistics (Kline, 2013; Schmidt, 1996; Thompson, 2002). For example, Meehl (1990, p. 207) reported that there is a statistically significant sex difference in the number of men and women who agree with the statement, "My hands and feet are usually warm enough." Although Meehl could reject the null hypothesis that the two groups were equal on this variable, there is no theoretical or practical value in knowing this fact, because this sex difference is trivial in importance. Thus, results can be statistically significant, but not important. Therefore, in a statistical and scientific context, you should never use the word "significant" to mean "important." Additionally, there are three kinds of significance in the social sciences (see Sidebar 8.3), meaning you should always specify "statistical significance" when referring to results in which the null hypothesis was rejected. Never use the words "significant" or "significance" alone (Thompson, 1996, 2002).

Sidebar 8.3 **Three kinds of significance**

In the social sciences, there are three types of significance: statistical significance, practical significance, and clinical significance. This sidebar will describe each one and include illustrative examples.

Statistical significance – as explained in the main text – is whether a null hypothesis has been rejected in an NHST procedure. If the null hypothesis is rejected, the results are statistically significant; if the null hypothesis has been retained, the results are statistically insignificant. As stated in the main text, the null hypothesis in this chapter's example was rejected, meaning that the difference between the height of modern American men and eighteenth-century French men is statistically significant.

Practical significance refers to the degree to which the differences observed between groups (or the strength of the relationship between variables) is practically useful in the real world. In other words, practical significance refers to the magnitude of an effect size and whether the results of the study matter to scientists, practitioners, or clients (Kirk, 1996). Therefore, if results are "practically significant," then the effect size is non-zero *and* the strength of the relationship has a practical impact in the real world. For example, the effect size of $d = .539$ in this chapter's main example indicates that American men are over one-half a standard deviation taller than French men born between 1725 and 1740. This effect size corresponds to 8.1 cm (3.19 inches), which is large enough of a difference in height that it would be noticeable to the casual observer. (That is, if we could transport the eighteenth-century men through time so that the casual observer could view both groups at once.)

Moreover, Komlos et al. (2003), as they recorded changes in men's height throughout the late French Renaissance, observed that adult men in France were taller when the weather was more favorable for agriculture during these people's childhood and teenage years – and that men from the upper classes were taller than the men from the peasant classes. These results indicated that height is a useful measure of nutrition quality and economic prosperity in early modern France. Therefore, Komlos and his colleagues (2003) felt justified in using height as a measure of France's economic conditions from 1666 to 1760 – a practically useful interpretation of the data for an economic historian like Komlos.

Finally, **clinical significance** refers to the degree to which a treatment moves people from a group that needs treatment to one that does not (Jacobson & Truax, 1991). For example, if 100 people are receiving treatment for depression and 5 of them achieve complete relief from their symptoms and the other 95 get slightly worse, then this treatment's effect would not be very clinically significant because it helps very few people (and hurts the vast majority!). Because clinical significance is concerned with the effectiveness of a treatment, most people who use the concept are in fields like medicine, clinical psychology, and counseling.

You may have already noticed that practical and clinical significance require subjective judgments. After all, whether an effect size is "practically" large enough or whether a clinical treatment is "helpful enough" for clients is a matter of opinion. This may be disconcerting to some students, but it is important to remember that some statistical judgments – such as choosing an α value or whether to conduct a one- or a two-tailed test – are subjective (Jacobson & Truax, 1991; Thompson, 2002).

At least practical significance and clinical significance make this subjectivity explicit, and readers are free to make their own subjective decisions. Additionally, practical and clinical significance tell research consumers (like clinicians and the public) what they want to know much more than does statistical significance – which merely states whether a null hypothesis (which the reader may not believe in the first place) was rejected.

Caveats for One-Sample *t*-Tests

Several cautions related to the *z*-test also apply to the one-sample *t*-test. These include the following:

- Type I and Type II errors are both possible with a one-sample *t*-test. Just like in a *z*-test, a Type I error occurs when the researcher rejects a null hypothesis that is actually true. A Type II error occurs when the researcher retains a null hypothesis that is actually false. Thus, it is important to remember that even if you reject the null hypothesis, this does not conclusively prove – once and for all – that the null hypothesis is wrong in the population (because you could have made a Type I error). Likewise, retaining the null hypothesis does not mean that there is no reliable mean difference between the sample and the population because a Type II error could have occurred.
- All NHST procedures, including the one-sample *t*-test, are sensitive to sample size, and it becomes easier to reject the null hypothesis as the sample size grows. In the example in this chapter, the null hypothesis would have been retained if n were only 26 or smaller (if $\alpha = .01$); any larger n results in a rejected null hypothesis. This is why it is necessary to calculate an effect size.
- One-sample *t*-tests also require the use of subjective decisions, including the value of α. Always be sure to justify your decisions when conducting a one-sample *t*-test.

Check Yourself!

- What does it mean when the results of an NHST are "statistically significant"?
- When using Appendix A2, what are the three possible results we can get for a *p*-value?
- Define a Type I error for a one-sample *t*-test.
- Define a Type II error for a one-sample *t*-test.

Confidence Intervals (CIs)

Problems with Estimating Population Parameters. In Chapter 4 we learned how to estimate population parameters, using sample data. Formulas 4.3 and 4.9 show how to calculate $\hat{\mu}$ and $\hat{\sigma}$, which are the estimates of the population mean and standard deviation calculated from sample data.

Figure 8.3 Visual schematic showing the relationship on a number line between a point estimate and a confidence interval (CI). The CI is a range of plausible values for the estimate of a population parameter – including the point estimate. The point estimate is the best possible estimate of the population parameter, given the sample data.

Given a set of sample data, these estimates are the best estimates possible for the population parameters. As such, we call them **point estimates**.

Paradoxically, although the point estimate is the best estimate for a population parameter, it is usually not equal to the actual population parameter. This is because of sampling error, which will make most samples' parameter estimates vary slightly from the true population parameter. (See Chapter 6 for an explanation of sampling error.) As a result of sampling error, when estimating population parameters, we find ourselves in the situation where our point estimates are the best possible parameter estimates, but are still most likely wrong. Yet, it is still more likely to be a better estimate for the parameter than any other value. To resolve this paradox, statisticians have created the **confidence interval**.

Description and Formula of Confidence Intervals. A confidence interval (CI) is a range of values that are plausible estimates for a population parameter, given the sample data (Thompson, Diamond, McWilliam, Snyder, & Snyder, 2005). This can be depicted visually in Figure 8.3, which shows a number line. The point estimate is one exact number on the number line, whereas the CI is a range of values. Figure 8.3 also shows that the CI will always include the point estimate. This makes sense because the point estimate is the best estimate for a population parameter, making it plausible.

Although CIs can be calculated for most sample statistics (e.g., Larsen & Warne, 2010), in this chapter we will focus on calculating the CI for a mean, which requires the following formula:

$$CI = \overline{X} \pm z^* \left(\frac{s_x}{\sqrt{n}} \right) \qquad \text{(Formula 8.4)}$$

In Formula 8.4, $\overline{X}$ stands for the sample mean, s_x symbolizes the sample standard deviation, and n is the sample size. The only new symbol is z^*, which is a number that corresponds to the width of the CI that the researcher has chosen.

CI widths are assigned a percentage, which means that, theoretically, CIs can range from 0% to 100%. In real research, though, there are a limited number of CI percentages. The most common percentages and their z^* values are shown in Table 8.2. Therefore, if you wish to calculate a 50% CI, you should use the value 0.68 for z^*. If you want to calculate a 90% CI, the proper value for z^* is 1.65. The most common CI width is the 95% CI, which has a z^* value of 1.96.

The z^* values in Table 8.2 are not the only possible CI widths. If you wish to find the z^* value for a CI width that is not in Table 8.2, you can use Appendix A1 to find the appropriate z^* value. To do this, first convert the percentage to a proportion and then divide it by 2. The next step is to find that value in column B. The number in column A in the same row is the appropriate z^* value. For example, if you wish to find the z^* value for an 80% CI, convert 80% to a proportion (.80). Dividing this number by 2 produces .40. The next step is to find .40 in the table in Appendix A4.

Table 8.2 z^* Values for common CI widths

CI width	z^* Value
50% CI	0.68
68% CI	1.00
90% CI	1.65
95% CI	**1.96**
98% CI	2.33
99% CI	2.57
100% CI	∞

Note. CI = confidence interval.
Note. The 95% CI is shown in boldface because it is the most common CI width in the social science research literature.
Note. Other CI z^* values can be found in Appendix A1. See text for details.

(The closest value without going over is .3997). Finally, the number in column A in this same row is the z^* value: 1.28.

Calculation Example. As an example of how to calculate a CI, we are going to calculate the 80% CI for $\hat{\mu}$ for the mean height of American men (CDC, 2012). Earlier in the chapter, we saw that $\overline{X} = 175.9$ cm, $s_x = 15.03$, and $n = 5,647$. From the previous paragraph we know that $z^* = 1.28$ for an 80% CI. Plugging these numbers into Formula 8.4 produces the following:

$$80\%CI = 175.9 \pm 1.28\left(\frac{15.03}{\sqrt{5,647}}\right)$$

Solving the piece inside of the parentheses simplifies the formula to:

$$80\%CI = 175.9 \pm 1.28(.20)$$

Multiplying 1.28 by .20 further simplifies the formula to:

$$80\%CI = 175.9 \pm .26$$

At this point we have to split the formula into two separate formulas because the $\pm$ symbol means we must subtract .26 and add .26 to the sample mean (175.9). This produces one equation that tells us the **lower limit** (i.e., minimal value) of the CI:

$$LL = 175.9 - .26$$

and another equation for the **upper limit** (i.e., maximum value) of the CI:

$$UL = 175.9 + .26$$

These equations produce two answers: LL = 175.64 cm and UL = 176.16 cm. In the notation for a CI, we bring these two results back into one equation like this:

$$80\%CI = [175.64, 176.16]$$

Always make sure that you state the width of the CI (e.g., 80% CI, in this example). You should also ensure that the CI limits are enclosed within square brackets and that they are separated by a comma and a space.

CIs are an effective way of providing unique descriptive information (e.g., regarding the precision of a point estimate for a parameter) that other statistics do not provide. When possible, it is a good idea to report a point estimate and a CI for statistics that function as estimates of population parameters. This is considered the "best reporting strategy" (APA, 2010, p. 34). However, it is best to remember that it is not essential to always report CIs, and when sample statistics are not serving as estimates for population parameters, a CI may not be necessary at all.

Correct Interpretations of CIs. So, what does this 80% CI mean? It means that although 175.9 cm is our point estimate for the mean height of the entire population of American men, our sample indicates that plausible values for μ range from 175.64 to 176.16 cm. This narrow width of the CI (only .52 cm) indicates that there are very few plausible values for μ. Therefore, we can trust our point estimate because if it is an inaccurate estimate for μ, it won't be far from the true value of the population mean (Thompson et al., 2005; Tukey, 1991).

In addition to quantifying the amount of trust we can place in a point estimate, CIs also state how often we can expect to create CIs that include the true population parameter. For example, if we were to take many random samples of 5,647 American men and calculate the 80% CI for each sample, then 80% of those samples would include the true population mean and 20% would not (Cumming, 2007; Cumming & Finch, 2005). Similarly, with many 95% CIs, we would expect that 95% would include the population parameter and 5% would not. In fact, this interpretation of CIs is why we use percentages to designate the width of CIs.

Incorrect Interpretations of CIs. Because the word "confidence" is in the name "confidence interval," some people believe that they are "95% confident" that the 95% CI includes the population parameter. This is an incorrect interpretation of CIs. Unless we already know μ, we do not really know how likely it is that a single CI includes the population parameter (Thompson, 2007; Thompson et al., 2005). In fact, there is absolutely no guarantee that a given CI includes the population parameter at all (Kline, 2013).

Another incorrect interpretation is that a given CI is a range of statistic values where 95% of future studies on the same topic (i.e., replication studies) will have a statistic inside the CI. This is simply not true. The percentage of future studies that have means within a prior study's CI is called the **capture percentage**. This is a different measurement than the CI, as is clear when you realize that – on average – the capture percentage of a 95% CI is only 83.4%, assuming all future studies have (1) the same *n* as the original, (2) μ is constant, and (3) *n* is large (Cumming & Maillardet, 2006). Under these conditions, a 99.44% CI has an average capture percentage of 95%. However, it is impossible to know the true capture percentage of any one CI without performing multiple replication studies, and some CIs will have a much lower capture percentage than 83.4% (Cumming & Maillardet, 2006).

Another incorrect interpretation of CIs is that they state how much "error" is in the study. In reality, CIs *only* quantify sampling error – and only for samples that are randomly selected from the population. If the study was not conducted well (e.g., a treatment group does not attend all the required therapy sessions), the variables were measured poorly, or the sample was not randomly selected, then CIs may not give an accurate picture of the plausible range of values for the population parameter (Kline, 2013).

Check Yourself!

- What is the difference between a point estimate and a CI?

- If a point estimate is the best estimate for a population parameter, why do we need CIs?

- Why do point estimates change from sample to sample, even if they are drawn from the same population?

- What is the correct interpretation of a 90% CI?

- What are the boundaries of a CI called?

Sidebar 8.4 CIs and NHST

The observant reader will look at Table 8.2 and think, "Some of those z^* values look familiar." In particular, the 90% CI z^* value (1.65) and 95% CI z^* value (1.96) were the critical values when $\alpha = .05$ for a one-tailed z-test and two-tailed z-test, respectively. Likewise, the 99% CI z^* value (2.57) is equal to the critical value for a two-tailed z-test when $\alpha = .01$. These similarities are not a coincidence. In fact, if the CI around the sample mean includes the population mean, then we would retain the null hypothesis if we conducted a one-sample t-test. Conversely, if the CI around $\overline{X}$ does not include μ, then we will reject the null hypothesis. This assumes that for $\alpha = .05$ we are using a 95% CI and that for $\alpha = .01$ we are using a 99% CI and a two-tailed test. (For any other α values, just convert α to a percentage and then subtract it from 100% to get the proper CI width. For a one-tailed test, you must double α, convert it to a percentage, and then subtract it from 100% to get the proper CI width.)

Because of this relationship between CIs and NHST results, we can use one method to check our results in the other because they will usually produce the same results (Hoenig & Heisey, 2001). To demonstrate this, I am going to calculate a 99% CI around the sample mean of the height of American men and then compare it to the μ value for the height of French men born in the 1700s.

According to Formula 8.4, the formula for a CI is:

$$CI = \overline{X} \pm z^* \left(\frac{s_x}{\sqrt{n}} \right)$$

In this example, $\overline{X} = 175.9$, $s_x = 15.03$, and $n = 5{,}647$. Because we performed a one-tailed test, when $\alpha = .01$, we should check our work by calculating a 98% CI, for which $z^* = 2.33$ (see Table 8.2). Putting these values into the CI formula produces the following:

$$98\% CI = 175.9 \pm 2.33 \left(\frac{15.03}{\sqrt{5{,}647}} \right)$$

Solving the portion in parentheses produces

$$98\% CI = 175.9 \pm 2.33(.20)$$

Multiplying .20 by z^* (i.e., 2.33), simplifies the formula to

$$98\% CI = 175.9 \pm .47$$

Splitting this formula into two parts in order to solve for the lower limit and the upper limit creates the following results:

$$\text{LL} = 175.9 - .47 = 175.43 \qquad \text{UL} = 175.9 + .47 = 176.37$$

Therefore, the 98% CI = [175.43, 176.37]. Remember that μ in this example was 167.8 cm. This value is outside the CI, which means we should reject the null hypothesis that $\overline{X}$ and μ are equal (i.e., $H_0 : \overline{X} = \mu$). This is exactly what we did when we followed the NHST steps in this chapter.

Some critics of NHST procedures (e.g., Cumming, 2014; Schmidt, 1996) advocate eliminating null hypothesis tests in favor of using CIs or other procedures. Although CIs do provide new information (e.g., on how much we can trust a point estimate), this exercise shows that using CIs to make decisions about the null hypothesis is just a different way of performing a null hypothesis test (García-Pérez, 2017; Kirk, 1996). Because of this, using CIs does not absolve a researcher from the need to report effect sizes or make subjective decisions about α. Thus, CIs seem unlikely to fully replace NHST (Abelson, 1997b; Savalei & Dunn, 2015).

Another Use of the One-Sample *t*-Tests

Although the main example in this chapter tests the null hypothesis that $\overline{X} = \mu$, the one-sample *t*-test can be used to test the null hypothesis that $\overline{X}$ is equal to any number – not just μ. This may be useful to researchers who are not interested in the null hypothesis and instead wonder if their sample is different from some other value. This requires a few modifications to the one-sample *t*-test procedure, but they are minor compared to the modifications needed to change a *z*-test into a one-sample *t*-test. This section of the chapter will show you how to conduct this type of one-sample *t*-test.

For this example, we will revisit Chapter 7's example from Vinten et al.'s (2009) sample of children who were exposed to an anti-seizure medication *in utero*. The researchers may not be interested in whether the children score lower on the VABS than average ($\mu = 100$). Rather, they may be interested in whether the children score low enough on the VABS to be candidates for a diagnosis of an intellectual disability (which requires a VABS score of 70 or lower). This may be interesting to Vinten et al. because people with intellectual disabilities have lifelong difficulty adapting to their environment and need frequent help with self-care. If the anti-seizure medication causes cognitive problems this severe, then that would be much more important than merely learning whether these children score lower on the VABS than the population mean. For this example, $\overline{X} = 76.7$, $s_x = 13.95$, and $n = 41$.

> **Step 1: Form Groups**. In this adaptation of a one-sample *t*-test, there aren't groups *per se*. Rather we have the sample and the score cutoff.
>
> **Step 2: Define the Null Hypothesis**. Because 70 is not the population's mean VABS score, the null hypothesis for this type of one-sample *t*-test is not $H_0 : \overline{X} = \mu$. Rather, it is $H_0 : \overline{X} = 70$ because 70 is replacing μ in our hypothesis test.
>
> **Step 3: Set Alpha**. The default α for all NHST procedures is .05. We don't have a good reason to change this, so we will keep this α value.
>
> **Step 4: Choose a One- or Two-Tailed Test, Which Determines the Alternative Hypothesis**. The basis for determining whether to conduct a one- or a two-tailed test is the same for this type of one-tailed *t*-test (i.e., whether there is previous research or theory). Also, there are only three alternative hypotheses: $H_1 : \overline{X} \neq 70$ for a two-tailed test, and $H_1 : \overline{X} > 70$ or $H_1 : \overline{X} < 70$ for a one-tailed test. Because we really don't know whether

the anti-seizure drug is so harmful that it may cause an intellectual disability, we will perform a two-tailed test, which means our alternative hypothesis is $H_1 : \overline{X} \neq 70$.

Step 5: Find the Critical Value. Finding the *t*-critical value in a one-sample *t*-test first requires calculating degrees of freedom. In this example there are 40 degrees of freedom (because $n = 41$, and $41 - 1 = 40$). According to Appendix A2, a two-tailed test when $\alpha = .05$ and with 40 degrees of freedom has *t*-critical values of ± 2.021.

Step 6: Calculate the Observed Value. The formula for finding the *t*-observed value is $t_{obs} = \dfrac{\overline{X} - \mu}{\left(\dfrac{s_x}{\sqrt{n}}\right)}$. (This was Formula 8.1.) However, because we are not concerned with μ in this type of one-sample *t*-test, we can replace μ with 70 and plug the remaining values into the formula. As a result, we get the following:

$$t_{obs} = \frac{76.7 - 70}{\left(\dfrac{13.95}{\sqrt{41}}\right)}$$

This produces a *t*-observed value of $+3.075$.

> **Step 7: Compare the observed and critical values and find *p*.** In this example, the *t*-critical value $= \pm 2.021$, and the *t*-observed value $= +3.075$. Therefore, the critical value is clearly within the rejection region, as shown in Figure 8.4. So, we can reject the hypothesis that these children's mean VABS score is equal to the threshold of diagnosis with an intellectual disability. Because their mean is higher (76.7) than that threshold value (70) and we rejected the null hypothesis that these two numbers are equal, we can conclude that there is not enough evidence in this sample to indicate that the anti-seizure medication harms the average child enough to be diagnosed with an intellectual disability.
>
> **Step 8: Calculate an Effect Size.** Ordinarily, for a one-sample *t*-test, the effect size would be calculated through Formula 8.3, which is $d = \dfrac{\overline{X} - \mu}{s_x}$. However, because we are not interested in μ in this example, we can replace it with 70. Replacing $\overline{X}$ and s_x with their values (76.7 and 13.95, respectively) produces:

$$d = \frac{76.7 - 70}{13.95}$$

This produces a Cohen's *d* value of .480. Therefore, we can conclude that the average child who was exposed to the anti-seizure medication while in the womb has a VABS score that is 0.480 standard deviation higher than the cutoff for an intellectual disability. Although the average child in the sample does not function as well as the average child in the population (as we saw when we conducted a *z*-test in Chapter 7), the impairment is not severe enough to warrant a disability diagnosis.

What About the *p*-Value and the CI? Although not required to conduct a one-sample *t*-test, we can still find a *p*-value and a CI. In fact, nothing about finding *p* or the CI changes with this type of one-sample *t*-test.

Because we rejected the null hypothesis when $\alpha = .05$, we know that *p* must be less than .05. However, we need to determine whether it is also less than .01, or whether it is between .05 and .01. To do this we need to determine whether we would reject the null hypothesis if α were equal to .01. Appendix A2 shows that when there are 40 degrees of freedom for a two-tailed test and $\alpha = .01$, the *t*-critical values are ± 2.704. With those critical values and a *t*-observed value of $+3.075$, we would still reject the null hypothesis, indicating that *p* must be less than .01.

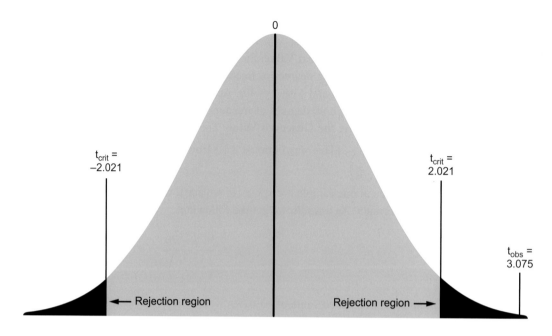

Figure 8.4 Schematic showing the decision to reject the hypothesis for the Vinten et al. (2009) data that $\overline{X} = 70$. Because the sample mean is higher than the threshold for diagnosis with an intellectual disability, we can conclude that the average child in the sample is not sufficiently impaired to have an intellectual disability.

The CI formula is $CI = \overline{X} \pm z^* \left(\frac{s_x}{\sqrt{n}} \right)$. Because μ is not part of the formula, nothing in the procedure of calculating a CI changes in this example. Because we conducted a two-tailed test where $\alpha = .05$, we should calculate a 95% CI, which is the equivalent to our NHST. According to Table 8.2, the appropriate z^* value is 1.96. Plugging in this value and the values for $\overline{X}$, s_x, and n produces the following:

$$CI = 76.7 \pm 1.96 \left(\frac{13.95}{\sqrt{41}} \right)$$

This formula produces a lower limit of 72.43 and an upper limit of 80.97. Therefore, 95% CI = [72.43, 80.97]. Notice that this CI does not include 70, showing that our decision to reject the null hypothesis was correct (see Sidebar 8.4).

Check Yourself!

- Why would someone want to perform a one-sample *t*-test that tests a hypothesis different from $H_0 : \overline{X} = \mu$?

- What is the effect size for a one-sample *t*-test where the hypothesis being tested is that the sample mean is equal to some score?

- In this type of one-sample *t*-test, how do you determine whether to reject or retain the null hypothesis?

Guided Practice 8.1

As part of my graduate school training in educational psychology, I was required to administer a short intelligence test to a first-grade class. These students ($n = 29$) had a mean score of 94.21 and a standard deviation of 13.78. The intelligence test was designed (much like the VABS) so that the population mean was equal to 100. Therefore, we can conduct a one-sample *t*-test to determine whether this class's mean score differed from the population mean of 100.

Step 1: Form Groups

In this case, the two groups are the population and the sample.

Step 2: Define the Null Hypothesis

Because we are comparing our sample mean ($\overline{X}$) to the population mean (μ), our null hypothesis is $H_0 : \overline{X} = \mu$.

Step 3: Set Alpha

The default α value in a one-sample *t*-test is .05. However, I want to guard against Type I error because there could be stigma for these students and their families if they are not seen as being as smart as average. Therefore, we are going to make it harder to reject the null hypothesis and set the α value at .01. This also makes it harder to determine whether the students are smarter than the average student in the population, but that is a price worth paying if it means preserving the dignity of these students and these families in case they score lower than average.

Step 4: Choose a One- or a Two-Tailed Test, Which Determines the Alternative Hypothesis

When I gave these intelligence tests, I did not know much about the school, so it is reasonable to perform a two-tailed test. Therefore, the alternative hypothesis is $H_1 : \overline{X} \neq \mu$.

Step 5: Find the Critical Values

To find the *t*-critical values for this example, we must first calculate the degrees of freedom. Because $n = 29$, we must have 28 degrees of freedom (df = $n - 1$; therefore, df = $29 - 1 = 28$). In Appendix A2, the row for 28 degrees of freedom in a two-tailed test when $\alpha = .01$ has a *t*-critical value of ± 2.763.

Step 6: Calculate the Observed Value

Formula 8.1 is the formula for calculating the *t*-observed value, which is $t_{obs} = \dfrac{\overline{X} - \mu}{\left(\dfrac{s_x}{\sqrt{n}}\right)}$. Plugging the example's sample mean, sample standard deviation, sample size, and population mean into this formula produces the following:

$$t_{obs} = \frac{94.21 - 100}{\left(\dfrac{13.78}{\sqrt{29}}\right)}$$

Solving for the numerator simplifies the formula to

$$t_{obs} = \frac{-5.79}{\left(\dfrac{13.78}{\sqrt{29}}\right)}$$

We can also solve the square root in the formula:

$$t_{obs} = \frac{-5.79}{\left(\dfrac{13.78}{5.385}\right)}$$

Solving the section of the parentheses is:

$$t_{obs} = \frac{-5.79}{2.559}$$

Finally, this produces a *t*-observed value of –2.263.

Step 7: Compare the Observed and Critical Values and Find *p*

In Step 5 we saw that the *t*-critical value = ±2.763. Step 6 showed us that the *t*-observed value = –2.263. When we compare the two, it is clear that the *t*-critical values are further from the center of the distribution (i.e., 0) than the *t*-observed value. Therefore, the latter value must be outside the rejection region. As a result, we should retain the null hypothesis.

Because we retained the null hypothesis when α was equal to .01, we know that *p* must be greater than .01. However, we do not know yet if it is greater than .05 or if *p* is between .01 and .05. To clarify this, we need to determine whether we would reject or retain the null hypothesis if *p* were equal to .05. According to Appendix A2, the *t*-critical value for a two-tailed test with 28 degrees of freedom, when α = .05, is ±2.048. With this *t*-critical value and a *t*-observed value of –2.263, we would reject the null hypothesis. Therefore, *p* must be between .01 and .05.

Step 8: Calculate an Effect Size

Formula 8.3 gives the formula for calculating an effect size (i.e., Cohen's *d*), which is:

$$d = \frac{\overline{X} - \mu}{s_x}$$

In this example the formula becomes the following when the symbols are replaced by numerical values:

$$d = \frac{94.21 - 100}{13.78}$$

Solving for the numerator produces:

$$d = \frac{-5.79}{13.78}$$

This produces a final Cohen's *d* result of –.420, meaning that the average child in this first-grade class is scoring 0.420 standard deviation lower than the average child in the population.

Optional: Calculate the 99% CI

Although not required for the NHST, it is still helpful to calculate a CI around this sample's mean. Because our one-sample *t*-test had an α value of .01 and was a two-tailed test, the corresponding CI will be 99%. As shown in Formula 8.4, the formula for a CI is $CI = \overline{X} \pm z^* \left(\frac{s_x}{\sqrt{n}}\right)$. Table 8.2 shows that the z^* value for a 99% CI is 2.57. Plugging this number into the formula, along with the sample mean, standard deviation, and sample size results in the following:

$$99\% CI = 94.21 \pm 2.57 \left(\frac{13.78}{\sqrt{29}}\right)$$

Solving the portion in parentheses produces:

$$99\% CI = 94.21 \pm 2.57(2.559)$$

Multiplying 2.57 and 2.559 results in:

$$99\% CI = 94.21 \pm 6.58$$

Splitting this formula into half to calculate the lower limit and the upper limit results in the following:

$$LL = 94.21 - 6.58 = 87.63 \qquad UL = 94.21 + 6.58 = 100.79$$

Therefore, the 99% CI is [87.63, 100.79].

General Linear Moment 8.2

When the GLM was introduced in Chapter 7, I stated that there were three characteristics of all GLM procedures:

1. All GLM procedures examine the relationships between independent and dependent variables. Another way of stating this point is that all GLM procedures are correlational in nature.

2. All GLM procedures apply weights to data during the analysis process.
3. All GLM procedures can produce an effect size.

In this General Linear Moment, we will explore how these three characteristics apply to the one-sample *t*-test. You will see that the characteristics of the GLM apply in the same way that they did to z-tests. If you read General Linear Moment 8.1 about how the one-sample *t*-test is a generalization of the z-test, these similarities will not surprise you.

Independent and Dependent Variables. In a z-test, the independent variable was the grouping variable that separated the data into the population and the sample. The dependent variable was the variable that was being used to calculate means. These are also the independent and dependent variables for a one-sample *t*-test. Therefore, the one-sample *t*-test is examining whether there is a relationship between these two variables. If there is no relationship, then the null hypothesis will be retained, and the two groups' means (i.e., $\overline{X}$ and μ) are equal. If there is a relationship between the independent and dependent variables, the null hypothesis will be rejected because members in one group tend to be different from members in the other group.

Weighting Data. Recall from General Linear Moment 7.1 that statistical weights are multiplied by the raw data to create statistical models. In a z-test, the Cohen's *d* was a statistical weight. For both a z-test and a one-sample t-test, if we multiply the person's score on the independent variable (0 = population member, 1 = sample member) by Cohen's *d*, the result is the predicted z-score for a person in that group. For example, in the height data in this chapter, Cohen's *d* was .539. Therefore, we can predict that American men in the sample will have a z-score of $(1)(.539) = .539$.

Effect Sizes. We have already seen in this chapter that the effect size for a one-sample *t*-test is Cohen's *d*. Like all GLM procedures, the one-sample *t*-test produces an effect size, and it is essential to report Cohen's *d* along with the results of your one-sample *t*-test.

Summary

A one-sample *t*-test is a new GLM member and NHST procedure which is appropriate when a z-test cannot be performed because the population standard deviation (σ) is unknown. The one-sample *t*-test follows all of the eight steps of the z-test, but because we don't have σ, some changes are required. The first is that the formulas that used σ (i.e., for the observed value and for Cohen's *d*) now use the sample standard deviation (s_x) instead. The second change is the requirement to calculate the degrees of freedom, the formula for which is $n - 1$. The last change is a new probability distribution (called a *t*-distribution), which means that we now use Appendix A2 to find the critical value.

In this chapter we also learned a little bit more about *p-values*. First, when *p* is lower than α, we will always reject the null hypothesis. Second, when *p* is higher than α, we will always retain the null hypothesis. As a result, we can determine whether *p* is smaller or larger than any given α merely by determining whether the null hypothesis was retained or rejected for a particular α.

A new concept in this chapter was CIs, which are a range of plausible values for a population parameter. CIs can vary in width, and it is important to remember that the researcher chooses the width of a CI. However, the 95% CI is the most common in social science research.

Finally, one-sample t-tests are flexible because they can be used to test the hypothesis that the sample mean is equal to any value (not just μ). This requires minimal adjustments to the one-sample t-test procedure.

Reflection Questions: Comprehension

1. Why do the z-test and the one-sample t-test share so many similarities?
2. When should you perform a one-sample t-test instead of a z-test?
3. How do we determine the range of a p-value in a one-sample t-test?
4. Explain the difference between "statistically significant" results and important results.
   a. Give an example of results that would be "statistically significant" but not important.
   b. Give an example of results that would be "statistically insignificant" and important.
5. How does the sampling distribution in a one-sample t-test differ from the sampling distribution in a z-test?
6. Explain what HARKing is and why it is considered a questionable research practice.
7. What are the three types of significance? How do they differ from one another?

Reflection Questions: Application

8. Calculate the degrees of freedom for the following sample sizes:
   a. 3
   b. 12
   c. 22
   d. 100
   e. 412
9. A student using Appendix A2 wants to find their t-observed value for a dataset with 113 degrees of freedom. Unfortunately, there is no row in the table displaying the z-observed value for 113 degrees of freedom.
   a. What should the student do whenever the exact number of degrees of freedom is not in the table?
   b. Which row should he or she use instead?
10. Conduct a one-sample t-test for a dataset where $\mu = 14.1$, $\overline{X} = 13.7$, $s_x = 0.8$, $n = 20$.
   a. What are the groups for this one-sample t-test?
   b. What is the null hypothesis for this one-sample t-test?
   c. What is the value of α?
   d. Should the researcher conduct a one- or a two-tailed test?
   e. What is the alternative hypothesis?
   f. What is the value for degrees of freedom?
   g. What is the t-observed value?
   h. What is(are) the t-critical value(s)?
   i. In view of the critical and observed values, should the researcher reject or retain the null hypothesis?
   j. What is the p-value for this example?

k.   What is the Cohen's *d* value for this example?

l.   If the α value were dropped to .01, would the researcher reject or retain the null hypothesis?

m.   Calculate a 68% CI around the sample mean.

n.   Calculate a 90% CI around the sample mean.

o.   Calculate a 98% CI around the sample mean.

11.   At a university, the mean grade-point average of all students is 2.84 (on a scale ranging from 0 to 4.0). A random sample of 24 anthropology students has a mean grade-point average of 3.14, with a standard deviation of 0.35. Conduct a one-sample *t*-test with these data.

a.   What are the groups for this one-sample *t*-test?

b.   What is the null hypothesis for this one-sample *t*-test?

c.   What is the value of α?

d.   Should the researcher conduct a one- or a two-tailed test?

e.   What is the alternative hypothesis?

f.   What is the value for degrees of freedom?

g.   What is the *t*-observed value?

h.   What is(are) the *t*-critical value(s)?

i.   Based on the critical and observed values, should the researcher reject or retain the null hypothesis? Does this mean that anthropology students have higher grades, equally high grades, or lower grades than the population of university students?

j.   What is the *p*-value for this example?

k.   What is the Cohen's *d* value for this example?

l.   If the α value were dropped to .01, would the researcher reject or retain the null hypothesis?

m.   Calculate a 68% CI around the sample mean.

n.   Calculate a 90% CI around the sample mean.

o.   Calculate a 98% CI around the sample mean.

12.   Daniel and Elise each conduct their own study. Daniel's study has an *n* of 412, and Elise's study has an *n* of 355. If both researchers have the same effect size, which researcher is more likely to reject the null hypothesis in a one-sample *t*-test? Why?

13.   Kathy and Becky are classmates who each conduct their own study. Kathy has a Cohen's *d* value of .104. Becky has a Cohen's *d* value of .401. If both researchers have the same sample size, which one is more likely to have statistically significant results?

14.   Use the formula for CI, $CI = \overline{X} \pm z^* \left(\frac{s_x}{\sqrt{n}} \right)$, to answer the following questions.

a.   What can a researcher do to z^* to make a CI narrower?

b.   What can a researcher do to *n* to make a CI wider?

c.   If a researcher wanted to maximize her chances of creating a CI that includes μ, what should she do to z^* and *n*?

15.   What is the appropriate z^* value for the following CI widths?

a.   40% CI?

b.   50% CI?

c.   62% CI?

d.   68% CI?

e.   81% CI?

f.   93% CI?

16.   The proper interpretation of a CI is that for a set of CIs that are all the same width (i.e., the same *x*% CI) for samples of the same *n* drawn from the same population, *x*% of CIs would include the population parameter μ. Given this interpretation, why is the z^* value for a 100% CI ∞?

17. Conduct a one-sample t-test for a dataset where $\mu = 74.2$, $\overline{X} = 75.1$, $s_x = 10.2$, and $n = 81$.
   a. What are the groups for this one-sample t-test?
   b. What is the null hypothesis for this one-sample t-test?
   c. What is the value of α?
   d. Is a one-tailed or a two-tailed test appropriate for this situation?
   e. What is the alternative hypothesis?
   f. What is the t-observed value?
   g. What is(are) the t-critical value(s)?
   h. Based on the critical and observed values, should the null hypothesis be rejected or retained?
   i. What is the p-value for this example?
   j. What is the Cohen's d value for this example?
   k. If the α value were dropped to .01, would the researcher reject or retain the null hypothesis?
   l. If α were .05 and the sample size were increased to 1,100, would the researcher reject or retain the null hypothesis?
   m. If α were .05 and the sample size were decreased to 18, would the researcher reject or retain the null hypothesis?
   n. If α were .05 and the sample size were decreased to 5, would the researcher reject or retain the null hypothesis?
   o. Calculate a 50% CI around the sample mean.
   p. Calculate a 69% CI around the sample mean.
   q. Calculate a 99% CI around the sample mean.
18. On a test called the MMPI-2, a score of 30 on the Anxiety Subscale is considered very low. Felipe participates in a yoga group at his gym and decides to give this subscale to 18 people in his yoga group. The mean of their scores is 35.2, with a standard deviation of 10.4. He wants to determine whether their anxiety scores are statistically equal to 30.
   a. What are the groups for this one-sample t-test?
   b. What is the null hypothesis for this one-sample t-test?
   c. What is the value of α?
   d. Should the researcher conduct a one- or two-tailed test?
   e. What is the alternative hypothesis?
   f. What is the value for degrees of freedom?
   g. What is the t-observed value?
   h. What is(are) the t-critical value(s)?
   i. Based on the critical and observed values, should Felipe reject or retain the null hypothesis? Does this mean that his yoga group has scores that are above 30, below 30, or statistically equal to 30?
   j. What is the p-value for this example?
   k. What is the Cohen's d value for this example?
   l. If the α value were dropped to .01, would Felipe reject or retain the null hypothesis?
   m. Calculate a 42% CI around the sample mean.
   n. Calculate a 79% CI around the sample mean.
   o. Calculate a 95% CI around the sample mean.

Software Guide

This Software Guide will show you how to conduct a one-sample *t*-test in Excel and SPSS. Like previous guides, this requires using Excel functions and SPSS point-and-click interface.

Excel

To conduct a one-sample *t*-test, you use an Excel function called TTEST, which has two formats:

- For a one-tailed one-sample *t*-test: "=TTEST(XX:XX,YY:YY,1,3)"
- For a two-tailed one-sample *t*-test: "=TTEST(XX:XX,YY:YY,2,3)"

In each of these formats, the "XX:XX" should be replaced with cells for the sample. The YY:YY should be replaced with a set of cells that all contain the mean of the population. The number of cells for XX:XX and YY:YY should be the same. Figure 8.5a shows how to use the function, and Figure 8.5b shows the results. The results in Excel are the *p*-values – not the *t*-observed values. If the *p*-value is less than alpha, the user should reject the null hypothesis. If the *p*-value is greater than alpha, the user should retain the null hypothesis.

Excel does not calculate Cohen's *d* as part of the one-sample *t*-test. Performing this requires a different function: "=(XX-YY)/ZZ." In this function YY is the population mean, ZZ is the sample standard deviation, and XX is the sample mean. Figure 8.5b shows that the Cohen's *d* value in this example is −.420.

SPSS

With the point-and-click interface in SPSS, conducting a one-sample *t*-test is easy. In the data window, the first step is to click "Analyze" → "Compare Means" → "One Sample T Test." This makes a new window appear that is labeled "One Sample T Test" (shown in Figure 8.6).

The next step is to select the variable desired for the one-sample *t*-test from the left side of the window (which is a list of the file's variables) and put it in the right side of the window. In the area labeled "Test Value," you should enter the value for μ. (If you are not testing the hypothesis $\overline{X}$ is equal to μ, then you can enter the threshold value into this area.) In this example (which has the same data as were used for Guided Practice 8.1), I am going to enter a test value of 100, which is the population mean for most IQ tests.

If you select the "Options" button, another window, called the options window, appears (shown in Figure 8.7). This allows you to select the width of the CI. The default is 95% (though I have changed it to 99% in this example). There is also an option for how the computer program should handle missing data. The default option is to "Exclude cases analysis by analysis." This means that if you perform more than one one-sample *t*-test at a time, the computer will only throw out cases that are missing data for each *t*-test. The second option, labeled, "Exclude cases listwise," means that for all *t*-tests that you perform at the same time the computer will throw out cases that are missing data on any variable. Because we are only performing one *t*-test, either option will produce the same results and use the same sample size.

(a)

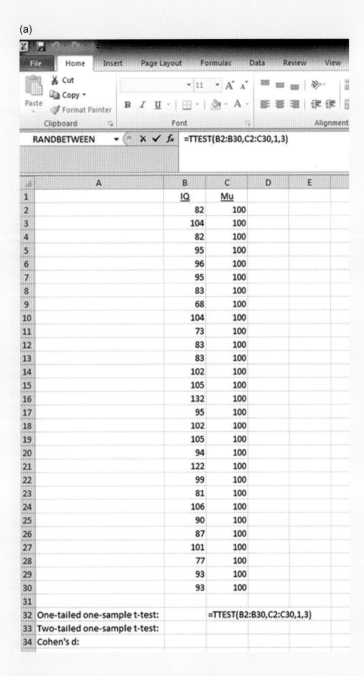

Figure 8.5a Screenshot from Microsoft Excel showing how to use the TTEST function to conduct a one-sample *t*-test. Notice the column of μ values necessary to conduct this test. The numbers in the second column do not have to be μ values, but they all must be equal.

After you select "Continue" in the options window and "OK" in the One Sample T Test window, the results appear in the output window. These results are shown in Figure 8.8. The first table provides basic descriptive statistics for the variable: the sample size, mean, standard deviation, and the standard error. (Notice that these values match the sample mean and standard deviation in Guided

(b)

	A	B	C	D
1		IQ	Mu	
2		82	100	
3		104	100	
4		82	100	
5		95	100	
6		96	100	
7		95	100	
8		83	100	
9		68	100	
10		104	100	
11		73	100	
12		83	100	
13		83	100	
14		102	100	
15		105	100	
16		132	100	
17		95	100	
18		102	100	
19		105	100	
20		94	100	
21		122	100	
22		99	100	
23		81	100	
24		106	100	
25		90	100	
26		87	100	
27		101	100	
28		77	100	
29		93	100	
30		93	100	
31				
32	One-tailed one-sample t-test:		0.015743	
33	Two-tailed one-sample t-test:		0.031487	
34	Cohen's d:		-0.42048	
35				

Figure 8.5b Screenshot from Microsoft Excel showing the results of the TTEST function and Cohen's *d*. The results for the one-sample *t*-tests (in cells C32 and C33) are *p*-values.

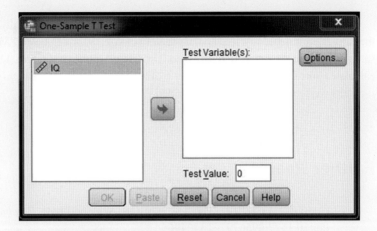

Figure 8.6 The One-Sample T Test window in SPSS.

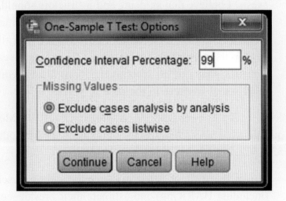

Figure 8.7 The options window for a one-sample *t*-test in SPSS.

One-Sample Statistics

	N	Mean	Std. Deviation	Std. Error Mean
IQ	29	94.21	13.777	2.558

One-Sample Test

	Test Value = 100					
					99% Confidence Interval of the Difference	
	t	df	Sig. (2-tailed)	Mean Difference	Lower	Upper
IQ	-2.264	28	.031	-5.793	-12.86	1.28

Figure 8.8 Results in SPSS of a one-sample *t*-test.

Practice 8.1.) The second table produces the *t*-value (labeled "t"), the degrees of freedom ("df"), and the two-tailed *p*-value (labeled "Sig"). Notice how this *p*-value is between .01 and .05, which is exactly what we found in Guided Practice 8.1. Again, if the *p*-value is less than alpha, the user should reject the null hypothesis. If the *p*-value is greater than alpha, the user should retain the null hypothesis.

Unfortunately, SPSS does not calculate Cohen's *d* automatically. But the tables provide all the information necessary to calculate the effect size: $\overline{X} - \mu$ (labeled "Mean Difference") and sample standard deviation (labeled "Std. Deviation" in the first table). Using these values to calculate Cohen's *d* produces $d = \frac{-5.793}{13.777} = .420$. This Cohen's *d* and the *p*-value are equal to the *d* and *p*-results we found in Excel and in Guided Practice 8.1.

Further Reading

- Cumming, G. (2014). The new statistics: Why and how. *Psychological Science, 25*, 7–29. doi:10.1177/0956797613504966

  * Cumming is one of today's leading detractors of NHST methods – including one-sample *t*-tests. I believe that students and instructors should be aware of his criticism about the value of NHST methods because they echo the criticisms that have been leveled against NHST procedures for decades. I do not agree with all of his opinions, but they have their supporters. Moreover, in this article Cumming gives recommendations for interpreting statistics. Many of his recommendations have become mainstream in psychology and other social sciences in the past 20 years.

- John, L. K., Loewenstein, G., & Prelec, D. (2012). Measuring the prevalence of questionable research practices with incentives for truth telling. *Psychological Science, 23*, 524–532. doi:10.1177/0956797611430953

  * This is an excellent article in which the authors describe questionable research practices (including HARKing) and estimate their prevalence among behavioral scientists. They also show that not all questionable research practices are equally serious, and they provide a useful ranking system to help the reader understand which questionable research practices are most harmful to scientific progress.

- Thompson, B. (2002). "Statistical," "practical," and "clinical": How many kinds of significance do counselors need to consider? *Journal of Counseling & Development, 80*, 64–71. doi:10.1002/j.1556–6678.2002.tb00167.x

  * Although it is just eight pages long, Thompson packs a lot of information into this article. In addition to explaining the three types of significance and clarifying misconceptions about them, he also explains the need for effect sizes, gives a classification scheme for some of the most common effect sizes, and then shows how these various effect sizes are related to one another. Thompson even gives information about a few effect sizes that are alternatives to Cohen's *d*, but which I don't discuss in this textbook.

9 Paired-Samples *t*-Tests

By now we have mastered two types of null hypothesis statistical significance tests (NHSTs) – the one-sample *t*-test and the *z*-test. Both of these have the same null hypothesis, which is that the sample mean ($\overline{X}$) is equal to the population mean (μ). Mathematically, we expressed this null hypothesis as $H_0 : \overline{X} = \mu$. Both of these NHST procedures are useful for determining whether the sample mean is statistically equal to the population mean.

However, that is rarely the research question that social scientists, practitioners, teachers, and therapists ask. Often this is because they do not know the population mean. Instead, they are often interested in whether two groups of sample members are similar or different. In Chapters 9 and 10 we will discuss two NHST procedures that answer this question. The first procedure – which this chapter covers – is called the **paired two-sample *t*-test**. This is useful for (1) investigating growth and change, and (2) comparing samples of data that are linked in some way.

Learning Goals

- Find appropriate uses for a paired two-sample *t*-test NHST procedure.
- Conduct a paired two-sample *t*-test.
- Calculate an effect size for a paired two-sample *t*-test.

When to Use the Paired Two-Sample *t*-Test

There are three situations in which it is appropriate to use the paired two-sample *t*-test. The first is when the investigator is interested in measuring growth or change. An example of this is a study conducted by Diefenbach, Abramowitz, Norberg, and Tolin (2007). These researchers wondered whether patients with obsessive-compulsive disorder had better quality of life after psychological therapy than they did before therapy. This required giving their patients a quality of life survey before they started therapy and then administering the same quality of life survey after therapy was finished.

The second appropriate situation for a paired two-sample *t*-test is when there are two samples, and each sample member has a clear connection with a member of the other sample. This connection (i.e., pairing) may occur naturally, as in family science research when husbands' scores can be paired with the scores of their wives. The connection can also be artificial, as when researchers match subjects on demographic variables (Zimmerman, 1997). For example, it is common in neuroscience studies for researchers to ensure that each group of subjects has the same number of males and females and the same number of left- and right-handed individuals. The easiest way to do this is to create pairs of individuals (one member of the pair in each group) who have the same gender and dominant hand. This artificial pairing of research subjects also requires a paired two-sample *t*-test to analyze the data.

The final situation that is appropriate for a paired two-sample *t*-test occurs when the same research participant provides multiple scores on the same variable. This often occurs in laboratory research in psychology, where each research participant is exposed to multiple stimuli in order to ascertain how the change in stimuli affects scores on the dependent variable. This research design is advantageous because it allows each person to function as their own control group member that they can be compared to.

There are two things to notice about these situations. First, all three scenarios involve a pairing of subjects' scores across samples; this is where the name "paired two-sample *t*-test" comes from. Second, neither of these scenarios involves the population data (only sample data), meaning that a *z*-test and a one-sample *t*-test cannot be used to analyze data from paired samples.

Sidebar 9.1   **Confusing terminology in statistics**

When I was in graduate school, one of my professors (Bruce Thompson, whom I cite periodically in this book) jokingly told my class that statisticians invent terminology with the intention of confusing students. As I have worked more with statistical methods, I have learned that his joke sometimes seems too true. While there is no evidence that statisticians are conspiring to confuse students, the terminology in statistics can be difficult to learn. There are a few reasons for this.

First, statistics is a field that embraced contributions from many areas, including biology, psychology, economics, and physics – and these fields sometimes adopt terminology that other fields do not share. Second, independent researchers have developed the same statistical procedures independently and without being aware of others' work (e.g., see Conroy, 2012). As a result, statistical terminology that one author uses depends on which "discoverer" the author used as their source for terminology.

The paired-samples *t*-test is an example of how terminology can be confusing. Two common alternative names for the paired samples *t*-test are the "dependent samples *t*-test" and the "two-sample dependent *t*-test." I avoid this terminology because I think that the term "dependent" is easily confused with the term "dependent variable," which is the outcome variable (see Chapter 1). Another term is the "related-samples *t*-test," which I avoid in this book because it can be confused with the term "relationship," which describes how scores on different variables appear together (see Chapters 7 and 12).

In this textbook I have tried to use the terminology that is most widespread in psychology, sociology, family science, anthropology, social work, and education. Most of this terminology is also applicable to other related fields, such as communications and business. (On the other hand, researchers in economics sometimes use a different terminology from that in the other social sciences.) Because you may encounter other terms for the same procedures or ideas, I have put some alternative terms in the glossary. These will direct you to the equivalent terminology used in this textbook.

Steps of a Paired-Samples *t*-Test

Like the *z*-test and the one-sample *t*-test, the paired-samples *t*-test is an NHST procedure and a member of the GLM. Therefore, conducting a paired-samples *t*-test requires following the same eight steps that we have seen in the previous two chapters. Those steps are:

1. Form groups in the data.
2. Define the null hypothesis (H_0). The null hypothesis is always that there is no difference between groups or that there is no relationship between independent and dependent variables.
3. Set alpha (α). The default alpha = .05.
4. Choose a one-tailed or a two-tailed test. This determines the alternative hypothesis (H_1).
5. Find the *critical* value, which is used to define the rejection region.
6. Calculate the *observed* value.
7. Compare the observed value and the critical value. If the observed value is more extreme than the critical value, the null hypothesis should be rejected. Otherwise, it should be retained.
8. Calculate an *effect size*.

However, because the paired-samples *t*-test does not involve the population mean (μ), some changes are required. The rest of this chapter is devoted to showing how to execute these eight steps in a paired-samples *t*-test and the implications of conducting an NHST without the use of μ.

As an example, we are going to revisit the data from the Waite et al. (2015) study on the relationship that subjects had with their siblings with autism and their siblings without autism. Waite et al. (2015) have two sets of ratings from the same people: one set of ratings relates to their sibling with autism, and the other set relates to their sibling without autism. Because each of these ratings comes from the same person, there is an obvious pairing between the sets of ratings. Additionally, each autistic sibling has another sibling in the non-autistic group – another way that the scores are paired across the two groups. Therefore, a paired-samples *t*-test is an appropriate way to analyze the data in this study.

Form Groups in the Data. This is the first step in an NHST. In the *z*-test and the one-sample *t*-test, the two groups were (1) the population and (2) the sample. But these cannot be the two groups in a paired-samples *t*-test because there are no population data; both of these groups of scores are sample data. Therefore, our groups in the data are (1) the first sample, and (2) the second sample. For the Waite et al. (2015) data, the first sample of scores is ratings about the sibling with autism, and the second sample is ratings about the typically developing sibling.

Define the Null Hypothesis. The second step in an NHST is to define a null hypothesis, which is always abbreviated H_0. For a *z*-test and the one-sample *t*-test, the null hypothesis was $H_0 : \overline{X} = \mu$ (see Formula 7.1). However, because we do not have any population data in a paired-samples *t*-test, we cannot use this null hypothesis (because it uses μ, which is the population mean). Therefore, we need a new null hypothesis. Getting to that new null hypothesis takes a few steps.

In Chapter 8, we replaced the population with a second sample. Therefore, it seems logical to do the same thing in this step; replacing μ with a sample mean ($\overline{X}$), which results in

$$H_0 : \overline{X}_1 = \overline{X}_2 \qquad \text{(Formula 9.1)}$$

In Formula 9.1, the two $\overline{X}$'s refer to the two sample means. There are also two subscript numbers (i.e., 1 and 2) in the formula. These numbers are just notation showing that $\overline{X}_1$ is the first sample's mean and that $\overline{X}_2$ is the second sample's mean. They do not serve any mathematical purpose.

However, this is not the correct null hypothesis for a paired-samples *t*-test. (We will revisit the null hypothesis in Formula 9.1 in the next chapter.) Because in Formula 9.1 $H_0 : \overline{X}_1 = \overline{X}_2$, we can subtract $\overline{X}_2$ from both sides of the equal sign. This results in:

$$H_0 : \overline{X}_1 - \overline{X}_2 = 0 \qquad \text{(Formula 9.2)}$$

Formula 9.2 is therefore mathematically equal to Formula 9.1, meaning it is still not the correct null hypothesis for a paired-samples *t*-test. So, we need to further adjust this null hypothesis. Because every score in the first group is paired with a score in the second group, we can test the null hypothesis that the difference between *every* pair of scores is 0 (not just the mean). In short,

$$X_{1i} - X_{2i} = D_i \qquad \text{(Formula 9.3)}$$

As in Formula 9.1, the subscripts (in this case 1*i* and 2*i*) are just for notation. This formula just means that for each pair of ratings we can find the difference between the two scores, and we call this difference D_i or just D. Therefore, if we find the difference for every pair of scores, we can examine the magnitude of the differences between the two sets of scores. But examining all of these difference scores (i.e., D values) would be difficult. Creating a statistical model that summarizes these difference scores would make it easier to understand the typical difference score. We use $\overline{D}$ as a statistical model that indicates the mean of the differences.

Finally, remember that the null hypothesis is always that there is no difference between groups or no impact of a treatment. In the context of a paired-samples *t*-test, this means that the typical D value (i.e., $\overline{D}$) is 0. Therefore, the null hypothesis for a paired-samples *t*-test is:

$$H_0 : \overline{D} = 0 \qquad \text{(Formula 9.4)}$$

In other words, the null hypothesis in a paired-samples *t*-test is a model that states that the average difference between a subject's scores in Group 1 and Group 2 is zero. In the Waite et al. (2015) example, this indicates that the mean difference between two scores in the same pair of sibling ratings is 0. If the statistical model of the null hypothesis fits the Waite et al. (2015) data, it indicates that subjects in the study rate their relationships with their siblings as being equally favorable, regardless of whether the sibling had autism or not.

General Linear Moment 9.1

In Chapter 6, I stated that all inferential statistics procedures in this textbook are members of the GLM, a group of statistical procedures that share several common characteristics. In Chapter 8, I discussed how many procedures of the GLM are special cases or generalizations of other procedures. This General Linear Moment will show you how the paired-samples *t*-test is a special case of the one-sample *t*-test.

This may sound odd. How can a paired-samples *t*-test be a type of one-sample *t*-test, when there are two sample scores in the former and only one sample score in the latter? The key is the difference score (*D*). Calculating a difference score collapses each pair of scores into one score.

With the difference score, we can now conduct a one-sample *t*-test. Chapter 8 showed that a one-sample *t*-test is flexible because it can be used to test the hypothesis that the sample mean is equal to any value (not just μ; see the last third of Chapter 8). This is precisely what we are doing in a paired-samples *t*-test when we test the null hypothesis $H_0 : \overline{D} = 0$. In other words, $\overline{D}$ is just another sample mean, and we are testing the null hypothesis that it is equal to the value of 0 – and this requires a one-sample *t*-test. With this knowledge and a mastery of the one-sample *t*-test, you should be able to master the paired-samples *t*-test.

In some of the earlier General Linear Moments, I showed how the three principles of the GLM apply to the *z*-test (General Linear Moment 7.1) and the one-sample *t*-test (General Linear Moment 8.2). Because a paired-samples *t*-test is just a one-sample *t*-test using difference scores, the same characteristics of the GLM in a one-sample *t*-test also apply to a paired-samples *t*-test. Therefore, the independent variable in a paired-samples *t*-test is the nominal variable that separates the scores into two groups, while the dependent variable is the variable that measures the scores that are used to calculate means. The statistical weights are the Cohen's *d* values, which are also the statistical weights in a paired-samples *t*-test. For a detailed explanation of how each of these issues applies to the GLM in a one-sample *t*-test, see General Linear Moment 8.2.

Set Alpha. Choosing an α value is the third step of any NHST procedure. The default value is .05, which means that the rejection region is 5% of the area of the sampling distribution. This alpha should only change if we have a legitimate reason, such as a very large sample size.

Check Yourself!

- What are paired samples? What is an example of a type of data that would have a paired structure?

- What is the null hypothesis for a paired-samples *t*-test?

- How is a paired-samples *t*-test similar to a one-sample *t*-test? How are the two tests different?

Choose a One-Tailed or a Two-Tailed Test. Step 4 in an NHST procedure is to choose between a one- or a two-tailed test. This determination is made on the basis of whether there is prior research or theory that can be used to predict the results of the NHST. If there is enough information in previous research or theory to permit an investigator to hazard an educated guess about the results, then they should choose a one-tailed test. Otherwise, a two-tailed test is appropriate. This is the same rule that determines, in a *z*-test and a one-sample *t*-test, whether to conduct a one-tailed or a two-tailed test.

As in a *z*-test and a one-sample *t*-test, the decision to conduct a one-tailed or a two-tailed test determines the alternative hypothesis. There are two possible alternative hypotheses for a one-tailed, paired-samples *t*-test:

$$H_1 : \overline{D} < 0 \qquad \text{(Formula 9.5)}$$

and

$$H_1 : \overline{D} > 0 \qquad \text{(Formula 9.6)}$$

Formula 9.5 is an appropriate alternative hypothesis if you believe that the mean of differences between paired scores will be less than 0. This means that you would be putting your entire rejection region on the left side of the sampling distribution, as in Figure 9.1a. Formula 9.6 is an appropriate alternative hypothesis if you believe that the mean of differences between paired scores will be greater than 0. This would put all of your rejection region on the right side of the distribution, as pictured in Figure 9.1b.

If you decide to conduct a two-tailed test, there is only one possible alternative hypothesis in a paired-samples *t*-test:

$$H_1 : \overline{D} \neq 0 \qquad \text{(Formula 9.7)}$$

If Formula 9.7 is your alternative hypothesis, then you are saying that you don't know whether $\overline{D}$ will be greater than or less than 0. That would require dividing the rejection region in half, as pictured in Figure 9.1c.

In their search of the previous literature about sibling relationships and autism, Waite et al. (2015) found that there was very little information that they could use to make an educated guess about their results. Therefore, a two-tailed test is appropriate for the paired data, and the correct alternative hypothesis is $H_1 : \overline{D} \neq 0$, which is Formula 9.7.

One characteristic of Figures 9.1a–9.1c is worth mentioning at this point because it is an important difference between the paired-samples *t*-test and the previous NHST procedures that we have discussed. All three figures show the sampling distribution for a paired-samples *t*-test. In a *z*-test and a one-sample *t*-test, the sampling distribution consisted of means, and that is why the center of the distributions was μ. (Recall from Chapter 6 that the mean of an infinite number of sample means is equal to μ, so the center of a sampling distribution of means will be μ.) However, *in a paired-samples t-test, our sampling distribution consists of differences between paired scores.* In theory, each *D* score is the difference of means selected from different population groups. When we subtract one score in the pair from another, we are estimating $\mu_1 - \mu_2$, and so our sampling

(a)

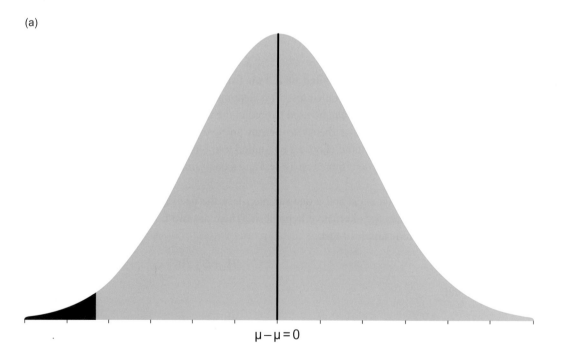

$$\mu - \mu = 0$$

Figure 9.1a A sampling distribution for a paired-samples *t*-test with the rejection region on the left side of the distribution. The alternative hypothesis for this distribution is $H_1 : \overline{D} < 0$. Notice that the distribution consists of differences between means – not sample means themselves (as in a *z*-test and one-sample *t*-test).

(b)

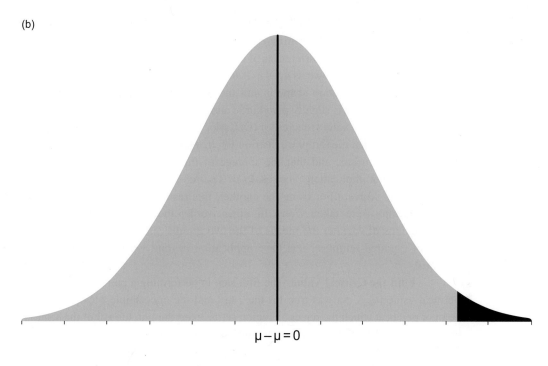

$\mu - \mu = 0$

Figure 9.1b A sampling distribution for a paired-samples *t*-test with the rejection region on the right side of the distribution. The alternative hypothesis for this distribution is $H_1 : \overline{D} > 0$. Notice that the distribution consists of differences between means – not sample means themselves (as in a *z*-test and one-sample *t*-test).

(c)

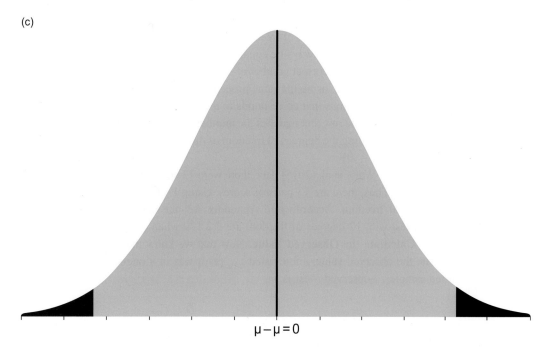

$\mu - \mu = 0$

Figure 9.1c A sampling distribution for a paired-samples *t*-test with the rejection region divided in half, with each portion put into each tail of the distribution. The alternative hypothesis for this distribution is $H_1 : \overline{D} \neq 0$. Notice that the distribution consists of differences between means – not sample means themselves (as in a *z*-test and one-sample *t*-test).

distribution of scores is actually a distribution of $\overline{D}$ values. If the null hypothesis is perfectly true, then $\mu_1 - \mu_2 = 0$, and this zero difference between population means will be the midpoint of the sampling distribution of the differences of means. This is why in Figures 9.1a–9.1c, the center of the sampling distribution is shown as $\mu_1 - \mu_2 = 0$. Although the sampling distribution no longer consists of $\overline{X}$ values, the distribution shape is still the same as for a one-sample *t*-test. This distribution (called a *t*-distribution) is slightly platykurtic and gradually becomes more normal as the number of scores (in this case $\overline{D}$ values) increases (DeCarlo, 1997).

The fact that the sampling distribution in a paired-samples *t*-test consists of the difference between sample means, and that the average of this sampling distribution is $\mu_1 - \mu_2 = 0$, has another important implication. The results of a paired-samples *t*-test do not merely tell us whether the two sets of scores differ from one another; this result also will generalize to the populations that the groups were taken from. In other words, the results of paired-samples *t*-tests are generalizations of whether the means of the two groups' parent populations are equal. Thus, the results of a paired-samples *t*-test have application beyond whether two specific sample groups are equal.

Find the Critical Value. The fifth step in performing a paired-samples *t*-test is to find the *t*-critical value (t_{crit}). As was true for the *z*-test and the one-sample *t*-test, the critical value is the point or points at which the rejection region starts; everything in the tail of the sampling distribution beyond the critical value is in the rejection region (see Figures 9.1a–9.1c).

Because a paired-samples *t*-test is nothing more than a special case of the one-sample *t*-test (see General Linear Moment 9.1), we can use the same table – Appendix A2 – to find the critical value. Again, this requires calculating the degrees of freedom for the test. The formula for this is:

$$\text{df} = n_{pairs} - 1 \qquad \text{(Formula 9.8)}$$

In Formula 9.8, df is the degrees of freedom for the paired-samples *t*-test, and n_{pairs} is the number of pairs of scores, which will always be equal to the number of difference scores in the sample.

After finding the correct number of degrees of freedom, you are ready to use Appendix A2 to find the *t*-critical value, using the same procedure, as in Chapter 8 for a one-sample *t*-test. That is, you use the set of columns that corresponds to the desired type of test (i.e., one-tailed or two-tailed test). Then you find the row that matches the number of degrees of freedom (or the highest row in the table without exceeding the degrees of freedom of the data). That row will display the *t*-critical value for $\alpha = .05$ and $\alpha = .01$.

For the Waite et al. (2015) data, there were 13 subjects, who each gave two ratings (one for each sibling). Thus, there are 13 pairs of scores. Using Formula 9.8, we find that there are $13 - 1 = 12$ degrees of freedom. According to Appendix A2, the critical values for a two-tailed, paired-samples *t*-test with 12 degrees of freedom are ± 2.179 when $\alpha = .05$.

Calculate the Observed Value. Now that we know the critical value, the sixth step is to calculate the observed value, abbreviated t_{obs} (as it was in a one-sample *t*-test). The formula for a paired-samples, *t*-observed *t*-test is:

$$t_{obs} = \frac{\overline{D}}{\left(\frac{s_D}{\sqrt{n_D}}\right)} \qquad \text{(Formula 9.9)}$$

In Formula 9.9, $\overline{D}$ symbolizes the mean of the difference scores, s_D refers to the standard deviation of difference scores, and n_D is the number of difference scores (i.e., number of pairs in the data).

Table 9.1 Level of agreement with the statement "I feel that my sibling understands me well"

Ratings on siblings with autism	Ratings on siblings without autism	Difference score
4	5	4 − 5 = −1
4	4	4 − 4 = 0
5	4	5 − 4 = 1
4	4	4 − 4 = 0
4	3	4 − 3 = 1
1	4	1 − 4 = −3
2	4	2 − 4 = −2
4	3	4 − 3 = 1
2	3	2 − 3 = −1
3	4	3 − 4 = −1
3	4	3 − 4 = −1
2	4	2 − 4 = −2
3	5	3 − 5 = −2

Note. The data in the first two columns are arranged in rows according to their pairings.

In the Waite et al. (2015) data, subjects were asked to rate how strongly they agreed with the statement, "I feel that my sibling understands me well," for one sibling with autism and another sibling without autism. This was a 5-point rating scale: 1 = strongly disagree, 2 = disagree, 3 = neutral, 4 = agree, and 5 = strongly agree. The data are shown in Table 9.1.

The first step in finding t_{obs} is to calculate difference scores for each pair of scores. The right column in Table 9.1 shows how this is done for each pair of scores for the Waite et al. (2015) data. Then we must calculate the mean (i.e., $\overline{D}$) and standard deviation (s_D) for the difference scores. For the mean:

$$\overline{D} = \frac{-1 + 0 + 1 + 0 + 1 - 3 - 2 + 1 - 1 - 1 - 1 - 2 - 2}{13} = \frac{-10}{13} = -0.769$$

This $\overline{D}$ value indicates that the average difference between scores in the sample is .769 points; the negative value indicates that the sibling without autism was rated higher on the statement, "My sibling understands me well," than the sibling with autism.

Calculating the standard deviation of difference scores is as follows:

$$s_D = \sqrt{\frac{\sum (D_i - \overline{D})^2}{n_D - 1}}$$

This is the same standard deviation formula that we saw earlier in Formula 4.9, but the X values have been replaced by D's to show that we are working with difference scores (not raw scores). The preliminary calculations for the standard deviation of D are shown in Table 9.2.

Table 9.2

D	Deviation score for *D*	Squared deviation score for *D*
−1	−1 − −0.769 = −0.231	$(-0.231)^2 = 0.053$
0	0 − −0.769 = 0.769	$(0.769)^2 = 0.592$
1	1 − −0.769 = 1.769	$(1.769)^2 = 3.130$
0	0 − −0.769 = 0.769	$(0.769)^2 = 0.592$
1	1 − −0.769 = 1.769	$(1.769)^2 = 3.130$
−3	−3 − −0.769 = −2.231	$(-2.231)^2 = 4.976$
−2	−2 − −0.769 = −1.231	$(-1.231)^2 = 1.515$
1	1 − −0.769 = 1.769	$(1.769)^2 = 3.130$
−1	−1 − −0.769 = −0.231	$(-0.231)^2 = 0.053$
−1	−1 − −0.769 = −0.231	$(-0.231)^2 = 0.053$
−1	−1 − −0.769 = −0.231	$(-0.231)^2 = 0.053$
−2	−2 − −0.769 = −1.231	$(-1.231)^2 = 1.515$
−2	−2 − −0.769 = −1.231	$(-1.231)^2 = 1.515$

Adding up the numbers in the right column produces:

$$0.053 + 0.592 + 3.130 + 0.592 + 3.130 + 4.976 + 1.515 + 3.130 + 0.053 + 0.053 + 0.053 + 1.515 + 1.515 = 20.308$$

Dividing this number by $n_D - 1$ results in:

$$\frac{20.308}{13-1} = \frac{20.308}{12} = 1.692$$

This is the variance of difference scores. The last step is to find the square root of this value:

$$s_D = \sqrt{1.692} = 1.301$$

Therefore, $\overline{D} = -0.769$, $s_D = 1.301$, and $n_D = 13$. To find t_{obs}, we must plug these values into Formula 9.9:

$$t_{obs} = \frac{\overline{D}}{\left(\dfrac{s_D}{\sqrt{n_D}}\right)} = \frac{-0.769}{\left(\dfrac{1.301}{\sqrt{13}}\right)}$$

Now we solve for t_{obs}:

$$t_{obs} = \frac{-0.769}{\left(\dfrac{1.301}{\sqrt{13}}\right)} = \frac{-0.769}{\left(\dfrac{1.301}{3.606}\right)} = \frac{-0.769}{.361} = -2.130$$

Therefore, $t_{obs} = -2.130$.

Compare the Observed Value and the Critical Value. The seventh step in a paired-samples *t*-test is to compare the t_{obs} and t_{crit} values. In the example from the Waite et al. (2015) study, $t_{crit} = \pm 2.179$ and $t_{obs} = -2.130$. This comparison is presented in visual form in Figure 9.2. The figure shows the rejection region (half of which is in each tail of the sampling distribution

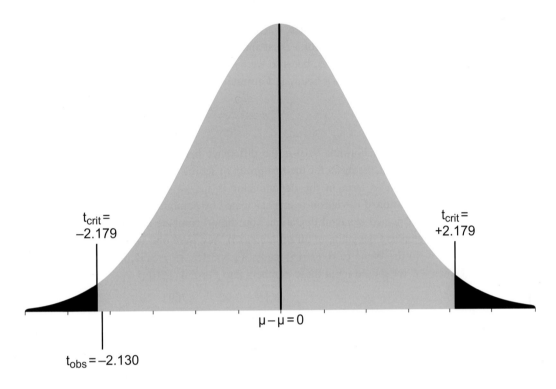

Figure 9.2 Visual schematic for the Waite et al. (2015) data. For this example $t_{crit} = \pm 2.179$ and $t_{obs} = -2.130$. Because t_{obs} is outside the rejection region (which is on the left side of the sampling distribution starting at -2.179 and going to $-\infty$), the null hypothesis ($H_0 : \overline{D} = 0$) should be retained.

because we are conducting a two-tailed test), which begins at the t_{crit} values of ± 2.179. The t_{obs} value of -2.130 is less extreme than one of the critical values (-2.179), and this means that it is outside the rejection region. As a result, we should retain the null hypothesis, which was $\overline{D} = 0$. We can thus conclude that the null hypothesis is a suitable model for our data. Practically, this means that subjects in the Waite et al. (2015) study felt that their sibling with autism and their sibling without autism knew them equally well.

Check Yourself!

- In a paired-samples *t*-test, how do you determine whether to conduct a one-tailed test or a two-tailed test?

- What is the statistic that the sampling distribution in a paired-samples *t*-test consists of?

- What does n_D symbolize in a paired-samples *t*-test?

- After finding the critical value and the observed value, how do you determine whether to reject or retain the null hypothesis?

Calculate an Effect Size. The eighth and final step of all NHST procedures is to calculate an effect size. Just as it was for a *z*-test and a one-sample *t*-test, the effect size for a paired-samples *t*-test is Cohen's *d*. However, because we have two sets of scores, the Cohen's *d* formula must be modified slightly, as shown below in Formula 9.10:

$$d = \frac{\overline{X}_1 - \overline{X}_2}{s_{pooled}} = \frac{\overline{D}}{s_{pooled}}$$ (Formula 9.10)

The numerator of Formula 9.10 is the difference between the two means of the two samples of scores (i.e., $\overline{X}_1$ is the mean for the first group of scores, and $\overline{X}_2$ is the mean for the second group of scores). The only term in the denominator is s_{pooled}, which is the pooled standard deviation. A **pooled standard deviation** is one calculated by combining the data from two or more samples. To find the pooled standard deviation, you should combine the two groups of scores together and find the standard deviation of all of them as if they were one sample.

In the Waite et al. (2015) study, $\overline{X}_1 = 3.15$, $\overline{X}_2 = 3.92$, and $s_{pooled} = 0.989$. To solve for Cohen's *d*, we should input these numbers into Formula 9.10:

$$d = \frac{3.15 - 3.92}{0.989} = \frac{-.769}{0.989} = -.778$$

This Cohen's *d* value indicates that – on average – the subjects in Waite et al.'s (2015) study gave ratings that were 0.778 standard deviation lower for their sibling with autism when asked whether their sibling understood them well. Another way of thinking about this effect size is that the mean ratings for the two groups are 0.778 standard deviation apart. Although this is a larger effect size than we often see in the social sciences, the sample size is so small that we still retained the null hypothesis.

Sidebar 9.2 **Effect size options**

There is some professional disagreement among social scientists and statisticians about the most appropriate effect size for a paired-samples *t*-test. The Cohen's *d* equation shown in Formula 9.10 is probably the most commonly reported effect size, but there are other options. In this sidebar I will discuss two other plausible options.

One alternative is to use the standard deviation of difference scores (i.e., s_D) in the denominator of Cohen's *d* instead of s_{pooled} (Volker, 2006). This would produce the following formula:

$$d = \frac{\overline{X}_1 - \overline{X}_2}{s_D} = \frac{\overline{D}}{s_D}$$

If we were to calculate this version of Cohen's *d* with the Waite et al. (2015) data (where $s_D = 1.301$), we would get the following result:

$$d = \frac{3.15 - 3.92}{1.301} = \frac{-.769}{1.301} = -.591$$

In this case, the equation that has the standard deviation of the difference scores in the denominator produces a Cohen's *d* that is noticeably smaller than the result of Formula 9.10 (which was *d* = −.778).

In studies that examine growth or change of individuals over time or the impact of a treatment or therapy, the pooled standard deviation and the standard deviation of difference scores are often inappropriate. This is because it is common in these types of studies for the standard deviation of individuals' scores to increase over time or after treatment. This increase in standard deviations is so common that one prominent social scientist called it the "First Law of Individual Differences" (Jensen, 1991, p. 178). Therefore, combining these standard deviations may distort effect size calculations. When a treatment is probably increasing the standard deviation of one group of scores, the preferred effect size is called **Glass's delta (Δ)**, the formula for which is:

$$\Delta = \frac{\overline{X}_1 - \overline{X}_2}{s_C}$$

(see Glass, 1976, 1977; M. L. Smith & Glass, 1977). Just as in Formula 9.10 and the other version of Cohen's *d* in this sidebar, the numerator is the difference between two sample means. The denominator of Glass's Δ, though, is the standard deviation of the group that has not received the treatment (i.e., a control group or a pre-treatment group). It is not appropriate to use Glass's Δ with the Waite et al. (2015) example because there was no treatment in that study, but Glass's Δ tends to produce effect sizes that are larger than Cohen's *d* with the pooled standard deviation in the denominator.

Because there are three possible options for calculating an effect size when conducting a paired-samples *t*-test, it is best practice to always specify which effect size you are reporting (i.e., Cohen's *d* or Glass's Δ), and how you calculated the effect size. This will make your results unambiguous and help your reader correctly interpret your statistics.

Finding *p*

Because the paired-samples *t*-test uses the same table as the one-sample *t*-test, it should be no surprise that finding a *p*-value is the same for both methods. With the tables in this textbook, it is not possible to calculate an exact *p*-value, but we can state whether *p* is greater than .05, between .01 and .05, or less than .01. The rules to determine *p* are:

- If the null hypothesis is retained when $\alpha = .05$, then $p > .05$.
- If the null hypothesis is rejected when $\alpha = .05$, but retained when $\alpha = .01$, then $.01 < p < .05$.
- If the null hypothesis is rejected when $\alpha = .01$, then $p < .01$.

For this chapter's example from Waite et al. (2015), we retained the null hypothesis when $\alpha = .05$. Thus, *p* must be greater than .05.

If we had rejected the null hypothesis, the next step would be to determine whether to reject the null hypothesis when $\alpha = .01$. You would determine this by finding the t_{crit} value in Appendix A2 and comparing that to the t_{obs} value of −2.130. If you reject the null hypothesis when $\alpha = .01$, then *p* must be less than .01. If you retain the null hypothesis when $\alpha = .01$, then *p* is between .01 and .05 (i.e., $.05 \geq p \geq .01$).

Old Concerns

The paired-samples *t*-test is another NHST method, meaning that the same concerns and caveats of other NHST methods are also applicable to the paired-samples *t*-test. These include concerns about Type I and Type II errors, sensitivity to sample size, and subjectivity of decisions.

Type I and Type II Errors. You may remember that a Type I error occurs when the researcher rejects a null hypothesis that is actually true. A Type II error occurs when the researcher retains a null hypothesis that is actually false. Unfortunately, we never know whether the null hypothesis is true or not. (If we did, there would be no need to test the null hypothesis!) Type I and Type II errors are both possible for the paired-samples *t*-test, but never at the same time.

Sidebar 9.3   **Mnemonic device**

When I first learned about Type I and Type II errors, I had difficulty remembering their definitions. Years later, one of my students taught me an effective mnemonic device to remember them:

- A Type I error occurs when you reject a null hypothesis that is right – "reject" and "right" both start with the letter *r*.
- A Type II error occurs when you fail to reject a false null hypothesis – "fail" and "false" both start with the letter *f*.

Sidebar 9.4   **Which is more serious: Type I or Type II error?**

I often have students ask me, "Which error is more serious: Type I or Type II error?" The answer is, "It depends."

As stated in this chapter (and Chapters 7 and 8), a Type I error occurs when a true null hypothesis is rejected. A Type II error is the reverse: retaining a false null hypothesis. Ideally, we would hope to never make mistakes, but sampling error means that Type I or Type II errors will happen from time to time.

The α value is the maximum probability of Type I error that we are willing to allow in our NHST procedure. Therefore, reducing α also reduces the probability of Type I error. Unfortunately, this also increases the probability of Type II error. On the other hand, raising α increases the probability of Type I error, but reduces the probability of Type II error. Although an α value of .05 is the default, there may be reasons to raise or lower α if the consequences of one type of error are very serious.

For example, in medicine a Type I error is called a "false positive," and a Type II error is called a "false negative." In medical tests the null hypothesis is that the person does *not* have a disease. In a false positive the test shows that a person has a disease when in reality they do not; a false negative shows that a person is healthy when they actually have a disease. Depending on the disease, a false positive or a false negative could have very serious consequences. A person who receives a false positive may be subjected to expensive, unnecessary (and sometimes painful) treatment. Even if a follow-up test indicates that the person does not have the disease, the patient could still be subjected to a lot of emotional turmoil and stress. On the other hand, a person who receives a false negative in their medical test would have their condition go untreated, which may be fatal. Increasing the α value will increase Type I errors (which would result in more unnecessary treatments), but will decrease Type II errors (and therefore prevent sick people from dying). The reverse is true: decreasing α would decrease Type I errors (and reduce unnecessary treatments), but will increase Type II errors (and result in more people avoiding treatment when they need it).

These are not hypothetical arguments. In medical research there is often discussion of the costs and benefits (in terms of money and lives saved) of medical tests, such as mammograms, magnetic resonance imaging, and ultrasound screening for diseases like breast cancer (Feig, 2010). Likewise, educators select students for admission to education programs using standardized tests (e.g., McBee, Peters, & Waterman, 2014). In this situation, a Type I error would be mistakenly admitting an unqualified student to a program, while a Type II error would occur when a qualified student is denied entry to an educational program. Knowing the consequences of Type I and Type II error rates of these medical or educational tests can help people make better decisions about patients' health or students' educational progress.

The ideal balance between Type I and Type II errors will depend on the consequences of each type of error. For example, an important British legal theorist once stated that it is "better that ten guilty persons escape, than one innocent party suffer" (Blackstone, 1765/1892, p. 713). This legal principle has been firmly established in most English-speaking countries and is designed to minimize Type I error (which would be imprisoning an innocent person), even if it results in a high rate of Type II error (which would be freeing a guilty person). But in situations where the consequences of an error are much less drastic, it may be better to find a balance that minimizes the type of either error simultaneously. McBee et al. (2014) did this in an article when they discussed the different methods of combining data to admit children to advanced academic programs. For many of these programs the decision to admit a child is not irreversible, and the consequences of mistakes (e.g., not admitting a qualified child or admitting an unqualified one) are rarely severe and lifelong. Thus, the authors argued that often the best course of action is to minimize both Type I and Type II errors in order to maximize correct decisions.

The important lesson to gather from these examples is that (1) we can never escape the possibility of Type I or Type II errors, and (2) the appropriate error rate depends greatly on the context of the NHST procedure or the decision to be made.

Statistical Significance. In the previous chapter, I discussed how the phrase "statistical significance" only refers to whether the null hypothesis was rejected or not. When results are "statistically significant," it means that the null hypothesis was rejected. When results are "statistically insignificant," the null hypothesis was retained. Remember that statistical significance has nothing to do with the importance of the results of a scientific study (see Sidebar 8.3).

Subjective Decisions. In Chapters 7 and 8, we saw how there are subjective decisions in NHST procedures, especially in the decision of α and whether to conduct a one- or a two-tailed test. All of these statements are true of the paired-samples t-test. Once again, you should always justify your decisions when conducting any NHST.

Sensitivity to Sample Size. As an NHST, the paired-samples t-test is sensitive to sample size. Like the one-sample t-test and the z-test, large sample sizes make it easier to reject the null hypothesis than small sample sizes do. For this reason, calculating an effect size is essential, because it is not susceptible to changes in the sample size.

Guided Practice 9.1

To provide another example of a paired-samples t-test, we are going to examine data from a study by Reyes and Asbrand (2005) of the effectiveness of play therapy for children who have been sexually abused. The authors measured the anxiety symptoms of 18 children before therapy and after 9 months of play therapy. A paired-samples t-test is appropriate in this example because all of the children have two scores: one taken before treatment and another collected after treatment.

Step 1: Form Groups

For Reyes and Asbrand (2005), the first group of scores was the pre-therapy scores, and the second group of scores was the post-therapy scores.

Step 2: Define the Null Hypothesis

The null hypothesis for a paired-samples *t*-test is always $H_0 : \overline{D} = 0$. This is a mathematical way of stating that the null hypothesis is that the mean difference between pre-treatment and post-treatment scores will be zero.

Step 3: Set Alpha

The default α value in a paired-samples *t*-test is .05. We really don't have a reason to change this α, so we are going to leave it at .05.

Step 4: Choose a One- or Two-Tailed Test, Which Determines the Alternative Hypothesis

Presumably, people in therapy should improve over time, so a one-tailed test seems appropriate. In Reyes and Asbrand's (2005) study, high numbers indicated stronger, more problematic symptoms. Therefore, people who are getting better after therapy should have higher scores before therapy and lower scores after therapy. That means that we would expect the difference scores to be positive because they are calculated by subtracting the post-therapy score from the higher pre-therapy score. Thus, the appropriate alternative hypothesis is $H_1 : \overline{D} > 0$.

Step 5: Find the Critical Values

To find the t_{crit} values for this example, we must first calculate the degrees of freedom. Formula 9.8 states that df $= n_{pairs} - 1$, where n_{pairs} is the number of pairs of scores. In Reyes and Asbrand's (2005) study, there are 18 children, each of whom has two scores. This means that there are 18 pairs of scores. Therefore, df $= 18 - 1 = 17$.

Now we must turn to Appendix A2 to find the t_{crit} value for a one-tailed test when df $= 17$ and $\alpha = .05$. According to Appendix A2, the critical value is either $+1.740$ or -1.740. We must choose one of these critical values. Because we believe that the difference scores should be positive (see Step 4), we should also have a positive critical value: $+1.740$.

Step 6: Calculate the Observed Value

According to Formula 9.9, the formula for calculating t_{obs} in a paired-samples *t*-test is $t_{obs} = \dfrac{\overline{D}}{\left(\dfrac{s_D}{\sqrt{n_D}} \right)}$. In Reyes and Asbrand's (2005) study, $\overline{D} = 8.39$, $s_D = 12.49$, and $n = 18$. Plugging these numbers into Formula 9.9 produces

$$t_{obs} = \frac{8.39}{\left(\dfrac{12.49}{\sqrt{18}}\right)}$$

The square root of 18 is 4.24, so replacing that in the formula results in:

$$t_{obs} = \frac{8.39}{\left(\dfrac{12.49}{4.243}\right)}$$

Solving for the fraction produces:

$$t_{obs} = \frac{8.39}{2.944}$$

which is equal to

$$t_{obs} = 2.850$$

Step 7: Compare the Observed and Critical Values and Find p

Step 5 showed us that $t_{crit} = 1.740$. Step 6 showed us that $t_{obs} = 2.850$. Drawing these critical and observed values will result in a diagram that resembles Figure 9.3. It is clear that if the rejection region starts at 1.740 (the critical value) and continues to $+\infty$, 2.85 (the observed value) must be inside the rejection region. Therefore, we should reject the null hypothesis, which was that the children would not improve at all from their pre-therapy scores to their post-therapy scores (i.e., $H_0 : \overline{D} = 0$).

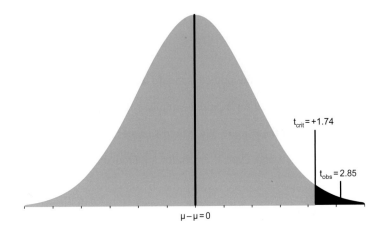

Figure 9.3 Visual schematic showing the sampling distribution for the Reyes and Asbrand (2005) study. The rejection region starts at the t_{crit} value of +1.74 and continues to $+\infty$ (shown in the shaded region). The t_{obs} value +2.85 is inside this rejection region, so it is appropriate to reject the null hypothesis, $H_0 : \overline{D} = 0$.

Step 8: Calculate an Effect Size

Using the version of Cohen's d found in Formula 9.10, we can find the effect size through the equation $d = \frac{\overline{X}_1 - \overline{X}_2}{s_{pooled}}$. According to Reyes and Asbrand (2005), $\overline{X}_1 = 59.11$, $\overline{X}_2 = 50.72$, and $s_{pooled} = 10.29$. Putting these values into Formula 9.10 produces:

$$d = \frac{59.11 - 50.72}{10.29}$$

The numerator is the difference between the two means. Solving for the numerator produces

$$d = \frac{8.39}{10.29}$$

giving a final answer of

$$d = 0.815$$

Thus, children who were victims of sexual abuse had an improvement of 0.815 standard deviation after therapy. Because this effect size is so large, the small sample size (i.e., 18) was no impediment to rejecting the null hypothesis.

Optional Practice: Finding *p*

Because we rejected the null hypothesis when $\alpha = .05$, we know that p must be less than .05. The remaining question is whether p is less than .01 or not. To determine this, we must ascertain the t_{crit} value in Appendix A2. This t_{crit} value is +2.567. Our t_{obs} value is equal to 2.85. Comparing these two values indicates that the t_{obs} value is still within the rejection region when $\alpha = .01$. Therefore, $p < .01$, and we can determine that the probability of Type I error would be less than 1% if the null hypothesis were perfectly true in the population.

Check Yourself!

- How do you calculate the pooled standard deviation?
- What is the effect size for a paired-samples *t*-test?
- How do you find the *p*-value in a paired-samples *t*-test?
- Define the Type I and Type II errors for a paired-samples *t*-test.

Summary

Social scientists are frequently interested in differences in paired scores. Paired scores occur when each score in one sample corresponds to a single score in another sample. Examples of paired scores include scores taken from the same individual (as in the main example in this chapter), scores from spouses, or scores taken from the same group of people at different times. Whenever paired scores occur, we can measure whether the difference between them is statistically significant through a paired-samples t-test.

A paired-samples t-test is very similar to a one-sample t-test. The major difference is that the sampling distribution consists of differences between group means. This necessitates a few minor changes to the t-test procedure. The eight steps of null hypothesis testing still hold for a paired-samples t-test. The major differences are:

- The null hypothesis for a paired-samples t-test is now $H_0 : \overline{D} = 0$, where $\overline{D}$ is the average difference between paired scores. This means that the alternative hypotheses have changed, too. For a one-tailed test, the alternative hypotheses are $H_1 : \overline{D} < 0$ or $H_1 : \overline{D} > 0$; for a two-tailed test or $H_1 : \overline{D} \neq 0$.
- n now refers to the number of *score pairs* (called n_{pairs}) in the data, not the number of scores.
- The Cohen's d formula has also changed slightly so that it is now $d = \frac{\overline{X}_1 - \overline{X}_2}{s_{pooled}}$, where the numerator is the difference between the two sample means and s_{pooled} is the pooled standard deviation, which is the standard deviation of both groups' data combined.

However, all of the other aspects of a paired-samples t-test are identical to a one-sample t-test, including the default α value, the rationale for selecting a one- or a two-tailed test, how to compare the observed and critical values in order to determine whether to reject the null hypothesis, and the interpretation of the effect size.

Because the paired-samples t-test is a null hypothesis statistical significance testing (NHST) procedure, the caveats of all NHSTs apply to paired-samples t-tests. These caveats include a sensitivity to sample size, the possibility of committing a Type I or Type II error, subjective decisions in NHST, and the fact that "statistical significance" is not synonymous with "importance."

Reflection Questions: Comprehension

1. Why do the one-sample t-test and the paired-samples t-test share so many similarities?
2. How do you calculate difference scores for a paired-samples t-test?
3. Explain the difference between a natural pairing and an artificial pairing of scores.
4. In a paired-samples t-test, how do you find the degrees of freedom?
5. How do we determine the range of a p-value for a paired-samples t-test?
6. Both Glass's Δ and Cohen's d are effect sizes, but how do the two differ?

Reflection Questions: Application

7. Calculate the degrees of freedom for the following numbers of score pairs:
   a. 11
   b. 28
   c. 97
   d. 123
   e. 412

8. A family science researcher is interested in whether families spend more time together after the parents take a parenting class. To measure the time families spend together, the researcher collects data on how many dinners per week the family eats together. The results for 16 families are below.

Family no.	Dinners Together Per Week (before classes)	Dinners Together Per Week (after classes)
1	2	5
2	4	5
3	6	6
4	4	4
5	1	3
6	0	3
7	2	2
8	1	3
9	3	2
10	3	2
11	4	4
12	5	5
13	7	6
14	1	4
15	0	3
16	4	5

a. Explain why these scores are considered paired data.
b. Find a difference score for each family.
c. Calculate the mean and standard deviation of the difference scores for the families.
d. If we conduct a paired-samples *t*-test for these data, what would the null hypothesis be?
e. What would the α value be for this NHST?
f. Is a one- or a two-tailed hypothesis appropriate for this scenario? Justify your response.
g. What is the alternative hypothesis for this paired-samples *t*-test?
h. Calculate the degrees of freedom in this example.
i. Find the t_{crit} value.
j. Calculate the t_{obs} value for the data.
k. Should you reject or retain the null hypothesis?
l. Calculate Cohen's *d* for these data. Use s_{pooled} in the standard deviation.
m. Calculate Cohen's *d* for these data, using the equation in Sidebar 9.2.
n. Calculate Glass's Δ for these data.
o. Why might Glass's Δ be an appropriate effect size for these data?
p. Find a *p*-value for these data.

9. In their study of children in play therapy (see Guided Practice 9.1), Reyes and Asbrand (2005) also measured the level of depression that the children had before and after therapy. They found that $\overline{D} = 7.89$, $s_D = 11.66$, and $n_D = 18$. These difference scores were calculated by taking the pre-therapy scores and subtracting the post-therapy scores.
a. Explain why these scores are considered paired data.

b. If we conduct a paired-samples t-test for these data, what would the null hypothesis be?
c. What would the α value be for this NHST?
d. Is a one- or a two-tailed hypothesis appropriate for this scenario? Justify your response.
e. What is the alternative hypothesis for this paired-samples t-test?
f. Calculate the degrees of freedom in this example.
g. Find the t_{crit} value.
h. Calculate the t_{obs} value for the data.
i. Should you reject or retain the null hypothesis?
j. Calculate Cohen's d for these data, using the equation in Sidebar 9.2.
k. Find a p-value for these data.

10. Reyes and Asbrand (2005) also measured unhealthy fantasy behaviors in child abuse victims before and after therapy. They found that $\overline{D} = 2.50$, $s_D = 8.16$, and $n_D = 18$. These difference scores were calculated by taking the pre-therapy scores and subtracting the post-therapy scores.
a. Explain why these scores are considered paired data.
b. If we conduct a paired-samples t-test for these data, what would the null hypothesis be?
c. What would the α value be for this NHST?
d. Is a one- or a two-tailed hypothesis appropriate for this scenario? Justify your response.
e. What is the alternative hypothesis for this paired-samples t-test?
f. Calculate the degrees of freedom in this example.
g. Find the t_{crit} value.
h. Calculate the t_{obs} value for the data.
i. Should you reject or retain the null hypothesis?
j. Calculate Cohen's d for these data, using the equation in Sidebar 9.2.
k. Find a p-value for these data.

11. Describe the relationship between the sample size and the decision to reject or retain the null hypothesis in a paired-samples t-test.

12. Javier is conducting a paired-samples t-test, and decides that he wants to avoid Type I errors as much as he can. Therefore, he sets his α value at .000001. "This way I will be sure that I won't make a mistake when I do my t-test," he says. What is the flaw in his logic?

13. Audrey is interested in studying twins. Knowing that members of a twin pair would have paired scores, she conducts a paired-samples t-test to determine whether identical twins have different levels of extraversion. For her data, she finds that $\overline{D} = 1.18$, $s_D = 2.04$, and $n_D = 34$.
a. What is the null hypothesis?
b. What would the α value be for this NHST?
c. Is a one- or a two-tailed hypothesis appropriate for this scenario? Justify your response.
d. What is the alternative hypothesis for this paired-samples t-test?
e. Calculate the degrees of freedom in this example.
f. Find the t_{crit} value.
g. Calculate the t_{obs} value for the data.
h. Should you reject or retain the null hypothesis?
i. Calculate Cohen's d for these data, using the equation in Sidebar 9.2.
j. Find a p-value for these data.
k. Interpret the results of the paired-samples t-test. In other words, do identical twins have, on average, the same level of extraversion? (Hint: remember your null hypothesis!)

14. Audrey also has a sample of fraternal twin pairs. She gives them the same test of extraversion to the fraternal twins and finds that $\overline{D} = 1.34$, $s_D = 2.40$, and $n_D = 15$.

a.   What is the null hypothesis?

b.   What would the α value be for this NHST?

c.   Is a one- or a two-tailed hypothesis appropriate for this scenario? Justify your response.

d.   What is the alternative hypothesis for this paired-samples *t*-test?

e.   Calculate the degrees of freedom in this example.

f.   Find the t_{crit} value.

g.   Calculate the t_{obs} value for the data.

h.   Should you reject or retain the null hypothesis?

i.   Calculate Cohen's *d* for these data, using the equation in Sidebar 9.2.

j.   Find a *p*-value for these data.

k.   Interpret the results of the paired-samples *t*-test. In other words, do identical twins have, on average, the same level of extraversion? (Hint: remember your null hypothesis!)

l.   Compare these results to the results from identical twins. What does that tell you about the similarities (or differences) in personalities among identical and fraternal twins?

15.   Conduct a paired-samples *t*-test if $\overline{D} = 28.20$, $s_D = 145.91$, and $n_D = 81$.

a.   What is the null hypothesis?

b.   What would the α value be for this NHST?

c.   Is a one- or a two-tailed hypothesis appropriate for this scenario? Justify your response.

d.   What is the alternative hypothesis for this paired-samples *t*-test?

e.   Calculate the degrees of freedom in this example.

f.   Find the t_{crit} value.

g.   Calculate the t_{obs} value for the data.

h.   Should you reject or retain the null hypothesis?

i.   Calculate Cohen's *d* for these data, using the equation in Sidebar 9.2.

j.   Find a *p*-value for these data.

Software Guide

The paired-samples *t*-test is similar to conducting a one-sample *t*-test in both Excel and SPSS. For each program there are some slight modifications to perform a paired-samples *t*-test, but performing and interpreting the *t*-test is still relatively simple.

Excel

To conduct a paired-samples *t*-test, you use an Excel function called TTEST, which has two formats:

- For a one-tailed, paired-samples *t*-test: "=TTEST(XX:XX,YY:YY,1,1)"
- For a two-tailed, paired-samples *t*-test: "=TTEST(XX:XX,YY:YY,2,1)"

In each of these formats, the "XX:XX" should be replaced with cells for the sample. The YY:YY should be replaced with a set of cells that all contain the mean of the population. The number of cells for XX:XX and YY:YY should be the same. Figure 9.4a shows how to use the function, and Figure 9.4b shows the results. The results in Excel are the *p*-values – not the t_{obs} values. If the *p*-value

(a)

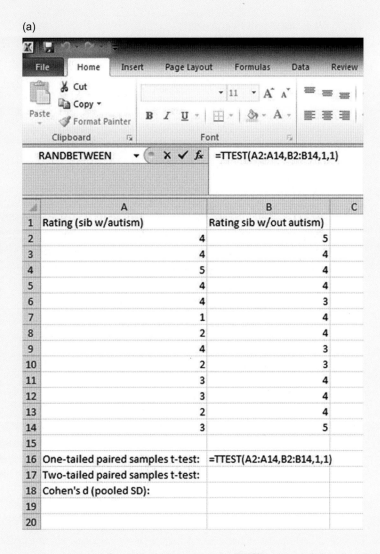

Figure 9.4a Screenshot from Microsoft Excel showing how to use the TTEST function to conduct a paired-samples *t*-test.

is less than alpha, the user should reject the null hypothesis. If the *p-v*alue is greater than alpha, the user should retain the null hypothesis.

Excel does not calculate Cohen's *d* as part of the paired-samples *t*-test. Performing this requires a different function: "=(XX-YY)/ZZ". In this function XX is the first sample's mean, YY is the second sample's mean, and ZZ is the standard deviation of both groups of scores combined. Figure 9.4b shows that Cohen's *d* value in this example is –.778.

SPSS

With the point-and-click interface in SPSS, conducting a paired-samples *t*-test is not difficult. In the data window, the first step is to click "Analyze" → "Compare Means" → "Paired-Samples T Test." This makes a new window appear that is labeled "Paired-Samples T Test" (shown in Figure 9.5).

(b)

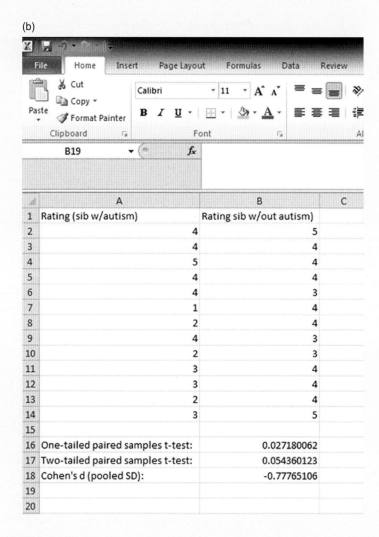

Figure 9.4b Screenshot from Microsoft Excel showing the results of the TTEST function and Cohen's *d*. The results for the paired-sample *t*-tests (in cells B16 and B17) are *p*-values.

In the Paired-Samples T Test window, you should select the variable you wish to use in the *t*-test and click the arrow to bring it into the "Paired Variables" column. When you put two variables in the same row, it means you are using the scores for those two variables to calculate a difference score. When both of these variables are selected sequentially, they will appear in the same row in the right column. This is pictured in Figure 9.6.

After you click "OK," the results appear in the output window. The relevant tables from the results are shown in Figure 9.7. The first table in the figure (labeled "Paired-Samples Statistics") provides the means, standard deviations, and number of pairs for the data. The second table (labeled "Paired-Samples Test") provides the results of the paired-samples *t*-test. In the last column, under the heading "Sig. (2-tailed)," SPSS displays the *p*-value for a two-tailed test. If this value is less than the α, you should reject the null hypothesis; if the *p*-value is greater than the α value, you should retain the null hypothesis.

Reflection Questions: Application   239

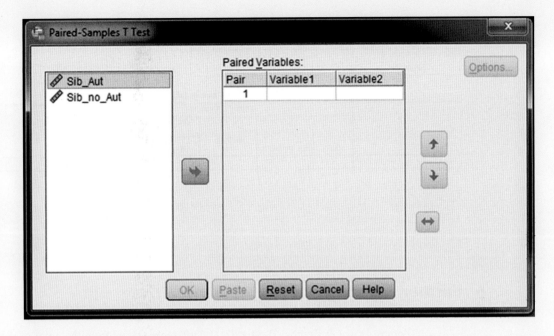

Figure 9.5 The Paired-Samples T Test window in SPSS.

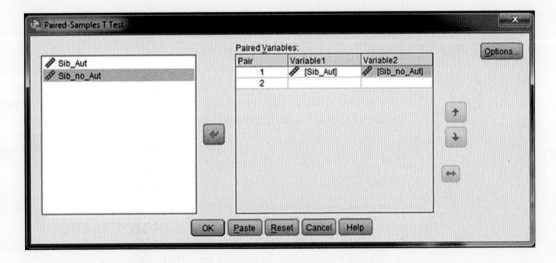

Figure 9.6 The Paired-Samples T Test window in SPSS with two variables selected for a paired-samples *t*-test.

SPSS does not automatically calculate an effect size. However, the information in these two tables can be used to calculate the effect sizes listed in this chapter. For example, for Cohen's *d* in Sidebar 9.2 ($d = \frac{\overline{D}}{s_D}$), you would use the mean and standard deviation labeled "Paired Differences" (in the lower table). SPSS does not conduct one-tailed tests for the paired-samples *t*-test. If you wish to conduct a one-tailed test, you should use the t_{obs} value (labeled "t" in the lower table in Figure 9.7) and compare this value to the t_{crit} value in Appendix A2.

Paired Samples Statistics

		Mean	N	Std. Deviation	Std. Error Mean
Pair 1	Sib_Aut	3.15	13	1.144	.317
	Sib_no_Aut	3.92	13	.641	.178

Paired Samples Test

		Paired Differences							
					95% Confidence Interval of the Difference				
		Mean	Std. Deviation	Std. Error Mean	Lower	Upper	t	df	Sig. (2-tailed)
Pair 1	Sib_Aut - Sib_no_Aut	-.769	1.301	.361	-1.555	.017	-2.132	12	.054

Figure 9.7 Results in SPSS of a paired-samples *t*-test.

Further Reading

- Thomas, D. R., & Zumbo, B. D. (2012). Difference scores from the point of view of reliability and repeated-measures ANOVA: In defense of difference scores for data analysis. *Educational and Psychological Measurement, 72*, 37–43. doi:10.1177/0013164411409929

  * One important consideration of paired-samples *t*-tests is that both scores in the pair have to be measures of the same variable. In other words, it does not make sense (in the paired-samples *t*-test context) to pair anxiety scores with depression scores. But it is fine to pair depression scores with depression scores as long as they are measured in the same manner. Thomas and Zumbo discuss the implications of finding difference scores for the same measures and for different measures.

- Zimmerman, D. W. (1997). Teacher's corner: A note on interpretation of the paired-samples *t* test. *Journal of Educational and Behavioral Statistics, 22*, 349–360. doi:10.3102/10769986022003349

  * Zimmerman explains the paired-samples *t*-test well in this article and explains the advantages and disadvantages of this method compared to the unpaired-samples *t*-test (which I discuss in Chapter 10). Zimmerman also shows how ignoring the paired nature of data can produce distorted results for NHST procedures.

10 Unpaired Two-Sample *t*-Tests

Social science students naturally have a lot of questions. Are college students majoring in the humanities more social than students majoring in the physical sciences? Are religious societies happier than secular societies? Do children with divorced parents have more behavioral problems than children with married parents? Are inmates who attended school in prison less likely to reoffend than inmates who do not receive education?

These questions compare two groups (e.g., children of divorced parents and children of married parents) and ask which group has a higher score on a variable (e.g., number of behavioral problems). These kind of questions are extremely common in the social sciences, so it should not surprise you that there is a statistical method developed to answer them. That method is the **unpaired two-sample *t*-test**, which is a comparison of scores from two different unrelated groups. The topic of this chapter is the unpaired two-sample *t*-test, one of the most common statistical methods in the social sciences.

Learning Goals

- Explain when an unpaired two-sample *t*-test is an appropriate NHST procedure.
- Conduct an unpaired two-sample *t*-test.
- Calculate an effect size (i.e., Cohen's *d*) for an unpaired two-sample *t*-test.
- Show how the unpaired two-sample *t*-test is a member of the general linear model (GLM).
- Correctly find and interpret a *p*-value.

Making Group Comparisons

Answering the questions at the beginning of the chapter requires comparing two scores. When these groups are unrelated to one another, an unpaired-samples *t*-test is an appropriate method of analyzing data. You may remember in Chapter 9 we paired scores, the two sets of scores formed pairs across the datasets (e.g., pre-test and post-test data, or scores about a pair of siblings). This allowed us to simplify the two sets of scores into one group of difference scores and to conduct a one-sample *t*-test with the difference scores.

However, in the social sciences our scores are often unrelated to one another. For example, a sociology student interested in the happiness levels in different societies would collect data on happiness levels from people in both religious and non-religious societies. After these data are collected, she would have two sets of scores – *but there would be no logical reason to pair individuals from one group with individuals from another group* because the people in the two groups had nothing to do with each other. Therefore, a paired-samples *t*-test would not make sense. In situations where the two groups of scores are unrelated to each other, an unpaired-samples *t*-test is an appropriate data analysis procedure.

Steps of an Unpaired-Samples *t*-Test

The unpaired-samples *t*-test is the fourth NHST procedure we have seen in this textbook. (The first three were the *z*-test, the one-sample *t*-test, and the paired-samples *t*-test.) Because all of these statistical tests are members of the GLM, they follow the same eight steps:

1. Form groups in the data.
2. Define the null hypothesis (H_0). The null hypothesis is always that there is no difference between groups or that there is no relationship between independent and dependent variables.
3. Set alpha (α). The default alpha = .05.
4. Choose a one-tailed or a two-tailed test. This determines the alternative hypothesis (H_1).
5. Find the *critical* value, which is used to define the rejection region.
6. Calculate the *observed* value.
7. Compare the observed value and the critical value. If the observed value is more extreme than the critical value, then the null hypothesis should be rejected. Otherwise, it should be retained.
8. Calculate an *effect size*.

As you have progressed through the textbook, you have probably noticed that even though the eight steps of NHST procedures always stay the same, there are changes in how some steps are executed. This pattern is also true for the unpaired-samples *t*-test. However, the changes are relatively modest. The rest of this chapter walks you through the eight steps of conducting an unpaired-samples *t*-test and compares these steps to the one-sample *t*-test (originally explained in Chapter 8).

To demonstrate how to conduct an unpaired-samples *t*-test, we will use data from a study conducted by Fox and Anderegg (2014). In this study the authors studied young adults' (mean age = 20.99 years, SD = 3.54 years) perceptions of appropriate online behavior as they form romantic relationships. Specifically, Fox and Anderegg (2014) were interested in differences across genders in online behavior in different stages of a relationship. The researchers asked 251 male and 265 female respondents whether they thought it was acceptable in the early stages of a relationship (i.e., after meeting face-to-face but before engaging in non-exclusive dating) to engage in passive strategies on Facebook to learn more about a potential romantic partner. These passive strategies included reading the person's Facebook profile, viewing pictures the person has posted online, or checking the person's relationship status. This was an important study because some people find this covert method of learning about a romantic partner acceptable, but others may see it as "Facebook stalking" or "creeping" (both terms used by the authors in the article). Indeed, their study has interesting implications in communications, family science, sociology, and psychology.

Fox and Anderegg (2014) used a 7-point scale to ask their respondents to rate how likely these behaviors were to occur after meeting a potential romantic partner face-to-face. On this scale, 1 represented "very unlikely" and 7 represented "very likely." Men gave a mean rating of 5.58 (SD = 1.42) to these passive strategies, and women gave a mean rating of 5.86 (SD = 1.13). An unpaired two-sample *t*-test is appropriate for this situation because the two gender groups in Fox and Anderegg's (2014) study are separate groups that have no connection to one another (e.g., they are not dating each other).

General Linear Moment 10.1

If you have been reading the General Linear Moment sections of the past few chapters, you know that the different NHST procedures in this book are all special cases or extensions of one another. Therefore, you may not be surprised to learn that the unpaired-samples *t*-test is a generalization of the one-sample *t*-test. Likewise, the one-sample *t*-test is a special case of the unpaired-samples *t*-test; this means that under certain conditions the unpaired-samples *t*-test simplifies to a one-sample *t*-test.

What are those conditions? Quite simply, when one of the groups in a two-sample *t*-test is a population and that population mean (i.e., μ) is known, then the two-sample *t*-test will produce the exact same answer as the one-sample *t*-test. If you compare the steps and equations in this chapter with those in Chapter 8, you will notice that the steps are generally the same. The differences between the two procedures arise from replacing μ with a second $\overline{X}$ or where having a second set of data required some other modifications (i.e., to the degrees of freedom equation and the addition of the pooled standard deviation term). But, in general, in this chapter we are actually doing the same procedure as a one-sample *t*-test, but it has been modified to accommodate a second set of sample data, instead of a population mean. If you keep that in mind as you read this chapter, you will learn more efficiently how to conduct an unpaired-samples *t*-test.

Form Groups in the Data. In any NHST procedure, the first step is to form groups with the data. In Fox and Anderegg's (2014) study, the two groups are gender groups (i.e., the 251 male and 265 female respondents). These are naturally existing groups, and using these pre-existing groups is common in the social sciences. However, it is also possible for the researcher to assign study participants to artificial groups, such as an experimental or control group. The way that these groups are created does not change the statistical procedures.

Define the Null Hypothesis. After creating the groups, in step 2, we must define the null hypothesis. Remember from previous chapters that in NHST procedures the null hypothesis is always that there is no difference between the two groups. In a paired two-sample *t*-test, we used the null hypothesis $H_0 : \overline{D} = 0$ (which was Formula 9.4). However, there are two reasons why calculating a difference score does not make sense for unpaired samples. First, there is no logical way to decide which scores in each group should be paired together to calculate the difference score. Second, it is very common with independent groups for the group sizes to be unequal, which would mean that any pairing would leave out some scores. This is the case in the Fox and Anderegg (2014) data, which include 14 more women than men. This is not a huge imbalance, but some studies have more uneven numbers across groups. For example, in a study of children with schizophrenia, the researchers divided their sample into individuals who developed schizophrenia before age 14 and those who developed it at 14 or older (Remschmidt, Schulz, Martin Warnke, & Trott, 1994). The older group had 162 individuals in it, while the younger group had 20 individuals – an 8:1 ratio.

Because Fox and Anderegg (2014) did not have paired scores that can be used to create a difference score, we cannot use the same null hypothesis as a paired-samples *t*-test. Instead, we will use the following null hypothesis:

$$H_0 : \overline{X}_1 = \overline{X}_2 \qquad \text{(Formula 10.1)}$$

This null hypothesis says that the mean for the first group ($\overline{X}_1$) is equal to the mean for the second group ($\overline{X}_2$). This is *always* the null hypothesis for an unpaired-samples *t*-test.[6]

The numbers assigned to the two groups (i.e., 1 and 2) are completely arbitrary. In other words, it doesn't matter which group is Group 1 and which is Group 2, because the "group membership" independent variable is always a nominal variable. (Remember from Chapter 2 that the numbers assigned to nominal data are inherently meaningless.) For the example in this chapter, we will assign females to Group 1 and males to Group 2.

Check Yourself!

- What is the difference between a paired-samples *t*-test and an unpaired-samples *t*-test?

- Is it possible to artificially create the groups (e.g., an experimental group and a control group) in an unpaired-samples *t*-test? Why or why not?

- What is always the null hypothesis in an unpaired-samples *t*-test?

Set Alpha. Choosing an α value is the third step of any NHST procedure. The default value is .05, which means that the rejection region is 5% of the area of the sampling distribution. This alpha should only change if we have a legitimate reason, such as a very large sample size. The Fox and Anderegg (2014) data have one of the largest sample sizes we have seen in this textbook, but it is not so large that we need to change alpha. Therefore, we will keep our alpha value at .05.

Choose a One-Tailed or Two-Tailed Test. Now that we have an alpha value, the fourth step in conducting an unpaired two-sample *t*-test is to choose whether to conduct a one- or a two-tailed test. Just as in the *z*-test, one-sample *t*-test, and paired-samples *t*-test, the decision of whether to conduct a one- or two-tailed test is based on whether there is enough theory or previous data to permit an educated guess about the results of the study. Like the previous NHST procedures we have discussed, there are three possible alternative hypotheses. For a one-tailed test there are two possible alternative hypotheses:

$$H_1 : \overline{X}_1 < \overline{X}_2 \qquad \text{(Formula 10.2)}$$

and

$$H_1 : \overline{X}_1 > \overline{X}_2 \qquad \text{(Formula 10.3)}$$

---

[6] Formula 10.1 is the same as Formula 9.1. In Chapter 9 it was used as an intermediate step to finding the null hypothesis for a paired-samples *t*-test, which is $H_0 : \overline{D} = 0$.

(a)

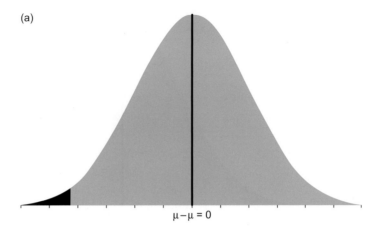

$\mu - \mu = 0$

Figure 10.1a A sampling distribution for an unpaired-samples *t*-test with the rejection region on the left side of the distribution. The alternative hypothesis for this distribution is $H_1 : \overline{X}_1 < \overline{X}_2$. Notice that the distribution consists of differences between means – not sample means themselves (as in a *z*-test and one-sample *t*-test). The sampling distribution for the paired-samples *t*-test was also a distribution of differences between means.

(b)

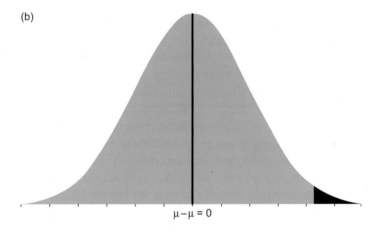

$\mu - \mu = 0$

Figure 10.1b A sampling distribution for an unpaired-samples *t*-test with the rejection region on the right side of the distribution. The alternative hypothesis for this distribution is $H_1 : \overline{X}_1 > \overline{X}_2$. Notice that the distribution consists of differences between means – not sample means themselves (as in a *z*-test and one-sample *t*-test). The sampling distribution for the paired-samples *t*-test was also a distribution of differences between means.

If there is enough information to use a one-tailed hypothesis and you expect that Group 1 will have the smaller mean, then Formula 10.2 is an appropriate alternative hypothesis in an unpaired-samples *t*-test. This alternative hypothesis corresponds to Figure 10.1a, which has the entire rejection region on the left side of the sampling distribution. If prior research or theory indicates that Group 2 will have the smaller mean, then Formula 10.3 is the correct alternative hypothesis. This one-tailed test would have the entire rejection region on the right side of the distribution, as shown in Figure 10.2b.

For an unpaired-samples *t*-test there is only one alternative hypothesis for a two-tailed test:

$$H_1 : \overline{X}_1 \neq \overline{X}_2 \qquad \text{(Formula 10.4)}$$

With the alternative hypothesis in Formula 10.4, half of the rejection region is in each tail of the sampling distribution, as shown in Figure 10.1c. Notice in all three figures that the sampling

(c)

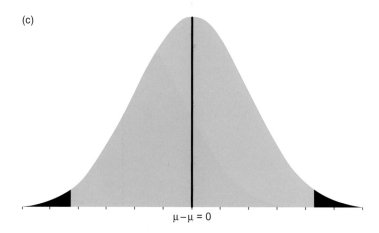

$\mu - \mu = 0$

Figure 10.1c A sampling distribution for an unpaired-samples *t*-test with half of the rejection region on each side of the distribution. The alternative hypothesis for this distribution is $H_1 : \overline{X}_1 \neq \overline{X}_2$. Notice that the distribution consists of differences between means – not sample means themselves (as in a *z*-test and one-sample *t*-test). The sampling distribution for the paired-samples *t*-test was also a distribution of differences between means.

distribution is made up of differences between sample means (and not the means themselves) – just as it was in the previous chapter.

Figures 10.1a–10.1c also show an important characteristic of the unpaired-samples *t*-test: the sampling distribution is made up of the differences between means. This was also true of the paired-samples *t*-test (see Chapter 9). Therefore, the sampling distribution for an unpaired-samples *t*-test will have the same shape as it did for the paired-samples *t*-test and the one-sample *t*-test. This sampling distribution of differences between means also implies that the results of an unpaired-samples *t*-test will apply to not just the difference between means of the scores in the two sample groups. Rather, the result will also generalize to the populations of groups. For the Fox and Anderegg (2014) example, this means that the results of the *t*-test will apply to the population of men and women, and we can learn whether the two populations' means are equal or not.

Fox and Anderegg (2014) cited an earlier article (Clark, Shaver, & Abrahams, 1999) showing that women, when forming romantic relationships, tend to use more passive strategies than men. It seems reasonable that these strategies would extend to social media, so we will conduct a one-tailed test. Because we expect women (i.e., Group 1) to score higher than men (i.e., Group 2) on these passive strategies, our alternative hypothesis should be $H_1 : \overline{X}_1 > \overline{X}_2$. Therefore, we will put the rejection region on the right side of the sampling distribution.

Check Yourself!

- What is alpha? What does it mean when $\alpha = .05$?

- How do you know how to choose a one-tailed or a two-tailed test in an unpaired two-sample *t*-test?

- What are the three possible alternative hypotheses in an unpaired two-sample *t*-test?

Find the Critical Value. With our alternative hypothesis chosen, the fifth step in performing an unpaired-samples *t*-test is to find the critical value, which is called t_{crit} (as it was in the one-sample *t*-test and the paired-samples *t*-test). Like all NHST procedures, the critical value in a paired-samples *t*-test is the point at which the rejection region starts (see Figures 10.1a–10.1c).

In the last section – and in Figures 10.1a–10.1c – we saw that the sampling distribution for the unpaired-samples *t*-test is made up of differences between means, just as in the paired-samples *t*-test. As a result, we will use the same table (i.e., Appendix A2, or the *t*-table) to find our critical values. Because the unpaired-samples *t*-test's sampling distribution also consists of differences between means, we will also use Appendix A2 to find the critical value for this NHST procedure.

The equation for the degrees of freedom in a paired-samples *t*-test is different from the equations in the prior chapters. For an unpaired-samples *t*-test, the degrees of freedom value is calculated as:

$$df = (n_1 - 1) + (n_2 - 1) = n_{Total} - 2 \qquad \text{(Formula 10.5)}$$

In Formula 10.5, n_1 refers to the sample size of the first group, and n_2 refers to the sample size of the second group. Again, it doesn't matter which group is labeled as Group 1 or Group 2, but you should keep the assignment consistent. An alternative, equivalent method of calculating the degrees of freedom is to take the total sample size of both groups combined (which is n_{Total}) and subtract 2.

In the Fox and Anderegg (2014) data, we assigned women to be Group 1 and men to be Group 2. Therefore, in this example, n_1 should be the number of women in the study, and n_2 should be the number of men in the study. As a result, $n_1 = 265$, and $n_2 = 251$. Plugging these numbers into Formula 10.5 produces $df = (265 - 1) + (251 - 1) = 514$ degrees of freedom.

With the degrees of freedom known, we can now look up the critical value in Appendix A2 in the same way that we did for the other *t*-tests. Because we are conducting a one-tailed test, we will use the columns on the left half of the table (which are labeled "One-Tailed Test"). Then we need to find the row that has the appropriate number of degrees of freedom. However, the table does not have a row for 514 degrees of freedom. Therefore, we should use the row that has the highest number of degrees of freedom but still less than 514, which is the row for 500 degrees of freedom. (This is another application of the *Price Is Right* rule from previous chapters.) Because $\alpha = .05$, the critical value will be in the second column: +/–1.648. However, we must use either +1.648 or –1.648, the selection of which is determined by examining the alternative hypothesis. In the example in this chapter, we decided on the alternative hypothesis $H_1 : \overline{X}_1 > \overline{X}_2$, which corresponded to a sampling distribution with the rejection region on the right side (i.e., Figure 10.1b). Because this rejection region is on the right side, and zero is in the middle of the distribution, the critical value will be positive. Therefore, +1.648 is the appropriate value for t_{crit}. (If men had been Group 1 and women had been Group 2, we would have had $H_1 : \overline{X}_1 < \overline{X}_2$ as an alternative hypothesis, and the rejection region would be on the left side of the sampling distribution. But all of the calculations would have been the same, and we would still reach the same conclusion about whether to reject the null hypothesis.)

Calculate the Observed Value. As with all other NHST procedures, the sixth step of an unpaired-samples *t*-test is to calculate the observed value. Before this can be done, though, it is necessary to calculate the pooled standard deviation (abbreviated s_{pooled}) for the two groups' scores. We learned in Chapter 9 that the pooled standard deviation of two sets of scores is the standard deviation of all the scores combined.

There are two ways to calculate the pooled standard deviation. The first is to combine all the data and calculate the standard deviation for all the scores in the typical way (see Formulas 4.7 and 4.9). The second method is to use the following formula:

$$s_{pooled} = \sqrt{\frac{s_1^2(n_1 - 1) + s_2^2(n_2 - 1)}{(n_1 - 1) + (n_2 - 1)}}$$
(Formula 10.6)

In Formula 10.6 n_1 refers to the sample size of Group 1, and n_2 refers to the sample size of Group 2 (just as in Formula 10.5). The abbreviation s_1^2 is the variance (i.e., the squared standard deviation) of Group 1, and s_2^2 is the variance of Group 2.

For the Fox and Anderegg (2014) example, Group 1 had a standard deviation of 1.13 and Group 2 had a standard deviation of 1.42. As stated above, $n_1 = 265$, and $n_2 = 251$. Plugging these numbers into Formula 10.6 produces:

$$s_{pooled} = \sqrt{\frac{1.13^2(265 - 1) + 1.42^2(251 - 1)}{(265 - 1) + (251 - 1)}}$$

We can now solve for the s_{pooled} value:

$$s_{pooled} = \sqrt{\frac{1.277(265 - 1) + 2.016(251 - 1)}{(265 - 1) + (251 - 1)}}$$

$$s_{pooled} = \sqrt{\frac{1.277(264) + 2.016(250)}{264 + 250}}$$

$$s_{pooled} = \sqrt{\frac{337.102 + 504.100}{264 + 250}}$$

$$s_{pooled} = \sqrt{\frac{841.202}{514}}$$

$$s_{pooled} = \sqrt{1.637}$$

$$s_{pooled} = 1.279$$

The pooled standard deviation will *always* be between the standard deviation values of the two groups. This fact will help you check yourself and determine whether you have obtained a realistic answer for your pooled standard deviation. In the Fox and Anderegg (2014) example, the females had a standard deviation of 1.13, and males had a standard deviation of 1.42. The pooled standard deviation value (1.279) was between both of these groups' standard deviations, so we know that our answer is a plausible pooled standard deviation for these data.

It is necessary to solve for the pooled standard deviation because it is part of the formula for the observed value (abbreviated t_{obs}):

$$t_{obs} = \frac{\overline{X}_1 - \overline{X}_2}{\sqrt{s_{pooled}^2\left(\frac{1}{n_1} + \frac{1}{n_2}\right)}}$$
(Formula 10.7)

where $\overline{X}_1$ symbolizes the mean for Group 1, and $\overline{X}_2$ symbolizes the mean for Group 2. Just like in Formulas 10.5 and 10.6, n_1 and n_2 refer to the sample sizes for Group 1 and Group 2, respectively.

You already know that s_{pooled} is the pooled standard deviation, but it is important to note that in Formula 10.7 this value is squared, which is why it appears as s^2_{pooled}. This makes the s^2_{pooled} value the **pooled variance**. Never forget to square the pooled standard deviation when calculating t_{obs}.[7]

The Fox and Anderegg (2014) groups had means of $\overline{X}_1 = 5.86$ and $\overline{X}_2 = 5.58$. Plugging in these numbers, the pooled standard deviation value, and the group sizes into Formula 10.7 produces:

$$t_{obs} = \frac{5.86 - 5.58}{\sqrt{1.279^2 \left(\frac{1}{265} + \frac{1}{251} \right)}}$$

We can now solve for this t_{obs} value.

$$t_{obs} = \frac{0.28}{\sqrt{1.279^2 \left(\frac{1}{265} + \frac{1}{251} \right)}}$$

$$t_{obs} = \frac{0.28}{\sqrt{1.637 \left(\frac{1}{265} + \frac{1}{251} \right)}}$$

$$t_{obs} = \frac{0.28}{\sqrt{1.637(0.003774 + 0.003984)}}$$

$$t_{obs} = \frac{0.28}{\sqrt{1.637(0.007758)}}$$

$$t_{obs} = \frac{0.28}{\sqrt{0.012696}}$$

$$t_{obs} = \frac{0.28}{0.112677}$$

$$t_{obs} = 2.485$$

Compare the Observed Value and the Critical Value. The seventh step in an unpaired-samples *t*-test is to compare the observed and critical values. As in the other NHST procedures we have learned so far, if the observed value (t_{obs}) is more extreme than the critical value (t_{crit}), you should reject the null hypothesis because that would mean that the observed value is inside the rejection region. On the other hand, if the observed value is outside the rejection region, the null hypothesis should be retained.

In the Fox and Anderegg (2014) data, $t_{crit} = 1.648$, and $t_{obs} = 2.485$. Figure 10.2 shows how these two values are compared to one another on the sampling distribution. It is clear from the figure that the t_{obs} value is inside the rejection region. Therefore, we should reject the null hypothesis of $H_0 : \overline{X}_1 = \overline{X}_2$. Instead, the alternative hypothesis is a better statistical model for the data. That alternative hypothesis is that females would have higher scores than males on the acceptability of

---

[7] In Chapter 4 we learned that the standard deviation of a variable is always the square root of its variance. The last step of calculating the s_{pooled} value is to take the square root. Therefore, the second-to-last number in the pooled standard deviation calculation is the pooled variance. For the example, that number was 1.637 (see above). Therefore, $s^2_{pooled} = 1.637$.

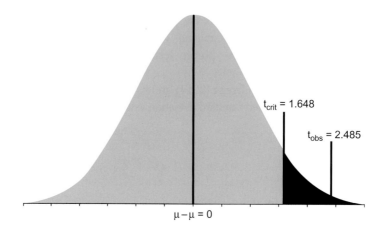

Figure 10.2 Visual representation of the sampling distribution for the Fox and Anderegg (2014) data about social media behavior of men and women. The critical value (t_{crit}), which is the point at which the rejection region begins, is equal to +1.648. The observed value (t_{obs}) is equal to +2.485, which is inside the rejection region. Therefore, it is appropriate to reject the null hypothesis that the two groups have equal mean scores (i.e., $H_0 : \bar{X}_1 = \bar{X}_2$).

passive strategies on social media to gather information about a prospective romantic relationship. Therefore, we can conclude that women engage in these behaviors at higher rates than men.

Check Yourself!

- What is the formula for degrees of freedom in an unpaired two-sample *t*-test?

- What should you do if Appendix A2 does not have a row for the exact number of degrees of freedom of your data?

- After calculating your observed value and your critical value, how do you know whether to retain or reject the null hypothesis?

Calculate an Effect Size. The eighth and final step of an unpaired-samples *t*-test is to calculate an effect size. You may remember from previous chapters that effect sizes are important in comparisons of means because they state how far apart two means are, whereas the NHST results only tell us whether the difference between the two means is statistically significant. For an unpaired-samples *t*-test, this effect size is Cohen's *d*:

$$d = \frac{\bar{X}_1 - \bar{X}_2}{s_{pooled}}$$ (Formula 10.8)

Again, the symbols $\bar{X}_1$ and $\bar{X}_2$ represent the means of Group 1 and Group 2, respectively. In the denominator s_{pooled} refers to the pooled standard deviation of the data (*not* the pooled variance).

We used these values in earlier formulas in this chapter. For the Fox and Anderegg (2014) example, $\bar{X}_1 = 5.86$, $\bar{X}_2 = 5.58$, and $s_{pooled} = 1.279$. Using these numbers in Formula 10.8 results in:

$$d = \frac{5.86 - 5.58}{1.279} = 0.219$$

Therefore, we can interpret this effect size as indicating that the average female in Fox and Anderegg's (2014) study gave a rating that was 0.219 standard deviation higher than the average male's rating when both groups were asked about the acceptability of passive strategies on social media to learn about a potential romantic partner. We could also interpret this Cohen's *d* value to indicate that, when compared to men, the average woman's *z*-score on this variable was 0.219 standard deviation higher. You may also remember from Chapter 8 that a Cohen's *d* of about 0.20 is noticeable to casual observers, meaning that this difference in social media behavior between men and women would be apparent in many people's everyday experience.

Sidebar 10.1 **Statistical power**

Whenever you have two sets of scores, there is the choice of whether to conduct a paired-samples *t*-test or an unpaired-samples *t*-test. Because there is the potential to confuse the two procedures, some people are tempted to always use the unpaired-samples *t*-test − even when it would be possible to conduct a paired-samples *t*-test. This approach does not violate any statistical assumptions because the data do not *have* to be unpaired when conducting an unpaired two-sample *t*-test. (However, for a paired-samples *t*-test, the data *must* be paired.)

But conducting an unpaired-samples *t*-test with paired data reduces the **statistical power** of an NHST. Statistical power (often just called "power") is the probability that an NHST will reject the null hypothesis when the null hypothesis is false. Studies with high statistical power have a lower probability of Type II error. This is because high power makes it easier to reject a false null hypothesis.

Statistical power is determined by four things: the effect size, the alpha value, the sample size, and the study design. All other things being equal, studies with stronger effect sizes, higher alpha values, or a larger sample size have greater statistical power (Cohen, 1992; Sedlmeier & Gigerenzer, 1989). Having high statistical power is a good thing for a study. In fact, if cost, time, and other practical considerations are not an issue, it is *always* better to have higher statistical power for a study than lower statistical power.

How can you increase statistical power in your studies? There are generally four possible ways:

- The easiest way is to increase alpha. Because alpha is always arbitrary, there's nothing special about the default alpha value of .05, so in theory researchers can change it − and they sometimes do (Cohen, 1992). However, because .05 is the default, people often get suspicious when alpha is raised because it looks like the researcher is "cheating" and trying to make it artificially easier to reject the null hypothesis.
- Studies with stronger effect sizes tend to have higher power. But changing the effect size is not a viable method of increasing statistical power because the magnitude of the effect size is almost always beyond the control of the researchers.
- Another − and often most feasible − way of increasing statistical power in a study is to increase the sample size (*n*) (Maxwell, 2004). In fact, a small *n* is a chronic problem in some branches of the social sciences. As a result, many studies have lower power, which makes it harder to reject a false null hypothesis. As if that were not enough of a problem, when a study has low statistical power, the possibility increases that any rejection of the null hypothesis is just a fluke. This is because the low statistical power makes it difficult to reject the null hypothesis. So, when we do reject the null

hypothesis, the result seems unstable. Low statistical power is the "worst of both worlds" because it increases Type II error and makes it harder to reject the null hypothesis, but it makes people suspicious when the null hypothesis actually is rejected (Schimmack, 2012). Unfortunately, for studies where the effect size is close to zero, the required sample size needed for high statistical power may be very large – often over 1,000 (Schmidt, 1996).

- The last way to increase statistical power is through the design of the study, and this is where the difference between paired and unpaired two-sample *t*-tests becomes relevant. Generally, NHST procedures that take advantage of data with a paired structure have higher power than procedures that use unpaired data. Therefore, *it is usually easier to detect a statistically significant difference between scores with paired data than with unpaired data* (Zimmerman, 1997). This is why – if you have paired data – it is usually better to use a paired two-sample *t*-test than an unpaired test (see Kline, 2013, p. 49, for the conditions where this generalization breaks down and unpaired data have higher statistical power). Indeed, scientific fields – like cognitive psychology – that frequently use multiple scores from the same subjects have higher power than fields – like social psychology – that rely more on unpaired data. As a result, studies in cognitive psychology are more replicable and seem more robust (Open Science Collaboration, 2015). Another feature of study design that increases statistical power is to have equally sized groups; if the total sample size stays constant, then studies with more unbalanced group sizes have lower statistical power (Kline, 2013).

Calculating power can be mathematically complex. There are several online calculators that do the process automatically. (I like the website powerandsamplesize.com.) Statistical power values always range from 0 to 1. Generally, you should try to obtain a statistical power level of .80 (Cohen, 1992). In this chapter's example from Fox and Anderegg (2014), the statistical power was .898 for a one-tailed test, showing that their study had sufficient power. Indeed, statistical power would have been .80 or higher as long as there was at least 190 people in each group.

At first glance, statistical power seems abstract and irrelevant. But studies with lower power that reject the null hypothesis by accident produce unstable "facts" that undermine the credibility of scientific research (Ioannidis, 2005). Other scientists who read these studies may waste time and effort trying to reproduce or build upon research that is of questionable quality (Fidler, 2010; Osborne, 2008; Schimmack, 2012). Additionally, a group of studies with low statistical power will have inconsistent results, and this is confusing and inhibits understanding (Maxwell, 2004). Unfortunately, statistical power in many branches of the social sciences tends to be low (Cohen, 1992), though it may be increasing in some fields of research (Osborne, 2008).

p and Type I and Type II errors

The procedure for finding *p* in an unpaired two-sample *t*-test is the same as with a one-sample *t*-test and a paired-samples *t*-test. This is because all three procedures use the same table in the textbook. As a reminder, the rules for determining *p* are as follows:

- If the null hypothesis is retained when $\alpha = .05$, then $p > .05$.
- If the null hypothesis is rejected when $\alpha = .05$, but retained when $\alpha = .01$, then $.01 < p < .05$.
- If the null hypothesis is rejected when $\alpha = .01$, then $p < .01$.

When we analyzed the Fox and Anderegg (2014) data, we rejected the null hypothesis when α was equal to .05 because $t_{crit} = 1.648$, and $t_{obs} = 2.485$ (see Figure 10.2). Therefore, *p* must be less than .05. The next question is whether *p* is also less than .01. To answer this, we need to find the critical value for $\alpha = .01$, which is in the same row (df = 500) in Appendix A2. This t_{crit} value is 2.334. Because t_{obs} is greater than this value, we still reject the null hypothesis if $\alpha = .01$. Therefore, *p* must be less than .01. This means that if the null hypothesis were perfectly true, we would expect to get results like ours less than 1 in every 100 studies. This is unlikely, but could still happen (see Sidebar 10.2). Therefore, we must worry about the possibility of Type I error because this error occurs when the null hypothesis is rejected when it should not be.

On the other hand, if we had retained the null hypothesis, then we would worry about Type II error. Just as in every other NHST procedure, a Type II error in an unpaired-samples *t*-test occurs when researchers retain a null hypothesis that is actually false. Remember, though, that we never really know whether the null hypothesis is true or not. (If we did, there would be no point in conducting any null hypothesis statistical significance test.) So, the possibility of these errors is something we must keep in mind.

Sidebar 10.2 **The surprising frequency of unlikely events**

Readers should realize that unlikely events (such as results with very small *p*-values) happen frequently due to chance. Consider the following highly unlikely events that actually occurred.

- On March 24, 2001, during a spring training pre-season game, professional baseball pitcher Randy Johnson threw a pitch which accidentally hit a bird that happened to be flying across the field. The bird died ("Bird 'explodes' after flying in path of fastball," 2001).
- Something similar happened almost exactly 14 years later on March 13, 2015. In another spring training pre-season game, professional baseball player James McCann hit a baseball that struck a bird resting on a net that protected spectators from errant baseballs. This bird survived (Townsend, 2015).
- A man in Indiana won the state lottery twice. In 2011 he was the winner of $1 million, and in 2015 he won $500,000 ("Orleans man wins Hoosier lottery – twice," 2015). Also in 2015 a British couple won the UK National Lottery for a second time in 20 months; they won £1 million both times (A. Jamieson, 2015). In fact, a Google News search for the phrase "won lottery twice" shows that these two cases are far from unique.
- Even your textbook author is not immune from unlikely occurrences. When I was in middle school (i.e., junior high school) I was randomly assigned the same locker two years in a row. In a school with over 1,500 lockers, this is a very improbable event.

There are many more examples of unlikely events in the news (e.g., people being struck by lightning twice in their life, the same sports fan catching an errant ball twice in a row, women giving birth to multiple sets of twins in the course of their lives). Although each of these events is unlikely at any given time, the fact that there are thousands of trials for these events every year means that unlikely events are bound to occur eventually. Therefore, even an extremely tiny *p*-value does not prove that the researcher is correct to reject the null hypothesis. With the thousands of studies that are conducted in the social sciences each year, it is likely that many studies are published each year in which the null hypothesis is incorrectly rejected (Greenwald, 1975; see Ioannidis, 2005, for a similar argument about medical research). Keep that in mind as you read published scientific articles.

If there were a contest for the most misinterpreted statistic, the *p-value* would probably be the winner. The correct interpretation of *p* is that it is the probability that a random sample of data from the same population would produce results that have the same observed value or a more extreme observed value *if the null hypothesis were perfectly true in reality* (Kenaszchuk, 2011; Wasserstein & Lazar, 2016).

For example, when we obtained a *p-value* of $< .01$ in the Fox and Anderegg (2014) example in this chapter, it meant that if the null hypothesis were perfectly true, then there would be less than a 1 in 100 probability of randomly selecting two unpaired sets of scores from the population that would have a t_{obs} value ≥ 2.485. In other words, the *p-value* represents the probability of making a Type I error *if the null hypothesis is perfectly true*.

But the *p-value* is also frequently misinterpreted. Here are some things to remember so that you can avoid common incorrect interpretations of *p*:

- The *p-value* does not give you the probability that you have made a Type I error in reality. The phrase "if the null hypothesis were perfectly true" is the key to avoiding this misinterpretation. If H_0 is not an absolutely perfect statistical model for reality (perhaps because of tiny differences between group means in the population, or just because the null is completely wrong), then the probability expressed in a *p-value* may not be accurate (Kirk, 1996). It is still a useful statistic, however, especially because it can help us make rational decisions about how well the null hypothesis matches the data in a study (Wasserstein & Lazar, 2016; Winch & Campbell, 1969).
- *p* says very little about the replicability or stability of results (Schmidt, 1996). Indeed, *p-values* fluctuate wildly across studies (Cumming, 2008). It is true, though, that (generally speaking) low *p-values* indicate that the null hypothesis may possibly be easier to reject in the future (Cumming & Maillardet, 2006). However, this assumes that the replications are conducted under precisely the same conditions as the original study, with every possible relevant (and irrelevant) factor perfectly replicated. In real life, a low *p-value* does not necessarily mean that you will get similar results if you conducted the same study again. In fact, attempts to replicate studies with low *p-values* often do not succeed (Open Science Collaboration, 2015). If the sample size is small or if the sample is not representative of the population in some way (as occurs frequently with nonrandom samples), the results may be unstable and not replicable, even if *p* is very low and the null hypothesis is strongly rejected. The best way to determine whether the results of a study will replicate is to conduct a replication.
- Remember that the *p-value* is the probability of obtaining our result if the null is perfectly true. However, many people get this idea reversed and incorrectly believe that *p* is the probability that the null hypothesis is true, given the data (Kirk, 1996; McCloskey & Ziliak, 2015; Rodgers, 2010). Another way of restating this incorrect understanding is that if the null hypothesis is rejected, people look at their low *p-value*, and say, "If *p* is less than .05, there is less than a 5% chance that my null is true." This is incorrect reasoning because a *p* value only tells a researcher whether the data fit the null hypothesis. The *p* value does *not* say anything about the probability that the null hypothesis is true because the *p-value* is calculated under the scenario that the null hypothesis is perfectly true (Fidler, 2010). As a result, *p* cannot tell us whether the null hypothesis is true because we had to assume it was true in the first place to calculate *p* (Haller & Krauss, 2002). Likewise, a *p-value* cannot tell us whether the alternative hypothesis is true because *p* is based on the assumption that the *null* hypothesis is perfectly true.
- Additionally, a *p-value* says nothing about *why* the null hypothesis is not a good model for the data – information which would be required to ascertain whether the null hypothesis is true or not

(Wasserstein & Lazar, 2016). Sampling error and individual study characteristics may result in data that differ greatly from what would be obtained from a random sample of data. Even if p is less than .05, there may be a much larger − or much smaller − probability that the null is true (e.g., Simmons, Nelson, & Simonsohn, 2011). It is correct to say, however, that the null hypothesis does not fit the data well when it is rejected, and that some alternative model (perhaps the alternative hypothesis) may fit the data better (E. S. Pearson, 1939).

- A closely related misinterpretation is the idea that the p-value is the probability of obtaining the results of a study "by chance alone." There are two problems with this thinking. First, the phrase "by chance alone" is nebulous and inexact. Many people use it to refer to sampling error, but there are other types of error (i.e., "chance") that can creep into a study (Kline, 2013). These other types of error can influence results. Even if someone is referring to just sampling error, they are still getting the logic of null hypothesis testing backwards. A p-value does not refer to the probability of getting the results of a study "by chance" or sampling error. It refers to the degree to which the data fit the null hypothesis. The formulas (or the computer) that give you a p-value do *not* know why the results occurred (e.g., whether it was "by chance" or because the null hypothesis is wrong). Instead, the formulas only help you understand whether the null hypothesis is a good statistical model for the data. The reasons why the null hypothesis is retained or rejected are beyond the ability of the formulas or software to tell.

- The p-value says *nothing* about the importance of findings (Kieffer, Reese, & Thompson, 2001). Remember that importance is an issue of practical significance − not statistical significance. There is nothing magical about an α value less than .05. Decisions about policy, psychological interventions, and other practical implications of research should be based on more than just a p-value. Such important decisions should not be based on a statistic that is vulnerable to changes in sample size and study conditions (Wasserstein & Lazar, 2016). See Sidebar 8.3 for more on this issue.

- Another common misinterpretation is that p-values indicate the size of an effect (e.g., the difference between means or the magnitude of the relationship between variables). For example, a researcher finding that p is greater than α (indicating that the null hypothesis should be retained) may decide that the results are "insignificant" or irrelevant. This confuses p-values with effect sizes. Effect sizes quantify the strength of mean group differences or variable relationships; p-values do not (Wasserstein & Lazar, 2016). If the sample size is small or the study has low statistical power, then there could be a large effect size that is worth discussing, even if p is too high to provide evidence to reject the null hypothesis (see Warne, 2016, for an example of this). Understanding the strength of relationships or the magnitude of group differences is important − and that is why it is essential to calculate and report an effect size to accompany a null hypothesis statistical significance test (American Psychological Association, 2010; Wasserstein & Lazar, 2016).

These misunderstandings are very common − even among professors (Haller & Krauss, 2002). Given how frequently people misinterpret p-values, I strongly urge you to be vigilant against these incorrect interpretations.

Assumptions of the Unpaired Two-Sample *t*-Test

We have seen in previous chapters that all statistical procedures have assumptions, which are requirements that the data must meet in order to produce interpretable results. Previous assumptions we have encountered include:

- Having interval- or ratio-level data in order to calculate a mean and standard deviation (see Chapter 4).
- The population mean (μ) and standard deviation (σ) must be known in a *z*-test (see Chapter 7).
- Scores can be paired across groups in the paired-samples *t*-test (see Chapter 9).

It is important to understand that the unpaired two-sample *t*-test also has assumptions. These are:

- The groups are mutually exclusive and exhaustive. This is because a nominal-level independent variable divides scores into the two groups.
- The variable that is used to calculate the mean scores is interval- or ratio-level. This should be unsurprising because we have known since Chapter 4 that means and standard deviations require at least interval-level data.
- A new assumption is **homogeneity of variance**, which means that the two groups have similar variance values.
- The two groups in an unpaired two-sample *t*-test also need to have similar sample sizes.

We have already discussed levels of data at length, so I will not expand upon the first two assumptions. However, the homogeneity of variance assumption is important because if one group's scores are much more variable than the other group's scores, then comparing the two means may be deceptive and simplistic. The assumption of similar sample sizes is key because when group sizes diverge it can inflate Type I error.

Both of these last two assumptions are not very strict. According to Fidell and Tabachnick (2003), the way to examine whether your data violate the homogeneity of variance assumption is to find the ratio between the larger variance and the smaller variance. If this ratio is less than or equal to 10:1, your data meet this assumption, and the results of an unpaired-samples *t*-test will not be distorted. The method of checking the assumption of similar group sizes is comparable: find the ratio of sample sizes between the larger group and the smaller group. If this ratio is less than or equal to 4:1, then your data meet this assumption. For both tests, a ratio of 1:1 indicates that the data perfectly meet each assumption (which is good).

We can examine the Fox and Anderegg (2014) data for a violation of these assumptions. The two variances were 2.016 and 1.277. (These values are each group's standard deviation squared.) The ratio between these values is 1.58:1 (because $2.016 \div 1.277 = 1.58$). The two sample sizes were 265 and 251, which have a ratio of 1.06:1 (because $265 \div 251 = 1.06$). Both of these values are well within Fidell and Tabachnick's (2003) guidelines. Therefore, we can conduct an unpaired two-sample *t*-test without worrying that the results are distorted because assumptions have been violated.

Guided Practice 10.1

The second example of an unpaired-samples *t*-test comes from a British study by Deary, Strand, Smith, and Fernandes (2007), who were interested in whether males or females had higher IQ scores. Their sample was 34,850 boys and 35,680 girls. After converting all IQ scores to *z*-scores, the mean male score was –0.007 (SD = 0.965). The mean female score was 0.004 (SD = 0.912). This Guided Practice will show how to conduct an unpaired-samples *t*-test with these data.

Step 1: Form Groups

In Deary et al.'s (2007) study, the two groups are gender groups (just as they were for the other example in this chapter): males and females.

Step 2: Define the Null Hypothesis

In an unpaired-samples *t*-test, the null hypothesis is always that there is no difference between the two group means. This is expressed mathematically as $H_0 : \overline{X}_1 = \overline{X}_2$ (see Formula 10.1). In this example we will label males Group 1 and females Group 2.

Step 3: Set Alpha

As with all other NHST procedures in the GLM, the default α value is .05. For the purposes of this example, we are going to maintain this α value.

Step 4: Choose a One- or a Two-Tailed Test, Which Determines the Alternative Hypothesis

Deary and his coauthors (2007) were not the first to investigate sex differences in intelligence. In fact, when they conducted their study, nearly a century of psychologists had investigated the topic (e.g., Terman et al., 1915; see Hollingworth, 1919, for an early literature review on the topic). In all this time there seemed to be no consistent pattern of one sex outscoring the other. In fact, in some studies there were no differences. As a result, a two-tailed hypothesis is appropriate because the evidence is not strong enough to favor a one-tailed hypothesis that one sex outscores the other on intelligence tests. Therefore, the alternative hypothesis for this unpaired-samples *t*-test is $H_1 : \overline{X}_1 \neq \overline{X}_2$, which is Formula 10.4.

Step 5: Find the Critical Values

Finding the critical value in an unpaired-samples *t*-test requires first calculating the degrees of freedom. To do this, you must use Formula 10.5, which is $df = (n_1 - 1) + (n_2 - 1)$. Because $n_1 = 34{,}850$, and $n_2 = 35{,}680$, calculating degrees of freedom produces:

$$df = (34850 - 1) + (35{,}680 - 1)$$

Solving for the parts of the formula inside the parentheses results in

$$df = 34{,}849 + 35{,}679 = 70{,}528$$

With the number of degrees of freedom known, we can now use Appendix A2 to find the critical value. However, the table in this example does not include a row for 70,528 degrees of freedom. The appropriate option instead is to use the row that has the highest degrees of freedom without exceeding the number of degrees of freedom at hand. This would be the row for 1,000 degrees of freedom. On that row the critical value for a two-tailed test when α = .05 is ± 1.962. It is important to keep the $\pm$ in mind because a two-tailed test will have two t_{crit} values. In this case the t_{crit} values are -1.962 and $+1.962$.

Step 6: Calculate the Observed Value

Before we can calculate t_{obs}, we must first find the pooled standard deviation (s_{pooled}). This requires using Formula 10.6, which is $s_{pooled} = \sqrt{\frac{s_1^2(n_1-1)+s_2^2(n_2-1)}{(n_1-1)+(n_2-1)}}$. Remember in this example that males are Group 1, and females are Group 2. Therefore, we need to plug in the male subjects' standard deviation (0.965) and sample size (34,850) into the s_1 and n_1 values in the formula. The s_2 and n_2 values should be replaced by the female subjects' standard deviation (0.912) and sample size (35,860) also. This results in:

$$s_{pooled} = \sqrt{\frac{0.965^2(34,850-1) + 0.912^2(35,860-1)}{(34,850-1) + (35,860-1)}}$$

Solving for the portions in the parentheses produces:

$$s_{pooled} = \sqrt{\frac{0.965^2(34,849) + 0.912^2(35,859)}{(34,849) + (35,859)}}$$

Squaring the two standard deviations produces the variances of the two groups and results in:

$$s_{pooled} = \sqrt{\frac{0.931(34,849) + 0.832(35,859)}{(34,849) + (35,859)}}$$

Solving for the denominator simplifies the equation to:

$$s_{pooled} = \sqrt{\frac{0.931(34,849) + 0.832(35,859)}{70,528}}$$

The next step is to multiply each variance by the number in the parentheses:

$$s_{pooled} = \sqrt{\frac{32,452.260 + 29,825.508}{70,528}}$$

Solving for the numerator results in:

$$s_{pooled} = \sqrt{\frac{62,277.768}{70,528}}$$

Now we need to solve for the fraction:

$$s_{pooled} = \sqrt{0.883}$$

You may want to note that 0.883 is the pooled variance (s_{pooled}^2). The last step in finding the pooled standard deviation is to square root this value:

$$s_{pooled} = \sqrt{0.883} = 0.940$$

With the pooled standard deviation known, we can use Formula 10.7 to solve for the observed value. This formula was $t_{obs} = \dfrac{\overline{X}_1 - \overline{X}_2}{\sqrt{s_{pooled}^2 \left(\dfrac{1}{n_1} + \dfrac{1}{n_2}\right)}}$. Remember that Group 1 is males and Group 2 is females, so $\overline{X}_1$ refers to the male mean (–0.007), and $\overline{X}_2$ refers to the female mean (0.004). As in the pooled standard deviation formula, n_1 and n_2 refer to the male and female sample sizes, respectively. For s_{pooled}^2 we can either use the pooled variance (0.883), or we can plug in the pooled standard deviation value (0.940) and square it. To make the arithmetic easier, I am going to use the pooled variance value. Plugging all these values into Formula 10.7 produces:

$$t_{obs} = \frac{-0.007 - 0.004}{\sqrt{0.883 \left(\dfrac{1}{34,850} + \dfrac{1}{35,860}\right)}}$$

Solving for the numerator:

$$t_{obs} = \frac{-0.011}{\sqrt{0.883 \left(\dfrac{1}{34,850} + \dfrac{1}{35,860}\right)}}$$

The next step is to solve for the fractions in the denominator. This requires more decimal places than we normally see in this book because the sample sizes are so large.

$$t_{obs} = \frac{-0.011}{\sqrt{0.883(0.0000287 + 0.0000279)}}$$

Adding up the values inside the parentheses results in:

$$t_{obs} = \frac{-0.011}{\sqrt{0.883(0.00005658)}}$$

Multiplying the pooled variance (i.e., 0.940) by the portion inside the parentheses produces:

$$t_{obs} = \frac{-0.011}{\sqrt{0.0000500}}$$

The next step is to solve for the denominator:

$$t_{obs} = \frac{-0.011}{0.0070684}$$

Finally, solving for the total fraction produces the final *t*-observed value:

$$t_{obs} = \frac{-0.011}{0.0070684} = -1.556$$

Step 7: Compare the Observed and Critical Values

Because of the calculations in steps 5 and 6, we know that $t_{crit} = +1.962$, and $t_{obs} = -1.556$. Figure 10.3 shows how these two values compare to one another on the sampling distribution.

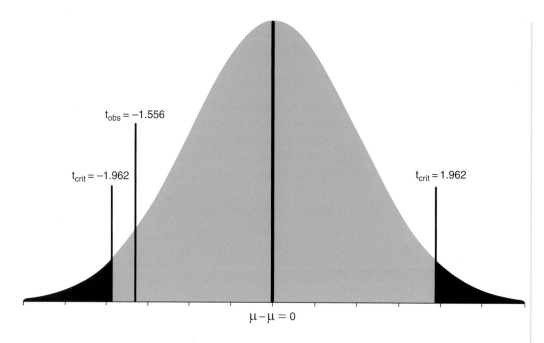

Figure 10.3 Visual diagram of the sampling distribution for the Deary et al. (2007) data. The rejection region (shaded in black) starts at the critical values of ±1.962. The observed value of −1.556 is outside the rejection region, indicating that the null hypothesis of $H_0 : \overline{X}_1 = \overline{X}_2$ should be retained.

As is clear in the figure, the observed value is outside the rejection region. Therefore, we should retain the null hypothesis (i.e., $H_0 : \overline{X}_1 = \overline{X}_2$) because we could not reject the model that males and females have equal intelligence scores. Because we retained the null hypothesis when $\alpha = .05$, p must be greater than .05.

Step 8: Calculate an Effect Size

Formula 10.8, which was $d = \frac{\overline{X}_1 - \overline{X}_2}{s_{pooled}}$, shows how to calculate the effect size – Cohen's d – for an unpaired two-sample *t*-test. Using the values for $\overline{X}_1$ (−0.007), $\overline{X}_2$ (0.004), and s_{pooled} (0.940) that we used for previous steps, our equation to find Cohen's d is:

$$d = \frac{-0.007 - 0.004}{0.940}$$

Solving for the numerator produces:

$$d = \frac{-0.011}{0.940}$$

The second step is to solve the fraction:

$$d = \frac{-0.011}{0.940} = -.012$$

This Cohen's d indicates that there is only 0.012 standard deviation between the means of males and females in Deary et al.'s (2007) study. This is a tiny difference that is nearly equal to zero – and never a difference that anyone would notice in daily life (see Chapter 8 for a reminder of how to interpret Cohen's *d* values).

Retaining the null hypothesis and finding a miniscule effect size that is almost exactly zero are both indications that males and females are equally intelligent in this study. We can also generalize these results to the population at large. As you have seen in previous chapters, it is easier to reject the null hypothesis with large samples than with small samples (all other things being equal). The fact that we couldn't reject the null hypothesis even with such a huge sample (total $n = 70{,}530$) is very compelling evidence that there is no real differences between these two groups in intelligence. Yet, there is still the possibility of Type II error.

Check Yourself!

- What is the effect size for an unpaired two-sample *t*-test? How is this effect size calculated?

- Is it better for a study to have high statistical power or low statistical power?

- Why is it always necessary in an unpaired two-sample *t*-test to worry about either Type I or Type II error?

- Explain the homogeneity of variance assumption.

General Linear Moment 10.1

We first encountered the principles of the GLM in Chapter 7. Those principles are as follows:

1. All GLM procedures examine the relationships between independent and dependent variables.
2. All GLM procedures apply weights to data during the analysis process.
3. All GLM procedures can produce an effect size.

This General Linear Moment will illustrate these points in detail to show how the unpaired two-sample *t*-test is part of the GLM.

Independent and Dependent Variables. As stated in this chapter, the independent variable in an unpaired two-sample *t*-test is a nominal variable that divides the sample members into two groups. The dependent variable is the variable for which we are calculating mean scores. (This is the same dependent variable that we have had for a *z*-test, a one-sample *t*-test, and a paired-samples *t*-test.)

The unpaired two-sample *t*-test examines the relationship between these two variables. The results can range from no relationship to a very strong relationship between variables. Figure 10.4 illustrates the distributions of the two groups under the conditions of no relationship, a moderate relationship, and a very strong relationship. When there is no relationship between the two, the null hypothesis ($H_0 : \overline{X}_1 = \overline{X}_2$) is a good statistical model for the data. In this case, the means would be equal and the distributions overlap completely. When there is a moderate relationship, there are

No relationship: Means are equal, and distributions
completely overlap.

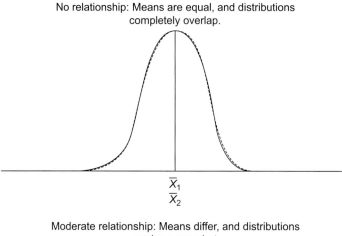

Moderate relationship: Means differ, and distributions
overlap somewhat.

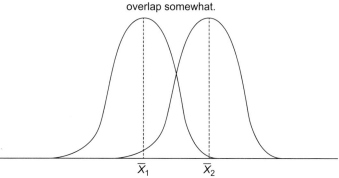

Extreme strong relationship: Large difference
between means, with no overlap
between distributions.

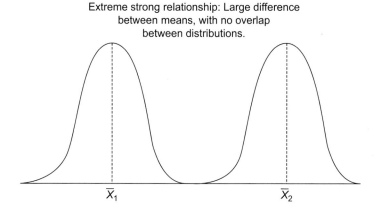

Figure 10.4 Schematic showing how the strength of the relationship between a nominal independent variable affects the overlap of the distributions of the two groups' dependent variable scores. When there is no relationship between group membership and the dependent variable, the two group means are equal and there is perfect overlap between the two distributions. In this case, the independent variable has no impact on dependent variable scores (see top third of the figure). As the relationship between variables increases, the two groups separate because the independent variable becomes a stronger predictor of scores (see middle part of figure). When the relationship between the independent and dependent variables is extremely strong, the two distributions are perfectly separated, and most or all members of one group have lower dependent scores than the members of the higher scoring group.

differences between means, and the dependent variable distributions have some overlap. But when the relationship is extremely strong, the difference between group means is very large and the two distributions have no overlap. Thus, the stronger the relationship between the independent (i.e., group) variable and the dependent variable, the more different the dependent variable scores in the two groups are. As the relationship between variables gets stronger, we can have more confidence that members of one group have lower scores than members of the other group.

Weighting Data. Just as with the NHST procedures in Chapters 7–9, Cohen's d functions as a statistical weight in the unpaired two-sample t-test. If we assign the two groups independent variable values of 0 and 1, then multiplying these scores by Cohen's d will produce a predicted dependent variable score for every sample member.

Effect Sizes. The effect size for the unpaired two-sample t-test is Cohen's d, which is calculated with Formula 10.8. As with the previous NHST procedures, Cohen's d refers to the number of standard deviations between group means.

Summary

One of the most frequent research designs in the social sciences is to make a comparison of two groups' scores. When every score in one group is paired with another score in the second group, a paired-samples t-test is appropriate. However, often there is no pairing between sets of scores. In this situation it is necessary to conduct an unpaired two-sample t-test. The steps of this NHST procedure are the same eight steps of the previous statistical tests we have learned about (i.e., z-test, one-sample t-test, paired two-sample t-test) because all of these are members of the GLM. There are a few modifications that make the unpaired two-sample t-test unique:

- The null hypothesis for an unpaired two-sample t-test is always $H_0 : \overline{X}_1 = \overline{X}_2$, which is that there is no difference between the means of two groups.
- The equation for the number of degrees of freedom is different: $df = (n_1 - 1) + (n_2 - 1)$, where n_1 is the sample size for Group 1 and n_2 is the sample size for Group 2.
- The formula to calculate the observed value (i.e., t_{obs}) is more complex:

$t_{obs} = \dfrac{\overline{X}_1 - \overline{X}_2}{\sqrt{s_{pooled}^2 \left(\dfrac{1}{n_1} + \dfrac{1}{n_2} \right)}}$. Also, to use this formula you must calculate the pooled standard

deviation (abbreviated as s_{pooled}), which is $s_{pooled} = \sqrt{\dfrac{s_1^2(n_1-1)+s_2^2(n_2-1)}{(n_1-1)+(n_2-1)}}$. In these formulas, n_1 is the sample size for Group 1, n_2 is the sample size for Group 2, s_1 is the standard deviation for Group 1, and s_2 is the standard deviation for Group 2. Finally, $\overline{X}_1$ is the mean for Group 1, and $\overline{X}_2$ is the mean for Group 2.

- The effect size for an unpaired two-sample t-test is still Cohen's d, but the formula has been modified slightly: $d = \dfrac{\overline{X}_1 - \overline{X}_2}{s_{pooled}}$. In this formula $\overline{X}_1$ is the mean for Group 1, and $\overline{X}_2$ is the mean for Group 2. The value in the denominator is the pooled standard deviation, the formula for which is in the previous bullet point.

Because the unpaired two-sample t-test is a member of the GLM, it shares many characteristics with other NHSTs. Among these are the sensitivity to sample size, the necessity of calculating an effect size, the arbitrary nature of selecting an α value, and the need to worry about Type I and Type II errors.

Reflection Questions: Comprehension

1. What does the phrase "unpaired data" mean?
2. What is the pooled standard deviation?
3. Explain the relationship between the pooled standard deviation and the pooled variance.
4. Define statistical power and explain why it is important in social science research.
5. What are the four things that determine statistical power?
6. How do we determine the range of a *p*-value for a paired-samples *t*-test?
7. What is the correct interpretation of the *p*-value?
8. What are the guidelines for ensuring that the data in an unpaired two-sample *t*-test meet the assumptions of homogeneity of variance and similar sample sizes?

Reflection Questions: Application

9. Calculate the degrees of freedom for the following sample sizes:
    a. Group 1: 10; Group 2: 15
    b. Group 1: 10; Group 2: 1,500
    c. experimental group: 35; control group: 35
    d. males: 18; females: 12
    e. children: 43; adults: 118
10. Grover, Biswas, and Avasthi (2007) studied people who had long-term delusions, and the authors were interested in whether individuals with another mental disorder had an earlier age of onset than individuals without any other mental disorder. The mean age of onset for the group with another diagnosis was 35.39 (SD = 13.77, *n* = 57). For the group without another diagnosis, the mean age of onset was 42.20 (SD = 17.65, *n* = 31).
    a. Explain why an unpaired-samples *t*-test is appropriate for these data.
    b. What is the null hypothesis for these data?
    c. What is the α for this example?
    d. Is a one- or a two-tailed hypothesis appropriate for this NHST?
    e. Given your response to item (d), what is the appropriate alternative hypothesis for this example?
    f. Calculate the degrees of freedom for the data.
    g. Find the t_{crit} value.
    h. Calculate the pooled standard deviation and the pooled variance for these data.
    i. Calculate the t_{obs} value for the data.
    j. Should you reject or retain the null hypothesis?
    k. Find a *p*-value for this example.
    l. Should you worry about Type I or Type II error in this example?
    m. Calculate and interpret Cohen's *d* for this example.
    n. Do the data in this example violate any assumptions? If so, which one(s)?
    o. The statistical power for this study was 0.858. Is that sufficient power for this study? If so, what does that mean, and why is it important?
11. Gagné and Gagnier (2004) studied the classroom behavior of children who were a year younger than their classmates and those who were a typical age for their grade. The children's teachers

rated each student's classroom conduct, with higher numbers indicating better behavior. The researchers found that the younger students had a mean score of 15.92 (SD = 5.33, n = 98). The students who were the typical age for their grade had a mean score of 15.01 (SD = 5.85, n = 1,723).

    a.   Explain why an unpaired-samples t-test is appropriate for these data.

    b.   What is the null hypothesis for these data?

    c.   What is the α for this example?

    d.   Several experts on grade skipping and early entrance to school recommend that a child be younger than their classmates only if the child already is well behaved. Given this knowledge, is a one- or a two-tailed hypothesis appropriate for this NHST? Justify your response.

    e.   Given your response to item (d), what is the appropriate alternative hypothesis for this example?

    f.   Calculate the degrees of freedom for the data.

    g.   Find the t_{crit} value.

    h.   Calculate the pooled standard deviation and the pooled variance for these data.

    i.   Calculate the t_{obs} value for the data.

    j.   Should you reject or retain the null hypothesis?

    k.   Find a p-value for this example.

    l.   Should you worry about Type I or Type II error in this example?

    m.   Calculate and interpret Cohen's d for this example.

    n.   Do the data in this example violate any assumptions? If so, which one(s)?

12. Jessi conducts a study to determine whether early voting in an election affects how informed the person is when they vote. She theorizes that people who vote early are more motivated to vote and will therefore spend more time becoming informed about the candidates. She divides her sample into early voters (n = 319) and non-early voters (n = 1,240). She asks each person how much time they spent learning about the candidates and finds that early voters spent an average of 2.4 hours (SD = 0.53) educating themselves, while the non-early voters spent an average of 2.2 hours (SD = 0.62) educating themselves.

    a.   Explain why an unpaired-samples t-test is appropriate for these data.

    b.   What is the null hypothesis for these data?

    c.   What is the α for this example?

    d.   Given Jessi's theory, is a one- or a two-tailed hypothesis appropriate for this NHST?

    e.   Given your response to item (d), what is the appropriate alternative hypothesis for this example?

    f.   Calculate the degrees of freedom for the data.

    g.   Find the t_{crit} value.

    h.   Calculate the pooled standard deviation and the pooled variance for these data.

    i.   Calculate the t_{obs} value for the data.

    j.   Should you reject or retain the null hypothesis?

    k.   Find a p-value for this example.

    l.   Should Jessi worry about Type I or Type II error?

    m.   Calculate and interpret Cohen's d for this example.

    n.   Do the data in this example violate any assumptions? If so, which one(s)?

13. Steven is an anthropology student who collected data on the behavior of children of immigrants and children of non-immigrants in a playground setting. He found that children of immigrants

spent an average of 16.2 minutes (SD = 20.2, n = 44) per hour playing with adults, while children of non-immigrants spent an average of 19.9 minutes (SD = 6.0, n = 113) per hour playing with adults.

   a.   Explain why an unpaired-samples *t*-test is appropriate for these data.
   b.   What is the null hypothesis for these data?
   c.   What is the α for this example?
   d.   Is a one- or a two-tailed hypothesis appropriate for this NHST?
   e.   Given your response to item (d), what is the appropriate alternative hypothesis for this example?
   f.   Calculate the degrees of freedom for the data.
   g.   Find the t_{crit} value.
   h.   Calculate the pooled standard deviation and the pooled variance for these data.
   i.   Calculate the t_{obs} value for the data.
   j.   Should you reject or retain the null hypothesis?
   k.   Find a *p-value* for this example.
   l.   Should Steven worry about Type I or Type II error?
   m. Calculate and interpret Cohen's *d* for this example.
   n.   Do the data in this example violate any assumptions? If so, which one(s)?

14. Conduct an unpaired two-sample *t*-test for the following data: $\overline{X}_1$ = 14.8, s_1 = 1.99, n_1 = 52, $\overline{X}_1$ = 13.2, s_2 = 2.89, n_2 = 233. For this problem, you should use an α value of .01.

   a.   Explain why an unpaired-samples *t*-test is appropriate for these data.
   b.   What is the null hypothesis for these data?
   c.   Is a one- or a two-tailed hypothesis appropriate for this NHST?
   d.   Given your response to item (c), what is the appropriate alternative hypothesis for this example?
   e.   Calculate the degrees of freedom for the data.
   f.   Find the t_{crit} value.
   g.   Calculate the pooled standard deviation and the pooled variance for these data.
   h.   Calculate the t_{obs} value for the data.
   i.   Should you reject or retain the null hypothesis?
   j.   Find a *p-value* for this example.
   k.   Should you worry about Type I or Type II error in this example?
   l.   Calculate and interpret Cohen's *d* for this example.
   m. Do the data in this example violate any assumptions? If so, which one(s)?

15. Jim found that the *p-value* in his study was less than .01. He says, "This means that my null hypothesis is false. My findings are strong enough to replicate."

   a.   Why are both of Jim's statements inaccurate?
   b.   Give a proper interpretation of Jim's *p-value*.

16. Answer the following questions about a scenario where the *p-value* is small (e.g., < .05 or < .01).

   a.   Why would it be incorrect to say that these results are important?
   b.   Why would it also be incorrect to say that these results prove that the null hypothesis is false?
   c.   Explain why it is impossible to know the replicability of the results based solely on the *p-value*.
   d.   Why is it also inaccurate to say that the *p-value* is the probability that the alternative hypothesis is wrong?
   e.   A small *p-value* means that, if the null hypothesis were perfectly true, the results would be unlikely to occur with a random sample of data from the population. Explain why "unlikeliness" is not a very good way to decide whether a hypothesis is true or not.

Software Guide

As the unpaired two-sample *t*-test is one of the most common statistical procedures in use, it is unsurprising that many computer programs are able to conduct this NHST easily.

Excel

In the Software Guides for Chapters 8 and 9, we used the TTEST function in Excel to conduct a one-sample *t*-test and a paired-samples *t*-test. We will use the same function to conduct the unpaired-samples *t*-test:

(a)

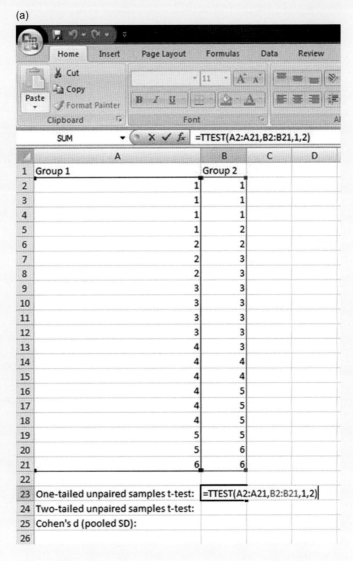

Figure 10.5a Screenshot from Microsoft Excel showing how to use the TTEST function to conduct an unpaired-samples *t*-test.

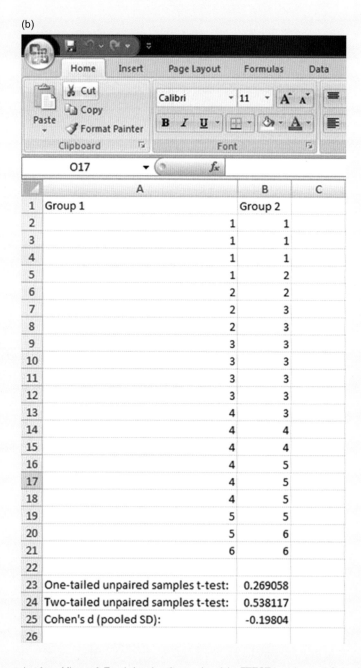

Figure 10.5b Screenshot from Microsoft Excel showing the results of the TTEST function and Cohen's *d*. The results for the unpaired two-sample *t*-tests (in cells B23 and B24) are *p*-values.

- For a one-tailed, paired-samples *t*-test: "=TTEST(XX:XX,YY:YY,1,2)"
- For a two-tailed, paired-samples *t*-test: "=TTEST(XX:XX,YY:YY,2,2)"

In each of these formats, the "XX:XX" should be replaced with cells for the sample. The YY:YY should be replaced with a set of cells that all contain the mean of the population. The number of cells for XX:XX and YY:YY do not have to be the same. Figure 10.5a shows how to use the function, and Figure 10.5b shows the results. The results in Excel are the *p*-values – not the t_{obs} values. If the *p*-value is less than alpha, the user should reject the null hypothesis. If the *p*-value is greater than alpha, the user should retain the null hypothesis.

Excel does not calculate Cohen's *d* as part of the unpaired two-sample *t*-test. Performing this requires a different function: "=(XX-YY)/ZZ". In this function XX is the first sample's mean, YY is the second sample's mean, and ZZ is the standard deviation of both groups of scores combined. Figure 10.5b shows that the Cohen's *d* value in this example is –.198.

SPSS

SPSS's point-and-click interface also makes conducting an unpaired two-sample *t*-test easy. In the data window, you must have at least two columns of data. One of these needs to be a variable that refers to group membership. The other variable needs to be the scores that will be used to calculate the group means. An example of this is shown in Figure 10.6. In this example, the column labeled "B0SEX" is the grouping variable. In this example, I will show how to compare IQ scores across the two groups. The IQ scores are in Figure 10.6 in the column labeled "IQ."

After the data are in the correct format, you should click "Analyze" → "Compare Means" → "Independent-Samples T Tests." This will result in a new window (labeled the "Independent-Samples T Tests" window) appearing, which is shown in Figure 10.7.

In the Independent-Samples T-Test window, you should put the grouping variable in the lower right area (labeled "Grouping Variable"). Figure 10.8 shows what the window looks like when a grouping variable has been selected.

The next step is to tell the computer which groups to compare. You should do this by clicking "Define Groups" on the right-hand side of the window. This causes a new window (labeled "Define Groups") to appear, as shown in Figure 10.9. In the top two areas you should type in the numbers that correspond to the groups' labels in the data window (Figure 10.6). Because the two groups are defined by a zero and a one in the data window, we need to type in the numbers 0 and 1. (If you used other numbers, like 1 and 2, in the data window, then you would type those into this window instead.)

The Define Groups window also permits you to divide your sample into two groups by selecting a cut point on a continuous variable. For example, if I wanted to compare tall subjects to short subjects, I could record their height in the data window, and then use the cut point option to select a height that divides the two groups. I could make 175 cm the cut point. The computer would then automatically define two groups: one for everyone with a height less than 175 cm, and another group containing everyone with a height greater than 175 cm.

After selecting the groups, you should click "Continue" in the Define Groups window. This will make the window disappear. The next step is to select the variable that will be compared across groups and move it into the upper-right area (labeled "Test Variable(s)"). See Figure 10.10 for an example of what this looks like. After both variables have been selected, you should click "OK."

After clicking "OK" in the Independent Samples T Test window, SPSS will produce the results of the unpaired-samples *t*-test as two tables in the output window. An example of this is shown in Figure 10.11. The first table provides the descriptive statistics (sample size, mean, and standard deviation) for each group.

The second table provides the results of the statistical test. These appear in two rows. The upper row is labeled "Equal variances assumed" and shows the results of the *t*-test that this chapter explained. The column labeled "t" is the t_{obs} value, and the "df" column displays the degrees of freedom. The column labeled "Sig. (2-tailed)" provides the *p*-value for the unpaired-samples *t*-test.

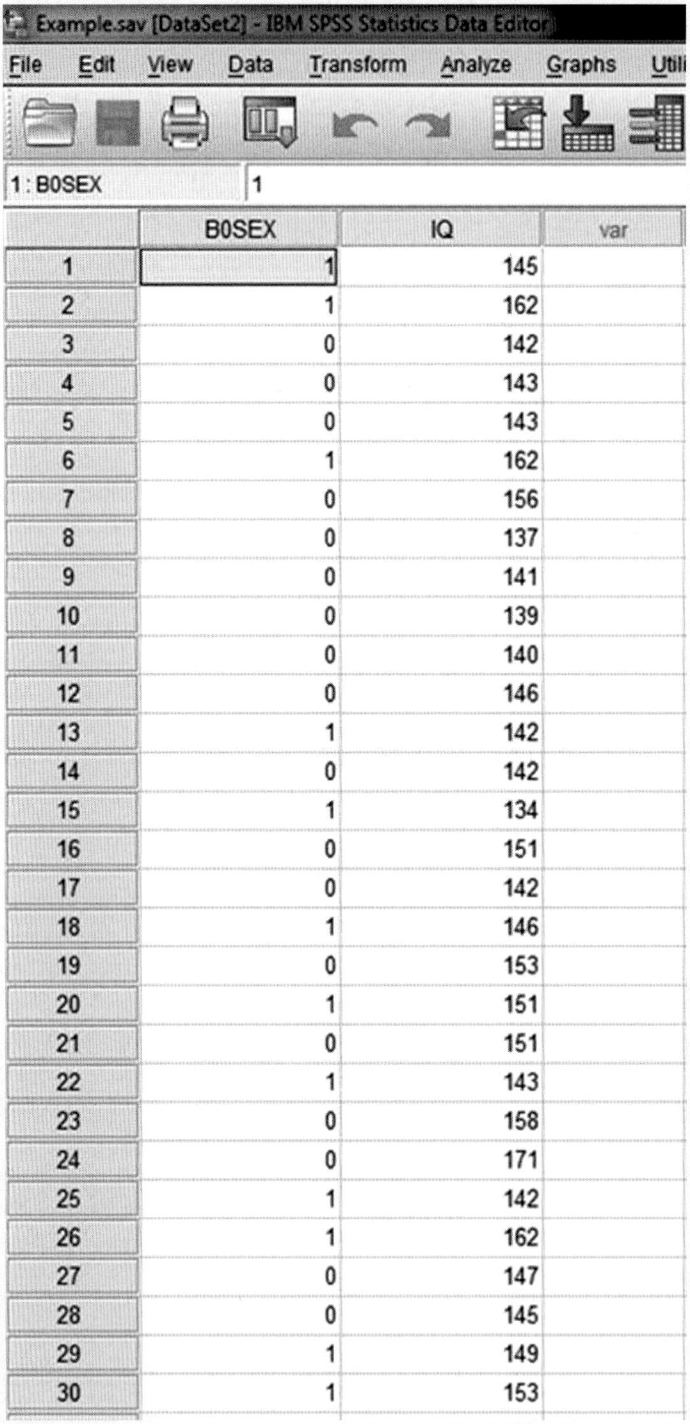

	B0SEX	IQ	var
1	1	145	
2	1	162	
3	0	142	
4	0	143	
5	0	143	
6	1	162	
7	0	156	
8	0	137	
9	0	141	
10	0	139	
11	0	140	
12	0	146	
13	1	142	
14	0	142	
15	1	134	
16	0	151	
17	0	142	
18	1	146	
19	0	153	
20	1	151	
21	0	151	
22	1	143	
23	0	158	
24	0	171	
25	1	142	
26	1	162	
27	0	147	
28	0	145	
29	1	149	
30	1	153	

Figure 10.6 Proper data format in SPSS for conducting an unpaired-samples *t*-test in SPSS. The far-left column is the numbered rows in the computer program. The middle column is the grouping variable (labeled B0SEX), and the right column (labeled IQ) is the variable that will be used to compare the two groups' means. Data from Warne and Liu (2017).

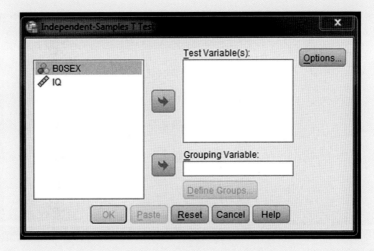

Figure 10.7 The Independent-Samples T-Test window in SPSS.

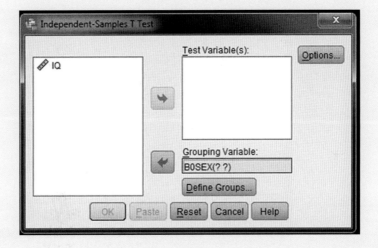

Figure 10.8 The Independent-Samples T Test window in SPSS after the grouping variable has been selected.

If this value is less than the α value, you should reject the null hypothesis; if p is greater than α, you should retain the null hypothesis. SPSS assumes that you want to do a two-tailed test; you can compare the t_{obs} value to the appropriate critical value in Appendix A2 if you wish to conduct a one-tailed test.

The lower row is an adaptation of the unpaired two-sample t-test that is appropriate when the homogeneity of variance assumption is violated. You should interpret the results in this row in the same way as the upper row. The column labeled "Sig. (2-tailed)" provides the p-value. Again, if this value is less than the α value, you should reject the null hypothesis; if p is greater than α, you should retain the null hypothesis. As in the other row, SPSS assumes that you want to do a one-tailed test; you can compare the t_{obs} value to the appropriate critical value in Appendix A2. The differences between these two rows in this example are very slight. This is because the standard deviations and variances of the two groups are very similar in this dataset. As the standard deviations of the two groups diverge, the results in these rows will also become different from one another.

Figure 10.9 The Define Groups window in SPSS. In the fields labeled "Group 1" and "Group 2," the numbers that define the two groups in the data window (Figure 10.6) have been entered in.

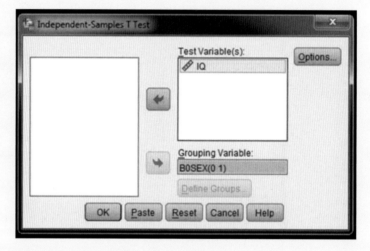

Figure 10.10 The Independent Samples T Test in SPSS window after both the grouping variable and the outcome variable have been selected.

Group Statistics

	BOSEX	N	Mean	Std. Deviation	Std. Error Mean
IQ	Male	856	146.54	9.217	.315
	Female	672	146.08	9.392	.362

Independent Samples Test

		Levene's Test for Equality of Variances		t-test for Equality of Means					95% Confidence Interval of the Difference	
		F	Sig.	t	df	Sig. (2-tailed)	Mean Difference	Std. Error Difference	Lower	Upper
IQ	Equal variances assumed	.221	.639	.976	1526	.329	.467	.479	-.472	1.407
	Equal variances not assumed			.973	1428.392	.331	.467	.480	-.475	1.409

Figure 10.11 Results in the SPSS output window for the unpaired two-sample *t*-test. The upper table shows descriptive statistics for the two groups. The lower table shows results for the unpaired two-sample *t*-test.

Further Reading

- Pearson, E. S. (1939). William Sealy Gosset, 1876–1937: (2) "Student" as statistician. *Biometrika*, *30*, 210–250. doi:10.1093/biomet/30.3-4.210

  * The *t*-test was invented by the Irish chemist William Sealy Gosset. In this article E. S. Pearson discusses the background and statistical contributions of Gosset, including how he realized the shortcomings of the *z*-test when working with small samples. I like this article because it humanizes Gosset and places his statistical discoveries in the context of his practical work as a brewer and chemist. Because I am a psychologist who is more interested in "getting things done" than in formulas and statistical proofs, I feel a connection with Gosset. The article's author was a prominent statistician and the son of Karl Pearson, who worked with Gosset in developing the *t*-test. Karl Pearson is most famous for creating the correlation coefficient, which is the topic of Chapter 12.

- Schimmack, U. (2012). The ironic effect of significant results on the credibility of multiple-study articles. *Psychological Methods*, *17*, 551–566. doi:10.1037/a0029487

  * Some people believe that the answer to unstable results from studies with low statistical power is to conduct a set of similar studies and publish them all together into one article. The logic behind this argument is that if six, eight, or more studies all produce the same effect, the result is likely to be stable. However, Schimmack shows how conducting several small studies with low statistical power is inferior to combining the resources and instead conducting one large study. This counterintuitive result shows the importance of high power and that under typical research circumstances no number of studies with low power can provide as much information as one study with high power – usually obtained from a large sample size.

- Skidmore, S. T., & Thompson, B. (2010). Statistical techniques used in published articles: A historical review of reviews. *Educational and Psychological Measurement*, *70*, 777–795. doi:10.1177/0013164410379320

  * The *t*-test (in all its various forms) is one of the most common statistical methods in the social sciences. In this article Skidmore and Thompson examine how common the *t*-test has been throughout the late twentieth century, and examine trends in the use of the *t*-test and other common statistical procedures that this textbook covers.

- Wasserstein, R. L., & Lazar, N. A. (2016). The ASA's statement on *p* values: Context, process, and purpose. *American Statistician*, *70*, 129–133. doi:10.1080/00031305.2016.1154108

  * This article is an official statement on *p*-values from the American Statistical Association. Written for a non-statistician audience, this short article explains correct interpretations of *p*-values and provides references to resources that provide in-depth discussions of correct and incorrect understanding of *p*.

11   Analysis of Variance

Until now we have only compared two means in our null hypothesis statistical significance tests. This is a useful procedure, but it has its limits. For example, one group of researchers were interested in levels of indecisiveness across three cultural groups: European Canadians, Mainland Chinese, and Hong Kong Chinese college students (Li, Masuda, & Jiang, 2016). An unpaired two-sample *t*-test is not appropriate for this situation because there are three groups. In this chapter we will discuss how to analyze data in situations like this (i.e., where there are more than two groups). We can use the methods in this chapter to determine whether the means from the groups are similar or if there are differences among groups.

Learning Goals

- Explain the problems of conducting multiple two-sample *t*-tests when comparing means from three or more groups.

- Make a Bonferroni correction to prevent Type I error inflation.

- Perform an analysis of variance.

- Calculate the effect size (η^2) for an analysis of variance.

- Identify when it is appropriate to conduct a *post hoc* test after an analysis of variance.

- Perform Tukey's *post hoc* test.

Comparing Means from Three or More Groups

Each chapter since Chapter 7 has been dedicated to a single null hypothesis statistical significance testing (NHST) procedure. As we have progressed from one chapter to another, these procedures have grown more complex. Among their common characteristics is the fact that the null hypothesis was always expressed as two means being equal. For example, the *z*-test (in Chapter 7) always has the null hypothesis of $H_0 : \mu = \overline{X}$, which states that the population mean (μ) is equal to the sample mean ($\overline{X}$). As another example, the unpaired-samples *t*-test (in Chapter 10) always has the null hypothesis of $H_0 : \overline{X}_1 = \overline{X}_2$, which is that sample means from two independent groups are equal.

However, it is common for social scientists to be interested in more than two groups at a time. This chapter opened with an example of such a study, where Li et al. (2016) studied levels of decisiveness across three cultural groups. If the researchers had used an unpaired-samples *t*-test (see Chapter 10), they would have compared the groups' means two at a time, requiring three *t*-tests:

- one *t*-test to compare the means for the European Canadian group and the Mainland Chinese group ($H_0 : \overline{X}_{EC} = \overline{X}_{MC}$)
- another *t*-test to compare the means for the European Canadian group and the Hong Kong Chinese group ($H_0 : \overline{X}_{EC} = \overline{X}_{HKC}$)
- a final *t*-test to compare the means for the Mainland Chinese group and the Hong Kong Chinese group ($H_0 : \overline{X}_{MC} = \overline{X}_{HKC}$).

After conducting all three of these unpaired-samples *t*-tests, the researchers could determine whether all three groups had similar means (if all three null hypotheses were retained), or if some means differed from others (if at least one null hypothesis were rejected).

In fact, whenever there are at least three groups, it would be necessary to perform multiple unpaired-samples *t*-tests to make all possible comparisons. These *t*-tests would all have to be conducted to detect the presence of group mean differences and understand the pattern of any differences among groups. The number of unpaired-samples *t*-tests will always be:

$$m = \frac{k(k-1)}{2}$$
(Formula 11.1)

In Formula 11.1 (which is from Tukey, 1991, p. 107, with the notation changed slightly), k is the number of groups in the independent variable and m is the number of statistical significance tests required. Therefore, for the Li et al. (2016) study, $k = 3$. Plugging 3 into Formula 11.1 shows that three unpaired-samples *t*-tests would be required (because $\frac{3(3-1)}{2} = \frac{3(2)}{2} = \frac{6}{2} = 3$), matching the list of the *t*-tests in the previous paragraph.

Problems with Multiple *t*-Tests

Although performing three *t*-tests is not very burdensome, the practice of conducting a series of two-sample *t*-tests has two drawbacks. One problem is that the number of *t*-tests can become very large. The second problem is that a series of *t*-tests has a greater Type I error rate than the Type I error probability of any single *t*-test. Both of these drawbacks merit some explanation.

Increasing Number of Tests. The first problem with conducting multiple unpaired-samples *t*-tests is that the number of tests rises quickly as the number of groups in the independent variable increases. According to Formula 11.1, three groups require three unpaired-samples *t*-tests to test all possible null hypotheses. With a fourth group, the number of required tests rises to six. Five groups require 10 unpaired-samples *t*-tests. This rapid rise in the number of required NHSTs can be seen in the second column of Table 11.1 (see also Tukey, 1991, p. 104).

Type I Error Inflation. The second problem is that conducting multiple NHSTs increases the risk of committing a Type I error. In other words, if $\alpha = .05$ for each of the three *t*-tests in the Li et al. (2016) data, the overall risk of committing a Type I error in any of the NHSTs in the group may be greater than .05. In fact, according to Hummel and Sligo (1971, p. 50), the actual maximum Type I error rate across a series of *t*-tests would be:

$$\alpha_{experimentwise} = 1 - \left(1 - \alpha_{testwise}\right)^m$$
(Formula 11.2)

In Formula 11.2, $\alpha_{testwise}$ represents the α level of each individual *t*-test (called the **testwise Type I error**), and $\alpha_{experimentwise}$ is the probability of making a Type I error at any point in the series of

Table 11.1 Required number of unpaired-samples t-tests and experimentwise Type I error rate for a given number of groups ($\alpha = .05$)

Number of groups	Required number of Tests	Uncorrected experimentwise Type I error rate	Testwise Type I error rate after Bonferroni correction
2	1	.05	.05 / 1 = .05
3	3	.143	.05 / 3 = .0167
4	6	.265	.05 / 6 = .0083
5	10	.401	.05 / 10 = .0050
6	15	.537	.05 / 15 = .0033
7	21	.659	.05 / 21 = .0024
8	28	.762	.05 / 28 = .0018
9	36	.842	.05 / 36 = .0014
10	45	.901	.05 / 45 = .0011
15	105	.995	.05 / 105 = .0005
20	190	.99994	.05 / 190 = .0003

t-tests, which is called the **experimentwise Type I error**. In a series of three t-tests where $\alpha = .05$ for each test, the maximum experimentwise Type I error rate would be:

$$\alpha_{experimentwise} = 1 - (1 - .05)^3 = 1 - .95^3 = 1 - .857375 = .142625$$

With a maximum experimentwise Type I error probability of .142625, we can conclude that even though the probability of making a Type I error for a particular t-test is 5% (because $\alpha_{testwise} = .05$), the probability of making a Type I error in any of the t-tests is 14.2625%. With the default maximum Type I error in the social sciences generally being 5%, an experimentwise Type I error rate of nearly 15% is often too high for comfort.[8] The third column in Table 11.1 shows how increasing the number of groups also increases the experimentwise Type I error rate.

Solutions to Problems of Multiple Comparisons

Although the second problem – that of Type I error inflation – is harder to understand, it is actually the easier problem to solve. Basically, if the Type I error is too high, the solution is to lower it by a **Bonferroni correction**. To perform a Bonferroni correction, you should use the following formula:

$$\alpha_{adjusted} = \frac{\alpha}{m} \qquad \text{(Formula 11.3)}$$

[8] This example shows experimentwise Type I error for a set of means from three or more groups. However, the exact same principles and formulas also apply to any set of null hypothesis tests – not comparisons of pairs of groups within a set of three or more independent variable groups. For example, if a sociologist is interested in levels of civic engagement across gender groups, she may measure males' and females' average scores on four variables: voting participation, time spent becoming informed about political issues, time spent volunteering for local organizations, and amount of money donated to civic causes. She could then conduct four unpaired-samples t-tests to compare males' and females' mean scores on each variable. Using Formula 11.2, we can see that if testwise $\alpha = .05$ for these four t-tests, experimentwise $\alpha = .185$.

Just as in Formula 11.1, m is the number of statistical significance tests to be performed. Therefore, if – as in the Li et al. (2016) example – there are three groups, then, to conduct an unpaired-samples t-test for each set of two group means (which requires $m = 3$ null hypothesis tests), the new testwise α after adjusting with the Bonferroni correction is .05 / 3 = .0167. If we set the testwise α to this value for each unpaired-samples t-test, the experimentwise α will be no greater than .05. This, therefore, controls for Type I error inflation (Dunn, 1961).

The Bonferroni correction has the advantage of being simple, elegant, and understandable. (In fact, after learning the problem of Type I error inflation, some of my students on their own suggest lowering the testwise α before they have even learned about the Bonferroni correction.) Because the logic behind a Bonferroni correction is intuitive, Bonferroni corrections are common in the social sciences (Warne et al., 2012). However, the Bonferroni correction has two problems. First, a Bonferroni correction is often too severe because it is based on the assumption that the maximum experimentwise Type I error is equal to the actual error rate. However, testwise and experimentwise Type I error rates are often below their maximum levels. When this happens, the Bonferroni correction will produce an actual experimentwise Type I error much lower than the desired .05 level (Warne, 2014a). Bonferroni corrections are also too severe when there are a large number of tests (Stevens, 2002). This is apparent in Table 11.1, which shows that the corrected testwise α values (in the far right column) can get so tiny that rejecting the null hypothesis for any individual NHST can become nearly impossible.

The second problem with the Bonferroni correction is that it doesn't address the problem of the increasing number of NHSTs. For this purpose the analysis of variance (ANOVA) was created. The rest of this chapter is devoted to explaining ANOVA, its assumptions, and related issues.

Check Yourself!

- What are the two shortcomings of using multiple unpaired-samples t-tests to compare means from more than two groups?
- Explain the difference between testwise Type I error and experimentwise Type I error.
- What is a Bonferroni correction, and how does it reduce Type I error?
- If a researcher wanted to compare means from five groups, how many two-sample t-tests would be required?

ANOVA

An ANOVA is a NHST procedure designed to make comparisons of three or more means. By making all comparisons of group means simultaneously, ANOVA avoids the need to conduct multiple unpaired-samples t-tests – a major time saver in the era before computers when the first versions of ANOVA were invented (the 1920s). Even in modern times an ANOVA is often simpler to interpret than a large number of unpaired-samples t-tests would be, which may be why ANOVA is one of the most common statistics used in the social sciences (Bangert & Baumberger, 2005;

Table 11.2 Raw data for ANOVA example: Stroop Test times (measured in seconds)

Group A	Group B	Group C	Group D
8	22	10	18
10	29	12	32
11	38	9	20

Note. For an explanation of the groups, see the text.

Baumberger & Bangert, 1996; Kieffer et al., 2001; Skidmore & Thompson, 2010; Warne et al., 2012; Zientek et al., 2008).

As another NHST procedure, conducting an ANOVA requires following the same eight steps as all null hypothesis tests:

1. Form groups in the data.
2. Define the null hypothesis (H_0). The null hypothesis is always that there is no difference between groups or that there is no relationship between independent and dependent variables.
3. Set alpha (α). The default alpha = .05.
4. Choose a one-tailed or a two-tailed test. This determines the alternative hypothesis (H_1).
5. Find the *critical* value, which is used to define the rejection region.
6. Calculate the *observed* value.
7. Compare the observed value and the critical value. If the observed value is more extreme than the critical value, then the null hypothesis should be rejected. Otherwise, it should be retained.
8. Calculate an *effect size*.

As you read through this chapter, I encourage you to compare the procedure for conducting an ANOVA with the procedure for an unpaired two-sample *t*-test. ANOVA is a generalization of the unpaired two-sample *t*-test (see General Linear Moment 11.1), meaning you should see similarities among the two that will help you learn ANOVA more easily. ANOVA can sometimes seem complex, but this is a small price to pay for conducting just one NHST and eliminating Type I error inflation.

To demonstrate ANOVA, I will be using the data from Table 11.2, which shows data that one of my students collected using a version of the Stroop (1935) Test. This is a very basic test of mental interference in which subjects are asked to name the color that a word is printed in. For Groups A and C in the table, the color of the word's ink matched the word's text (e.g., the word "red" was printed in red ink, the word "orange" was printed in orange ink, etc.). Groups B and D read words where the color of the word's ink did not match the word's text (e.g., the word "red" was printed in blue ink," the word "orange" was printed in red ink, etc.). Each word list consisted of 24 color words, and the student timed how long it took each person to read the entire list of words. Groups A and B were males, and Groups C and D were females. In studies using the Stroop method, almost everyone takes longer to read the list of words where the text and ink are mismatched. Later studies have shown that the Stroop Test is useful for diagnosing brain damage because people with brain damage often take longer than the general population to name the color of words (Golden, 1976). Even in healthy populations, people who do well on the Stroop Test tend to have better cognitive functioning (Brydges, Reid, Fox, & Anderson, 2012).

Form Groups in the Data. In ANOVA (and in the two-sample *t*-test), the groups in the data (i.e., Group A, Group B, Group C, and Group D) are formed with the nominal-level independent variable. The dependent variable is the outcome variable, which we use to compare means across the groups. In the example data (displayed in Table 11.2), there are four groups for the independent variable. The dependent variable scores for each individual in the sample are displayed as the numbers in the table.

Define the Null Hypothesis. In all NHST procedures the second step is to define the null hypothesis. In the previous chapter the null hypothesis was that the two group means were equal (i.e., $H_0 : \overline{X}_1 = \overline{X}_2$). This null hypothesis doesn't work for ANOVA because there are more than two groups in ANOVA. Therefore, we need to alter this null hypothesis to add more groups. For three groups you can expand the null hypothesis to $H_0 : \overline{X}_1 = \overline{X}_2 = \overline{X}_3$. With four groups you can alter this null hypothesis further to $H_0 : \overline{X}_1 = \overline{X}_2 = \overline{X}_3 = \overline{X}_4$. Thus, it is apparent that creating a null hypothesis for ANOVA requires stating that all the group means are equal.

There is an alternative way to write the null hypothesis that applies to any number of groups. That formula is:

$$H_0 : \overline{X}_1 = \overline{X}_2 = \ldots = \overline{X}_k \qquad \text{(Formula 11.4)}$$

In this formula, k is the number of groups (as it was in Formula 11.1). Therefore, Formula 11.4 says that the null hypothesis (H_0) is that the first group's mean ($\overline{X}_1$) is equal to the second group's mean ($\overline{X}_2$). These means are, in turn, equal to the next group's mean and the next group's mean, until all k groups are included in the null hypothesis. When you state the null hypothesis for an ANOVA, it does not matter whether you write Formula 11.4, or whether you write out all the $\overline{X}$'s (e.g., $H_0 : \overline{X}_1 = \overline{X}_2 = \overline{X}_3 = \overline{X}_4$ for four groups).

Set Alpha. After formulating the null hypothesis, the third step in conducting an ANOVA is to set alpha. Once again, .05 is the default α value in ANOVA, although it may be sensible to increase or decrease alpha. We already know that a small sample size makes it hard to reject the null hypothesis, so lowering alpha for the example ANOVA would not be a good idea because the sample size is already very small ($n_{Total} = 12$). Conversely, increasing α is also not a good idea. Other researchers are often suspicious when α is greater than .05 because it looks like the person is trying to make it artificially easy to reject the null hypothesis. Therefore, we are going to keep α at .05 for this example ANOVA.

Sidebar 11.1 **When to adjust alpha levels**

You have seen in every chapter since Chapter 7 that the default α value is .05, meaning that the size of the rejection region is 5% of the entire area of the sampling distribution. This is – by far – the most common α value in the social sciences. However, there is nothing special about .05, and if it suits the needs of your study you may choose another α value (Rosnow & Rosenthal, 1989). *If you choose to change alpha, you should be able to justify your decision.* The purpose of this sidebar is to explain in more detail when it would be justified to change α.

Lowering Alpha. Lowering α makes it harder to reject the null hypothesis, because the rejection region is smaller. One common reason to lower α is a large sample size. As sample size grows, it becomes easier to reject the null hypothesis. This leads some people to claim that NHSTs are basically a measure of sample size: rejecting the null hypothesis means you have a large sample size, because with a large sample size you can reject almost any null hypothesis (Thompson, 1992). Therefore, researchers with a large sample size will often lower α in order to mitigate the influence of the sample size on their likelihood of rejecting the null hypothesis.

Another reason to lower α is a large number of null hypotheses in the study. Remember that as the number of statistical significance tests increases, the experimentwise Type I error also increases. Therefore, many authors who plan to conduct many NHSTs often lower α in an effort to control Type I error inflation. As an extreme example, in studies of genetic influences on behavior, researchers often conduct hundreds of NHSTs as they examine each gene's influence on behavior. Because they often investigate hundreds of genes at once, these studies are very vulnerable to Type I errors. Therefore, these researchers often reduce the α value, perhaps with a Bonferroni correction. But lowering the α to handle hundreds of NHSTs often leads to tiny α values, such as Okbay et al.'s (2016) α value of .00000005. (Despite the miniscule α value, the researchers still found genes that had a statistically significant relationship with personality traits.)

Lowering α is also a good idea in **exploratory research**, which is not driven by pre-existing hypotheses or theory. People who conduct this research are often conducting some of the first studies on a topic, so they are frequently performing many NHSTs in order to determine what variables are related to one another. Discovering these relationships can lead researchers to develop a theoretical model that can serve as a foundation for future studies. However, results from exploratory data analysis can be unstable and unreplicable (Ioannidis, 2005). Exploratory research can also produce results that are surprising or don't make theoretical sense, as when Google Correlate results showed that people in US states with lower average IQs conduct more Internet searches for Hello Kitty (McDaniel, Pesta, & Gabriel, 2015). Reducing α can reduce the likelihood of producing weird, fluky, unreplicable results.

Raising Alpha. Lowering α is much more common than raising alpha, because most researchers usually expect to reject their null hypothesis. Therefore, taking any steps that would make it easy to reject the null hypothesis is sometimes perceived as "cheating" or manipulating the data to produce the results that the researcher wants.

However, it is sometimes justifiable to raise α. One of these situations may occur if getting a large sample size is difficult or impossible, as when studying a rare population or if a study is very expensive or time-consuming. For example, when I was a graduate student, I performed a study that took 18 months to collect data at multiple time points from children (Warne, 2011a, 2014b). In this situation it was justified to raise α to .10 because the sample was too small to make testing the null hypothesis when α = .05 meaningful, and it was too time-consuming and expensive to expand the sample.

Raising α is also defensible in situations where the costs of Type I error are much lower than those of a Type II error. For example, a medical researcher testing a new drug may be searching for possible side effects. If α is higher, she will be less likely to miss any potentially harmful consequences of the drug. Raising α in this case could save lives.

Choose a One-Tailed or a Two-Tailed Test. With α set, the fourth step in conducting an NHST is to select a one- or a two-tailed test. This is a particularly easy step in ANOVA because the sampling distribution, called an *F*-distribution, is always one-tailed. Like the *t*-distribution (see Chapter 8), the *F*-distribution changes shape as the number of degrees of freedom changes. Figure 11.1 shows several forms that the *F*-distribution can take. All of these have one long tail to the right of the distribution, making them positively skewed. We will see later (in step 6 of ANOVA) that observed values are always at least zero for ANOVA. Because we never get a negative value in our *F*-distribution, we never have to worry about the negative side of the number line in an ANOVA. Therefore, the rejection region in an ANOVA is always on the right side of the *F*-distribution. That is why we only perform one-tailed tests with ANOVA.

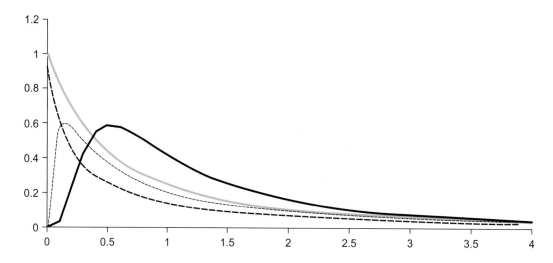

Figure 11.1 Examples of *F*-distributions. The *F*-distribution is the sampling distribution for analysis of variance. Notice that all *F*-distributions are positively skewed and that all values in an *F*-distribution have a minimum of zero (as shown on the horizontal axis).

Because only one-tailed tests with the rejection region on the right side of the sampling distribution are possible with ANOVA, there is also only one possible alternative hypothesis for an ANOVA. That is:

$$H_1 : \overline{X} \neq \overline{X}, \text{for any two means} \qquad \text{(Formula 11.5)}$$

In other words, to reject the null hypothesis, which states that all group means are equal (see Formula 11.4), we merely need to find any two means that are not statistically equal to one another. It does not matter at all which two means differ.

Check Yourself!

- What level of data is the independent variable in an ANOVA?

- When is it appropriate to raise α for a null hypothesis test? When is it appropriate to lower α?

- What is the null hypothesis for an ANOVA?

- Why is an ANOVA always a one-tailed test of the null hypothesis?

Sidebar 11.2 **Why ANOVA's sampling distribution is called the *F*-distribution**

In Sidebar 9.1, I explained how the terminology in statistics can sometimes be confusing. The *F*-distribution and the *F*-table (i.e., Appendix A3), which are both needed to perform an ANOVA, are examples of the confusing terminology in statistics. After all, a *z*-test uses the *z*-distribution and the *z*-table; the *t*-tests use the t-distribution and the t-table. But there is no ANOVA distribution, and the table in Appendix A3 of this textbook is not called the ANOVA table. Why are they called the F-distribution and the F-table?

They are called this because the earliest form of ANOVA was created by Sir Ronald Fisher in the 1920s. In the next decade the statistician George W. Snedecor created the F-table and gave it that name to honor Fisher. Few statisticians deserved the honor of having something named after them as much as Fisher. He is probably the most influential statistician who ever lived. His work revolutionized the social sciences, and he also made major contributions to agriculture and genetics. In 1952 he became one of a small handful of statisticians to be knighted when Queen Elizabeth II bestowed that honor upon him.

Find the Critical Value. This is step 5. With previous NHSTs, we found the critical value by using the tables in the appendices of the book. This is also how to find the critical value, called F_{crit}, in an ANOVA. For this NHST, we use Appendix A3. This table is called the F-table, and it is more complex than previous tables in the appendices.

To use Appendix A3, you must know the $df_{Between}$ and df_{Within}, requiring the following formulas:

$$df_{Between} = k - 1 \qquad \text{(Formula 11.6)}$$

$$df_{Within} = n_{Total} - k \qquad \text{(Formula 11.7)}$$

where k is the number of groups and n_{Total} is the total sample size (for all groups combined).

With these two df values, we can use Appendix A3 to find the F_{crit} value. The table in this appendix has a column for each $df_{Between}$ (up to 15) and a row for each df_{Within} (up to 500). You should find the row that corresponds to the number of $df_{Between}$ in the data and the column that corresponds to the number of df_{Within} in the data. Where this column and row meet, there will be two numbers. One will be in **boldface**, and the other will be in *italics*. The number in boldface is the F_{crit} value for $\alpha = .05$, and the number in italics is the F_{crit} value for $\alpha = .01$.

In the Stroop Test example, $df_{Between} = 3$ (because $k = 4$, and $4 - 1 = 3$) and $df_{Within} = 8$ (because $n = 12$, and $12 - 4 = 8$). Therefore, we should find the column labeled "3" and the row labeled "8." Where this column and row meet, there are two numbers. The number 4.066 is in boldface, and the number 7.591 is in italics. Because the boldface number corresponds to our α value (i.e., .05), the correct F_{crit} value for our data is 4.066.

Find the Observed Value. Step 6 in any NHST is to find the observed value (called F-observed, and abbreviated F_{obs}). Calculating this value is a multistep process that requires two tables. Table 11.3 displays the first table needed to calculate F_{obs}. This table is called the **information table**. There are four rows in the information table that require calculation. These are:

- The sum of scores on the dependent variable, which is $\sum Y$.
- The sum of the squared scores on the dependent variable, which is shown in Table 11.3 as $\sum (Y^2)$.
- The number of sample members, which is n.
- The mean score ($\overline{Y}$) for the dependent variable.

Each of these values is calculated separately for each group and for the entire sample. For example, finding the sum of dependent variable scores for Group A requires adding together all of Group A's scores ($8 + 10 + 11 = 29$). The process is repeated for the other groups (e.g., for Group B the

Table 11.3 Information table for ANOVA example: Stroop Test times (measured in seconds)

	Group A	Group B	Group C	Group D	Total
	8	22	10	18	
	10	29	12	32	
	11	38	9	20	
$\sum Y$	29	89	31	70	219
$\sum (Y^2)$	285	2,769	325	1,748	5,127
N	3	3	3	3	12
$\overline{Y}$	$9\frac{2}{3}$	$29\frac{2}{3}$	$10\frac{1}{3}$	$23\frac{1}{3}$	$18\frac{1}{4}$

Note. For an explanation of the groups, see the text.

sum of the scores is $22 + 29 + 38 = 89$). After all of the groups' summed scores are found, these $\sum Y$ values are added together to produce the value in the Total column (that is, $29 + 89 + 31 + 70 = 219$).

The next row, labeled $\sum (Y^2)$, requires the scores in each group to be squared first and then added together. For Group A, this is:

$$8^2 + 10^2 + 11^2 = 64 + 100 + 121 = 285$$

For Group B:

$$22^2 + 29^2 + 38^2 = 484 + 841 + 1444 = 2,769$$

For Group C:

$$10^2 + 12^2 + 9^2 = 100 + 144 + 81 = 325$$

And for Group D:

$$18^2 + 32^2 + 20^2 = 324 + 1,024 + 400 = 1,748$$

To find the total value for that row, you should just add up the values for each group in the row. This results in:

$$285 + 2,769 + 325 + 1,748 = 5,127$$

The third row in the information table is labeled *n*. For each group, this is the number of scores within the group. For Table 11.3 there are three people per group (i.e., $n_{Group} = 3$ for all four groups). Adding together these group sizes produces a total sample size (n_{Total}) of 12. The final row of the table, which has the label $\overline{Y}$, is the mean for each group. We calculated this in Group A by finding the sum of the scores (which was 29) and dividing by the number of scores in Group A (which was 3). This produces a mean of $9\frac{2}{3}$ (because $29 \div 3 = 9\frac{2}{3}$). The means for all the other groups and the total sample are calculated the same way.

With the information table completed, we can now move on to the second table, which is called the **ANOVA table**. An ANOVA table with the formulas needed for each cell is displayed in Table 11.4. The ANOVA table divides the dependent variable variance of the data into two portions. One portion is variance between the independent variable groups, while the other portion is variance

Table 11.4 ANOVA table with formulas

	SOS	df	MS	F_{obs}
Between	Formula 11.8	$k-1$	$\frac{SOS_{Between}}{df_{Between}}$	$\frac{MS_{Between}}{MS_{Within}}$
Within	Formula 11.9	$n_{Total}-k$	$\frac{SOS_{Within}}{df_{Within}}$	
Total	Formula 11.10	$n_{Total}-1$		

Note. SOS = sum of squares, df = degrees of freedom, MS = mean square, F_{obs} = F-observed value.

within the independent variable groups. These two pieces of variance add up to the total variance. For this reason, there are three rows in the ANOVA table, labeled "Between," "Within," and "Total."

The first step to completing the ANOVA table is to calculate the sum of squares (SOS) for each row. The formulas for the sum of squares are:

$$SOS_{Between} = \sum\left(\frac{\left(\sum Y_{Group}\right)^2}{n_{Group}}\right) - \frac{\left(\sum Y_{Total}\right)^2}{n_{Total}} \qquad \text{(Formula 11.8)}$$

$$SOS_{Within} = \sum_{k=1}^{k}\left(\sum\left(Y_i - \overline{Y}_{Group}\right)^2\right) \qquad \text{(Formula 11.9)}$$

$$SOS_{Total} = \sum Y_{Total}^2 - \frac{\left(\sum Y_{Total}\right)^2}{n_{Total}} \qquad \text{(Formula 11.10)}$$

Most of the information needed to calculate the three SOS values is in the information table (i.e., Table 11.3). The first part of the $SOS_{Between}$ formula, which is $\sum\left(\frac{\left(\sum Y_{Group}\right)^2}{n_{Group}}\right)$, can be replaced with a series of fractions, each with the sum of a group's scores squared and then divided by the number of scores in each group. If we use the Stroop Test example data, this becomes:

$$SOS_{Between} = \frac{29^2}{3} + \frac{89^2}{3} + \frac{31^2}{3} + \frac{70^2}{3} - \frac{\left(\sum Y_{Total}\right)^2}{n_{Total}}$$

The number of fractions in this section of the $SOS_{Between}$ formula will always be equal to the number of groups in the independent variable. In this example, there are four groups, so there are four fractions. The second section of the $SOS_{Between}$ formula, $\frac{\left(\sum Y_{Total}\right)^2}{n_{Total}}$, is the squared sum of all groups scores divided by the total number of scores in the entire sample. Both of these numbers are available in the "Total" column of the information table. Plugging them into the $SOS_{Between}$ formula produces:

$$SOS_{Between} = \frac{29^2}{3} + \frac{89^2}{3} + \frac{31^2}{3} + \frac{70^2}{3} - \frac{219^2}{12}$$

Once these numbers are in place, some arithmetic produces a final $SOS_{Between}$ value.

$$SOS_{Between} = \frac{841}{3} + \frac{7,921}{3} + \frac{961}{3} + \frac{4,900}{3} - \frac{47,961}{12}$$

$$SOS_{Between} = 280\frac{1}{3} + 2,640\frac{1}{3} + 320\frac{1}{3} + 1,633\frac{1}{3} - 3,996\frac{3}{4}$$

$$SOS_{Between} = 4,874\frac{1}{3} - 3,996\frac{3}{4}$$

$$SOS_{Between} = 877.583$$

The SOS_{Within} formula also has two parts to it. The first, $\sum\left(Y_i - \overline{Y}_{Group}\right)^2$, means that we need to find the sum of all the squared deviation scores for each group. To do this, we need to first find $Y_i - \overline{Y}_{Group}$, which is each score minus the *mean for that group* (not the mean for the entire sample). Each individual in the dataset will get a $Y_i - \overline{Y}_{Group}$ value. We then add these values together for each group. For Group A of the Stroop example data, which has a group mean of $9\frac{2}{3}$, these deviation scores would be:

$$8 - 9\frac{2}{3} = -1\frac{2}{3}$$

$$10 - 9\frac{2}{3} = \frac{1}{3}$$

$$11 - 9\frac{2}{3} = 1\frac{1}{3}$$

The next step is to square all of these scores:

$$\left(-1\frac{2}{3}\right)^2 = 2\frac{7}{9}$$

$$\left(\frac{1}{3}\right)^2 = \frac{1}{9}$$

$$\left(1\frac{1}{3}\right)^2 = 1\frac{7}{9}$$

Then, we add these numbers together:

$$2\frac{7}{9} + \frac{1}{9} + 1\frac{7}{9} = 4\frac{2}{3}$$

The process is then repeated for Group B, which has a mean of $29\frac{2}{3}$:

$$\left(22 - 29\frac{2}{3}\right)^2 = \left(-7\frac{2}{3}\right)^2 = 58\frac{7}{9}$$

$$\left(29 - 29\frac{2}{3}\right)^2 = \left(-\frac{2}{3}\right)^2 = \frac{4}{9}$$

$$\left(38 - 29\frac{2}{3}\right)^2 = \left(8\frac{2}{3}\right)^2 = 69\frac{4}{9}$$

$$58\frac{7}{9} + \frac{4}{9} + 69\frac{4}{9} = 128\frac{2}{3}$$

Likewise, we do the same for Group C, which has a mean of $10\frac{2}{3}$:

$$\left(10 - 10\frac{1}{3}\right)^2 = \left(-\frac{1}{3}\right)^2 = \frac{1}{9}$$

$$\left(12 - 10\frac{1}{3}\right)^2 = \left(1\frac{2}{3}\right)^2 = 2\frac{7}{9}$$

$$\left(9 - 10\frac{1}{3}\right)^2 = \left(-1\frac{1}{3}\right)^2 = 1\frac{7}{9}$$

$$\frac{1}{9} + 2\frac{7}{9} + 1\frac{7}{9} = 4\frac{2}{3}$$

And also for Group D, which has a mean of $23\frac{1}{3}$:

$$\left(18 - 23\frac{1}{3}\right)^2 = \left(-5\frac{1}{3}\right)^2 = 28\frac{4}{9}$$

$$\left(32 - 23\frac{1}{3}\right)^2 = \left(8\frac{2}{3}\right)^2 = 75\frac{1}{9}$$

$$\left(20 - 23\frac{1}{3}\right)^2 = \left(-3\frac{1}{3}\right)^2 = 11\frac{1}{9}$$

$$28\frac{4}{9} + 75\frac{1}{9} + 11\frac{1}{9} = 114\frac{2}{3}$$

With all of the squared deviation scores for each group calculated, we can now handle the first Σ in SOS_{Within} formula. For this part of the formula we add up the numbers we calculated in the previous step (i.e., squared deviation scores for each group). In the Stroop example data this is:

$$SOS_{Within} = 4\frac{2}{3} + 128\frac{2}{3} + 4\frac{2}{3} + 114\frac{2}{3} = 252\frac{2}{3}$$

Finally, calculating the SOS_{Total} is similar to the other sum of squares formulas because it also requires using numbers from the information table in the formula (in this case, Formula 11.10). The first half of the formula ($\sum Y^2_{Total}$) is just the sum of all of the squared scores across all groups. In the Stroop Test example data, this value was 5,127 (which we can obtain from Table 11.3). The second half of the formula, which is $\frac{\left(\sum Y_{Total}\right)^2}{n_{Total}}$, is a fraction where the numerator is the squared sum of all scores in the sample, and the denominator is n_{Total}. For the example data in Table 11.3, this fraction would be $\frac{219^2}{12}$. Plugging these values from the example into the SOS_{Total} formula produces:

$$SOS_{Total} = 5,127 - \frac{219^2}{12}$$

which simplifies to:

$$SOS_{Total} = 5,127 - \frac{47,961}{12}$$

$$SOS_{Total} = 5,127 - 3996\frac{3}{4}$$

$$SOS_{Total} = 1130.25$$

Table 11.5 Partially completed ANOVA table (using Stroop Test data)

	SOS	df	MS	F_{obs}
Between	877.583	3		
Within	252.667	8		
Total	1,130.25	11		

Note. SOS = sum of squares, df = degrees of freedom, MS = mean square, F_{obs} = F-observed value.

With the SOS values calculated, the next step in completing the ANOVA table is to find the degrees of freedom for each row. As Table 11.4 shows, $df_{Between} = k - 1$ (which is Formula 11.6), $df_{Within} = n_{Total} - k$ (which is Formula 11.7), and $df_{Total} = n_{Total} - 1$. Remember that k is the number of groups (in our example, $k = 4$), and n_{Total} is the total sample size (which is 12 in the example data). Therefore,

$$df_{Between} = 4 - 1 = 3$$

$$df_{Within} = 12 - 4 = 8$$

$$df_{Total} = 12 - 1 = 11$$

With the degrees of freedom and SOS values, we can complete the left half of the ANOVA table. These numbers are shown in Table 11.5.

Sidebar 11.3 **Hints for completing the ANOVA table**

Because there are so many steps in the arithmetic of completing an ANOVA table, it is easy to make a mistake. Here are a few tips for reducing errors and checking yourself as you calculate these values.

- The last fraction in both the $SOS_{Between}$ formula and the SOS_{Total} formula is the same: $\frac{\left(\sum Y_{Total}\right)^2}{n_{Total}}$. In the Stroop Test example, this fraction was $\frac{219^2}{12} = \frac{47,961}{12} = 3,996\frac{3}{4}$.
- All SOS values should *always* be positive. If you get a negative SOS value, you have definitely made an error in your arithmetic.
- The numbers in the SOS_{Total} formula *all* come from the column in the information table labeled "Total."
- The $SOS_{Between}$ value and SOS_{Within} value should *always* add up to the SOS_{Total} value. This is a simple way to check your math. In the Stroop Test example $SOS_{Between} = 877.583$, $SOS_{Within} = 252.667$, and $SOS_{Total} = 1130.25$. A little arithmetic shows that $877.583 + 252.667 = 1130.25$.
- Likewise, the $df_{Between}$ value and df_{Within} value should *always* add up to the df_{Total} value. In the Stroop Test example, $df_{Between} = 3$, $df_{Within} = 8$, and $df_{Total} = 11$. Because $3 + 8 = 11$, we know that our degrees of freedom values are all correct.

Check Yourself!

- Explain the difference between the information table and the ANOVA table.

- How do you find the $\sum Y$ value in an information table?

- How do you calculate the number of degrees of freedom between groups?

- Which sum of squares value will always be the largest?

The next step in completing the ANOVA table is to find the mean square (MS) values. For the Between and Within rows, calculating the MS values requires dividing the sum of squares value in a row by the degrees of freedom value in that same row (see Table 11.4). In the Stroop Test example, $MS_{Between}$ is:

$$MS_{Between} = 877.583 \div 3 = 292.528$$

And for MS_{Within}:

$$MS_{Within} = 252.667 \div 8 = 31.583$$

The last portion of the ANOVA table requires finding F_{obs}, which you may remember is the F-observed value. To calculate F_{obs}, you only need to take the $MS_{Between}$ and divide by MS_{Within}:

$$F_{obs} = 292.528 \div 31.583 = 9.262$$

With the F_{obs} value found, step 6 is complete, and we can move on to the next step, which is to find the critical value. The completed ANOVA table is shown in Table 11.6.

Compare the Observed Value and the Critical Value. Armed with the F_{obs} and F_{crit} values, we can now perform the seventh step of an ANOVA, which is to compare the critical and observed values in order to determine whether to reject or retain the null hypothesis. If the F_{crit} value is more extreme than the F_{obs} value, we retain the null hypothesis. On the other hand, if the F_{obs} value is more extreme than the F_{crit} value, we reject the null hypothesis. This is the rule about rejecting or retaining the null hypothesis in an ANOVA because if F_{obs} is greater than the F_{crit} value, then F_{obs} would be in the rejection region.

The location of the F_{obs} and F_{crit} values in the sampling distribution of the Stroop example data is shown in Figure 11.2. Like all F-distributions, the sampling distribution in this example is positively skewed, and the horizontal axis (i.e., x-axis) values begin at 0. The rejection region is shaded in this figure, and it totals 5% of the area of the sampling distribution because $\alpha = .05$. As you can see, the F_{obs} value is inside the rejection region because F_{obs} is greater than the F_{crit} value. Therefore, we should reject the null hypothesis that all four groups' means are equal (i.e., $H_0 : \overline{X}_1 = \overline{X}_2 = \overline{X}_3 = \overline{X}_4$). This means the alternative hypothesis (i.e., $H_1 : \overline{X} \neq \overline{X}$, for any two means) is a better statistical model for our data than the null hypothesis.

Calculate an Effect Size. The eighth snd final step in conducting an ANOVA is to calculate the effect size. Until now all of our effect sizes have been differences between two means: either Cohen's d or Glass's Δ. However, these effect sizes are not very useful for ANOVA because we have more than two groups. If we were to calculate Cohen's d or Glass's Δ for every pair of

—

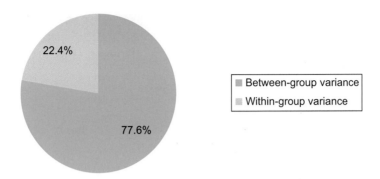

Table 11.6 Fully completed ANOVA table (using Stroop Test data)

	SOS	df	MS	F_{obs}
Between	877.583	3	292.528	9.262
Within	252.667	8	31.583	
Total	1,130.250	11		

Note. SOS = sum of squares, df = degrees of freedom, MS = mean square, F_{obs} = F-observed value.

Figure 11.2 Diagram of the F-distribution ($df_{Between}$ = 3 and df_{Within} = 8) for the example Stroop ANOVA data. For this example, F_{crit} = 4.066, and the rejection region (which is 5% of the entire sampling distribution because α = .05) is shaded in black. Because F_{obs} = 9.262 and is inside the rejection region, the null hypothesis ($H_0 : \overline{X}_1 = \overline{X}_2 = \ldots = \overline{X}_k$) should be rejected.

groups, we would have more than one effect size. Because the number of effect sizes would increase faster than the number of groups (just as with the number of unpaired-samples t-tests with more than two groups, see Formula 11.1 and Table 11.1), this quickly becomes complicated – and tedious to calculate.

Instead, ANOVA uses a new effect size, called η^2 – **eta-squared**. (η is the Greek letter eta and is pronounced "EIGHT-uh.") The formula for calculating η^2 is:

$$\eta^2 = \frac{SOS_{Between}}{SOS_{Total}} \qquad \text{(Formula 11.11)}$$

Thus, η^2 is a ratio of the sum of squares between groups and the total sum of squares. In our Stroop ANOVA example, $SOS_{Between}$ = 877.583 and SOS_{Total} = 1130.25 (see the completed ANOVA table in Table 11.6). Therefore, to find η^2, we should divide the first number by the second:

$$\eta^2 = \frac{877.583}{1130.25} = .776$$

Figure 11.3 The division of the dependent variable's variance into a portion associated with the nominal grouping independent variable (i.e., the between-group variance) and the portion unrelated to the independent variable (i.e., the within-group variance). The effect size η^2 is equal to the size of the between-group variance proportion. In the Stroop data example, η^2 is equal to 77.6% or .776. This means that 77.6% of the differences among scores can be attributed to group differences. The remaining 22.4% is unrelated to group-level differences.

Because the $SOS_{Between}$ will always be smaller than the SOS_{Total}, η^2 will always be a value between 0 and 1.

But what does η^2 *mean*? When I introduced the ANOVA table, I stated that the ANOVA table divides the dependent variable's variance of the data into two portions: variance between groups and variance within groups. These add up to the total variance of the dependent variable. The variance between groups is the variance associated with the independent variable – which in ANOVA is the grouping variable. This means that η^2 is the proportion of dependent variable variance that is shared or associated with the independent variable. In other words, some of the variance of the dependent variable (i.e., the scores in the information table) is related to the group that individuals belong to (i.e., the independent variable), and η^2 tells us how strongly related these variables are.

Figure 11.3 shows an example of how dependent variable variance is partitioned in the Stroop Test example. Because $\eta^2 = .776$, we know that 77.6% of the variance in individuals' scores on the Stroop Test (which was the dependent variable) is associated with the group they belonged to (which was the independent variable). This means that the group that the person belongs to is strongly associated with their Stroop Test score.

Another way to interpret η^2 is in the context of prediction. The bottom row of the information table (Table 11.3) displays the mean of the scores in each group. It also displays the mean for all of the scores (in the "Total" column), which is called the **grand mean**. The group means in this row are the predicted values of a sample member's dependent variable score. For example, in the Stroop example, if we know that someone belongs to Group A, we predict that their time on the Stroop Test will be $9\frac{2}{3}$ seconds, because that is the mean for Group A. On the other hand, if we have no knowledge about a person's group (or if we ignore group membership), then we will predict that they will have a score equal to the grand mean, which is 18.25 seconds in the Stroop Test example. The effect size η^2 measures how much better the predictions from the group means are compared to predictions from the grand mean. In the Stroop Test example, the predictions using group means will be – on average –77.6% more accurate than predictions made with the grand mean.

Therefore, another way of thinking about η^2 is as a measure of overall prediction accuracy. We can also measure accuracy of prediction for individual sample members with the following formula:

Table 11.7 Residuals for the Stroop Test times (measured in seconds) calculated with group means

Group A ($\bar{Y} = 9\frac{2}{3}$)	Group B ($\bar{Y} = 29\frac{2}{3}$)	Group C ($\bar{Y} = 10\frac{1}{3}$)	Group D ($\bar{Y} = 23\frac{1}{3}$)
$8 - 9\frac{2}{3} = -1\frac{2}{3}$	$22 - 29\frac{2}{3} = -7\frac{2}{3}$	$10 - 10\frac{1}{3} = -\frac{1}{3}$	$18 - 23\frac{1}{3} = -5\frac{1}{3}$
$10 - 9\frac{2}{3} = \frac{1}{3}$	$29 - 29\frac{2}{3} = -\frac{2}{3}$	$12 - 10\frac{1}{3} = 1\frac{2}{3}$	$32 - 23\frac{1}{3} = 8\frac{2}{3}$
$11 - 9\frac{2}{3} = 1\frac{1}{3}$	$38 - 29\frac{2}{3} = 8\frac{1}{3}$	$9 - 10\frac{1}{3} = -1\frac{1}{3}$	$20 - 23\frac{1}{3} = -3\frac{1}{3}$

Note. For an explanation of the groups, see the text.

Table 11.8 Residuals for the Stroop Test times (measured in seconds) calculated with the grand mean ($\bar{Y} = 18.25$)

Group A	Group B	Group C	Group D
$8 - 18.25 = -10.25$	$22 - 18.25 = 3.75$	$10 - 18.25 = -8.25$	$18 - 18.25 = -0.25$
$10 - 18.25 = -8.25$	$29 - 18.25 = 10.75$	$12 - 18.25 = -6.25$	$32 - 18.25 = 13.75$
$11 - 18.25 = -7.25$	$38 - 18.25 = 19.75$	$9 - 18.25 = -9.25$	$20 - 18.25 = 1.75$

Note. For an explanation of the groups, see the text.

$$e_i = Y_i - \hat{Y}_i \qquad \text{(Formula 11.12)}$$

Formula 11.12 says that the individual accuracy (called the **residual**, or **error**, and abbreviated e_i) is the difference between the person's predicted dependent variable score ($\hat{Y}_i$) and their actual dependent variable score (Y_i). The i subscript indicates that each person in a sample will have their own residual. Table 11.7 shows how the residuals were calculated for each individual in the Stroop Test data, using Formula 11.12. It is apparent in the table that some individuals' predictions were very accurate (as indicated by small residuals close to zero), but were relatively inaccurate for other individuals (as indicated by larger residual values).

The residuals calculated in Table 11.7 can be compared with the residuals calculated for each person on the basis of the grand mean. These are shown in Table 11.8. Although some people in the sample (such as the first person in Group D) have smaller residuals when we use the predictions based on the grand mean, generally people's residuals are smaller with the predictions made on the basis of the group means. In other words, predicting that people will have a score equal to their group's mean will generally be more accurate than predicting that everyone will score at the grand mean.

To find an exact measure of prediction accuracy, we can take the square of the residual (to get rid of the negatives) and then sum each group of squared residuals. These values are shown in Table 11.9.

The value in the left column of Table 11.9 – which is based on residuals calculated from the group means – is smaller than the value in the right column. This is because the predicted dependent variable scores based on group means are more accurate than predicted dependent variable scores based on grand means. In fact, the number on the left is exactly 77.6% smaller than the number of the right:

Table 11.9

Individual	Squared residual (using group means)	Squared residual (using grand means)
Group A, person no. 1	$\left(8 - 9\frac{2}{3}\right)^2 = \left(-1\frac{2}{3}\right)^2 = 2\frac{7}{9}$	$\left(8 - 18\frac{1}{4}\right)^2 = \left(-10\frac{1}{4}\right)^2 = 105\frac{1}{16}$
Group A, person no. 2	$\left(10 - 9\frac{2}{3}\right)^2 = \left(\frac{1}{3}\right)^2 = \frac{1}{9}$	$\left(10 - 18\frac{1}{4}\right)^2 = \left(-8\frac{1}{4}\right)^2 = 68\frac{1}{16}$
Group A, person no. 3	$\left(11 - 9\frac{2}{3}\right)^2 = \left(1\frac{1}{3}\right)^2 = 1\frac{7}{9}$	$\left(11 - 18\frac{1}{4}\right)^2 = \left(-7\frac{1}{4}\right)^2 = 52\frac{9}{16}$
Group B, person no. 1	$\left(22 - 29\frac{2}{3}\right)^2 = \left(-7\frac{2}{3}\right)^2 = 58\frac{2}{3}$	$\left(22 - 18\frac{1}{4}\right)^2 = \left(3\frac{3}{4}\right)^2 = 14\frac{1}{16}$
Group B person no. 2	$\left(29 - 29\frac{2}{3}\right)^2 = \left(-\frac{2}{3}\right)^2 = \frac{4}{9}$	$\left(29 - 18\frac{1}{4}\right)^2 = \left(10\frac{3}{4}\right)^2 = 115\frac{9}{16}$
Group B, person no. 3	$\left(38 - 29\frac{2}{3}\right)^2 = \left(8\frac{1}{3}\right)^2 = 69\frac{4}{9}$	$\left(38 - 18\frac{1}{4}\right)^2 = \left(19\frac{3}{4}\right)^2 = 390\frac{1}{16}$
Group C, person no. 1	$\left(10 - 10\frac{1}{3}\right)^2 = \left(-\frac{1}{3}\right)^2 = \frac{1}{9}$	$\left(10 - 18\frac{1}{4}\right)^2 = \left(-8\frac{1}{4}\right)^2 = 68\frac{1}{16}$
Group C, person no. 2	$\left(12 - 10\frac{1}{3}\right)^2 = \left(1\frac{2}{3}\right)^2 = 2\frac{7}{9}$	$\left(12 - 18\frac{1}{4}\right)^2 = \left(-6\frac{1}{4}\right)^2 = 39\frac{1}{16}$
Group C, person no. 3	$\left(9 - 10\frac{1}{3}\right)^2 = \left(-1\frac{1}{3}\right)^2 = 1\frac{7}{9}$	$\left(9 - 18\frac{1}{4}\right)^2 = \left(-9\frac{1}{4}\right)^2 = 85\frac{9}{16}$
Group D, person no. 1	$\left(18 - 23\frac{1}{3}\right)^2 = \left(-5\frac{1}{3}\right)^2 = 28\frac{4}{9}$	$\left(18 - 18\frac{1}{4}\right)^2 = \left(-\frac{1}{4}\right)^2 = \frac{1}{16}$
Group D, person no. 2	$\left(32 - 23\frac{1}{3}\right)^2 = \left(8\frac{2}{3}\right)^2 = 75\frac{1}{9}$	$\left(32 - 18\frac{1}{4}\right)^2 = \left(13\frac{3}{4}\right)^2 = 189\frac{1}{16}$
Group D, person no. 3	$\left(20 - 23\frac{1}{3}\right)^2 = \left(-3\frac{1}{3}\right)^2 = 11\frac{1}{9}$	$\left(20 - 18\frac{1}{4}\right)^2 = \left(1\frac{3}{4}\right)^2 = 3\frac{1}{16}$
Sum of the squared residuals in column	252.667	1130.250

$$\frac{1130.250 - 252.667}{1130.250} = \frac{877.583}{1130.250} = .776$$

This shows that the η^2 effect size measures how much more accurate the predictions are when based on group means than when based on the grand mean. In the Stroop Test example, the squared residuals based on the group means are – on average – 77.6% smaller than the squared residuals based on the grand mean, meaning that predictions based on group means are 77.6% more accurate than predictions based on the grand mean. That is why η^2 functions as a measure of prediction accuracy.

This example illustrates one other aspect of ANOVA: the nature of the SOS values in the ANOVA table. If you look in the bottom row of Table 11.9, the sums of the squared residuals in the columns above should look familiar. That is because the number on the left is the SOS within groups (SOS_{Within}), and the number on the right is the SOS total value (SOS_{Total}). Therefore, the SOS values refer to the sum of squared residuals around either the group mean (in the case of SOS_{Within}) or the grand mean (for SOS_{Total}). In fact, this is precisely why the statistic is called the "sum of squares."

Check Yourself!

- How do you determine whether to reject or retain the null hypothesis in an ANOVA?

- Why does ANOVA have its own effect size, instead of using Cohen's *d*?

- How do you calculate the effect size for ANOVA?

- What is a residual?

- Define the grand mean.

- What are the two ways to interpret the effect size of ANOVA?

Sidebar 11.4 **Cohen's benchmarks for effect sizes**

Now that we have discussed three different effect sizes, it is important to take a moment to discuss effect size interpretation. Effect size reporting has grown more popular, but researchers are not always interpreting their effect sizes correctly or fully. One of the most pernicious habits in the social sciences is to just label an effect size as "small," "medium," or "large," based purely on its numerical value. Many people do this because of recommendations from Jacob Cohen in an influential book (1988) he wrote on statistical power (see Sidebar 10.1 for an explanation of statistical power). In his book, Cohen chose values that he considered to be "small," "medium," and "large" effect sizes. For example, for Cohen's *d* he stated that .20 was small, .50 was medium, and .80 was large. Cohen (1988) produced similar guidelines, popularly called **Cohen's benchmarks**, for several other effect sizes.

However, merely labeling an effect size as "small," "medium," or "large" is not a sufficient interpretation for three reasons. First, the magnitude of an effect size sometimes is unrelated to the importance of the effect (see Sidebar 8.3). Some tiny effect sizes can have massive consequences for individuals (Abelson, 1985). For example, in a study on the effects of aspirin on people at risk of heart attack, the effect size was $\eta^2 = .039$, which, according to Cohen (1988), would be "small." However, the outcome of this study was whether the person survived a heart attack or not – a very important outcome. In fact, this "small" effect size meant that individuals who took aspirin regularly had *double* the survival rate of those taking a placebo (The Steering Committee of the Physicians' Health Study Research Group, 1988). That's pretty powerful for a "small" effect size!

Another reason that labeling an effect size is not a sufficient interpretation is that Cohen himself said that his benchmarks were not universally applicable. In his book Cohen (1988) explicitly stated over 10 times that his benchmarks were only appropriate in situations where there was little previous research on a topic (see also Durlak, 2009; Huberty, 2002; Thompson, 2007; Volker, 2006; Warne et al., 2012). Indeed, some authors have found that the typical effect size in some social science fields is smaller than the standard for Cohen's "medium" effect size (e.g., P. E. Morris & Fritz, 2013), while others have found typical effect sizes larger than the threshold for a "medium" effect size (Osborne, 2008). To complicate matters further, some topics of research *within the same field* have widely different typical effect sizes (Schmitt, 2015).

Finally, it is important to realize that Cohen's (1988) recommendations are subjective. There is nothing in the formulas for any effect size – whether it is Cohen's *d*, η^2, or any other effect size – that sanctions a particular value as a dividing line between "small" and "medium" or between "medium" and "large." In fact, Cohen changed his opinion over the years about what constituted a "small," "medium," or "large" effect size (compare the benchmarks in Cohen, 1962, with the benchmarks in Cohen, 1988). What is "large" or "small" is a matter of opinion, and it is best to make judgments and form opinions on your own, rather than just slapping a label on an effect size (Murray & Dosser, 1987; Sedlmeier & Gigerenzer, 1989; Zientek, Yetkiner, & Thompson, 2010).

Instead of blindly using Cohen's benchmarks, here is how each effect size you have learned so far should be interpreted:

- Cohen's *d* refers to the size of the difference between two group means, as expressed in standard deviation units. Cohen's *d* can also describe the *z*-score of the average person in one group, compared to the average member in the other group.
- Glass's Δ describes the amount of improvement in a treatment group (in standard deviation units), when compared to the control group. In other words, Glass's Δ is the average *z*-score for a person in the treatment group, when compared to the control group (which would have a mean *z*-score of 0 in Glass's Δ). Like Cohen's *d*, Glass's Δ can be conceptualized as the size of the difference between two group means, as expressed in standard deviation units, though in Glass's Δ the standard deviation units are calculated with the control group's data, instead of the data for all sample members (see Sidebar 9.2).
- There are two ways to interpret η^2. The first is that η^2 is the percentage of variance in the dependent variable that is related to the independent variable. An alternative interpretation is that η^2 is the percentage of improvement of a model's predictions, when compared to predictions based on the grand mean.

In addition to these proper interpretations, it is always important to consider the context of your effect sizes. Are they typical when compared to other studies, or are they larger or smaller? How important is the outcome for your study's participants? Do the group differences cause problems in people's lives? Is the effect large enough to notice in daily life? Is the effect size large enough to support one theory or treatment over another? Is the effect size large enough to support or disprove a theory? Answering questions like these can help provide context and make your interpretations more thoughtful than merely labeling an effect size.

p and Type I and Type II Errors

Finding an exact *p*-value is not possible with just the tables in this textbook. However, we can still find a range of values for *p* using the same rules that we have used in Chapters 8–10:

- If the null hypothesis is retained when $\alpha = .05$, then $p > .05$.
- If the null hypothesis is rejected when $\alpha = .05$, but retained when $\alpha = .01$, then $.01 < p < .05$.
- If the null hypothesis is rejected when $\alpha = .01$, then $p < .01$.

In the Stroop Test example, we found that when $\alpha = .05$, we rejected the null hypothesis that the four groups all have equal means. Therefore, $p < .05$ because when the null hypothesis is rejected in an ANOVA (or any other null hypothesis statistical significance test), p must be less than α.

Using Appendix A3, we can also determine whether p is less than or greater than .01. We can do this by finding the F_{crit} value when $\alpha = .01$ and determining whether F_{obs} is within the new

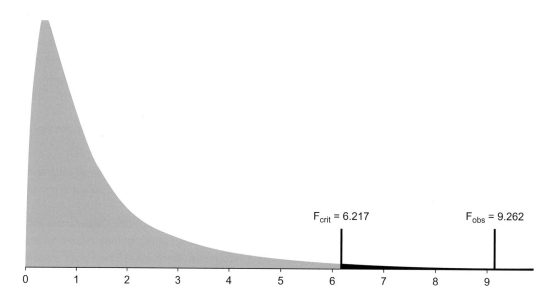

Figure 11.4 Diagram of the F-distribution ($df_{Between}$ = 3 and df_{Within} = 8) for the example Stroop ANOVA data. For this example, F_{crit} = 6.217, and the rejection region (which is 1% of the entire sampling distribution because α = .01) is shaded in black. Because F_{obs} = 9.262 and is inside the rejection region, the null hypothesis ($H_0 : \overline{X}_1 = \overline{X}_2 = \ldots = \overline{X}_k$) should be rejected. As a result, $p < .01$.

rejection region. If we reject the null hypothesis when α = .01, then p is less than .01. If we retain the null hypothesis when α = .05, then .05 $< p <$ .01. F_{obs} in the Stroop Test example was 9.262. According to Appendix A3, when $df_{Between}$ = 3 and df_{Within} = 8 and α = .01, the F_{crit} value is equal to 6.217. If we create a diagram to show where the F_{obs} value is in relation to this new F_{crit} value and the smaller rejection region, we will find that we should reject the null hypothesis (see Figure 11.4). Therefore, in the Stroop Test example, $p < .01$.

The rules for determining whether Type I or Type II error is a potential problem are the same for all NHSTs, including ANOVA. To recap, a Type I error occurs when the data analyst rejects a true null hypothesis. A Type II error occurs when the data analyst retains a false null hypothesis. Because we rejected the null hypothesis in the Stroop Test example, we have to worry about Type I error. Remember, though, that it is impossible to know whether the null hypothesis is actually true. Therefore, we never do know whether we are making an error when we reject or retain the null hypothesis.

Additional Thoughts on ANOVA

Although mastering the eight steps of ANOVA is enough to perform an ANOVA in a satisfactory manner, there are some other aspects of ANOVA that your instructor may believe are beneficial for you to know. These are the assumptions of ANOVA, the logic of ANOVA, and *post hoc* tests.

Assumptions of ANOVA. Like all statistical methods, ANOVA has assumptions that the data must meet in order for the procedure to have credible results. The four statistical assumptions of ANOVA are:

- The membership of the groups is separate and non-overlapping. In other words, the independent variable that divides your data into three or more groups must be a nominal-level variable with three or more mutually exclusive and exhaustive categories.
- The dependent variable is interval- or ratio-level so that means, variances, and residuals can be calculated with its data.
- The homogeneity of variance assumption applies to ANOVA. In Chapter 10 we saw that the homogeneity of variance assumption requires the variance of the groups to be similar.
- Groups in an ANOVA need to have similar sample sizes.

If these assumptions look familiar to you it is because these are the exact same assumptions for the unpaired-samples t-test. This should be unsurprising because ANOVA was created to perform comparisons of several group means without inflating Type I error and without conducting multiple NHSTs. Indeed, both the unpaired two-sample t-test and ANOVA are members of the GLM. General Linear Moment 11.1 in this text explains the relationship between the two procedures.

General Linear Moment 11.1

If you have been paying close attention to these General Linear Moment boxes, you know that all null hypothesis tests are closely related because they are all members of the GLM. The same is true with ANOVA because it is a generalization of the unpaired two-sample t-test. Therefore, *an unpaired two-sample t-test is just an ANOVA with two groups*. This is demonstrated when conducting an ANOVA with only two groups. In the previous chapter we became familiar with the example from Fox and Anderegg's (2014) study about appropriate behavior on social media. When we performed an unpaired two-sample t-test in Chapter 10, we decided to reject the null hypothesis ($H_0 : \overline{X}_1 = \overline{X}_2$). Performing an ANOVA with the same data also results in a rejected null hypothesis – because they have the same null hypothesis when there are only two groups in an ANOVA. The decision to reject the null hypothesis for both NHSTs is not unique to this example. When there are two groups, ANOVA and the unpaired two-sample t-test will always produce the same decision about the null hypothesis. This is because when there are only two groups, the ANOVA will simplify to an unpaired two-sample t-test.

There is one important difference: in the unpaired two-sample t-test, $d = .219$, but in ANOVA, $\eta^2 = .0118$. However, these effect sizes are not directly comparable because of the two different ways they are calculated and two different interpretations of them. However, there is a formula (modified from Durlak, 2009, p. 928) that converts one effect size to the other:

$$\eta^2 = \left(\frac{d}{\sqrt{d^2 + 4}} \right)^2$$

Plugging the Cohen's d value into this equation produces:

$$\eta^2 = \left(\frac{.219}{\sqrt{.219^2 + 4}} \right)^2 = \left(\frac{.219}{\sqrt{.047961 + 4}} \right)^2 = \left(\frac{.219}{\sqrt{4.047961}} \right)^2 = \left(\frac{.219}{2.011955} \right)^2 = .108849^2$$

$$\eta^2 = .108849^2 = .0118$$

This example demonstrates that unpaired two-sample t-tests and ANOVA always produce the same results when there are only two groups in the data. This is exactly what we would expect because the unpaired two-sample t-test is a special case of ANOVA in the GLM.

Comparing the t-table and the F-table also shows how the unpaired-samples t-test is related to the F-test. The degrees of freedom values in the t-table are the same as the $df_{Between}$ in the F-table, and if an ANOVA is conducted with two groups, then the $df_{Between} = 1$. Therefore, if you choose a number from the first column on the F-table, it should correspond to the number in the two-tailed t-table with the same α and same df as the df_{Within} for its row in the F-table. In fact, any number in a t-table is the square root of the number in the F-table with 1 $df_{Between}$ and the same number of df_{Within} as the df in the t-table. For example, in the F-table the critical value for a test that has 1 df_{Within} and 15 $df_{Between}$ and α = .05 is 4.543. In the t-table, the critical value for a two-tailed test with 15 degrees of freedom and α = .05 is +2.131. To make these two numbers equivalent, you should square the value from the t-table: $+2.131^2 =$ 4.541. (The slight difference between this number and the F_{crit} value (4.543) is due to rounding error.)

Logic of ANOVA. When I first learned about ANOVA – and for years afterwards – the logic seemed confusing to me. The null hypothesis in an ANOVA is that group means are equal (i.e., $H_0 : \overline{X}_1 = \overline{X}_2 = \ldots = \overline{X}_k$). I could not understand why we would analyze *variance* in order to test a null hypothesis about group *means*. After all, one is a measure of variability, while the other is a measure of central tendency (see Chapter 4).

The answer is that ANOVA is really about examining the relationship between an independent variable (a nominal variable that categorizes sample members into groups) and a dependent variable (which is interval- or ratio-level). This is because ANOVA is a member of the GLM, and all members of the GLM investigate the relationships among variables – a fact we have seen in the General Linear Moments since Chapter 7. Therefore, if the group that sample members belong to (i.e., the independent variable) were unrelated to individuals' scores on the dependent variable, then there would be a lot of overlap among the groups – and their means would be very similar. This would happen when the null hypothesis is a good statistical model for the data.

On the other hand, if the group means were very different, then scores in the different groups would not overlap much (or at all). In this situation the null hypothesis of an ANOVA would be rejected because the null hypothesis is that all group means are equal. Therefore, to ascertain whether group means are similar, it makes sense to determine how much variability there is between and within groups. If variability is high between groups and low within groups, the means will be different and the null hypothesis will be rejected. If variability is low between groups and high within groups, the means will be similar and the null hypothesis retained.

This relationship between variability and the null hypothesis of an ANOVA is apparent in the Stroop Test example. Figure 11.5 shows the scores on the Stroop Test for each member of the sample. The sample members have been arranged in vertical columns so that the variability within each group is apparent. Notice that Group A and Group B have no overlap in the range of their scores. This indicates that variability between these groups is high, but that there is less variability within each group's scores, especially for Group A. Because the overall difference between Group A and Group B is high, it is not feasible to use the null hypothesis as a model for these groups – because the null hypothesis is that all group means are equal.

The opposite situation is displayed in Figure 11.6. In this diagram there is little variability between groups because all their group means are similar. Therefore, the null hypothesis would be

Figure 11.5 A diagram showing the variability between and within groups from the Stroop Test data. The differences between groups (i.e., between-group variability) is high and the differences among sample members within the same group (i.e., within-group variability) is low. Therefore, the null hypothesis – which is that all group means are equal – does not fit the data because average group differences are sometimes very large.

Figure 11.6 Diagram showing the variability between and within groups for simulated Stroop Test data. The differences between groups (i.e., between-group variability) is low, and the differences among sample members within the same group (i.e., within-group variability) is higher. Therefore, the null hypothesis – which is that all group means are equal – is a good statistical model for the data because average group differences are very small.

retained. For Figure 11.6, within-group variability seems to matter much more in determining individuals' scores than between-group variability. Therefore, the independent variable (i.e., group membership) does not have a strong – if any – relationship with dependent variable scores.

General Linear Moment 11.2

We first learned in Chapter 7 (and have had it reiterated in every chapter since) that there are three principles of the GLM:

1.   All GLM procedures examine the relationships between independent and dependent variables.
2.   All GLM procedures apply weights to data during the analysis.
3.   All GLM procedures can produce an effect size.

This General Linear Moment will illustrate these points in detail to show how ANOVA is part of the GLM.

Independent and Dependent Variables. The section in this chapter on the logic of ANOVA makes it clear how ANOVA investigates the relationship between a nominal-level independent variable and an interval- or ratio-level dependent variable. To reiterate, if the two variables are unrelated, then all group means will be similar, and the variation within the groups will be much larger than the variation between groups. When the independent and dependent variables are related, then at least one group mean will have a statistically significant difference with at least one other mean, and the null hypothesis will be rejected.

Weighting Data. The way statistical weights operate in ANOVA can be difficult to see. In Chapters 7–10, Cohen's d operated as a statistical weight, which was multiplied by the nominal independent variable's scores of 0 and 1 for the two groups. In ANOVA, we can extend this procedure to more than two groups. Instead of a single nominal variable, we can imagine multiple nominal variables where each group takes a turn being assigned a value of 1. Each group's value of 1 can then be multiplied by its group mean to produce a predicted value for the dependent variable for each group. (See Chapter 15, especially Table 15.3 for more information about this method of assigning 1's and 0's to groups.) Because (group mean) (1) = group mean, this just means that members of each group are predicted to have a dependent variable value equal to their group's mean.

Effect Size. As stated in this chapter, the effect size for ANOVA is η^2, which is the percentage of total variance that is shared with the independent variable's variance. General Linear Moment 11.1 shows how this η^2 is related to Cohen's d. Chapters 12 and 13 will show further connections between η^2 and other effect sizes.

Post Hoc Tests

Because it saves us from performing many unpaired-samples t-tests and eliminates Type I error inflation, ANOVA is one of the most frequently performed null hypothesis tests in the social sciences. However, its usefulness has limits. The null hypothesis in an ANOVA is that all the group means are equal (i.e., $H_0 : \overline{X}_1 = \overline{X}_2 = \ldots = \overline{X}_k$). Retaining the null hypothesis means that there are no statistically significant differences among group means.

Rejecting the null hypothesis tells us that the alternative hypothesis is a better statistical model for the data. That alternative hypothesis is $H_1 : \overline{X} \neq \overline{X}$, for any two means. The problem with ANOVA is that when the null hypothesis is rejected, we don't know which group means differ from one another. All ANOVA tells the researcher is that a difference exists – but neither the location of the difference nor the number of mean differences are explained in the alternative hypothesis.

To provide this information, statisticians have created ***post hoc* tests**. These are statistical procedures that we use to determine where differences among means exist. There are many types of *post hoc* tests (see Sidebar 11.5), but in this section we will see how to conduct the most common one, which is Tukey's *post hoc* test. The formula for comparing a pair of means via Tukey's *post hoc* test is:

$$HSD = \frac{\overline{X}_1 - \overline{X}_2}{\sqrt{\left(\dfrac{MS_{Within}}{\sum \dfrac{1}{n_{Group}}}\right)}}$$

(Formula 11.13)

In Formula 11.13, HSD refers to the "honestly significant difference." The HSD is a statistic that we will use to determine if the null hypothesis in ANOVA was rejected because of a large difference between a particular pair of means. In this formula MS_{Within} is the mean square within groups (from the ANOVA table), and $\overline{X}_1$ and $\overline{X}_2$ are a pair of group means. $\dfrac{k}{\sum \dfrac{1}{n_{Group}}}$ is the

harmonic mean, which is a special measure of central tendency that gives a disproportionate weight to smaller group sizes. In the harmonic mean, k is the number of groups (as it was for all the other formulas in this chapter), and n_{Group} is the number of scores within each group. After the HSD is found for each pair of means, the HSD values are then compared to the appropriate critical value in Appendix A4. The rest of this section will show how to perform Tukey's *post hoc* test with the Stroop Test example data.

The harmonic mean for the Stroop Test data is calculated as follows:

$$\frac{k}{\sum \dfrac{1}{n_{Group}}} = \frac{4}{\dfrac{1}{3} + \dfrac{1}{3} + \dfrac{1}{3} + \dfrac{1}{3}} = \frac{4}{\dfrac{4}{3}} = 3$$

When all of the group sizes are equal, the harmonic mean will be equal to each group's *n*, as it is in this example. When sample sizes differ, the harmonic mean will always be a value between the largest and smallest group sizes.

Plugging the harmonic mean and the MS_{Within} (which is 31.583; see the ANOVA table in Table 11.6) into Formula 11.13, we get:

$$HSD = \frac{\overline{X}_1 - \overline{X}_2}{\sqrt{\dfrac{31.583}{3}}} = \frac{\overline{X}_1 - \overline{X}_2}{\sqrt{\dfrac{31.583}{3}}} = \frac{\overline{X}_1 - \overline{X}_2}{\sqrt{10.528}} = \frac{\overline{X}_1 - \overline{X}_2}{3.245}$$

The next step is to calculate an HSD for each pair of means. For the means for Groups A and B, this is:

$$HSD_{\overline{X}_A - \overline{X}_B} = \frac{9\frac{2}{3} - 29\frac{2}{3}}{3.245} = \frac{20}{3.245} = 6.164$$

For Groups A and C, the HSD is:

$$HSD_{\overline{X}_A - \overline{X}_C} = \frac{9\frac{2}{3} - 10\frac{1}{3}}{3.245} = \frac{\frac{-2}{3}}{3.245} = 0.205$$

For the other pairs of groups the HSD values are:

$$HSD_{\overline{X}_A - \overline{X}_D} = \frac{9\frac{2}{3} - 23\frac{1}{3}}{3.245} = \frac{-13\frac{2}{3}}{3.245} = -4.212$$

$$HSD_{\overline{X}_B - \overline{X}_C} = \frac{29\frac{2}{3} - 10\frac{1}{3}}{3.245} = \frac{19\frac{1}{3}}{3.245} = 5.959$$

$$HSD_{\overline{X}_B - \overline{X}_D} = \frac{29\frac{2}{3} - 23\frac{1}{3}}{3.245} = \frac{6\frac{1}{3}}{3.245} = 1.952$$

$$HSD_{\overline{X}_C - \overline{X}_D} = \frac{10\frac{1}{3} - 23\frac{1}{3}}{3.245} = \frac{-13}{3.245} = -4.007$$

Knowing all the HSD values, we can now find the critical value for Tukey's *post hoc* test. This critical value is called q, and can be found in Appendix A4. Finding the q value in Appendix A4 is the same as finding the F_{crit} value in Appendix A3. The columns of the table are labeled with differing $df_{Between}$ values, and the rows are organized according to their df_{Within} values. Just as with the F-table, you should find the column that corresponds to your $df_{Between}$ value and the row that corresponds to the data's df_{Within} value. In the cell where that column and that row meet, there will be two numbers, one in **boldface** and the other in *italics*. The number in boldface is the q value for an α value of .05, and the number in italics is the q value for an α value of .01. For the Stroop Test data, $df_{Between} = 3$ and $df_{Within} = 8$. In the cell for these two df values, we find two numbers: 4.29 in boldface and 6.20 in italics. Because $\alpha = .05$, the correct q value for this example is 4.529.

To complete Tukey's *post hoc* test, we now need to identify all HSD values that are outside the range of ± 4.529. These HSD values will correspond to the pairs of means that are statistically significantly different. In the Stroop Test example, there are two HSD values that are outside the ± 4.529 range. These are for the difference between the means for Groups A and B ($HSD_{\overline{X}_A - \overline{X}_B} = 6.164$) and Groups B and C ($HSD_{\overline{X}_B - \overline{X}_C} = 5.959$). Therefore, the null hypothesis in the ANOVA was rejected because Groups A and B had a statistically significant mean differences, as did Groups B and C.

In this chapter's example, Group A comprised males who had matching text and color on the Stroop Test; Group B, males who did not have matching text and color; Group C, females who had matching text and color on the Stroop Test; and Group D, females who did not have matching text and color. The results from Tukey's *post hoc* test show that the null hypothesis in ANOVA was rejected because males who did not have matching text and color on the Stroop Test (i.e., Group B) had longer average times than males with matching text and color (i.e., Group A) and females with matching text and color (i.e., Group C). This shows that – at least for males in this very small sample – having words printed in a mismatched ink color slows the time needed to name the color of ink that the words were printed in.

Performing Tukey's *post hoc* test is easier than conducting ANOVA, so students sometimes ask why they have to perform ANOVA at all. To them, it would seem easier and more logical to just perform Tukey's *post hoc* test. However, this reasoning overlooks two important contributions of ANOVA. The first is that ANOVA provides information needed to calculate an effect size, η^2. Tukey's *post hoc* test can produce an effect size, but it would be an effect size for each pair of means (like Cohen's *d*), not a single effect size for the overall relationship between the independent variable and the dependent variable – which is more important. Second, ANOVA provides information for making predictions and calculating residuals for individual members of each group. Tukey's *post hoc* test does not provide this information. Apart from these advantages, it is worth noting that Formula 11.13 requires the MS_{Within} value – which can only be found in the ANOVA table. Therefore, performing Tukey's *post hoc* test requires information from an ANOVA anyway.

As this section on Tukey's *post hoc* test comes to a close, it is important to mention that Tukey's *post hoc* test relies on the assumption that it is desirable to compare every possible combination of mean pairs in the data. However, this is not always the case. Sometimes researchers have pairs of groups that are irrelevant to their theory or that would provide nonsensical comparisons. For example, a family science student may have three groups of individuals: unmarried subjects, married subjects, and recently divorced subjects. If the student is examining group differences in attitudes following major life stressors, it may not make sense to compare the unmarried subjects with the other two groups if most married and divorced subjects' stressors are marriage related (e.g., divorce, giving birth, custody battles). In this case, Tukey's *post hoc* test may not be desirable, and one of the other *post hoc* tests may be a more sensible choice (see Sidebar 11.5).

It is also relevant to note that there is another family of follow-up tests called **planned contrasts**. These are comparisons of individual groups that are driven by theory, instead of being driven by the fact that the null hypothesis was rejected. Planned contrasts usually involve fewer statistical significance tests, and thereby are not as susceptible to the risks of Type I error inflation as performing a large number of *t*-tests would be. On the other hand, by not testing the difference between every possible pair of means, individuals who conduct planned contrasts sometimes risk missing a statistically significant group difference because it was not in their pre-planned data analysis scheme. Therefore, in planned contrasts it is not unusual to reject the null hypothesis in an ANOVA and then fail to find any statistically significant differences between means in the planned mean comparisons.

Sidebar 11.5 **Other *post hoc* tests**

This chapter explained how to perform a Tukey's *post hoc* test, which is the most common *post hoc* test in the social sciences (e.g., Warne et al., 2012). However, there are over a dozen *post hoc* tests to choose from. This sidebar provides a brief explanation of some of the most common.

- The **Bonferroni–Dunn *post hoc* test** is merely a series of unpaired-samples *t*-tests with a Bonferroni correction. When performed on every possible pair of means, the testwise α may get so tiny that it becomes very difficult to determine why the null hypothesis in an ANOVA was rejected (see Table 11.1). It also defeats the entire purpose of performing an ANOVA because ANOVA reduces the number of NHSTs that a researcher needs to perform and controls for Type I error inflation without having a tiny α for each test. Therefore, this strategy is often illogical (Warne et al., 2012). However, in a planned contrast the

Bonferroni–Dunn test does not have to include every pair of means; this makes it easier to reject the null hypothesis when comparing pairs of group means. But this strategy also risks missing statistically significant mean pair differences because they were not in the planned contrast strategy.

- Like Tukey's *post hoc* test, **Scheffé's *post hoc* test** compares every possible group of mean pairs. However, Scheffé's *post hoc* test also compares group means with means from combinations of groups. For example, in the Stroop data, a Scheffé *post hoc* test would not only compare Group A and Group B's means, but also Group A's mean with the mean of the combined Groups B and D. Combining Groups B and D makes sense in this case, because both groups received the version of the Stroop Test where the word's text and the ink color did not match. Therefore, a comparison of the mean of Group A with the mean of the combined Groups B and D may be useful. If combining groups makes sense, then Scheffé's *post hoc* test is a better choice than Tukey's *post hoc* test. However, if combining groups is theoretically nonsensical, then Scheffé's *post hoc* test should not be used because it is not as good at identifying mean differences between pairs of single groups.
- **Dunnett's test** is a planned contrast, not a *post hoc* test, but it is still useful to mention in this context. In Dunnett's test a comparison group – usually a control group or baseline group of some sort – is chosen, and all the other groups' means are only compared to that comparison group's mean. For example, imagine there are three groups in a study on depression therapies: (1) a control group that receives no therapy, (2) a group that receives a drug therapy, and (3) a group that receives a psychological therapy. Dunnett's test would first compare the mean of Group 1 with the mean of Group 2 and then compare the mean of Group 1 with the mean of Group 3. However, the means from groups 2 and 3 would not be compared. This set of comparisons makes sense in a context where the research question is whether each individual treatment works better than a control group. (On the other hand, if the purpose of the study is to also determine which treatment is more effective, then the two treatment groups' means must be compared, and Dunnett's test is not appropriate.) Dunnett's test is only suitable when there is a clear baseline group.

There are several other options for conducting *post hoc* tests and planned contrasts (see Figure 11.19). Often multiple options are viable for a given situation. When you conduct a *post hoc* test, it is always necessary to explain which *post hoc* test (or planned contrast) you have chosen and to justify this decision. As you can imagine, not explaining which test(s) you perform after a statistically significant ANOVA can be very confusing for your reader.

Check Yourself!

- If the null hypothesis in an ANOVA is about testing group *means*, why is it an analysis of *variance*?
- What are the statistical assumptions that data must meet in order for a researcher to conduct an ANOVA?
- After conducting an ANOVA, when should you use a *post hoc* test?
- What is the purpose of conducting a *post hoc* test?
- What is the difference between a *post hoc* test and a planned contrast?

Guided Practice 11.1

For another example of an ANOVA, we will examine data from three groups of college students who participated in a study on stress relief. The first group (labeled Group A) was taking yoga classes to learn how to relax more quickly. The second group (Group B) was told to use quiet music to relax. The last group (Group C) did not receive any stress relief interventions. The researchers collected scores that measured the college students' relaxation levels during final exams, with higher numbers indicating more relaxed subjects. The students' scores were:

Group A	Group B	Group C
9	4	1
12	6	3
4	8	4
8	2	5
7	10	2

With three groups in this study, an unpaired two-sample *t*-test is not appropriate. It would take three *t*-tests to examine every possible pair of groups. Additionally, performing three *t*-tests would either inflate experimentwise Type I error or require a Bonferroni correction that would reduce testwise α.

Step 1: Form Groups

The independent variable in this study is the nominal group membership variable that divides the subjects into three groups. We will be comparing the means from the three groups in the ANOVA.

Step 2: Define the Null Hypothesis

In an ANOVA, the null hypothesis is that all of the groups will have equal means. We can write this as $H_0 : \overline{X}_1 = \overline{X}_2 = \ldots = \overline{X}_k$ (as in Formula 11.4) or as $H_0 : \overline{X}_1 = \overline{X}_2 = \overline{X}_3$. This null hypothesis means that all of the group means are statistically equal.

Step 3: Set Alpha

The default α level is .05. Although there may be reasons to change this α (see Sidebar 11.1), none of them apply to this situation.

Step 4: Choose a One- or a Two-Tailed Test, Which Determines the Alternative Hypothesis

Because an *F*-distribution is always positively skewed with one long tail (see Figure 11.1), ANOVAs are always one-tailed, and the alternative hypothesis is always $H_1 : \overline{X} \neq \overline{X}$, for any two means.

Step 5: Find the Critical Values

To find the critical value for an ANOVA, we must first find the degrees of freedom between groups and within groups. As Table 11.4 shows, $df_{Between} = k - 1$, and $df_{Within} = n_{Total} - k$, where k is the number of groups and n_{Total} is the sample size for all groups. In this example $k = 3$, and $n_{Total} = 15$. Therefore, $df_{Between} = 3 - 1 = 2$, and $df_{Within} = 15 - 3 = 12$. Appendix A3 shows that for these degrees of freedom and $\alpha = .05$, $F_{crit} = 3.885$.

Step 6: Calculate the Observed Value

Finding F_{obs} requires filling out the information table. The first row, $\sum Y$, is the sum of scores for each group. For Group A this value is $9 + 12 + 4 + 8 + 7 = 40$. For Group B this value is $4 + 6 + 8 + 2 + 10 = 30$. Finally, Group C's $\sum Y$ is $1 + 3 + 4 + 5 + 2 = 15$.

Finding the values for the second row, labeled $\sum(Y^2)$, requires squaring each score first and then adding them together. For Group A this number is:

$$9^2 + 12^2 + 4^2 + 8^2 + 7^2 = 81 + 144 + 16 + 64 + 49 = 354$$

For Group B:

$$4^2 + 6^2 + 8^2 + 2^2 + 10^2 = 16 + 36 + 64 + 4 + 100 = 220$$

And for Group C:

$$1^2 + 3^2 + 4^2 + 5^2 + 2^2 = 1 + 9 + 16 + 25 + 4 = 55$$

The next row is n, which is the number of individuals in each group. For this example, $n = 5$ for all three groups. Finally, the last row is to find the mean $(\overline{Y})$ for each group. This requires finding the sum of the scores within each group and then dividing by the number of scores within each group. For Group A the mean is:

$$40 \div 5 = 8$$

For Group B:

$$30 \div 5 = 6$$

And for Group C:

$$15 \div 5 = 3$$

The last step in completing the information table is to find the numbers in the "Total" column. For the top three rows, this requires adding together the numbers in the corresponding row. For the first row this is:

$$40 + 30 + 15 = 85$$

For the second row:

$$354 + 220 + 55 = 629$$

And for the third row:

$$5 + 5 + 5 = 15$$

Summing the numbers in the row will not give you the correct number for the last number in the bottom row, which is the grand mean. For that, you should find the sum of all the scores (which is the top number in the "Total" column) and divide by the number of scores in the entire sample (which is the third number in the "Total" column). In this example, the equation for finding the grand mean is:

$$85 \div 15 = 5\frac{2}{3}$$

All of these numbers are displayed in the completed information table (Table 11.10).

Table 11.10

	Group A	Group B	Group C	Total
$\sum Y$	40	30	15	85
$\sum (Y^2)$	354	220	55	629
n	5	5	5	15
$\overline{Y}$	8	6	3	$5\frac{2}{3}$

Now, we have all the information needed to complete the ANOVA table. The first step is to find the $SOS_{Between}$ with Formula 11.8, which was $SOS_{Between} = \sum \left(\frac{\left(\sum Y_{Group} \right)^2}{n_{Group}} \right) - \frac{\left(\sum Y_{Total} \right)^2}{n_{Total}}$. The first part of the formula will create three fractions (one for each group) that are added together. This is:

$$\frac{40^2}{5} + \frac{30^2}{5} + \frac{15^2}{5}$$

The second part of the formula requires plugging in numbers from the total column:

$$\frac{85^2}{15}$$

Putting the two pieces together gives us the entire $SOS_{Between}$ formula:

$$SOS_{Between} = \frac{40^2}{5} + \frac{30^2}{5} + \frac{15^2}{5} - \frac{85^2}{15}$$

Now we can solve for $SOS_{Between}$:

$$SOS_{Between} = \frac{1600}{5} + \frac{900}{5} + \frac{225}{5} - \frac{7225}{15} = \frac{2725}{5} - \frac{7225}{15} = 545 - 481\frac{2}{3}$$

$$SOS_{Between} = 63\frac{1}{3}$$

The next step is to find SOS_{Within} using Formula 11.9, which was $SOS_{Within} = \sum_{k=1}^{k} \left(\sum \left(Y_i - \overline{Y}_{Group} \right)^2 \right)$. This requires finding a group mean deviation score for every score in the sample (Table 11.11).

Table 11.11

	Deviation score	**Squared deviation score**
Group A, person no. 1	9 – 8 = 1	1^2 = 1
Group A, person no. 2	12 – 8 = 4	4^2 = 16
Group A, person no. 3	4 – 8 = –4	$–4^2$ = 16
Group A, person no. 4	8 – 8 = 0	0^2 = 0
Group B, person no. 5	7 – 8 = –1	$–1^2$ = 1
Group B, person no. 1	4 – 6 = –2	$–2^2$ = 4
Group B, person no. 2	6 – 6 = 0	0^2 = 0
Group B, person no. 3	8 – 6 = 2	2^2 = 4
Group B, person no. 4	2 – 6 = –4	$–4^2$ = 16
Group B, person no. 5	10 – 6 = 4	4^2 = 16
Group C, person no. 1	1 – 3 = –2	$–2^2$ = 4
Group C, person no. 2	3 – 3 = 0	0^2 = 0
Group C, person no. 3	4 – 3 = 1	1^2 = 1
Group C, person no. 4	5 – 3 = 2	2^2 = 4
Group C, person no. 5	2 – 3 = –1	$–1^2$ = 1
Sum of squared deviation scores, which is SOS_{Within} =		84

Therefore, this example's SOS_{Within} value is 84.

Finding the SOS_{Total} requires using Formula 11.10, which is $SOS_{Total} = \sum Y_{Total}^2 - \frac{\left(\sum Y_{Total}\right)^2}{n_{Total}}$. The first part is finding the sum of the squared scores for all individuals in the sample. This number, 629, is in the information table in the second row of the last column. The second portion of the SOS_{Total} formula is also the second portion of the $SOS_{Between}$ formula. This was $\frac{85^2}{15}$. Therefore, to find the SOS_{Total} we calculate:

$$SOS_{Total} = 629 - \frac{85^2}{15} = 629 - 481\frac{2}{3}$$

$$SOS_{Total} = 147\frac{1}{3}$$

The next column in the ANOVA table is for the degrees of freedom. We have already calculated $df_{Between}$ (2) and df_{Within} (12) in order to find F_{crit} in the previous step. The formula for df_{Total} is $n_{Total} - 1$. Therefore, df_{Total} for our example is 15 – 1 = 14.

The third column in the ANOVA table is to find the mean square between groups and the mean square within groups. For $MS_{Between}$, the formula is $SOS_{Between} \div df_{Between}$. For this example, this is:

$$MS_{Between} = \frac{63\frac{1}{3}}{2} = 31\frac{2}{3}$$

The formula for MS_{Within} is $SOS_{Within} \div df_{Within}$. From the numbers that we have so far for the ANOVA table, the MS_{Within} value is:

$$MS_{Within} = \frac{84}{12} = 7$$

The last cell in the ANOVA table is the F_{obs} value, the formula for which is $\frac{MS_{Between}}{MS_{Within}}$. Therefore, the F_{obs} value in this example is:

$$F_{obs} = \frac{31\frac{2}{3}}{7} = 4.524$$

Step 7: Compare the Observed and Critical Values

With the observed and critical values known, we can now compare them and determine whether to reject or retain the null hypothesis. $F_{crit} = 3.885$, and $F_{obs} = 4.524$. The critical value is where the rejection region starts; the rejection region continues to $+\infty$. Because the observed value (4.524) is between 3.885 and ∞, it is in the rejection region (as shown in Figure 11.7). Therefore, we should reject the null hypothesis.

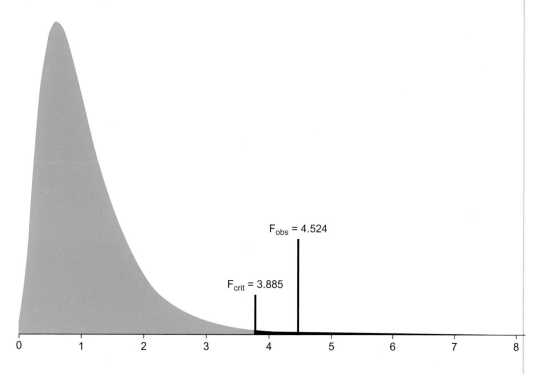

Figure 11.7 Sampling distribution showing the relative location of the *F*-critical and *F*-observed values in this Guided Practice example. $F_{crit} = 3.885$, and the rejection region is the shaded region (in black) and totals 5% of the area of the sampling distribution. $F_{obs} = 4.524$, which is inside the rejection region. Therefore, when $\alpha = .05$, the null hypothesis should be rejected.

Step 8: Calculate an Effect Size

The effect size for ANOVA is η^2, which is calculated as $\frac{SOS_{Between}}{SOS_{Total}}$. The $SOS_{Between}$ value for these data is $63\frac{1}{3}$, and the SOS_{Total} value for these data is $147\frac{1}{3}$. By this formula, the effect size for this example is

$$\eta^2 = \frac{63\frac{1}{3}}{147\frac{1}{3}} = .430$$

Therefore, 43% of the variance in the subjects' relaxation scores is associated (or shared) with the group membership variable. Another way to interpret this η^2 effect size is that predictions made on the basis of group means will generally be 43% more accurate than predictions on the basis of the grand mean.

Finding *p*

Because the null hypothesis was rejected when $\alpha = .05$, *p* must be less than .05. We can also determine whether *p* is greater or less than .01 by determining whether the null hypothesis is rejected when $\alpha = .01$. To do this, we must find F_{crit} when $\alpha = .01$. Given our data's degrees of freedom ($df_{Between} = 2$ and $df_{Within} = 12$), the corresponding F_{crit} is 6.927. The relationships between this F_{crit} and the F_{obs} value (4.524) is shown in Figure 11.8. As Figure 11.8 shows, this critical value is more extreme than the observed value, indicating that the null hypothesis should be retained when $\alpha = .01$.

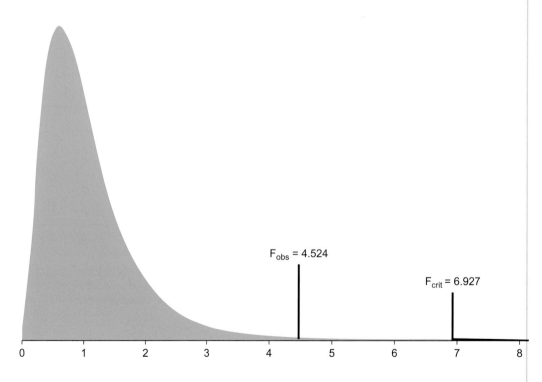

Figure 11.8 Sampling distribution showing the relative location of the *F*-critical and *F*-observed values in the Guided Practice example when $\alpha = .01$ and $F_{crit} = 6.927$, which is the point where the rejection region (shaded in black) begins. $F_{obs} = 4.524$, which is outside the rejection region. Therefore, when $\alpha = .01$, the null hypothesis should be retained. As a result, $p > .01$ in this example, but (as shown in Figure 11.7), *p* is also less than .05.

Tukey's *post hoc* Test

With the null hypothesis rejected, we know that the group means are not statistically equal. However, we do not know *which* means differ from other means. To determine this, we conduct a Tukey's *post hoc* test. This requires finding the HSD for each pair of group means. Finding the HSD requires Formula 11.13, which is $\dfrac{\bar{X}_1 - \bar{X}_2}{\sqrt{\dfrac{MS_{Within}}{\left(\sum \dfrac{k}{\frac{1}{n_{Group}}}\right)}}}$. The denominator of this formula will be

the same for each pair of group means. Using the MS_{Within} value (7), k (3), and n_{Group} (5 for all groups) from this example, we can find the value of this denominator:

$$\sqrt{\frac{MS_{Within}}{\left(\sum \dfrac{k}{\frac{1}{n_{Group}}}\right)}} = \sqrt{\frac{7}{\left(\dfrac{3}{\frac{1}{5}+\frac{1}{5}+\frac{1}{5}}\right)}} = \sqrt{\frac{7}{5}} = \sqrt{1.4} = 1.183$$

We can now plug this value into the HSD formula and then create a formula for each pair of group means from the information table. This gives us three HSD values:

$$HSD_{\bar{X}_A - \bar{X}_B} = \frac{8-6}{1.183} = \frac{2}{1.183} = 1.690$$

$$HSD_{\bar{X}_A - \bar{X}_C} = \frac{8-3}{1.183} = \frac{5}{1.183} = 4.226$$

$$HSD_{\bar{X}_B - \bar{X}_C} = \frac{6-3}{1.183} = \frac{3}{1.183} = 2.535$$

These values should then be compared to the q values in Appendix A4. For $df_{Between} = 2$ and $df_{Within} = 12$ and $\alpha = .05$, the critical q value is 3.773. Any value greater than 3.773 (or less than −3.773) would be statistically significant. Only the HSD for the means for Groups A and C is this large. Therefore, the null hypothesis in the ANOVA was rejected because these two groups had a large enough difference for the null hypothesis to be rejected. This shows that the group that had yoga classes (Group A) was statistically more relaxed than the control group (Group C). However, there were no statistically significant differences between the group that listened to quiet music (Group B) and the other two groups.

Summary

All the NHSTs that we have discussed before this chapter are designed to compare two means. However, social scientists often have more than two groups to compare. In this case it is possible to use unpaired two-sample *t*-tests for each pair of group means, but there are two problems with this strategy. First, as the number of groups increases, the number of *t*-tests required increases even faster. Second, the risk of Type I error increases with each additional *t*-test. This latter problem can be fixed by reducing the α value for each test until the overall α is equal to the desired level.

The analysis of variance (called ANOVA), though, fixes both problems. Its null hypothesis is that all of the group means are equal. The alternative hypothesis is that at least two means among the groups are unequal. ANOVA follows the same eight steps as the other NHST procedures in this textbook, though the calculations are more complex than previous NHSTs. ANOVA requires completing an information table and an ANOVA table in order to find the observed value. ANOVA also produces an effect size, η^2 (called "eta-squared"). The η^2 effect size ranges from 0 to 1 and can be interpreted in two ways. First, η^2 quantifies the percentage of dependent variable variance that is shared with the independent variable's variance. Second, η^2 measures how much better the group mean functions as a predicted score when compared to the grand mean.

ANOVA has the shortcoming of only saying whether a difference exists – not which means differ from other means. To do this, one must perform either a *post hoc* test or a planned contrast. The most common procedure is Tukey's *post hoc* test, which compares the group means one pair at a time to determine which means are statistically significantly different from one another. This helps researchers identify the source of the rejection of the null hypothesis.

Reflection Questions: Comprehension

1. What is Type I error inflation, and why is it a problem when conducting multiple NHSTs?
2. What is the purpose of a Bonferroni correction?
3. Some of the formulas in this chapter use the abbreviation *k*. What does *k* signify?
4. The effect size for ANOVA is η^2. What are the two interpretations of this effect size?
5. In an ANOVA the null hypothesis is that all of the group means are equal to one another. If the null hypothesis is rejected, how do we determine *which* group mean(s) differ from other mean(s)?
6. Explain the connection between the unpaired two-sample *t*-test and ANOVA.
7. What is the benefit of calculating group means in the information table?
8. Explain why labeling effect sizes as "small," "medium," or "large" without any further interpretation is problematic.
9. In an ANOVA we can use the information table to make predictions. How do we measure
   a. individual prediction accuracy?
   b. overall prediction accuracy?
10. How do you find a critical value in an ANOVA?

Reflection Questions: Application

11. Dana wants to compare the grade-point averages (GPAs) for freshman, sophomore, junior, and senior sociology students. If she chooses not to use an ANOVA,
    a. how many unpaired two-sample *t*-tests will she need to conduct?
    b. what would be her experimentwise Type I error if she makes each test have an α value of .05?
    c. what would be her testwise Type I error if she performs a Bonferroni correction in order to maintain the experimentwise Type I error rate at .05?

d. what would be her testwise Type I error if she performs a Bonferroni correction in order to maintain the experimentwise Type I error rate at .01?

e. What would be the advantages of performing an ANOVA compared to performing a number of unpaired two-sample t-tests?

12. Dave's university has students from six different Canadian provinces. He surveys a representative sample of students to learn how many hours per week they study. Jim wants to know if there are any differences among students from the six provinces in the average number of hours they study per week. If he chooses not to use an ANOVA,

a. how many unpaired two-sample t-tests will he need to conduct?

b. what would be his experimentwise Type I error if he makes each test have an α value of .05?

c. what would be his testwise Type I error if he performs a Bonferroni correction in order to maintain the experimentwise Type I error rate at .05?

d. what would be his testwise Type I error if he performs a Bonferroni correction in order to maintain the experimentwise Type I error rate at .01?

e. what would be the advantages of performing an ANOVA compared to performing a number of unpaired two-sample t-tests?

13. Liliana collected data about the happiness level of teenagers, young adults, and elderly individuals, with a score of 1 being "very unhappy" and a score of 5 being "very happy."

a. Why is an ANOVA an appropriate statistical procedure for Liliana to use?

b. What are the groups in this ANOVA?

c. What is the null hypothesis for this dataset?

d. Should she perform a one- or a two-tailed test with her data? Justify your response.

e. Find the F_{crit} value for this ANOVA if α = .05.

f. Complete the information table below.

	Teenagers	Young adults	Elderly adults	Total
Score:	2	5	4	
Score:	4	5	5	
Score:	4	1	4	
Score:	5	2	2	
Score:	3	3	1	
Score:	1	4	3	
$\sum Y$				
$\sum (Y^2)$				
N				
$\bar{Y}$				

g. Complete the ANOVA table below.

	SOS	df	MS	F_{obs}
Between				
Within				
Total				

   h. Given the F_{obs} value, should she reject or retain the null hypothesis?

   i. What is the p-value for this ANOVA?

   j. Calculate *and interpret* the η^2 value for these data.

   k. Should she conduct a *post hoc* test of the data? Why or why not?

   l. Find the critical q value for Tukey's *post hoc* test for these data.

   m. Find the HSD values in Tukey's *post hoc* test for each pair of groups and interpret the HSD values.

   n. Find the residuals (based on the group means) for each score in the dataset.

14. Nicole is a psychology student interested in the social dynamics of solving problems. She divided her sample into three groups: people who solved problems alone (Group A), people forced to solve problems together (Group B), and people who could choose whether to solve problems in groups (Group C). She then measured how many minutes it took for each problem to be solved.

   a. Why is an ANOVA an appropriate statistical procedure for Nicole to use?

   b. What are the groups in this ANOVA?

   c. What is the null hypothesis for this dataset?

   d. Should she perform a one- or a two-tailed test with her data? Justify your response.

   e. Find the F_{crit} value for this ANOVA if $\alpha = .05$.

   f. Complete the information table below.

	Group A	Group B	Group C	Total
Score:	8	13	7	
Score:	12	10	15	
Score:	16	9	10	
Score:	7	14	15	
Score:	11	16	12	
Score:	19		4	
Score:	14			
Score:	6			
$\sum Y$				
$\sum (Y^2)$				
n				
$\overline{Y}$				

   g. Complete the ANOVA table below.

	SOS	df	MS	F_{obs}
Between				
Within				
Total				

h. Given the F_{obs} value, should she reject or retain the null hypothesis?
i. What is the *p*-value for this ANOVA?
j. Calculate *and interpret* the η^2 value for these data.
k. Should she conduct a *post hoc* test of the data? Why or why not?
l. Find the critical *q* value for Tukey's *post hoc* test for these data.
m. Find the HSD values in Tukey's *post hoc* test for each pair of groups and interpret the HSD values.
n. Find the residuals (based on the group means) for each score in the dataset.

15. Oi-mon is a sociology student interested in how groups of people choose to travel long distances. He asked four groups of travelers how much they enjoyed long journeys. The four groups were plane travelers, train travelers, car travelers, and bus travelers. In his data higher numbers indicated more enjoyment in their trips.
   a. Why is an ANOVA an appropriate statistical procedure for Oi-mon to use?
   b. What are the groups in this ANOVA?
   c. What is the null hypothesis for this dataset?
   d. Should he perform a one- or a two-tailed test with his data? Justify your response.
   e. Find the F_{crit} value for this ANOVA if $\alpha = .05$.
   f. Complete the information table below.

	Plane	Train	Car	Bus	Total
Score:	4	5	6	4	
Score:	6	5	4	3	
Score:	3	6	2	3	
Score:	1	4	5	5	
Score:	5	2	6	1	
Score:	6	3			
Score:	5	2			
Score:		4			
$\sum Y$					
$\sum (Y^2)$					
N					
$\overline{Y}$					

g. Complete the ANOVA table below.

	SOS	df	MS	F_{obs}
Between				
Within				
Total				

h. Given the F_{obs} value, should he reject or retain the null hypothesis?
i. What is the *p*-value for this ANOVA?

j.   Calculate *and interpret* the η^2 value for these data.

k.   Should he conduct a *post hoc* test of the data? Why or why not?

l.   Find the critical q value for Tukey's *post hoc* test for these data.

m.   Find the HSD values in Tukey's *post hoc* test for each pair of groups and interpret the HSD values.

n.   Find the residuals (based on the group means) for each score in the dataset.

16. Davita is an anthropology student who measures the level of trust in her subjects. In her data higher numbers indicate greater trust of strangers and lower numbers indicate less trust. She divided her subjects into three groups: (1) residents of the capital city, (2) residents of suburbs, and (3) residents of rural areas.

a.   Why is an ANOVA an appropriate statistical procedure for Davita to use?

b.   What are the groups in this ANOVA?

c.   What is the null hypothesis for this dataset?

d.   Should she perform a one- or a two-tailed test with her data? Justify your response.

e.   Find the F_{crit} value for this ANOVA if $\alpha = .05$.

f.   Complete the information table below.

	Capital city	Suburbs	Rural	Total
Score:	10	7	1	
Score:	3	10	8	
Score:	2	4	9	
Score:	7	6	5	
Score:	6	7	7	
Score:	5	2	6	
Score:	8	5	4	
Score:	2	9	8	
$\sum Y$				
$\sum (Y^2)$				
n				
$\overline{Y}$				

g.   Complete the ANOVA table below.

	SOS	df	MS	F_{obs}
Between				
Within				
Total				

h.   Given the F_{obs} value, should she reject or retain the null hypothesis?

i.   What is the *p*-value for this ANOVA?

j.   Calculate *and interpret* the η^2 value for these data.

k.   Should she conduct a *post hoc* test of the data? Why or why not?

l. Find the critical q value for Tukey's *post hoc* test for these data.

m. Find the HSD values in Tukey's *post hoc* test for each pair of groups and interpret the HSD values.

n. Find the residuals (based on the group means) for each score in the dataset.

17. Zachary is a psychology student who is interested in the degree of control that people feel they have in their lives. He has five groups in his dataset: (a) police officers, (b) victims of violent crime, (c) victims of non-violent personal crime, (d) victims of vandalism and other property crime, and (e) non-crime victims. In his data the higher numbers indicate greater control, and lower numbers indicate lower control.

a. Why is an ANOVA an appropriate statistical procedure for Zachary to use?

b. What are the groups in this ANOVA?

c. What is the null hypothesis for this dataset?

d. Should he perform a one- or a two-tailed test with his data? Justify your response.

e. Find the F_{crit} value for this ANOVA if $\alpha = .05$.

f. Complete the information table below.

	Group A	Group B	Group C	Group D	Group E	Total
Score:	4	3	5	8	2	
Score:	6	1	6	7	6	
Score:	2	4	5	8	4	
Score:	7	5	4	6	8	
Score:	6	5	4	1	6	
Score:	7	9	8	3	7	
Score:	8	2	7	4	9	
Score:		4	9	6	9	
Score:		7	3	8	8	
Score:			4	8	7	
$\sum Y$						
$\sum (Y^2)$						
N						
$\overline{Y}$						

g. Complete the ANOVA table below.

	SOS	df	MS	F_{obs}
Between				
Within				
Total				

h. Given the F_{obs} value, should he reject or retain the null hypothesis?

i. What is the p-value for this ANOVA?

j. Calculate *and interpret* the η^2 value for these data.

k. Should he conduct a *post hoc* test of the data? Why or why not?

l. Find the critical q value for Tukey's *post hoc* test for these data.

m. Find the HSD values in Tukey's *post hoc* test for each pair of groups and interpret the HSD values.

n. Find the residuals (based on the group means) for each score in the dataset.

18. Mason is a sociology student who is interested in how city size influences how people interact with their neighbors. He has three groups in his dataset: (1) inner city dwellers, (2) suburban residents, and (3) rural residents. In his data the higher numbers indicate that people interact with their neighbors more.

a. Why is an ANOVA an appropriate statistical procedure for Mason to use?

b. What are the groups in this ANOVA?

c. What is the null hypothesis for this dataset?

d. Should he perform a one- or a two-tailed test with his data? Justify your response.

e. Find the F_{crit} value for this ANOVA if $\alpha = .05$.

f. Complete the information table below.

	Group A	Group B	Group C	Total
Score:	9	3	5	
Score:	11	1	6	
Score:	7	4	5	
Score:	12	5	4	
Score:	11	5	4	
$\sum Y$				
$\sum (Y^2)$				
N				
$\overline{Y}$				

g. Complete the ANOVA table below.

	SOS	df	MS	F_{obs}
Between				
Within				
Total				

h. Given the F_{obs} value, should he reject or retain the null hypothesis?

i. What is the *p*-value for this ANOVA?

j. Calculate *and interpret* the η^2 value for these data.

k. Should he conduct a *post hoc* test of the data? Why or why not?

l. Find the critical q value for Tukey's *post hoc* test for these data.

m. Find the HSD values in Tukey's *post hoc* test for each pair of groups and interpret the HSD values.

n. Find the residuals (based on the group means) for each score in the dataset.

Software Guide

Because ANOVA is merely an extension of the unpaired two-sample *t*-test, it should be unsurprising that both Microsoft Excel and SPSS can perform an ANOVA. This software guide provides step-by-step instructions for conducting an ANOVA in each program.

Excel

With the default settings, Microsoft Excel cannot conduct an ANOVA quickly. However, with the Analysis ToolPak add-in installed, it is easy to conduct an ANOVA. To install the Toolpak, click the "File" ribbon and then select "Options" (see Figure 11.9).

Figure 11.9 First step in installing the Analysis ToolPak in Microsoft Excel. This is the file ribbon. After clicking this, the user should then click "Options." In this version of Microsoft Excel, it is the second item from the bottom.

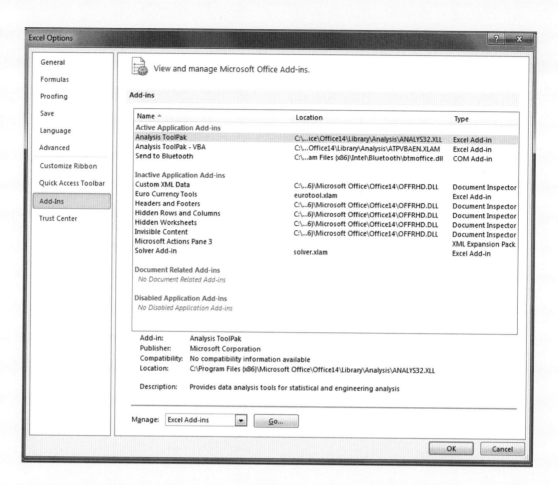

Figure 11.10 The Excel Options window.

A new window, called the Excel Options window, will appear. This is shown in Figure 11.10. On the left side of the window, you should select "Add-ins." On the right-hand side, you should click the button that says, "Go."

After selecting "Go" in the Excel Options window, a new window appears, called the Add-Ins window. This is shown in Figure 11.11. To install the Analysis ToolPak, you should check the boxes next to "Analysis ToolPak" and "Analysis Toolpak – VBA." The next step is to click the button labeled "OK." This will install the Analysis Toolpak.

With the Analysis ToolPak installed, you can now conduct an ANOVA. To do this, the data should first be entered into the spreadsheet in Excel. Figure 11.12 shows the data from this chapter's Stroop Test example. After the data have been entered, you should click the "Data" ribbon and then the "Data Analysis" button (at the top right of the screen, as shown in the figure). This causes a new window to appear.

Figure 11.13 shows the new window, called the Data Analysis window. This window gives a list of statistical procedures that the Analysis Toolpak can perform. To perform an ANOVA, you should select "Anova: Single Factor" from the list and then click "OK."

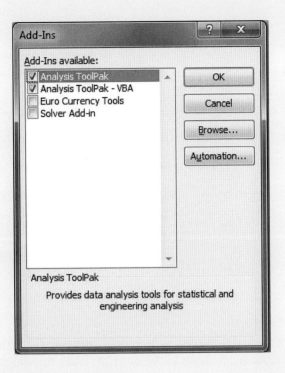

Figure 11.11 The Add-Ins window in Microsoft Excel.

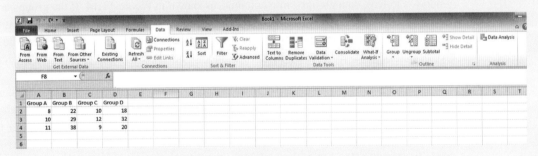

Figure 11.12 A spreadsheet with data for an ANOVA entered.

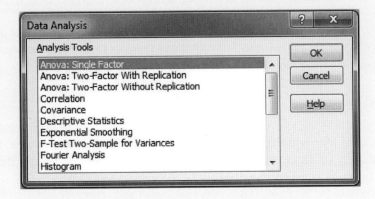

Figure 11.13 The Data Analysis window. The option for conducting an ANOVA is highlighted on the left side of the window.

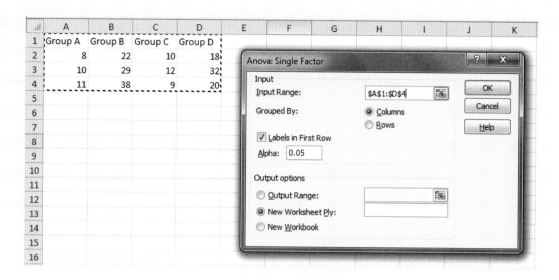

Figure 11.14 The Anova: Single Factor window and the ANOVA data in Microsoft Excel.

Yet another window appears after clicking "OK." This is the called the Anova: Single Factor window and is shown in Figure 11.14. When this window appears, you should use the computer mouse to select the data from the spreadsheet. The default in the Anova: Single Factor window is to have data grouped into columns, as shown in Figure 11.14. If the groups are arranged in rows, you select "Rows" in the Anova: Single Factor window. Also, please note that the box on the left of the Anova: Single Factor window is checked. This tells the computer that the top row of the selected cells has the group labels in it – and not actual data. Finally, you should click "OK" on the right side of the Anova: Single Factor window.

Completing the previous step makes the results of the ANOVA display on the computer screen. This is shown in Figure 11.15. The upper table is the information table, although it does not contain $\sum(Y^2)$, which is the sum of the squared dependent variable scores. The lower table is the ANOVA table, which contains the results of the ANOVA. Notice the column in the ANOVA table that is labeled "P value." This p-value refers to the F-observed value, which is also displayed in the ANOVA table. As with previous analyses in Microsoft Excel, if the p-value is less than the α value, the null hypothesis should be rejected. If the p-value is greater than the α value, the null hypothesis should be retained.

Finally, it is important to recognize that Microsoft Excel does not calculate the effect size (η^2). You have to calculate η^2 by hand (see Formula 11.11). Excel also cannot perform any *post hoc* tests, requiring those to be performed manually as well.

SPSS

Unlike Microsoft Excel, SPSS has a built-in tool that performs an ANOVA easily. For SPSS, though, the data must be entered into the data window in the manner shown in Figure 11.16. The first column contains the data for the independent variable, which is the group membership variable. In this figure Group A is represented as 1, Group B as 2, etc. The dependent variable

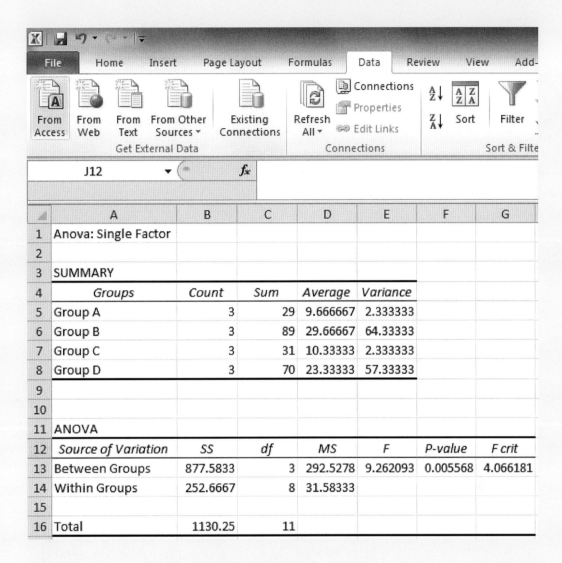

Figure 11.15 The results of ANOVA performed in Microsoft Excel.

scores (in Stroop Test scores) are the numbers in the second column. Each person in the dataset is represented by a row.

To perform the ANOVA, click the "Analyze" menu at the top of the screen, and then "Compare Means" and then "One-Way ANOVA." A new window, called the One-Way ANOVA window, will appear, as shown in Figure 11.17. The variables in the dataset are listed on the left. The independent variable (i.e., the group membership variable) should be selected and then placed in the lower window labeled "Factor." The dependent variable (in this example, Stroop scores), should be selected and put in the upper-right window labeled "Dependent list." Figure 11.18 shows what the window looks like with the variable names put in these windows.

The next step is to click the "Post Hoc" button on the right. This makes a new window appear, as shown in Figure 11.19. This window provides all of the options for 18 different *post hoc* tests. In Figure 11.19 Tukey's *post hoc* test option has been selected. If you examine the figure you

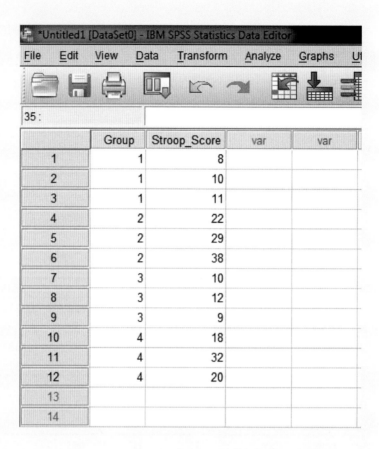

Figure 11.16 SPSS data window with the Stroop Test example data entered in. The first column refers to the group an individual belongs to, while the second column displays their score.

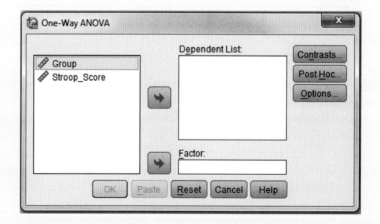

Figure 11.17 The One-Way ANOVA window in SPSS.

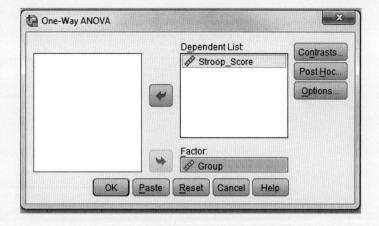

Figure 11.18 The One-Way ANOVA window in SPSS with the independent and dependent variables selected for the ANOVA.

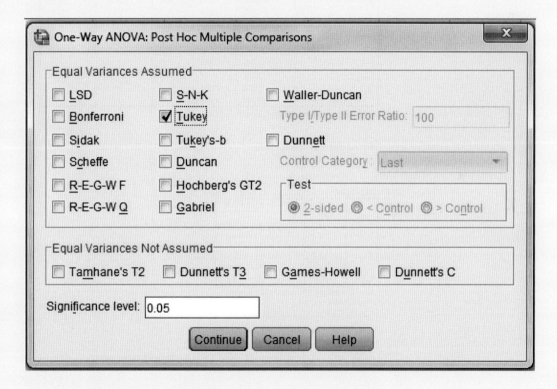

Figure 11.19 SPSS window showing options for *post hoc* tests. Tukey's *post hoc* test has been selected.

can see that Scheffé's *post hoc* test and Dunnett's test are also options available in SPSS. After selecting a post hoc test, you should select "Continue" in this window and then "OK" in the One-Way ANOVA window.

The next window to appear is the output window, which shows the results of the ANOVA and the *post hoc* test. These results are in Figure 11.20. The first table is the ANOVA table, which

ANOVA

Stroop_Score

	Sum of Squares	df	Mean Square	F	Sig.
Between Groups	877.583	3	292.528	9.262	.006
Within Groups	252.667	8	31.583		
Total	1130.250	11			

Post Hoc Tests

Multiple Comparisons

Dependent Variable: Stroop_Score

Tukey HSD

(I) Group	(J) Group	Mean Difference (I-J)	Std. Error	Sig.	95% Confidence Interval	
					Lower Bound	Upper Bound
1	2	-20.000*	4.589	.010	-34.69	-5.31
	3	-.667	4.589	.999	-15.36	14.03
	4	-13.667	4.589	.069	-28.36	1.03
2	1	20.000*	4.589	.010	5.31	34.69
	3	19.333*	4.589	.013	4.64	34.03
	4	6.333	4.589	.544	-8.36	21.03
3	1	.667	4.589	.999	-14.03	15.36
	2	-19.333*	4.589	.013	-34.03	-4.64
	4	-13.000	4.589	.084	-27.69	1.69
4	1	13.667	4.589	.069	-1.03	28.36
	2	-6.333	4.589	.544	-21.03	8.36
	3	13.000	4.589	.084	-1.69	27.69

*. The mean difference is significant at the 0.05 level.

Homogeneous Subsets

Stroop_Score

Tukey HSD[a]

Group	N	Subset for alpha = 0.05	
		1	2
1	3	9.67	
3	3	10.33	
4	3	23.33	23.33
2	3		29.67
Sig.		.069	.544

Means for groups in homogeneous subsets are displayed.

a. Uses Harmonic Mean Sample Size = 3.000.

Figure 11.20 SPSS output showing the results of the ANOVA example. The top table is the ANOVA table. The second and third tables show the results of Tukey's *post hoc* test.

appears the same as in Excel and in this book chapter. The next table shows the result of Tukey's *post hoc* test. This table shows the group differences for every possible pair of groups. The table shows this information by labeling groups as Groups I and J. It then shows the difference between their means, as calculated as Group I – Group J. The column labeled "Sig." is the *p*-value for that group's difference. For these group differences (and for the *p*-value, labeled "Sig." in the ANOVA table), any *p*-value less than the α value indicates that the null hypothesis (of no mean group differences) should be rejected. A *p*-value greater than the α value indicates that the null hypothesis should be retained. SPSS marks all *p*-values less than .05 with an asterisk (*). The results of this *post hoc* test indicate that the differences between Groups A and B and Groups B and C are statistically significant, which is precisely what we found when we performed the Tukey's *post hoc* test manually with these data. Therefore, it is because of these group differences that the null hypothesis in the ANOVA was rejected (as indicated by the small *p*-value in the ANOVA table).

Finally, the bottom table is a supplementary table that helps in interpreting the *post hoc* results. Each column in this table represents a group of means from the data. Groups that are placed in the same column are means that do not statistically differ from one another. Figure 11.20 indicates that Groups A, C, and D all belong to the same group, while Groups B and D belong to a different group. Notice that Group D belongs to both groups, indicating that there are no statistically significant differences between Group D and any other group mean. This happens frequently and should be no cause of concern. The row labeled "Sig." displays a *p*-value indicating the differences among the means within a single group. This value will always be larger than .05 (the default α in SPSS); if this value were smaller than .05, the means would not all belong to the same group.

Further Reading

- Kieffer, K. M., Reese, R. J., & Thompson, B. (2001). Statistical techniques employed in *AERJ* and *JCP* articles from 1988 to 1997: A methodological review. *Journal of Experimental Education*, *69*, 280–309. doi:10.1080/00220970109599489

  * In this article Kieffer and his coauthors tabulated the most popular statistical methods in leading journals in two different areas: education and psychology. They found that ANOVA was the most common statistical procedure in the education journal and third most common in the psychology journal. This is typical of articles of this kind, which are useful because they help students and instructors know which statistical procedures are most important to learn.

- Thompson, B. (2007). Effect sizes, confidence intervals, and confidence intervals for effect sizes. *Psychology in the Schools*, *44*, 423–432. doi:10.1002/pits.20234

  * If you want to take your effect size reporting one step further, include a confidence interval. In this article Thompson explains the value of calculating confidence intervals for effect sizes and how to calculate them.

- Warne, R. T. (2014a). A primer on multivariate analysis of variance (MANOVA) for behavioral scientists. *Practical Assessment, Research & Evaluation*, *19*(17), 1–10.

  * ANOVA eliminates Type I error inflation from multiple unpaired-samples *t*-tests, but conducting multiple ANOVAs when there are multiple dependent variables also inflates Type I error. I wrote this article to explain multivariate analysis of variance

(MANOVA), which is a statistical procedure designed to eliminate Type I error and bypass the need to conduct multiple ANOVAs (see Chapter 15). It is a more complex procedure than anything in this textbook, but the only thing needed to understand it is a solid grasp of ANOVA. There is no hand calculation in the article, just instructions on how to use SPSS to conduct a MANOVA and the logic behind MANOVA as a statistical procedure.

12 Correlation

Video games are one of the most popular forms of multimedia entertainment available today. Because of their popularity, social scientists have been studying the effects of video games for over 30 years. However, for the first 20 years or so, this research was focused on the negative effects of video gaming, such as a theorized link between playing violent video games and engaging in aggressive behavior in the real world (e.g., Browne & Hamilton-Giachritis, 2005). But since the turn of the millennium more social scientists have recognized the potentially positive benefits of video games. These researchers have found evidence that playing video games may increase players' ability to shift their focus of attention (e.g., Bavelier, Achtman, Mani, & Föcker, 2012), foster collaboration among players, and improve planning and goal-directive behavior (Granic, Lobel, & Engels, 2014).

One intriguing finding is that people who obtain high scores on some video games have higher intelligence test scores (e.g., Ángeles Quiroga et al., 2015; Foroughi, Serraino, Parasuraman, & Boehm-Davis, 2016). Two of my students decided to test this finding for themselves, and so they collected two variables from a sample. The first variable was the average score on a simple video game, and the second variable was the subjects' scores on a brief intelligence test. When my students wanted to analyze their data, they discovered that they couldn't use an ANOVA or an unpaired-samples t-test. These statistical analysis methods require a nominal independent variable that divides the sample into groups. However, one variable that my students collected (video game scores) was ratio-level, and the second variable (intelligence test scores) was interval-level. Therefore, they needed a different analysis method to analyze their data. That statistical method is called the correlation, and it is the topic of this chapter.

Learning Goals

- Explain the purpose of a correlation and when it is appropriate to use.
- Calculate Pearson's r to measure the strength of the relationship between two variables.
- Interpret the effect size (r^2) for a correlation.

Purpose of the Correlation Coefficient

My students' example of video game scores and intelligence test scores is typical of the types of data that social scientists calculate correlations for. Since both variables are interval-level data, it is usually not feasible to use any previous NHST procedures because there are not discrete groups (e.g., two sets of scores created by a nominal data) with interval-level data. Rather, what is needed is a statistic that describes the relationship between two variables without using any nominal groups. That statistic is the correlation coefficient.

Definition of a Correlation

A **correlation coefficient** is a statistic that measures the strength of the relationship between two variables. If two variables have a relationship between them, we say that they are correlated. In fact, the word "related" is in the word cor*related*; the "cor-" prefix means "together," indicating that correlation occurs when two things (in this case, variables) are related to one another. When there is a strong correlation between two variables, there is a somewhat consistent pattern in the way that scores from each variable occur together. When there is a weak correlation between two variables, the pattern of how scores occur together is inconsistent. If there is no pattern with the way that variable scores occur together, we say that there is no correlation, or a zero correlation, between variables.

There are several types of correlation (e.g., see General Linear Moment 13.1), but the one that we discuss in this chapter is called Pearson's r, and it is one of the most common statistics in the social sciences (Skidmore & Thompson, 2010; Warne et al., 2012). Pearson's r is an appropriate statistic when both variables consist of interval- or ratio-level data, as is true of video game scores and intelligence test scores.

Calculating Pearson's r

The formula for Pearson's r (sometimes called a correlation coefficient) is

$$r = \frac{\frac{\sum (x_i - \overline{X})(y_i - \overline{Y})}{n - 1}}{s_x \cdot s_y} \qquad \text{(Formula 12.1)}$$

In the first part of the formula (which comes from K. Pearson, 1896, p. 265, with slight notation changes), x_i and y_i are the scores *from the same individual* for variables X and Y; $\overline{X}$ is the mean of variable X, and $\overline{Y}$ is the mean of variable Y. The symbol n is the sample size (i.e., the number of individuals in the sample). The symbols s_x and s_y are the standard deviations of the two variables.

To demonstrate how to find a Pearson's r value with Formula 12.1, we will use data from my students' video game study. Table 12.1 shows the data from the first 10 people in their sample. In this example, the X variable is the subjects' video game scores, and the Y variable is the individuals' intelligence test scores. Finding Pearson's r will tell us whether these individuals' scores on these two variables are related.

Preparatory Steps: Descriptive Statistics. Before we can use Formula 12.1, we need to find the mean and standard deviation of each variable. For the X variable, the mean is:

$$\overline{X} = \frac{\sum x_i}{n} = \frac{6{,}000 + 4{,}900 + 4{,}700 + 7{,}200 + 4{,}700 + 5{,}600 + 4{,}800 + 6{,}200 + 3{,}500 + 5{,}400}{10}$$

$$\overline{X} = \frac{53{,}000}{10} = 5300$$

For the Y variable, the mean is:

$$\overline{Y} = \frac{\sum y_i}{n} = \frac{26 + 22 + 21 + 28 + 20 + 28 + 29 + 32 + 30 + 36}{10} = \frac{272}{10} = 27.2$$

Table 12.1 Video game and intelligence scores for 10 individuals

ID number	Video game scores (X variable)	Intelligence test scores (Y variable)
1	6,000	26
2	4,900	22
3	4,700	21
4	7,200	28
5	4,700	20
6	5,600	28
7	4,800	29
8	6,200	32
9	3,500	30
10	5,400	36

Table 12.2

ID number	Deviation score (for X)	Squared deviation score (for X)
1	$6,000 - 5,300 = 700$	$700^2 = 490,000$
2	$4,900 - 5,300 = -400$	$-400^2 = 160,000$
3	$4,700 - 5,300 = -600$	$-600^2 = 360,000$
4	$7,200 - 5,300 = 1,900$	$1900^2 = 3,610,000$
5	$4,700 - 5,300 = -600$	$-600^2 = 360,000$
6	$5,600 - 5,300 = 300$	$300^2 = 90,000$
7	$4,800 - 5,300 = -500$	$-500^2 = 250,000$
8	$6,200 - 5,300 = 900$	$900^2 = 810,000$
9	$3,500 - 5,300 = -1,800$	$-1800^2 = 3,240,000$
10	$5,400 - 5,300 = 100$	$100^2 = 10,000$

Calculating the standard deviation of X requires first finding a deviation score $(x_i - \overline{X})$ for each individual and then squaring that deviation score (Table 12.2).

The next step is to add the squared deviation scores:

$$490,000 + 160,000 + 360,000 + 3,610,000 + 360,000 + 90,000 + 250,000$$
$$+ 810,000 + 3,240,000 + 10,000 = 9,380,000$$

and then divide by $n - 1$ and take the square root. The result is the standard deviation of X.

$$\frac{9,380,000}{10 - 1} = \frac{9,380,000}{9} = 1,042,222.222$$

$$\sqrt{1,042,222.222} = 1,020.893$$

$$s_x = 1,020.893$$

Repeating the same steps for the y variable produces the following (Table 12.3):

Table 12.3

ID	Deviation score (for Y)	Squared deviation score (for Y)
1	26 – 27.2 = –1.2	–1.2^2 = 1.44
2	22 – 27.2 = –5.2	–5.2^2 = 27.04
3	21 – 27.2 = –6.2	–6.2^2 = 38.44
4	28 – 27.2 = 0.8	0.8^2 = 0.64
5	20 – 27.2 = –7.2	–7.2^2 = 51.84
6	28 – 27.2 = 0.8	0.8^2 = 0.64
7	29 – 27.2 = 1.8	1.8^2 = 3.24
8	32 – 27.2 = 4.8	4.8^2 = 23.04
9	30 – 27.2 = 2.8	2.8^2 = 7.84
10	36 – 27.2 = 8.8	8.8^2 = 77.44

Table 12.4

ID	Deviation score (for X)	Deviation score (for Y)
1	700	–1.2
2	–400	–5.2
3	–600	–6.2
4	1,900	0.8
5	–600	–7.2
6	300	0.8
7	–500	1.8
8	900	4.8
9	–1,800	2.8
10	100	8.8

$$1.44 + 27.04 + 38.44 + 0.64 + 51.84 + 0.64 + 3.24 + 23.04 + 7.84 + 77.44 = 231.6$$

$$\frac{231.6}{10-1} = \frac{231.6}{9} = 25.733$$

$$\sqrt{25.733} = 5.073$$

$$s_y = 5.073$$

Finding Pearson's r. With the descriptive statistics for both variables in hand, we can now use Formula 12.1 to calculate Pearson's r. The first step in using the formula is to find the deviation scores for the scores on both variables for each individual. We already had to calculate the deviation scores when we found the standard deviation. Those scores were as shown in Table 12.4.

The top part of the Pearson's r formula – that is, $\sum(x_i - \overline{X})(y_i - \overline{Y})$, in Formula 12.1 – requires us to multiply the deviation score for X by the same individual's deviation score for Y (Table 12.5).

Table 12.5

ID	Deviation score (for X)	Deviation score (for Y)	Multiplied deviation scores
1	700	−1.2	$(700)(-1.2) = -840$
2	−400	−5.2	$(-400)(-5.2) = 2{,}080$
3	−600	−6.2	$(-600)(-6.2) = 3{,}720$
4	1,900	0.8	$(1900)(0.8) = 1{,}520$
5	−600	−7.2	$(-600)(-7.2) = 4{,}320$
6	300	0.8	$(300)(0.8) = 240$
7	−500	1.8	$(-500)(1.8) = -900$
8	900	4.8	$(900)(4.8) = 4{,}320$
9	−1,800	2.8	$(-1800)(2.8) = -5{,}040$
10	100	8.8	$(100)(8.8) = 880$

After multiplying the deviation scores by one another, we sum the numbers:

$$-840 + 2{,}080 + 3{,}720 + 1{,}520 + 4{,}320 + 240 + -900 + 4{,}320 + -5{,}040 + 880 = 10{,}300$$

Then, we divide by $n-1$. Remember that n is the number of individuals in the data – not the number of scores. There are 10 individuals in this example data, so $n = 10$. Therefore, $n - 1$ is equal to 9.

$$\frac{10{,}300}{9} = 1{,}144.44$$

The final step is to divide this number by the two standard deviations multiplied by each other:

$$r = \frac{1{,}144.44}{s_x \cdot s_y} = \frac{1{,}144.44}{1{,}020.893 \cdot 5.073} = \frac{1{,}144.44}{5{,}178.789} = .221$$

$$r = +.221$$

Therefore, for this dataset, the correlation between video game scores and intelligence test scores is $r = +.221$.

Sidebar 12.1 Alternative formula for *r*

There is an alternative formula for Pearson's *r* that does not require calculating the mean and standard deviation for the two variables. The formula is:

$$r = \frac{n(\sum XY) - (\sum X)(\sum Y)}{\sqrt{\left[n(\sum X^2) - (\sum X)^2\right]\left[n(\sum Y^2) - (\sum Y)^2\right]}} \qquad \text{Formula 12.2}$$

Given the same set of data, Formulas 12.1 and 12.2 will produce the same results. This will be demonstrated below by using the same video game data as the example in this chapter.

First, *n* in this example is equal to 10, so we can replace the three *n*'s in the formula with 10's:

$$r = \frac{10(\sum XY) - (\sum X)(\sum Y)}{\sqrt{\left[10(\sum X^2) - (\sum X)^2\right]\left[10(\sum Y^2) - (\sum Y)^2\right]}}$$

Table 12.6

ID	X score	Y score	XY (cross-product)
1	6,000	26	156,000
2	4,900	22	107,800
3	4,700	21	98,700
4	7,200	28	201,600
5	4,700	20	94,000
6	5,600	28	156,800
7	4,800	29	139,200
8	6,200	32	198,400
9	3,500	30	105,000
10	5,400	36	194,400

The ΣX in the formula is equal to the sum of all of the scores on variable X, which is equal to 53,000. The ΣY signifies the sum of all the Y scores, which is equal to 272. We can now plug these numbers into the formula:

$$r = \frac{10(\sum XY) - (53,000)(272)}{\sqrt{\left[10(\sum X^2) - (53,000)^2\right]\left[10(\sum Y^2) - (272)^2\right]}}$$

The portion of the XY in the formula is called the "cross-product," and to find it, you must multiply each person's X score by their Y score (Table 12.6).

After we have found all these cross-products, we must add them together to get ΣXY:

156,000 + 107,800 + 98,700 + 201,600 + 94,000 + 156,800 + 139,200 + 198,400 +105,000 + 194,400 = 1,451,900

Then we can plug this number into the formula:

$$r = \frac{10(1,451,900) - (53,000)(272)}{\sqrt{\left[10(\sum X^2) - (53,000)^2\right]\left[10(\sum Y^2) - (272)^2\right]}}$$

The next step is to find ΣX^2 and ΣY^2, which are the squared scores for each variable (Table 12.7).

The sum of these columns are $\Sigma X = 290,280,000$ and $\Sigma Y = 7,630$. We can now plug these values into the formula:

$$r = \frac{10(1,451,900) - (53,000)(272)}{\sqrt{\left[10(290,280,000) - (53,000)^2\right]\left[10(7,630) - (272)^2\right]}}$$

Now the formula is ready to be solved:

$$r = \frac{14,519,000 - 14,416,000}{\sqrt{\left[10(290,280,000) - (53,000)^2\right]\left[10(7,630) - (272)^2\right]}}$$

Table 12.7		
ID	Squared *X* score	Squared *Y* score
1	$6,000^2 = 36,000,000$	$26^2 = 676$
2	$4,900^2 = 24,010,000$	$22^2 = 484$
3	$4,700^2 = 22,090,000$	$21^2 = 441$
4	$7,200^2 = 51,840,000$	$28^2 = 784$
5	$4,700^2 = 22,090,000$	$20^2 = 400$
6	$5,600^2 = 31,360,000$	$28^2 = 784$
7	$4,800^2 = 23,040,000$	$29^2 = 841$
8	$6,200^2 = 38,440,000$	$32^2 = 1,024$
9	$3,500^2 = 12,250,000$	$30^2 = 900$
10	$5,400^2 = 29,160,000$	$36^2 = 1,296$

$$r = \frac{14,519,000 - 14,416,000}{\sqrt{\left[10(290,280,000) - (53,000)^2\right]\left[10(7,630) - (272)^2\right]}}$$

$$r = \frac{103,000}{\sqrt{\left[10(290,280,000) - (53,000)^2\right]\left[10(7,630) - (272)^2\right]}}$$

$$r = \frac{103,000}{\sqrt{[10(290,280,000) - 2,809,000,000][10(7,630) - 73,984]}}$$

$$r = \frac{103,000}{\sqrt{(2,902,800,000 - 2,809,000,000)(76,300 - 73,984)}}$$

$$r = \frac{103,000}{\sqrt{(93,800,000)(2,316)}}$$

$$r = \frac{103,000}{\sqrt{217,240,800,000}}$$

$$r = \frac{103,000}{466,090.978}$$

$$r = +.221$$

This example shows that both formulas provide the same answer. Use the formula that you think makes the most sense or is easiest to work with. Some people prefer Formula 12.2 because they can avoid calculating the mean and standard deviation for each variable, a process which may make it easy to make a mistake. On the other hand, if you don't mind calculating descriptive statistics, then Formula 12.1 is probably easiest to work with. My personal preference is to use Formula 12.1 because it appears simpler and I am less likely to confuse the symbols in the equation. Formula 12.1 also has some conceptual advantages, which I describe in Sidebar 12.2.

Interpreting Pearson's *r*

Interpreting Pearson's *r* requires interpreting two aspects of the *r* value: the sign and the number. The sign refers to whether the *r* value is positive or negative. When *r* is positive, that means that the individuals who have high scores on the *X* variable tend to have high scores on the *Y* variable. Also when *r* is positive, individuals who have low scores on the *X* variable tend to have low scores on the *Y* variable. When *r* is positive, we say that there is a **positive correlation** or **direct correlation** between the two variables. Conversely, when *r* is negative, individuals with high scores on *X* tend to have low scores on *Y* (and vice versa: individuals with low scores on *X* tend to have high scores on *Y*). When *r* is negative, we say that there is a **negative correlation** – or **inverse correlation** – between the two variables. Finally, when *r* = 0, there is no relationship between the variables. In this case, scores on the *X* variable do not form a pattern with scores on *Y*. This usually indicates that these variables are unrelated.

The second aspect of Pearson's *r* to interpret is the value of the number. Values that are further from 0 indicate stronger relationships between variables. Mathematically, the limits of Pearson's *r* are –1 and +1. Values close to –1 and +1 indicate strong relationships where the pattern of scores (e.g., high scores on *X* being paired with high scores on *Y*) is consistent. Values close to zero indicate weak relationships. When a correlation is weak, there are often exceptions to the general pattern of how scores on *X* and *Y* are paired together.

Now that we know that interpreting Pearson's *r* requires examining the sign and the number, we can interpret the *r* = +.221 value from the video game data example. Because the correlation is greater than 0 (as indicated by the positive sign), we know that – generally – people with high video game scores have high intelligence test scores. The positive correlation value also means that people with low video game scores tend to have lower intelligence test scores.

However, if you examine Table 12.1, you will see that there are exceptions to this general pattern. This is supported by the value of the correlation coefficient, which is .221. This value is close to 0, which indicates that the pattern between these two variables is relatively inconsistent. For example, Person 9 had the lowest video game score, but had the third highest intelligence test score. Therefore, the +.221 correlation coefficient can be interpreted as a weak positive correlation. Table 12.8 lists examples of Pearson's *r* values in real research, providing some context of this correlation. Most of these examples are from the social sciences, although I have included a few examples from biology and earth science for comparison purposes. The +.221 correlation in the video game example is almost the same as the +0.21 correlation between husbands' and wives' level of neuroticism (i.e., negative personality traits). Both of these are weak positive correlations, but they are not nearly as strong as the relationship between high-school grades and first-year college grades (*r* = +0.36), height and weight in adults (*r* = +0.44), intelligence scores in childhood and in old age (*r* = + 0.63), or the level of religiousness of husbands and wives (*r* = +0.75).

Also, notice that the relationship in the example data between video game scores and intelligence test scores was positive, but there is a negative correlation between ADHD symptoms and creativity (*r* = –0.17), depression and job satisfaction (*r* = –0.43), and a nation's corruption level and the effectiveness of its legislature (*r* = –0.81). Finally, you should notice that the stronger correlations in Table 12.8 are the sort of relationships that you would notice in daily life, such as the correlation between height and weight (*r* = +0.44) or the relationship between closeness to the equator and temperature (*r* = +0.60). However, correlations closer to zero are much subtler and may represent non-existent relationships, such as the correlation between sugar consumption and behavioral changes in children (*r* = +0.01). Another possibility is that correlations close to zero indicate relationships that are only apparent with careful observation and statistical analysis, such as the correlation between ADHD and creativity level (*r* = –0.17).

Table 12.8 Examples of Pearson's r values		
Variables	***r***	**Reference**
A nation's corruption level and the effectiveness of its legislature	−0.81	Klomp & de Haan, 2008
Talking speed and schizophrenia symptom severity (among people with schizophrenia)	−0.61	Alpert, Kotsaftis, & Pouget, 1997
Anxiety and performance on a difficult academic test	−0.45	Sommer & Arendasy, 2014
Depression and job satisfaction	−0.43	Faragher, Cass, & Cooper, 2005
Elevation above sea level and daily temperature (US locations)	−0.34	Meyer et al., 2001
ADHD symptoms and creativity level	−0.17	Paek et al., 2016
Sugar consumption and children's behavior changes	+0.01	Wolraich, Wilson, & White, 1995
Husbands' and wives' level of neuroticism (i.e., negative personality traits)	+0.21	Watson, Klohnen, Casillas, Simms, Haig, & Berry, 2004
High-school grades and first-year college grades (US students)	+0.36	Kobrin, Patterson, Shaw, Mattern, & Barbuti, 2008
Length (i.e., height) at birth and height in adulthood (Sweden)	+0.40	Karlberg & Luo, 2000
Height and weight (US adults)	+0.44	Meyer et al., 2001
Closeness to the equator and average daily temperature (US locations)	+0.60	Meyer et al., 2001
Intelligence at age 11 and intelligence at age 77 (Scotland)	+0.63	Deary, Whalley, Lemmon, Crawford, & Starr, 2000
Extraversion personality scores when measured 1.7 years apart in the same individuals	+0.73	Viswesvaran & Ones, 2000
Husbands' and wives' religiousness	+0.75	Watson et al., 2004
Weight in kilograms and weight in pounds	+1.00	–

Check Yourself!

- What is the purpose of a correlation?

- What does the sign of a correlation indicate?

- How do you determine the strength of a correlation?

- What are the highest and lowest possible values for Pearson's *r*?

Sidebar 12.2 Correlation is a standardized measure

When calculating Pearson's r, I prefer Formula 12.1 to Formula 12.2 because the former shows that the correlation coefficient is a standardized measure of the relationship between variables. When I say "standardized," I mean that Pearson's r is expressed in terms of z-scores. You may remember that the formula for z-scores is:

$$z_i = \frac{x_i - \overline{X}}{s_x} \qquad \text{(Formula 5.7)}$$

The first step in calculating a z-score is to find the deviation score by subtracting the mean from the raw score $(x_i - \overline{X})$, and the second step is to divide by the standard deviation. Both of these steps are embedded in Formula 12.1:

$$r = \frac{\frac{\sum (x_i - \overline{X})(y_i - \overline{Y})}{n - 1}}{s_x \cdot s_y} \qquad \text{(Formula 12.1)}$$

The first step in calculating a correlation coefficient is to calculate the deviation score for both variables: $(x_i - \overline{X})$ and $(y_i - \overline{Y})$. The final step in Formula 12.1 is to divide by the two standard deviations $(s_x \cdot s_y)$. Thus, by calculating a Pearson's r value, we are automatically converting all of the data into z-scores. This is what makes Pearson's r a standardized statistic.

Knowing that Pearson's r converts data to z-scores makes it possible to conceptualize another interpretation of correlations. We can imagine Pearson's r as being the expected number of standard deviations on the Y variable between the scores of two individuals who were 1 SD apart on the X variable. For example, in the video game data, because $r = +.221$, we would expect that two people who had a 1 SD difference in their video game scores will have – on average – a 0.221 SD difference in their intelligence test scores.

Similarly, we can see that in Table 12.8 the correlation between depression and job satisfaction is $r = -0.43$. This would indicate that two people who are 1 SD apart in their level of depression would be expected to be 0.43 SD apart in their level of job satisfaction. However, in this example the negative correlation indicates that the person with the higher level of depression would have the lower level of job satisfaction. The reverse would also be true: the person with the lower level of depression should have the higher level of job satisfaction.

Although standardizing variables makes a correlation easier to interpret, sometimes it is beneficial to keep the variables unstandardized. This is done by calculating the **covariance**, abbreviated $cov(x,y)$, which follows the same steps as Formula 12.1, with the exception of the final step of dividing by $s_x \cdot s_y$, as seen below:

$$r = \frac{\frac{\sum (x_i - \overline{X})(y_i - \overline{Y})}{n - 1}}{s_x \cdot s_y} = \frac{cov(x, y)}{s_x \cdot s_y}$$

Just like a correlation, the covariance is a measure of the relationship between two variables, but – unlike the correlation – it has not been standardized by converting all scores into z-scores. Therefore, covariance values can usually not be compared to one another.

Visualizing Correlations

If you prefer diagrams and visual aids as you learn, you may wish to use a scatterplot to create a visual model of your correlational data. We first learned about scatterplots in Chapter 3. In that chapter we saw that each sample member in a dataset is represented in a scatterplot with a dot which is placed at the coordinates that correspond to the person's X score and Y score. A scatterplot for the video game data is shown below in Figure 12.1. We can see, for example, that the person with the lowest video game score (3,500) had an intelligence test score of 30. That person's data are represented by the left-most dot, which is at coordinates (3,500, 30). The other individuals' dots are plotted in the same way.

The appearance of a scatterplot will vary in accordance with the sign and value of the correlation coefficient. First, the value of the correlation indicates how tightly packed the dots in the

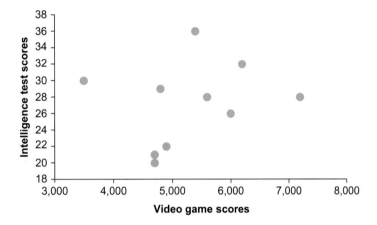

Figure 12.1 Scatterplot for the chapter example data. The horizontal axis represents the *X* variable, which is video game scores. The vertical axis represents the *Y* variable, which is intelligence test scores. Each dot in the scatterplot is an individual in the dataset. See Chapter 3 for a description of how scatterplots are created.

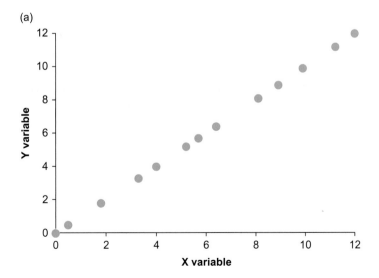

Figure 12.2a A scatterplot where r = +1.00.

(b)

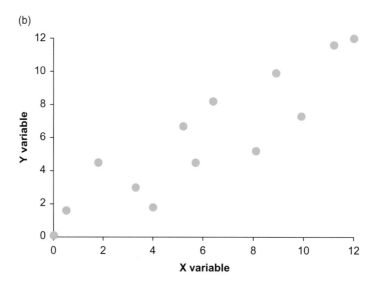

Figure 12.2b A scatterplot where *r* = +0.90.

(c)

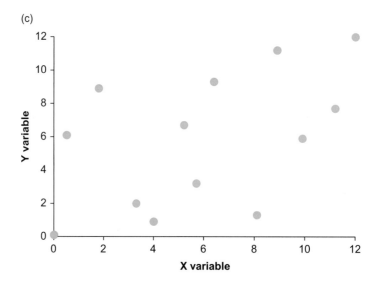

Figure 12.2c A scatterplot where *r* = +0.50.

scatterplot are around a straight line. Figures 12.2a–12.2d show scatterplots for datasets with correlations of decreasing strength from *r* = +1.00 to *r* = 0.00. When the correlation is +1.00, all the data points in the scatterplot are arranged in a perfectly straight line. As the correlation weakens, the dots spread out more and more from a straight line. When the correlation is zero, the dots in a scatterplot are distributed more-or-less randomly throughout the scatterplot. You can see this pattern in Figures 12.2a–12.2d; as the correlation goes down, the dots are less tightly packed around a straight line.

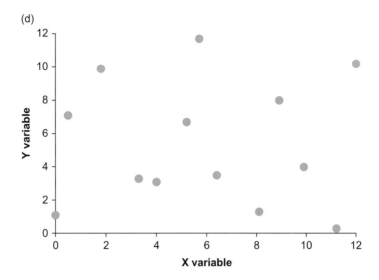

Figure 12.2d A scatterplot where $r = +0.00$.

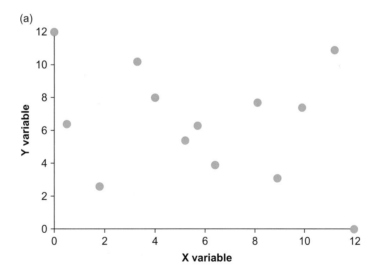

Figure 12.3a A scatterplot where $r = -0.30$.

The sign of the correlation coefficient also has an impact on the appearance of the scatterplot. This can be seen by comparing Figures 12.2a–12.2c to Figures 12.3a–12.3d. In the first series of scatterplots, the dots generally fall into the bottom-left and the top-right quadrants of the scatterplot. This is because all of these scatterplots are visual models for positive correlations. This makes sense if you remember that individuals with low scores on the X variable tend to have low scores on the Y variable, meaning that the dots representing these people's data will be in the bottom-left quadrant of the scatterplot. If r is positive, people with high scores on the X variable generally have high scores on the Y variable. These sample members' dots will generally be in the top-right quadrant of the scatterplot.

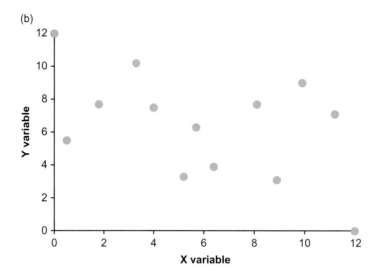

Figure 12.3b A scatterplot where $r = -0.50$.

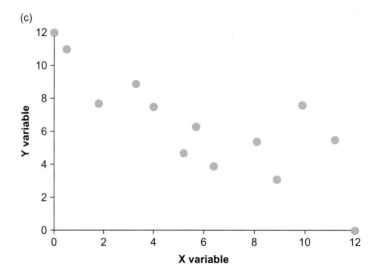

Figure 12.3c A scatterplot where $r = -0.80$.

On the other hand, if r is negative, as in Figures 12.3a–12.3d, the dots will generally be in the top-left and bottom-right quadrants. Again, this is logical, because in a negative correlation people with a high score on the X variable will have low scores on the Y variable, making their dots appear in the bottom-right quadrant. Likewise, in negative correlations, people with low scores on the X variable will have high scores on the Y variable. This results in dots that appear in the top-left quadrant.

In sum, there are two ways that the correlation coefficient can influence the appearance of the scatterplot. The first is in the sign correlation coefficient. Positive Pearson's r values produce a pattern of dots covering the lower-left to the upper-right portions of the scatterplot. Negative

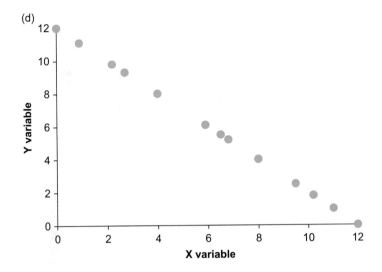

Figure 12.3d A scatterplot where *r* = −1.00.

correlation coefficients result in a visual model where the dots are in the upper-left and lower-right portions of the scatterplot. The second way that the correlation coefficient influences the scatterplot is that the strength of the correlation (i.e., the numerical value of Pearson's *r*) influences how spread apart the dots are. Weaker correlations with values closer to zero result in scatterplots with very widely spaced dots. Stronger correlation values (with values closer to +1 or −1) produce scatterplots that have dots tightly spaced together.

Check Yourself!

- When building a scatterplot, how do you determine where to place the dot that represents a person's *X* and *Y* scores?

- What is the difference between the appearance of scatterplots that represent positive and negative correlations?

- Some scatterplots have widely spaced dots, and others have more closely spaced dots. What does this indicate about their correlation coefficients?

Pearson's *r* in the Null Hypothesis Testing Context

The Pearson's *r* statistic is excellent at providing a measure of the strength of the relationship between two variables. Often this is useful information in its own right, and testing a null hypothesis may not be relevant to a scientist's research question, as in situations when a researcher is interested in the strength of a relationship, not a yes/no question of whether a relationship exists (e.g., Strenze,

2007; Warne, 2016). However, it is useful to understand how the correlation fits into the general linear model (GLM) and how to test a null hypothesis with Pearson's *r*. This section of the chapter explains how to conduct a null hypothesis statistical significance test (NHST) with Pearson's *r*. Because all null hypothesis tests are members of the GLM, the process follows the same eight steps that we have encountered in every NHST:

1. Form groups in the data.
2. Define the null hypothesis (H_0). The null hypothesis is always that there is no difference between groups or that there is no relationship between independent and dependent variables.
3. Set alpha (α). The default alpha = .05.
4. Choose a one-tailed or a two-tailed test. This determines the alternative hypothesis (H_1).
5. Find the *critical* value, which is used to define the rejection region.
6. Calculate the *observed* value.
7. Compare the observed value and the critical value. If the observed value is more extreme than the critical value, the null hypothesis should be rejected. Otherwise, it should be retained.
8. Calculate an *effect size*.

Form Groups in the Data. In prior chapters, we formed groups with our data, either by defining the groups as the sample and the population (for the *z*-test and the one-sample *t*-test) or by using the categories of the nominal independent variable to define the groups (for the paired-samples *t*-test, unpaired-samples *t*-test, and ANOVA). However, with Pearson's *r*, interval- or ratio-level data do not form separate groups because the data are continuous. Rather, instead of two or three discrete groups of data, we can consider the independent variable as having a continuum of categories, from low to high. In this view, the number for the independent variable quantifies how much the individual belongs to one extreme or the other.

Figure 12.4 shows how this idea works with the video game data from the beginning of the chapter. Under the horizontal axis, I added a label showing that the video game scores can arrange

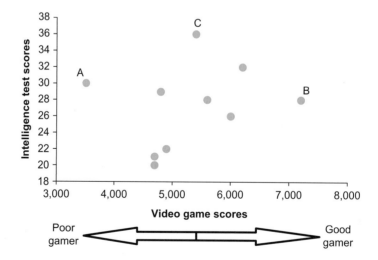

Figure 12.4 Example video game data. Interval- and ratio-level data do not form discrete categories. But you can think of the horizontal axis as representing a continuum of categories which each person in the dataset belongs to in varying degrees. Here, Person A mostly belongs to the "poor gamer" category, while Person B belongs mostly to the "good gamer" category. Person C belongs about equally to both. This is how groups are formed in an NHST performed with Pearson's *r*.

people in categories ranging from "poor gamer" to "good gamer." In the scatterplot, Person A belongs almost entirely to the "poor gamer category," while Person B belongs almost entirely to the "good gamer category." Person C belongs partially to both categories. This way of collecting and understanding data allows for much more nuance than separating the individuals into two separate categories, because people can be ranked and we can quantify the degree to which they belong to each extreme group.

Define the Null Hypothesis. When we test the statistical significance of a correlation coefficient, the null hypothesis is that there is no relationship between the X and Y variables. As we saw earlier in this chapter, when there is no relationships between variables, $r = 0$. Therefore, the null hypothesis for Pearson's r is:

$$H_0 : r = 0 \qquad \text{(Formula 12.3)}$$

Formula 12.3 is always the null hypothesis when performing a statistical significance test of a correlation coefficient.

Set Alpha. The third step of any NHST is to set the alpha level. Like previous null hypothesis tests, the default alpha for testing a correlation coefficient is .05. There are often reasons to increase or decrease the alpha value, and these are largely the same reasons as we have seen in previous chapters (e.g., large sample size). See Sidebar 11.1 for details.

Choose a One-Tailed or a Two-Tailed Test. After setting the alpha value, the fourth step is to choose a one- or a two-tailed test. In choosing the type of test to perform, it is important to consider the sampling distribution of Pearson's r. When the population correlation (abbreviated by the Greek letter *rho*, which is symbolized as ρ) is equal to zero, the sampling distribution of sample correlation coefficients is normal and centered on ρ = 0.

Given this normal sampling distribution for the null hypothesis of Pearson's r, it is possible to perform a one- or a two-tailed test for Pearson's r. A one-tailed test is appropriate when there is prior research or theory that would lead you to believe that a correlation should be positive or negative. On the other hand, when there is no prior research or theory about whether a correlation would be positive or negative, a two-tailed test is appropriate. There are two possible null hypotheses for a one-tailed test:

$$H_0 : r > 0 \qquad \text{(Formula 12.4)}$$
$$H_0 : r < 0 \qquad \text{(Formula 12.5)}$$

For a two-tailed test, there is only one possible alternative hypothesis:

$$H_0 : r \neq 0 \qquad \text{(Formula 12.6)}$$

In the example of the video game data, my students were aware of prior research that showed that there are positive correlations between intelligence scores and some video game scores (Ángeles Quiroga et al., 2015; Foroughi et al., 2016). Therefore, it seems rational to expect that the correlation between these two variables in my students' data would be positive. In this situation a one-tailed test is appropriate with an alternative hypothesis of H_0: $r > 0$.

Find the Critical Value. After we decide whether to conduct a one- or a two-tailed test, the fifth step in performing the NHST of a correlation coefficient is to find the critical value. Like the prior NHSTs (except the z-test), it is necessary to calculate the degrees of freedom. The formula for this is:

$$\text{df} = n - 2 \qquad \text{(Formula 12.7)}$$

In Formula 12.7, n is the number of sample members. In the video game example, $n = 10$, meaning that there are 8 degrees of freedom.

After calculating the degrees of freedom, the critical value, abbreviated r_{crit}, is found by looking it up in Appendix A5. The table provides critical values in the sampling distribution for one- and two-tailed tests for up to 1,000 degrees of freedom. This sampling distribution is made up of sample correlation values and is normally distributed when the population correlation between the two variables is $\rho = 0$ (i.e., when the null hypothesis is perfectly true).[9] Finding the critical value is the exact same procedure as finding the critical value in the t-table (i.e., Appendix A2). The left columns are for one-tailed tests and the right columns are for two-tailed tests. In the appropriate set of columns, you should find the row that corresponds to the number of degrees of freedom in the data and the column that corresponds to the alpha level of the null hypothesis test. The cell where that row and column meet contains the critical value for the NHST. In the video game data example, there were 8 degrees of freedom for a one-tailed test and $\alpha = .05$. Appendix A5 shows that the critical value under these conditions is either +0.550 or –0.550. Because the alternative hypothesis is that H_0: $r > 0$, the positive critical value (i.e., +0.550) is the correct option for this example.

Find the Observed Value. This is step 6. When we test the null hypothesis of Pearson's correlation, the observed value is equal to the actual Pearson's r value. The equation for this statistic is shown in Formulas 12.1 and 12.2. There is no additional critical value to calculate. In the video game example, the correlation was $r = +.221$.

Compare the Observed Value and the Critical Value. Step 7 in conducting the NHST of a correlation coefficient is to compare the observed and critical values on the sampling distribution. Just as with all prior NHSTs, we should reject the null hypothesis if the observed value falls within the rejection region. This occurs when the observed value is more extreme than the critical value. On the other hand, when the observed value is closer to the center of the distribution (i.e., zero) than the critical value, you should retain the null hypothesis.

The video game example data have an r_{crit} value of +0.550 and an r_{obs} value of +0.221. Figure 12.5 shows the sampling distribution for the NHST and where these two values are in relationship to the rejection region and the center of the distribution. In the figure it is clear that the rejection region starts at +0.550 and goes to the end of the distribution (i.e., $r = +1.000$). That means that our observed value of +0.221 is outside the rejection region. Therefore, it is appropriate to retain the null hypothesis in this example.

Calculate an Effect Size. The eighth and final stage of this NHST is to calculate an effect size. For Pearson's r, the effect size is called r-squared (r^2), and it is calculated as:

$$r^2 = r \cdot r \qquad \text{(Formula 12.8)}$$

where r is the Pearson's r value for the sample data. In the video game example data, the Pearson's r is +0.221. Therefore, r^2 is:

$$r^2 = (0.221)(0.221) = 0.049$$

---

[9] The sampling distribution for the null hypothesis is normally distributed, as is the sampling distribution of correlation coefficients when the population correlation is $\rho = 0$. When the population coefficient is not zero, the sampling distribution becomes skewed, with the longer tail pointing towards zero. This skewness increases as the population correlation coefficient gets stronger. When $\rho > 0$, the distribution of sample correlation coefficients is negatively skewed. When $\rho < 0$, the distribution of sample correlation coefficients is positively skewed.

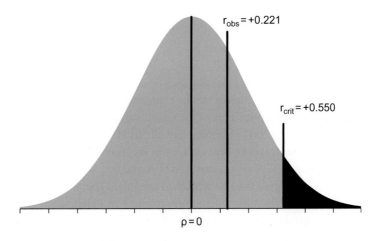

Figure 12.5 A sampling distribution of correlation coefficients in a population where the correlation between two variables is ρ = 0. The rejection region (shaded in black) is on the right side of the sampling distribution and begins at *r* = +0.550. The observed sample correlation is *r* = +0.221, which is outside the rejection region. Therefore, it is best to retain the null hypothesis in this example.

There are two possible interpretations of r^2. The first is that r^2 is the proportion of dependent variable variance (i.e., Y variable variance) that is shared or associated with the independent variable (i.e., the X variable). In other words, some of the variance of the dependent variable (i.e., the IQ test scores) is related to the individuals' independent variable scores (i.e., video game scores). The effect size r^2 tells us how strongly related these variables are. In this interpretation, because r^2 is equal to 0.049 we can understand that 4.9% of IQ test score variance is related to video game score variance.

The second interpretation of r^2 is in terms of prediction. As we learned in the last chapter, we can measure how accurate our model's predictions are by calculating a residual for each person. For ANOVA, the residual was

$$e_i = Y_i - \hat{Y}_i \qquad \text{(Formula 11.10)}$$

This formula is the same for all members of the GLM – including the correlation coefficient. The effect size r^2 tells us how much the squared residuals decrease when we make predictions based on the statistical model compared to the **baseline model**, which is the worst model that would still fit the data. This baseline model is the model that we would use to make predictions if we did not know anything about our sample members. For both ANOVA and Pearson's *r*, the baseline model is that every sample member will achieve a score equal to the grand mean (i.e., the mean of all the dependent variable scores in the data). Therefore, r^2 is also a measure of average prediction improvement compared to the baseline model. Chapter 13 discusses how to make predictions on the basis of Pearson's *r*.

General Linear Moment 12.1

Discussing the interpretation of r^2 gives me *déjà vu* because we have encountered these two interpretations of an effect size before. If you look back at Chapter 11, you will see that the two interpretations of r^2 are the exact same as the two interpretations of η^2, which is the effect size for ANOVA. These two effect sizes have the same interpretations because of the following formula:

$$r^2 = \eta^2 \qquad\qquad\qquad \text{(Formula 12.9)}$$

In light of Formula 12.9, it should be clear why the interpretations of r^2 and η^2 are the same: the two statistics are equal.

But why would the two statistics be equal? The method of calculating r^2 and the method of calculating η^2 are very different, so the connection between them is not obvious. The answer lies in the GLM. One of the principles of the GLM is that all analyses are correlational in nature (Vacha-Haase & Thompson, 2004), meaning that all NHSTs examine whether there is a correlation between two variables. In calculating Pearson's r, this fact is obvious, but it is not so clear with other NHSTs. However, Formula 12.9 shows that ANOVA and Pearson's r are designed to detect the degree of association (i.e., correlation) between two variables. The only difference is the level of data for the two procedures. Performing an ANOVA requires an independent variable with nominal-level data; Pearson's r requires interval- or ratio-level data for the independent variable. Therefore, both *ANOVA and Pearson's* r *are the same procedure adapted to different levels of data in the independent variable*. Because the other NHSTs discussed so far in this book are all special cases of ANOVA, it is logically true that the z-test, one-sample t-test, unpaired-samples t-test, and paired-samples t-test are also correlations that have been adapted to different forms of data.

This principle applies to all members of the GLM – even those far beyond the scope of this textbook. Indeed, this is the power of the GLM. If you remember that everything is a correlation of some sort, you will be able to learn new NHSTs very quickly. It will also be easier to comprehend the usage of many statistical procedures when you come across them in research articles, even if you have not learned all the nuances of a statistical procedure.

Check Yourself!

- What is the null hypothesis when conducting an NHST on a Pearson's r value?

- When comparing a Pearson's r value to the r_{crit} value, how do you know whether to reject or retain the null hypothesis?

- What is a residual?

Sidebar 12.3 **Obtaining stable correlations**

The example video game data in this chapter contain only the first 10 individuals in the dataset. (I did this to make the calculations in this chapter manageable.) The Pearson's r value calculated from the entire sample of 61 people is $r = +0.523$, which is strong enough to reject the null hypothesis ($p < .01$). This is probably surprising because the correlation with just 10 individuals was much smaller: $+0.221$. This discrepancy occurred because Pearson's r values are unstable when sample sizes are small – a characteristic that r shares with every other sample statistic.

Therefore, to obtain stable correlations you must have a large sample size. Stronger correlations stabilize with smaller samples than do weaker correlations. Larger sample sizes are also required for researchers who have less tolerance of sampling error (and therefore require more stability in their correlation coefficients). With these reservations in mind, Schönbrodt and Peruigini (2013) recommend that "the sample size should approach 250 for stable estimates" (p. 609). Although this guideline is not appropriate in all situations, it is a nice starting point for estimating the necessary sample size to conduct a study.

Warning: Correlation Is Not Causation

A correlation quantifies the strength of a relationship between an independent and a dependent variable. It is because of this function of a correlation that we can interpret the Pearson's r values in Table 12.8 and understand the strength and direction of a correlation between two variables.

There is a temptation, though, to interpret a relationship between two variables as an indication that changes in the independent variable *cause* changes in the dependent variable. For example, Table 12.8 indicates that the correlation between depression and job satisfaction is $r = -0.43$ (Faragher et al., 2005), meaning that people with higher levels of depression tend to be less satisfied with their jobs. Some readers may believe that this correlation indicates that higher levels of depression cause individuals to be less satisfied with their jobs.

Although this interpretation is seductive, it is not the only possible interpretation of a correlation. There are three different interpretations (i.e., models) that a correlation can support. These possible interpretations are shown in Figure 12.6. The first possibility is that the changes in the independent variable (X) cause changes in the dependent variable (Y). The second possibility is that changes in the dependent variable (Y) cause changes in the independent variable (X). The final possibility is that a third, unknown variable (Z) can cause changes in X and Y. This latter possibility is called the **third variable problem**. If all we know is the correlation between two variables, it is not possible to conclude which interpretation in Figure 12.6 is correct. This leads to the widespread use of a phrase that has almost become a cliché in the social sciences: *correlation is not causation*. In other words, you cannot draw conclusions about the cause of a relationship solely from the existence of a correlation.

Although the warning against interpreting correlations in terms of cause is widespread, it is not unusual to see interpretations of correlational data that imply that one variable causes another. One example is a famous study by Hart and Risley (2003) in which the authors wanted to learn why pre-schoolers from high-income families had larger vocabularies than pre-schoolers from medium- or low-income families. They observed families' interactions with their children from when the children were 8–36 months old. Hart and Risley found that in families in higher income groups the parents spoke more to their children. Therefore, Hart and Risley observed a correlation between the number of words that parents spoke (the independent variable) and the size of their children's vocabulary (the dependent variable). The researchers then suggested that gap in vocabulary sizes could be reduced or closed by exposing low-income children to more verbal communication. The problem with this suggestion is that it is reliant on a cause-and-effect relationship between the independent and dependent variables – that increasing the number of words that parents speak will cause an increase in their children's vocabulary size.

But Hart and Risley (2003) did not consider the other two possibilities in Figure 12.6. For example, it is possible that children with larger vocabularies talk more to their parents, who respond

Possibility 1:

Possibility 2:

Possibility 3:

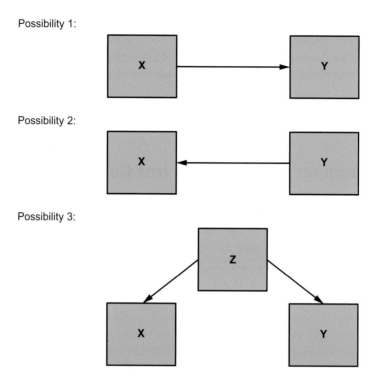

Figure 12.6 Three possible interpretations of a correlation coefficient. In this diagram *X* signifies an independent variable, *Y* signifies a dependent variable, and *Z* refers to a third variable. The first possibility is that a correlation between two variables could be the result of changes in *X* causing changes in *Y*. The second possibility is that changes in *Y* cause changes in *X*. The third possibility is that changes in a third, unknown variable *Z* cause changes in both *X* and *Y*.

by speaking more words than they would to a child with a smaller vocabulary. (This would be possibility 2 in Figure 12.6.) Another interpretive model for their data is that some unknown third variable – such as the family's income level, or genetic factors – causes the correlation between *X* and *Y*. (This would be possibility 3 in Figure 12.6.)

To be fair, Hart and Risley's suggestion of how to close the vocabulary gap is not unreasonable. The problem is that its success is dependent on a causal relationship between the number of words the parents speak and the children's vocabulary size. But the researchers have no way of knowing whether that causal relationship is the reason their independent and dependent variables are correlated. Always be careful not to infer a cause-and-effect relationship between two correlated variables.

Sidebar 12.4 **Establishing cause-and-effect relationships**

The Hart and Risley (2003) example may be dismaying to some readers. It seems intuitive that some children in the study have larger vocabularies because their parents speak to them more. Yet, because a correlation does not imply causation, we cannot draw this conclusion from the correlational data. So, how do scientists determine whether changes in one variable cause changes in another?

The answer is that they conduct an **experiment**. An experiment requires the experimenter to randomly assign sample members to two groups. Usually a group called the **control group** receives no treatment, while the other group, called the **experimental group**, receives the treatment. (Sometimes there are multiple treatment groups; they may receive different treatments, or different levels of the strength of the intervention.) **Random assignment** of individuals to groups balances the two groups so that any differences at the end of the study are the result of the treatment.

An experiment with random assignment and a control group is the only way to establish a causal relationship between two variables where changes in the independent variable cause changes in the dependent variable. Without all these components, it is impossible to talk about cause-and-effect relationships between variables. This is why Hart and Risley (2003) were incorrect in stating that an intervention in which parents talk more to their children would cause increases in their children's vocabulary. Because the researchers did not randomly assign parents and their children to an experimental group, they could not determine which of the possible interpretations in Figure 12.6 was the proper explanation for their data.

Check Yourself!

- Why does a correlation between two variables not imply that the independent variable causes the dependent variable?

- Explain what the third variable problem is.

Summary

Pearson's correlation is a statistic that quantifies the relationship between two interval- or ratio-level variables. It is calculated with Formula 12.1: $r = \dfrac{\frac{\sum (x_i-\bar{X})(y_i-\bar{Y})}{n-1}}{s_x \cdot s_y}$. There are two components of the Pearson's r value to interpret. The first is the sign of the correlation coefficient. Positive values indicate that individuals who have high X scores tend to have high Y scores (and that individuals with low X scores tend to have low Y scores). A negative correlation indicates that individuals with high X scores tend to have low Y scores (and that individuals with low X scores tend to have high Y scores). The second component of a correlation coefficient that is interpreted is the number, which indicates the strength of the relationship and the consistency with which the relationship is observed. The closer an r value is to +1 or −1, the stronger the relationship between the variables. The closer the number is to zero, the weaker the relationship.

For many purposes, calculating the r value is enough to answer the research questions in a study. But it is also possible to test a correlation coefficient for statistical significance, where the null hypothesis is $r = 0$. Such a null hypothesis statistical significance test (NHST) follows the same steps of all NHSTs. The effect size for Pearson's r is calculated by squaring the r value (r^2).

The data used to calculate Pearson's r can be visualized with a scatterplot, which was introduced in Chapter 3. In a scatterplot each sample member is represented as a dot plotted in a position corresponding to the individual's X and Y scores. Scatterplots for strong correlations tend to have a group of dots that are closely grouped together. Weak correlations are represented in scatterplots by a cloud of dots that are widely spaced apart. Positive correlations tend to have dots that cluster in the lower-left and upper-right quadrants of a scatterplot. Conversely, negative correlations are represented in scatterplots that tend to have dots concentrated in the upper-left and lower-right quadrants of a scatterplot.

You should remember that a correlation between two variables does not imply a causal relationship between the two. There are three reasons that a correlation could occur: (1) changes in the independent variable could cause changes in the dependent variable, (2) changes in the dependent variable could cause changes in the independent variable, and (3) changes in a third variable could cause changes in both the independent and dependent variables. If only the correlation is known, it is not possible to ascertain which of these three explanations is correct.

Reflection Questions: Comprehension

1. Which correlation value is the strongest and which is the weakest: (a) +0.42, (b) –0.87, (c) +0.59, (d) –0.34.
2. Which correlation coefficient is the strongest? (a) –0.21, (b) –0.62, (c) +0.04, (d) +0.33, (e) +0.49.
3. What are the two interpretations of r^2?
4. Explain the relationship between Pearson's r and the unpaired-samples t-test in terms of the GLM.
5. Samantha found that the correlation between income and self-reported happiness is $r = +0.39$. She concludes that if more people were wealthy they would be happier. What is the problem with her logic?
6. Explain the third variable problem.

Reflection Questions: Application

7. Explain whether the following relationships are positive correlations or negative correlations.
   a. People with larger families tend to have better support systems in a crisis.
   b. Individuals who brush their teeth more usually have fewer cavities.
   c. Factory workers who spend more time doing a job usually make fewer errors.
   d. People with higher salaries usually take more expensive vacations.
   e. Children who watch TV more tend to have lower grades in school.
   f. Societies where women have more human rights tend to have lower birthrates.
   g. Children who receive more vaccinations have fewer serious illnesses.
   h. Romantic couples who spend more time together say that their relationship is stronger.
   i. People who consume more calories tend to have greater body weights.
   j. Musicians who practice their instrument are usually better performers.
8. Draw a scatterplot for the following correlations:
   a. $r = -0.82$
   b. $r = -0.61$
   c. $r = -0.22$

d. $r = 0.00$
e. $r = +0.45$
f. $r = +0.66$
g. $r = +0.79$
h. $r = +1.00$

9.   Find the correlation value between the two variables below.

ID	X	Y
1	6	5
2	4	5
3	1	7
4	2	4
5	5	4
6	9	2

10. Tomás is a sociology student who collected data on two variables: perceived level of racism in society (x) and willingness to sign a political petition (y). Below are the scores from the first 8 people in his sample:

ID	x	y
1	4	9
2	2	4
3	8	5
4	7	4
5	5	6
6	1	1
7	2	1
8	5	6

Note. Higher numbers on both variables indicate higher levels on each variable.

a.   Calculate the correlation for Tomás's data.
b.   What is the null hypothesis for these data?
c.   What is the degrees of freedom value for these data?
d.   If Tomás conducts a two-tailed test and $\alpha = .05$, what should the critical values for an NHST be?
e.   Should Tomás reject or retain the null hypothesis?
f.   Is the *p*-value (a) greater than .05, (b) between .01 and .05, or (c) less than .01?
g.   What is the r^2 value?
h.   Draw the scatterplot for Tomás's data.
i.   Can Tomás correctly state that perceiving racism in society causes people to be more willing to participate in political change? Why or why not?

11. Leigh is an anthropology student who has measured the diameter of clay pots found at an archeological site (x) and the volume of those pots (y). Below are the scores for both variables for the 12 pots found at the site:

ID	x	y
1	12.8	342.1
2	10.6	244.9
3	7.8	199.1
4	15.2	252.0
5	12.2	190.6
6	9.9	120.1
7	14.4	218.9
8	10.9	111.6
9	12.8	212.5
10	14.0	308.9
11	15.0	355.0
12	16.2	391.2

Note. X scores measured in cm. Y scores measured in cc.

    a.   Calculate the correlation for Leigh's data.
    b.   What is the null hypothesis for these data?
    c.   What is the degrees of freedom value for these data?
    d.   Because both variables are part of a pot's physical measurements, it is reasonable to expect them to be positively correlated. If Leigh conducts a one-tailed test, what should the critical values for an NHST be?
    e.   Should Leigh reject or retain the null hypothesis?
    f.   Is the *p*-value (a) greater than .05, (b) between .01 and .05, or (c) less than .01?
    g.   What is the r^2 value?
    h.   Draw a scatterplot that represents these data.

12. Angelica collected data on people's anxiety levels (*x*) and life satisfaction (*y*). The scores are below:

ID	x	y
1	4	5
2	6	2
3	7	3
4	10	9
5	1	6
6	2	8
7	5	1
8	4	2
9	9	9
10	8	6
11	7	5
12	1	9

a. Calculate the correlation for Angelica's data.
b. What is the null hypothesis for these data?
c. What is the degrees of freedom value for these data?
d. If Angelica conducts a two-tailed test, what should the critical values for an NHST be?
e. Should she reject or retain the null hypothesis?
f. Is the p-value (a) greater than .05, (b) between .01 and .05, or (c) less than .01?
g. What is the r^2 value?
h. Draw a scatterplot that represents these data.

13. Eliza, a family science student, asks married couples to count the number of arguments they have in a month (x) and rate their children's happiness on a scale from 1 to 7 (y), higher numbers indicating greater unhappiness. The data are below:

ID	x	y
1	1	3
2	3	3
3	2	5
4	8	7
5	7	6
6	11	3
7	2	2
8	4	4
9	1	7
10	14	2
11	6	5
12	2	7

a. Calculate the correlation for Eliza's data.
b. What is the null hypothesis for these data?
c. What is the degrees of freedom value for these data?
d. If Eliza conducts a two-tailed test, what should the critical values for an NHST be?
e. Should she reject or retain the null hypothesis?
f. Is the p-value (a) greater than .05, (b) between .01 and .05, or (c) less than .01?
g. What is the r^2 value?
h. Draw a scatterplot that represents these data.

14. Peggy collects data for the restaurant where she works. In a sample of regular customers, she collected data on the number of restaurant visits per week (x) and customer satisfaction (y). Both variables are on a 0–7 scale, with higher numbers indicating more frequent visits to the restaurant and greater levels of satisfaction. Her data were:

ID	x	y
1	1	6
2	7	7
3	2	6

ID	x	y
(cont.)		
4	3	7
5	5	6
6	5	5
7	3	6
8	4	6
9	1	7
10	4	5
11	6	5
12	2	7
13	1	6
14	1	4
15	2	5

a. Calculate the correlation for Peggy's data.
b. What is the null hypothesis for these data?
c. What is the degrees of freedom value for these data?
d. If Peggy conducts a two-tailed test, what should the critical values for an NHST be?
e. Should she reject or retain the null hypothesis?
f. Is the p-value (a) greater than .05, (b) between .01 and .05, or (c) less than .01?
g. What is the r^2 value?
h. Draw a scatterplot that represents these data.

Software Guide

As Pearson's r is one of the most common statistical analysis procedures in the social sciences, it should be no surprise that both SPSS and Excel can calculate a correlation. This process is relatively simple in both programs.

Excel

Calculating r and r^2. The Excel function for a correlation is CORREL. To use it, you should type "=CORREL(XX:XX,YY:YY)" where XX:XX is the range of cells for the independent variable and YY:YY is the range of cells for the dependent variable. Figure 12.7a shows how this appears in Excel, using the example video game data.

Excel does not automatically calculate the effect size (r^2) for a correlation. However, this is an easy calculation to perform, using the function "=XX^2" where XX is the cell containing the correlation value. This is shown in Figure 12.7b.

Creating a Scatterplot. Excel has a built-in capability of creating scatterplots. The first step is to highlight the scores that contain the scores for the X and Y variables. After the scores are

(a)

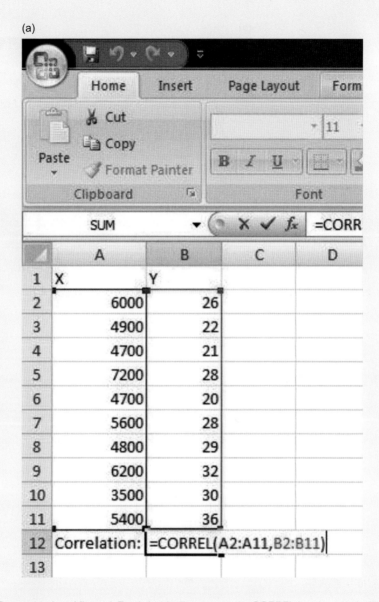

Figure 12.7a Screenshot from Microsoft Excel showing how to use the CORREL function to calculate a correlation. The correlation value is $r = +0.221$.

selected, click the "Insert" ribbon at the top of the screen and then the icon labeled "Scatter." This is shown in Figure 12.7c. After you click the "Scatter" icon, a small group of new icons appears (not shown in a screenshot). Selecting the first one makes the scatterplot in Figure 12.7d appear.

You can alter the appearance of the scatterplot in several ways. I like to use the "Chart Tools" ribbon, which appears after the user clicks on the scatterplot. This ribbon is shown at the top of Figure 12.7e. Clicking some of these options will change the cosmetic features of the scatterplot. The icons on the right will change the color of the dots in the scatterplot. To the left of those options is a series of defaults that will add or change axis lines, charts, axis labels, etc. I recommend

(b)

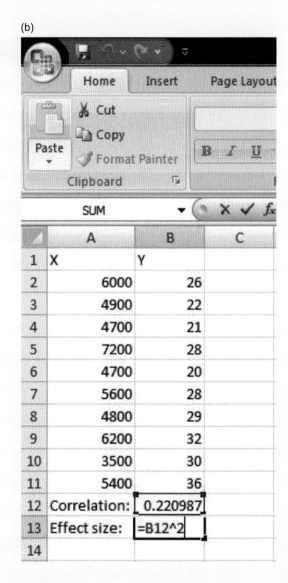

Figure 12.7b Screenshot from Microsoft Excel showing how to calculate the effect size r^2. The effect size value is $r^2 = 0.0488$.

exploring some of these options so you can find a scatterplot that strikes the right balance between providing sufficient information and not overwhelming the viewer with detail.

Another way to change the appearance of a scatterplot is to right-click each element of the scatterplot and to change its appearance manually with the "Format" option in the menu that appears. For example, changing the shape of the dots in the scatterplot is done by right-clicking the dots and then selecting "Format Data Series" from the menu that appears. Right-clicking an axis will allow the user to set a range of values for the horizontal or vertical axes. Again, I recommend that readers experiment with the options in order to create an aesthetically pleasing and informative scatterplot.

(c)

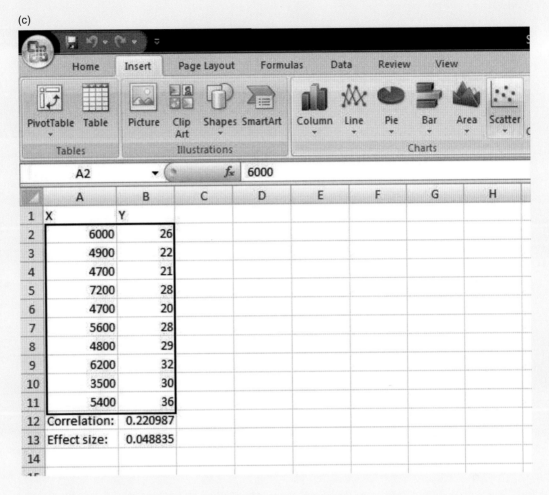

Figure 12.7c A screenshot from Microsoft Excel, which shows the scores for both variables selected. The "Insert" ribbon has also been selected, and the appropriate icon (labeled "Scatter") is highlighted on the far right of the screenshot.

SPSS

Calculating r and r^2. Like all other statistical features in SPSS, calculating a Pearson's r correlation coefficient requires the user to enter the data into the SPSS data file. For the sake of simplicity, the screenshots in this Software Guide will only show how to calculate a single correlation coefficient when there are only two variables in a dataset. However, the figure captions will explain how to calculate multiple correlations at once from larger datasets. Figure 12.8a shows a screenshot of what the data looks like in the SPSS data window.

To calculate a correlation, click "Analyze" → "Correlate" → "Bivariate" from the menus at the top of the screen. This causes a new window called the Bivariate Correlations window to appear. On the left side is the list of variables. Select the variables that you want to correlate and move them to the right side of the window in the space labeled "Variables." The Bivariate Correlations window is shown in Figure 12.8b with the variables already selected.

(d)

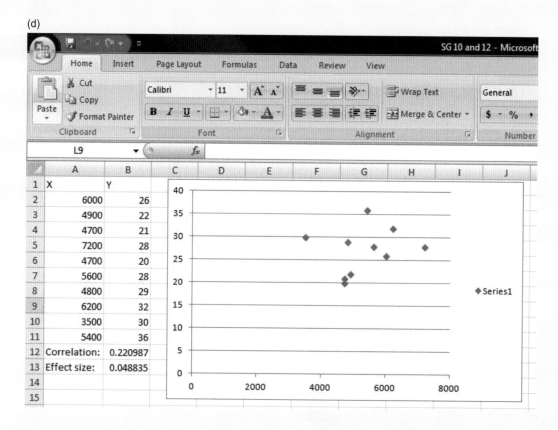

Figure 12.7d The default appearance of a scatterplot in Microsoft Excel.

(e)

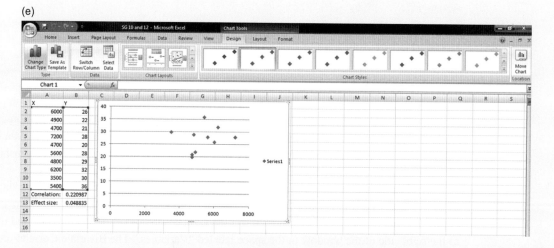

Figure 12.7e A screenshot from Microsoft Excel showing the options to change the appearance of the scatterplot.

(a)

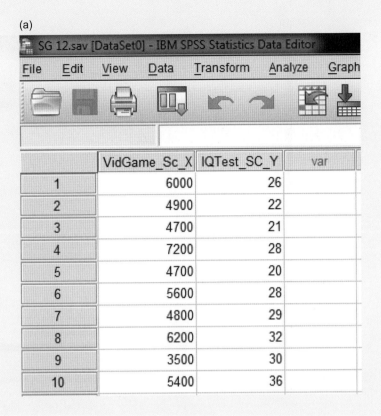

Figure 12.8a Screenshot of an SPSS data file with the example video game data entered in. Each row represents a sample member, and each column represents a variable. Datasets with more variables will have more columns with data in them.

The Bivariate Correlations window also provides several options. The default correlation is "Pearson" (checked in Figure 12.8b), which uses Formula 12.1 or Formula 12.2 in its calculation. The other two options, Kendall's tau-b and Spearman, are appropriate for ordinal data. (See Chapter 15 for an explanation of the Spearman's ρ correlation.) The "Test of Significance" option shows how to select a one- or a two-tailed test of the null hypothesis. Finally, the box labeled "Flag significant correlations" should be checked if you would like the computer to automatically put an asterisk (*) next to correlation coefficients for which the null hypothesis (which is H_0: $r = 0$) is rejected. Figure 12.8b shows the SPSS defaults for each of these options.

If you click the "Options" button, a new window (shown in Figure 12.8c) appears. Selecting the first checkbox (labeled "Means and standard deviations") gives you the choice of calculating descriptive statistics for the variables selected in the Bivariate Correlations window. Another option, labeled "Cross-product deviations and covariances," provides an unstandardized measure of the strength of the relationship between variables. This is based on the formula $\frac{\sum(x_i-\overline{X})(y_i-\overline{Y})}{n-1}$, which is the same as Formula 12.1, except without the division by the two multiplied standard deviations ($s_x \cdot s_y$). There are also two options for handling individuals who are missing data in the variables. The "Exclude cases pairwise" option (which is the default in SPSS) throws individuals out of the correlation calculation if they are missing data on either variable in a particular

(b)

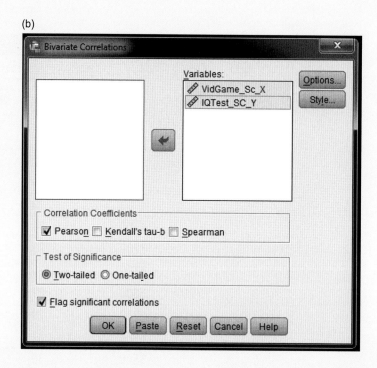

Figure 12.8b The SPSS Bivariate Correlations window with the variables already selected (as shown by their presence in the right side of the window). Users who desire to calculate more than one correlation at a time should move all variables that they want correlations for into the right side of the window. Default options shown as selected.

correlation coefficient. In the "Exclude cases listwise" option, individuals who are missing data on *any* variable in the list in the Bivariate Correlations window are eliminated from all Pearson's *r* calculations. When there are two variables selected in the Bivariate Correlations window or when there are no missing data, these options produce identical results. However, when there are more than two variables or when there are missing data, SPSS may throw sample members out of a particular correlation coefficient – even if a sample member is not missing any data on either variable – because the sample member is missing data on another variable in the list. The "Exclude cases pairwise" option maximizes the sample size for each Pearson's *r* value, while "Exclude cases listwise" ensures a consistent sample size across all correlation coefficients. Both options have their advantages and disadvantages.

After selecting all the desired options, clicking "OK" in the Bivariate Correlations window will cause the SPSS output window to appear. Figure 12.8d shows two tables produced by SPSS in the output window. The first table, labeled "Descriptive Statistics," shows the means, standard deviations, and sample size for each variable. The second table is called a **correlation table**. The columns and rows of the correlation table will be labeled with the names of the variables that were selected in the Bivariate Correlations window. Apart from the labels, the correlation table will always be a square with the same number of rows and columns as there were variables selected in the Bivariate Correlations window. Figure 12.8d's correlation table is a 2×2 table because there were two variables used to produce this output. Each box within the correlation table is called a cell.

(c)

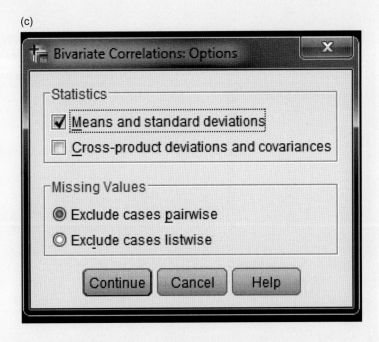

Figure 12.8c The Bivariate Correlations: Options window in SPSS. The first checked box will produce descriptive statistics for the selected variables. It is unchecked in SPSS's defaults.

(d)

Descriptive Statistics

	Mean	Std. Deviation	N
VidGame_Sc_X	5300.00	1020.893	10
IQTest_SC_Y	27.20	5.073	10

Correlations

		VidGame_Sc_X	IQTest_SC_Y
VidGame_Sc_X	Pearson Correlation	1	.221
	Sig. (2-tailed)		.540
	N	10	10
IQTest_SC_Y	Pearson Correlation	.221	1
	Sig. (2-tailed)	.540	
	N	10	10

Figure 12.8d The tables produced by SPSS in the output window. The lower table is the correlation table. When more than two variables have been selected from the Bivariate Correlations window, this table will be larger and will display the correlation for every possible pair of variables. The number of rows and columns in the correlation table will be equal to the number of variables selected in the Bivariate Correlations window. Regardless of the size of the correlation table, a diagonal of cells in the table – extending from top left to bottom right – will all display a correlation of 1. The cells above this diagonal will be a mirror image of the cells below it.

(e)

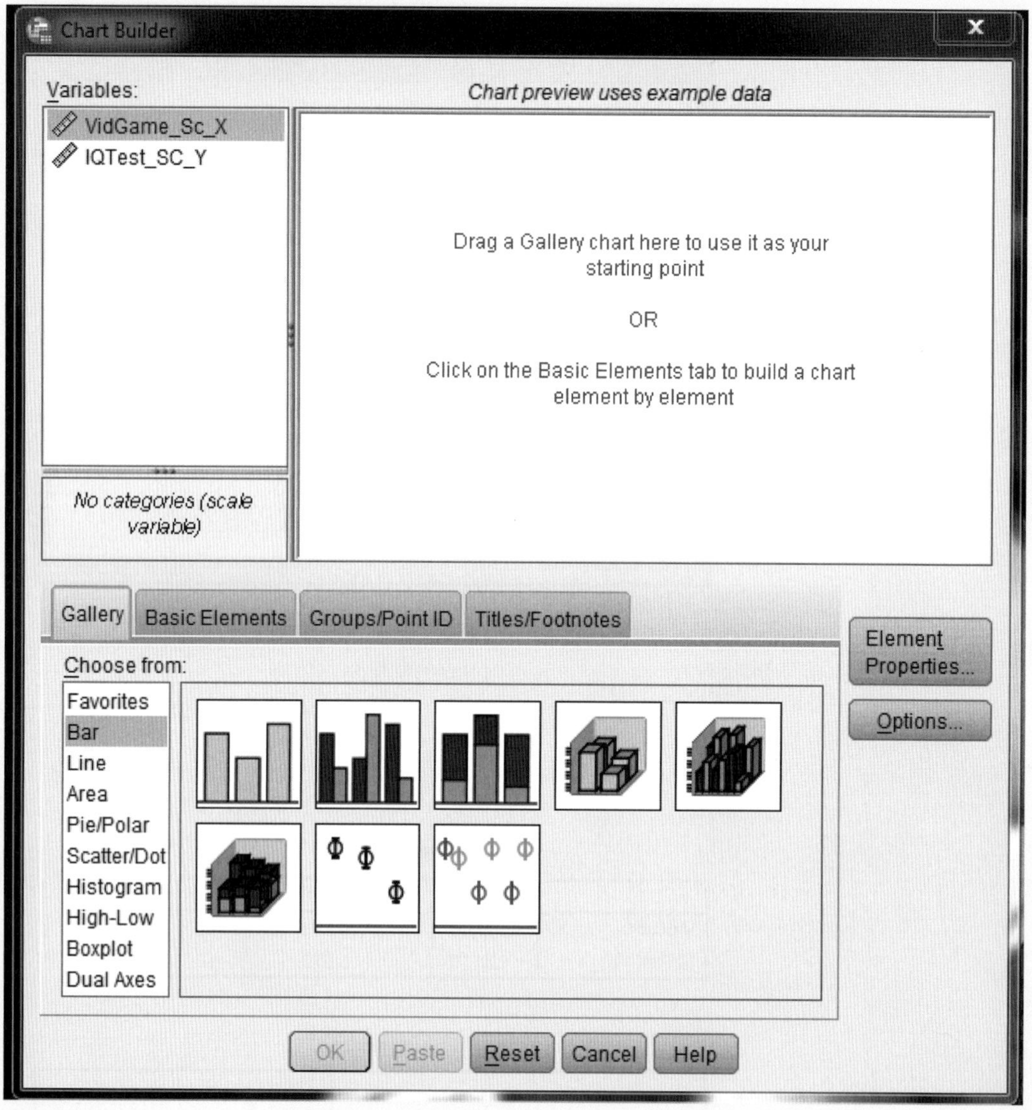

Figure 12.8e The SPSS Chart Builder window as it appears when first opened.

Whatever the size of the correlation table, it will always have a set of cells that run diagonally from the top left to the bottom right in which the correlation is 1. This is because these cells represent each variable's correlation with itself – which will always be $r = +1.00$. The cells above the diagonal will always be a mirror image of the cells below the diagonal, and it does not matter which set of cells the user chooses to interpret or report. In the correlation coefficient in Figure 12.8d, between the video game scores and IQ test scores, is $r = +0.221$, which is labeled in SPSS as "Pearson Correlation." The value labeled "Sig. (2-tailed)" is the p-value for a two-tailed test of the null hypothesis (H_0: $r = 0$), which in this case is .540. The last number in the cell represents the sample size that SPSS used to calculate the correlation coefficient, which is $n = 10$ in this

(f)

Figure 12.8f The SPSS Chart Builder window as it appears after the Scatter/Dot option has been selected.

example. If this correlation coefficient were statistically significant, the *p*-value would have been less than .05 and there would be an asterisk (*) next to the Pearson's *r* value. Because the asterisk is missing, the correlation is not statistically significant, and we should retain the null hypothesis that this correlation is statistically equal to 0.

Creating a Scatterplot and Regression Line. The SPSS Chart Builder can create a scatterplot. To open the Chart Builder, select the "Graphs" menu and then "Chart Builder." The Chart Builder menu (shown in Figure 12.8e) will appear. To create a scatterplot, select "Scatter/Dot"

(g)

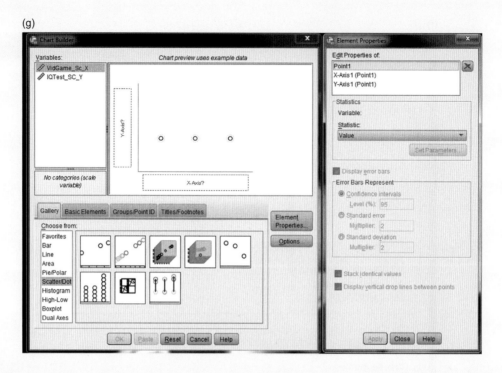

Figure 12.8g The SPSS Chart Builder window as it appears after the top-left icon has been dragged into the upper-right region of the window.

(h)

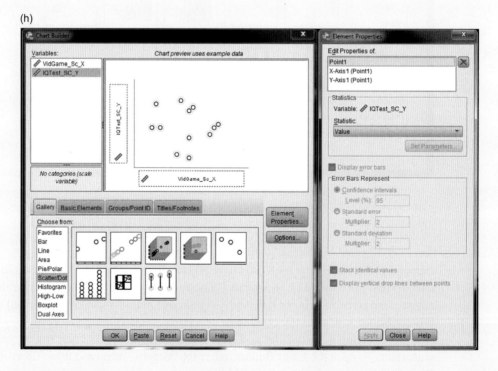

Figure 12.8h The SPSS Chart Builder window as it appears after the variables have been selected from the list on the left side of the window. The independent variable name is now on the horizontal axis, while the dependent variable name is now on the vertical axis.

(i)

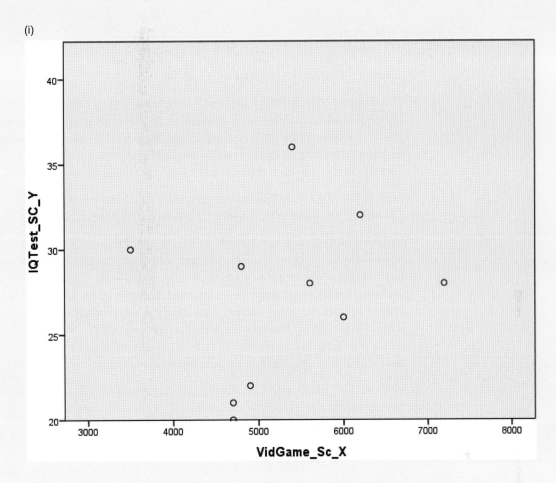

Figure 12.8i The scatterplot that SPSS produced showing the example video game and intelligence test data.

in the bottom left of the window. The icons at the bottom of the window will change to their appearance in Figure 12.8f.

The next step is to select the top-left icon and to drag it into the white space in the top right of the window. This result is shown in Figure 12.8g. Some dots appear in the scatterplot, but these do not actually represent the final appearance of the scatterplot.

The next step is to drag the variables from the list on the left side of the window to the scatterplot. You should put the independent (X) variable on the horizontal axis on the bottom of the diagram and the dependent (Y) variable on the vertical axis on the left side of the diagram. The result is shown in Figure 12.8h. This is the last step in building a scatterplot, and the user is now ready to press the "OK" button on the window.

After you press "OK," the SPSS Chart Builder window will disappear, and the finished correlation coefficient will appear in the SPSS output window. Figure 12.8i shows the final scatterplot for the example data in this chapter.

Further Reading

- *Guess the Correlation*: www.guessthecorrelation.com

  * This website by Omar Wagih is a simple computer game in which players are shown a scatterplot and asked to guess the correlation. Points are awarded for more accurate guesses, and players lose "lives" when guesses are inaccurate. This game is surprisingly addictive, and it helps students gain experience in interpreting scatterplots. I like to have a contest in my class each semester to see who can obtain the highest score.

- Pearson, E. S. (1936). Karl Pearson: An appreciation of some aspects of his life and work: Part I: 1857–1906. *Biometrika*, *28*, 193–257. doi:10.1093/biomet/28.3–4.193

  * Statistical methods and formulas do not appear out of thin air. Rather, they are created by people who are trying to understand their data better. An excellent illustration of this fact is shown in this article by Egon S. Pearson, which is the first half of a biography of his father, Karl Pearson, and it shows how the latter invented his correlation because of a need to advance the infant science of genetics. An added bonus of the article is that it shows the breadth of Pearson's scholarly interests and touches on his contributions to descriptive statistics (see Chapter 4) and the chi-squared test (see Chapter 14). The second half of the biography is in E. S. Pearson (1938).

- Schönbrodt, F. D., & Perugini, M. (2013). At what sample size do correlations stabilize? *Journal of Research in Personality*, *47*, 609–612. doi:10.1016/j.jrp.2013.05.009

  * The authors of this article show how unstable correlation coefficients can be when sample sizes are small. They do this by recalculating the Pearson's *r* value for a dataset after adding one individual to the sample, and then repeating this process until the correlation coefficient stabilizes. This article also provides useful guidelines for estimating the needed sample size to obtain a stable correlation coefficient.

13 Regression

In the previous chapter, we learned about how Pearson's *r* can be used to describe the strength and nature of the relationship between two variables. In addition to describing the relationship between variables, it is also possible to use the correlation coefficient to make predictions. Therefore, we could take the +0.221 correlation between video game scores and intelligence test scores (in Chapter 12) to use individuals' scores from one variable to predict scores on the other variable. We could use this information, for example, to predict individuals' intelligence test scores if we know their video game scores. Making predictions about human traits and behavior is a powerful tool of the social sciences.

To take more examples from the previous chapter, we could use the correlation coefficients in Table 12.8 and predict individuals' job satisfaction from their depression scores, or predict first-year college students' grades on the basis of their high-school grades. In fact, correlation coefficients are often used to make predictions. The purpose of this chapter is to show you how to use correlation coefficients to make predictions in the social sciences.

Learning Goals

- Make a prediction on the basis of a correlation coefficient.

- Describe how violations of the assumptions of Pearson's *r* and linear regression can distort correlation coefficients and statistical predictions.

- Illustrate how the phenomenon of restriction of range has practical, real-world implications.

Using Pearson's *r* to Make Predictions

Any time we use a statistical model to make predictions of a sample member's dependent variable value, it is called **regression**. Using Pearson's *r*, we can use two types of equations to make predictions through a special type of regression called **linear regression**, which uses an equation to build a model to make predictions. Two equations can be used for linear regression, and both of them produce a straight line on the scatterplot. The first is the standardized regression equation, and the second is the unstandardized regression equation.

Standardized Regression Equation. The simpler method of making predictions is to use the standardized regression equation, which is:

$$\hat{z}_y = rz_x \qquad \text{(Formula 13.1)}$$

In this equation, $\hat{z}_y$ is the predicted z-score for an individual on the dependent variable (i.e., the Y variable), r is the correlation coefficient between the two variables, and z_x is the same sample member's z-score on the independent variable (i.e., the X variable).

Formula 13.1 is easy to use if the correlation is already known. In the example video game data for this chapter, r = +0.221. Therefore, we can make a prediction for someone who has a z_x score of +1.3 in the following way:

$$\hat{z}_y = (0.221)1.3$$

$$\hat{z}_y = 0.2873$$

This means that if an individual has a z-score on the independent variable of +1.3, we would predict that they have a z-score of +.2873 on the dependent variable. As another example, a person with a z-score on the independent variable of –0.7 would be predicted to have a z-score on the dependent variable of (0.221)(–0.7) = –0.1547.

Unstandardized Regression Equation. The standardized regression equation is only appropriate if both variables are expressed as z-scores. If either the X or the Y variable (or both) is not converted to z-scores, you must use the unstandardized regression equation, which is

$$\hat{y}_i = bx_i + a \qquad \text{(Formula 13.2)}$$

where $\hat{y}_i$ is the individual's predicted score on the dependent variable and x_i is the sample member's actual observed score. The b value is calculated as

$$b = r\frac{s_y}{s_x} \qquad \text{(Formula 13.3)}$$

and a is calculated as

$$a = \overline{Y} - b\overline{X} \qquad \text{(Formula 13.4)}$$

In the video game example data, $\overline{X}$ = 5300, s_x = 1,020.893, $\overline{Y}$ = 27.2, s_y = 5.073, and r = +0.221. We can plug these numbers into Formula 13.3 to find b:

$$b = (0.221)\frac{5.073}{1,020.893}$$

$$b = (0.221)0.004969$$

$$b = 0.001098$$

The next step is to calculate a with Formula 13.4:

$$a = 27.2 - (0.001098)(5300)$$

$$a = 27.2 - 5.8198$$

$$a = 21.3802$$

With a known a and b, we can plug numbers into Formula 13.2:

$$\hat{y}_i = (0.001098)x_i + 21.3802$$

The only thing missing now is x_i, which is an individual's independent variable score. We can plug in the sample members' actual scores to find predicted scores on the dependent variable:

Table 13.1 Predicted Y scores for individuals in the video game datasets

ID	X Score	Predicted Y score ($\hat{y}_i$)
1	6,000	$(0.001098)(6,000) + 21.3802 = 27.97$
2	4,900	$(0.001098)(4,900) + 21.3802 = 26.76$
3	4,700	$(0.001098)(4,700) + 21.3802 = 26.54$
4	7,200	$(0.001098)(7,200) + 21.3802 = 29.29$
5	4,700	$(0.001098)(4,700) + 21.3802 = 26.54$
6	5,600	$(0.001098)(5,600) + 21.3802 = 27.53$
7	4,800	$(0.001098)(4,800) + 21.3802 = 26.65$
8	6,200	$(0.001098)(6,200) + 21.3802 = 28.19$
9	3,500	$(0.001098)(3,500) + 21.3802 = 25.22$
10	5,400	$(0.001098)(5,400) + 21.3802 = 27.31$

In addition to calculating $\hat{y}_i$ scores for each sample member, we can make predictions for individuals who do not belong to the sample. For example, if a person has an x_i score of 5,000, we can predict that they would have a score on the dependent variable of:

$$\hat{y}_i = (0.001098)(5000) + 21.3802 = 26.87$$

The Regression Line

Visually, we can display the standardized regression equation or the unstandardized regression equation as a visual model that can be added to a scatterplot. This visual model takes the form of a straight line called the **regression line**. You may remember from Chapter 1 that models are simplified versions of reality. Therefore, we can think of the regression line as an attempt to simplify the data so that the relationship between the independent and dependent variable is easier to discern.

Regression Line Derived from the Unstandardized Regression Equation. The unstandardized regression equation can be used to graph a straight line on top of the scatterplot. This line represents the predicted dependent variable values for any x_i score on the horizontal axis of the scatterplot. The first step of creating the regression line is to select two x-values and to estimate the scores on the dependent variable for both values. After that, you should plot the points on the scatterplot and then connect them with a straight line.

Figure 13.1a shows the result of this process. The circles in the scatterplot are the data points from the video game example data, which is why the dots in Figures 12.1 and 13.1a are the same (the two scatterplots were created with the same data). The two white squares ($\square$) in the scatterplot correspond to the predicted scores for the individuals with the video game scores of 6,000 and 4,900 (who are the first two people in Table 13.1). The regression line connects the two dots and extends through the entire length of the scatterplot.

Figure 13.1a shows the regression line drawn with the predicted scores for the first two people in the example video game dataset. But it does not matter which two points are selected to draw the regression line. This is shown in Figure 13.1b, which shows the predicted intelligence test

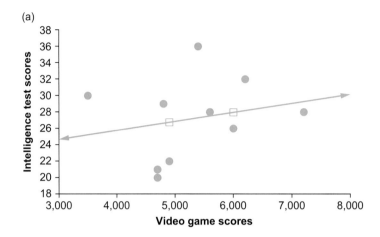

Figure 13.1a The scatterplot for the example video game data with the regression line. The two white squares represent the points (6,000, 27.97) and (4,900, 26.76). The *Y* value for these two points is the predicted value for these two *X* values using the unstandardized regression equation.

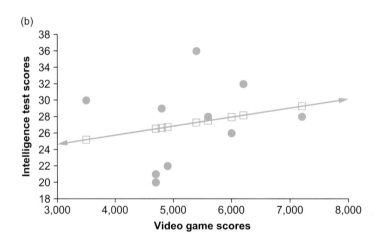

Figure 13.1b The scatterplot for the example video game data with the regression line. The white squares correspond to each individual's predicted score on the dependent variable. All predicted scores for the dependent variable (even if they do not correspond to a sample member) will be on the regression line.

scores for each person in the data. (This information comes from Table 13.1.) Figure 13.1b clearly shows that all of these predicted scores are on the regression line.

Regression Line Derived from the Standardized Regression Equation. A regression line can also be created with a standardized regression equation (i.e., Formula 13.1), which requires the *x*-scores to be expressed as *z*-scores. Table 13.2 shows the *z*-scores for each individual and their *z*-score for the dependent variable. Each person's *z*-score for the two variables has been plotted on a scatterplot in Figure 13.2a. It is enlightening to compare Figure 13.2a, which displays the video game data as raw scores, with Figure 12.1, which displays the video game data as *z*-scores. Notice

Table 13.2 Predicted standardized *Y* scores for individuals in the video game datasets

ID	Standardized *X* score	Standardized *Y* score	Standardized predicted *Y* score ($\hat{y}_i$)
1	+0.69	−0.24	(+0.69)(0.221) = +0.15
2	−0.39	−1.03	(−0.39)(0.221) = −0.09
3	−0.59	−1.22	(−0.59)(0.221) = −0.13
4	+1.86	+0.16	(+1.86)(0.221) = +0.41
5	−0.59	−1.42	(−0.59)(0.221) = −0.13
6	+0.29	+0.16	(+0.29)(0.221) = +0.06
7	−0.49	+0.35	(−0.49)(0.221) = −0.11
8	+0.88	+0.95	(+0.88)(0.221) = +0.19
9	−1.76	+0.55	(−1.76)(0.221) = −0.39
10	+0.10	+1.73	(+0.10)(0.221) = +0.02

(a)

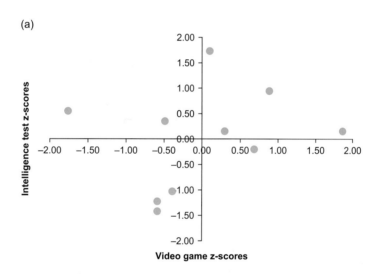

Figure 13.2a Scatterplot of the video game data with all scores converted to *z*-scores. Notice that converting the data to *z*-scores has only changed the axes of the scatterplot, and not the pattern of the dots in the scatterplot or the relative position of the dots in comparison to one another. This is because the conversion of raw data to *z*-scores is a linear transformation, and linear transformations never change the pattern of scores within a dataset (see Chapter 5).

how in both figures the pattern of the dots is the same. The only thing that has changed is the location and scale of the horizontal axis and the vertical axis. This is because converting scores to *z*-scores is a special type of linear transformation, which, as we learned in Chapter 5, does not change the pattern of scores within a dataset. Linear transformations only change the axis of the data.

Table 13.2 also displays prediction of the *z*-score on the dependent variable, which was calculated via Formula 13.1 ($\hat{z}_y = rz_x$). These scores have been plotted onto Figure 13.2b as white squares and used to create the regression line. Just as in the Figure 13.1b, all of these predicted scores fall on the regression line.

(b)

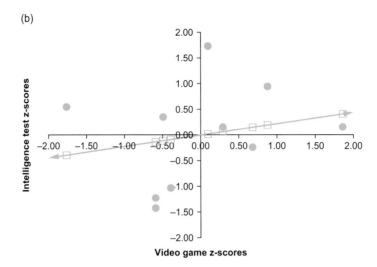

Figure 13.2b Scatterplot of the video game data with all scores converted to z-scores. The figure also includes each individual's predicted score on the outcome variable (shown as a white square) and the regression line. Notice that converting the data to z-scores has only changed the axes of the scatterplot (compare this figure to Figure 13.1b), and not the pattern of the dots in the scatterplot. This is because the conversion of raw data to z-scores is a linear transformation, and linear transformations never change the pattern of scores within a dataset (see Chapter 5).

Sidebar 13.1 **Common links between the two regression line equations**

Figures 13.1a and 13.2a are very similar, but it can be difficult to understand why. In this section, I will compare the two regression equations and show why both of these equations produce a straight line and why these lines appear so similar in the two figures.

The best way to understand the standardized and unstandardized regression equations is to see how both of them can be used to graph a straight line. You may remember from your algebra class that the equation for a straight line is

$$y = mx + b \qquad \text{(Formula 13.5)}$$

In this formula, m is the slope of the line and b is the y-intercept. Each of the four components of this equation (slope, y-intercept, x-value, and y-value) has a corresponding portion in both the standardized and unstandardized regression equation. This is apparent in Figure 13.3, which shows all three equations and the portion of each one that represents the slope, the y-intercept, the x-value, and the y-value. In fact, it is because the standardized and unstandardized regression equations both produce a straight line that this procedure is called *linear regression*.

Figure 13.3 has a few implications. First, it is clear that the standardized and unstandardized regression equations are just different ways to graph a straight line. Their only substantive differences are in notation. Second, it is apparent that the y-intercept, which is defined as the value for x when $y = 0$, of the standardized regression equation is always 0. Therefore, the standardized regression line must always pass through (0, 0). You can see this, for example, in Figure 13.2b. Because the mean of a set of scores will always have a z-score of 0, the standardized regression equation's (0, 0) point must correspond to the point $(\overline{X}, \overline{Y})$. Therefore, the unstandardized regression equation must pass through $(\overline{X}, \overline{Y})$.

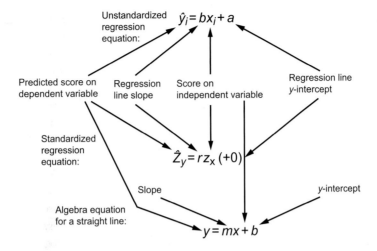

Figure 13.3 Commonalities among the standardized and unstandardized regression equations and the algebraic equation for a straight line. All three equations have four components: a *y*-variable score, a line slope, an *x*-variable score, and the line's *y*-intercept.

Check Yourself!

. What is the purpose of regression?

. How do you know when to use the standardized or unstandardized regression equation?

. How is the regression line a model for the data in the scatterplot?

. What point will a regression line always pass through?

Measuring Prediction Individual Accuracy. In Chapters 11 and 12, we learned about the residual, which is a measurement of the accuracy of the prediction for an individual. The residual is calculated as $e_i = Y_i - \hat{Y}_i$ (Formula 11.10), where Y_i is the person's actual score on the dependent variable and $\hat{Y}_i$ is the person's predicted score on the dependent variable. We can obtain the $\hat{Y}_i$ value for each person by plugging their *x*-score into the unstandardized regression equation. These predicted dependent variable scores and the actual dependent variable scores can then be used with Formula 11.10 to calculate a residual for each sample member. Table 13.3 shows how to calculate the residual for each person in the video game dataset. Negative residuals indicate that the person scored lower on the *Y* variable than predicted, while positive residuals indicate that the person scored higher on the dependent variable than predicted. Residuals in a dataset will always add up to zero.

The scatterplot can also be used to visualize the residual. Figure 13.4 shows the scatterplot for the example video game data. The figure shows that the residual is the vertical distance between a sample member's actual (i.e., observed) score on the *Y* variable and the individual's predicted score on the regression line. It is apparent when you examine the figure

Table 13.3 Residuals for individuals in the video game datasets

ID	Y score	Predicted Y score ($\hat{y}_i$)	Residual ($Y_i - \hat{Y}_i$)
1	26	27.97	26 − 27.97 = −1.97
2	22	26.76	22 − 26.76 = −4.76
3	21	26.54	21 − 26.54 = −5.54
4	28	29.29	28 − 29.29 = −1.29
5	20	26.54	20 − 26.54 = −6.54
6	28	27.53	28 − 27.53 = 0.47
7	29	26.65	29 − 26.65 = 2.35
8	32	28.19	32 − 28.19 = 3.81
9	30	25.22	30 − 25.22 = 4.78
10	36	27.31	36 − 27.31 = 8.69

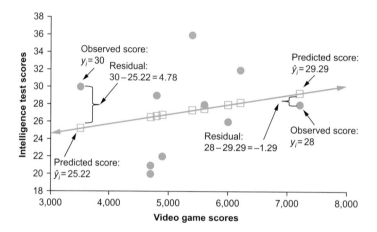

Figure 13.4 Scatterplot of the video game data with residuals (marked with white squares) and the regression line. For two selected individuals in the dataset, the observed and predicted scores are marked. The residual (i.e., $Y_i - \hat{Y}_i$) is the vertical distance between the person's observed and predicted scores.

that positive residuals indicate that a person's Y variable score exceeded their predicted Y score, while negative residuals indicate the reverse.

Whether calculated with the standardized regression equation (Formula 13.1) or the unstandardized regression equation (Formula 13.2), the regression line is the straight line that minimizes the size of the residuals and makes them as small as possible. No other straight line can result in smaller residuals for the entire sample. This is why the regression line is sometimes called the **line of best fit**. We can use the residuals to estimate how much the regression line has minimized the residuals of the sample members, by comparing the residuals derived from the regression line to the residuals from the **baseline model**. The equation that defines the baseline model is:

$$\hat{y}_i = \bar{y} \qquad \text{(Formula 13.6)}$$

Formula 13.6 says that the predicted score (i.e., $\hat{y}_i$) for every sample member is equal to the grand mean of all the dependent variable scores (i.e., $\bar{y}$). You can think of the baseline model as the worst possible model that still fits the data. To see how much better the regression line is at making

Table 13.4 Residuals for individuals in the video game datasets

ID	Y	Residual (derived from regression line)	Residual (derived from baseline model)
1	26	26 − 27.97 = −1.97	26 − 27.2 = −1.2
2	22	22 − 26.76 = −4.76	22 − 27.2 = −5.2
3	21	21 − 26.54 = −5.54	21 − 27.2 = −6.2
4	28	28 − 29.29 = −1.29	28 − 27.2 = 0.8
5	20	20 − 26.54 = −6.54	20 − 27.2 = −7.2
6	28	28 − 27.53 = 0.47	28 − 27.2 = 0.8
7	29	29 − 26.65 = 2.35	29 − 27.2 = 1.8
8	32	32 − 28.19 = 3.81	32 − 27.2 = 4.8
9	30	30 − 25.22 = 4.78	30 − 27.2 = 2.8
10	36	36 − 27.31 = 8.69	36 − 27.2 = 8.8
Sum		0	0

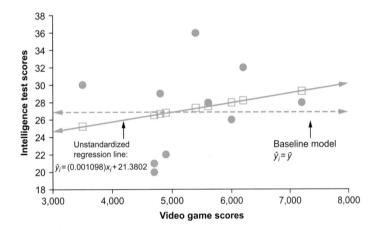

Figure 13.5 Scatterplot of the example video game data with the regression line (in solid blue) and the line representing the baseline model (the dashed line). The residual for a model is the vertical distance between the individual's observed score – represented by the black dot – and the straight line representing the model. The lines represented by the two models cross at the point $(\overline{X}, \overline{Y})$, which is always where the regression line and the line representing the baseline model intersect.

predictions than the baseline model, we can compare the two sets of residuals. This is done in Table 13.4. Notice how both sets of residuals sum to zero.

The two models and the predictions based on them are shown visually in Figure 13.5. Again, the residual is the vertical distance between the person's observed score (represented as the blue dot) and the straight line representing the model. For the regression line, this straight line is shown in solid blue. The baseline model is shown as the dashed line. For some of these people (e.g., individuals 4 and 9) the residual derived from the baseline model is smaller than the residual derived from the regression line. However, for the majority of sample members, the residuals are smaller. In Table 13.4 this is shown by the smaller numbers in the second column from the right. In Figure 13.5 this is represented visually by the fact that most dots are closer to the solid line (i.e., the regression line) than to the dashed line (i.e., the baseline model).

Table 13.5 Residuals for individuals in the video game datasets

ID	Squared residual (derived from regression line)	Residual (derived from baseline model)
1	$-1.97^2 = 3.88$	$-1.2^2 = 1.44$
2	$-4.76^2 = 22.66$	$-5.2^2 = 27.04$
3	$-5.54^2 = 30.70$	$-6.2^2 = 38.44$
4	$-1.29^2 = 1.65$	$0.8^2 = 0.64$
5	$-6.54^2 = 42.79$	$-7.2^2 = 51.84$
6	$0.47^2 = 0.22$	$0.8^2 = 0.64$
7	$2.35^2 = 5.52$	$1.8^2 = 3.24$
8	$3.81^2 = 14.53$	$4.8^2 = 23.04$
9	$4.78^2 = 22.82$	$2.8^2 = 7.84$
10	$8.69^2 = 75.52$	$8.8^2 = 77.44$
Sum of squared residuals:	220.29	231.60

Table 13.5 shows how we calculate the degree of improvement from using the base line model to make predictions to making predictions from the regression line. The first step is to square all of the residuals. Then each set of residuals is summed.

After summing the residuals, the difference between the residuals is calculated:

$$231.60 - 220.29 = 11.31$$

That number is then divided by the sum of the squared residuals derived from the baseline model:

$$\frac{11.31}{231.60} = 0.04884$$

This means that the squared residuals are – on average – 4.884% smaller when calculated from the regression line than when calculated from the baseline model. If this number seems familiar, that is because it is the same as the r^2 value for these data ($0.221 \cdot 0.221 = 0.04884$). This demonstrates that the effect size r^2 *is the degree of improvement in the predictions when compared to the baseline model*. This also shows that if $r^2 = 0$, the model provides no useful information because the baseline model (which does not use any information about the independent variable X) makes equally useful predictions. On the other hand, if $r^2 = 1.00$, all predictions based on the regression line are perfectly accurate and all residuals are equal to zero. Any r^2 between 0 and 1 will contain some error, and there will be some improvement compared to the baseline model.

Sidebar 13.2 **Ordinary Least-Squares Regression**

The explanation of how r^2 is a measure of the improvement in predictions shows that the regression line is an attempt to produce the most accurate predictions possible from the data in a sample. We saw that linear regression produces these predictions by minimizing the sum of the squared residuals for the dataset. Because every regression line created through the method described in this book will make these squared residuals as small as possible, this type of regression is often called **ordinary least-squares (OLS) regression**. There are other types of regression, but OLS is the most common type in the social sciences.

Guided Practice 13.1

In this Guided Practice, we will use data on vaccination rates in children and adults in the United States (CDC, 2016) to construct a standardized and an unstandardized regression equation and to make predictions based on these statistical models.

The independent variable in this example is the adult influenza vaccination rates at the state level, and the dependent variable is the child influenza vaccination rate. The mean state vaccination rate for adults in 2015–2016 was 42.55% (SD = 4.19%). For children, the mean state vaccination rate was 59.74% (SD = 8.04%). The correlation between the two variables is $r = 0.626$.

Standardized Regression Equation. To create a standardized regression equation, we should use Formula 13.1, which was $\hat{z}_y = rz_x$. Creating a standardized regression equation that we can make predictions from requires replacing r with the correlation between the two variables (0.626):

$$\hat{z}_y = 0.626z_x$$

We can now use this equation to make predictions. For example, a state that has an adult influenza rate that is 1 SD above average (i.e., $z_x = +1.0$) will be predicted to have the following z-score for its child influenza vaccination rate:

$$\hat{z}_y = 0.626(1.0) = 0.626$$

Similarly, a state with an adult influenza vaccination rate that is 1.5 SD below average will be expected to have a child influenza vaccination rate z-score of:

$$\hat{z}_y = 0.626(-1.5) = -0.939$$

Unstandardized Regression Equation. Using the information above ($\overline{X} = 42.55, s_x = 4.19, \overline{Y} = 59.74, s_y = 8.04, r = 0.626$), we can also construct an unstandardized regression equation based on Formula 13.2 ($\hat{y}_i = bx_i + a$). This requires using Formula 13.3 ($b = r\frac{s_y}{s_x}$) to find b and Formula 13.4 ($a = \overline{Y} - b\overline{X}$). First, to find b, we need to replace r, s_y, and s_x with the values above:

$$b = 0.626\frac{8.04}{4.19}$$
$$b = 0.626(1.919)$$
$$b = 1.201$$

Likewise, finding a requires replacing $\overline{Y}$, b, and $\overline{X}$ in Formula 13.4 with the values above:

$$a = 59.74 - 1.201(42.55)$$
$$a = 59.74 - 51.111$$
$$a = 8.629$$

Finally, we can put these b and a values into Formula 13.2 to produce:

$$\hat{y}_i = 1.201x_i + 8.629$$

And we can use this equation to make predictions. For example, for a state that has half of its adults vaccinated against influenza ($x_i = 50$), we can predict that the child vaccination rate will be:

$$\hat{y}_i = 1.201(50) + 8.629$$
$$\hat{y}_i = 60.060 + 8.629$$
$$\hat{y}_i = 68.69$$

Or, in a state where 65% of adults are vaccinated against influenza, we can predict that the childhood vaccination rate will be:

$$\hat{y}_i = 1.201(65) + 8.629$$
$$\hat{y}_i = 78.078 + 8.629$$
$$\hat{y}_i = 86.71$$

Creating Regression Lines. With the standardized regression equation, we can create a regression line showing the linear relationship between the two variables. This requires knowing any two $(z_x, \hat{z}_y)$ points and plotting these on the scatterplot. Then the points should be connected with a straight line. Only two points are necessary because all $(X, \hat{Y})$ values you obtain from these equations will be on the regression line, and it only takes two points to define a line. If you remember that the standardized regression line must pass through $(0, 0)$, you can use that as one of the points that defines your regression line.

If you wish to create a visual model of the unstandardized regression equation, you should plot any two $(X, \hat{Y})$ points on the scatterplot and then connect these two points with a straight line. Again, only two points are necessary because all $(X, \hat{Y})$ values you obtain from these equations will be on the regression line, and it only takes two points to define a line in geometry (see Figures 13.1a and 13.1b). One convenient point that can help you draw the regression line is $(\overline{X}, \overline{Y})$, through which the regression line will always pass.

Regression Towards the Mean

Definition. Although not the only possible method, the regression line is the most common method of making predictions based on correlation coefficients in the social sciences. However, it results in a fascinating phenomenon: **regression towards the mean**, which occurs when a sample member's predicted values on a dependent variable (i.e., the Y variable) is less extreme than the person's score on the independent variable (i.e., the X variable). This means that each individual is predicted to be more average on the dependent variable than they were on the independent variable.

A real example of regression towards the mean can be seen in Table 13.6. This table shows the X scores and the predicted Y scores for the 10 individuals from the video game dataset. These scores have been converted to z-scores for convenience because this makes both variables have the same scale. The standardized predicted Y scores (i.e., $\hat{z}_y$ values) were calculated with Formula 13.1. Notice that in Table 13.6 the z-scores for the independent variable range from -1.76 to $+1.86$. However, the predicted dependent variable scores range from -0.39 to $+0.41$. Additionally, each individual's predicted Y score is closer to zero than their X score. This is regression towards the mean.

Table 13.7 shows how the severity of regression towards the mean depends on (1) a sample member's score on the independent variable, and (2) the strength of the correlation coefficient (Rambo-Hernandez & Warne, 2015). When we compare the differences between the z_x and $\hat{z}_y$

Table 13.6 Standardized observed X scores and predicted Y scores for individuals in the video game dataset

ID	Standardized X score (i.e., z-scores)	Standardized predicted Y score (i.e., z-scores)
1	+0.69	+0.15
2	−0.39	−0.09
3	−0.59	−0.13
4	+1.86	+0.41
5	−0.59	−0.13
6	+0.29	+0.06
7	−0.49	−0.11
8	+0.88	+0.19
9	−1.76	−0.39
10	+0.10	+0.02

Note. Data are derived from Table 13.2.

Table 13.7 Magnitude of regression towards the mean with various correlation coefficients

z_x Score	$\hat{z}_y(r = +1.0)$	$\hat{z}_y\ (r = +.70)$	$\hat{z}_y\ (r = +.40)$	$\hat{z}_y\ (r = +.10)$
−3.00	−3.00	−2.10	−1.20	−0.30
−2.50	−2.50	−1.75	−1.00	−0.25
−2.00	−2.00	−1.40	−0.80	−0.20
−1.50	−1.50	−1.05	−0.60	−0.15
−1.00	−1.00	−0.70	−0.40	−0.10
−0.50	−0.50	−0.35	−0.20	−0.05
0.00	0.00	0.00	0.00	0.00
+0.50	+0.50	+0.35	+0.20	+0.05
+1.00	+1.00	+0.70	+0.40	+0.10
+1.50	+1.50	+1.05	+0.60	+0.15
+2.00	+2.00	+1.40	+0.80	+0.20
+2.50	+2.50	+1.75	+1.00	+0.25
+3.00	+3.00	+2.10	+1.20	+0.30

scores, it is apparent that the differences are greater for z_x scores furthest from the mean of x. For example, when $r = +.40$ and $z_x = −3.00$, the $\hat{z}_y$ value is −1.20. This difference of 1.8 SD is much larger than the 0.3 SD difference that we would expect for a person when $r = +.40$, $z_x = +0.50$, and $\hat{z}_y = +0.20$.

The table also shows that regression towards the mean is largest when a correlation coefficient is weak. For example, when $r = +0.70$, a person with a z_x score of +3.00 will have a $\hat{z}_y$ score of +2.10 – a difference of only .90 SD. On the other hand, when $r = +0.10$, that same person's $\hat{z}_y$ score is +0.30 – a difference of 2.70 SD.

Table 13.7 shows that there is no regression towards the mean when the correlation between two variables is perfect, as when $r = −1.0$ or $+1.0$ (Bland & Altman, 1994a; Pearson,

1896; Stigler, 1997). This is apparent in the first two columns, showing that there is no difference in z_x and $\hat{z}_y$ scores when two variables are perfectly correlated. Also, there is no regression towards the mean when a person's score on the independent variable is already equal to the mean. This can be clearly seen in the middle row of Table 13.7, showing that when $z_x = 0.00$, $\hat{z}_y$ is always equal to zero.

Examples of Regression Towards the Mean. Sir Francis Galton (1822–1911) was the first to observe this phenomenon when he noticed, in the 1880s, that both short and tall parents tended to have children who were closer to average height than their parents (Bland & Altman, 1994a; Galton, 1886; Senn, 2011; Stigler, 1986, 1997). Since Galton's time, scientists have noticed regression towards the mean in many fields. For example, educational programs that are designed to help struggling students often appear highly effective because students' scores increase from the first testing (before enrolling in the program) to the second testing (after experiencing the program). However, because these students' first test scores were often very low, we would expect their second test scores to be higher solely because of regression towards the mean. Thus, these programs often look more effective than they really are – a fact that social scientists have known for a long time (e.g., Jensen, 1969; Thorndike, 1942). This tendency for members of extreme groups to appear more average also appears in medical research of unhealthy groups, such as individuals with high blood pressure (Bland & Altman, 1994b), many of whom appear to have improved health even when taking a placebo. Regression towards the mean also occurs in business and economics, where corporations that perform poorly in one year will usually have a better performance in the following year. Likewise, years with strong earnings will often be followed by relatively more average years (G. Smith, 2016).

Aside from scientific interests, regression towards the mean appears in daily life. Several writers (e.g., G. Smith, 2016) have commented on the *Sports Illustrated* curse, which is the apparent poorer performance that many athletes display immediately after appearing on the cover of *Sports Illustrated*. When an athlete has performed strongly enough to appear on the cover, their subsequent performance will return to an average level for that athlete because of regression towards the mean. Likewise, regression towards the mean also explains why most movie sequels are worse than their preceding film. Usually, only popular movies get a sequel. Because of regression towards the mean, we should expect that the sequel will have a more average quality than the original film.

Why does regression to the mean occur? Stigler (1997) has an intuitive explanation in which each score can be considered to have two components: (1) the person's real score level, and (2) "luck," which is often called "error" (e.g., Crocker & Algina, 2008). This "luck" can raise or lower the person's score in a random fashion. If a person scores very high on a variable, it may be a combination of an above-average score plus some "luck" that raised their score even higher. However, we should not expect their luck to continue every time we collect data on that person. Eventually, the person's "luck" will run out and their score will return to a more average level (see also Thorndike, 1942).

Caveats. Regression towards the mean does not mean that *every* member of a sample will have a dependent variable score closer to the mean than their score on the independent variable. Rather, there is a tendency for *most* people's dependent variable scores to be closer to the mean, but there will almost always be a portion of sample members that have more extreme scores on the dependent variables than on the independent variable. This means, for example, that not every movie sequel is awful. A few movie sequels are better than their preceding film. (My students often name *The Empire Strikes Back, The Dark Knight*, and *Toy Story 2* as examples of superior sequels.) Likewise, there are some athletes who continue their excellent performance after appearing on the cover of *Sports Illustrated*; 50 appearances on the cover of the magazine were not damaging to Michael Jordan's sports career (Burt, 2015).

It is also important to remember that regression towards the mean is a statistical phenomenon; it does not have any real cause beyond an imperfect correlation between variables. For example, Galton's (1886) observation that the children of short people tended to be taller than their parents is not because of some force of human genetics. This can be seen by predicting parents' height from the height of their children: in this case, parents of very tall or very short children tend to be more average in height (Bland & Altman, 1994a; Senn, 2011). There is no genetic cause that can explain both examples of regression towards the mean (from parental height to children's height and vice versa).

Another caveat about the concept of regression towards the mean is that it assumes that the population of scores does not change (Bland & Altman, 1994a). Therefore, if an athlete's performance is really declining (e.g., because of injury or advancing age), it is unrealistic to expect their performance to return to their old average after a particularly bad game.

Finally, because of regression towards the mean, it is difficult to predict the appearance of outliers. This is apparent in Table 13.7 – you may notice that in the right three columns there are no extreme z-scores (i.e., –3.0 or + 3.0). But outliers *do* occur; Table 13.7 just shows that regression often cannot make accurate predictions of who will be an outlier (Taylor & Russell, 1939). This is why psychologists are not good at predicting exactly which patients will attempt suicide (Meyer et al., 2001), or which children will grow up to win a Nobel Prize (Ackerman, 2014). Both of these outcomes are rare in the general population and are therefore difficult to predict (McGrath & Meyer, 2006).

Check Yourself!

- At the individual level, how do we judge the quality of the predictions based on the regression line?
- At the group level, how do we judge the quality of the predictions based on the regression line?
- Define the baseline model and explain how it is used to measure prediction quality.
- Define regression towards the mean and explain why it occurs.

Assumptions of Regression and Correlation

As with all statistical methods, there are assumptions that data must meet in order for Pearson's *r* and linear regression to produce results that are not distorted. These assumptions are: (1) a linear relationship between variables, (2) homogeneity of residuals, (3) absence of a restriction of range, (4) lack of outliers/extreme values that distort the relationship between variables, (5) equivalent subgroups within the sample, and (6) interval- or ratio-level data for both variables. With the exception of the final assumption (which I discussed in Chapter 12), I will discuss each of these assumptions briefly.

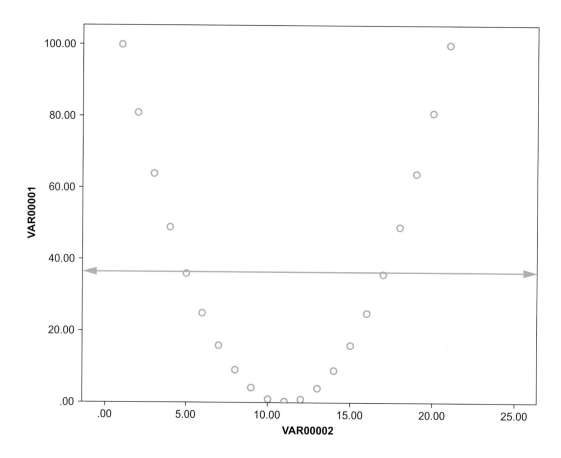

Figure 13.6 A nonlinear relationship between variables. The independent and dependent variables are clearly related. However, the straight regression line in the scatterplot indicates that $r = 0$. This is an example of a violation of the linear relationship assumption, which is why Pearson's r and the regression line are not appropriate in this situation.

Linear Relationship. One vital assumption of Pearson's r is that there is a linear relationship between the independent and dependent variables. The term "linear relationship" indicates that a straight regression line is a suitable model, which is why the procedure is called linear regression (see Sidebar 13.1). If the relationship is better represented by a curved line (e.g., in Figure 13.6), Pearson's r will produce distorted results. In a situation where a curved line fits the data better than a straight regression line, we say that there is a **nonlinear relationship** between the variables. For example, Werblow and Duesbery (2009) found a nonlinear relationship in their investigation of high-school size and students' math achievement scores. These researchers found that students in the high schools with the smallest enrolments (less than 674 students) and the largest enrolments (more than 2,592 students) had the highest math scores. But students in medium-sized high schools had lower math scores. This is an example of a nonlinear relationship because as high-school enrolment increases, it is associated first with lower math scores. But as high-school enrolment continues to increase, this trend reverses and students in larger high schools tend to be associated with high math scores.

Homogeneity of residuals. The second assumption of Pearson's r and linear regression is the homogeneity of residuals. This assumption states that there is no correlation between the

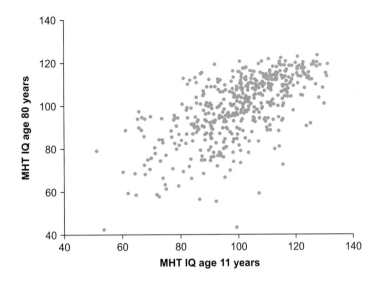

Figure 13.7 A correlation between intelligence test scores at ages 11 and 80. This scatterplot represents a correlation of $r = +0.66$. This scatterplot violates the homogeneity of residuals assumption because the dots are more tightly packed in the upper-right portion of the scatterplot and spread out in the bottom-left portion of the scatterplot. Additionally, instead of an oval, the dots form a fan shape, with the wider portion in the lower-left quadrant of the scatterplot. This scatterplot also violates the assumption of an absence of a restriction of range (explained in the text). *Source:* Deary, Whiteman, Starr, Whalley, and Fox (2004, p. 135).

independent variable and the residuals. When this occurs, the dots in the scatterplot form more or less an oval shape around the regression line, with scatterplots representing stronger correlations having tighter, narrower ovals. You can see several scatterplots that meet this assumption in Figures 12.2a–12.3d. The scatterplot for the example video game data also meets this assumption (see Figure 12.1).

On the other hand, Figure 13.7 shows a real dataset where this assumption is violated. The dots are more tightly packed together in the upper-right portion of the scatterplot and further apart in the lower-left part of the scatterplot. Another indication of a violation of the homogeneity of residuals assumption is that the dots do not form a symmetrical ellipse (or oval). Instead, the dots make more of a fan shape, with the narrow part of the fan in the top-right quadrant of the scatterplot; the wide part of the fan is in the bottom-right portion of the scatterplot.

Although these graphical tests of the assumption are useful, the best method is to calculate the correlation between the independent variables and the residuals in the sample. This is done by using Formula 12.1 and replacing the dependent variable (i.e., Y variable) data with the residual scores. When this assumption is met, the correlation will be zero, and the correlation will be larger and statistically significant when the assumption is violated. In the example video game data, the correlation is exactly $r = +0.00042$. This is extremely close to zero and indicates that the homogeneity of residuals definition is met in this example.

Absence of restriction of range. The third assumption of Pearson's r and linear regression is that there is no restriction of range. **Restriction of range** occurs when the data do not include the entire range of scores in either the independent or dependent variables. Restriction of range generally drives correlations closer to zero, although there are situations where restriction of range can inflate a correlation coefficient (Steinemann, 1963). Figure 13.7 shows an example of restriction of range because sample members earned a maximum score on the test that was used to measure intelligence. This is why the scores seem to pile up at about 120 or 130, which was the maximum score on the test. It is likely that some of these individuals could have scored higher on the test, but the test's maximum score does not allow us to have access to the full range of possible scores.[10]

Restriction of range is especially apparent in elite samples. For example, fans of American football may be surprised to learn that the correlation[11] between a linebacker's weight and the number of tackles he has in the regular National Football League (NFL) season is $r = -0.02$. This may seem astonishing to many people who know anything about American football because the linebackers are some of the largest, heaviest members of a team. They need bulk to be effective at their job, which is to physically overpower and tackle players on the opposing team. But this correlation implies that weight does not matter on the playing field. It seems counterintuitive in a physical game of strength, like American football, to ignore the size and strength of players. So why is the correlation so low?

The answer is restriction of range. The NFL linebackers in this sample all weigh between 225 and 290 pounds (102.1 to 131.5 kg). Their average weight is 246.3 pounds (111.7 kg), and the standard deviation is only 12.5 pounds (5.7 kg). In contrast, the average American adult male weighs 195.5 pounds (88.7 kg), and the standard deviation is about 48 pounds (21.7 kg; Centers for Disease Control, 2012). This means that the weights of football linebackers have only 26% of the variability that the general population has; clearly this reduces (i.e., restricts) the range of data for this variable.

But weight is not the only variable that has a restriction of range in this example. All of these linebackers are professional athletes because they were excellent tacklers on previous teams (e.g., on college, high-school, or childhood teams). Although there are no data on the number of tackles the average American is capable of making each year, it is a certain fact that NFL linebackers are elite tacklers and that there is much less variability in their performance than there would be in the general population. It is because of restriction of range on both variables – weight and number of tackles – that this correlation is so low.

If we were to remove this restriction of range by assigning all linebackers on all teams in every league in the United States randomly to teams, the correlation would increase. Figure 13.8 shows the scatterplot that we would expect from data that included all linebackers randomly assigned to teams. As is apparent, the correlation between weight and tackles is not perfect (I estimate that $r = +0.36$ in the general population), but it is positive and noteworthy.[12]

[10] Although it is much less apparent by examining the scatterplot in Figure 13.7, Deary et al. (2004) also had to deal with restriction of range from another source: individuals who had lower intelligence test scores in childhood were less likely to survive to old age. Thus, Deary et al. (2004) had restriction of range that reduced the number of high scorers and the number of low scorers in their study. They estimated that if there were no restriction of range from either source the correlation would rise from $r = +0.66$ to $r = +0.73$.

[11] Data calculated by the author. Sample size was $n = 135$ and included every NFL linebacker who played in at least 15 regular season games during 2015. (There are 16 regular season games each year; if only players who participated in every game are included, the Pearson's $r = -0.06$, which does not substantively change this discussion of restriction of range.)

[12] This estimate is made by correcting for the restriction of range with the formula given by Wiberg and Sundström (2009, p. 4). The selected sample's weight SD was estimated to be 26% of the population's weight SD. The selected sample's tackle SD was estimated to be 10% of the population's tackle SD. The restricted sample's correlation estimate was reset to $r = +0.01$ because using the value $r = -0.02$ would make the corrected correlation negative, which is probably not true for the population correlation between weight and tackles.

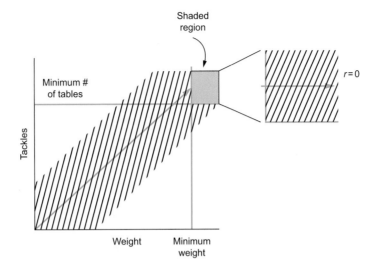

Figure 13.8 A scatterplot for an entire population of linebackers showing the correlation between their weight (on the *x*-axis) and number of tackles (on the *y*-axis). The correlation in the overall population is r = +0.36. However, selecting a subsample of individuals who meet a minimum weight requirement (represented as a vertical line) and a requirement for a minimum number of tackles (represented as a horizontal line), and calculating a separate correlation for them produces a result of r = −0.02. The scatterplot for this subsample (at right) also shows no relationship between weight and tackles among the subsample.

Two lines have been added to the scatterplot to represent the restriction of range in this example where only players who can achieve a minimum number of tackles *and* who meet a minimum weight requirement are selected. The shaded region is the group of linebackers who are good enough at tackling and heavy enough to play in the NFL. Within this group the correlation drops to nearly zero, and the scatterplot (on the right side of the figure) resembles the scatterplot for a zero correlation.

Restriction of range has been recognized as a problem in other professional sports (Abelson, 1985) and areas of social science research where individuals are selected based on a test score, as in college admission (Zwick, 2006) or employment testing (Sireci & Hambleton, 2009; Vernon, 1947). It also occurs in studies that track people's change over the course of years – called longitudinal studies – because often the individuals still in the study when it ends are less variable than the group that started the study, due to deaths or dropouts in the sample (W. Johnson, Brett, Calvin, & Deary, 2016).

Outliers Do Not Distort the Relationship. We saw in Chapter 4 that outliers can distort the values of means and standard deviations. Because means and standard deviations are also part of the Pearson's *r* formula (see Formula 12.1), the potential exists for outliers to also distort correlation coefficients and linear regression models. However, you should be aware that outliers do not always distort correlation coefficients and linear regression models.

Figures 13.9a–13.9c show an example of a scatterplot without an outlier (a) and after an outlier has been added (b and c). Besides the outlier in the last two scatterplots, the data are all the same. In the scatterplot in Figure 13.9a, the correlation between the two variables is r = +0.30. The outlier added to Figure 13.9b has singlehandedly increased the

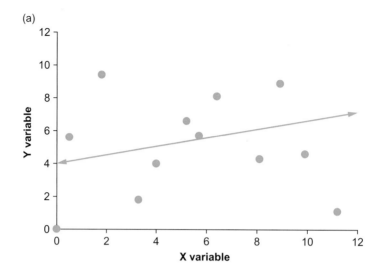

Figure 13.9a A scatterplot with *r* = +0.30 and the accompanying regression line.

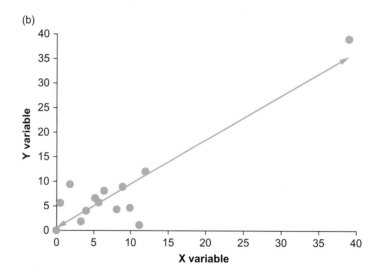

Figure 13.9b Scatterplot with an outlier added that distorts the correlation. Without the outlier, the correlation would be *r* = +0.30 (see Figure 13.9a). With this outlier included, the correlation is *r* = +0.90.

correlation to $r = +0.90$. However, the outlier added to Figure 13.9c has not changed the correlation at all.

Whether an outlier distorts the correlation of a set of data depends on the outlier's residual. Remember that the regression line is the line that makes every residual as small as possible. Therefore, the degree to which an outlier alters the correlation depends directly on how large the outlier's residual would be for the regression line calculated without the outlier. This is apparent in

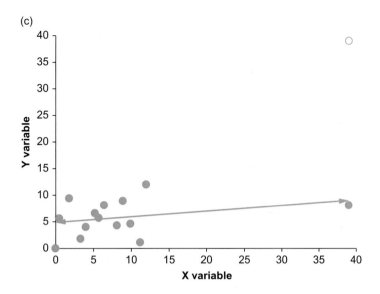

Figure 13.9c Scatterplot with an outlier added that does not distort the correlation. Without the outlier, the correlation would be $r = +0.30$ (see Figure 13.9a). With this outlier included, the correlation is still $r = +0.30$, and the regression line is not altered. The white circle in the upper-right hand corner represents the location of the outlier in Figure 13.9b that distorted the correlation.

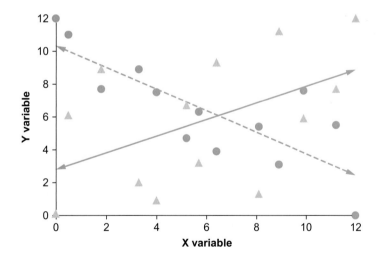

Figure 13.10 A sample consisting of two subgroups with different correlation coefficients. The subgroup represented by circles has a correlation coefficient of $r = -0.80$ (represented by the dashed regression line). The subgroup represented by triangles has a correlation coefficient of $r = +0.50$ (represented by the solid regression line). When their data are combined and a single correlation coefficient calculated for the entire sample, the Pearson's r value is $r = -0.08$, a value that is not appropriate for either subgroup.

Figure 13.9c; the outlier represented by a black dot is very close to the regression line, which is why it did not alter the correlation coefficient of $r = +0.30$. Figure 13.9c also shows the location of the outlier (as a white circle) from Figure 13.9b. Compared to the regression line from Figure 13.9a, this outlier has a very large residual. When the outlier was added to the data (in Figure 13.9b), the regression line had to move much closer to the outlier in order to minimize its residual. Therefore, outliers influence correlation coefficients when they have large residuals compared to the regression line that would be calculated without the outlier.

Equivalent Subgroups. The fifth assumption of Pearson's r is that the sample is homogeneous and that if separate correlation coefficients are calculated from sample subgroups, then those correlation values will be equal. Figure 13.10 shows an example of a violation of this assumption. Overall, the correlation coefficient calculated from all the data is $r = -0.08$. There are two subgroups in the sample, one represented by circles, and the other by triangles. When correlation coefficients for these groups are calculated separately, the circles have a correlation of $r = -0.80$ (represented by the dashed regression line), and the triangles have a correlation of $r = +0.50$ (represented by the solid regression line). Combining these groups' data produces an overall correlation coefficient and a regression line that does not represent either group well. This comparison of subgroups' correlation coefficients is common in evaluations of psychological tests to ensure that the test functions similarly for different groups of people, such as language groups, gender groups, or age groups (Warne, Yoon, et al., 2014; see Cleary, 1968, for an early example of this type of study). It also appears when a researcher is interested in whether the strength of the relationship varies under different conditions, a situation that will be explored more in Chapter 15 in the discussion on interactions.

General Linear Moment 13.1

The sixth assumption of Pearson's r and regression is that both variables are interval- or ratio-level data. We saw in General Linear Moment 12.1 that all procedures in the GLM are correlational in nature and that the only difference is the level of data of the variables in each procedure. Thus, if both variables are not interval- or ratio-level data, another procedure is appropriate. When the independent variable is nominal and dichotomous, the usual statistical procedure is the unpaired-samples t-test (see Chapter 10).

However, there is an alternative procedure that can be used when the independent variable is nominal and dichotomous. That procedure is the **point-biserial correlation** (abbreviated r_{pb}), which was proposed by K. Pearson (1910). Just like Pearson's r, it is calculated with Formula 12.1 or Formula 12.2. Because the independent variable is nominal, a number must be assigned to each category. (The values are arbitrary, but 0 and 1 are the most common choices.) Once the r_{pb} value is calculated, it can be converted to Cohen's d with the following formula (from Durlak, 2009, p. 928):

$$r_{pb} = \frac{d}{\sqrt{d^2 + 4}}$$

As we have seen in other General Linear Moments in this textbook, the different procedures in the GLM are all interrelated. The equation is just one more demonstration of the connection between different GLM methods – in this case the unpaired-samples t-test and correlation statistics.

Check Yourself!

- Why do we have to worry about the assumptions of Pearson's r?

- What does a scatterplot look like when the homogeneity of residuals assumption is violated?

- Why is it important that subgroups within a sample have similar regression lines before we examine the regression line of the entire dataset?

Summary

After finding the correlation coefficient, it is possible to make predictions of dependent variable values. This procedure of making predictions is called linear regression. There are two equations that can be used to perform regression: the standardized regression equation and the unstandardized regression equation. The former is used when both variables are converted to z-scores; the latter is appropriate when one (or both) variables are not in z-score format. Both regression equations produce a straight line that can be included in the scatterplot. This line is called the regression line or the line of best fit, and it represents the predicted value on the dependent variable ($\hat{Y}$) for a sample member with a given X variable value. The difference between a person's predicted dependent variable value and the actual value (i.e., $\hat{Y} - Y$) is called the residual. The regression line is the line that makes all the squared residuals as small as possible.

One statistical phenomenon to be aware of when making predictions is regression towards the mean. This arises because using the regression equations to make a prediction will result in a predicted dependent variable value that will always be closer to the mean of the dependent variable than the person's score on the independent variable was to the mean of the independent variable. This means that outliers and rare events can be difficult (sometimes impossible) to predict via the regression equations.

It is important to be aware of the assumptions of Pearson's r and regression. These are (1) a linear relationship between variables, (2) homogeneity of residuals, (3) an absence of a restriction of range, (4) a lack of outliers/extreme values that distort the relationship between variables, (5) subgroups within the sample are equivalent, and (6) interval- or ratio-level data for both variables. Violating any of these assumptions can distort the correlation coefficient.

Reflection Questions: Comprehension

1. Every time she makes a regression equation, Jocelyn converts all her data to z-scores and then uses the standardized regression equation to create the line of best fit. She notices that her regression line always passes through the point (0, 0). Why is this?
2. Dallin is a sports fan. As he tracks the performance of different teams, he notices that teams that were poor performers 10 years ago tend to be better teams now,

whereas teams that were excellent 10 years ago tend to be worse teams now. Dallin says this is because bad teams make changes that help them improve, and good teams become stagnant. What statistical phenomenon would be a better explanation for this observation?

3. Explain why regression is not able to make predictions of outliers or of rare events.
4. What assumption does the scatterplot below violate?

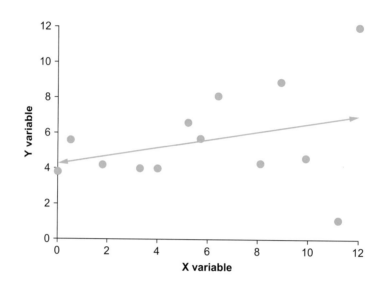

5. Many professions (e.g., medicine, law, architecture) require job applicants to pass a licensing test of basic skills and knowledge in order to work in that field. Examinees who do not pass the test are denied jobs, and some people who pass the test are offered jobs. Janine examined the correlation between test scores on the architecture licensing test and ratings of the quality of the architects' work. She was surprised to find that the correlation was $r = +0.05$. Why is this correlation so low?
6. What does a scatterplot look like when the homogeneity of residuals assumption is violated?
7. How do you determine whether an outlier is distorting the relationship between two variables?
8. Describe why some outliers distort the regression line and others do not.

Reflection Questions: Application

9. Using the standardized regression equation of $\hat{z}_y = rz_x$, find the predicted dependent variable z-scores of individuals with the following individuals if $r = -0.72$:
    a. $z_x = -4.0$
    b. $z_x = -2.9$
    c. $z_x = -1.2$
    d. $z_x = -0.4$
    e. $z_x = 0.0$
    f. $z_x = +0.6$
    g. $z_x = +1.9$

h. $z_x = +2.5$

i. $z_x = +3.2$

j.   Explain why the predicted dependent variable z-scores are less variable than the z_x scores.

10. Using the unstandardized regression equation of $\hat{y}_i = bx_i + a$

   a.   find the values for b and a if $r = +0.35$, $\overline{X} = 4.2$, $s_x = 1.5$, $\overline{Y} = 3.0$, and $s_y = 2.1$.

   b.   find the predicted dependent variable scores for the following independent variable scores.

x_i	$\hat{y}_i$
0	
1.8	
3.0	
4.2	
5.8	
5.9	
10.0	

11. Using the standardized regression equation of $\hat{z}_y = rz_x$, find the predicted dependent variable z-scores if $r = +0.10$:

   a. $z_x = -3.5$

   b. $z_x = -2.8$

   c. $z_x = -2.5$

   d. $z_x = -0.8$

   e. $z_x = 0.0$

   f. $z_x = +0.4$

   g. $z_x = +1.2$

   h. $z_x = +2.8$

   i. $z_x = +3.5$

   j.   Explain why the predicted dependent variable z-scores are less variable than the z_x scores.

12. Using the unstandardized regression equation of $\hat{y}_i = bx_i + a$

   a.   find the values for b and a if $r = -0.45$, $\overline{X} = 6.9$, $s_x = 0.8$, $\overline{Y} = 10.6$, and $s_y = 1.4$.

   b.   find the predicted dependent variable scores for the following independent variable scores.

x_i	$\hat{y}_i$
0	
1.8	
3.0	
4.2	
5.8	
5.9	
10.0	

13. What assumption does the scatterplot below violate?

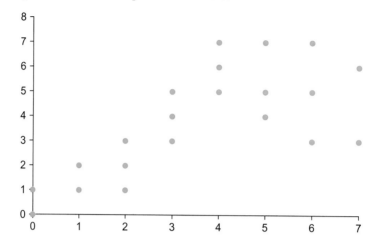

14. Jane is interested in health psychology, so for a project she collects data on the number of hours that college students watch television per day (x) and the number of hours that they exercise per week (y). Her data are below:

ID	x	y
1	3	9
2	5	4
3	3	5
4	4	9
5	2	2
6	1	5
7	0	8
8	4	7
9	6	2
10	1	12

   a.   Find the correlation between these two variables.
   b.   Write the standardized regression equation for these data.
   c.   Calculate b and a for the unstandardized regression equation for these data.
   d.   Write the unstandardized regression equation for these data.
   e.   Draw the scatterplot and regression line for these data.
   f.   Do the data violate any assumptions?
   g.   Using the standardized regression equation, make a prediction for the following z_x values

z_x	$\hat{z}_y$
−3	
−2.5	
−1	

z_x	$\hat{z}_y$
(cont.)	
0	
1.8	
2.0	
3.5	

h. Using the unstandardized regression equation, make a prediction for the following x values.

x	$\hat{y}$
0	
1	
2	
3	
4	
5	
6	

i. Use the predictions in question 14h to calculate the residual for each x value in the dataset.

ID	x	y	Residual
1	3	9	
2	5	4	
3	3	5	
4	4	9	
5	2	2	
6	1	5	
7	0	8	
8	4	7	
9	6	2	
10	1	12	

j. Which individual has the largest residual? Which individual has the smallest residual?

15. Camilla collected data on the quality of day care (x) and the child's grades in kindergarten (y). Her data are below:

ID	x	y
1	3.8	3.5
2	1.9	4.8
3	0.5	5.2
4	1.6	7.0
5	4.8	2.2
6	5.2	5.1
7	6.1	4.0
8	4.3	6.5
9	2.6	2.3
10	1.2	4.1
11	3.5	5.8
12	4.6	6.8
13	6.2	7.2
14	2.1	6.9
15	0.3	1.4

a. Find the correlation between these two variables.
b. Write the standardized regression equation for these data.
c. Calculate b and a for the unstandardized regression equation for these data.
d. Write the unstandardized regression equation for these data.
e. Draw the scatterplot and regression line for these data.
f. Do the data violate any assumptions?
g. Using the standardized regression equation, make a prediction for the following z_x values

z_x	$\hat{z}_y$
−3	
−2	
−0.8	
0	
0.6	
1.2	
2.4	

h. Using the unstandardized regression equation, make a prediction for the following x values.

x	$\hat{y}$
0	
1	
2	
3	
4	
5	
6	

i. Calculate the residual predicted dependent variable score and residual for each individual in the dataset.

ID	y	$\hat{y}_i$	Residual
1	3.5		
2	4.8		
3	5.2		
4	7.0		
5	2.2		
6	5.1		
7	4.0		
8	6.5		
9	2.3		
10	4.1		
11	5.8		
12	6.8		
13	7.2		
14	6.9		
15	1.4		

j. Which individual has the largest residual? Which individual has the smallest residual?

16. For the unstandardized equation, b is the slope of the regression line. Given the equation for b (which is $b = r\frac{s_y}{s_x}$), explain why r is the slope of the regression line when the independent and dependent variable scores are expressed as z-scores.

17. For the unstandardized equation, a is the y-intercept of the regression line. Given the equation for a (which is $a = \overline{Y} - b\overline{X}$), explain why the y-intercept of the regression line is always 0 when the independent and dependent variable scores are expressed as z-scores.

18. If $d = 1.0$, what is the equivalent point-biserial correlation value?

Software Guide

The purpose of this chapter's software guide is to show how to add a regression line to a scatterplot. If you need to review how to create a scatterplot, please see the Software Guide in Chapter 12.

Excel

To add a regression line to a scatterplot in Excel, right-click any dot in the scatterplot and then select "Add Trendline" from the menu that appears. The line will automatically appear along with a window called the Format Trendline window. This is shown in Figure 13.11. Excel's default is to have the regression line extend only from the minimum X-variable to the maximum X-variable value in the dataset.

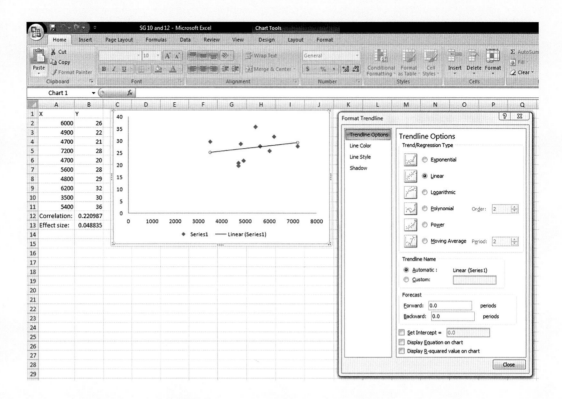

Figure 13.11 The appearance of a scatterplot with the regression line added. When the regression line is first added, Excel automatically opens the Format Trendline window, where the appearance of the regression line can be altered.

In the Format Trendline window, there are options that can alter the appearance of the trendline. For example, to create a nonlinear trendline, you can select one of the other options (like "exponential" or "polynomial") on the right side of the window. To extend the trendline through the entire length of the scatterplot, enter numbers into the two blanks in the "Forecast" section of the window (towards the bottom). The numbers indicate the number of units beyond the highest X-variable value (for the "Forward" blank) and the lowest X-variable value (for the "Backward blank) that you wish to extend the regression line. The Format Trendline window also has options for naming the regression line, and displaying the unstandardized regression equation and the r^2 value (the check boxes towards the bottom of the window). Cosmetic aspects of the line, such as making the regression line dotted, dashed, thick, or boldface, or a different color, can be altered in the Format Trendline window. Other options allow you to modify the ends of the regression line to become arrows, squares, or circles. Again, I recommend that you experiment with some of the options to create regression lines that enhance the appearance of scatterplots.

SPSS

Figure 13.12 shows a scatterplot in the output window in SPSS. To add the regression line, double-click the scatterplot, which causes the Chart Editor window (also shown in Figure 13.12) to appear.

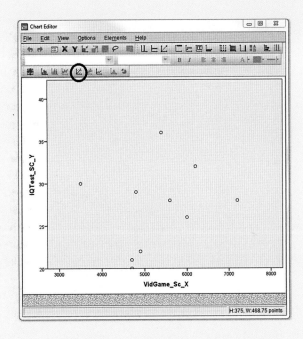

Figure 13.12 The SPSS Chart Editor window. The icon needed to add a regression line is circled.

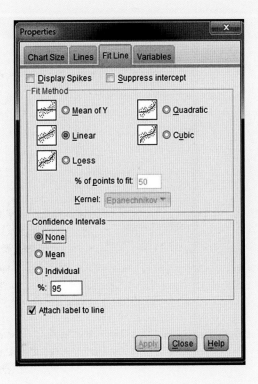

Figure 13.13 The Properties window for a scatterplot on SPSS. If the user wishes to add a linear regression line, this window can be closed. However, the user can choose other visual models for their data instead. "Mean of Y" will show the baseline model. The "Loess," "Quadratic," and "Cubic" options will produce nonlinear trend lines in the scatterplot.

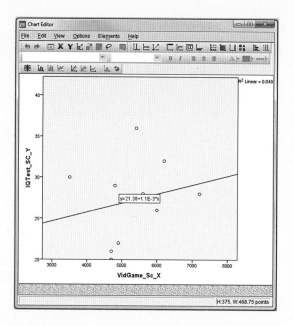

Figure 13.14 The scatterplot's default appearance in SPSS after the trend line has been added. SPSS automatically adds the unstandardized regression equation (shown in the box in the middle of the scatterplot) and the r^2 value (shown at the top right outside of the scatterplot).

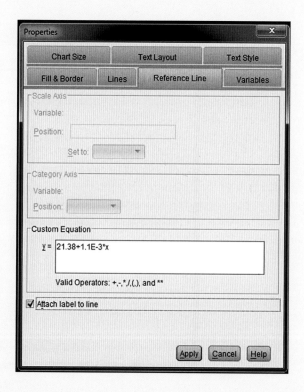

Figure 13.15 The Properties window for the regression line. To remove the unstandardized regression equation from the scatterplot, uncheck "Attach label to line" and then click "Apply."

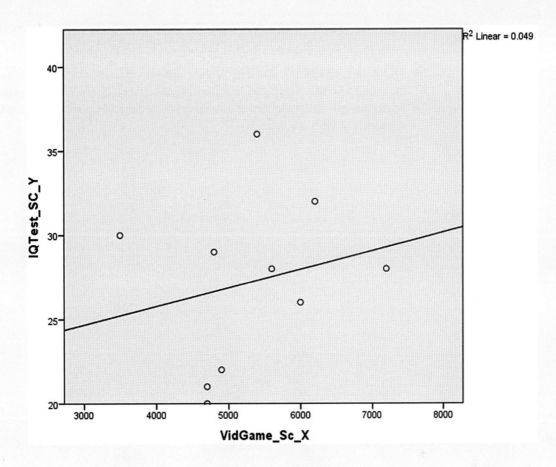

Figure 13.16 The final scatterplot and regression line produced by SPSS.

In the Chart Editor window, you should click the icon that is circled in Figure 13.12, which causes yet another window to appear. This is called the Properties window, and it is shown in Figure 13.13. This window can be closed immediately.

Figure 13.14 shows the appearance of the scatterplot in SPSS after the trendline has been added. SPSS automatically displays the unstandardized regression equation (in the box in the middle of the scatterplot) and the r^2 value (at the top right outside the scatterplot). Some people find the unstandardized regression equation annoying (especially if it covers up dots). To remove this, double-click it. This causes another Properties window to appear, as shown in Figure 13.15. To get rid of the regression equation, just uncheck the box labeled "Attach label to line" and then click "Apply."

The last step is to close the Chart Editor. The final product is shown in Figure 13.16.

Further Reading

- Senn, S. (2011). Francis Galton and regression to the mean. *Significance*, *8*, 124–126. doi:10.1111/j.1740–9713.2011.00509.x

  * This accessibly written article describes the history of regression towards the mean. Senn explains that the placebo effect is often just a manifestation of regression towards the mean.

- Stigler, S. M. (1997). Regression towards the mean, historically considered. *Statistical Methods in Medical Research*, *6*, 103–114. doi:10.1177/096228029700600202

  * This is an excellent article that gives three different explanations of regression towards the mean: a verbal explanation, a mathematical explanation, and a visual explanation. Stigler also provides examples of how other people have fallen victim to misinterpreting regression towards the mean.

14 Chi-Squared Test

One of the most famous ocean disasters was the sinking of the *RMS Titanic* on April 15, 1912. This catastrophe has captured the imaginations of millions of people for the past century through books, films, documentaries, and other works inspired by the infamous "unsinkable ship." When I first learned about the *Titanic* years ago, I heard that the first-class passengers – the wealthiest passengers – were more likely to survive than the people in second class (less wealthy passengers) and third class (the poorest group of passengers), and that third-class passengers were the most likely to die. This seemed odd to me because, of the 498 surviving passengers, approximately one-third were from each group. I thought that if first-class passengers really were the most likely to survive, there would be more survivors from that group than any other. (I was wrong, and you will see why later in this chapter.)

To determine whether a group of individuals is more likely to experience an outcome – surviving or dying in the example of the *Titanic* – it is necessary to look beyond the raw numbers and instead conduct a statistical test. This test is called the chi-squared test. In this chapter, I will explain the chi-squared test, which is named after the Greek letter χ, which is pronounced to rhyme with "fly." We will also use the chi-squared test to determine whether first-class passengers on the *Titanic* were more likely to survive than less wealthy passengers.

Learning Goals

- Determine the appropriate situation for a one-way or two-way chi-squared test.
- Conduct a one-variable chi-squared test and two-variable chi-squared test.
- Calculate and interpret an effect size for a chi-squared test: the odds ratio and relative risk.

Nominal Outcomes

Every null hypothesis test discussed so far in this textbook has had a dependent variable that was either interval- or ratio-level data. This was necessary either to calculate a correlation coefficient (in Chapter 12) or test a null hypothesis that means were equal (in Chapters 7–11). However, dependent variables (i.e., outcomes) are not always interval- or ratio-level data. The *Titanic* is a perfect example of an outcome of this sort: whether a passenger survived or perished is a nominal variable. Because nominal variables cannot sensibly be used to calculate means or correlation coefficients, data with a nominal dependent variable cannot be used in any of the NHSTs that we have learned so far in this book. However, in Chapter 2 we learned that nominal data can be used to calculate proportions (see Table 2.1). We can use proportions to conduct a chi-squared test, which is just an NHST designed (by K. Pearson, 1900) to handle nominal outcomes.

One-Variable Chi-Squared Test

The most basic type of chi-squared test involves a single nominal variable. This is called a **one-variable chi-squared test** and involves testing whether the proportions of sample members in each group are equal to a theorized proportion. For example, in the *Titanic* data, I assumed that first-, second-, and third-class would each be one-third of the passengers. We can conduct a one-variable chi-squared test to check this assumption. Just as with any NHST, there are eight steps to conducting a one-variable chi-squared test. These steps are:

1. Form groups in the data.
2. Define the null hypothesis (H_0). The null hypothesis is always that there is no difference between groups or that there is no relationship between independent and dependent variables.
3. Set alpha (α). The default alpha = .05.
4. Choose a one-tailed or a two-tailed test. This determines the alternative hypothesis (H_1).
5. Find the *critical* value, which is used to define the rejection region.
6. Calculate the *observed* value.
7. Compare the observed value and the critical value. If the observed value is more extreme than the critical value, the null hypothesis should be rejected. Otherwise, it should be retained.
8. Calculate an *effect size*.

Form Groups in the Data. This is step 1. With all of the previous NHSTs, the groups in the data were formed with the independent variable. This variable denoted:

- whether the sample members belonged to the population or the sample (for the *z*-test and one-sample *t*-test),
- which of two or more sample groups sample members belonged to (for the paired-samples *t*-test, unpaired-samples *t*-test, or ANOVA), or
- the degree to which sample members belonged to a particular sample group (for Pearson's *r*).

For a chi-squared test, the independent variable is nominal-level data, just as it was for the *z*-test, the one-sample *t*-test, the paired-samples *t*-test, the unpaired-samples *t*-test, and ANOVA. In the *Titanic* example, the passenger class is the nominal variable that we are using to divide our data into groups. According to Frey, Savage, and Torgler (2011, p. 39), of the 1,316 passengers, 325 were in first class, 285 were in second class, and 706 were in third class. (We are only going to use passenger data because the exact number of crew and staff on the *Titanic* is not known.)

Define the Null Hypothesis. This is step 2. In a one-variable chi-squared test, the null hypothesis is that the groups have proportions equal to their theorized proportions. There is no convenient way to write this mathematically, so we have to express this null hypothesis as words. In the *Titanic* example, we would say that the null hypothesis is that first-class passengers make up one-third of the sample, that second-class passengers make up one-third of the sample, and that third-class passengers make up one-third of the sample. Although all of these proportions are the same size in this example, the proportions do not have to be equal in a one-variable chi-squared test null hypothesis.

Set Alpha. This is step 3. As in all NHSTs, the default alpha is .05. Just as in the other null hypothesis tests we have encountered, alpha denotes the size of the rejection region in the sampling distribution. For a one-variable chi-squared test, the choice of alpha is completely arbitrary, and there may be reasons to alter it. We are going to keep the alpha for the *Titanic* example at .05.

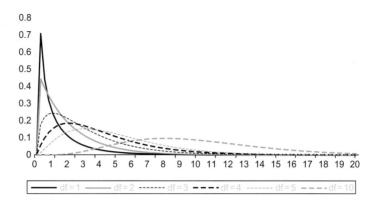

Figure 14.1 Examples of χ^2 distributions. A χ^2 distribution is the sampling distribution for a chi-squared test. Notice that all χ^2 distributions are positively skewed and that the peak of the distribution is further from zero as the number of degrees of freedom increases. Additionally, all χ^2 distributions have a minimum value of zero (as shown in the horizontal axis).

Choose a One-Tailed or a Two-Tailed Test. Step 4 of any NHST is to select a one-tailed or a two-tailed test. The sampling distribution for a chi-squared test is called the χ^2 distribution, and, as in the t-distribution and F-distribution, its shape changes as the number of degrees of freedom changes. This is shown in Figure 14.1, which displays six different χ^2 distributions. Regardless of their exact shape, all χ^2 distributions are positively skewed – this was also true of F-distributions. As a result, a one-tailed test (with the rejection region on the right side of the sampling distribution) is the only possible test to conduct for a chi-squared test.

Find the Critical Value. The fifth step in NHST is to find the critical value. Like all previous NHSTs, we can find the critical value via a table – in this case, the one in Appendix A6. This table is called the χ^2-table, and reading it is the same as reading Appendix A2 (which was the t-table). To find the appropriate chi-squared critical value, it is necessary to first calculate the degrees of freedom. For a one-variable chi-squared test, the formula for degrees of freedom is as follows:

$$df = (k - 1) \qquad\qquad \text{(Formula 14.1)}$$

where k is the number of groups. Therefore, in the *Titanic* example, the degrees of freedom are equal to 2 (because $k = 3$, and $3 - 1 = 2$).

Once df is known, the χ^2 critical value is the number in the cell that corresponds to the row for the correct degrees of freedom and the column for the chosen alpha level. In the *Titanic* example, df = 2, and $\alpha = .05$. Therefore, $\chi^2_{crit} = 5.991$.

Check Yourself!

- Why is it appropriate to use one of the other NHSTs when the variable consists of nominal-level data?

- What is the null hypothesis for a one-variable chi-squared test?

- Why is the chi-squared test always a one-tailed test?

- How do you find the degrees of freedom for a one-variable chi-squared test?

Find the Observed Value. This is step 6. After calculating the χ^2 critical value, it is necessary to calculate the χ^2 observed value. The formula for doing so is:

$$\chi^2_{obs} = \sum \left(\frac{(obs - exp)^2}{exp} \right) \qquad \text{(Formula 14.2)}$$

In Formula 14.2, *obs* refers to the observed count of sample members in a category, and *exp* refers to the theorized expected count of sample members in the same category. Formula 14.2 shows that there is a fraction created for each category in a one-variable chi-squared test, and that these fractions are then summed together.

In the *Titanic* example, there were 325 passengers in first class, 285 in second class, and 706 in third class. These numbers are the observed counts.[13] To find the expected counts, we must ascertain the theorized proportion of sample members who belong to each group. In this example, this proportion is one-third for each category. To find the expected count, we use Formula 14.3:

$$exp = proportion(n_{Total}) \qquad \text{(Formula 14.3)}$$

where n_{Total} is the entire sample size. In this example, $n_{Total} = 1,316$. Therefore, for all three groups, the expected count is:

$$exp = .33\overline{3}(1,316) = 438.667$$

This is the exact number of sample members we would expect to see in each group if the groups were the same size. If we retain the null hypothesis, the differences between the observed counts and the expected counts are small and not statistically significant; if we reject the null hypothesis, it indicates that the groups are not the same size (within sampling error).

With the expected and observed values known for all three groups, Formula 14.2 requires building a fraction for each group in the data. Each fraction consists of the $\frac{(obs - exp)^2}{exp}$ information from each group, and those fractions are then added together. For the *Titanic* example, the χ^2_{obs} equation is:

$$\chi^2_{obs} = \frac{(325 - 438.667)^2}{438.667} + \frac{(285 - 438.667)^2}{438.667} + \frac{(706 - 438.667)^2}{438.667}$$

$$\chi^2_{obs} = \frac{(-113.667)^2}{438.667} + \frac{(-153.667)^2}{438.667} + \frac{(267.333)^2}{438.667}$$

$$\chi^2_{obs} = \frac{12,920.111}{438.667} + \frac{23,613.444}{438.667} + \frac{71,467.111}{438.667}$$

$$\chi^2_{obs} = 29.453 + 53.830 + 162.919$$

$$\chi^2_{obs} = 246.202$$

In this example we had three fractions in the χ^2_{obs} formula because we had three groups. It is also worth noting that the expected counts (and, therefore, the denominators of the fractions in the χ^2_{obs}

---

[13] The *obs* in Formula 14.1 refers to the observed number of sample members in a category. This is different from the χ^2 observed value, which is the final result of Formula 14.2 and which we will compare with the χ^2 critical value in order to determine whether to reject or retain the null hypothesis. It is important that you don't confuse these two concepts – even though they both have the word "observed" in their names.

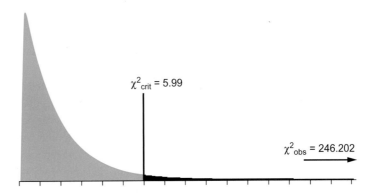

Figure 14.2 The χ^2 sampling distribution for the *Titanic* example, which tests the null hypothesis that the three groups of passengers (i.e., first class, second class, and third class) are equally sized. The χ^2_{crit} value, which is where the rejection region – shaded in black – begins is 5.991. The χ^2_{obs} value is equal to 246.202. Because the χ^2_{obs} value is inside the rejection region, the null hypothesis is rejected, and we should believe that the groups were different sizes.

formula) are all equal because we hypothesized that the groups would be the same size. If we had hypothesized groups that were of differing sizes, the expected counts would not be equal.

Compare the Observed Value and the Critical Value. This is step 7. Now that we know the χ^2_{crit} and χ^2_{obs} values, we can compare them in order to reject or retain the null hypothesis. Just as with the previous null hypothesis tests we have learned, if the observed value is more extreme than the critical value, the null hypothesis will be rejected (because the observed value will be inside the rejection region). Conversely, if the observed value is less extreme than the critical value, then the null hypothesis will be retained (because the observed value will be outside of the rejection region).

For the *Titanic* example, we can draw the χ^2 sampling distribution to determine whether the null hypothesis should be rejected. This is shown in Figure 14.2. The sampling distribution shows that the rejection region starts at the χ^2_{crit} value of 5.991 and includes all of the right tail beyond that value. The χ^2_{obs} value is 246.202, which is so extreme that it is beyond the range shown in Figure 14.2. This means that the observed value is inside the rejection region and that the null hypothesis should be rejected. Thus, we can dispense with the belief that the three groups of passengers on the *Titanic* were the same size. As a consequence, we cannot determine whether one group was more likely to survive the sinking than another group solely by comparing the number of survivors, because the different group sizes may influence the total number of survivors.

Rejecting the null hypothesis has two implications. First, the *p*-value for this example must be smaller than alpha, which was .05. (Indeed, the χ^2_{crit} value when $\alpha = .01$ is 9.210, indicating that p is also less than .01, because the null hypothesis would still be rejected when $\alpha = .01$.) The second implication of rejecting the null hypothesis is that we need to worry about Type I error. After all, it is possible that the *Titanic* passengers are an unusual sample that is not representative of the population of steamship passengers. Conversely, we do not need to worry about Type II error because it is only possible to make a Type II error when the null hypothesis is retained.

Sidebar 14.1 **The *p*-value is continuous**

Null hypothesis statistical significance testing (NHST) results in a dichotomous yes/no decision about whether the null hypothesis is a model that fits the data. One of the criticisms of NHST is that this yes/no decision does not fit the reality of *p*-values. This is because the *p*-value, which is a measure of how well (or poorly) the data fit the null hypothesis, is continuous. Therefore, there is no natural firm line where a *p*-value suddenly provides much stronger evidence of the incorrectness of the null hypothesis than a slightly larger *p*-value does. Therefore, it does not make sense to treat a *p*-value of .049 as somehow being a better result than a *p*-value of .051 or .060.

One memorable way of thinking about this concept was stated by Rosnow and Rosenthal (1989, p. 1277): "surely God loves the .06 [*p*-value] nearly as much as the .05." Less theologically, Gelman and Stern stated, "The difference between 'significant' and 'not significant' is not itself statistically significant" (2006, p. 328). What these authors mean is that it is illogical to treat results with a *p* = .05 as being far better than results with a *p* of slightly larger value. Both results produce evidence of the incorrectness of the null hypothesis, and for both sets of results this evidence is nearly equally strong. This fact becomes even more obvious when you remember that *p*-values are extremely sensitive to sample size, with larger samples resulting in smaller *p*-values, with all other study characteristics held constant (see Chapter 7). So, there is nothing much more special about a *p*-value of .05 than there is of a *p*-value of .06.

Unfortunately, many people – including published researchers – get hung up on the yes/no decision of null hypothesis testing, and they judge whether their study is successful or their results correct solely on whether *p* is smaller than .05. There are several major consequences to this illogical thinking. One consequence is the temptation for researchers to engage in "*p*-hacking," a questionable research practice in which researchers – sometimes unwittingly – tweak their study until their *p*-values dip below .05. (See Sidebar 8.1 for more discussion of questionable research practices.) This tweaking can make the results match the researcher's theory or beliefs, but these results are less stable and more difficult to replicate.

Another consequence of an overemphasis on dichotomous thinking is that studies that retain the null hypothesis are less likely to be published. As a result, we do not have full access to the research literature; what we do have access to is a nonrepresentative subset of the studies that have been conducted on a topic. This is called the "**file drawer problem**" (Rosenthal, 1979, p. 638; also called **publication bias**), referring to researchers' file drawers full of unpublished studies. As a result of the file drawer problem, scientific knowledge about a topic is distorted – sometimes severely (Bouter et al., 2016; see Vadillo, Hardwick, & Shanks, 2016, for a good example of the literature on a topic being severely distorted by publication bias). Some methodologists have discussed this problem for decades (e.g., Lane & Dunlap, 1978; Sterling, 1959), but only recently have rank-and-file social scientists realized the magnitude of the problem.

Why are studies that retain the null hypothesis less likely to get published? One reason is that many researchers do not write up their studies in which the null hypothesis is retained, or, if they do, they do not submit the studies to a journal. Even if the researcher sends the study to a journal, the journal's editor (who decides whether to publish the study) or the peer reviewers (who advise the editor) often believe that studies that retain the null are not interesting, important, or correct – and therefore should not be published. In other words, the people who determine whether a study is published are engaging in this illogical dichotomous thinking about *p*-values and null hypothesis testing.[14]

---

[14] This discussion of the file drawer problem is not theoretical. While I was writing this textbook, I performed a study in which the null hypothesis was retained. The editor at one journal rejected the study without even sending it to peer reviewers because the main *p*-value was too large, and I retained the null hypothesis. Another journal I sent it to rejected the study because the editor and peer reviewers thought that a study that retains the null hypothesis couldn't be very important. Even after I informed the latter journal that their behavior contributes to the file drawer problem, the editor said in an email, "I don't expect that there will be much change at [the journal] for a while." Thus, the file drawer problem continues – at least in psychology. (The study was later published as Warne & Liu, 2017.)

A final negative result of improper dichotomous thinking is that some scientists have decided that the NHSTs are fatally flawed or should be banned completely (e.g., Cumming, 2014; Kline, 2013; Trafimow, 2014; Trafimow & Marks, 2015). While abuses and misinterpretations of NHSTs and *p-values* abound (see Sidebar 10.3), I believe that NHSTs are valuable. They are excellent tools, for example, in comparing statistical models to one another and making dichotomous decisions (e.g., "Is a new therapy more effective than the alternative therapy?"). In my view, the problem is not NHSTs themselves – but incorrect thinking about NHST results (especially *p-values*). Much of this incorrect thinking can be traced to an obsession with the dichotomous results that a null hypothesis provides (Abelson, 1997a).

Here are my tips for avoiding illogical, dichotomous thinking about null hypothesis tests. I have included references to other sections of this textbook so that you can learn more about each point.

- Remember that *p-values* are very susceptible to the influence of sample size. If a study has a very large sample size, a small *p-value* may merely indicate that the sample size is large. Having a large sample size is a finding that is usually not very interesting (Thompson, 1992). For more details, see Chapter 7.
- Do not confuse "statistical significance" with "importance." The former merely indicates that the null hypothesis was rejected – which may or may not have anything to do with the latter. See Chapter 8, including Sidebar 8.3.
- When interpreting results, give more emphasis to effect sizes than to *p-values* or the reject/retain decision for the null hypothesis. Effect sizes are not sensitive to sample size, and they do a better job at answering the important questions (e.g., "What is the strength of the relationship between variables?") than NHSTs do. See Chapter 7.
- Pay more attention to studies that have high statistical power. In Sidebar 10.1 we learned that statistical power is the ability of a study to reject a false null hypothesis. Studies with low statistical power tend to produce unstable results, even if their *p-values* are very low.
- When available, interpret confidence intervals because they provide information unavailable in NHSTs. Confidence intervals state the precision of a statistic, and a narrow confidence interval indicates that there is a narrow range of plausible values for a population parameter, which is a good thing. Wide confidence intervals indicate a large degree of uncertainty of the value of a parameter. See Chapter 8.
- Periodically review the correct interpretation of a *p-value* and guard vigilantly against the incorrect interpretations of *p* in Sidebar 10.3.
- Interpret effect sizes in the context of the real world and of other studies. This means avoiding firm rules about the numerical value that an effect size must have to be "strong" or "large," such as Cohen's benchmarks (see Sidebar 11.4). As Thompson (2001, pp. 82–83) stated, "if people interpreted effect sizes [using Cohen's benchmarks] with the same rigidity that $\alpha = .05$ has been used in statistical testing, we would merely be being stupid in another metric." Instead, consider whether the size of the effect is large enough to affect people's daily lives or is consistent with past studies.

Following these guidelines will make you a smart, mature consumer of research. And if you ever conduct your own research studies, these guidelines will also help you avoid common pitfalls when interpreting NHSTs. They will also help show a thoughtful understanding of statistical results.

Calculate an Effect Size. Finally, in step 8, we can calculate an effect size to quantify the degree to which a group deviates from the theorized proportion in the one-variable chi-squared test. This effect size is called an odds ratio (OR) and is calculated as:

$$\text{OR} = \frac{obs}{exp} \qquad \text{(Formula 14.4)}$$

Each group gets its own effect size, and the effect size is calculated from the group's observed count (abbreviated *obs* in Formula 14.4) and expected count (abbreviated *exp*).

In the *Titanic* data, the first-class passengers' effect size would be calculated as:

$$OR = \frac{325}{438.667} = 0.741$$

This value indicates that there were 0.741 times as many first-class passengers as we would expect if they were exactly one-third of the passengers on the *Titanic*. For second-class passengers, the odds ratio is:

$$OR = \frac{285}{438.667} = 0.650$$

meaning that there were 0.650 times as many passengers in second class as we would expect if all the groups were the same size. Finally, for third-class passengers, the odds ratio is:

$$OR = \frac{706}{438.667} = 1.609$$

which indicates that this group was 1.609 times larger than would be expected if all the passenger groups were equally sized.

When the odds ratio is exactly equal to 1.0, the expected and observed values are precisely the same, and the group is as large as hypothesized. When all groups' odds ratios are exactly 1.0, the null hypothesis is a perfect statistical model for the data. When the odds ratio for a group is less than 1.0, the group is smaller than hypothesized (as occurred with the first-class and second-class passengers on the *Titanic*). However, if the odds ratio for a group is greater than 1.0, the group is larger than hypothesized (as was true for the third-class passengers on the *Titanic*).

Check Yourself!

- In the χ^2_{obs} equation, how do you know how many fractions you will need to create to use the formula?

- How do you know whether to reject or retain the null hypothesis in a one-variable chi-squared test?

- What does it mean when the odds ratio in a one-variable chi-squared test is greater than 1.0?

- What does it mean when the odds ratio in a one-variable chi-squared test is less than 1.0?

Guided Practice 14.1

In a student satisfaction study a university drew a sample of 520 students that consisted of 140 freshmen, 133 sophomores, 129 juniors, and 118 seniors. Because some students drop out of college, the university student body as a whole is 30% freshmen, 26% juniors, 24% juniors, and 20% seniors. The study creators are interested in having a representative sample of students in their sample. This Guided Practice example will show how to conduct a one-variable chi-squared test to determine whether the sample is representative of the population.

Step 1: Form Groups

The groups in this example are formed by the nominal variable. In this case, the groups are freshmen, sophomores, juniors, and seniors.

Step 2: Define the Null Hypothesis

The null hypothesis is that each group has the same proportion in the sample as it does in the population. Another way of stating this is that the proportion of freshmen in the sample will be .30, the proportion of sophomores in the sample will be .26, the proportion of juniors in the sample will be .24, and the proportion of seniors in the sample will be .20.

Step 3: Set Alpha

The default alpha in any NHST is .05. We do not have a good reason to change alpha for this example, so we will keep it at that value.

Step 4: Choose a One- or a Two-Tailed Test

Figure 14.1 shows that the chi-squared sampling distribution is always positively skewed. This means we will always conduct a one-tailed test and put the rejection region on the right side of the sampling distribution.

Step 5: Find the Critical Value

Finding the critical value first requires calculating the degrees of freedom in the data. According to Formula 14.1, $df = (k - 1)$, where k is the number of groups in the data. In this example, $k = 4$. As a result, there must be three degrees of freedom in the data (because $4 - 1 = 3$).

After calculating the degrees of freedom, we can use Appendix A6 to find the χ^2_{crit} value. The column labeled $\alpha = .05$ and the row labeled 3 degrees of freedom intersect at a cell that contains the number 7.815. This is the χ^2_{crit} value.

Step 6: Calculate the Observed Value

Before calculating the χ^2_{obs} value, we must find the expected count for each group using Formula 14.3, which is $exp = \text{proportion}(n_{Total})$. For freshmen, this value would be:

$$.30(520) = 156$$

The expected count for sophomores is:

$$.26(520) = 135.2$$

And for juniors:

$$.24(520) = 124.8$$

Finally, for seniors the expected count is:

$$.20(520) = 104$$

We can use these values to create the χ^2_{obs} value, using Formula 14.2:

$$\chi^2_{obs} = \frac{(140-156)^2}{156} + \frac{(133-135.2)^2}{135.2} + \frac{(129-124.8)^2}{124.8} + \frac{(118-104)^2}{104}$$

$$\chi^2_{obs} = \frac{(-16)^2}{156} + \frac{(-2.2)^2}{135.2} + \frac{(4.2)^2}{124.8} + \frac{(14)^2}{104}$$

$$\chi^2_{obs} = \frac{256}{156} + \frac{4.84}{135.2} + \frac{17.64}{124.8} + \frac{196}{104}$$

$$\chi^2_{obs} = 1.641 + 0.036 + 0.141 + 1.885$$

$$\chi^2_{obs} = 3.703$$

Notice that there were four fractions in this χ^2_{obs} value because there were four groups in the data.

Step 7: Compare the Observed and Critical Values

We can now compare the χ^2_{obs} and χ^2_{crit} values in order to determine whether to reject or retain the null hypothesis. Remember that $\chi^2_{crit} = 7.815$ and $\chi^2_{obs} = 3.703$. Graphing these on the sampling distribution produces Figure 14.3. According to the figure, the χ^2_{obs} value is outside the rejection region because it is less extreme than the χ^2_{crit} value. Therefore, we should retain the null hypothesis in this example. As a result, we can conclude that the sample does not differ from the proportions of each group in the university population. This means that the sample is likely representative of the population (which is a good thing). Because the null hypothesis was retained when $\alpha = .05$, we know that $p > .05$. Additionally, we must worry about Type II error.

Step 8: Calculate an Effect Size

In a one-variable chi-squared test, there should be one effect size for each group. The effect size for this situation is an odds ratio, and it is calculated via Formula 14.4, which is $OR = \frac{obs}{exp}$. Using the observed and expected counts for each groups, the effect sizes are:

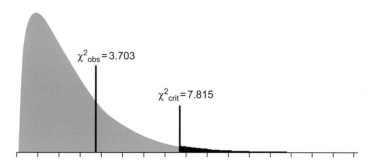

Figure 14.3 The χ^2 distribution for the example data of university students. In this dataset, χ^2_{crit} = 7.815 and χ^2_{obs} = 3.703, meaning that the null hypothesis should be retained.

$$OR_{fresh} = \frac{140}{156} = 0.897 \quad OR_{soph} = \frac{133}{135.2} = 0.984 \quad OR_{jun} = \frac{129}{124.8} = 1.034 \quad OR_{sen} = \frac{118}{104} = 1.135$$

These odds ratios show that there are slightly fewer freshmen and sophomores in the sample than what we would expect if the sample were perfectly representative of the university population (as indicated by the odds ratio value less than 1.0). Likewise, the numbers of juniors and seniors in the sample are slightly greater than what we would expect from a perfectly representative sample, as is shown by the odds ratio values greater than 1.0. However, retaining the null hypothesis shows that these differences are not large enough to be statistically significant, which makes sense because these odds ratios are all very close to 1.0.

General Linear Moment 14.1

The one-variable chi-squared test is another member of the general linear model (GLM), which is why conducting it requires following the same eight steps as the other statistical tests we have learned about so far. Indeed, it most closely resembles the one-sample t-test (see Chapter 8). In both of these tests, a sample's statistic is compared to a theorized population parameter or a chosen score threshold. In the one-sample t-test, the sample statistic was the sample mean and the other value was either the population parameter (when H_0: $\overline{X} = \mu$) or an arbitrarily chosen score (when H_0: $\overline{X} = a$, where a is some number). In Chapter 8 we saw examples of both types of one-sample t-tests.

In a one-variable chi-squared test we cannot find sample or population means because the variable is not interval- or ratio-level data. But we can compare counts and proportions because both of these can be calculated with nominal-level data. Therefore, in a one-variable chi-squared test, we compare the proportions of the group members either to a theorized proportion – as we did in the *Titanic* example – or to the population proportion (as we would do if the population proportion for each group were known). This shows that *a one-variable chi-squared test is just a one-sample t-test applied to nominal data.*

Two-Variable Chi-Squared Test

Although the one-variable chi-squared test is valuable, it is not the most common statistical test using proportion and count data. A much more common procedure is to examine two nominal variables to determine whether a relationship exists between them. This is called the **two-variable chi-squared test**. This portion of the chapter will demonstrate how to conduct a two-variable test.

Sidebar 14.2 **Terminology**

The name two-variable chi-squared test is often shortened to **chi-squared test** because it is much more common than the one-variable chi-squared test. However, as you explore the published research in the social sciences, it is important that you recognize that the term "chi-squared test" can refer to either the one-variable chi-squared test or the two-variable chi-squared test. Additionally, there are other, more complex statistical procedures that use the chi-squared sampling distribution in order to reject or retain the null hypothesis. This group of statistical tests – which includes the one- and two-variable chi-squared tests – are sometimes just called "chi-squared tests" for convenience. As if that weren't confusing enough, the spelling "chi-square" (without the d) is very common.

As an example for this section of the chapter, we will return to the *Titanic* data. Table 14.2 shows the fate of the 1,316 passengers on the *Titanic*: 498 passengers survived, and 818 passengers perished. This is an example of a **contingency table**, which displays all possible combinations of the independent and dependent variables and the number of sample members who have each combination of variable values. In the contingency table, we have two variables: the type of ticket the person purchased (i.e., first-, second-, or third-class) and voyage outcome (i.e., whether the person survived or perished). The purpose of this two-variable chi-squared test is to determine whether there is a relationship between these two nominal variables. If there is a relationship between the two variables, it would indicate that some types of passengers were more likely to survive than others. If we retain the null hypothesis and find that there is no relationship between variables, it would indicate that first-, second-, and third-class passengers were equally likely to survive the *Titanic*.

Because a two-variable chi-squared test is another NHST and another member of the GLM, there are eight steps to conducting a null hypothesis test. These eight steps are the same steps that we have seen for every NHST so far in this textbook.

Form Groups in the Data. This is step 1. Just as with nearly every NHST we have discussed so far, the groups in the data are formed by the independent variable values. In the *Titanic* example, the independent variable is the passenger group that a person belonged to, and the dependent variable is the voyage outcome. Therefore, in this example we have three groups in the independent variable: first-class passengers, second-class passengers, and third-class passengers.

Define the Null Hypothesis. This is step 2. In a two-variable chi-squared test, the null hypothesis is that the two variables are unrelated to one another. Again, there is no convenient way to express this mathematically, meaning we express it as words. For a two-variable chi-squared test, we would say that the null hypothesis is that the independent variable and the dependent variable are unrelated.

Set Alpha. This is step 3. As in all NHSTs, alpha in a two-variable chi-squared test is the size of the rejection region in the sampling distribution. The default alpha value for any NHST is

Table 14.1 Contingency table showing the observed counts of *Titanic* passengers, categorized by group and voyage outcome

Passenger group	Survived	Perished	Total
First class	202	123	325
Second class	118	167	285
Third class	178	528	706
Total	498	818	1,316

.05, though there are reasons to change alpha. For the *Titanic* example data, we may decide that the folk belief that first-class passengers were more likely to survive is so ingrained that we should be skeptical, which would mean lowering alpha to .01.

Choose a One-Tailed or a Two-Tailed Test. This is step 4. We saw in Figure 14.1 that the chi-squared sampling distribution is always positively skewed. As a result, the one-variable chi-squared test always uses a one-tailed test. The two-variable chi-squared test also uses the positively skewed chi-squared sampling distribution, which means that its test is always one-tailed.

Find the Critical Value. The fifth step in conducting a two-variable chi-squared test is to find the critical value. Earlier in this chapter I introduced Appendix A6, and this same χ^2-table is also used to find the critical value for a two-variable chi-squared test. Again, this requires finding the row for the correct degrees of freedom and then finding the column with the correct alpha value. The cell where the appropriate row and the correct column intersect contains the χ^2 critical value.

However, a two-variable chi-squared test has a different formula for degrees of freedom:

$$df = (n_{rows} - 1)(n_{columns} - 1) \qquad \text{(Formula 14.5)}$$

The term n_{rows} refers to the number of rows in the contingency table, whereas $n_{columns}$ refers to the number of columns in the contingency table. It is important to note that when counting rows and columns, you should *not* count the column or row labeled "Total." For the *Titanic* data in Table 14.1, there are three rows for the independent variable (i.e., first class, second class, and third class) and two columns in the dependent variable (i.e., survived and perished). Therefore, the number of degrees of freedom is:

$$df = (3 - 1)(2 - 1)$$
$$df = (2)(1)$$
$$df = 2$$

Knowing that there are 2 degrees of freedom and that $\alpha = .01$, we can see that the χ^2 critical value is 9.210.

Find the Observed Value. This is step 6. The same equation (Formula 14.2) provides the chi-squared observed value for both the one-variable and two-variable chi-squared tests. Again, the equation creates a series of fractions. For a two-variable chi-squared test, the number of fractions will be equal to the number of cells in the contingency table (not counting the cells in the "Total" row or columns). Creating these fractions requires identifying the observed count and expected count for each cell. Just as for a one-variable chi-squared test, the observed count is equal to the number of sample members who appeared in each cell.

Calculating Expected Counts for Cells

Step 1: Find the
proportion of sample
members who belong
to the "first-class" category

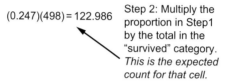

Passenger Group	Survived	Perished	Total	
First Class:	202	123	325	$\dfrac{325}{1,316} = 0.247$
Second Class:	118	167	285	
Third Class:	178	528	706	
Total:	498	818	1,316	

$(0.247)(498) = 122.986$

Step 2: Multiply the
proportion in Step1
by the total in the
"survived" category.
*This is the expected
count for that cell.*

Figure 14.4 The two-step process for calculating expected counts in cells for a two-variable chi-squared test. For the top-left cell, the expected count is $\left(\frac{325}{1,316}\right)(498) = (.247)(498) = 122.986$. Alternatively, it is possible to find the proportion of the individuals in the cell's column and multiplying it by the total number of individuals in the row (see Sidebar 14.3). This would be $\left(\frac{498}{1,316}\right)(325) = (.378)(325) = 122.986$.

Finding the expected count for a cell is slightly more complex. It requires calculating the proportion of sample members who belong to one of the cell's categories and multiplying it by the total number of sample members who belong to the cell's other category. Figure 14.4 shows an example of this for the top-left cell of the contingency table (i.e., first-class survivors). The proportion of individuals who belong to the first-class category is $\frac{325}{1,316} = .247$. This number should be multiplied by the total for the column that the cell belongs in, which is 498 in this example: $(.247)(498) = 122.986$. This is the expected count for the top-left cell of first-class survivors.

Finding the expected count for the top-right cell (i.e., first-class passengers who perished) is similar:

$$\left(\frac{325}{1,316}\right)(818) = (.247)(818) = 202.014$$

The expected count for the cell representing second-class passengers who survived is:

$$\left(\frac{285}{1,316}\right)(498) = (.217)(498) = 107.850$$

For the cell representing the second-class passengers who perished, the expected count is:

$$\left(\frac{285}{1,316}\right)(818) = (.217)(818) = 177.150$$

The bottom-left cell (for third-class passengers who survived) has an expected count of:

$$\left(\frac{706}{1,316}\right)(498) = (.536)(498) = 267.164$$

Table 14.2 Observed and expected counts of *Titanic* passengers, categorized by group and voyage outcome

Passenger group	Survived	Perished	Total
First class	202 (122.986)	123 (202.014)	325
Second class	118 (107.850)	167 (177.150)	285
Third class	178 (267.164)	528 (438.836)	706
Total	498	818	1,316

Note. Observed counts are outside parentheses. Expected counts are inside parentheses.

Finally, the bottom-right cell, which represents third-class passengers who perished, has an expected count of:

$$\left(\frac{706}{1,316}\right)(818) = (.536)(818) = 438.836$$

Table 14.2 shows the contingency table with both the observed counts and the expected counts in each cell. These expected counts represent the number of individuals who would be in each cell if the null hypothesis were perfectly true. In other words, if there were no relationship between the independent and dependent variables, the number of sample members in each cell would be precisely equal to the expected counts.

Sidebar 14.3 Three methods of calculating expected counts

There are three possible methods of calculating expected counts. Figure 14.4 shows one method: to calculate the proportion of row members who are in the sample and multiply it by the total in the cell's column. The second method is to do the reverse: for a given cell, find the proportion of sample members who belong to the column and multiply the proportion by the total in the cell's row. For the top-left cell in Table 14.1, this is $\left(\frac{498}{1,316}\right)(325) = (.378)(325) = 122.986$.

The third method relies on the fact that all of the expected counts in a row or column will sum to that row or column's total. For example, the top row of expected counts in Table 14.2 is 122.986 + 202.014 = 325, which is the exact number of first-class passengers on the *Titanic*. Likewise, the expected counts in the left column sum to 122.986 + 107.850 + 267.164 = 498, which is the number of passengers who survived the shipwreck. Therefore, the expected count for the final cell in a row or column can be found by subtracting all other expected counts from that row or column's total. For the top-right cell in Table 14.2, after finding the top-left cell's expected count (which was 122.986), we can subtract that expected count from the row's total (which was 325). This produces 325 − 122.986 = 202.014, which is equal to the expected value calculated via the first method (see the text above).

It does not matter which of the three methods is used to find expected counts because they all produce the same results. Although I have a preferred method, I sometimes like to check my results by using a different procedure.

After finding the expected counts for each cell, we can plug these expected counts and the observed counts into Formula 14.2:

$$\chi^2_{obs} = \frac{(202 - 122.986)^2}{122.986} + \frac{(123 - 202.014)^2}{202.014} + \frac{(118 - 107.850)^2}{107.850} + \frac{(167 - 177.150)^2}{177.150}$$

$$+ \frac{(178 - 267.164)^2}{267.164} + \frac{(528 - 438.836)^2}{438.836}$$

$$\chi^2_{obs} = \frac{(79.014)^2}{122.986} + \frac{(-79.014)^2}{202.014} + \frac{(10.150)^2}{107.850} + \frac{(-10.150)^2}{177.150} + \frac{(-89.164)^2}{267.164} + \frac{(89.164)^2}{438.836}$$

$$\chi^2_{obs} = \frac{6,243.161}{122.986} + \frac{6,243.161}{202.014} + \frac{103.032}{107.850} + \frac{103.032}{177.150} + \frac{7,950.243}{267.164} + \frac{7,950.243}{438.836}$$

$$\chi^2_{obs} = 50.763 + 30.905 + 0.955 + 0.582 + 29.758 + 18.117$$

$$\chi^2_{obs} = 131.079$$

Check Yourself!

- How is a one-variable chi-squared test related to a one-sample t-test?

- What is the null hypothesis for a two-variable chi-squared test?

- How do we find the degrees of freedom value for a two-variable chi-squared test?

- What is the method for calculating the expected count for a cell?

Compare the Observed Value and the Critical Value. This is step 7. Now that we know the chi-squared critical and chi-squared observed values, we can compare them on the sampling distribution. With a χ^2 critical value of 9.210 and a χ^2 observed value of 131.080, the null hypothesis should be rejected because the observed value is more extreme than the critical value (where the rejection region starts). This is shown in Figure 14.5, which indicates that the χ^2_{obs} is inside the

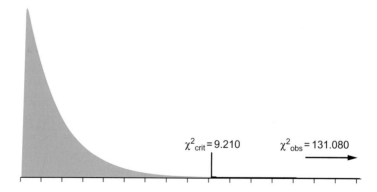

Figure 14.5 The χ^2 sampling distribution for the *Titanic* example, which tests the null hypothesis that a passenger's group (i.e., first class, second class, and third class) is unrelated to individuals' voyage outcome. The χ^2_{crit} value, which is where the rejection region – shaded in black – begins is 9.210. The χ^2_{obs} value is equal to 131.080. Because the χ^2_{obs} value is inside the rejection region, the null hypothesis is rejected, and we should believe that some groups were more likely to survive the sinking than others.

rejection region. Thus, we can ascertain that there is a relationship between a passenger's ticket type and whether they survived or perished in the sinking of the *Titanic*.

General Linear Moment 14.2

General Linear Moment 14.1 showed how the chi-squared test is basically a one-sample *t*-test for nominal-level dependent variables. Another way in which the chi-squared test is related to other members of the GLM is through the shape of sampling distributions. In Chapter 6 we learned that because of the central limit theorem, we can expect a sampling distribution of sample means to be normally distributed. This normal distribution is used in the *z*-test (where it is called a *z*-distribution), and when $\alpha = .05$, the *z*-critical values in a two-tailed test are ± 1.96. When $\alpha = .01$, the *z*-critical values in a two-tailed test are ± 2.58. The chi-squared distribution, though, is the theoretical sampling distribution for an infinite number of samples' variances. Calculating variances requires squaring the deviation scores (see Formula 4.11), and this results in a non-symmetrical, positively skewed distribution, as shown in Figure 14.1. What does all this mean for the GLM? When df = 1, the χ^2-critical value for $\alpha = .05$ is 3.841, and the χ^2-critical value for $\alpha = .01$ is 6.635. These values are the same within rounding error as the squared critical values for the *z*-test:

$$\sqrt{3.841} = 1.96$$
$$\sqrt{6.635} = 2.58$$

The *F*-distribution (which is the sampling distribution for an ANOVA; see Chapter 11) is also related to the chi-squared distribution. This is because the *F*-distribution is a distribution of ratios between two variances (see the explanation accompanying Appendix A3), which is $F = \frac{\sigma^2_{Between}}{\sigma^2_{Within}}$. Because each variance will have a chi-squared distribution, the *F*-distribution must be a ratio of two chi-squared distributions.

Thus, the chi-squared distribution is built around the central limit theorem – just as the *z*- and *t*-distributions are, except now this sampling distribution is a theoretical distribution of sample variances. This squaring is also why χ^2 values can never be negative (because squaring gets rid of any negative values) and why χ^2 tests are always one-tailed. This explanation of how the distribution shapes relate to one another is also just one more way that the members of the GLM are all interrelated.

Calculate an Effect Size. The eighth and final step in conducting a two-variable chi-squared test is to calculate an effect size, which in this case is an odds ratio. Calculating an odds ratio in a two-variable chi-squared test is more complex than it was for a one-variable chi-squared test, and it requires making some decisions. First, it is necessary to choose a baseline independent variable group. The **baseline group** will serve as the group that the other groups of sample members (formed by the categories in the independent variable) will be compared to. These other groups are called non-baseline groups. It is also necessary to choose an **outcome of interest** and a **baseline outcome**. The outcome of interest is the outcome that we are most concerned about as we investigate the differences in the dependent variable across groups. The baseline outcome is the other outcome (which we are sometimes less interested in). Once these groups and outcomes have been chosen, the equation for calculating an odds ratio is:

$$OR = \frac{(obs_{BB})(obs_{NB})}{(obs_{BI})(obs_{NI})} \qquad \text{(Formula 14.6)}$$

With one non-baseline group, one baseline group, one outcome of interest, and one baseline outcome, there are four possible combinations of groups and outcomes. These will correspond to four cells in the table used to conduct the two-variable chi-squared test. In Formula 14.6,

- obs_{BB} refers to the observed count in the cell for the baseline group and the baseline outcome;
- obs_{BI} is the observed count for the cell that corresponds to the baseline group and the outcome of interest;
- obs_{NI} refers to the observed count in the cell that corresponds to the non-baseline group and outcome of interest;
- obs_{NB} is the observed count in the cell for the non-reference group and the baseline outcome.

Another way of thinking about calculating an odds ratio is to collapse the contingency table into a smaller table with two rows and two columns:

	Baseline outcome	Outcome of interest
Baseline group:	a	b
Non-baseline group:	c	d

In this smaller contingency table, the letters a–d are observed counts for each combination of outcomes and groups. With this notation, Formula 14.6 is expressed as:

$$OR = \frac{ad}{bc}$$

In the *Titanic* data, I may decide that I am interested in learning how much more likely first-class passengers were to survive the sinking than third-class passengers. In this case, the baseline group is third-class passengers because I am comparing another group to their outcomes. This means that first-class passengers are the non-baseline group. The outcome of interest is surviving the sinking, which makes the baseline outcome perishing in the sinking. According to Table 14.1, there were:

- 528 third-class passengers that died in the sinking (obs_{BB}, or a)
- 202 first-class passengers that survived (obs_{NI}, or d)
- 178 third-class passengers that survived (obs_{BI}, or b)
- 123 first-class passengers that perished (obs_{NB}, or c).

Plugging these numbers into Formula 14.6 produces:

$$OR = \frac{(528)(202)}{(178)(123)}$$

$$OR = \frac{106,656}{21,894}$$

$$OR = 4.871$$

When the odds ratio is equal to 1, the outcome of interest is equally likely for both groups. When an odds ratio is greater than 1, the outcome is more likely for the non-baseline group. As a result, we can interpret an odds ratio of 4.871 as indicating that first-class passengers were 4.871 times more likely to survive than third-class passengers.

On the other hand, an odds ratio less than 1 indicates that the outcome of interest is more likely for the baseline group. We can see this in an odds ratio when we switch the baseline and non-baseline groups:

$$OR = \frac{(123)(178)}{(202)(528)}$$

$$OR = \frac{21,894}{106,656}$$

$$OR = 0.205$$

This indicates that first-class passengers were 0.205 times as likely to perish. This number is the reciprocal of the first odds ratio we calculated (1 / 4.871 = 0.205).

Guided Practice 14.2

Another common belief about the *Titanic* sinking is that there was a policy of putting "women and children first" into the lifeboats. Just as we could test whether first-class passengers were more likely to survive the sinking, we can also test whether women and children were more likely to survive the *Titanic* than men were. The numbers of individuals from each group who survived or died is listed in Table 14.3.

Step 1: Form Groups

The independent variable in this example is the passenger group that people belonged to (i.e., whether they were men, women, or children).

Step 2: Define the Null Hypothesis

The null hypothesis in a two-variable chi-squared test is that the independent variable and dependent variables are unrelated. With this *Titanic* example, the null hypothesis would indicate

Table 14.3 Contingency table containing observed counts of *Titanic* passengers, categorized by group and voyage outcome

Passenger group	Survived	Perished	Total
Men	146	659	805
Women	296	106	402
Children	56	53	109
Total	498	818	1,316

that whether a passenger was a man, woman, or child had no relationship to whether they survived the sinking or not.

Step 3: Set Alpha

The default α value in a two-variable chi-squared test is .05. Because the belief in "women and children first" on the Titanic is so prominent and the sample size is very large, we would be justified in lowering the alpha value to .01.

Step 4: Choose a One- or a Two-Tailed Test

You may remember from earlier in the chapter that the chi-squared sampling distribution is always positively skewed (see Figure 14.1), which means that we will always conduct a one-tailed test with the rejection region on the right side of the χ^2 sampling distribution.

Step 5: Find the Critical Value

We must use Appendix A6 to find the χ^2_{crit} value. This value will be in the cell where the row for the degrees of freedom and the column for the α value meet. According to Formula 14.5, the degrees of freedom is calculated as: df $= (n_{rows} - 1)(n_{columns} - 1)$. For this example, $n_{rows} = 3$ and $n_{columns} = 2$. Therefore,

$$\text{df} = (3 - 1)(2 - 1)$$
$$\text{df} = (2)(1)$$
$$\text{df} = 2$$

This is the exact same df value as in the last *Titanic* example because the contingency table has the same number of rows and columns. Appendix A6 indicates that when $\alpha = .01$ and df $= 2$, the χ^2_{crit} value is 9.210.

Step 6: Calculate the Observed Value

Before we can find the χ^2_{obs} value, we must first calculate the expected count for each of the cells in Table 14.3. Using the process shown in Figure 14.4, we can find the values of these expected counts. For the top-left cell in Table 14.3, the expected count is:

$$exp = \left(\frac{805}{1,316}\right)(498) = 304.628$$

For the top-right cell, the expected count is:

$$exp = \left(\frac{805}{1,316}\right)(818) = 500.372$$

For the left cell in the second row, we can calculate the expected count:

$$exp = \left(\frac{402}{1,316}\right)(498) = 152.125$$

The right cell in the second row has an expected count of:

$$exp = \left(\frac{402}{1,316}\right)(818) = 249.875$$

The expected count for the left cell in the bottom row is:

$$exp = \left(\frac{109}{1,316}\right)(498) = 41.248$$

Finally, the expected count for the bottom right cell is:

$$exp = \left(\frac{109}{1,316}\right)(818) = 67.752$$

We can now put the expected counts in the table next to the observed counts in each cell.

Table 14.4 Contingency table with observed and expected counts of *Titanic* passengers, categorized by group and voyage outcome

Passenger group	Survived	Perished	Total
Men	146 (304.628)	659 (500.372)	805
Women	296 (152.125)	106 (249.875)	402
Children	56 (41.248)	53 (67.752)	109
Total	498	818	1,316

Note. Observed counts are outside parentheses. Expected counts are inside parentheses.

These values can then be put into Formula 14.2 to calculate the χ^2_{obs} value:

$$\chi^2_{obs} = \frac{(146 - 304.628)^2}{304.628} + \frac{(659 - 500.372)^2}{500.372} + \frac{(296 - 152.125)^2}{152.125} + \frac{(106 - 249.875)^2}{249.875}$$
$$+ \frac{(56 - 41.248)^2}{41.248} + \frac{(53 - 67.752)^2}{67.752}$$

$$\chi^2_{obs} = \frac{(-158.628)^2}{304.628} + \frac{(158.628)^2}{500.372} + \frac{(143.875)^2}{152.125} + \frac{(-143.875)^2}{249.875} + \frac{(14.752)^2}{41.248} + \frac{(-14.752)^2}{67.752}$$

$$\chi^2_{obs} = \frac{25,162.734}{304.628} + \frac{25,162.734}{500.372} + \frac{20,700.125}{152.125} + \frac{20,700.125}{249.875} + \frac{217.630}{41.248} + \frac{217.630}{67.752}$$

$$\chi^2_{obs} = 82.602 + 50.288 + 136.073 + 82.842 + 5.276 + 3.212$$

$$\chi^2_{obs} = 360.293$$

Step 7: Compare the Observed and Critical Values

In this example, $\chi^2_{crit} = 9.210$ and $\chi^2_{obs} = 360.293$. Figure 14.6 shows the location of these two values on the chi-squared sampling distribution. The rejection region starts at the χ^2_{crit} value, which means that the χ^2_{obs} value is inside the rejection region. As a result, we should reject the null hypothesis. Therefore, the passenger groups were *not* equally likely to survive the sinking of the *Titanic*. Because we rejected the null hypothesis when $\alpha = .01$, we know that $p < .01$. Additionally, we should still be aware of the possibility of Type I error, even though the null hypothesis was strongly rejected.

Step 8: Calculate an Effect Size

Because we have more than two passenger groups, we have a few options of how to calculate an odds ratio. One option is to eliminate a group and to calculate the odds ratio with Formula 14.6 for the remaining two groups. This is what we will do for this example by using women as the baseline group and survival as the outcome of interest. With men as the non-baseline group (and eliminating the children from the data for now), the odds ratio is:

$$OR = \frac{(146)(106)}{(296)(659)}$$

$$OR = \frac{15,476}{195,064}$$

$$OR = 0.079$$

This indicates that men were 0.079 times as likely to survive the sinking of the *Titanic* as women were. Because this value is so much lower than 1.0, it indicates that men were *much* less likely to survive than women.

We can also calculate an effect size stating the likelihood that children would survive compared to women (with men eliminated from the calculation):

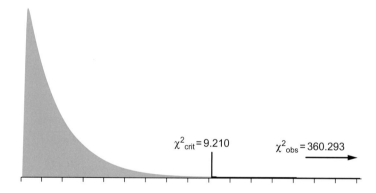

Figure 14.6 A χ^2 sampling distribution showing the critical and observed values for the second *Titanic* example. The $\chi^2_{crit} = 9.210$, which is where the rejection region begins. The χ^2_{obs} value of 360.293 is so extreme that it cannot be shown on the figure. This observed value is inside the rejection region, indicating that we should reject the null hypothesis.

$$OR = \frac{(106)(56)}{(296)(53)}$$

$$OR = \frac{5,936}{15,688}$$

$$OR = 0.378$$

With this odds ratio, it is clear that children were less likely to survive than women (again, because the odds ratio is less than 1.0). By comparing the odds ratios, we can see that the most likely group to survive the *Titanic* was women, followed by children and then men. Therefore, we can conclude that it really was "women and children first" on the *Titanic*.

Information About Odds Ratios

Odds ratios are very different from the other effect sizes we have encountered before. In addition to the formula for calculating an odds ratio, it is important to understand other aspects of the odds ratio: the interpretation, being aware of the groups, how to calculate odds ratios for multiple groups, and a relationship with a statistic called relative risk. This section of the chapter will explore each of these issues.

Interpretation. What does an odds ratio *mean*? Some students don't realize that they have heard examples of the odds ratio before. This is usually in the context of sports match-ups. For example, if in a soccer game, Team A has 2-to-1 odds of beating Team B, it indicates that Team A is twice as likely to win the game as Team B is. This is an odds ratio of 2.0 favoring Team A. (The reciprocal of this is 1 / 2 = 0.5, an odds ratio indicating that Team B is half as likely to win as Team A.) In the example data, where the odds ratio was 4.871, this indicates that if we were to take a first-class passenger and a third-class passenger from the *Titanic* knowing that only one would survive, the odds would be 4.871-to-1 that the first-class passenger would survive.

Another way of thinking about the odds ratio is to imagine the 2-to-1 soccer match-up where the two teams would play each other three times. Team A would be expected to win twice, and Team B would be expected to win once. This would indicate a 66.7% probability that Team A would win any given game (2 / 3 = .667, or 66.7%), while Team B would have a probability of 33.3% (1 / 3 = .333, or 33.3%) of winning a game. These predicted probabilities are found via the following formula:

$$\hat{\pi} = \frac{OR}{1 + OR} \qquad \text{(Formula 14.7)}$$

where $\hat{\pi}$ is the predicted probability for the non-baseline group to experience the outcome of interest, and OR is the corresponding odds ratio. For the *Titanic* example, the predicted probability that a first-class passenger would survive the sinking (compared to a third-class passenger) is:

$$\hat{\pi} = \frac{4.871}{1 + 4.871}$$

$$\hat{\pi} = \frac{4.871}{5.871}$$

$$\hat{\pi} = 0.830$$

Be Aware of the Groups. When you interpret an odds ratio, it is important to keep the baseline and non-baseline groups in mind. Because these are arbitrary choices, mixing up groups can result in incorrect results. For example, reversing the baseline and non-baseline groups produces opposite results – as we saw in the previous paragraph. Therefore, if we confuse which group is the baseline group, we risk coming to a conclusion that is the exact opposite of the real conclusion. However, one convenient aspect of odds ratios is that if we wish to change the baseline group, we should find the reciprocal of the odds ratio. There is no need to start over and completely recalculate the odds ratio.

Sidebar 14.4 **Meta-analysis**

As the General Linear Moments throughout this book have shown, every NHST procedure has an effect size. These effect sizes permit readers to compare the results of studies to one another. An additional benefit of effect sizes is that they can be used to combine results from different studies as if they were one large study, a procedure called **meta-analysis**. There are several advantages of meta-analysis. The first is that prior methods of synthesizing research did a poor job at providing strong answers to research questions. One method was the **literature review**, which requires a researcher to read all the studies done on a topic, describe these studies, and reach a general conclusion about them. Although literature reviews will always have a place in the social sciences, they are susceptible to the author's preconceived notions of what the research literature means and what types of studies are trustworthy. Another method is "vote counting," which involves tallying up the number of studies that reject the null hypothesis or retain the null hypothesis in order to determine the most likely overall result. Vote counting sounds like a good method, but it is inherently flawed, especially when the file drawer problem distorts the literature (Vadillo et al., 2016), when researchers engage in questionable research practices (see Sidebar 8.1; Schimmack, 2012), or when sample sizes are small (Nuijten, van Assen, Veldkamp, & Wicherts, 2015).

The second advantage of meta-analysis is that pooling many studies together increases the combined sample size. As a result, the results are more stable and precise, with greater statistical power (see Sidebar 10.1). The third advantage of meta-analysis is that it can resolve contradictions in the scientific literature. For example, for many years the research on the effectiveness of psychological tests in selecting people for jobs was inconsistent. However, an early meta-analysis (Schmidt & Hunter, 1977) showed that when these studies were combined it was very clear that psychological tests were an effective means of screening for people for jobs. Earlier inconsistencies were due to low statistical power and restriction of range in correlation coefficients, among other factors.

A fourth advantage of meta-analyses is that they can show whether certain characteristics of studies have an impact on the strength of the results (i.e., the magnitude of the effect sizes). This was apparent in a meta-analysis my student performed, where cognitive therapy was found to be more effective than play therapy for children who were survivors of abuse (Slade & Warne, 2016). Similarly, the very first meta-analysis (originally reported in Glass, 1976, and later expanded in M. L. Smith & Glass, 1977) showed that subjective measures of patient outcomes – which are easier for clients or therapists to fake or influence than objective measures – tended to produce results that made therapy appear more effective.

Finally, recent developments in meta-analysis have made it possible to sometimes estimate the impact of the file drawer problem (see Sidebar 14.1). Because the file drawer problem distorts the research literature, it can also distort the results of a meta-analysis – which is, by definition, based on the research literature. New procedures have made it possible to estimate the presence and severity of this distortion (e.g., Vadillo et al., 2016), though the methods are not perfect, especially when the number of studies is small.

For all of these reasons meta-analyses are popular in the social and medical sciences today. Although they are not perfect, by pooling together the effect sizes from many studies, a meta-analysis produces results that are much stronger than could ever occur in a single study. The next time you have to read scientific articles about a topic for a class, I suggest you find a meta-analysis to read. The article will likely be more informative and methodologically sound than a single study.

Odds Ratio for More Than Two Groups. Formula 14.6 can only calculate an odds ratio with two independent variable groups and two dependent variable outcomes. When there are more than two groups in either the independent or dependent variables, there are two options available for calculating an odds ratio. The first option is to select two groups and two outcomes and eliminate the rest of the data. This is what we did above when we calculated the odds ratio that compared first- and third-class passengers' outcomes. We threw out the data from the second-class passengers in order to calculate the odds ratio for the other two groups. The disadvantage of this method is that it requires multiple odds ratios in order to understand the data. For the *Titanic* data, we can also calculate an odds ratio that compares the likelihood that second-class passengers would survive when compared with first-class passengers. This would be:

$$OR = \frac{(528)(118)}{(178)(167)}$$

$$OR = \frac{62,304}{29,726}$$

$$OR = 2.096$$

This odds ratio indicates that second-class passengers were 2.096 times more likely to survive than third-class passengers. With both of these odds ratios known, we can confidently state that first-class passengers had the highest likelihood of survival, followed by second-class passengers; third-class passengers were the least likely to survive.

The second option when there are more than two groups for either variable is to combine the data from multiple groups until there are only two remaining groups. For example, we can add the observed counts for first- *and* second-class passengers who survived (202 + 118 = 320) and the observed counts for first- *and* second-class passengers who died (123 + 167 = 290). We can then use these values to calculate an odds ratio that would represent the likelihood that a first- *or* second-class passenger would survive compared to a third-class passenger:

$$OR = \frac{(528)(320)}{(178)(290)}$$

$$OR = \frac{168,960}{51,620}$$

$$OR = 3.273$$

The downside with combining data is that it is not always clear which groups should be combined, and sometimes different choices will produce very different odds ratio results.

Relationship with Relative Risk. Another possible method of interpreting two-variable chi-squared data is to calculate the **relative risk**, which is an effect size that quantifies the probability of an outcome for one group compared to another. The formula for relative risk is:

$$RR = \frac{obs_{NI} \div (obs_{NI} + obs_{NB})}{obs_{BI} \div (obs_{BI} + obs_{BB})} = \frac{d \div (d + c)}{b \div (b + a)} \qquad \text{(Formula 14.8)}$$

The relative risk quantifies the probability of the outcome of interest occurring for the non-baseline group compared to the baseline group. The numerator is the probability of the outcome of interest happening for the non-baseline group, while the denominator is the probability of the outcome of interest happening in the baseline group. Using the example data, the relative risk (where first-class passengers on the *Titanic* are the non-reference group and third-class passengers are the reference group, with survival being the outcome of interest) would be:

$$RR = \frac{202 \div (202 + 123)}{178 \div (178 + 528)}$$

$$RR = \frac{202 \div 325}{178 \div 706}$$

$$RR = \frac{0.622}{0.252}$$

$$RR = 2.465$$

This relative risk value compares only individuals who experience the outcome of interest. The numerator is the proportion of non-baseline group individuals who experienced the outcome of interest. The denominator is the proportion of baseline group members who experienced the outcome of interest. The relative risk value is the ratio between these two proportions. In this example, the proportion of first-class passengers who survived the *Titanic* is 2.465 times greater than the proportion of third-class passengers who survived the sinking.

As with an odds ratio, when the relative risk is equal to 1.0, the outcome of interest is equally likely for both groups. Values smaller than 1 indicate that the outcome is more likely for the baseline group, while values larger than 1 indicate that the outcome is more likely for the non-baseline group. Although the interpretations are similar, the same data may not necessarily produce the same relative risk and odds ratio values. This is because relative risk is based on proportions of group members who experience an outcome of interest, while the odds ratio is based on the odds of an occurrence of an outcome of interest (Agresti, 2007).

Most researchers in the social sciences prefer to use the odds ratio. However, the relative risk is frequently found in medical research where a baseline group would be a control group and the non-baseline group would be an experimental group. In this framework, relative risk is used in measuring the effectiveness of a medicine or the frequency of symptoms of patients experiencing different types of therapy. For example, in a study cited in Chapter 11 on the impact of aspirin on the survival of people suffering heart attacks, the relative risk of having a fatal heart attack for individuals taking aspirin was 0.25 when compared to the control group (Steering Committee of the Physicians Health Study Group, 1988). This indicates that the proportion of individuals who were taking aspirin that later had a fatal heart attack was 0.25 times as large as the proportion of individuals in the control group that later had a fatal heart attack. The decision of whether to use an odds ratio or relative risk is often one of personal preference. Given the four needed observed counts, it is possible to calculate both effect sizes. The odds ratio has some benefits when considered in the context of more complex statistics, like multiple regression (discussed in Chapter 15).

General Linear Moment 14.3

Since Chapter 7, I have reiterated that all NHST procedures are members of the GLM with three characteristics:

1. All GLM procedures examine the relationships between independent and dependent variables. Another way of stating this point is that all GLM procedures are correlational in nature. (See Chapter 12 for an explanation of correlation.)
2. All GLM procedures apply weights to data during the analysis process.
3. All GLM procedures can produce an effect size.

In this General Linear Moment, I will illustrate how the two-variable chi-squared test has these three characteristics.

Independent and Dependent Variables. A two-variable chi-squared test by definition has two variables: an independent and a dependent variable, both of which are nominal. The null hypothesis for this NHST is that the two variables are unrelated or uncorrelated. Therefore, it should not surprise you that a two-variable chi-squared test is also a form of correlation. We can see this in the null hypothesis for the two-variable chi-squared test, which is that the independent and dependent variables are unrelated (i.e., uncorrelated) with one another. Therefore, *we can view the two-variable chi-squared test as being a correlation for two nominal variables*. In fact, for this reason there is a correlation coefficient designed for two dichotomous variables:

$$\phi = \frac{(obs_{BB})(obs_{NI}) - (obs_{BI})(obs_{NB})}{\sqrt{(obs_{BB} + obs_{BI})(obs_{BI} + obs_{NI})(obs_{NB} + obs_{NI})(obs_{BB} + obs_{NB})}} \qquad \text{(Formula 14.9)}$$

which is equal to

$$\phi = \sqrt{\frac{\chi^2_{obs}}{n}} \qquad \text{(Formula 14.10)}$$

This correlation coefficient, ϕ (which is the Greek letter *phi*, pronounced "fee") ranges from 0 to 1 and is interpreted the same way as Pearson's *r*. Also like Pearson's *r*, it can be squared to produce an effect size. Despite these advantages, it is not as common as the odds ratio because it cannot be used with more than two categories in each variable, and ϕ can sometimes have an artificially low value when the four *obs* counts are not approximately equally sized.

The correlation coefficient ϕ is a special case of another measure of correlation, called **Cramér's *V***, which is calculated as:

$$V = \sqrt{\frac{\chi^2_{obs}}{n(df_{less})}} \qquad \text{(Formula 14.11)}$$

Cramér's *V* is the same formula as ϕ, except the denominator is the sample size (*n*) multiplied by the lesser of $(n_{rows} - 1)$ and $(n_{columns} - 1)$, which were the two values needed to calculate the degrees of freedom value in Formula 14.5. Although Cramér's V is a generalization of the ϕ correlation, Cramér's V values cannot be directly compared to a Pearson's r or a ϕ value because varying numbers of variable categories (especially in the variable that has the smaller number of categories) can inflate or depress the value of V (Volker, 2006). This can make Cramér's V challenging to interpret, and is (in my opinion) a problem with the statistic.

Compared to the odds ratio and the relative risk, ϕ and Cramér's V are not as commonly reported in social science research. Therefore, I will not show the details of how to calculate either value in this textbook, though the algebra required by Formulas 13.10 and 13.11 is not difficult. However, they do have value in showing that the two-variable chi-squared test is a form of a correlation, thereby strengthening the χ^2 test's links to other members of the GLM.

Weighting Data. As is typical, this is the hardest of the three characteristics of the GLM to see. The key is the expected counts, which Figure 14.4 shows is calculated by multiplying proportions for a group by total counts for outcomes. The proportions used to calculate the expected counts – and therefore the χ^2_{obs} value – are the statistical weights in the two-variable chi-squared test.

Effect Size. It should be clear as you read this chapter that chi-squared tests produce effect sizes. In addition to the odds ratio, data analysts also have the option of using the relative risk effect size, ϕ, and Cramér's V.

Check Yourself!

- How do you interpret an odds ratio?

- How do you convert an odds ratio to a predicted probability?

- What is a meta-analysis?

Summary

When the dependent variable consists of nominal data, it is not possible to use any of the null hypothesis statistical significance tests (NHSTs) that we have learned before. Instead we must use a chi-squared test, of which there are two types: the one-variable chi-squared test and the two-variable chi-squared test. The former procedure uses the same eight steps as all NHSTs and tests the null hypothesis that each group formed by the independent variable is equal to a hypothesized proportion. The two-variable chi-squared test has the null hypothesis that the two variables are unrelated to one another.

The most common effect size for chi-squared tests is the odds ratio. Calculating an odds ratio requires choosing a baseline group and a non-baseline group, and an outcome of interest and a baseline outcome. When an odds ratio is equal to 1.0, the outcome of interest is equally likely for both groups. For odds ratios greater than 1.0, the outcome of interest is more likely for the non-baseline group. When the odds ratio is less than 1.0, the outcome of interest is more likely for the baseline group. The easiest way to imagine the odds ratio is to think of the "odds" in a gambling or sports context, where the odds of an event are, for example, 2-to-1, which would correspond to an odds ratio of 2.0 and indicate that the event is twice as likely to occur for the first group as for the second group. When there are more than two groups or two outcomes, calculating an odds ratio requires either (1) calculating more than one odds ratio, or (2) combining groups together. The odds ratio can also be converted to predicted probabilities that the outcome of interest will occur for the groups. Another effect size option is the relative risk, which is a ratio of the proportions of members in two group that experience an outcome.

Reflection Questions: Comprehension

1. Which odds ratio indicates that the baseline group and the non-baseline group are equally likely to experience the outcome of interest? (a) 0.45, (b)1.00, (c)1.33, or (d) 2.05.
2. Explain the relationship between a one-variable chi-squared test and a one-sample t-test.
3. What is the relationship between a two-variable chi-squared test and Pearson's r?
4. Define relative risk.
5. What is the "file drawer problem," and why is it a problem in the social sciences?
6. Name the four benefits of meta-analysis.

Reflection Questions: Application

7. Dante gave a survey to the anthropology students in his department. He had 42 female respondents and 31 male respondents. In his department the entire population of students is 59% female and 41% male. Conduct a one-variable chi-squared test to determine whether the proportion of male and female respondents in Dante's study is representative of the population of anthropology students.
   a. What is the null hypothesis for this study?
   b. Is a one- or a two-tailed test appropriate for this example? Why?
   c. How many degrees of freedom are in Dante's data?
   d. If $\alpha = .05$, what is the χ^2_{crit} value for the data?
   e. Calculate the χ^2_{obs} value.
   f. Compare the χ^2_{crit} value and the χ^2_{obs} value. Should you reject or retain the null hypothesis in this example?
   g. Calculate an odds ratio for each of the gender groups. Interpret these odds ratios.
8. Kathryn's sample consists of patients at a psychiatric clinic. In the clinic population, 40% of patients have depression, 28% have anxiety disorders, 15% have eating disorders, 10% have intellectual disabilities, and 7% have another diagnosis. Kathryn's sample has 55 individuals with depression, 35 with anxiety disorders, 19 with eating disorders, 5 with intellectual disabilities, and 16 with another diagnosis. Conduct a statistical test to determine whether the proportion of individuals with each diagnosis in Kathryn's study is representative of the population of clinic patients.
   a. What is the null hypothesis for this study?
   b. Is a one- or a two-tailed test appropriate for this example? Why?
   c. How many degrees of freedom are in Kathryn's data?

    d.   If $\alpha = .05$, what is the χ^2_{crit} value for the data?

    e.   Calculate the χ^2_{obs} value.

    f.   Compare the χ^2_{crit} value and the χ^2_{obs} value. Should you reject or retain the null hypothesis in this example?

    g.   Calculate an odds ratio for each of the diagnosis groups. Interpret these odds ratios.

9.   Maddie is a sociology student who found that individuals with high levels of social support were more likely to graduate from college than individuals with low levels, as indicated by the odds ratio value of 1.5.

    a.   Convert this odds ratio to an odds ratio where the individuals with high levels of social support are the new baseline group. (Hint: this switches which group is the baseline group and which group is the non-baseline group.)

    b.   Convert the odds ratio of 1.5 into a predicted probability that an individual with high levels of social support will graduate from college.

10. In a study of the effectiveness of a new vaccine, a researcher found that the relative risk of developing a disease is 0.31 for individuals who have had the vaccine. In the same study, it was apparent that the relative risk of experiencing side effects was 1.0 for individuals who had the vaccine.

    a.   Interpret both of these relative risk values.

    b.   Given these results, is the vaccine effective? Is it safe for patients?

11. Barnsley, Thompson, and Barnsley (1985, p. 24) examined the birth months of National Hockey League players in the United States and Canada. They hypothesized that traditional rules stating that a player must be born before January 1 to join the youth hockey team for a particular age group would mean that older players would be put on better teams because they were bigger and more physically developed. This would give them an advantage in their youth sports training over younger players. According to their data, professional hockey players were born in the following months. The null hypothesis for their study was that players were equally likely to be born each month, which would produce an equal number of players born each month (with a proportion of 1/12 or .083 born each month).

Jan	Feb	Mar	Apr	May	Jun	Jul	Aug	Sep	Oct	Nov	Dec	Total
81	69	79	72	78	63	46	45	66	38	45	33	715

    a.   How many degrees of freedom are in Barnsley et al.'s (1985) data?

    b.   If $\alpha = .05$, what is the χ^2_{crit} value for the data?

    c.   Calculate the χ^2_{obs} value.

    d.   Compare the χ^2_{crit} value and the χ^2_{obs} value. Should you reject or retain the null hypothesis in this example?

    e.   Calculate an odds ratio for each month.

    f.   Interpret these odds ratios.

12. In a study of second language learning, Researcher A found that individuals whose parents were bilingual were 2.5 times more likely to be fluent in a second language by age 21 than children whose parents were not bilingual. However, Researcher B read the study and interpreted the results to indicate that children of monolingual parents were 0.40 times as likely to become bilingual by age 21. Why do both researchers have a correct understanding of the study results?

13. Logan's favorite sports team has an 80% chance of winning their next game. Convert this value into an odds ratio where his team is the non-baseline group and the outcome of interest is a victory.

14. In a university political science department, there are 90 students enrolled, 36 males and 54 females. Of the 36 males, 28 eventually graduated, while 8 did not. Of the 54 females, 42 graduated, while 12 did not. Conduct a chi-squared test to determine whether there is a relationship between student gender and graduate status.

   a. What is the null hypothesis for this study?
   b. Is a one- or two-tailed test appropriate for this example? Why?
   c. How many degrees of freedom are in the data?
   d. If $\alpha = .05$, what is the χ^2_{crit} value for the data?
   e. Create the contingency table with the observed and expected counts.
   f. Calculate the χ^2_{obs} value.
   g. Compare the χ^2_{crit} value and the χ^2_{obs} value. Should you reject or retain the null hypothesis in this example?
   h. Calculate an odds ratio for the data.
   i. Interpret the odds ratio in question 14h.

15. Customers of four companies were surveyed and placed into three categories: repeat customers, non-repeat satisfied customers, and non-repeat/dissatisfied customers.

Company	Repeat customers	Non-repeat satisfied customers	Non-repeat/dissatisfied customers	Total
A	42	22	10	74
B	18	15	7	40
C	61	45	15	121
D	50	26	6	82
Total	171	108	38	317

   a. What is the null hypothesis for this study?
   b. Is a one- or a two-tailed test appropriate for this example?
   c. How many degrees of freedom are in the data?
   d. If $\alpha = .05$, what is the χ^2_{crit} value for the data?
   e. Create the contingency table with expected values.
   f. Calculate the χ^2_{obs} value.
   g. Compare the χ^2_{crit} value and the χ^2_{obs} value. Should you reject or retain the null hypothesis in this example?
   h. Calculate and interpret an odds ratio where Company A is the baseline group and being a repeat customer is the outcome of interest. Combine the other groups together and the other outcomes together in order to calculate a single odds ratio.
   i. Interpret the effect size in question 15h.

16. A university collected data on the number of scholarship students that donated to the same scholarship fund when they were alumni. There were three groups of alumni: those receiving athletic scholarships, those receiving academic scholarships, and those receiving citizenship

scholarships. The numbers in each group that donated or did not donate are listed in the contingency table below.

Student groups	Donated	Did not donate	Total
Athletics	13	16	29
Academic	22	28	50
Citizenship	9	12	21
Total	44	56	100

a. What is the null hypothesis for this example?
b. Is a one- or two-tailed test appropriate for this example? Why?
c. How many degrees of freedom are in the data?
d. If $\alpha = .05$, what is the χ^2_{crit} value for the data?
e. Create the contingency table with the expected counts.
f. Calculate the χ^2_{obs} value.
g. Compare the χ^2_{crit} value and the χ^2_{obs} value. Should you reject or retain the null hypothesis in this example?
h. Calculate an odds ratio where alumni who received an athletic scholarship are the baseline group and *not* donating is the baseline outcome, with alumni who received an academic scholarship as the non-baseline group. (This requires eliminating the citizenship group of alumni from the calculation.)
i. Interpret the effect size in question 16h.

Software Guide

As with most NHSTs, it is possible to conduct chi-squared tests in both Excel and SPSS. This Software Guide will show how to conduct a one-variable and two-variable chi-squared test using the main example of *Titanic* data in this chapter. Given the way these two computer programs function, it is easier to show how to conduct a two-variable chi-squared test and then explain how to adapt the procedure to the one-variable chi-squared test.

Excel

Two-Variable Chi-Squared Test. The first step to conducting a two-variable chi-squared test in Microsoft Excel is to enter the contingency table into the worksheet. This is shown in Figure 14.7. Notice that the user must enter both the observed counts and the expected counts. Excel does not calculate the expected counts. The user must calculate those manually or enter a mathematical formula to calculate the expected counts. Also, the expected and observed counts cells must be in the same order. This is apparent in Figure 14.7, where the survivors are in the left column of each set of counts, and the victims are in the right column. Likewise, the top row in the table consists of first-class passengers, the second row is the count of second-class passengers, and the bottom row is the count of third-class passengers.

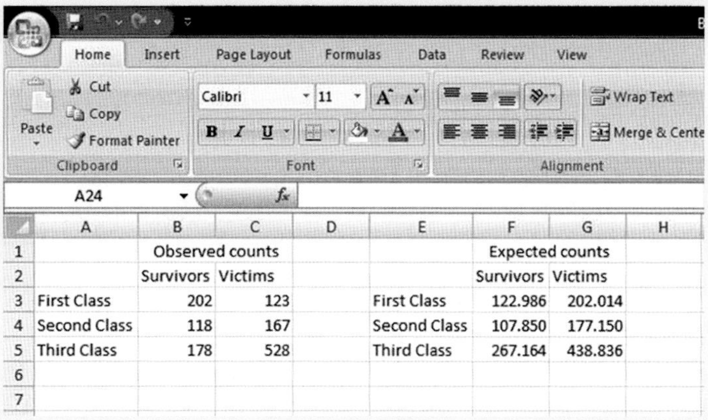

Figure 14.7 Screenshot of Microsoft Excel showing how to set up the contingency table.

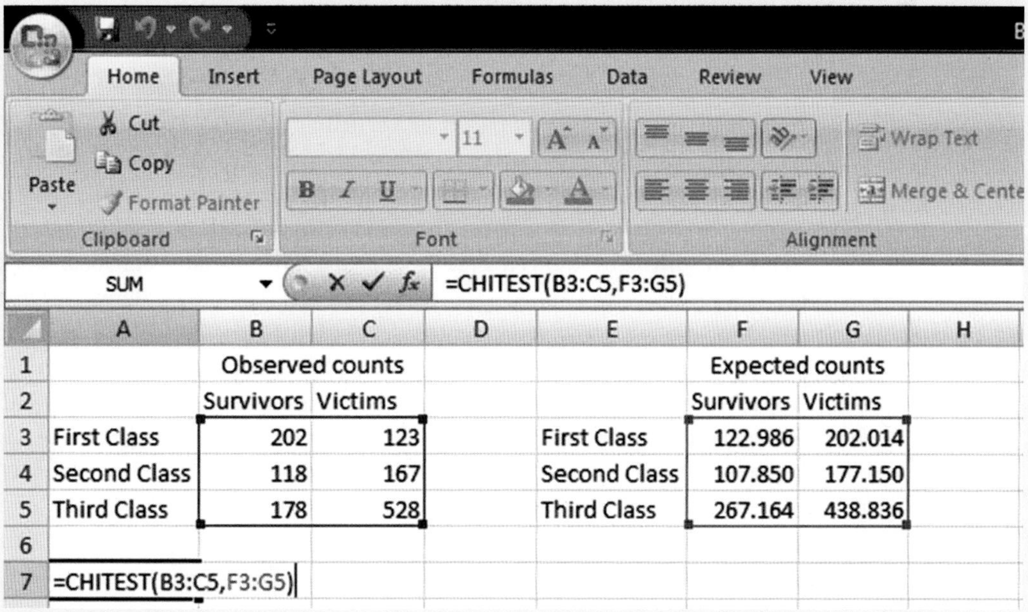

Figure 14.8 Screenshot in Microsoft Excel showing how to use the CHITEST function.

After the data are entered, the proper Excel function to conduct a two-variable chi-squared test is =CHITEST(XX:XX,YY:YY), where XX:XX is the set of cells for the observed counts, and YY:YY stands for the cells that contain the expected counts. Figure 14.8 shows how this function is used for the *Titanic* data.

After entering the CHITEST function, press the "enter" key, which will produce the *p*-value for the chi-squared test. A *p*-value less than the α value indicates that the null hypothesis should be rejected. Conversely, if the *p*-value is greater than the α value, the null hypothesis should be retained. Figure 14.9 shows the result of the two-variable chi-squared test. The *p*-value

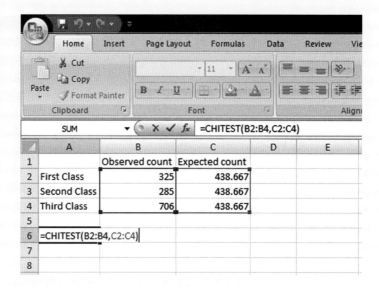

Figure 14.9 Screenshot from Microsoft Excel showing how to conduct a one-variable chi-squared test. After you enter the CHITEST function, pressing "enter" will produce the NHST's *p*-value.

in this example is so tiny that Excel puts it into scientific notation. The "3.4388E-29" is 3.4388×10^{-29}, which is a decimal point followed by 28 zeros and then 34388 (i.e., $p = .0000000000000000000000000000034388$). This is clear evidence that the null hypothesis should be rejected. Excel does not calculate an odds ratio.

One-Variable Chi-Squared Test. Conducting a one-variable chi-squared test is almost the exact same as the two-variable chi-squared test. The only difference is that there is only one column of observed and expected counts in the data. This is shown in Figure 14.9. The figure also shows that the Excel function CHITEST is also used to conduct a one-variable chi-squared test. With this example data, the statistical test produced a *p*-value of 3.45054×10^{-54}, which is smaller than α, indicating that the null hypothesis that the groups are the same size should be rejected.

SPSS

Two-Variable Chi-Squared Test. For a two-variable chi-squared test, there are two ways that the data can be organized. Figure 14.10 shows the simpler method, which organizes the observed values from Table 14.1. The first column represents the independent variable, which is the class of passenger that each person was. In this column, 1 represents first-class passengers, 2 represents second-class passengers, and 3 represents third-class passengers. (Because this is a nominal variable, the value of the numbers does not matter. But these values are very convenient.) The second column is the dependent variable, which is whether the person survived or perished in the voyage of the *Titanic*. In this column, 0 represents perishing in the sinking, and 1 represents surviving the sinking. The final columns display the observed count for each combination of independent variable values. When the data are in this format, the number of rows in the data will be the same as the number of cells in the table. This is why there are six rows in Figure 14.10 (which correspond to the six rows in Table 14.1).

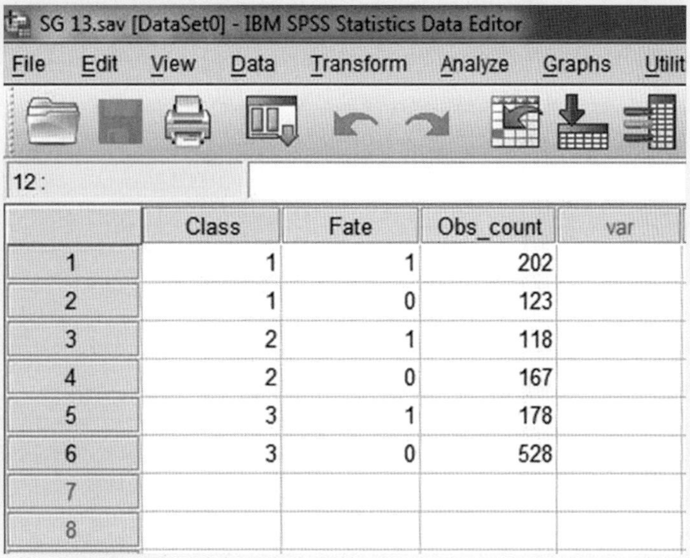

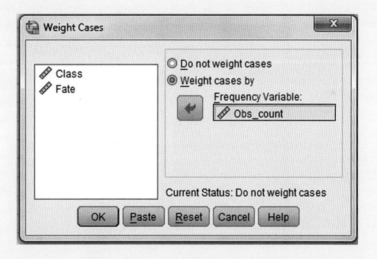

Figure 14.10 SPSS data window showing one method of organizing data to conduct a two-variable chi-squared test.

Figure 14.11 The SPSS Weight Cases window. With the "Obs_count" variable selected and moved into the right-hand side of the window, the computer will understand that the Obs_count column contains count data and is not a separate variable.

Now click the "Data" menu and then select "Weight Cases." This makes the Weight Cases window appear. In this window the user selects the button labeled "Weight cases by." Then the user selects the variable that represents the observed counts and moves it into the open space on the right side of the window. The result is Figure 14.11. Doing this tells the computer that the "Obs_count" variable contains count data and is not a third variable.

The next step is to select the "Analyze" menu and then select "Descriptive Statistics" ➔ "Crosstabs." This makes the window in Figure 14.12 appear. The purpose of this

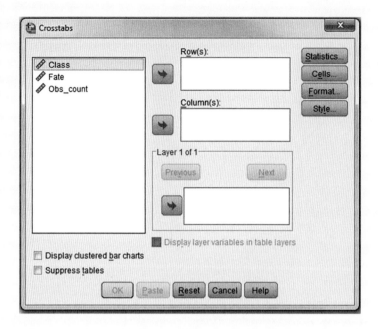

Figure 14.12 The SPSS Crosstabs window as it first appears.

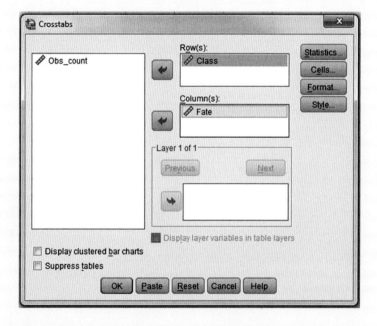

Figure 14.13 The SPSS Crosstabs window with the row and column for the contingency table selected.

window is to tell the computer which variable in the data window corresponds to the rows and the columns in Table 14.1. This is done by selecting a variable name from the left and putting it into either the "Row(s)" or "Column(s)" area on the right side of the window. The result is shown in Figure 14.13.

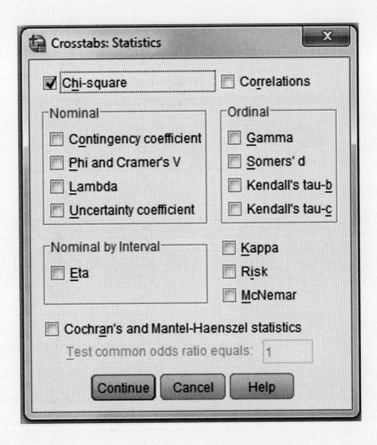

Figure 14.14 The Crosstabs: Statistics window in SPSS. This window is where the user tells the computer to conduct the two-variable chi-squared test in the upper-left corner.

The Crosstabs window in Figures 14.12 and 14.13 only tells SPSS to create the contingency table for the data. To tell the computer to conduct a chi-squared test, select the "Statistics" button in the top-right corner of the window. This causes a new window, as shown in Figure 14.14, to appear. This is called the "Crosstabs: Statistics" window. To get the chi-squared test result, check the box labeled "Chi-square." Then click "Continue" in the Crosstabs: Statistics window and "OK" in the Crosstabs window. This causes the results to appear in the output window, as shown in Figure 14.15.

In Figure 14.15, there are two tables that SPSS produced. The first is the contingency table, which is identical to Table 14.1. The second table shows the results of the statistical analysis. The chi-squared observed value is the top number in the "Value" column. The degrees of freedom for the statistical test is the top number in the "df" column. Finally, the column at right, which is labeled "Asymp. Sig. (2-sided)," displays the p-values. The p-value in Figure 14.15 appears to be .000, but this is an impossible p-value. (In fact, in this example, $p = 3.43 \times 10^{-29}$, which is a decimal point, followed by 28 zeros and then 343.) SPSS displays it this way because it is rounding the p-value. When this occurs, it is proper to report that "$p < .001$" (American Psychological Association, 2010). As in the previous Software Guides, the null hypothesis should be rejected when $p < \alpha$, and the null hypothesis should be retained when $p > \alpha$. SPSS does not calculate an odds ratio automatically when conducting a chi-squared test.

Class * Fate Crosstabulation

Count

		Fate		
		0	1	Total
Class	1	123	202	325
	2	167	118	285
	3	528	178	706
Total		818	498	1316

Chi-Square Tests

	Value	df	Asymp. Sig. (2-sided)
Pearson Chi-Square	131.079[a]	2	.000
Likelihood Ratio	130.694	2	.000
Linear-by-Linear Association	130.503	1	.000
N of Valid Cases	1316		

a. 0 cells (0.0%) have expected count less than 5. The minimum expected count is 107.85.

Figure 14.15 Tables in SPSS's output window showing the results of a two-variable chi-squared test. The upper table is the contingency table. The lower table shows the chi-squared observed value (as the top number in the "Value" column) and the *p-value* (the top number in the far-right column). Note that even though the *p-value* appears to be zero (i.e., .000), it is impossible to obtain a *p-value* of 0 (see Sidebar 7.3). It merely appears this way because SPSS rounds the *p-values*.

One last note deserves mention. At the beginning of this section of the software guide, I said that there are two ways to organize the data. Figure 14.10 shows the first method. The second method is to enter data in a format that gives a row to each individual in the dataset. For example, for the 202 first-class passengers who survived the *Titanic*, there would be 202 rows that have a "1" in the class column and a "1" in the fate column. Likewise, for the 123 first-class passengers, there would be 123 rows that have a "1" in the class column and a "0" in the fate column. The data entry would continue in this fashion until there are 1,316 rows – one for each sample member. If you decide to enter the data into SPSS this way, there is no need to have an "Obs_count" column or to use the Weight Cases function (in Figure 14.11). All of the other steps in conducting a chi-squared test are the same.

One-Variable Chi-Squared Test. Conducting a one-variable chi-squared test in SPSS is the same as a two-variable chi-squared test. The only difference is how the data are set up. To create the one-variable chi-squared test, the data must be structured as two variables and a count – just as in Figure 14.10. However, the columns have a different meaning, and they are shown in Figure 14.16. Just as in Figure 14.10, "Class" refers to whether the individuals are first-, second-, or third-class passengers. The "Data" column refers to whether the data are observed counts (labeled as "1") or expected counts (labeled as "0"). The "Count" column is the actual observed or expected counts for each group. Note that SPSS does not calculate the

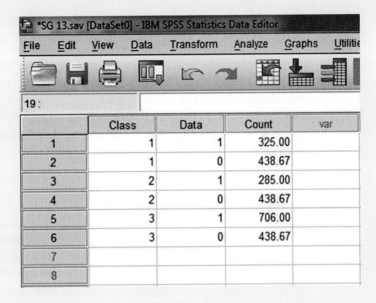

Figure 14.16 A view of the data window in SPSS for a one-variable chi-squared test. The first column corresponds to the classification variable in the dataset. The second column is a variable that states whether the data are observed or expected counts. The final column is the actual observed or expected counts for each group in the data.

expected counts automatically. The user must calculate these. Once the data are set up in this fashion, you can follow the same instructions for a two-variable chi-squared test to conduct your one-variable chi-squared test.

Further Reading

- Plackett, R. L. (1983). Karl Pearson and the chi-squared test. *International Statistical Review, 51*, 59–72. doi:10.2307/1402731

  * Karl Pearson's 1900 paper in which he introduced the chi-squared test is an extraordinarily difficult paper to read and understand – even by the standards of statistical writing. Plackett's article is a time-saving guide to understanding Pearson's paper. Moreover, Plackett's work is interesting in its own right (and much easier to read than Pearson's prose).

- Rosenthal, R. (1979). The file drawer problem and tolerance for null results. *Psychological Bulletin, 86*, 638–641. doi:10.1037//0033-2909.86.3.638

  * In this famous article Rosenthal described the "file drawer problem" and its implications in the social sciences. Although Rosenthal was not the first person to discuss the problem of a bias against the null hypothesis, his term "file drawer problem" stuck in the social science collective consciousness, and his article is now regarded as a classic.

- Standley, J. M. (1996). A brief introduction to meta-analysis. *Journal of Research in Music Education, 44,* 101–104. doi:10.2307/3345664

  * This excellent introduction to meta-analysis is appropriate for undergraduates. Standley explains the basic purposes and steps of a meta-analysis, which have not changed since Gene Glass performed the first meta-analysis in the mid-1970s. There are some developments in meta-analysis that have occurred since Standley's article was published (especially in the assessment of publication bias), but this article covers the basics well and is accessibly written.

- Steenbergen-Hu, S., & Olszewski-Kubilius, P. (2016). How to conduct a good meta-analysis in gifted education. *Gifted Child Quarterly, 60,* 134–154. doi:10.1177/0016986216629545

  * After readers have mastered Standley's (1996) article, this piece by Steenbergen-Hu and Olszewski-Kubilius is a good resource for those who want a more detailed explanation of meta-analysis and a step-by-step guide that meets modern methodological standards. It is designed for people working in education and educational psychology, but all of the explanations and guidelines apply to the social sciences as a whole.

15 Applying Statistics to Research, and Advanced Statistical Methods

As you have progressed through this book, you have learned seven inferential statistics methods. However, even the most mathematically savvy student can sometimes have difficulty applying what they have learned to real-life research situations. Students – and some professionals – often have two challenges in applying these statistical methods:

- Selecting an appropriate statistical method to analyze their data.
- Understanding complex statistical methods.

This chapter is designed to help you overcome these two hurdles to using statistics with real data. As a result, it is structured differently from the other chapters in this textbook. Rather than a thorough exploration of relevant statistical procedures, this chapter is designed to be a reference guide that students can turn to when they are using statistics to analyze their own data. Therefore, this chapter does not include the mathematical, step-by-step procedures; instead, it relies more on interpretation and the use of software. You will also notice that the software guides in this chapter are dispersed throughout the chapter – rather than being placed at the end.

Learning Goals

- Select an appropriate statistical method for a given research question.

- Explain how multiple regression fits into the general linear model (GLM).

- Interpret multiple regression results.

- Define nonparametric statistics and recognize when their use is appropriate.

- Distinguish between univariate and multivariate statistical methods.

How to Choose a Statistical Method

With the seven statistical methods that we have discussed so far in this textbook – and with the many more methods available – sometimes one of the biggest challenges is just to know which statistical procedure to use. Many students are surprised to learn that the choice of statistical methods depends mostly on two characteristics of the data: (1) the number of independent and dependent variables, and (2) the levels of data for the different variables. Yet, this makes sense because, as we have progressed from one null hypothesis test to another (Chapters 7–13), we have had to tweak the eight steps of statistical significance testing to accommodate different types of data.

Figure 15.1 is a chart to guide you through the process of choosing an appropriate statistical analysis procedure. The first five columns of boxes represent the characteristics of the

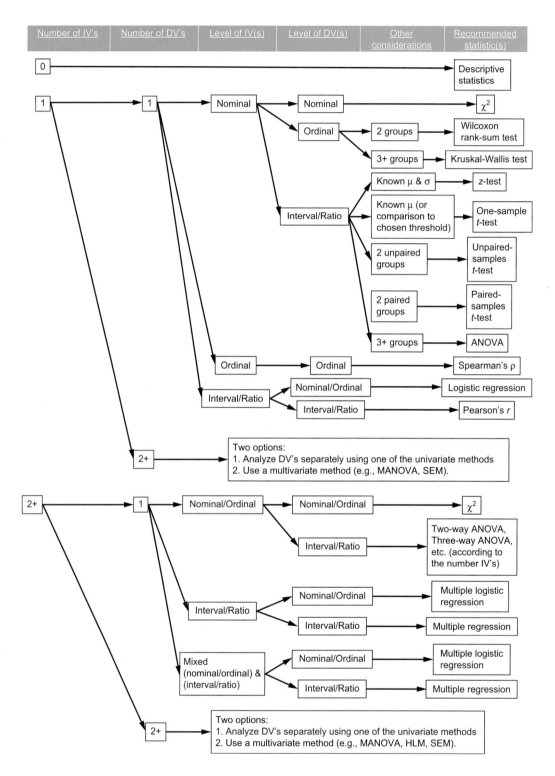

Figure 15.1 Decision process to determine the correct statistical procedure to analyze data. IV: independent variable; DV: dependent variable.

data that influence what statistical procedure to adopt. The far-right column shows the appropriate statistical method, given the specified characteristics of the data. For example, with one interval-level independent variable and one interval-level dependent variable, the appropriate statistical method is Pearson's *r*.

This chart is a visual representation of the overarching themes of this chapter. It also links the statistical methods in previous chapters with those discussed in this chapter: multiple regression, two-way and three-way ANOVA, logistic regression, multiple logistic regression, and multivariate methods. As each section of this chapter introduces a new statistical procedure, I recommend that you refer to Figure 15.1 to understand when each method is appropriate.

Sidebar 15.1 **Plan ahead!**

A lot of things can go wrong during the course of a social science research project. To increase the chances of successfully completing a project, it is best to plan the study in as much detail as possible *before* starting any data collection. That includes choosing a statistical method. Here is a simple schematic for the process of planning a study:

Formulate research questions ➔ Choose methodology ➔ Plan statistical analysis

In this scheme, the first step is to formulate research questions. These research questions determine your methodology and how you will collect data. The characteristics of the data (i.e., number of independent and dependent variables and the level of measurement they are collected at) determine the appropriate statistical procedure for the data analysis.

Conducting any of these steps out of order makes it harder to create coherent research or to successfully finish a study. In extreme cases, I have seen people who collected data that were not analyzable or that did not answer their research questions. Planning the details of a study is usually not very exciting. (Once I get an idea it can be very tempting to just dive into collecting data.) But it is worth it to spend time planning your study so that the later steps in the research project proceed more smoothly and the chances of success for the study increase.

This chapter will also be more intelligible if you remember that every statistical method is a member of the GLM. Thus, all of these procedures exist for one purpose: to examine relationships between independent and dependent variables. As members of the GLM, each procedure also produces an effect size and uses statistical weights. These will be recurring themes in the sections of this chapter.

Check Yourself!

- What are the two main characteristics of data that determine which statistical procedure is appropriate?

- Using Figure 15.1, determine which statistical procedure is best with one nominal independent variable with three groups and an interval-level dependent variable.

- When should you choose a statistical method while designing a study?

Multiple Regression and Related Procedures

Multiple Regression. The easiest way to understand the next methods discussed in this chapter (on two-way and three-way ANOVA, logistic regression, and multiple logistic regression) is that they are special cases of **multiple regression** (Cohen, 1968). Therefore, this section will explain multiple regression and then show how the methods I explain in the next two sections are merely simplifications of multiple regression. In turn, the last section on complex methods discusses methods that are all generalizations of multiple regression. In a way, multiple regression is the key to moving beyond the basic statistical methods explained in most of this book to the more advanced methods that you may learn in future classes. As such, multiple regression occupies an important place within the GLM.

Now that we see that multiple regression is important, the question becomes: what is multiple regression? The answer is that it is a regression model with two or more independent variables. You may remember from Chapter 13 that the unstandardized regression formula to make a prediction for an individual's dependent variable score is:

$$\hat{y}_i = bx_i + a \qquad \text{(Formula 13.2)}$$

where $\hat{y}_i$ is the predicted dependent variable score for individual i, b is the slope of the regression line, a is the intercept of the regression line, and x_i is an individual's score on the independent variable x. Multiple regression is merely the extension of this formula to accommodate more than one independent variable. The mathematical formula for multiple regression with two independent variables is:

$$\hat{y}_i = b_1 x_{1i} + b_2 x_{2i} + a \qquad \text{(Formula 15.1)}$$

In this formula, $\hat{y}_i$ is still the predicted dependent variable score for individual i, and a is still the intercept. The symbol b_1 is a slope value for independent variable 1, and x_{1i} is the individual i's score on independent variable 1. Likewise, b_2 is a slope value for independent variable 2, and x_{2i} is the individual i's score on independent variable 2. Thus, the multiple regression model can be used to make predictions of dependent variable values by using more than one independent variable. This usually makes the predictions more accurate than they would be with either variable alone.

Indeed, we can keep adding variables to the multiple regression model in order to improve our statistical models. Unless an independent variable is perfectly uncorrelated with all other variables in the statistical model, the addition of more independent variables will always improve the accuracy of predictions. The general form of a multiple regression equation is:

$$\hat{y} = b_1 x_1 + b_2 x_2 + \ldots + b_j x_j + a \qquad \text{(Formula 15.2)}$$

The new piece of this equation $(+ \ldots + b_j x_j)$ just means that we keep adding slope parameters and independent variables until we reach the last variable in the model with its accompanying slope parameter (symbolized as $b_j x_j$).

In Formulas 15.1 and 15.2, the b's are called statistical weights. We have seen in the General Linear Moments since Chapter 7 that a statistical weight is a number that is multiplied by a variable score. All other things being equal, when a variable's statistical weight is high, it indicates that the variable is weighted more heavily in the statistical model. This means that it is more important in estimating dependent variable values. If a statistical weight is zero, the independent variable does not contribute any information to a statistical model or in the estimation of the dependent variable value.

Table 15.1 Correlation table among health variables in the Add Health dataset

	Felt sick	Trouble sleeping	Trouble relaxing	Felt depressed
Felt sick	1			
Trouble sleeping	.279	1		
Trouble relaxing	.319	.500	1	
Felt depressed	.300	.395	.540	1

One benefit of multiple regression models is that they allow us to compare the relative importance or impact of independent variables. To do this, we must standardize all of the independent variables and the dependent variable into z-score format. This allows us to compare the independent variables to one another, which is only permitted when the independent variables are all in the same scale. To show that all the variables have been converted into z-scores, we change the notation of Formula 15.2 to the following:

$$\hat{y}_z = \beta_1 x_1 + \beta_2 x_2 + \ldots + \beta_j x_j \qquad \text{(Formula 15.3)}$$

In Formula 15.3, $\hat{y}_z$ is the predicted z-score on a dependent variable, while the β values ("beta values") are the standardized (i.e., expressed in z-score format) statistical weights, and the x values are independent variable z-scores.

An example of a multiple regression model can be seen in the National Longitudinal Study of Adolescent and Adult Health, which is sometimes abbreviated as "Add Health." This is an American study that started when its subjects were adolescents in 1994–1995, and which has periodically collected more data in the ensuing two decades. When the subjects were adolescents, they were asked whether in the previous month they had felt depressed, had difficulty relaxing (i.e., anxiety), had trouble sleeping, or were physically ill. The correlation table (i.e., Table 4.1) shows the correlation among these variables, all of which are statistically significant ($p < .001$) when testing the null hypothesis that H_0: $r = 0$. The r^2 values for these correlations range from .078 to .292.

If we want to predict a subject's level of depression, Table 15.1 shows that the single best variable for predicting depression is whether the individual had difficulty relaxing ($r = .540$), and the r^2 value is .292. That is a respectable effect size, but not overwhelming. However, if we include the other two variables (i.e., "Felt sick" and "Trouble sleeping"), we get the following equation:

$$\hat{y} = .155(Sick) + .145(Sleep) + .465(Relaxing) + .419$$

In this equation, the first three numbers are the b regression weight values (see Formula 15.2), and the words in parentheses represent the variables. Each variable's b value represents the expected difference in dependent variable scores when comparing two sample members who have a 1-point difference in an independent variable score, *but are equal in all other independent variables scores*. For example, if two subjects have equal scores on the "Trouble sleeping" and the "Trouble relaxing" variables, but a difference of 1 point on the "Felt sick" variable, we would expect a difference of .155 points in their depression variable scores. Similarly, when holding the other independent variables constant, a 1-point difference in "Trouble relaxing" corresponds to a .465 point difference in depression. The last number (+.419) is the y-intercept for the line – i.e., the a value. The y-intercept is not a statistical weight; it is just a number we have to add to the formula in order for $\hat{y}$ values to be on the same scale as the original data's dependent variable values.

Although the statistical model above is useful information, we cannot compare the relative impact of these independent variables to one another because they are not on the same scale. To do this, we must first convert all the variables to z-scores, which produces the following equation:

$$\hat{y}_z = .123(Sick) + .145(Sleep) + .429(Relaxing)$$

In this equation, the numbers are the standardized weights (i.e., β values) after all the variables are converted to z-scores. These β values represent the expected difference in depression scores if an independent variable score changed by 1 SD (i.e., 1 point in z-scores) with all other variables held constant. Thus, if there are two people with the same "Sick" and "Sleep" scores, but their "Relaxing" scores were 1 SD apart, we would expect their dependent variable scores to be .429 SD apart. With all the scores in the same metric, we can now compare their β values. Because the "Trouble relaxing" variable has the highest β value (i.e., .429), we can conclude that it has the strongest relationship with the dependent variable. On the other hand, the other two variables' β values are similar, though the "Trouble sleeping" variable's β value is slightly larger (.145), indicating that its influence on the depression score is slightly more powerful.

The null hypothesis in multiple regression is that each independent variable has no relationship with the dependent variable when all other independent variable values are held constant. Mathematically, this means that the null hypothesis for multiple regression is:

$$H_0 : b = 0 \qquad \text{(Formula 15.4)}$$

for each independent variable. When all variables are standardized (i.e., converted to z-scores), the null hypothesis becomes

$$H_0 : \beta = 0 \qquad \text{(Formula 15.5)}$$

Therefore, every independent variable's statistical weight has its own null hypothesis statistical significance test. When the null hypothesis is rejected (i.e., when $p < \alpha$), it indicates that the independent variable has a statistically significant relationship with the dependent variable, when all the other independent variables are held constant. On the other hand, if a null hypothesis for an independent variable is retained (i.e., when $p > \alpha$), the variable has no statistically significant relationship with the dependent variable. Usually this indicates that the independent variable can be dropped from the multiple regression model without any major loss of information, though there is the occasional exception (see R. L. Smith, Ager, & Williams, 1992). If you choose to alter a multiple regression model by adding or subtracting variables, you should always recalculate the model.

Like all members of the GLM, multiple regression produces an effect size. In this case, the effect size is called R^2 (pronounced "multiple r-squared"). As with the effect size r^2 in Chapters 12 and 13, there are two ways to interpret R^2. The first is as the degree of improvement in prediction accuracy compared to the baseline model of $\hat{y}_i = \bar{y}$, which has no predictor variables in it. (This equation is Formula 13.6.) The second way of interpreting R^2 is as the percentage of dependent variable variance that is shared with the entire set of independent variables. R^2 can range from 0 to 1. In the Add Health example, the R^2 value was .325 – which is higher than any of the r^2 values derived from the correlations. This shows that making predictions based on all three variables will produce more accurate results than predictions based on any one particular independent variable. The R^2 value indicates that the sum of the squared residuals based on this multiple regression model will be 32.5% smaller than the sum of the squared residuals derived from the baseline model.

You may notice that the interpretations of r^2 and R^2 are identical and that both effect sizes have the same range of values. This is because Pearson's r and linear regression are a special case of multiple regression in the GLM. In other words, when there is only one independent variable in the multiple regression model, it simplifies to a correlation and the regression equations in Formulas 13.1 and 13.2. One implication is that the correlation coefficient is just a standardized regression weight (i.e., β value) when used to make dependent variable predictions. As a result of these similarities, both effect sizes – r^2 and R^2 – are really just the same statistic, but adapted to handle differing numbers of independent variables.

In addition to handling multiple independent variables, multiple regression can be used to investigate interactions. An **interaction** occurs when the impact of an independent variable varies according to the value of another independent variable. In other words, when an interaction is present, an independent variable may have a stronger impact on a dependent variable for some individuals than others. An interaction can also be understood in contrast to a **main effect**, which is the overall average effect that an independent variable has on a dependent variable. When there is no interaction, the subjects' dependent variable scores can be predicted just by adding together the independent variable's main effects. Interactions are important to investigate because sometimes the best average treatment may not be the best treatment for a particular individual – or for any individuals (Cronbach, 1957). Researchers who study interactions can learn how to best customize medical, psychological, educational, and other treatments for individuals, which can improve outcomes for clients.

Investigating interactions in multiple regression requires creating a new variable by multiplying the scores of two existing variables. This new variable can be inserted into Formula 15.2 (or converted into a z-score and then inserted into Formula 15.3) like any other variable. If the b value (or the β value) for the new interaction variable is statistically significant, an interaction effect is present. If it is not, there is no interaction between those two variables in the data. In the Add Health data example, the standardized regression equation (i.e., after all variables have been converted into z-scores) produces the following:

$$\hat{y}_z = \textbf{.125}(Sick) + \textbf{.191}(Sleep) + \textbf{.486}(Relaxing) - .044(Sick{*}Sleep\_int) - .058(Sick{*}Anx\_int)$$
$$- \textbf{.137}(Sleep{*}Anx\_int) + \textbf{.148}(Sick{*}Sleep{*}Anx\_int)$$

The bold numbers indicate statistically significant p-values (all $\leq$ .008). The β values for the main effects are similar to the prior results (when there were no interactions in the statistical model). But two of the interactions – between sleep and anxiety and among all three independent variables – were statistically significant. The negative β value for the sleep × anxiety interaction (pronounced "sleep by anxiety interaction") indicates that individuals who have higher values on the difficulty sleeping variable and anxiety variable have slightly lower depression levels than what we would expect without the interaction. On the other hand, the statistically significant interaction among all three independent variables indicates that a combination of high scores on the three variables produce even higher depression scores than what we would expect based on just the main effects. The two interactions that were not statistically significant (between the sick and sleep variables and between the sick and anxiety variables) could likely be dropped from the model without a meaningful change in the R^2 value.

Beware of multicollinearity!

Because adding variables (including interactions) to a multiple regression model can never make predictions worse, it can be tempting to throw in every independent variable imaginable. After all, if some variables do not improve the model (by raising the R^2 value), they are superfluous, and their presence does not make the model worse.

However, multiple regression models with many variables may suffer from a problem called **multicollinearity**, which occurs when independent variables are too highly correlated with one another. As a result some independent variables are redundant in the model. When this occurs, it can be difficult for the statistical model to "decide" which variable should get any credit for improving predictions. This can sometimes cause a computer program to make important variables appear to be non-statistically significant (i.e., the p-values for the b weights or β may be too high), which would incorrectly indicate that the variables should be dropped from the statistical model.

Multicollinearity does not affect the R^2 value of a multiple regression model, nor does it alter the b or β for the redundant independent variables – or any other variables for that matter (J. D. Morris & Lieberman, 2015). But it does distort p-values and results in misleading judgments about the statistical significance of independent variables. SPSS has an automatic method of checking for multicollinearity that produces two statistics: the variance inflation factor (VIF) and tolerance. These two statistics produce the exact same results because tolerance = 1 / VIF, and VIF = 1 / tolerance. A general rule of thumb is that multicollinearity is not a problem when VIF is less than 10 or if tolerance is greater than 0.1.

Another way to prevent multicollinearity is to avoid what I call "kitchen sink statistics," where variables are thrown into a model without justification. If you have a theoretical justification for the inclusion of every model in your data (including interactions), then multicollinearity is rarely a serious problem because theoretically justified models tend to have nonredundant variables. Theoretically justified models also usually have fewer variables, providing fewer opportunities for independent variables to accidentally correlate with one another.

Software Guide 15.1

This software guide will show the steps of conducting and interpreting a multiple regression with the Add Health data. Figure 15.2 shows the data window in SPSS. As usual, each column represents a variable, while each row represents a sample member. Note that some individuals are missing data; these missing scores are represented as periods. SPSS will automatically eliminate any sample member who is missing data on any variable used in the multiple regression model. To create the multiple regression model, click the "Analyze" menu, then "Regression" → "Linear." This causes the Linear Regression window to appear, as shown in Figure 15.3.

The next step is to select variables by highlighting a variable from the left side of the window and moving it to the right side. The dependent variable goes in the top field on the right

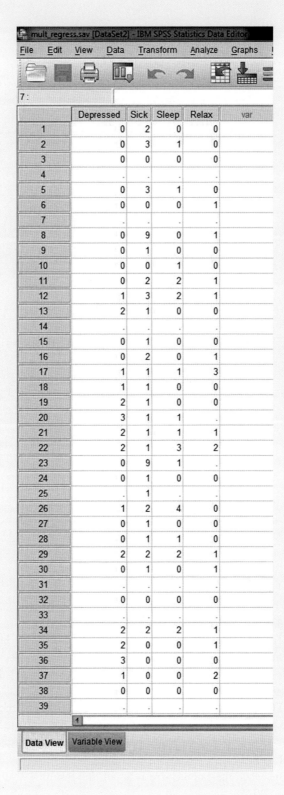

	Depressed	Sick	Sleep	Relax	var
1	0	2	0	0	
2	0	3	1	0	
3	0	0	0	0	
4	.	.	.	.	
5	0	3	1	0	
6	0	0	0	1	
7	.	.	.	.	
8	0	9	0	1	
9	0	1	0	0	
10	0	0	1	0	
11	0	2	2	1	
12	1	3	2	1	
13	2	1	0	0	
14	.	.	.	.	
15	0	1	0	0	
16	0	2	0	1	
17	1	1	1	3	
18	1	1	0	0	
19	2	1	0	0	
20	3	1	1	.	
21	2	1	1	1	
22	2	1	3	2	
23	0	9	1	.	
24	0	1	0	0	
25	.	1	.	.	
26	1	2	4	0	
27	0	1	0	0	
28	0	1	1	0	
29	2	2	2	1	
30	0	1	0	1	
31	.	.	.	.	
32	0	0	0	0	
33	.	.	.	.	
34	2	2	2	1	
35	2	0	0	1	
36	3	0	0	0	
37	1	0	0	2	
38	0	0	0	0	
39	.	.	.	.	

Figure 15.2 Data window in SPSS showing the data in the multiple regression example. Cells with a period in them represent missing data.

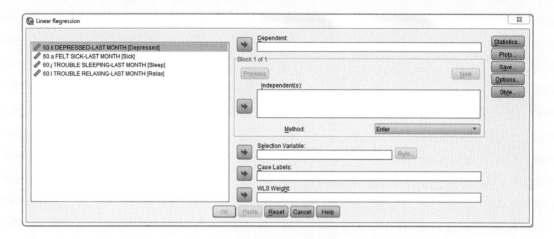

Figure 15.3 The Linear Regression window as it first appears in SPSS.

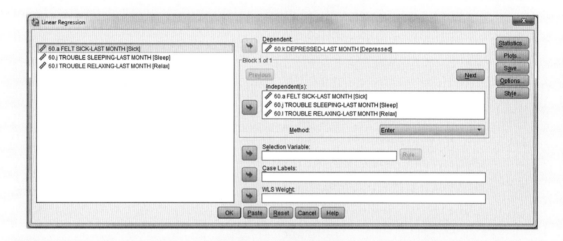

Figure 15.4 The SPSS Linear Regression window with the variables selected.

(which is labeled "Dependent"). The independent variables should be moved into the area labeled "Independent(s)." The result is shown in Figure 15.4.

To get multicollinearity statistics, click the button labeled "Statistics." This makes a new window appear, as shown in Figure 15.5. Check the box labeled "Collinearity diagnostics" and then click "Continue." Finally, click "OK" in the SPSS Linear Regression window (in Figure 15.4).

The output window will then show the results of the multiple regression, as shown in Figure 15.6. There are four tables in this output. The first one provides the R^2 value (.325 in this example). This table also provides an R^2 value that is adjusted for the sample size. When the sample size is large (as in this example), the R^2 and the adjusted R^2 will be equal or very similar. But when the sample size is small, the results will diverge more (see Skidmore & Thompson, 2011).

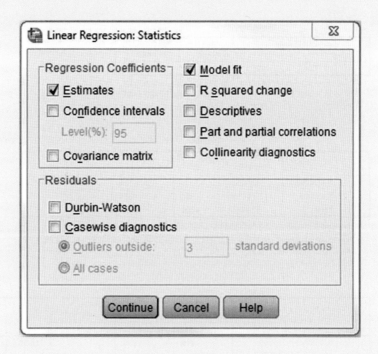

Figure 15.5 The Linear Regression Statistics window in SPSS. To receive multicollinearity statistics, click the box labeled "Collinearity diagnostics."

The next table in the output window is an ANOVA table, which only provides one unique piece of information: the p-value for the entire multiple regression model, which is labeled "Sig." If the null hypothesis in Formula 15.4 or 15.5 is rejected for any variable, or if the combination of independent variables is statistically significant, this p-value will also be statistically significant. In this case, the table displays a p-value of .000. However, this does not indicate that $p = 0$. SPSS rounds p-values to three decimal places. Instead, p is less than .001. (See Sidebar 7.3.)

The third table in the output window shows the b and β weight values for each variable. The b weights are under the column labeled "B," while the β weights are in the column labeled "Beta." The right three columns are also relevant. The one labeled "Sig." is the p-value for each independent variable's null hypothesis test (see Formulas 15.4 and 15.5). The last two columns are the multicollinearity statistics, all of which indicate that multicollinearity is not a problem in this example. The last table provides more information about multicollinearity, and it is rarely necessary to analyze this table in a detailed manner.

If you wish to include an interaction in your statistical model, it is necessary to create a new variable. Do this by selecting the "Transform" menu and then "Compute Variable." This makes the Compute Variable window appear, as shown in Figure 15.7. This window basically functions like a calculator. In the top-right area (labeled "Numeric Expression"), you can enter the equation needed to calculate the new interaction variable. Figure 15.7 shows how to calculate the interaction between the "Sick" and "Sleep" variables. The top-left area is

Model Summary

Model	R	R Square	Adjusted R Square	Std. Error of the Estimate
1	.570[a]	.325	.325	.980

a. Predictors: (Constant), 60.l TROUBLE RELAXING-LAST MONTH, 60.a FELT SICK-LAST MONTH, 60.j TROUBLE SLEEPING-LAST MONTH

ANOVA[a]

Model		Sum of Squares	df	Mean Square	F	Sig.
1	Regression	2020.662	3	673.554	701.030	.000[b]
	Residual	4194.880	4366	.961		
	Total	6215.541	4369			

a. Dependent Variable: 60.k DEPRESSED-LAST MONTH

b. Predictors: (Constant), 60.l TROUBLE RELAXING-LAST MONTH, 60.a FELT SICK-LAST MONTH, 60.j TROUBLE SLEEPING-LAST MONTH

Coefficients[a]

Model		Unstandardized Coefficients		Standardized Coefficients	t	Sig.	Collinearity Statistics	
		B	Std. Error	Beta			Tolerance	VIF
1	(Constant)	.419	.025		16.563	.000		
	60.a FELT SICK-LAST MONTH	.155	.017	.123	9.256	.000	.880	1.137
	60.j TROUBLE SLEEPING-LAST MONTH	.145	.014	.145	9.999	.000	.735	1.360
	60.l TROUBLE RELAXING-LAST MONTH	.465	.016	.429	29.203	.000	.717	1.394

a. Dependent Variable: 60.k DEPRESSED-LAST MONTH

Collinearity Diagnostics[a]

Model	Dimension	Eigenvalue	Condition Index	Variance Proportions			
				(Constant)	60.a FELT SICK-LAST MONTH	60.j TROUBLE SLEEPING-LAST MONTH	60.l TROUBLE RELAXING-LAST MONTH
1	1	3.065	1.000	.03	.03	.03	.03
	2	.428	2.675	.18	.22	.22	.27
	3	.284	3.284	.02	.04	.70	.66
	4	.223	3.711	.77	.72	.05	.04

a. Dependent Variable: 60.k DEPRESSED-LAST MONTH

Figure 15.6 SPSS output for multiple regression.

where you must type the name of the new variable. Once all the interactions of interest are created as new variables, analyzing the new multiple regression model is the same as explained above, except the interactions are added to the variable list in the Linear Regression window (shown in Figure 15.4).

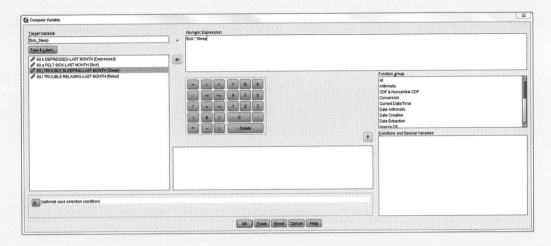

Figure 15.7 The Compute Variable Window in SPSS. This example shows how to calculate an interaction between the "Sleep" and "Sick" variables. This window also can be used to create other variables derived from existing ones.

Check Yourself!

- Why is multiple regression an important procedure to understand?

- What is the null hypothesis in multiple regression?

- What is the effect size for multiple regression, and how do you interpret it?

- What is an interaction?

Two-Way and Three-Way ANOVAs. Chapter 11 introduced analysis of variance (ANOVA) and showed that this procedure is used to compare means for three or more groups. This type of ANOVA is called a **one-way ANOVA** because it has only one nominal-level independent variable. In ANOVAs, sometimes an independent variable is called a **way**. By this logic, we can extend the ANOVA procedure to encompass two nominal-level independent variables; this is called a **two-way ANOVA** because it is an ANOVA with two independent variables.

Consider an example of a two-way ANOVA from the Add Health dataset. In this example there were two independent variables: (1) the gender of the participants, and (2) whether the individual was born inside the United States. Both of these are nominal variables with two conditions in each variable. Thus, there are four possible combinations of the variables that subjects could have, as shown in Table 15.2. Therefore, some researchers would label this as a 2 × 2 ANOVA (pronounced "two-by-two ANOVA"). The numbers in this terminology merely refer to the number of conditions in each variable, and we know that there are two independent variables (i.e., ways) because there are two digits in this label. If there were three conditions in one independent variable and four conditions in the other independent variable, we would label this a 3 × 4 ANOVA.

Table 15.2 Means, standard deviations, and sample sizes for each combination of conditions in a 2 × 2 ANOVA

	Males	Females	Total
Subjects born in US	M = 35.49 SD = 7.54 n = 514	M = 32.61 SD = 9.23 n = 463	M = 34.12 SD = 8.50 n = 977
Subjects born outside US	M = 34.36 SD = 8.77 n = 55	M = 35.38 SD = 6.991 n = 52	M = 34.86 SD = 7.93 n = 107
Total	M = 35.38 SD = 7.66 n = 569	M = 32.89 SD = 9.06 n = 515	M = 34.20 SD = 8.44 n = 1,084

Data source: National Longitudinal Study of Adolescent and Adult Health (i.e., Add Health).

The dependent variable in this 2 × 2 ANOVA example is the length of time participants had activity in their physical education class – a ratio-level variable. Table 15.2 shows the number of means, standard deviations, and group sizes for each combination of conditions in the data.

An alternative to conducting a two-way ANOVA would be to conduct two separate one-way ANOVAs. The downside with this course of action is that it would inflate experimentwise Type I error – just as conducting multiple unpaired-samples *t*-tests inflates experimentwise Type I error. We could correct for this by performing a Bonferroni correction and dividing α by the number of ANOVAs (i.e., the number of independent variables). In the example shown in Table 15.2, the adjusted α would be .05/2 = .025 because the two independent variables would require two ANOVAs to investigate separately. The downside to performing multiple ANOVAs is that it does not permit the investigation of an interaction between independent variables. One-way ANOVAs can only investigate main effects; they cannot investigate interactions.

Table 15.2 is an example of an interaction taken from the Add Health database. The two independent variables in this example are the subjects' sex (male or female) and their location of birth (inside the United States or outside the United States), which makes this a 2 × 2 ANOVA. The dependent variable is the duration of activity in their physical education classes (measured in minutes). The results of the 2 × 2 ANOVA indicate that the main effect for sex was not statistically significant ($p = .276$). This means that there is no overall difference in the duration of physical activity across males and females. Similarly, the main effect for the subjects' location of birth was not statistically significant ($p = .332$), indicating that native-born and overseas-born adolescents had similar values on the dependent variable.

However, the interaction between the two independent variables is statistically significant ($p = .022$). A statistically significant interaction indicates that at least one of the four groups has a mean that cannot be explained via the overall impacts (i.e., the main effects) of independent variables. Rather, there is a nonlinear effect, where some combinations of the variables have larger impacts than others. This can be seen graphically in Figure 15.8. In the graph it is apparent that among subjects born in the United States, males had more activity time in physical education classes than females did. However, among subjects born outside the United States, this tendency was reversed, with females

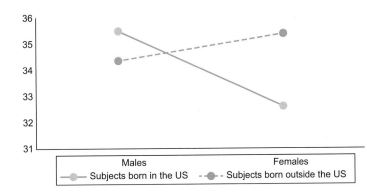

Figure 15.8 Visual model of a statistical interaction. In this graph each dot represents a group mean from Table 15.2, and the solid line connects the means representing subjects born in the US, while the dotted line corresponds to groups of subjects born outside the US. When an interaction is present in an ANOVA, the lines in a graph like this will be nonparallel. If no interaction were present, the lines would be approximately parallel.

having more physical activity in their classes than males. This is why the lines in Figure 15.8 cross. It is important to note, though, that when an interaction is present the lines will be nonparallel, though they may not cross. If an interaction were not present, the lines would be approximately parallel.

When an interaction is present, it is impossible to get an accurate interpretation of the data without considering both independent variables and the interaction. Again, this is shown in the physical activity example: we cannot say uniformly that males spend more time in activity in their physical education class, even though (as shown in Table 15.2) the average for all males is higher than the average for all females. Rather, we have to have a more nuanced interpretation: that some males (i.e., those born in the United States) spend more time in activity in their physical education class, while some females (i.e., those born outside the United States) spend more time in activity in their physical education class. This example shows that interactions make interpreting data more complex – but more accurate.

Interactions are common. For example, Caspi et al. (2007) found that the impact of breast-feeding on a child's intelligence varied according to which version of a gene (called an allele) that the child had. This is an example of an environment–gene interaction. Such environment–gene interactions are probably common and may contribute to an understanding of why people react to the same situation (e.g., a natural disaster, life trauma, special academic treatment) in different ways. As another example, Spinath, Freudenthaler, and Neubauer (2010) found an interaction between subjects' sex and their level of extraversion when studying the impact of both variables on school grades. They found that female students with high levels of extraversion earned higher grades in language arts and foreign language classes, while boys with high levels of extraversion had lower grades in these subjects. Thus, it is not possible to accurately say overall whether extraversion is associated with higher grades. For some students (girls) it is associated with higher grades, while for other students (boys) it is associated with lower grades.

After you see how a two-way ANOVA is performed and interpreted, this procedure can be extended to three nominal-level independent variables (i.e., a three-way ANOVA) or even more independent variables (e.g., a four-way ANOVA, a five-way ANOVA, etc.). Likewise, with modern computers it is relatively easy to create statistical models to investigate interactions among three or more variables (called "three-way interactions," "four-way interactions," etc.). However, in practice, researchers rarely investigate or conduct interactions with more than three variables because these become extremely difficult to interpret, and the results often do not replicate in other samples. When a statistical model includes every main effect and every possible interaction, we call it a **factorial model**. Thus, the example in Table 15.2 is a 2 × 2 factorial ANOVA because it investigates both main effects and their interaction.

Software Guide 15.2

The purpose of this section is to describe how to conduct a two-way ANOVA in SPSS. The data in this example are taken from the Add Health database that was used as an example in this chapter. Readers who wish to conduct a three-way or four-way ANOVA will find that the process is almost entirely the same and merely requires changing a few options.

The first step is to click the "Analyze" menu and then "General Linear Model" → "Univariate." This makes the Univariate window in SPSS appear, as shown in Figure 15.9.

The list of all variables in the dataset is on the left. To include these variables in the ANOVA model, select a variable from the left and move it into one of the areas on the right. The "Dependent Variable" field is where the model's outcome variable should be put. The independent variables should be placed in either the "Fixed Factor(s)" or the "Random Factor(s)" fields. If an independent variable covers all possible values of interest, it should be placed in the "Fixed Factor(s)" field. Otherwise, the independent variable should be placed in the "Random Factor(s)" field. In the Add Health example, both independent variables include all possible values of interest. The sex variable comprises both males and females; the birth variable consists of individuals born inside and outside the United States. There are no other possible groups that these variables do not include. The Univariate window with the variables placed in the appropriate fields is shown in Figure 15.10.

The default option in SPSS is to conduct an ANOVA with a factorial model. This is a sensible choice when there are two or three independent variables, but when there are more independent variables, these models can become complex and difficult to interpret. To create a different type of model, click the "Model" button, which makes a new window appear, called the Univariate: Model window. This is shown in Figure 15.11. To do this, click the button labeled

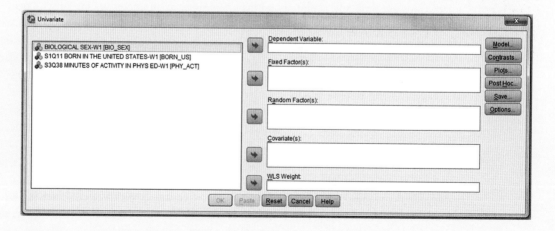

Figure 15.9 The Univariate window in SPSS as it first appears.

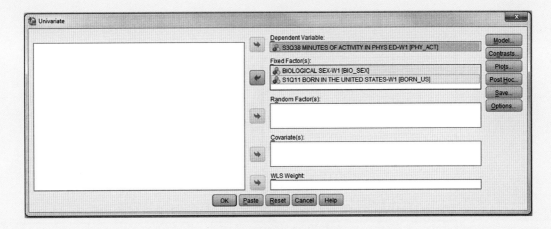

Figure 15.10 The SPSS Univariate window with a dependent variable and two independent variables selected. The independent variables are selected and have been placed in the "Fixed Factor(s)" area because they comprise all of the sex and birth location groups that would be of interest.

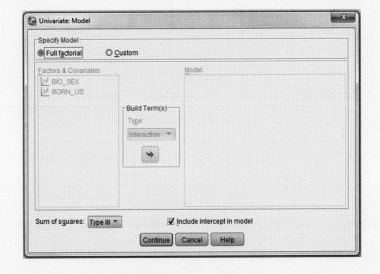

Figure 15.11 The Univariate: Model window in SPSS.

"Custom." Then, select the variables that you want to include in the statistical model and move them to the right side of the screen. The menu in between will allow you to select whether you want a variable included in the model as a main effect or an interaction. Once you have built a model, click the "Continue" button.

Once the model is created, select "OK" in the Univariate window. This causes the results of the ANOVA to appear in the output window. This is shown in Figure 15.12. The first table is a count of the number of sample members who appear in each group. Because this is a 2×2 ANOVA, there are four groups listed in this table. If you compare the numbers in Figure 15.12 to the numbers in Table 15.1, you will notice that these counts are from the "Total" row and "Total"

Between-Subjects Factors

		Value Label	N
BIOLOGICAL SEX-W1	1	Male	569
	2	Female	515
S1Q11 BORN IN THE UNITED STATES-W1	0	No	107
	1	Yes (skip to Q.15)	977

Tests of Between-Subjects Effects

Dependent Variable: S3Q38 MINUTES OF ACTIVITY IN PHYS ED-W1

Source	Type III Sum of Squares	df	Mean Square	F	Sig.
Corrected Model	2090.516[a]	3	696.839	10.020	.000
Intercept	457683.540	1	457683.540	6580.883	.000
BIO_SEX	82.614	1	82.614	1.188	.276
BORN_US	65.453	1	65.453	.941	.332
BIO_SEX * BORN_US	365.216	1	365.216	5.251	.022
Error	75111.237	1080	69.547		
Total	1344900.000	1084			
Corrected Total	77201.753	1083			

a. R Squared = .027 (Adjusted R Squared = .024)

Figure 15.12 Results of a 2 × 2 ANOVA as they appear in the SPSS output window.

column in Table 15.1. Therefore, in this example, the counts are the total numbers of males, females, individuals born in the United States, and individuals born outside the United States. It does not list the number of individuals in each combination of groups.

The second table is an ANOVA table describing the results. The most important part is the footnote of the table, which shows the R^2 effect size for the entire model. In this example, the effect size is .027 (or .024 after adjusting for the sample size). This R^2 is equal to the η^2 value, and it really doesn't matter whether you call the effect size R^2 or η^2. Another important piece of information is the p-values of the main effects and interaction in the table. These are in the variable labeled "Sig." The top row refers to the "Corrected Model," which is the p-value of the entire model (i.e., the total impact of all variables and interactions combined). The next row, labeled "Intercept," is not substantially meaningful. It is just a value needed for scaling purposes and can always be ignored. The rest of the values in the "Sig." column are the p-values for each main effect and the interaction in the model. In this example, neither of the main effects is statistically significant ($p = .276$ and .332), but the interaction is statistically significant ($p = .022$). This matches the results described in the text and shown in Figure 15.2.

Table 15.3 Example of dummy coding a nominal variable with five conditions into four dichotomous variables

	Variable 1	Variable 2	Variable 3	Variable 4
African-Americans have scores of	1	0	0	0
Asian/Pacific Islanders have scores of	0	1	0	0
Hispanics have scores of	0	0	1	0
Other racial/ethnic groups have scores of	0	0	0	1
Whites have scores of	0	0	0	0

It is difficult to see at first glance, but the two-way ANOVA and other more complex ANOVAs are all special cases of multiple regression. Using Formulas 15.2 or 15.3 with nominal data requires some data preparation. Typically, when we record data, we put all the scores in the same column in a computer program. However, if you want to use nominal variables in a multiple regression equation, you must create $k - 1$ new variables, where k is the number of groups in the original nominal variable. For example, in one study I conducted (Warne, Nagaishi, et al., 2014), I had a nominal variable for my subjects' race/ethnicity, and that nominal variable had five categories: African-American, Asian/Pacific Islander, Hispanic, White, and other race/ethnicity. Therefore, I created four new variables via a scheme called "dummy coding." There are other methods of coding nominal data, but dummy coding is the easiest to learn and interpret.

In dummy coding, the data analyst picks a baseline group that all other groups will be compared to. This group will receive the value "0" in all of the new variables. The other, non-baseline groups each receive a score of "1" for a particular variable and a "0" for all other variables. The result is $k - 1$ dichotomous variables. Table 15.3 shows how, in my study, I created the four new variables:

The choice of the baseline group does not matter in dummy coding. I like to pick either the largest group (as in the example in Table 15.3) or the theoretically most important group, such as a control group. When these variables are used in a multiple regression model in Formula 15.2 (i.e., $\hat{y} = b_1x_1 + b_2x_2 + \ldots + b_jx_j + a$), the result is a b weight value for each dummy variable that quantifies the difference between a particular group's mean and the baseline group's mean on the dependent variable. In using dummy-coded variables (or any nominal variables, for that matter) in multiple regression, the β values in Formula 15.3 are much harder to interpret than the b values in Formula 13.2. This is because Formula 15.3 converts all the data to z-scores, and nominal data cannot be used sensibly in the z-score formula (because the formula requires being able to calculate a mean and a standard deviation). On the other hand, in comparing the relative strength of a nominal variable with other variables in an ANOVA or a multiple regression model, the standardized β are required (as explained above in the section on multiple regression).

There is one final note relevant to dummy coding. ANOVA (whether the one-way ANOVAs in Chapter 11 or the more complex ANOVAs in this chapter) requires all independent variables to be nominal-level data. If any independent variables are not nominal-level, you cannot use ANOVA. Instead, you must use multiple regression and recode all the nominal variables so that they are dichotomous. On the other hand, if all the variables are nominal-level data and you use multiple regression anyway, the results will be the same as if an ANOVA had been conducted. (Note that performing a factorial ANOVA with multiple regression requires creating all the necessary interaction variables first.)

Check Yourself!

- What does it mean if a study is said to be a $3 \times 2 \times 3$ ANOVA?

- Figure 15.8 shows an interaction between two independent variables. What would the visual model look like if there were no interaction present?

- What is a factorial model?

Logistic Regression and Multiple Logistic Regression. In almost every NHST explained in this book so far, the dependent variable has been interval- or ratio-level data. (The chi-squared test is the only exception.) These methods work for many situations, but not in cases where the dependent variable (i.e., the outcome) is nominal- or ordinal-level data. For example, in medical research the outcome of a study may be whether a patient lives or dies – definitely a nominal variable! In the social sciences other nominal or ordinal outcomes include whether:

- a couple divorces or not
- a patient maintains a therapeutic regimen or stops treatment
- a child graduates from high school or not
- a person is diagnosed with a psychological disorder or not
- a college student is on the dean's list, is otherwise in good academic standing, or is on academic probation.

Because it is impossible to calculate a meaningful average for nominal outcome variables, previous NHST procedures that compare means are not appropriate for these dependent variables.

Logistic regression was created to solve this problem and permit null hypothesis tests of nominal outcome variables. The solution (derived by Berkson, 1944) is to ignore the impact of the independent variable directly on the dependent variable, but rather to convert the dependent variable to a **logit** (pronounced "LOW-jit," and also called a log-odds). Mathematically, the logit for a particular outcome of interest is calculated as

$$logit(p) = ln\left(\frac{p}{1-p}\right) \qquad \text{(Formula 15.6)}$$

In this formula, p is the proportion of sample members who had experienced the outcome of interest. Thus, $\left(\frac{p}{1-p}\right)$ is an odds ratio, with values greater than 1 indicating that the majority of sample members experience the outcome of interest. (Conversely, values less than 1 indicate that a minority of sample members experience the outcome of interest.) The ln refers to the natural log function, which converts proportion p into a form that can be used for null hypothesis testing.

When it is used as the dependent variable in regression, we can make a prediction of a nominal variable, using a single independent variable with the following equation:

$$ln\left(\frac{p}{1-p}\right) = bx_i + a \qquad \text{(Formula 15.7)}$$

Table 15.4 Multiple logistic regression example predicting the likelihood that a child would be labeled "gifted"

Variable	B Value	Odds ratio (e^B)	p
African-American (dummy coded)	0.798	2.985	< .001
Asian-American (dummy coded)	1.093	2.222	.022
Hispanic (dummy coded)	1.046	2.846	< .001
Multiracial (dummy coded)	0.404	1.499	.135
Native American (dummy coded)	0.432	1.540	.489
Pacific Islander (dummy coded)	1.526	4.598	< .001
Low SES (dummy coded)	-0.047	0.954	.594
Math Scores	0.067	1.069	< .001
Reading Scores	0.071	1.074	< .001

Note. Race/ethnicity group variables dummy coded with Whites as the baseline group. "Low SES" is a nominal variable defined by whether students were classified as qualifying for a subsidized lunch at school. Students who were not eligible for a subsidized lunch were the baseline group.
Source: Warne, Anderson, & Johnson (2013).

where $ln\left(\frac{p}{1-p}\right)$ is the log odds, x_i is a sample member's score on independent variable x, b is the slope of the regression line (which also functions as an unstandardized regression weight), and a is the y-intercept. You may notice that the part of the formula on the right side of the equal sign looks familiar. That is because it is the same as in Formula 13.2, which was the unstandardized regression equation with one independent variable. Thus, logistic regression is just a regression procedure used to predict nominal outcomes via the logit.

Comparing this formula to the multiple regression Formula 15.1 makes it clear that **logistic regression** is just a method of predicting the logit of the nominal dependent variable, instead of a mean dependent variable score. The principles of how to make this prediction (i.e., on the basis of b weights multiplied by independent variable x-scores) are the same.

At the beginning of this chapter, we saw that traditional regression (which we learned about in Chapter 12) can be converted into multiple regression by adding independent variables to the statistical model. The same is true of logistic regression. When there are two or more independent variables in a regression model and one nominal outcome variable, we use the term **multiple logistic regression** to describe the statistical procedure.

An example of multiple logistic regression can be found in an article that I published with two of my students (Warne, Anderson, & Johnson, 2013) where we were interested in variables that predicted whether a student would be labeled as being "gifted" in their local schools. This is a nominal dependent variable with two possible outcomes (being labeled as "gifted" or "not gifted"). For the independent variables we used race/ethnicity (with seven groups: African-Americans, Asian-Americans, Hispanics, Native Americans, Pacific Islanders, Whites, and multiracial individuals), socioeconomic status (SES), reading test scores, and mathematics test scores. The race variable was dummy coded (with Whites as the baseline group). The results are shown in Table 15.4.

The column labeled "b Value" quantifies the expected impact of a 1-point change in an independent variable on the dependent variable's logit while holding all other independent variables constant. For example, a 1-point change in math scores is associated with a 0.067 point change in the dependent variable logit value.

Interpreting logits can be hard to understand, so many people convert the independent variable β values to an odds ratio effect size with the following formula:

$$e^{\beta} = OR \qquad \text{(Formula 15.8)}$$

where e is a mathematical constant equal to approximately 2.718, β is the β value for an independent variable, and OR is the odds ratio for that variable. For example, in Table 15.4, the odds ratio for math scores is:

$$e^{0.067} = OR$$
$$2.718^{0.067} = OR$$
$$1.069 = OR$$

Thus, in our study, students whose math scores were 1 point higher than other students' math scores were 1.069 times more likely to be labeled as "gifted," if all other variables were held constant. Likewise, Table 15.4 shows that Hispanic students were 2.846 times more likely to be labeled as "gifted" than white students.

If we are interested in identifying the expected change from a larger number of points, we should raise the odds ratio to the power of the number of points. For example, if we are interested in the impact of a 10-point change in math scores, we would take the odds ratio for that variable (1.069) and raise it to the 10th power: $1.069^{10} = 1.949$. This tells us that a 10-point increase in math scores nearly doubles a child's likelihood of being labeled "gifted."

The last column in Table 15.4 lists *p-v*alues for each independent variable. These *p-v*alues are for a statistical test for the null hypothesis that the independent variable β = 0. From the traditional α value of .05, it is apparent that all of the independent variables were statistically significant, except the multiracial dummy code variable, the Native American dummy code variable, and the socioeconomic status dummy code variable. Thus, these variables did not have a detectable relationship with the dependent variable (after all the other variables were held constant).

Sidebar 15.3 **Simpson's paradox**

The article that Table 15.4 is taken from displays an interesting phenomenon. My student coauthors and I built the multiple logistic regression model in Table 15.4 by running the model, adding a variable or two, running the model again, and then adding variables until the final model in Table 15.4 was created. (Adding variables in this fashion is called a step-up procedure.) In the earliest model, which consisted of only the race/ethnicity dummy code variables, three of the groups had negative β values: African-Americans (β = −.209), Hispanics (β = −0.055), and Native Americans (β = −0.614). Although none of these β values were statistically significant from zero, they did indicate that these groups would be less likely to be labeled "gifted" than white students (Warne, Anderson, & Johnson, 2013). Yet, when additional variables were added to the model, all three of these groups' β values flipped from negative to positive and became statistically significant. In any regression model, when β values switch from negative to positive (or vice versa) as independent variables are added to the model, it indicates that the relationship between the dependent and independent variables switches from a negative to a positive as other variables are added to the model. This is called **Simpson's paradox**, and it seems counterintuitive because most people believe that relationships between variables should stay positive or stay negative as variables are added to a statistical model. So, how does Simpson's paradox happen?

One way of thinking of Simpson's paradox is that it arises because the relationship between the independent and dependent variable was not constant for all subjects. In the example in Table 15.4, there was either a negative or zero relationship between the variables for lower academic achievement score levels. But for students with above-average test scores, the smaller numbers of African-American, Hispanic, and Native American students were disproportionately more likely to be identified as "gifted" than white students. The larger numbers of African-American, Hispanic, and Native American students' scores at lower score levels (who were unlikely to be labeled "gifted") overwhelmed the influence of the smaller numbers of students with high scores (who were *more* likely to be labeled "gifted"). Because the relationship between race and the "gifted" label was not constant across all academic achievement score levels, this complex relationship between these three variables cannot be ascertained without examining all three variables. This varying relationship between race and the dependent variable across different test score levels is an example of an interaction. Therefore, this example shows how leaving an interaction out of a statistical model can provide distorted and misleading results of that model (Goltz & Smith, 2010; Simpson, 1951).

Another way to think about Simpson's paradox is in terms of probabilities. In the example above, the overall probability that an African-American student would be labeled "gifted" (instead of an equivalent white student) was only .448. (The β value for these students was $-.209$, which corresponds to an odds ratio of $e^{-.209} = 0.811$. Converting this odds ratio into a predicted probability results in $0.811 / (1 + 0.811)$ $= 0.811 / 1.811 = 0.448$.) This overall probability for the entire group experiencing the outcome of interest is called the **marginal probability**. On the other hand, Table 15.4 shows that adding the other independent variables into the model produces a β value of 0.798, which corresponds to an odds ratio of $e^{0.798} = 2.222$. Converting this odds ratio into a probability produces the result of $2.222 / (1 + 2.222) =$ $2.222 / 3.222 = 0.690$. This probability is *not* the overall probability that any African-American student would be identified as "gifted." Rather, it represents the probability that, of two students – one African-American and the other white – who are equal on all other independent variables, the African-American student would be identified as "gifted" instead of the white student. Because this probability depends on equal scores on all other independent variables, it is called the **conditional probability**. Simpson's paradox occurs when marginal and conditional probabilities vary after adding the other independent variables to a model (Agresti, 2007).

Although Simpson's paradox has been known to social scientists for a long time (e.g., Glass, 1977) and to statisticians for even longer (Simpson, 1951; Yule, 1903), it is still often poorly understood. One challenge with Simpson's paradox is that it is often difficult to know when it lurks in the data without adding the right independent variables to a statistical model. This can be seen in my study of identification in gifted education programs; previously there were dozens of studies on the relative likelihood that students from different racial groups would be selected for gifted programs in the United States, and almost all showed a lower probability for African-Americans being selected for these programs (e.g., Konstantopoulous, Modi, & Hedges, 2001). Only when my students and I added variables of academic achievement did we notice the paradox: that even though, overall, African-Americans were less likely to be labeled "gifted," African-Americans with high educational test scores were more likely to be selected for these programs than white students. No one else had ever noticed these results because no other researchers added variables that interacted with race (i.e., academic achievement) to their regression models.

How important is Simpson's paradox? Because it can produce results that are the exact opposite of the actual statistical relationship between variables, the consequences of ignoring

Simpson's paradox can be drastic. Goltz and Smith (2010) recounted examples from education, sociology, and public safety, some of which give counterintuitive results if Simpson's paradox is not considered. For example, one study they discussed showed that a country with a longer average lifespan can have a higher death rate than a country with a shorter lifespan! This is counterintuitive because one would expect countries in which people live longer to have lower death rates. But when an additional variable – the average age of each nation – was taken into consideration, this surprising result disappears, and the discrepancy is resolved. In reality, the country with the shorter lifespan had a younger mean age, which depresses its death rate; the nation with the longer lifespan had an older mean age, and these elderly citizens inflated the country's death rate. Additionally, people who apply research to real-world situations may often be misled if they do not realize that Simpson's paradox is distorting a statistical analysis. This may lead to policies or therapies that are ineffective and do not improve people's lives. The result may be frustration, wasted resources, and a stunting of scientific and social progress (Warne, Anderson, & Johnson, 2013).

Software Guide 15.3

The first step in conducting a logistic regression or multiple logistic regression in SPSS is to click the "Analyze" menu and then "Regression" ➔ "Binary Logistic." This causes the Logistic Regression window to appear in SPSS. This window is shown in Figure 15.13.

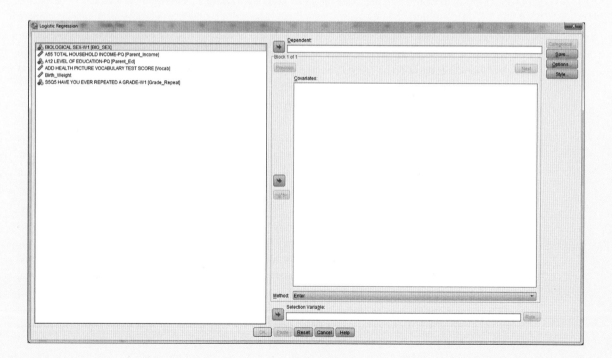

Figure 15.13 The Logistic Regression window in SPSS as it first appears.

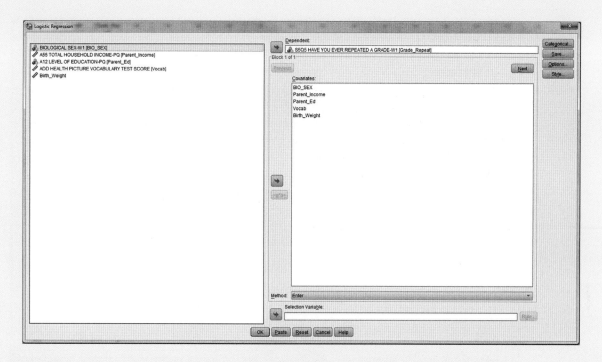

Figure 15.14 The SPSS Logistic Regression window with five independent variables and one dependent variable.

In this window, the next step is to select independent and dependent variables and put them in the section labeled "Covariates" (for independent variables) or "Dependent" (for the dependent variable). In this example, we will use the Add Health data to estimate the likelihood of a subject repeating a year of school based on their scores from five independent variables: sex (males = 1, females = 2), household income, parental level of education, vocabulary, and birth weight. (Note that this is a multiple logistic regression model. To create a logistic regression model, limit yourself to one independent variable.) After these variables were selected, Figure 15.14 shows the appearance of the Logistic Regression window.

If any independent variables are nominal-level data, click the "Categorical" button in the top right of the Logistic Regression window, which makes a new window appear, as shown in Figure 15.15. This window is called the Logistic Regression: Define Categorical Variables window. When it appears, select any nominal variables and move them to the right side of the window. As the variable is highlighted, you have the option of selecting whether to make the baseline category (called the "Reference Category" in SPSS) the group with the lowest score on the variable or the highest score. This tells the computer to automatically create dummy codes with the designated baseline group. Other coding options are available by selecting the pull-down menu labeled "Contrast." Dummy coding (which SPSS labels "contrast coding") is the default, and it works for many purposes. After designating nominal variables and a coding scheme, select "Continue." Then push "OK" in the Logistic Regression window.

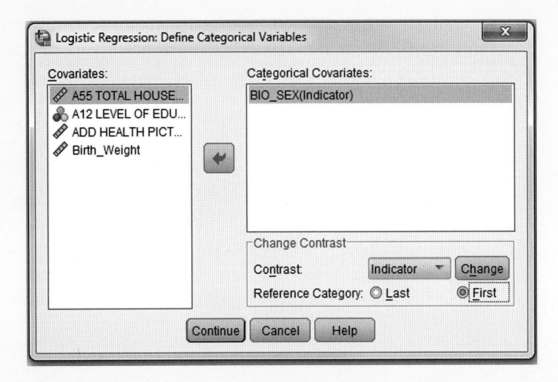

Figure 15.15 The Logistic Regression: Define Categorical Variables window in SPSS. This window is used to designate categorical variables and to tell the computer how to code the variables.

Three tables are shown in Figure 15.16; this is not the entire SPSS output, but it is the most relevant. The top table is labeled "Model Summary," and lists two possible R^2 values: the Cox and Snell R^2 (.090 in this example) and the Nagelkerke R^2 (.145). Logistic regression does not create a true R^2 effect size. These two values are approximations; neither is better than the other, and I recommend that researchers report both values.

The second table in Figure 15.15 is a classification table that shows how well the model can classify sample members' scores on the outcome variables. In this example, the table shows that the model correctly classifies 97.9% of individuals who had never repeated a grade and 5.7% of individuals who had repeated a grade. Overall, this means that 80.4% of sample members were correctly classified by the model.

The last table shows the b values, odds ratios, and p-values for each independent variable in the model. The b values are in the column labeled "b," and in this example indicate the change in likelihood that a subject would repeat a grade if they had a 1-point increase in the independent variable if all other independent variables were held constant. For example, the sex variable indicates that females had a lower likelihood of repeating a grade, as indicated by the negative b weight ($b = -.638$). Notice that the other variables' b values are all negative, indicating that as parental income, parental education, vocabulary, and birth weight increased, the subject's probability of repeating a grade decreased. The p-value of each variable is in the "Sig." category, and all are below the customary α value of .05,

Model Summary

Step	-2 Log likelihood	Cox & Snell R Square	Nagelkerke R Square
1	3742.197[a]	.090	.145

a. Estimation terminated at iteration number 5 because parameter estimates changed by less than .001.

Classification Table[a]

			Predicted		
			S5Q5 HAVE YOU EVER REPEATED A GRADE-W1		
	Observed		No (skip to Q. 7)	Yes	Percentage Correct
Step 1	S5Q5 HAVE YOU EVER REPEATED A GRADE-W1	No (skip to Q.7)	3381	72	97.9
		Yes	764	46	5.7
	Overall Percentage				80.4

a. The cut value is .500

Variables in the Equation

		B	S.E.	Wald	df	Sig.	Exp(B)
Step 1[a]	BIO_SEX(1)	-.638	.084	57.655	1	.000	.528
	Parent_Income	-.005	.002	11.292	1	.001	.995
	Parent_Ed	-.147	.020	53.042	1	.000	.863
	Vocab	-.032	.003	111.365	1	.000	.968
	Birth_Weight	-.005	.002	5.195	1	.023	.995
	Constant	3.691	.378	95.254	1	.000	40.088

a. Variable(s) entered on step 1: BIO_SEX, Parent_Income, Parent_Ed, Vocab, Birth_Weight.

Figure 15.16 SPSS output for a multiple logistic regression model.

indicating that all of these independent variables are statistically significant predictors (even when all other independent variables are held constant) of whether a person would repeat a grade. Finally, the Exp(B) column gives the odds ratio for a 1-point change in each independent variable. For example, the 0.995 odds ratio for the birth weight variable indicates that for every 1-ounce (28.3 grams) difference in birth weight between individuals, we can expect that the child whose birth weight was higher to be 0.995 times as likely to repeat a grade as the child whose birth weight was lower. This may not seem like much, but a child who was born 1 pound (16 ounces, or 453.6 grams) heavier than another child is $0.995^{16} = 0.923$ times as likely to repeat a grade. For a 2-pound difference (32 ounces, or 907.2 grams), this odds ratio becomes $0.995^{32} = 0.852$. Clearly, low birth weight is a risk factor for a child needing to repeat a grade.

Check Yourself!

- Why does logistic regression first require calculating a logit?

- What is the difference between logistic regression and multiple logistic regression?

- How do you compare the relative influence of independent variables on one another in multiple logistic regression?

- What is Simpson's paradox?

Nonparametric Statistics

One family of statistics that some individuals prefer to use is **nonparametric statistics**, which are statistical procedures that make fewer assumptions about the shape of the distribution of the population that the sample is taken from. Nonparametric statistics are in opposition to **parametric statistics**, which frequently require strict assumptions about the population having a normally distribution shape (and often homogeneity of variance). Almost all statistical procedures I have discussed in this book so far are parametric statistics. The only exceptions are the chi-squared tests, both of which are nonparametric (see Chapter 13).

Nonparametric procedures are often based on nominal or ordinal data. In fact, many nonparametric procedures were created as ordinal-level alternatives to existing procedures that required interval- or ratio-level data. Because ordinal-level data are more basic, nonparametric statistics are more versatile and can be used in more situations than traditional parametric methods. On the other hand, this versatility comes at a cost. Nonparametric statistics have less statistical power than parametric statistics, which usually means that sample sizes must be larger than for corresponding parametric procedures (Anderson, 1961). See Sidebar 10.1 for an explanation of statistical power.

This section of the chapter will describe three basic nonparametric procedures and how they relate to parametric procedures discussed in previous chapters of this book. I have also included references where interested readers can learn more about these procedures and how to conduct and interpret them.

Spearman's ρ. The nonparametric version of Pearson's r is called Spearman's ρ (rho), and it is appropriate when both the independent and dependent variables are ordinal-level data. Proposed by Charles Spearman (1906), this nonparametric correlation coefficient uses the exact same formula as Pearson's r (see Formulas 12.1 and 12.2). But in Spearman's ρ, the variables either (1) both were collected as ordinal level data, or (2) one or both variables were collected as interval- or ratio-level data and then changed into ordinal-level data by ranking the sample members' scores on the variable(s).

Spearman himself (1904a, 1906) recognized that converting the data from a higher level down to ordinal-level data resulted in some loss of information. However, Spearman's ρ has the advantage of not being distorted by outliers – another insight that Spearman had into his own method. Because converting data into ranks forces distributions to have similar shapes, sometimes two interval-level variables will have stronger correlations when calculated via Spearman's ρ than with Pearson's r. For more information about Spearman's ρ, including how to test the null hypothesis that $\rho = 0$, see Zar (2005).

Software Guide 15.4

SPSS. To calculate Spearman's ρ in SPSS, follow nearly the same procedures outlined in Chapter 12's Software Guide. The only difference is shown in Figure 12.8b. Spearman's ρ requires checking the box labeled "Spearman." The default in SPSS is to calculate Pearson's r. This default is shown in Figure 12.8b, where the box labeled "Pearson" is checked.

Excel. Like SPSS, calculating Spearman's ρ in Microsoft Excel requires a slight modification to the Pearson's r calculation procedure. In this case, it is necessary to create a new set of scores for each individual's independent and dependent variable scores. To do this, use the Excel function =RANK(XX,YY:ZZ), where XX is the original score for an individual, and YY:ZZ represents the range of scores on the same variable. Once the rankings are created, following the steps in Chapter 12's Software Guide to find the correlation between the rankings will produce Spearman's ρ value.

Note that Microsoft Excel gives ranks scores in descending order. This means that high scores are given low rankings and low scores are given high rankings. In other words, the highest score will be given a ranking of 1, the second highest score receives a ranking of 2, and so forth. This does not change the Spearman's ρ value, nor does it alter the interpretation of Spearman's ρ.

Wilcoxon rank-sum test. When two samples consist of ordinal-level data, it is inappropriate to conduct a two-sample t-test, because calculating the means for each group would be an "illegal statistic" (Stevens, 1946, p. 679) with ordinal data. However, a nonparametric analog, called the Wilcoxon rank-sum test, allows comparisons of two groups of ordinal data. Although the Wilcoxon rank-sum test is appropriate for comparing two groups, it does *not* test a null hypothesis that the two groups' measures of central tendency (e.g., the median) are equal. This is an important difference between the Wilcoxon rank-sum test and the two-sample t-test, the latter of which *does* test a null hypothesis that two models of central tendency are equal (i.e., that H_0: $\overline{X}_1 = \overline{X}_2$).

Instead, the Wilcoxon rank-sum test compares the rankings of all possible pairs of scores in the two groups and finds the differences in these ranks. The Wilcoxon rank-sum test compares this median rank difference to the null hypothesis. The null hypothesis of a Wilcoxon rank-sum test is that this median rank difference is zero. If the two distributions overlap perfectly, the data will perfectly fit this null hypothesis model. When there is little overlap or when the two distributions have very different frequencies of each rank, the null hypothesis is more likely to be rejected.

In addition to testing the null hypothesis, some computer programs that perform the Wilcoxon rank-sum test also present a statistic that states the probability that a randomly chosen member of one group will have a higher rank than a randomly chosen member of the second group. This statistic, which is sometimes called **AUC** (which stands for the "area under the receiver operating characteristic curve"), is a useful nonparametric effect size. The AUC is also mathematically related to a statistic called the Mann–Whitney U statistic:

$$AUC = \frac{U}{n_1 n_2} \qquad \text{(Formula 15.9)}$$

where U is the Mann–Whitney U statistic, and n_1 and n_2 are the sample sizes for the two groups in the statistical test. The denominator $n_1 n_2$ is the number of possible pairs of scores that one could draw from the two groups. The AUC is a measure of the probability that a randomly selected person from the higher scoring group will rank higher than a randomly selected person from the lower scoring group. AUC values can range from 0 to 1. An AUC of 0.5 indicates that the groups' rankings overlap completely (and that the independent variable has no relationship to the dependent ordinal variable). Numbers closer to 0 and 1 indicate a greater separation between groups, less overlap in their distributions, and a stronger relationship between the independent and dependent variables.

Most of this description of the Wilcoxon rank-sum test is based on my favorite article on the concept, which was written by Conroy (2012). He not only explains what the Wilcoxon rank-sum test is, but also clarifies the common misconception that the null hypothesis in that test is that the two groups' medians are equal. Conroy also provides an excellent history of this nonparametric procedure, including the strange way it gets "discovered" again and again by researchers who do not realize that it already exists.

Check Yourself!

- What is an advantage of using nonparametric statistics? What is a disadvantage?
- How do you know when to use Spearman's ρ?
- What is the null hypothesis of the Wilcoxon rank-sum test?
- What is the effect size of the Wilcoxon rank-sum test?

Software Guide 15.5

This Software Guide will show how to conduct a Wilcoxon rank-sum test, using the Add Health dataset. The independent variable in this example is the sample member's sex, while the dependent variable is whether the sample member said they had been depressed in the previous month. This is a 5-point rating scale, with higher numbers indicating more frequent depression. The level of data in rating scales can be ambiguous (see Sidebar 2.3), so this example shows how to compare responses on an ordinal-level scale.

The first step to performing a Wilcoxon rank-sum test is to click "Analyze" → "Nonparametric Tests" → "Legacy Dialogs" → "2 Independent Samples." This produces a window shown in Figure 15.17, which is called the Two-Independent Samples Tests window.

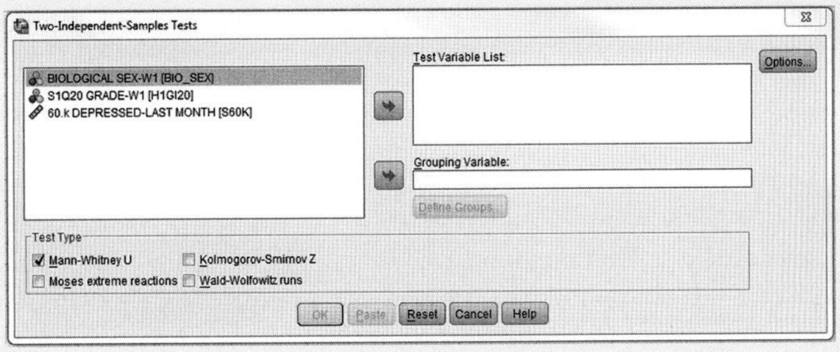

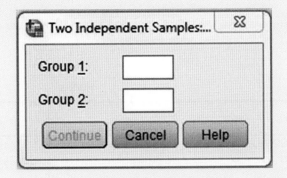

Figure 15.17 The Two-Independent Samples Tests window in SPSS as it first appears.

Figure 15.18 The Two Independent Samples: Define Groups window in SPSS.

The next step is to select the ordinal dependent variable and place it in the upper-right portion of the window (in the area labeled "Test Variable List"). Then, select the nominal independent variable from the left side of the window and place it into the area in the lower-right portion of the window, which is labeled "Grouping variable." After doing this, click the button labeled "Define Groups." This causes the image in the window shown in Figure 15.18 to appear. This is called the Two Independent Samples: Define Groups window. In this window, the user must state which numbers in the variable correspond to the groups. In the Add Health dataset, males were given a value of 1 and females were given a value of 2. Therefore, in the window, I entered the numbers "1" and "2" into the two fields and then clicked "Continue." This makes the window disappear, leaving the Two-Independent-Samples-Tests window, which now appears as shown in Figure 15.19. The final step is to click "OK" in this window.

The results of a Wilcoxon rank-sum test are in Figure 15.20. There are two tables in the output. The first shows the number of individuals in each group (in the column N), the mean rank of individuals within each group, and the sum of all ranks within a group. The last two are not very useful pieces of information because ordinal data cannot be summed or averaged sensibly (see Chapter 2).

The second table produces a Mann–Whitney U and Wilcoxon W statistic values. Neither of these is an effect size. The easiest way to calculate an effect size is to use the Mann–Whitney U value and Formula 15.9. For this example, the AUC value is:

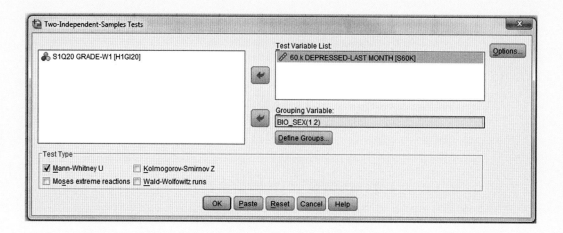

Figure 15.19 The Two-Independent-Samples Tests window in SPSS with independent and dependent variables selected.

Ranks

	BIOLOGICAL SEX-W1	N	Mean Rank	Sum of Ranks
60.k DEPRESSED-LAST MONTH	Male	2049	1919.11	3932248.50
	Female	2376	2466.45	5860276.50
	Total	4425		

Test Statistics[a]

	60.k DEPRESSED-LAST MONTH
Mann-Whitney U	1832023.500
Wilcoxon W	3932248.500
Z	-14.817
Asymp. Sig. (2-tailed)	.000

a. Grouping Variable: BIOLOGICAL SEX-W1

Figure 15.20 SPSS output showing the results of a Wilcoxon rank-sum test.

$$AUC = \frac{1,832,023.5}{(2049)(2376)}$$

$$AUC = \frac{1,832,023.5}{4,868,424}$$

$$AUC = 0.376$$

This AUC value indicates that a randomly chosen male would have a 37.6% chance of having a higher rank than a randomly chosen female in the Add Health sample. (If the two groups had identical distributions of ranks, the AUC would be .500. This would indicate a 50% chance that a randomly selected member of one group would score higher than a randomly selected person from the other group.) Therefore, it is likely that males in the Add Health sample generally had lower levels of depression than females. The Z value is a nonparametric version of the z-observed value in a z-test (see Chapter 7). The number in "Asymp. Sig. (2-tailed)" is the p-value for the test of the null hypothesis that the two groups have identical distributions of ranks. In Figure 15.19, the p-value is listed as .000, but it is important to remember that p can never equal zero. Instead, SPSS is rounding the p-value. This should be reported as $p < .001$. (See Sidebar 7.3.)

Kruskal–Wallis Test. In parametric statistics ANOVA is a generalization of the unpaired-samples t-test (for three or more groups, instead of just two groups). Nonparametric statistics has a similar extension of the Wilcoxon rank-sum test. This is called the **Kruskal–Wallis test**, and it is appropriate for three or more groups of ordinal data.

As with the Wilcoxon rank-sum test, a common misconception of the Kruskal–Wallis test is that it tests a null hypothesis of equal group medians. This is not true, even though this error appears in textbooks and scientific articles. Rather, the null hypothesis is that the distributions of ranks for all groups are equal (Ruxton & Beauchamp, 2008), which is very different from an ANOVA (where the null hypothesis is that all central tendency values in the groups are equal). When the null hypothesis is rejected in the Kruskal–Wallis test, it indicates that the distribution of ranks across groups is different. Therefore, a randomly chosen member of one group will generally have a higher rank than a randomly chosen member of one of the other groups in the data (Vargha & Delaney, 1998). This is the same interpretation as a rejected null hypothesis in the Wilcoxon rank-sum test, except it has been extended to three or more groups.

The Kruskal–Wallis test is easily misinterpreted, and it requires some strict assumptions about the distribution of ranks in the groups. As a result, I urge readers to consult a detailed treatment that is free from the common errors about the Kruskal–Wallis test (e.g., Ruxton & Beauchamp, 2008; Vargha & Delaney, 1998).

There is no clear effect size for a Kruskal–Wallis test, and η^2 (the effect size for ANOVA) is not appropriate with ordinal data. AUC can only be calculated with two groups, so it does not work well for the Kruskal–Wallis test. There are three options; the first is to calculate a series of AUC values for each pair of groups. This can create a problem, though, because the number of possible AUC values will be $\frac{k(k-1)}{2}$, where k is the number of groups. For six groups, this would indicate 15 AUC values. Another option is to calculate fewer AUC values. For example, you can choose only theoretically important group comparisons. In the Add Health example, we may choose to compare each grade level to a baseline group, like the youngest subjects in Grade 7.

The final effect size option for a Kruskal–Wallis test would be to calculate one AUC value per group. In each AUC, the comparison would be between a given group and the data from all other groups combined. Regardless of the selection of effect size strategy, any of these AUC values would have to be calculated via a Wilcoxon rank-sum test.

Guided Practice 15.6

Conducting a Kruskal–Wallis test in SPSS is similar to conducting a Wilcoxon rank-sum test in the same program. In this example, we will use the Add Health data to investigate the relationship between an ordinal independent variable with six categories and a dependent ranking variable. The independent variable was the school grade that the subject was enrolled in (ranging from 7 to 12), and the dependent variable was whether the sample member said they had been depressed in the previous month. Just as in Software Guide 15.5, this is a 5-point rating scale that could be considered ordinal data.

The first step to performing a Wilcoxon rank-sum test is to click "Analyze" → "Non-parametric Tests" → "Legacy Dialogs" → "K Independent Samples." This produces a window shown in Figure 15.21, which is called the Tests for Several Independent Samples window.

As with most SPSS windows, the dataset's variables are listed on the left, and it is necessary to move the dependent variable to the upper-right field labeled "Test Variable List." The independent variable also needs to be moved to the field labeled "Grouping Variable" (in the lower right area of the window). The next step is to click the "Define Range" variable.

This makes a window called the Several Independent Samples: Define Range window appear, as shown in Figure 15.22. There are two fields, labeled "Minimum" and "Maximum." In these fields the user must enter the numbers that correspond to the lowest and highest score categories for the independent variables. Because the subjects in the Add Health were in grades 7–12, the number "7" is entered into the "Minimum" field, while the number "12" is entered into the "Maximum" field. (See Figure 15.22 as an example.) This makes the window disappear. Note that SPSS does not permit users to skip categories. If the user wishes to use nonconsecutively numbered categories, he or she should change the numerical values assigned to some of the categories so that only consecutive categories are included in the Kruskal–Wallis test.

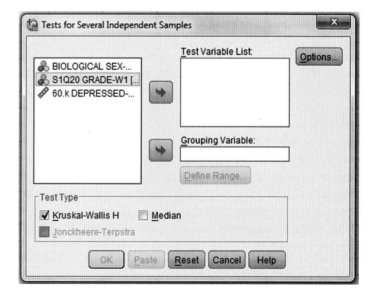

Figure 15.21 The Tests for Several Independent Samples window in SPSS as it first appears.

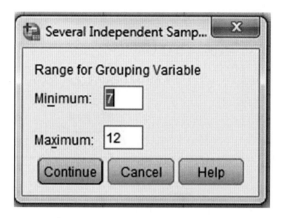

Figure 15.22 The Several Independent Samples: Define Range window in SPSS. The numbers represent the lowest and the highest score categories for the independent variable.

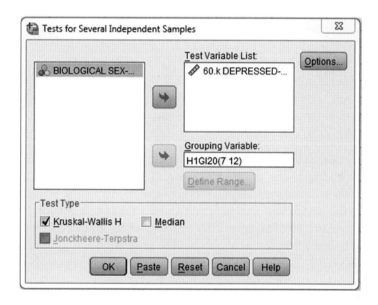

Figure 15.23 The Tests for Several Independent Samples window in SPSS in its final appearance before finishing the Kruskal–Wallis test.

After the values are entered into the field, the user should click "Continue." This makes the Several Independent Samples: Define Range window disappear, leaving the Tests for Several Independent Samples window. The last step in a Kruskal–Wallis test is to click "OK" in this window. Figure 15.23 shows its final appearance before this last step.

The SPSS output for a Kruskal–Wallis test is shown in Figure 15.24. There are two tables in the output. The first one is labeled "Ranks," and it shows the number of sample members in each group and the mean rank for each group. This latter statistic is not very useful because it is an average of ordinal data, which is not sensible (see Chapter 2). The second table shows the results of the Kruskal–Wallis test, which is a χ^2 observed statistic, labeled as "Chi-Square" in the table. The next number is the degrees of freedom, which is always $k - 1$, where k is the number of groups

Ranks

	S1Q20 GRADE-W1	N	Mean Rank
60.k DEPRESSED-LAST MONTH	7th grade	631	1842.36
	8th grade	669	2044.19
	9th grade	786	2168.74
	10th grade	820	2253.92
	11th grade	793	2374.60
	12th grade	675	2373.54
	Total	4374	

Test Statistics[a,b]

	60.k DEPRESSED -LAST MONTH
Chi-Square	98.121
df	5
Asymp. Sig.	.000

a. Kruskal Wallis Test

b. Grouping Variable: S1Q20 GRADE-W1

Figure 15.24 SPSS output for a Kruskal–Wallis test.

in the independent variable. Finally, the last number – labeled "Asymp. Sig." – is the p-value corresponding to the χ^2 observed value. If this value is smaller than α, it indicates that the distribution of ranks across groups is not equal. If this p-value is higher than α, we retain the null hypothesis that the distribution of ranks among the groups is equal. In Figure 15.24 the p-value is displayed as ".000," because SPSS has rounded the p-value. Sidebar 7.3 showed us that p can never be equal to 0, so this result would be reported as $p < .001$.

Sidebar 15.4 **Meta-analytic thinking**

No research study can ever produced a scientific fact that is beyond doubt. Perhaps the researchers unknowingly made a Type I or Type II error. Or maybe questionable research practices (see Sidebar 8.1) distorted the results. It is also possible that the researchers unwittingly made a mistake in the procedure or that the sample was full of outliers.

It takes multiple studies on the same topic before scientific results are trustworthy. Therefore, it is important that researchers and students engage in **meta-analytic thinking**, which is a mode of thought that considers studies in the wider research context. The term is derived from "meta-analysis," which is a type of quantitative research study that combines results from previous research into one analysis that produces an overall effect size (see Sidebar 14.4). The point of meta-analytic thinking is not necessarily to conduct meta-analyses. Rather, it is to think like a meta-analyst by looking at the big picture and ensuring that a study can join the larger research conversation about a topic.

Meta-analytic thinking can take several forms, and there is no "one right way" to engage in it. Thompson (2002b) claimed that researchers can engage in meta-analytic thinking procedures during the planning and execution of a study or that research consumers can do it when reading, considering, and applying past research.

Researchers who use meta-analytic thinking when designing and conducting studies have several tactics at their disposal to ensure that their study can more easily fit into the larger body of scientific literature. One of these tactics is to report as much detailed statistical information as possible, such as reporting confidence intervals, effect sizes, and detailed descriptive statistics (Thompson, 2002b; Zientek & Thompson, 2009). This ensures that results from different studies can be compared to one another and that there is enough information for a study to be included in a future meta-analysis. As a result, the position of a study in the greater body of scientific literature on a topic is clearer.

Another tactic of meta-analytic thinking is to report the procedures used to perform the study with enough detail that a reader could replicate the study independently. In recent years it has become clear that there are many research studies in the scientific literature that are not replicable (Open Science Collaboration, 2015). Sometimes this is because of vague reporting. But poor replicability can also occur because of questionable research practices, low statistical power (see Sidebar 10.1), and the file drawer problem (see Sidebar 14.1). Replication is one of the foundational principles of science because nonreplicable findings have no real meaning outside the laboratory and sometimes do not represent meaningful phenomena – or anything real at all. Unfortunately, replications – even when they are conducted – have historically been neglected in many fields of research (Makel & Plucker, 2014). These facts make meta-analytic thinking harder to engage in, and they distort the scientific knowledge base. Fortunately, the research community is taking steps to improve the replicability of research (e.g., Moore, 2016) and encouraging the publication of replication studies (e.g., McBee & Matthews, 2014). These are important practices that make meta-analytic thinking more common in the social sciences because replication is based on the idea that no one study is definite.

What all the procedures in meta-analytic thinking have in common is an overall philosophy of research that prioritizes the accumulation of knowledge across many studies, rather than reliance on a single study that may be flawed. I encourage you to engage in meta-analytic thinking as you read studies or perform your own research. For example, after you read a study, you can search for other work that either supports or contradicts it (or even a meta-analysis on the same topic). You could also conduct a replication of the study, which is a great way to gain experience in research and strengthen the knowledge in the field (Warne, 2014c).

Check Yourself!

- When is it appropriate to use a Kruskal–Wallis test?

- Explain the similarities between the Kruskal–Wallis test and the Wilcoxon rank-sum test.

- What is meta-analytic thinking?

- What are two ways you can engage in meta-analytic thinking?

Multivariate Methods

Until now, all the statistical methods discussed in this book have fallen into the family of **univariate statistics**, which are statistical procedures that have a single dependent variable. However, sometimes we may be interested in more than one dependent variable. When this occurs, there are two options. The easier option is to analyze each dependent variable separately, using univariate procedures. For example, if a psychologist wants to investigate a set of independent variables' relationship with (1) physical aggression, (2) emotionally manipulatively behavior, and (3) disregard for personal safety, she could create three multiple regression models. The first would investigate the independent variables' relationship with physical aggression, while the second model would investigate the independent variables' relationship with emotionally manipulative behavior. The last model would investigate the independent variables' relationship with a disregard for one's personal safety.

However, creating three regression models assumes that the dependent variables are uncorrelated and conceptually unrelated to each other (Warne, 2014a). For many real-world dependent variables, this assumption may be unrealistic because in humans many dependent variables are correlated or related to one another (Meehl, 1990). For example, physical aggression, emotionally manipulative behavior, and disregard for personal safety are sometimes seen in the same people, and it may not make sense to study these dependent variables in isolation. Indeed, these are three of the symptoms of antisocial personality disorder, and, for individuals with the disorder, these behaviors often occur in clusters – not in isolation.

The other option is to use a statistical procedure that considers all dependent variables at once. These **multivariate statistics** are a family of statistical procedures that are designed to analyze two or more dependent variables at the same time (Hidalgo & Goodman, 2013). These procedures sometimes combine the observed dependent variables into at least one **latent variable**, which is an underlying variable theorized to be the common source of individuals' scores on the observed dependent variables. For example, a psychologist may believe that physical aggression, emotionally manipulatively behavior, and disregard for personal safety are all symptoms of antisocial personality disorder. Therefore, she may theorize that these observed variables are caused by the latent variable "antisocial personality." If this theorizing is correct, then multivariate methods would be beneficial because these methods would assume that all the dependent variables are separate and unrelated; only multivariate methods take into account the common underlying connections among the dependent variables. Using multivariate statistics, the psychologist could investigate the latent variable of antisocial personality – which is more interesting anyway – via the observed symptoms.

Another advantage of multivariate methods is that they require fewer NHSTs than does creating multiple univariate statistical models. By creating a single statistical model, we can control the Type I error inflation that would occur from having two or more univariate analyses. If this rationale for the use of multivariate statistics sounds familiar, it is because it is the same justification in Chapter 12 for using ANOVA instead of a series of unpaired-samples t-tests (Warne, 2014a).

The next few subsections give a brief description of a few of the most common multivariate procedures. It is intended to be a short introduction for students who want a concise reference guide to methods they may find in articles. Additionally, students who intend to take a second or third semester of statistics may also find these descriptions to be a helpful preparation for more in-depth study of these procedures. If you do wish to learn these procedures, I suggest you consult the references I cite or take a course in multivariate statistics. Before readers try to learn any of these procedures in depth, I recommend that they gain some practical experience with multiple regression. This will help make the transition to multivariate methods easier. Because this section is meant to be a first taste of multivariate methods (and not a comprehensive guide), I have decided to omit the software guides, which would be either far too long or so oversimplified that they would not be useful for most research situations.

Multivariate Analysis of Variance. A procedure called **multivariate analysis of variance (MANOVA)** is a generalization of ANOVA for two or more dependent variables. MANOVA can handle independent variables of any type, as long as the dependent variables are interval- or ratio-level data. The null hypothesis in MANOVA is that the independent variable(s) have no statistical relationship with the combination of dependent variables. When the null hypothesis is rejected, it is appropriate to follow up with a **descriptive discriminant analysis**. This is the multivariate version of rejecting the null hypothesis in an ANOVA and then following up with a *post hoc* test. See Warne (2014a) for a practical guide on how to conduct a MANOVA in SPSS. A more detailed treatment is available in Stevens (2002).

Factor Analysis. It is not unusual for social scientists to have a larger number of variables than they can easily analyze. **Factor analysis** was designed (by Spearman, 1904b) to reduce a large number of observed variables into a smaller number of latent variables, which are often easier to understand and analyze. There are two types of factor analysis. Exploratory factor analysis is an atheoretical method that attempts to place observed variables into groups (called factors, which are like latent variables) according to how well they correlate with one another. Confirmatory factor analysis starts with theory of how observed variables "should" group together, and then it examines how well the data fit that theory. Factor analysis is common in the creation and interpretation of psychological and educational tests because testing experts often are not interested in individual responses to items. Therefore, they group the items together in order to have a smaller number of latent variables to analyze because the test items are theorized to measure these latent variables. (See Costa and McCrae, 2008, for an example of a psychological test being created via this method.) For readers interested in factor analysis, I suggest the book by Thompson (2004). Another authoritative source is the book by Gorsuch (1983).

Structural Equation Modeling. It is not just dependent variables that can be used to create latent variables. Independent variables can also be combined to form latent variables. Often when we investigate relationships between independent and dependent variables, the best statistical procedure available is **structural equation modeling** (SEM). SEM is the most versatile statistical method in the GLM because it is the most general procedure in the GLM and encompasses all simpler methods – univariate and multivariate. Therefore, SEM can examine complex relationships among latent variables, observed variables, and even a mix of the two types of variables. Readers with a strong grasp of multiple regression (and perhaps other multivariate methods) can benefit from Kline's (2005) book about structural equation modeling. Recently, Asparouhov and Muthén (2009) created a generalization of SEM – called exploratory structural equation modeling – that is even more flexible, though my personal experience is that exploratory SEM can produce results that are hard to interpret.

Check Yourself!

- How do multivariate methods differ from univariate methods?
- What is the *post hoc* test for a MANOVA?
- What is the purpose of conducting a factor analysis?
- SEM occupies a special place in the GLM. What is that place?

Reflection Questions: Comprehension

1. What does it mean if a study is said to be a 4×2 ANOVA?
2. Describe the relationship between correlation (or Pearson's r) and multiple regression.
3. Kyla and Joan are classmates analyzing the same set of data. There are two nominal independent variables and one interval-level dependent variable. Kyla chooses to conduct a two-way ANOVA, while Joan dummy codes the independent variable and conducts a multiple regression analysis. Why do the two students get the same effect size from their different analyses?
4. What is the difference between exploratory factor analysis and confirmatory factor analysis?
5. How can you practice meta-analytic thinking as you read research in your field?
6. Why can it be difficult to detect Simpson's paradox?
7. The following questions are about multicollinearity.
   a. What is multicollinearity?
   b. Why is multicollinearity a problem in multiple regression?
   c. What can a data analyst do to reduce the chance of problems with multicollinearity?
8. Explain when it would be beneficial to calculate Spearman's ρ instead of Pearson's r.
9. When there are two independent variables and a single dependent variable, why is it better to conduct a 2×2 ANOVA instead of two separate one-way ANOVAs?

Reflection Questions: Application

10. Christine has a single, independent, nominal-level variable with two categories and three dependent variables.
    a. What is the appropriate multivariate statistical procedure for this situation?
    b. If she wishes to use univariate procedures instead, what is the appropriate analysis strategy?
11. Pablo's data consist of a nominal independent variable with four groups and a dependent interval-level variable. What is the appropriate statistical procedure for Pablo's data?
12. A nominal variable records the major of students in a sample of (1) sociology students, (2) social work students, and (3) anthropology students.
    a. How many new variables would have to be created in a dummy coding system based on this nominal variable?

b.   Create a dummy coding system for this variable, with sociology students as the baseline group.

13. Ahmed has four variables in his data. Three are independent variables: a nominal-level variable and two ratio-level variables. He also has an interval-level dependent variable. What is the appropriate statistical procedure for Ahmed's data?

14. Interpret the following R^2 values:
   a.   0.744
   b.   0.312
   c.   0.004.

15. Aaron has two interval-level independent variables and an interval-level dependent variable. His R^2 value is 0.110.
   a.   Aaron adds another independent variable, and this increases the R^2 to 0.155. What does this say about the contribution of the new variable?
   b.   Aaron adds a fourth independent variable to the statistical model, and this does not increase the R^2 value any further, and the null hypothesis for the new variable's β value is not rejected. What does this say about the contribution of this additional new variable?

16. Emily is a sociology student who uses a Wilcoxon rank-sum test to compare the levels of interest in political activity among college students and non-college students. She finds that college students are more interested in political activity, and the AUC value is 0.62. What does this AUC mean?

17. Interpret the following AUC values:
   a.   0.922
   b.   0.713
   c.   0.500
   d.   0.412
   e.   0.331
   f.   0.012

18. Elias conducts a 3 × 3 ANOVA. His independent variables are socioeconomic status and education level, and his dependent variable is the willingness of a subject to donate to charity. He finds that there is an interaction between the two independent variables.
   a.   What would the presence of an interaction indicate?
   b.   Draw a possible visual model showing this interaction.

Further Reading

•   Cohen, J. (1968). Multiple regression as a general data-analytic system. *Psychological Bulletin*, *70*, 426–443. doi:10.1037/h0026714

   *   In this classic article, Cohen explains how multiple regression encompasses all other, more basic univariate methods in the GLM. He also shows the benefits of understanding statistics in a GLM framework, explains the details of coding, and shows how interactions are important in statistical analysis.

•   Kline, R. B. (2013). *Beyond significance testing: Statistics reform in the behavioral sciences* (2nd ed.). Washington, DC: American Psychological Association.

* Readers who enjoy getting into the weeds of complex methods may appreciate Rex Kline's book, which is a scathing critique of parametric statistics. Kline argues that the assumptions behind parametric techniques are so strict that most real-life data violate them, producing distorted results. He is also a critic of null hypothesis testing, and instead wishes for it to be replaced with more robust procedures, confidence intervals, and a family of statistics called Bayesian methods. I do not agree with all of Kline's arguments, but his viewpoint has its vocal proponents. Students who intend to become researchers would profit from learning more about the weaknesses of traditional statistics.

- Lovie, A. D. (1995). Who discovered Spearman's rank correlation? *British Journal of Mathematical and Statistical Psychology, 48*, 255–269. doi:10.1111/j.2044–8317.1995.tb01063.x

   * Because many statistics (e.g., Kruskal–Wallis test, Bonferroni correction) are named after statisticians, students can get the impression that progress in statistics is linear. This is because it often appears that a person invents a statistic, names it after themselves, and then the statistic is adopted. In reality, most statisticians do not name their statistics after themselves, and the history of the invention of statistical methods is more complex. I like Lovie's article because it uses Spearman's ρ as a case study for how statistics are invented, named, and popularized. The story is much messier (and more interesting) than a straightforward tale of Spearman inventing a formula.

- Warne, R. T. (2011b). Beyond multiple regression: Using commonality analysis to better understand R^2 results. *Gifted Child Quarterly, 55*, 313–318. doi:10.1177/0016986211422217

   * The effect size R^2 is the most common way of understanding the strength of the relationship of a collection of independent variables. However, another way to consider multiple regression results is to divide the R^2 into pieces that correspond to the contributions of different independent variables. This process is called commonality analysis and can provide a great deal of detail about how much unique or overlapping information each independent variable provides to the statistical model.

Appendix A1   *z*-Table

Explanation. This table shows the proportion of the area in the normal distribution that – for a given *z*-score (in column A) – is between the mean and a *z*-value (column B). The last column (column C) shows the proportion of the area in the tail of the normal distribution beyond the value in column B. Because the normal distribution is symmetrical, each row has values for both a positive and a negative *z*-value. Note that a *z*-value can be either a *z*-score (for Chapter 5) or a *z*-observed value (for Chapter 7).

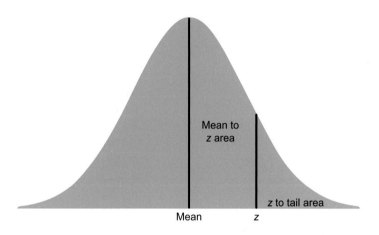

A *z*-value	B Mean to *z*	C *z* to tail
± 0.00	0.0000	0.5000
± 0.01	0.0040	0.4960
± 0.02	0.0080	0.4920
± 0.03	0.0120	0.4880
± 0.04	0.0160	0.4840
± 0.05	0.0199	0.4801
± 0.06	0.0239	0.4761
± 0.07	0.0279	0.4721
± 0.08	0.0319	0.4681
± 0.09	0.0359	0.4641
± 0.10	0.0398	0.4602
± 0.11	0.0438	0.4562
± 0.12	0.0478	0.4522
± 0.13	0.0517	0.4483
± 0.14	0.0557	0.4443
± 0.15	0.0596	0.4404

A z-value	B Mean to z	C z to tail
± 0.16	0.0636	0.4364
± 0.17	0.0675	0.4325
± 0.18	0.0714	0.4286
± 0.19	0.0753	0.4247
± 0.20	0.0793	0.4207
± 0.21	0.0832	0.4168
± 0.22	0.0871	0.4129
± 0.23	0.0910	0.4090
± 0.24	0.0948	0.4052
± 0.25	0.0987	0.4013
± 0.26	0.1026	0.3974
± 0.27	0.1064	0.3936
± 0.28	0.1103	0.3897
± 0.29	0.1141	0.3859
± 0.30	0.1179	0.3821
± 0.31	0.1217	0.3783
± 0.32	0.1255	0.3745
± 0.33	0.1293	0.3707
± 0.34	0.1331	0.3669
± 0.35	0.1368	0.3632
± 0.36	0.1406	0.3594
± 0.37	0.1443	0.3557
± 0.38	0.1480	0.3520
± 0.39	0.1517	0.3483
± 0.40	0.1554	0.3446
± 0.41	0.1591	0.3409
± 0.42	0.1628	0.3372
± 0.43	0.1664	0.3336
± 0.44	0.1700	0.3300
± 0.45	0.1736	0.3264
± 0.46	0.1772	0.3228
± 0.47	0.1808	0.3192
± 0.48	0.1844	0.3156
± 0.49	0.1879	0.3121
± 0.50	0.1915	0.3085
± 0.51	0.1950	0.3050
± 0.52	0.1985	0.3015
± 0.53	0.2019	0.2981
± 0.54	0.2054	0.2946
± 0.55	0.2088	0.2912
± 0.56	0.2123	0.2877

(cont.)

	(cont.)	
A z-value	**B Mean to z**	**C z to tail**
± 0.57	0.2157	0.2843
± 0.58	0.2190	0.2810
± 0.59	0.2224	0.2776
± 0.60	0.2257	0.2743
± 0.61	0.2291	0.2709
± 0.62	0.2324	0.2676
± 0.63	0.2357	0.2643
± 0.64	0.2389	0.2611
± 0.65	0.2422	0.2578
± 0.66	0.2454	0.2546
± 0.67	0.2486	0.2514
± 0.68	0.2517	0.2483
± 0.69	0.2549	0.2451
± 0.70	0.2580	0.2420
± 0.71	0.2611	0.2389
± 0.72	0.2642	0.2358
± 0.73	0.2673	0.2327
± 0.74	0.2704	0.2296
± 0.75	0.2734	0.2266
± 0.76	0.2764	0.2236
± 0.77	0.2794	0.2206
± 0.78	0.2823	0.2177
± 0.79	0.2852	0.2148
± 0.80	0.2881	0.2119
± 0.81	0.2910	0.2090
± 0.82	0.2939	0.2061
± 0.83	0.2967	0.2033
± 0.84	0.2995	0.2005
± 0.85	0.3023	0.1977
± 0.86	0.3051	0.1949
± 0.87	0.3078	0.1922
± 0.88	0.3106	0.1894
± 0.89	0.3133	0.1867
± 0.90	0.3159	0.1841
± 0.91	0.3186	0.1814
± 0.92	0.3212	0.1788
± 0.93	0.3238	0.1762
± 0.94	0.3264	0.1736
± 0.95	0.3289	0.1711
± 0.96	0.3315	0.1685
± 0.97	0.3340	0.1660

(cont.)		
A z-value	**B Mean to z**	**C z to tail**
± 0.98	0.3365	0.1635
± 0.99	0.3389	0.1611
± 1.00	0.3413	0.1587
± 1.01	0.3438	0.1562
± 1.02	0.3461	0.1539
± 1.03	0.3485	0.1515
± 1.04	0.3508	0.1492
± 1.05	0.3531	0.1469
± 1.06	0.3554	0.1446
± 1.07	0.3577	0.1423
± 1.08	0.3599	0.1401
± 1.09	0.3621	0.1379
± 1.10	0.3643	0.1357
± 1.11	0.3665	0.1335
± 1.12	0.3686	0.1314
± 1.13	0.3708	0.1292
± 1.14	0.3729	0.1271
± 1.15	0.3749	0.1251
± 1.16	0.3770	0.1230
± 1.17	0.3790	0.1210
± 1.18	0.3810	0.1190
± 1.19	0.3830	0.1170
± 1.20	0.3849	0.1151
± 1.21	0.3869	0.1131
± 1.22	0.3888	0.1112
± 1.23	0.3907	0.1093
± 1.24	0.3925	0.1075
± 1.25	0.3944	0.1056
± 1.26	0.3962	0.1038
± 1.27	0.3980	0.1020
± 1.28	0.3997	0.1003
± 1.29	0.4015	0.0985
± 1.30	0.4032	0.0968
± 1.31	0.4049	0.0951
± 1.32	0.4066	0.0934
± 1.33	0.4082	0.0918
± 1.34	0.4099	0.0901
± 1.35	0.4115	0.0885
± 1.36	0.4131	0.0869
± 1.37	0.4147	0.0853
± 1.38	0.4162	0.0838

A *z*-value	B Mean to *z*	C *z* to tail
± 1.39	0.4177	0.0823
± 1.40	0.4192	0.0808
± 1.41	0.4207	0.0793
± 1.42	0.4222	0.0778
± 1.43	0.4236	0.0764
± 1.44	0.4251	0.0749
± 1.45	0.4265	0.0735
± 1.46	0.4279	0.0721
± 1.47	0.4292	0.0708
± 1.48	0.4306	0.0694
± 1.49	0.4319	0.0681
± 1.50	0.4332	0.0668
± 1.51	0.4345	0.0655
± 1.52	0.4357	0.0643
± 1.53	0.4370	0.0630
± 1.54	0.4382	0.0618
± 1.55	0.4394	0.0606
± 1.56	0.4406	0.0594
± 1.57	0.4418	0.0582
± 1.58	0.4429	0.0571
± 1.59	0.4441	0.0559
± 1.60	0.4452	0.0548
± 1.61	0.4463	0.0537
± 1.62	0.4474	0.0526
± 1.63	0.4484	0.0516
± 1.64	0.4495	0.0505
± 1.65	0.4505	0.0495
± 1.66	0.4515	0.0485
± 1.67	0.4525	0.0475
± 1.68	0.4535	0.0465
± 1.69	0.4545	0.0455
± 1.70	0.4554	0.0446
± 1.71	0.4564	0.0436
± 1.72	0.4573	0.0427
± 1.73	0.4582	0.0418
± 1.74	0.4591	0.0409
± 1.75	0.4599	0.0401
± 1.76	0.4608	0.0392
± 1.77	0.4616	0.0384
± 1.78	0.4625	0.0375
± 1.79	0.4633	0.0367

(cont.)

(cont.)		
A z-value	**B Mean to z**	**C z to tail**
± 1.80	0.4641	0.0359
± 1.81	0.4649	0.0351
± 1.82	0.4656	0.0344
± 1.83	0.4664	0.0336
± 1.84	0.4671	0.0329
± 1.85	0.4678	0.0322
± 1.86	0.4686	0.0314
± 1.87	0.4693	0.0307
± 1.88	0.4699	0.0301
± 1.89	0.4706	0.0294
± 1.90	0.4713	0.0287
± 1.91	0.4719	0.0281
± 1.92	0.4726	0.0274
± 1.93	0.4732	0.0268
± 1.94	0.4738	0.0262
± 1.95	0.4744	0.0256
± 1.96	0.4750	0.0250
± 1.97	0.4756	0.0244
± 1.98	0.4761	0.0239
± 1.99	0.4767	0.0233
± 2.00	0.4772	0.0228
± 2.01	0.4778	0.0222
± 2.02	0.4783	0.0217
± 2.03	0.4788	0.0212
± 2.04	0.4793	0.0207
± 2.05	0.4798	0.0202
± 2.06	0.4803	0.0197
± 2.07	0.4808	0.0192
± 2.08	0.4812	0.0188
± 2.09	0.4817	0.0183
± 2.10	0.4821	0.0179
± 2.11	0.4826	0.0174
± 2.12	0.4830	0.0170
± 2.13	0.4834	0.0166
± 2.14	0.4838	0.0162
± 2.15	0.4842	0.0158
± 2.16	0.4846	0.0154
± 2.17	0.4850	0.0150
± 2.18	0.4854	0.0146
± 2.19	0.4857	0.0143
± 2.20	0.4861	0.0139

(cont.)		
A z-value	**B Mean to z**	**C z to tail**
± 2.21	0.4864	0.0136
± 2.22	0.4868	0.0132
± 2.23	0.4871	0.0129
± 2.24	0.4875	0.0125
± 2.25	0.4878	0.0122
± 2.26	0.4881	0.0119
± 2.27	0.4884	0.0116
± 2.28	0.4887	0.0113
± 2.29	0.4890	0.0110
± 2.30	0.4893	0.0107
± 2.31	0.4896	0.0104
± 2.32	0.4898	0.0102
± 2.33	0.4901	0.0099
± 2.34	0.4904	0.0096
± 2.35	0.4906	0.0094
± 2.36	0.4909	0.0091
± 2.37	0.4911	0.0089
± 2.38	0.4913	0.0087
± 2.39	0.4916	0.0084
± 2.40	0.4918	0.0082
± 2.41	0.4920	0.0080
± 2.42	0.4922	0.0078
± 2.43	0.4925	0.0075
± 2.44	0.4927	0.0073
± 2.45	0.4929	0.0071
± 2.46	0.4931	0.0069
± 2.47	0.4932	0.0068
± 2.48	0.4934	0.0066
± 2.49	0.4936	0.0064
± 2.50	0.4938	0.0062
± 2.51	0.4940	0.0060
± 2.52	0.4941	0.0059
± 2.53	0.4943	0.0057
± 2.54	0.4945	0.0055
± 2.55	0.4946	0.0054
± 2.56	0.4948	0.0052
± 2.57	0.4949	0.0051
± 2.58	0.4951	0.0049
± 2.59	0.4952	0.0048
± 2.60	0.4953	0.0047
± 2.61	0.4955	0.0045

(cont.)		
A z-value	**B Mean to z**	**C z to tail**
± 2.62	0.4956	0.0044
± 2.63	0.4957	0.0043
± 2.64	0.4959	0.0041
± 2.65	0.4960	0.0040
± 2.66	0.4961	0.0039
± 2.67	0.4962	0.0038
± 2.68	0.4963	0.0037
± 2.69	0.4964	0.0036
± 2.70	0.4965	0.0035
± 2.71	0.4966	0.0034
± 2.72	0.4967	0.0033
± 2.73	0.4968	0.0032
± 2.74	0.4969	0.0031
± 2.75	0.4970	0.0030
± 2.76	0.4971	0.0029
± 2.77	0.4972	0.0028
± 2.78	0.4973	0.0027
± 2.79	0.4974	0.0026
± 2.80	0.4974	0.0026
± 2.81	0.4975	0.0025
± 2.82	0.4976	0.0024
± 2.83	0.4977	0.0023
± 2.84	0.4977	0.0023
± 2.85	0.4978	0.0022
± 2.86	0.4979	0.0021
± 2.87	0.4979	0.0021
± 2.88	0.4980	0.0020
± 2.89	0.4981	0.0019
± 2.90	0.4981	0.0019
± 2.91	0.4982	0.0018
± 2.92	0.4982	0.0018
± 2.93	0.4983	0.0017
± 2.94	0.4984	0.0016
± 2.95	0.4984	0.0016
± 2.96	0.4985	0.0015
± 2.97	0.4985	0.0015
± 2.98	0.4986	0.0014
± 2.99	0.4986	0.0014
± 3.00	0.49865	0.00135
± 3.10	0.49903	0.00097
± 3.20	0.49931	0.00069

A z-value	B Mean to z	C z to tail
(cont.)		
± 3.30	0.49952	0.00048
± 3.40	0.49966	0.00034
± 3.50	0.49977	0.00023
± 3.60	0.49984	0.00016
± 3.70	0.49989	0.00011
± 3.80	0.49993	0.00007
± 3.90	0.49995	0.00005
± 4.00	0.49997	0.00003
± 4.50	0.499997	0.000003
± 5.00	0.4999997	0.0000003

Appendix A2 *t*-Table

Explanation. This table shows the value at which the area in the tail of the *t*-distribution is equal to either 1% (for α = .01) or 5% (for α = .05) of the total area in the distribution. For one-tailed tests, use the set of columns on the left-hand side. For two-tailed tests, use the set of columns on the right-hand side. Because the *t*-distribution is symmetrical, each row has values for both positive and negative *t*-values.

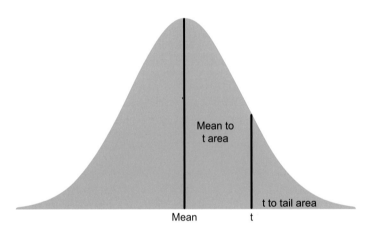

One-tailed Test			Two-tailed Test		
df	α = 0.05	α = 0.01	df	α = 0.05	α = 0.01
1	+/–6.314	+/–31.821	1	+12.706	+63.657
2	+/–2.920	+/–6.965	2	+4.303	+9.925
3	+/–2.353	+/–4.541	3	+3.182	+5.841
4	+/–2.132	+/–3.747	4	+2.776	+4.604
5	+/–2.015	+/–3.365	5	+2.571	+4.032
6	+/–1.943	+/–3.143	6	+2.447	+3.707
7	+/–1.895	+/–2.998	7	+2.365	+3.499
8	+/–1.860	+/–2.896	8	+2.306	+3.355
9	+/–1.833	+/–2.821	9	+2.262	+3.250
10	+/–1.812	+/–2.764	10	+2.228	+3.169
11	+/–1.796	+/–2.718	11	+2.201	+3.106
12	+/–1.782	+/–2.681	12	+2.179	+3.055
13	+/–1.771	+/–2.650	13	+2.160	+3.012
14	+/–1.761	+/–2.624	14	+2.145	+2.977
15	+/–1.753	+/–2.602	15	+2.131	+2.947
16	+/–1.746	+/–2.583	16	+2.120	+2.921

(cont.)

	One-tailed Test			Two-tailed Test	
df	α = 0.05	α = 0.01	df	α = 0.05	α = 0.01
17	+/–1.740	+/–2.567	17	+2.110	+2.898
18	+/–1.734	+/–2.552	18	+2.101	+2.878
19	+/–1.729	+/–2.539	19	+2.093	+2.861
20	+/–1.725	+/–2.528	20	+2.086	+2.845
21	+/–1.721	+/–2.518	21	+2.080	+2.831
22	+/–1.717	+/–2.508	22	+2.074	+2.819
23	+/–1.714	+/–2.500	23	+2.069	+2.807
24	+/–1.711	+/–2.492	24	+2.064	+2.797
25	+/–1.708	+/–2.485	25	+2.060	+2.787
26	+/–1.706	+/–2.479	26	+2.056	+2.779
27	+/–1.703	+/–2.473	27	+2.052	+2.771
28	+/–1.701	+/–2.467	28	+2.048	+2.763
29	+/–1.699	+/–2.462	29	+2.045	+2.756
30	+/–1.697	+/–2.457	30	+2.042	+2.750
31	+/–1.696	+/–2.453	31	+2.040	+2.744
32	+/–1.694	+/–2.449	32	+2.037	+2.738
33	+/–1.692	+/–2.445	33	+2.035	+2.733
34	+/–1.691	+/–2.441	34	+2.032	+2.728
35	+/–1.690	+/–2.438	35	+2.030	+2.724
36	+/–1.688	+/–2.434	36	+2.028	+2.719
37	+/–1.687	+/–2.431	37	+2.026	+2.715
38	+/–1.686	+/–2.429	38	+2.024	+2.712
39	+/–1.685	+/–2.426	39	+2.023	+2.708
40	+/–1.684	+/–2.423	40	+2.021	+2.704
41	+/–1.683	+/–2.421	41	+2.020	+2.701
42	+/–1.682	+/–2.418	42	+2.018	+2.698
43	+/–1.681	+/–2.416	43	+2.017	+2.695
44	+/–1.680	+/–2.414	44	+2.015	+2.692
45	+/–1.679	+/–2.412	45	+2.014	+2.690
50	+/–1.676	+/–2.403	50	+2.009	+2.678
55	+/–1.673	+/–2.396	55	+2.004	+2.668
60	+/–1.671	+/–2.390	60	+2.000	+2.660
70	+/–1.667	+/–2.381	70	+1.994	+2.648
80	+/–1.664	+/–2.374	80	+1.990	+2.639
90	+/–1.662	+/–2.368	90	+1.987	+2.632
100	+/–1.660	+/–2.364	100	+1.984	+2.626
110	+/–1.659	+/–2.361	110	+1.982	+2.621
120	+/–1.658	+/–2.358	120	+1.980	+2.617
130	+/–1.657	+/–2.355	130	+1.978	+2.614
140	+/–1.656	+/–2.353	140	+1.977	+2.611
150	+/–1.655	+/–2.351	150	+1.976	+2.609

(cont.)

	One-tailed Test			Two-tailed Test	
df	$\alpha = 0.05$	$\alpha = 0.01$	df	$\alpha = 0.05$	$\alpha = 0.01$
200	+/−1.653	+/−2.345	200	+1.972	+2.601
250	+/−1.651	+/−2.341	250	+1.969	+2.596
500	+/−1.648	+/−2.334	500	+1.965	+2.586
1,000	+/−1.646	+/−2.330	1,000	+1.962	+2.581
∞	+/−1.645	+/−2.326	∞	+1.960	+2.576

Appendix A3 *F*-Table

Explanation. This table shows the value at which the area in the *F*-distribution is equal to either 1% (for $\alpha = .01$) or 5% (for $\alpha = .05$) of the total area in the distribution. *F*-distributions are sampling distributions of ratios of two variances, the variance between groups and the variance within groups: $F = \frac{\sigma^2_{Between}}{\sigma^2_{Within}}$. Because of this, *F*-distributions have two different degrees of freedom values, one for the number of degrees of freedom in the numerator (i.e., $df_{Between}$), and another for the degrees of freedom in the denominator (i.e., df_{Within}). The columns are for the number of $df_{Between}$, while the rows are for the number of degrees of freedom df_{Within}. To find the appropriate *F* value, identify the column that corresponds to the number of degrees of freedom between groups for your data. Then, identify the row that corresponds to your data's degrees of freedom within groups. There will be two cells that belong to that row and column. The cell text is **boldface** for the *F* value that corresponds to $\alpha = .05$. The cell text is *italicized* for the *F* value that corresponds to $\alpha = .01$.

	Degrees of freedom in denominator (i.e., degrees of freedom within groups, or df_{Within})	Degrees of freedom in numerator (i.e., degrees of freedom between groups, or $df_{Between}$)														
α	df_{Within}	1	2	3	4	5	6	7	8	9	10	11	12	13	14	15
.05	1	161.448	199.500	215.707	224.583	230.162	233.986	236.768	238.883	240.543	241.882	242.983	243.906	244.690	245.364	245.950
.01	1	4052.181	4999.500	5403.352	5624.583	5763.650	5858.986	5928.356	5981.070	6022.473	6055.847	6083.317	6106.321	6125.865	6142.674	6157.285
.05	2	18.513	19.000	19.164	19.247	19.296	19.330	19.353	19.371	19.385	19.396	19.405	19.413	19.419	19.424	19.429
.01	2	98.503	99.000	99.166	99.249	99.299	99.333	99.356	99.374	99.388	99.399	99.408	99.416	99.442	99.428	99.433
.05	3	10.128	9.552	9.277	9.117	9.013	8.941	8.887	8.845	8.812	8.786	8.763	8.745	8.729	8.715	8.703
.01	3	34.116	30.817	29.457	28.710	28.237	27.911	27.672	27.489	27.345	27.229	27.133	27.052	26.983	26.924	26.872
.05	4	7.709	6.944	6.591	6.388	6.256	6.163	6.094	6.041	5.999	5.964	5.936	5.912	5.891	5.873	5.858
.01	4	21.198	18.000	16.694	15.977	15.522	15.207	14.976	14.799	14.659	14.546	14.452	14.374	14.307	14.249	14.198
.05	5	6.608	5.786	5.409	5.192	5.050	4.950	4.876	4.818	4.772	4.735	4.704	4.678	4.655	4.636	4.619
.01	5	16.258	13.274	12.060	11.392	10.967	10.672	10.456	10.289	10.158	10.051	9.963	9.888	9.825	9.770	9.722
.05	6	5.987	5.143	4.757	4.534	4.387	4.284	4.207	4.147	4.099	4.060	4.027	4.000	3.976	3.956	3.938
.01	6	13.745	10.925	9.780	9.148	8.746	8.466	8.260	8.102	7.976	7.874	7.790	7.718	7.657	7.605	7.559
.05	7	5.591	4.737	4.347	4.120	3.972	3.866	3.787	3.726	3.677	3.637	3.603	3.575	3.550	3.529	3.511
.01	7	12.246	9.547	8.451	7.847	7.460	7.191	6.993	6.840	6.719	6.620	6.538	6.469	6.410	6.359	6.314
.05	8	5.318	4.459	4.066	3.838	3.687	3.581	3.500	3.438	3.388	3.347	3.313	3.284	3.259	3.237	3.218
.01	8	11.259	8.649	7.591	7.006	6.632	6.371	6.178	6.029	5.911	5.814	5.734	5.667	5.609	5.559	5.515
.05	9	5.117	4.256	3.863	3.633	3.482	3.374	3.293	3.230	3.179	3.137	3.102	3.073	3.048	3.025	3.006
.01	9	10.561	8.022	6.992	6.422	6.057	5.802	5.613	5.467	5.351	5.257	5.178	5.111	5.055	5.005	4.962
.05	10	4.965	4.103	3.708	3.478	3.326	3.217	3.135	3.072	3.020	2.978	2.943	2.913	2.887	2.865	2.845
.01	10	10.044	7.559	6.552	5.994	5.636	5.386	5.200	5.057	4.942	4.849	4.772	4.706	4.650	4.601	4.558
.05	11	4.844	3.982	3.587	3.357	3.204	3.095	3.012	2.948	2.896	2.854	2.818	2.788	2.761	2.739	2.719
.01	11	9.646	7.206	6.217	5.668	5.316	5.069	4.886	4.744	4.632	4.539	4.462	4.397	4.342	4.293	4.251
.05	12	4.747	3.885	3.490	3.259	3.106	2.996	2.913	2.849	2.796	2.753	2.717	2.687	2.660	2.637	2.617
.01	12	9.330	6.927	5.953	5.412	5.064	4.821	4.640	4.499	4.388	4.296	4.220	4.155	4.100	4.052	4.010
.05	13	4.667	3.806	3.411	3.179	3.025	2.915	2.832	2.767	2.714	2.671	2.635	2.604	2.577	2.554	2.533
.01	13	9.074	6.701	5.739	5.205	4.862	4.620	4.441	4.302	4.191	4.100	4.025	3.960	3.905	3.857	3.815

α	df															
.05	14	**4.600**	**3.739**	**3.344**	**3.112**	**2.958**	**2.848**	**2.764**	**2.699**	**2.646**	**2.602**	**2.565**	**2.534**	**2.507**	**2.484**	**2.463**
.01	14	*8.862*	*6.515*	*5.564*	*5.035*	*4.695*	*4.456*	*4.278*	*4.140*	*4.030*	*3.939*	*3.864*	*3.800*	*3.745*	*3.698*	*3.656*
.05	15	**4.543**	**3.682**	**3.287**	**3.056**	**2.901**	**2.790**	**2.707**	**2.641**	**2.588**	**2.544**	**2.507**	**2.475**	**2.448**	**2.424**	**2.403**
.01	15	*8.683*	*6.359*	*5.417*	*4.893*	*4.556*	*4.318*	*4.142*	*4.004*	*3.895*	*3.805*	*3.730*	*3.666*	*3.612*	*3.564*	*3.522*
.05	16	**4.494**	**3.634**	**3.239**	**3.007**	**2.852**	**2.741**	**2.657**	**2.591**	**2.538**	**2.494**	**2.456**	**2.425**	**2.397**	**2.373**	**2.352**
.01	16	*8.531*	*6.226*	*5.292*	*4.773*	*4.437*	*4.202*	*4.026*	*3.890*	*3.780*	*3.691*	*3.616*	*3.553*	*3.498*	*3.451*	*3.409*
.05	17	**4.451**	**3.592**	**3.197**	**2.965**	**2.810**	**2.699**	**2.614**	**2.548**	**2.494**	**2.450**	**2.413**	**2.381**	**2.353**	**2.329**	**2.308**
.01	17	*8.400*	*6.112*	*5.185*	*4.669*	*4.336*	*4.102*	*3.927*	*3.791*	*3.682*	*3.593*	*3.519*	*3.455*	*3.401*	*3.353*	*3.312*
.05	18	**4.414**	**3.555**	**3.160**	**2.928**	**2.773**	**2.661**	**2.577**	**2.510**	**2.456**	**2.412**	**2.374**	**2.342**	**2.314**	**2.290**	**2.269**
.01	18	*8.285*	*6.013*	*5.092*	*4.579*	*4.248*	*4.015*	*3.841*	*3.705*	*3.597*	*3.508*	*3.434*	*3.371*	*3.316*	*3.269*	*3.227*
.05	19	**4.381**	**3.522**	**3.127**	**2.895**	**2.740**	**2.628**	**2.544**	**2.477**	**2.423**	**2.378**	**2.340**	**2.308**	**2.280**	**2.256**	**2.234**
.01	19	*8.185*	*5.926*	*5.010*	*4.500*	*4.171*	*3.939*	*3.765*	*3.631*	*3.523*	*3.434*	*3.360*	*3.297*	*3.242*	*3.195*	*3.153*
.05	20	**4.351**	**3.493**	**3.098**	**2.866**	**2.711**	**2.599**	**2.514**	**2.447**	**2.393**	**2.348**	**2.310**	**2.278**	**2.250**	**2.225**	**2.203**
.01	20	*8.096*	*5.849*	*4.938*	*4.431*	*4.103*	*3.871*	*3.699*	*3.564*	*3.457*	*3.368*	*3.294*	*3.231*	*3.177*	*3.130*	*3.088*
.05	30	**4.171**	**3.316**	**2.922**	**2.690**	**2.534**	**2.421**	**2.334**	**2.266**	**2.211**	**2.165**	**2.126**	**2.092**	**2.063**	**2.037**	**2.015**
.01	30	*7.562*	*5.390*	*4.510*	*4.018*	*3.699*	*3.473*	*3.304*	*3.173*	*3.067*	*2.979*	*2.906*	*2.843*	*2.789*	*2.742*	*2.700*
.05	40	**4.085**	**3.232**	**2.839**	**2.606**	**2.449**	**2.336**	**2.249**	**2.180**	**2.124**	**2.077**	**2.038**	**2.003**	**1.974**	**1.948**	**1.924**
.01	40	*7.314*	*5.179*	*4.313*	*3.828*	*3.514*	*3.291*	*3.124*	*2.993*	*2.888*	*2.801*	*2.727*	*2.665*	*2.611*	*2.563*	*2.522*
.05	50	**4.034**	**3.183**	**2.790**	**2.557**	**2.400**	**2.286**	**2.199**	**2.130**	**2.073**	**2.026**	**1.986**	**1.952**	**1.921**	**1.895**	**1.871**
.01	50	*7.171*	*5.057*	*4.199*	*3.720*	*3.408*	*3.186*	*3.020*	*2.890*	*2.785*	*2.698*	*2.625*	*2.562*	*2.508*	*2.461*	*2.419*
.05	75	**3.968**	**3.119**	**2.727**	**2.494**	**2.337**	**2.222**	**2.134**	**2.064**	**2.007**	**1.959**	**1.919**	**1.884**	**1.853**	**1.826**	**1.802**
.01	75	*6.985*	*4.900*	*4.054*	*3.580*	*3.272*	*3.052*	*2.887*	*2.758*	*2.653*	*2.567*	*2.494*	*2.431*	*2.377*	*2.329*	*2.287*
.05	100	**3.936**	**3.087**	**2.696**	**2.463**	**2.305**	**2.191**	**2.103**	**2.032**	**1.975**	**1.927**	**1.886**	**1.850**	**1.819**	**1.792**	**1.768**
.01	100	*6.895*	*4.824*	*3.984*	*3.513*	*3.206*	*2.988*	*2.823*	*2.694*	*2.590*	*2.503*	*2.430*	*2.368*	*2.313*	*2.265*	*2.223*
.05	150	**3.904**	**3.056**	**2.665**	**2.432**	**2.274**	**2.160**	**2.071**	**2.001**	**1.943**	**1.894**	**1.853**	**1.817**	**1.786**	**1.758**	**1.734**
.01	150	*6.807*	*4.749*	*3.915*	*3.447*	*3.142*	*2.924*	*2.761*	*2.632*	*2.528*	*2.441*	*2.368*	*2.305*	*2.251*	*2.203*	*2.160*
.05	200	**3.888**	**3.041**	**2.650**	**2.417**	**2.259**	**2.144**	**2.056**	**1.985**	**1.927**	**1.878**	**1.837**	**1.801**	**1.769**	**1.742**	**1.717**
.01	200	*6.763*	*4.713*	*3.881*	*3.414*	*3.110*	*2.893*	*2.730*	*2.601*	*2.497*	*2.411*	*2.338*	*2.275*	*2.220*	*2.172*	*2.129*
.05	300	**3.873**	**3.026**	**2.635**	**2.402**	**2.224**	**2.129**	**2.040**	**1.969**	**1.911**	**1.862**	**1.821**	**1.785**	**1.753**	**1.725**	**1.700**
.01	300	*6.720*	*4.677*	*3.848*	*3.382*	*3.079*	*2.862*	*2.699*	*2.571*	*2.467*	*2.380*	*2.307*	*2.244*	*2.190*	*2.142*	*2.099*
.05	400	**3.865**	**3.018**	**2.627**	**2.394**	**2.237**	**2.121**	**2.032**	**1.962**	**1.903**	**1.854**	**1.813**	**1.776**	**1.745**	**1.717**	**1.691**
.01	400	*6.699*	*4.659*	*3.831*	*3.366*	*3.063*	*2.847*	*2.684*	*2.556*	*2.452*	*2.365*	*2.292*	*2.229*	*2.175*	*2.126*	*2.084*
.05	500	**3.860**	**3.014**	**2.623**	**2.390**	**2.232**	**2.117**	**2.028**	**1.957**	**1.899**	**1.850**	**1.808**	**1.772**	**1.740**	**1.712**	**1.686**
.01	500	*6.686*	*4.648*	*3.821*	*3.357*	*3.054*	*2.838*	*2.675*	*2.547*	*2.443*	*2.356*	*2.283*	*2.220*	*2.166*	*2.117*	*2.075*

Appendix A4 Q-table (Tukey's *Post Hoc* Test)

Explanation. This table shows the critical value at which the honestly significant difference (HSD) values in Tukey's *post hoc* tests are statistically significant for α values of .01 or .05. Like the *F*-distribution, this distribution (technically called the Studentized range distribution) has two different degrees of freedom values: one for the number of degrees of freedom in the numerator (i.e., $df_{Between}$), and another for the degrees of freedom in the denominator (i.e., df_{Within}). The columns are for the number of $df_{Between}$, while the rows are for the number of degrees of freedom df_{Within}. To find the appropriate q value, identify the column that corresponds to the number of degrees of freedom between groups for your data. Then, identify the row that corresponds to your data's degrees of freedom within groups. Two cells will belong to that row and column. The cell text is **boldface** for the q value that corresponds to α = .05. The cell text is *italicized* for the q value that corresponds to α = .01. These values are taken from Harter (1960, pp. 1134, 1138).

Degrees of freedom in denominator (i.e., degrees of freedom within groups, or df_{Within})

Degrees of freedom in numerator (i.e., degrees of freedom between groups, or $df_{Between}$)

α	df_{Within}	2	3	4	5	6	7	8	9	10	11	12	13	14	15	16
.05	1	17.97	26.98	32.82	37.08	40.41	43.12	45.40	47.36	49.07	50.59	51.96	53.20	54.33	55.36	56.32
.01	1	90.03	135.0	164.3	185.6	202.2	215.8	227.2	237.0	245.6	253.2	260.0	266.2	271.8	277.0	281.8
.05	2	6.085	8.331	9.798	10.88	11.74	12.44	13.03	13.54	13.99	14.39	14.75	15.08	15.38	15.65	15.91
.01	2	14.04	19.02	22.29	24.72	26.63	28.20	29.53	30.68	31.69	32.59	33.40	34.13	34.81	35.43	36.00
.05	3	4.501	5.910	6.825	7.502	8.037	8.478	8.853	9.177	9.462	9.717	9.946	10.15	10.35	10.53	10.69
.01	3	8.261	10.62	12.17	13.33	14.24	15.00	15.64	16.20	16.69	17.13	17.53	17.89	18.22	18.52	18.81
.05	4	3.927	5.040	5.757	6.287	6.707	7.053	7.347	7.602	7.826	8.027	8.208	8.373	8.525	8.664	8.794
.01	4	6.512	8.120	9.173	9.958	10.58	11.10	11.55	11.93	12.27	12.57	12.84	13.09	13.32	13.53	13.73
.05	5	3.635	4.602	5.218	5.673	6.033	6.330	6.582	6.802	6.995	7.168	7.324	7.466	7.596	7.717	7.828
.01	5	5.702	6.976	7.804	8.421	8.913	9.321	9.669	9.972	10.24	10.48	10.70	10.89	11.08	11.24	11.40
.05	6	3.461	4.339	4.896	5.305	5.628	5.895	6.122	6.319	6.493	6.649	6.789	6.917	7.034	7.143	7.244
.01	6	5.243	6.331	7.033	7.556	7.973	8.318	8.613	8.869	9.097	9.301	9.485	9.653	9.808	9.951	10.08
.05	7	3.344	4.165	4.681	5.060	5.359	5.606	5.815	5.998	6.158	6.302	6.431	6.550	6.658	6.759	6.852
.01	7	4.949	5.919	6.543	7.005	7.373	7.679	7.939	8.166	8.368	8.548	8.711	8.860	8.997	9.124	9.242
.05	8	3.261	4.041	4.529	4.886	5.167	5.399	5.597	5.767	5.918	6.054	6.175	6.287	6.389	6.483	6.571
.01	8	4.746	5.635	6.204	6.625	6.960	7.237	7.474	7.681	7.863	8.027	8.176	8.312	8.436	8.552	8.659
.05	9	3.199	3.949	4.415	4.756	5.024	5.244	5.432	5.595	5.739	5.867	5.983	6.089	6.186	6.276	6.359
.01	9	4.596	5.428	5.957	6.348	6.658	6.915	7.134	7.325	7.495	7.647	7.784	7.910	8.025	8.132	8.232
.05	10	3.151	3.877	4.327	4.654	4.912	5.124	5.305	5.461	5.599	5.722	5.833	5.935	6.028	6.114	6.194
.01	10	4.482	5.270	5.769	6.136	6.428	6.669	6.875	7.055	7.213	7.356	7.485	7.603	7.712	7.812	7.906
.05	11	3.113	3.820	4.256	4.574	4.823	5.028	5.202	5.353	5.487	5.605	5.713	5.811	5.901	5.984	6.062
.01	11	4.392	5.146	5.621	5.970	6.247	6.476	6.672	6.842	6.992	7.128	7.250	7.362	7.465	7.560	7.649
.05	12	3.082	3.773	4.199	4.508	4.751	4.950	5.119	5.265	5.395	5.511	5.615	5.710	5.798	5.878	5.953
.01	12	4.320	5.046	5.502	5.836	6.101	6.321	6.507	6.670	6.814	6.943	7.060	7.167	7.265	7.356	7.441
.05	13	3.055	3.735	4.151	4.453	4.690	4.885	5.049	5.192	5.318	5.431	5.533	5.625	5.711	5.789	5.862
.01	13	4.260	4.964	5.404	5.727	5.981	6.192	6.372	6.528	6.667	6.791	6.903	7.006	7.101	7.188	7.269
.05	14	3.033	3.702	4.111	4.407	4.639	4.829	4.990	5.131	5.254	5.364	5.463	5.554	5.637	5.714	5.786

α	df_{within}	2	3	4	5	6	7	8	9	10	11	12	13	14	15	16
.01	14	4.210	4.895	5.322	5.634	5.881	6.085	6.258	6.409	6.543	6.664	6.772	6.871	6.962	7.047	7.126
.05	**15**	**3.014**	**3.674**	**4.076**	**4.367**	**4.595**	**4.782**	**4.940**	**5.077**	**5.198**	**5.306**	**5.404**	**5.493**	**5.574**	**5.649**	**5.720**
.01	15	4.168	4.836	5.252	5.556	5.796	5.994	6.162	6.309	6.439	6.555	6.660	6.757	6.845	6.927	7.003
.05	**16**	**2.998**	**3.649**	**4.046**	**4.333**	**4.557**	**4.741**	**4.897**	**5.031**	**5.150**	**5.256**	**5.352**	**5.439**	**5.520**	**5.593**	**5.662**
.01	16	4.131	4.786	5.192	5.489	5.722	5.915	6.079	6.222	6.349	6.462	6.564	6.658	6.744	6.823	6.898
.05	**17**	**2.984**	**3.628**	**4.020**	**4.303**	**4.524**	**4.705**	**4.858**	**4.991**	**5.108**	**5.212**	**5.307**	**5.392**	**5.471**	**5.544**	**5.612**
.01	17	4.099	4.742	5.140	5.430	5.659	5.847	6.007	6.147	6.270	6.381	6.480	6.572	6.656	6.734	6.806
.05	**18**	**2.971**	**3.609**	**3.997**	**4.277**	**4.495**	**4.673**	**4.824**	**4.956**	**5.071**	**5.174**	**5.267**	**5.352**	**5.429**	**5.501**	**5.568**
.01	18	4.071	4.703	5.094	5.379	5.603	5.788	5.944	6.081	6.201	6.310	6.407	6.497	6.579	6.655	6.725
.05	**19**	**2.960**	**3.593**	**3.977**	**4.253**	**4.469**	**4.645**	**4.794**	**4.924**	**5.038**	**5.140**	**5.231**	**5.315**	**5.391**	**5.462**	**5.528**
.01	19	4.046	4.670	5.054	5.334	5.554	5.735	5.889	6.022	6.141	6.247	6.342	6.430	6.510	6.585	6.654
.05	**20**	**2.950**	**3.578**	**3.958**	**4.232**	**4.445**	**4.620**	**4.768**	**4.896**	**5.008**	**5.108**	**5.199**	**5.282**	**5.357**	**5.427**	**5.493**
.01	20	4.024	4.639	5.018	5.294	5.510	5.688	5.839	5.970	6.087	6.191	6.285	6.371	6.450	6.523	6.591
.05	**24**	**2.919**	**3.532**	**3.901**	**4.166**	**4.373**	**4.541**	**4.684**	**4.807**	**4.915**	**5.012**	**5.099**	**5.179**	**5.251**	**5.319**	**5.381**
.01	24	3.956	4.546	4.907	5.168	5.374	5.542	5.685	5.809	5.919	6.017	6.106	6.186	6.261	6.330	6.394
.05	**30**	**2.888**	**3.486**	**3.845**	**4.102**	**4.302**	**4.464**	**4.602**	**4.720**	**4.824**	**4.917**	**5.001**	**5.077**	**5.147**	**5.211**	**5.271**
.01	30	3.889	4.445	4.799	5.048	5.242	5.401	5.536	5.653	5.756	5.849	5.932	6.008	6.078	6.143	6.203
.05	**40**	**2.858**	**3.442**	**3.791**	**4.039**	**4.232**	**4.389**	**4.521**	**4.635**	**4.735**	**4.824**	**4.904**	**4.977**	**5.044**	**5.106**	**5.163**
.01	40	3.825	4.367	4.696	4.931	5.114	5.265	5.392	5.502	5.599	5.686	5.764	5.835	5.900	5.961	6.017
.05	**60**	**2.829**	**3.399**	**3.737**	**3.977**	**4.163**	**4.314**	**4.441**	**4.550**	**4.646**	**4.732**	**4.808**	**4.878**	**4.942**	**5.001**	**5.056**
.01	60	3.762	4.282	4.595	4.818	4.991	5.133	5.253	5.356	5.447	5.528	5.601	5.667	5.728	5.785	5.837
.05	**120**	**2.800**	**3.356**	**3.685**	**3.917**	**4.096**	**4.241**	**4.363**	**4.468**	**4.560**	**4.641**	**4.714**	**4.781**	**4.842**	**4.898**	**4.950**
.01	120	3.702	4.200	4.497	4.709	4.872	5.005	5.118	5.214	5.299	5.375	5.443	5.505	5.562	5.614	5.662
.05	**∞**	**2.772**	**3.317**	**3.633**	**3.858**	**4.030**	**4.170**	**4.286**	**4.387**	**4.474**	**4.552**	**4.622**	**4.685**	**4.743**	**4.796**	**4.845**
.01	∞	3.643	4.120	4.403	4.603	4.757	4.882	4.987	5.078	5.157	5.227	5.290	5.348	5.400	5.448	5.493

Degrees of freedom in denominator (i.e., degrees of freedom within groups, or df_{Within})

Degrees of freedom in numerator (i.e., degrees of freedom between groups, or $df_{Between}$)

Appendix A5　Critical Values for *r*

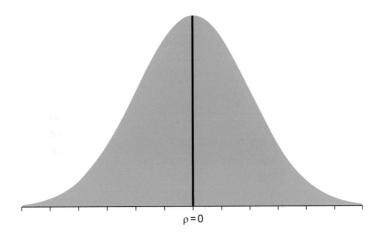

$\rho = 0$

The sampling distribution of correlation coefficients is normally distributed when the population correlation is $\rho = 0$. When the population correlation coefficient is not zero, the sampling distribution will be skewed, with the longer tail closer to zero. The critical values in this table are for the null hypothesis that $r = 0$. The columns on the left are for a one-tailed test, while the columns on the right are for a two-tailed test. When a sample's correlation coefficient is closer to zero than the critical value in the table, the null hypothesis should be rejected. When the correlation coefficient is more extreme than the critical value, the null hypothesis should be rejected. The formula for the degrees of freedom is Formula 12.7: df $= n - 2$.

One-tailed test			Two-tailed test		
df	$\alpha = 0.05$	$\alpha = 0.01$	df	$\alpha = 0.05$	$\alpha = 0.01$
1	+/−0.988	+/−0.9995	1	+0.997	+0.9999
2	+/−0.900	+/−0.980	2	+0.950	+0.990
3	+/−0.805	+/−0.934	3	+0.878	+0.959
4	+/−0.729	+/−0.882	4	+0.811	+0.917
5	+/−0.669	+/−0.833	5	+0.754	+0.875
6	+/−0.621	+/−0.789	6	+0.707	+0.834
7	+/−0.582	+/−0.750	7	+0.666	+0.798
8	+/−0.550	+/−0.716	8	+0.632	+0.765
9	+/−0.521	+/−0.686	9	+0.603	+0.735
10	+/−0.498	+/−0.659	10	+0.576	+0.708
11	+/−0.477	+/−0.634	11	+0.553	+0.684
12	+/−0.458	+/−0.613	12	+0.533	+0.662
13	+/−0.441	+/−0.593	13	+0.514	+0.642

(*cont.*)

	One-tailed test			Two-tailed test	
df	α = 0.05	α = 0.01	df	α = 0.05	α = 0.01
14	+/−0.426	+/−0.575	14	+0.498	+0.623
15	+/−0.413	+/−0.558	15	+0.483	+0.606
16	+/−0.401	+/−0.543	16	+0.469	+0.590
17	+/−0.389	+/−0.529	17	+0.456	+0.576
18	+/−0.379	+/−0.516	18	+0.444	+0.562
19	+/−0.369	+/−0.504	19	+0.433	+0.549
20	+/−0.360	+/−0.493	20	+0.423	+0.537
21	+/−0.352	+/−0.482	21	+0.414	+0.526
22	+/−0.344	+/−0.472	22	+0.405	+0.516
23	+/−0.337	+/−0.463	23	+0.397	+0.506
24	+/−0.330	+/−0.454	24	+0.389	+0.496
25	+/−0.324	+/−0.446	25	+0.381	+0.487
26	+/−0.318	+/−0.438	26	+0.374	+0.479
27	+/−0.312	+/−0.430	27	+0.368	+0.471
28	+/−0.307	+/−0.423	28	+0.362	+0.463
29	+/−0.301	+/−0.416	29	+0.356	+0.456
30	+/−0.296	+/−0.410	30	+0.350	+0.449
31	+/−0.292	+/−0.404	31	+0.344	+0.443
32	+/−0.287	+/−0.398	32	+0.339	+0.436
33	+/−0.283	+/−0.392	33	+0.334	+0.430
34	+/−0.279	+/−0.387	34	+0.330	+0.424
35	+/−0.275	+/−0.381	35	+0.325	+0.419
36	+/−0.271	+/−0.376	36	+0.321	+0.413
37	+/−0.268	+/−0.372	37	+0.317	+0.408
38	+/−0.264	+/−0.367	38	+0.313	+0.403
39	+/−0.261	+/−0.363	39	+0.309	+0.398
40	+/−0.258	+/−0.358	40	+0.305	+0.394
41	+/−0.255	+/−0.354	41	+0.301	+0.389
42	+/−0.252	+/−0.350	42	+0.298	+0.385
43	+/−0.249	+/−0.346	43	+0.294	+0.381
44	+/−0.246	+/−0.342	44	+0.291	+0.377
45	+/−0.243	+/−0.339	45	+0.288	+0.373
50	+/−0.231	+/−0.322	50	+0.274	+0.355
55	+/−0.221	+/−0.308	55	+0.261	+0.339
60	+/−0.211	+/−0.295	60	+0.251	+0.325
70	+/−0.196	+/−0.274	70	+0.232	+0.302
80	+/−0.183	+/−0.257	80	+0.218	+0.283
90	+/−0.173	+/−0.243	90	+0.205	+0.268
100	+/−0.164	+/−0.231	100	+0.195	+0.254
110	+/−0.157	+/−0.220	110	+0.186	+0.243
120	+/−0.150	+/−0.211	120	+0.178	+0.233

	One-tailed test			Two-tailed test	
df	$\alpha = 0.05$	$\alpha = 0.01$	df	$\alpha = 0.05$	$\alpha = 0.01$
130	+/–0.144	+/–0.203	130	+0.171	+0.224
140	+/–0.139	+/–0.196	140	+0.165	+0.216
150	+/–0.134	+/–0.189	150	+0.160	+0.209
200	+/–0.116	+/–0.164	200	+0.138	+0.181
250	+/–0.104	+/–0.146	250	+0.124	+0.162
500	+/–0.073	+/–0.104	500	+0.088	+0.115
1,000	+/–0.052	+/–0.073	1,000	+0.062	+0.081

(cont.)

Appendix A6 χ^2-Table

Explanation. This table shows the value at which the area in the χ^2 distribution is equal to either 1% (for $\alpha = .01$) or 5% (for $\alpha = .05$) of the total area in the distribution. As explained in General Linear Moment 14.1, the χ^2 distribution is a sampling distribution that consists of sample variances. This results in a distribution made of data that have been squared (see Formula 4.11), and this makes the χ^2 distribution always positively skewed. As a result, all of the critical values are always positive.

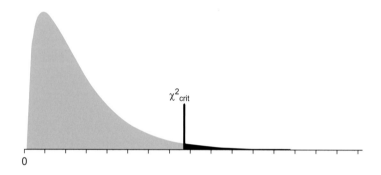

df	$\alpha = 0.05$	$\alpha = 0.01$
1	3.841	6.635
2	5.991	9.210
3	7.815	11.345
4	9.488	13.277
5	11.070	15.086
6	12.592	16.812
7	14.067	18.475
8	15.507	20.090
9	16.919	21.666
10	18.307	23.209
11	19.675	24.725
12	21.026	26.217
13	22.362	27.688
14	23.685	29.141
15	24.996	30.578
16	26.296	32.000
17	27.587	33.409
18	28.869	34.805
19	30.144	36.191
20	31.410	37.566

df	α = 0.05	α = 0.01
(cont.)		
21	32.671	38.932
22	33.924	40.289
23	35.172	41.638
24	36.415	42.980
25	37.652	44.314
26	38.885	45.642
27	40.113	46.963
28	41.337	48.278
29	42.557	49.588
30	43.773	50.892
31	44.985	52.191
32	46.194	53.486
33	47.400	54.776
34	48.602	56.061
35	49.802	57.342
36	50.998	58.619
37	52.192	59.893
38	53.384	61.162
39	54.572	62.428
40	55.758	63.691
41	56.942	64.950
42	58.124	66.206
43	59.304	67.459
44	60.481	68.710
45	61.656	69.957
50	67.505	76.154
55	73.311	82.292
60	79.082	88.379
70	90.531	100.425
80	101.879	112.329
90	113.145	124.116
100	124.342	135.807
110	135.480	147.414
120	146.567	158.950
130	157.610	170.423
140	168.613	181.840
150	179.581	193.208
200	233.994	249.445
250	287.882	304.940
500	553.127	576.493
1,000	1,074.679	1,106.969

Glossary

Alpha (α): The size of a rejection region in a null hypothesis statistical significance test. See also null hypothesis statistical significance testing (NHST) and rejection region.

Alternative hypothesis: The hypothesis that the data support if the null hypothesis is rejected in NHST. See also null hypothesis and null hypothesis statistical significance testing (NHST).

Analysis of variance (ANOVA): NHST in which the null hypothesis is that all independent variable groups have equal means. A member of the general linear model, ANOVAs are conducted when there are three or more groups in a nominal variable and the dependent variable is interval- or ratio-level data. ANOVA is an extension of the unpaired-samples t-test; if there are only two groups in the ANOVA, the procedure simplifies to an unpaired-samples t-test. See also ANOVA table, eta-squared (η^2), F-distribution, general linear model, information table, interval data, Kruskal–Wallis test, mean, nominal data, null hypothesis, null hypothesis statistical significance testing, one-way ANOVA, *post hoc* test, ratio data, two-way ANOVA, unpaired-samples t-test, and way.

Analytical probability distribution: See probability distribution.

ANOVA table: The second of two tables required for calculating the observed value for analysis of variance. The data needed for the ANOVA table come from the information table. See also analysis of variance (ANOVA), information table, and observed value.

Assumption: A requirement that data must meet in order for a statistical procedure to be used without producing distorted or inaccurate results.

AUC: A nonparametric effect size for the Wilcoxon rank-sum test. AUC stands for "area under the receiver operator characteristic curve." AUC is a probability that a randomly selected person from the higher scoring group will rank higher than a randomly selected person from the lower scoring group. AUC values always range between 0 and 1. See also effect size, parametric statistics, probability (definition 2), and Wilcoxon rank-sum test.

Average: See mean.

Baseline group: A group within a sample that all other groups in the sample are compared to. Baseline groups are formed by nominal independent variables. See also nominal data.

Baseline model: In the context of regression, the worst model fitting the data. It is also the model that would be used to make predictions if nothing were known about the data. For analysis of variance and regression, the baseline model is that every sample member will obtain a score equal to the grand mean. See also analysis of variance (ANOVA), eta-squared (η^2), grand mean, r^2, and regression.

Baseline outcome: A dependent variable group that an outcome of interest is compared to when interpreting an odds ratio in a chi-squared test. See also odds ratio and outcome of interest.

Bell curve: See normal distribution.

Bessel's correction: The adjustment in the denominator from n to $n - 1$ in using sample data to estimate the population standard deviation. Bessel's correction is necessary because using the sample size (n) produces an estimate of the population standard deviation that is too small. Bessel's correction is named after the German astronomer and mathematician Friedrich Bessel.

Bimodal: A distribution or histogram that has two peaks. See also histogram and unimodal.

Bonferroni correction: A method of correcting experimentwise Type I error inflation in a set of NHSTs by dividing the testwise alpha value by the number of NHSTs performed. Named for the Italian mathematician Carlo Emilio Bonferroni.

Also called a Bonferroni–Dunn correction. See also alpha (α), Bonferroni–Dunn *post hoc* test, experimentwise Type I error, testwise Type I error, and Type I error.

Bonferroni–Dunn correction: See Bonferroni correction.

Bonferroni–Dunn *post hoc* test: A *post hoc* test that is conducted after an ANOVA to determine the pair(s) of group means that resulted in the rejection of the ANOVA's null hypothesis. The Bonferroni–Dunn correction is performed by conducting a series of unpaired-samples *t*-tests with a Bonferroni correction applied to the alpha value of each *t*-test. Named for the Italian mathematician Carlo Emilio Bonferroni and the American statistician Olive Jean Dunn. See also analysis of variance (ANOVA), Bonferroni correction, null hypothesis statistical significance testing (NHST), and *post hoc* test.

Capture percentage: The percentage of replication studies having a population statistic that falls within the confidence interval of a previous study. For a 95% confidence interval, the mean capture percentage is actually 83.4%. See also confidence interval.

Central limit theorem: The statistical law that, for a continuous, randomly determined variable, as the number of trials approaches infinity, the distribution of sample means will have a shape that converges towards normality. This distribution of sample means is called a sampling distribution, and with an infinite number of samples, it will have a mean that converges on the population mean, and a standard deviation that converges on the standard error. See also sampling distribution.

Central tendency: The location on a number line which tends to be the center of a distribution or histogram. See also harmonic mean, histogram, mean, median, mode, and trimmed mean.

Chi-squared test: (1) Any null hypothesis statistical significance test which uses the chi-squared distribution as the sampling distribution. This includes the one-variable chi-squared test and the two-variable chi-squared test, among other, more complex procedures. (2) The two-variable chi-squared test. Regardless of the definition,

chi-squared tests are nonparametric tests that require nominal-level data to be performed correctly. See also nonparametric statistics, null hypothesis statistical significance testing (NHST), odds ratio, one-variable chi-squared test, and two-variable chi-squared test.

Clinical significance: The degree to which treatment moves people from a group that needs treatment to one that does not (i.e., the degree to which a treatment makes people well enough to no longer need treatment). See also practical significance and statistical significance.

Coefficient of determination: See r^2.

Cohen's benchmarks: A label of "small," "medium," or "large" based on guidelines originally propagated by the American psychologist and statistician Jacob Cohen. These labels are not a sufficient interpretation of effect sizes, and Cohen himself stated that they should only be used in areas of research where there were little or no previous studies to provide guidance about typical effect sizes. See also effect size.

Cohen's *d*: An effect size that measures the standardized distance between two means. The metric of Cohen's *d* is standard deviations (i.e., it is expressed as a *z*-score). A Cohen's *d* of 0 means that two means are exactly equal. Values further from zero (including negative values) indicate larger differences between the two means. Cohen's *d* is named for the American psychologist and statistician Jacob Cohen. See also effect size, point-biserial correlation, standard deviation, and *z*-score.

Conditional probability: The probability that a group of sample members will experience an outcome, given (i.e., conditional upon) their values on at least one other independent variable. See also marginal probability and probability (definition 2).

Confidence interval (CI): A range of estimates that are plausible values for a population parameter. See also generalization (definition 1), lower limit, point estimate, and upper limit.

Confirmatory factor analysis: See factor analysis.

Constant: A characteristic that is the same for all members of the population or sample.

In quantitative data a constant is represented by the same number for all population or sample members.

Contingency table: A table that shows every possible combination of values for a nominal independent variable and a nominal dependent variable. A contingency table also shows the number of sample members who have each combination of variable scores. Contingency tables are commonly used in chi-squared tests.

Continuous data: Data that permit a wide range of scores with no gaps at any point along the scale. See also discrete data.

Control group: The group in an experiment that receives no treatment. Random assignment to experimental and control groups is necessary to perform an experiment and establish a causal relationship between variables. See also experiment, experimental group, random assignment, and relationship.

Correlation: A standardized measurement of the relationships between two variables. If two variables are related, it is said that they are correlated. Strong correlations mean that there is a high degree of consistency in scores on the two variables. Weak correlations indicate a low degree of consistency between two variables. See also correlation coefficient, correlation table, covariance, direct correlation, general linear model, inverse correlation, and Pearson's *r*.

Correlation coefficient: A statistic quantifying the strength of the relationship (i.e., correlation) between two variables. See also correlation, correlation table, Cramér's *V*, Pearson's *r*, phi (ϕ), point-biserial correlation, and Spearman's rho (ρ).

Correlation table: A table of correlation coefficients between a set of variables. With *m* variables, a correlation table will have *m* rows and *m* columns. All correlation tables have a diagonal of cells extending from the upper-left corner to the bottom-right corner in which all correlations are 1.0. The correlation coefficients above this diagonal are a mirror image of the correlation coefficients below the diagonal. See also correlation and correlation coefficient.

Covariance: An unstandardized measure of association or relationship between two interval- or ratio-level variables. Standardizing the covariance (by dividing by the product of the two variables' standard deviations) converts the covariance into the Pearson's *r* correlation. See also correlation and Pearson's *r*.

Cramér's *V*: A correlation coefficient that is a generalization of the phi correlation for nominal independent and dependent variables. Cramér's *V* values can only range from 0 (no association between variables) to 1 (a perfect association between variables). See also chi-squared test, correlation, correlation coefficient, generalization, and phi (ϕ). Named for the Swedish statistician Carl Harald Cramér.

Critical value: The point in the sampling distribution at which the rejection region starts in a null hypothesis statistical significance test (NHST). See also null hypothesis statistical significance test (NHST), observed value, rejection region, and sampling distribution.

Cumulative frequency: In a frequency table, the frequency in a row plus the frequency in all higher rows. See also frequency and frequency table.

Curvilinear relationship: See nonlinear relationship.

Data: See datum.

Dataset: A compilation of data. Most datasets are arranged so that sample members are displayed as rows, and variables or constants are displayed as columns. However, some complex datasets may deviate from this pattern.

Datum: A piece of information about a person's characteristics on a variable or a constant. To conduct statistical analysis, we must convert a datum to a number. Plural: data.

Degrees of freedom: A statistic (abbreviated df) referring to the number of data points that can vary given the results of the sample statistics.

Dependent samples *t*-test: See paired-samples *t*-test.

Dependent variable: The outcome variable in a study. See also variable and independent variable.

Descriptive discriminant analysis: The *post hoc* test for a rejected null hypothesis in a multivariate analysis of variance. See also *post hoc* test and multivariate analysis of variance (MANOVA).

Descriptive statistics: The branch of statistics concerned with describing the data that a researcher has on hand.

Deviation score: The difference between an individual score and the mean of the sample or population.

Direct correlation: See positive correlation.

Discrete data: Data that have a limited number of possible values or have large gaps in the possible scores on the scale. See also continuous data.

Dunnett's test: A planned contrast after the null hypothesis has been rejected in an ANOVA. In Dunnett's test a baseline or control group's mean is compared to the mean of every other group, one at a time. However, no comparisons of other groups' means occur. Named for the Canadian statistician Charles W. Dunnett. See also analysis of variance (ANOVA), null hypothesis statistical significance testing (NHST), and planned contrast.

Effect size: A statistic that quantifies the degree to which the null hypothesis is wrong. Effect sizes can also describe the strength of the relationship between two variables. The most common effect sizes are Cohen's d, r^2, R^2, η^2, and the odds ratio. Some people also consider Pearson's r to be an effect size. See also AUC, Cohen's benchmarks, Cohen's d, eta-squared (η^2), Glass's delta (Δ), odds ratio, Pearson's r, r^2, R^2, and relative risk.

Empirical probability: A probability calculated from a number of repeated, independent observations. See also probability (definition 2) and theoretical probability.

Empirical probability distribution: See probability distribution.

Error: See residual.

Eta-squared (η^2): An effect size in ANOVA that is calculated by finding the ratio between the sum of squares between groups and the total sum of squares. η^2 is interpreted as (1) the amount of variance in the dependent variable that is shared with the independent variable (i.e., the nominal grouping variable), or (2) the percentage of the size of the decrease in squared residuals in comparing predictions made with the regression line to predictions made with the baseline model. Because ANOVA is a special case of correlation and regression in the general linear model, η^2 is algebraically equal to the r^2 effect size in Pearson's r, and both effect sizes are interpreted the same way. See also analysis of variance (ANOVA), baseline model, effect size, general linear model, grand mean, Pearson's r, r^2, regression, residual, special case, and sum of squares.

Experiment: A study in which a scientist randomly assigns sample members to treatment and control groups in order to ascertain the presence of a causal relationship between variables. See also control group, experimental group, random assignment, and relationship.

Experimental group: The group in an experiment that receives treatment. Random assignment to experimental and control groups is necessary to perform an experiment and establish a causal relationship between variables. Also called treatment group. See also control group, experiment, random assignment, and relationship.

Experimentwise Type I error: The probability of making a Type I error in any one of the series of null hypothesis tests. See also alpha (α), Bonferroni correction, testwise Type I error, and Type I error. Also called familywise Type I error rate.

Exploratory factor analysis: See factor analysis.

Exploratory research: Research that is not governed by pre-existing theory or hypotheses, usually because little pre-existing research exists on a topic. Exploratory research can be difficult to replicate because of the potential for Type I error inflation. See also replication and Type I error inflation.

Extension: See generalization (definition 2).

Extreme value: See outlier.

Factor analysis: A multivariate procedure which reduces a set of observed variables into a smaller number of latent variables called factors. There are two types of factor analysis. (1) Exploratory factor analysis is an atheoretical procedure in which variables are grouped together into factors. (2) In confirmatory factor analysis, the grouping of variables into factors is specified in advance, and the data are tested against this theory. See also latent variable and multivariate statistics.

Factorial model: A statistical model that includes every possible main effect and interaction. See also main effect and interaction.

False negative: See Type II error.

False positive: See Type I error.

Familywise Type I error rate: See experimentwise Type I error rate.

F-distribution: The sampling distribution for an analysis of variance (ANOVA). The F-distribution is always positively skewed, and critical and observed values on the distribution must be 0 or greater. Named by the American statistician George W. Snedecor in honor of the British biologist and statistician Sir Ronald Fisher, who developed the earliest version of ANOVA. See also analysis of variance (ANOVA) and sampling distribution.

File drawer problem: The tendency for studies that retain the null hypothesis not to be published and instead languish in researchers' file drawers. The file drawer problem contributes to publication bias in scientific literature. See also publication bias.

Frequency: The number of times that a value appears for a single variable in a dataset. See also cumulative frequency and frequency table.

Frequency polygon: A visual model similar to a histogram that has an x-axis representing a variable's values and a y-axis representing the frequency. In a frequency polygon, a dot is plotted in the center of each interval at the height of the frequency for that interval. The dots are then connected with a solid line. By convention, frequency polygons should start and end with an interval that has a frequency of zero. See also frequency, histogram, interval, and line graph.

Frequency table: A table showing (1) all of the values for a variable in a dataset, and (2) the frequency of each of those responses. Some frequency tables also show a cumulative frequency and proportions of responses. See also cumulative frequency, frequency, and proportion.

Gaussian distribution: See normal distribution.

General linear model (GLM): A family of statistical procedures that (1) are all correlational in nature, (2) apply weights to data during the analysis process, and (3) produce an effect size. See also

correlation, null hypothesis statistical significance testing (NHST), and effect size.

Generalization (definition 1): The process of drawing conclusions about the entire population based on data from a sample. See confidence interval, inferential statistics, and point estimate.

Generalization (definition 2): In the general linear model, a statistical procedure that encompasses at least one other statistical procedure that is a special case. For example, a one-sample t-test is a generalization of a z-test. See also special case.

Glass's delta (Δ): An effect size that is calculated by subtracting two means from one another and dividing by the standard deviation of the control/pre-test group. This is similar to Cohen's d, except it only uses one sample's standard deviation in the denominator. Named for the American educational psychologist Gene Glass. See also Cohen's d and effect size.

Grand mean: The mean of all the scores from a dataset, including scores belonging to any subgroups. In an ANOVA and regression, the grand mean is the predicted dependent variable score for all individuals, regardless of their independent variable, in the baseline model. See also baseline model and regression.

HARKing: An acronym for *H*ypothesizing *A*fter the *R*esults are *K*nown, HARKing is a questionable research practice which entails creating or altering a research hypothesis after data have been collected. See also hypothesis, questionable research practice, and research hypothesis.

Harmonic mean: A special measure of central tendency that gives a disproportionate weight to smaller group sizes. See also central tendency.

Histogram: A visual model that shows how frequent each response is in a dataset. The width bars of a histogram represent a range of possible variable values, and the height of the bars represents the frequency (i.e., number of times) that values inside the interval occurred in the dataset. See also frequency, frequency polygon, and interval.

Homogeneity of variance: A statistical assumption in unpaired and paired two-sample t-tests and ANOVA that the groups' variances are approximately equal. Fidell and Tabachnick

(2003) state that these NHST procedures are robust to violations of this assumption as long as the ratio between the largest group variance and the smallest group variance is no more than 10:1. See also assumption.

Honestly significant difference (HSD): See Tukey's *post hoc* test.

Hypothesis: A supposition or belief about the world that a scientific study is designed to test. To be scientific, a hypothesis must be falsifiable, which means that it must be possible to disprove the hypothesis. See also null hypothesis and research hypothesis.

Independent samples *t*-test: See unpaired-samples *t*-test.

Independent variable: The variable that is believed to cause changes in the dependent variable. See also dependent variable and variable.

Inferential statistics: The branch of statistics concerned with drawing conclusions about an entire population based solely on sample data. See generalization (definition 1).

Information table: A requirement for calculating the observed value in an ANOVA, this table compiles all the information needed to calculate the sum of squares values. These sum of square values are part of the ANOVA table. See also analysis of variance (ANOVA), ANOVA table, and observed value.

Interaction: A statistical anomaly that occurs when the relationship between an independent variable and a dependent variable varies according to the subject's values on a second independent variable. Thus, an interaction's impact is different from the sum of the impact of the main effects. The nonadditive impact may occur, for example, when a treatment is more effective for older adults than for young adults. See also factorial model, main effect, and Simpson's paradox.

Interquartile range: A model of variability that is calculated by finding the scores that encompass the middle 50% of scores for a variable in the dataset. The interquartile range is the highest quartile minus the lowest quartile. See also quartile and variability.

Interval: In a histogram, the width of a bar. The interval represents a range of possible values for a variable. See histogram.

Interval data: The level of data in which the numbers assigned to mutually exclusive and exhaustive categories indicates a rank order, and the distance between numbers on the scale is constant along the entire length of the scale. See also levels of data.

Inverse correlation: See negative correlation.

Joint probability: The probability of a trial resulting in a combination of two outcomes. See also conditional probability, probability (definition 2), and marginal probability.

Kruskal–Wallis test: A nonparametric test that compares ordinal-level rank data from three or more groups. The null hypothesis of the Kruskal–Wallis test is that the groups all have the same distribution of ranks. The test is an extension of the nonparametric Wilcoxon rank-sum test, and it is analogous to the parametric analysis of variance. Named for the American statisticians William Henry Kruskal and Allen Wallis. See also analysis of variance (ANOVA), nonparametric statistics, and Wilcoxon rank-sum test.

Kurtosis: A measurement of the height of the parts of a distribution in relationship to the height of a normal distribution. See also leptokurtic, mesokurtic, normal distribution, and platykurtic.

Latent variable: An underlying variable that is assumed to be the cause of individuals' scores on a set of observed variables.

Left skewed: See negatively skewed.

Leptokurtic: A label describing the shape of a histogram or distribution. A leptokurtic distribution has a taller peak, taller tails, and shorter shoulders than a normal distribution. See also kurtosis, mesokurtic, and platykurtic.

Levels of data: A system created by Stevens (1946) for organizing the characteristics of numerical data into one of four categories, which are – from most basic to most advanced – nominal, ordinal, interval, and ratio data. Also called levels of measurement. See also interval data, measurement, nominal data, ordinal data, and ratio data.

Levels of measurement: See levels of data.

Line graph: A visual model that is created by plotting data points on two axes and connecting the sequential dots with a series of straight line segments. Line graphs can be used to show trends across time or across nominal or ordinal categories. See also frequency polygon and visual model.

Line of best fit: See regression line.

Linear regression: A regression model that can be expressed mathematically as a standardized or unstandardized regression equation that produces a straight line in a scatterplot. See also regression, regression line, standardized regression equation, and unstandardized regression equation.

Linear transformation: The process of performing the same arithmetic function (i.e., adding, subtracting, multiplying, and dividing) with a constant for every score in a dataset. Linear transformations change the axis or scale of the data, but do not change the pattern of data (i.e., histogram shape or scatterplot pattern of dots). Converting data to z-scores is a special linear transformation. See z-scores.

Literature review: A type of research synthesis where a person reads most or all of the studies on a topic and then describes the studies and provides a general judgment on their meaning as a whole. See also meta-analysis.

Logistic regression: A null hypothesis statistical significance testing procedure that examines the relationship between an independent variable and a nominal dependent variable. Conducting a logistic regression requires a logit as the dependent variable. See also logit, multiple logistic regression, null hypothesis statistical significance testing (NHST), and regression.

Logit: The natural log of the odds ratio of a nominal level outcome. The logit is the dependent variable in logistic regression and is calculated because the nominal outcome variable in a logistic regression cannot be used in many null hypothesis statistical significance testing procedures. See also logistic regression.

Log-odds: See logit.

Lower limit: The minimal value within a confidence interval. See also confidence interval and upper limit.

Main effect: The overall average effect that an independent variable has on a dependent variable. When there is no interaction between independent variables present, the predicted score for a group is the sum of the independent variables' main effects. See also factorial model and interaction.

Mann–Whitney U test: See Wilcoxon rank-sum test.

Marginal probability: The overall probability of a group of sample members experiencing an outcome, without any regard for any other independent variables. See also conditional probability and probability (definition 2).

Mean: A number at the point where all deviation scores from a dataset sum to 0. The mean is calculated by adding the scores in a dataset and dividing by the number of scores. Also called the average. See also deviation score.

Measurement: "The assignment of numerals to objects or events according to rules" (Stevens, 1946, p. 677). See also levels of data.

Median: The middle score for a variable when the scores of that variable are put in order from the smallest to the greatest (or from the greatest to the smallest). Calculating a median requires data that are at least ordinal level. See also central tendency and ordinal data.

Mesokurtic: A label describing the shape of a histogram or distribution. A mesokurtic distribution has a peak, tails, and shoulders that are as tall as the same parts of a normal distribution. See also kurtosis, leptokurtic, and platykurtic.

Meta-analysis: A type of study in which results from previous studies about the same topic are combined. The goal of most researchers who conduct a meta-analysis is to calculate an average effect size that applies to all the studies under consideration. See also effect size, literature review, and meta-analytic thinking.

Meta-analytic thinking: A mode of thinking about research that considers studies in the wider research context.

Mode: The most frequently occurring score in a dataset. The mode is the most basic model of central tendency and requires at least nominal data to calculate. See also central tendency and ordinal data.

Model: A simplified version of reality that a researcher uses in order to understand the phenomenon under investigation. See also statistical model, theoretical model, and visual model.

Multicollinearity: A condition where independent variables in a statistical model are correlated so highly with one another that one is redundant and provides little – if any – unique information.

Multiple logistic regression: A statistical procedure in the general linear model that is appropriate with two or more independent variables and a single nominal-level dependent variable. See also logistic regression and multiple regression.

Multiple regression: A regression model that includes more than one independent variable. Multiple regression is a member of the general linear model. Pearson's r is a special case of multiple regression, as are ANOVA (including two-way ANOVA and more complex ANOVA methods), all t-tests, the z-test, and the chi-squared test. See also general linear model, R^2, and regression.

Multiple R-squared: See R^2.

Multivariate analysis of variance (MANOVA): A generalization of analysis of variance which tests the null hypothesis that the independent variable(s) is/are unrelated to a set of two or more dependent variables. When the null hypothesis of a MANOVA is rejected, it is appropriate to follow up with a *post hoc* descriptive discriminant analysis. See also analysis of variance, multivariate statistics, and *post hoc* test.

Multivariate statistics: Statistical procedures that analyze relationships between at least one independent variable and two or more dependent variables. See also factor analysis, multivariate analysis of variance (MANOVA), structural equation modeling, and univariate statistics.

Negative correlation: A relationship between variables in which individuals with high scores on one variable tend to have low scores on the other variable. Correlation coefficient values for negative correlations are positive). See also correlation and positive correlation.

Negatively skewed: A label describing the shape of a distribution or histogram. Negatively skewed distributions have a peak on the right side of the distribution and an elongated tail on the left. See also positively skewed, skewness, and unskewed.

NHST: See null hypothesis statistical significance testing.

Nominal data: The simplest level of data, in which objects are assigned a number based on the category they belong to. Nominal data require that categories be mutually exclusive and exhaustive. See also levels of data.

Nonlinear relationship: A relationship between variables that is poorly represented by a straight regression line. Rather, a nonlinear relationship is best represented by a curved line. Also called a curvilinear relationship. See also regression and regression line.

Nonparametric statistics: A family of statistical procedures that do not make assumptions about the shape of the distribution of the population that was the source of sample data. See also AUC, chi-squared test, Kruskal–Wallis test, parametric statistics, Spearman's rho (ρ), and Wilcoxon rank-sum test.

Normal distribution: A unimodal symmetrical distribution that serves as a model for the distribution of a randomly determined, continuous variable. Also called the Gaussian distribution (after the German mathematician and astronomer Johann Carl Friedrich Gauss, though Gauss was not the first to write about it) or – informally – the "bell curve." The latter name is based on the resemblance of the normal distribution to a bell. See also central limit theorem.

Null hypothesis: A hypothesis stating that there is no relationship between two variables (i.e., that they are perfectly uncorrelated, or that there is no difference between groups). In null hypothesis statistical significance testing procedures, rejecting the null hypothesis indicates that it is not a good statistical model for the data, while retaining it indicates that the null hypothesis fits the data and may be a viable model. See also alternative hypothesis, hypothesis, null hypothesis statistical significance testing, and research hypothesis.

Null hypothesis statistical significance testing (NHST): A statistical procedure that tests the null hypothesis to determine whether a relationship exists between two variables. All NHST procedures are members of the general linear model. See also alpha (α), alternative hypothesis, correlation, general linear model, null hypothesis, and statistical significance.

Observed value: A statistic that quantifies the location of a sample statistic on a sampling distribution. In NHST procedures a researcher must compare the locations of the observed and critical values; if an observed value is more extreme than the critical value (and therefore in the rejection region), the null hypothesis should be rejected. See also critical value, rejection region, and null hypothesis statistical significance testing.

Odds ratio: An effect size for a chi-squared test indicating the likelihood that a group of interest will experience an outcome of interest compared to the baseline group. Odds ratios must always be greater than 0, but have no upper limit. An odds ratio of 1.0 indicates that the outcome of interest is equally likely for both groups. See also chi-squared test, effect size, and relative risk.

One-sample *t*-test: A null hypothesis statistical significance test that tests the null hypothesis that a sample mean and population mean are equal when the population mean is not known. The effect size for a one-sample *t*-test is Cohen's *d*. See Cohen's *d* and null hypothesis statistical significance testing (NHST).

One-tailed test: A null hypothesis statistical significance test in which the entire rejection region is on one side of the sampling distribution. One-tailed tests are possible in *z*-tests, one-sample *t*-tests, unpaired-samples *t*-tests, and paired-samples *t*-tests. See also null hypothesis statistical significance testing, rejection region, sampling distribution, and two-tailed test.

One-variable chi-squared test: A null hypothesis statistical significance test that examines whether the proportion of sample members who belong to various nominal categories matches a hypothesized proportion or the population proportion for that category. The effect size for a one-variable chi-squared test is the odds ratio. See also chi-squared test, null hypothesis statistical significance testing (NHST), odds ratio, and two-variable chi-squared test.

One-way ANOVA: An analysis of variance (ANOVA) with one independent variable. See also analysis of variance (ANOVA), two-way ANOVA, and way.

Operationalization: The process of defining a variable in a way that makes it measurable so that quantitative data can be collected.

Ordinal data: The level of data in which the numbers assigned to mutually exclusive and exhaustive categories indicate a rank order. The order of numbers in ordinal data indicates in varying degrees that some groups possess more of the variable than other groups. See also levels of data.

Ordinary least squares (OLS) regression: A type of regression model that is designed to minimize the squared residuals for each sample member, thereby maximizing overall prediction accuracy for the sample. See also regression and residual.

Outcome of interest: The dependent variable group that is of interest in interpreting an odds ratio. See also baseline outcome, odds ratio, and relative risk.

Outlier: An unusual member of a dataset because the sample member's score is much higher or much lower than the vast majority of scores in the dataset. Outliers can distort the results of some statistical calculations, such as the mean or Pearson's *r*.

***p*-Value:** The probability that the results of a study would occur if the null hypothesis were perfectly true. See also null hypothesis and Type I error.

Paired-samples *t*-test: An inferential statistical procedure that tests the null hypothesis that the mean difference between pairs of scores is zero. The paired-samples *t*-test is a null hypothesis statistical significance test, and it is sometimes called a dependent samples *t*-test or two-sample dependent *t*-test. See also null hypothesis and null hypothesis statistical significance test (NHST).

Parameter: A statistical model that describes some aspect of the data from a population. See also population, statistic, and statistical model.

Parametric statistics: A family of statistical procedures that rely on assumptions about the shape of the population that the sample data were taken from. Most parametric statistical procedures assume that the underlying population is normally distributed, though some also assume homogeneity of variance among groups or that residuals are normally distributed (as opposed to the population). See also homogeneity of variance and nonparametric statistics.

Pearson's *r*: A standardized correlation coefficient that describes the relationship between two interval- or ratio-level variables. Pearson's *r* can range from –1 to +1, with relationships becoming stronger and more consistent as the numbers move further from 0. Named after the British statistician, biologist, mathematician, geneticist, biographer, and scholar of German culture Karl Pearson. (He also made contributions to evolutionary biology, physical anthropology, and epidemiology.) See also correlation, correlation coefficient, covariance, direct correlation, inverse correlation, point-biserial correlation, Spearman's ρ (rho), and restriction of range.

Phi (ϕ): A correlation coefficient that is a special case of Cramér's *V* correlation for nominal independent and dependent variables in a chi-squared test. Values of ϕ can only range from 0 (no association between variables) to 1 (a perfect association between variables). See also chi-squared test, correlation, correlation coefficient, Cramér's *V*, and special case.

Pie chart: A visual model that is most useful for showing percentages and proportions. The whole dataset or sample is represented as a circle, and the portions of the sample represented by each percentage are displayed as wedges in the circle, resembling pieces of a pie. See also percentage, proportion, and visual model.

Planned contrasts: Pre-planned comparisons of group means to be conducted after an ANOVA. This is in contrast to *post hoc* tests, which were not planned and are only conducted after the null hypothesis is rejected in an ANOVA. See also analysis of variance (ANOVA), Dunnett's test, null hypothesis statistical significance testing

(NHST), *post hoc* test, and Tukey's *post hoc* test.

Platykurtic: A label describing the shape of a histogram or distribution. A platykurtic distribution has a shorter peak, shorter tails, and taller shoulders than a normal distribution. See also kurtosis, leptokurtic, and mesokurtic.

Point-biserial correlation: A correlation calculated from data that have a nominal and dichotomous independent variable and interval- or ratio-level data. The point-biserial correlation is calculated with the same formula as Pearson's *r* and can be converted into a Cohen's *d* effect size. See also effect size, Cohen's *d*, correlation coefficient, levels of data, and Pearson's *r*.

Point estimate: The best estimate of a population parameter, given a set of sample data. See also confidence interval, generalization (definition 1), and parameter.

Pooled standard deviation: A standard deviation calculated by combining the data from two or more samples. The pooled standard deviation is the square root of the pooled variance. See also pooled variance and standard deviation.

Pooled variance: A pooled variance calculated by combining the data from two or more samples. The pooled variance is the square of the pooled standard deviation. See also pooled standard deviation and variance.

Population: The entire set of people, items, or events that a researcher studies. Most populations in the social sciences consist of people. The population size is abbreviated *N*.

Positive correlation: A relationship between variables in which individuals with high scores on one variable tend to have high scores on the other variable. Likewise, individuals with low scores on one variable tend to have low scores on the other variable. Positive correlations have correlation coefficients greater than zero. See also correlation and inverse correlation.

Positively skewed: A label describing the shape of a distribution or histogram. Positively skewed distributions have a peak on the left side of the distribution and an elongated tail on the right. See also negatively skewed, skewness, and unskewed.

Post hoc test: A statistical test that is conducted after rejecting the null hypothesis in an ANOVA, in which the researcher attempts to ascertain which group means differ from one another. *Post hoc* tests are not planned in advance, but a planned contrast is. See also analysis of variance (ANOVA), Bonferroni–Dunn *post hoc* test, descriptive discriminant analysis, null hypothesis statistical significance testing (NHST), planned contrast, Scheffé's *post hoc* test, and Tukey's *post hoc* test.

Power: See statistical power.

Practical significance: The degree to which the differences observed between groups (or the strength of the relationship between variables) is practically useful in the real world. See also clinical significance and statistical significance.

Prediction: See regression.

Probability (definition 1): A branch of mathematics concerned with the likelihood of various outcomes for an event.

Probability (definition 2): The likelihood of any particular outcome of a trial, such as the likelihood that the roll of a die will be a 4. See also conditional probability, empirical probability, marginal probability, theoretical probability, and trial.

Probability distribution: A histogram of probabilities of possible outcomes of a trial. Probability distributions can be analytical (i.e., estimated mathematically) or empirical (i.e., produced from observations of many trials). See also probability (definitions 1 and 2) and trial.

Proportion: A value – usually expressed as a fraction or a decimal – that indicates the ratio of the number at hand (such as a frequency of a response) to the total number of objects (e.g., responses, persons, variance). Proportions always range from 0 to 1, and can be converted to a percentage by multiplying by 100. See also pie chart.

Publication bias: The tendency for the published literature to be a nonrepresentative subset of studies that have been conducted on a topic. See also file drawer problem.

Qualitative research: A family of research methods in which non-numeric data are collected and analyzed in an attempt to understand the experience of the sample member or broader themes and influences on the person's behavior (e.g., culture, power structures).

Quantitative research: A family of research methods in which a researcher converts data into numbers for the purpose of statistical analysis. This is the dominant method of conducting research in the social sciences.

Quartiles: The three scores that divide a distribution into four equal-sized areas. Note that a quartile does not refer to one-fourth of the scores in a distribution and that there are only three quartiles – not four. The interquartile range is the range of scores between the lowest and the highest quartile. See also interquartile range.

Questionable research practice: A research practice that is inappropriate because it may distort the conducting or reporting of social science research. HARKing is an example of a questionable research practice.

r^2: Effect size that quantifies (1) the percentage of variance in a dependent variable that is shared with the independent variable in a correlation, or (2) the percentage of the size of the decrease in squared residuals when comparing predictions made with the regression line to predictions made with the baseline model. The effect size for ANOVA, η^2, is mathematically equivalent to r^2, and both are interpreted the same way. Also called a coefficient of determination. See also baseline model, correlation, effect size, eta-squared (η^2), grand mean, Pearson's r, R^2, regression, and residual.

R^2: The effect size for multiple regression. R^2 quantifies (1) the percentage of variance in a dependent variable that is shared with the set of independent variables in a regression model, or (2) the percentage of the size of the decrease in squared residuals in comparing predictions made with the regression line to predictions made with the baseline model. R^2 (for multiple regression) shares many common features with r^2 (for Pearson's r) because Pearson's r is a special case of multiple regression in the general linear model. See also effect size, general linear model, multiple regression, r^2, and special case.

Random assignment: The process of randomly assigning samples to an experimental or control group in an experiment. In theory, random assignment balances out the groups so that any differences between them at the end of the study are solely the result of the treatment. See also control group, experiment, and experimental group.

Range: A measure of variability that is calculated by subtracting the lowest score in a dataset from the highest score. See also variability.

Ratio data: The highest level of data in which data form mutually exclusive and exhaustive categories, have rank order, and possess equal intervals between numbers across the entire length of the scale, and in which zero represents the complete absence of the quality being measured. See also levels of data.

Reference group: See baseline group.

Regression: The use of a statistical model to make a prediction of a sample member's dependent variable value. See also logistic regression, multiple logistic regression, multiple regression, nonlinear regression, ordinary least squares (OLS) regression, regression line, and regression towards the mean.

Regression line: A statistical model that can be used to make predictions of an outcome variable. The regression line is produced with the standardized regression equation or the unstandardized regression equation. Individual prediction accuracy of the regression line is measured via residuals, while overall prediction accuracy is measured by either the r^2 or η^2 effect size. See also effect size, eta-squared (η^2), linear regression, nonlinear regression, r^2, regression towards the mean, standardized regression equation, and unstandardized regression equation.

Regression towards the mean: The tendency for sample members' predicted dependent variable values (as derived from a regression model) to be closer to the mean of the dependent variable than the same sample members' independent variable scores were to the mean of the independent variable. Thus, regression models predict that sample members will be "more average" on a dependent variable than they were on the independent variable. Regression towards the mean will occur whenever Pearson's $r \neq +1.0$. See also mean and regression.

Rejection region: An arbitrarily chosen area in the sampling distribution, starting at the critical value, that defines whether a null hypothesis will be rejected. If the observed value falls within the rejection region, the null hypothesis is rejected. If the observed value Falls outside the rejection region, the null hypothesis is retained. The rejection region starts at the critical value and continues to the extremes of the sampling distribution. See also critical value, null hypothesis statistical significance testing, and observed value.

Related-samples t-test: See paired-samples t-test.

Relative risk: An effect size for the chi-squared test that is the ratio between the proportions of two groups that experience an outcome of interest. See also chi-squared test, effect size, odds ratio, outcome of interest, and two-variable chi-squared test.

Research hypothesis: A supposition or belief that a researcher has about the outcome of a study. Research hypotheses are sometimes based on theories or previous research. See also hypothesis and null hypothesis.

Residual: In regression, the amount of individual inaccuracy for a particular sample member's predicted dependent variable score. Each individual in a sample will have their own residual. See also eta-squared (η^2), ordinary least squares (OLS) regression, r^2, R^2, and regression.

Restriction of range: A situation where the data do not encompass the full range of scores in an independent or dependent variable. Restriction of range generally (though not always) attenuates (i.e., reduces) correlation coefficients. See also correlation coefficient.

Right skewed: See positively skewed.

Sample: A selection of population members that a researcher collects data from. Often researchers use sample data because it is not feasible to collect data from every population member. See also population and sample size.

Sample size: The number of subjects (in the social sciences, usually people) who are in a dataset. The abbreviation for sample size is n. See also population and sample.

Sampling distribution: A distribution of sample statistics which can be used to generate a probability distribution. See also central limit theorem, probability distribution, and rejection region.

Sampling error: The natural variation in sample statistics that results from the random sampling process. Sampling error arises because the composition of samples will vary somewhat from sample to sample, producing differences in statistics among samples.

Scattergram: See scatterplot.

Scatterplot: A visual model which displays data from two variables at a time – each variable represented on an axis. In a scatterplot each sample member is represented by a dot that is at the coordinates corresponding to the person's scores on both variables. Often a scatterplot includes a regression line. See also regression line and visual model.

Scheffé's *post hoc* test: A *post hoc* test that is conducted after an ANOVA to determine the group mean(s) that resulted in the rejection of the ANOVA's null hypothesis. Like the Tukey's and Bonferroni–Dunn *post hoc* tests, Scheffé's test permits comparisons of pairs of means. However, Scheffé's *post hoc* test also allows groups to be combined, the mean of one group being compared to the combined means of two or more other groups. Named for the American statistician Henry Scheffé. See also analysis of variance (ANOVA), null hypothesis statistical significance testing (NHST), and *post hoc* test.

Significance: See clinical significance, practical significance, and statistical significance.

Simpson's paradox: An occurrence when a relationship between an independent variable and a dependent variable switches from being positive to negative (or negative to positive) by the addition of another independent variable to a statistical model. This occurs when an interaction between two independent variables results in differing marginal and conditional probabilities for at least one group of subjects in a sample. Named for the British statistician Edward H. Simpson. Also called the Yule–Simpson paradox to honor the British statistician George Udny Yule, who was the first person to identify it. See also interaction.

Skewness: The degree to which a distribution or histogram is non-symmetrical. See also negatively skewed, positively skewed, and unskewed.

Spearman's ρ (rho): A nonparametric statistical procedure that can be used to find a correlation between two ordinal-level variables. Spearman's ρ uses the same formula as Pearson's r, except the data were either collected as ordinal data, or were interval- or ratio-level data that had been converted to ranks. Named for the British psychologist and military officer Charles Spearman. See also correlation, correlation coefficient, nonparametric statistics, and Pearson's r.

Special case: In the general linear model, a special case is a procedure that is a simplification occurring under the special circumstances of a more complicated procedure. For example, a two-sample t-test is a simple case of analysis of variance when the independent variable has only two groups. See also generalization (definition 2).

Standard deviation: A model of variability that is the square root of the mean of the squared deviation scores. The standard deviation is the square root of the variance, and both are statistical models of variability. See also Bessel's correction, generalization (definition 1), pooled standard deviation, variability, and variance.

Standard error: The standard deviation of the sampling distribution. The standard error is used to create confidence intervals, and the standard error for the sampling distribution of means is used to estimate the population standard deviation.

Standardized regression equation: A mathematical equation that produces the regression line when the independent and dependent variables are standardized into z-score format. The standardized regression line can also be used to make predictions of dependent variable z-scores. See also regression, regression line, unstandardized regression equation, and *z*-scores.

Standardized scores: See *z*-scores.

Statistic: A number that describes some aspect of the data from a sample. See also parameter and statistical model.

Statistical methods: The science of quantitative data analysis. See also statistic, descriptive statistics and inferential statistics.

Statistical model: A model expressed through mathematical notation that describes mathematically some aspect of the data or the phenomenon under study. Any number or equation that is the result of statistical analysis can be considered a statistical model. See also model and theoretical model.

Statistical power: The probability that NHST will reject a false null hypothesis. Statistical power is determined by the effect size, alpha value, and sample size. All other things being equal, studies with stronger effect sizes, higher alphas, larger sample sizes, and paired data designs have greater statistical power and are most likely to be able to reject the null hypothesis.

Statistical significance: A descriptive term indicating that a null hypothesis has been rejected. See also clinical significance, null hypothesis, null hypothesis statistical significance testing (NHST), and practical significance.

Statistical weight: A number that is multiplied by a score to create statistical models. See general linear model.

Stem-and-leaf plot: A visual model that can be used to represent subjects' scores. In a stem-and-leaf plot, the digits in a score are separated so that the leading digits (e.g., the first digit in a two-digit number) are on the left side of the image, called "the stem." The trailing digits (e.g., the last digit in a two-digit number) are on the right side, with scores having the same leading digit placed in the same row. See also histogram and visual model.

Structural equation modeling (SEM): The most versatile and most general member of the general linear model. SEM is an appropriate multivariate method for examining relationships among latent variables or among latent and observed variables. See also latent variable and multivariate statistics.

Testwise Type I error: In a sequence of NHSTs, the testwise Type I error is equal to the alpha (α) of each NHST procedure. See also alpha (α), Bonferroni correction, experimentwise Type I error, and Type I error.

Theoretical model: A model which represents a hypothesized causal explanation for a phenomenon under study. Theoretical models are described non-mathematically. See also model, statistical model, and theory.

Theoretical probability: A probability estimated without conducting and observing trials. Theoretical probabilities are estimated by dividing the number of possible trials resulting in an outcome by the total number of trials. See also empirical probability and probability (definition 2).

Theoretical probability distribution: See probability distribution.

Theory: A system of principles that are believed to explain phenomena in the world in a wide range of contexts. Theories give rise to theoretical models. See also theoretical model.

Third variable problem: The possibility that a relationship between two variables, X and Y, is caused by the presence of an unknown variable, labeled Z.

Treatment group: See experimental group.

Trial: A particular event. In probability mathematics, researchers try to estimate the likelihood (also called the probability) of a given event. With a set of independent trials, the outcome of any one trial has no influence on the outcome of any other trial. See also probability (definition 2).

Trimmed mean: A model of central tendency that is calculated by eliminating the same number of scores from the top and the bottom of the distribution and then calculating the mean for the remaining scores. See also central tendency and mean.

Tukey's *post hoc* test: A *post hoc* test conducted after a statistically significant ANOVA, which tests whether a pair or pairs of group means in a set of groups has or have differences large enough to result in the null hypothesis of an ANOVA being rejected. Also called Tukey's honestly significant difference (HSD) test. Named for the American statistician John W. Tukey. See also analysis of variance (ANOVA), null hypothesis statistical significance testing (NHST), and *post hoc* test.

Two-sample *t*-test: See unpaired-samples *t*-test.

Two-tailed test: A null hypothesis statistical significance test in which one-half of the rejection region is on each side of the sampling distribution. See also null hypothesis statistical significance testing, one-tailed test, and rejection region.

Two-variable chi-squared test: A null hypothesis statistical significance test in which the null hypothesis is that two nominal-level variables are unrelated. The effect sizes for a two-variable chi-squared test are the odds ratio, relative risk, phi, and Cramér's *V*. Sometimes the two-variable chi-squared test is called just the "chi-squared test." See also chi-squared test, Cramér's *V*, null hypothesis statistical significance testing (NHST), odds ratio, one-variable chi-squared test, Spearman's rho), and relative risk.

Two-way ANOVA: An analysis of variance (ANOVA) with two independent variables. See also analysis of variance (ANOVA), one-way ANOVA, and way.

Type I error: An error in null hypothesis statistical significance testing in which the researcher rejects a null hypothesis that is actually true. In reality, researchers never know whether they have made a Type I error. However, the probability that a Type I error occurred if the null hypothesis were perfectly true is the *p*-value. See also experimentwise Type I error, *p*-value, testwise Type I error, and Type II error.

Type II error: An error in null hypothesis statistical significance testing in which the researcher retains a null hypothesis that is actually false. In reality, researchers never know whether they have made a Type II error. The probability of Type II error can be reduced by increasing statistical power. See also statistical power and Type I error.

Uniform distribution: A distribution or histogram of data where all of the intervals are of the same height. See also histogram and interval.

Unimodal: A word used to describe distributions that have one peak. See also bimodal and histogram.

Univariate statistics: Statistical procedures that analyze relationships between at least one independent variable and a single dependent variable. See also multivariate statistics.

Unpaired-samples *t*-test: A general linear model procedure to test the null hypothesis that the difference between mean groups is zero. In an unpaired-samples *t*-test, the scores from one group do not have a connection to scores in another group (as they do in the paired-samples *t*-test). The effect size for the unpaired-samples *t*-test is Cohen's *d*. The unpaired-samples *t*-test is a NHST procedure, and it is sometimes called an independent samples *t*-test or two-sample *t*-test. See also Cohen's *d*, null hypothesis statistical significance testing (NHST), and paired-samples *t*-test.

Unskewed: A label describing the shape of a distribution or histogram. Unskewed distributions are symmetrical. See also negatively skewed, positively skewed, and skewness.

Unstandardized regression equation: A mathematical equation that produces the regression line when the independent or dependent variable is not standardized into *z*-score format. The unstandardized regression line can also be used to predict dependent variable scores. See also regression, regression line, standardized regression equation, and *z*-scores.

Upper limit: The maximum value in a confidence interval. See also confidence interval and lower limit.

Variability: The degree to which the scores of a variable are spread out from one another. See also interquartile range, range, standard deviation, and variance.

Variable: A characteristic in which members of the sample or population differ from one another. In quantitative data, a variable is apparent because some subjects' data values are different from the values of other subjects. See also independent variable and dependent variable.

Variance: A measure of variability or scores and the square of the standard deviation. See also standard deviation and variability.

Visual model: A simplified visual representation of data, which can take the form of a chart (e.g., a histogram, a bar graph, scatterplot) or a schematic. See also model.

Way: A nominal independent variable in the context of analysis of variance (ANOVA). See also analysis of variance, independent variable, nominal data, one-way ANOVA, and two-way ANOVA.

Weight: See statistical weight.

Wilcoxon rank-sum test: A nonparametric statistical test that is appropriate for comparing the distributions of ranks of two samples of ordinal data. This test produces an effect size called the area under the receiver operator characteristic curve (AUC). Named for the American chemist Frank Wilcoxon. The Wilcoxon rank-sum test is sometimes called the Mann–Whitney U test. See also AUC, Kruskal–Wallis test, and nonparametric statistics.

z-Scores: Scores that have a mean of 0 and a standard deviation of 1. Also called standardized scores. Raw data are converted to z-scores through a linear transformation. See also linear transformation, mean, and standard deviation.

z-Test: The simplest form of null hypothesis statistical significance testing. The z-test is used to determine whether a sample is representative or typical of the population that it was drawn from when the population mean and standard deviation are known. See also mean, null hypothesis statistical significance testing (NHST), population, and standard deviation.

Answer Key

Chapter 1

1. It is very difficult to have data from an entire population. Some people may refuse to participate, for example. Or possibly the population is too large to get all data from.
2. Other researchers may be mistaken about their data, so an independent evaluation is important to avoid perpetuating errors.
3. They are all simplifications of reality, and all models are wrong in some way.
4. Most research is quantitative in the social sciences, and that research uses statistics to describe, analyze, and summarize findings.
5. A model is a simplified version of reality constructed in order to understand the world better. The scientific understanding of models is more formal. Everyday and formal models both emphasize some aspects of phenomena at the expense of others.
6. a. Because the simplification process reduces accuracy.
   b. Models explain and demonstrate relationships among variables. They make complex realities easier to understand.
   c. Models are judged on the basis of whether they are useful.
7. To separate good research from bad; evaluate the conclusions of researchers; communicate findings to others; and interpret research to create practical, real-world results.
8. Carl's hypothesis is not scientific because it is not falsifiable.
9. N/A
10. "Heart rate" is a dependent variable because it is an outcome of the study.
11. Operationalization.
12. a. Select independent and dependent variables.
    b. The independent variable is the number of posts that a person uses the word "I." The dependent variable is the selfishness test score.
    c. Correlational design.

13. a. Theory.
    b. Theoretical model.
14. a. All votes cast by legislators.
    b. The votes that the student selects for their study.
15. a. The frequency of quizzes.
    b. The number of hours per week students study.
    c. The number of hours per week students study.
    d. Experimental design.

Chapter 2

1. It depends on how the test scores are designed and interpreted. If 0 on a test represents the absence of what is measured, test scores may be ratio-level data. If there is reason to believe that the scores have equal intervals between them, they may be interval-level data. If either (or both) of these characteristics are absent, then test scores may be ordinal-level data.
2. Operationalization is a necessary part of the quantitative research process. Although it sometimes means that researchers are not studying what they "really" want to measure, it makes quantitative research possible.
3. Interval or ratio.
4. Nominal.
5. Collect data at the highest level possible.
6. a. Ratio.
   b. Ratio.
   c. Ratio.
   d. Ratio.
   e. Nominal.
   f. Nominal.
   g. Ordinal.
   h. Interval.
   i. Nominal.
   j. Ordinal.
   k. Nominal.
   l. Ratio.
   m. Ratio.
   n. Nominal.

o. Interval.

7. a. Continuous.
   b. Continuous.
   c. Continuous.
   d. Continuous.
   e. Discrete.
   f. Discrete.
   g. Discrete
   h. Continuous.
   i. Discrete.
   j. Discrete.
   k. Discrete.
   l. Continuous.
   m. Continuous.
   n. Discrete.
   o. Continuous.

8. a. Ordinal.
   b. Yes, because you can always convert data to a lower level of data. He would make this conversion by rearranging the numbers for the categories so they lose their order.
   c. No, because it is never possible to convert data to a more complex level.

9. Ordinal.
   a. Ratio.
   b. 9b (i.e., ratio-level data on the number of years someone has taught).

10. a. Nominal.
    b. Interval.
    c. Nominal.
    d. Ratio.
    e. Interval.
    f. Interval.

Chapter 3

1. Both have the frequency of a variable on the vertical axis (i.e., *y*-axis) and use the height of bars to show how common a score is. The main difference is that gaps between bars in a histogram represent scores that have a frequency of zero, while gaps in a bar graph represent the fact that the variable is nominal-level data.

2. Unimodal.

3. Symmetry.

4. Platykurtic distributions have shorter peaks and tails and taller shoulders than a normal distribution. Leptokurtic distributions have taller peaks and tails and shorter shoulders than a normal distribution.

5. Skewness = 0, kurtosis = 0.

6. Scatterplots can show relationships between variables and show groupings of sample members.

7. Because the interval width represents a range of scores that appear in the dataset. Even if the dataset only includes whole numbers, if the data were measured more precisely, the scores would probably not be precisely equal to the whole number. Having the interval span a range of values shows that the interval encompasses more precise values than the whole numbers displayed in the dataset.

8. a. Because the bottom row of the dataset will always be equal to the proportion of the total sample size that is in the data.
   b. Because $n / n = 1.000$.
   c. Calculating a proportion from this sample size will always be 1.000 because all proportions must add up to 1.000.

9.
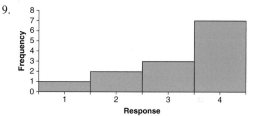

Score	Frequency	Frequency Proportion	Cumulative Frequency	Cumulative Proportion
1	1	1/13 = 0.769	1	1/13 = 0.769
2	2	2/13 = 0.154	3	3/13 = 0.231
3	3	3/13 = 0.231	6	4/13 = 0.308
4	7	7/13 = 0.538	13	13/13 = 1.000
Total	13	13/13 = 1.000	13	13/13 = 1.000

10. a. The histogram will have a distinct elongated left tail and a somewhat tall peak.
    b. Negatively skewed and leptokurtic.

11. a. The histogram will have a distinct elongated right tail and a slightly shorter peak.
    b. Positively skewed and slightly platykurtic.

12. a. The histogram will be almost exactly symmetrical and have a peak, shoulders, and tails that are as tall as a normal distribution.
    b. Unskewed and mesokurtic.

13.1 0138889
   2 11
   3 0778

14.

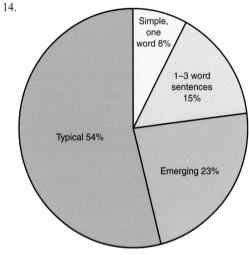

15.a.

Height	Frequency	Frequency Proportion	Cumulative Frequency	Cumulative Proportion
56	1	0.038	1	0.038
57	0	0.000	1	0.038
58	0	0.000	1	0.038
59	1	0.038	2	0.077
60	1	0.038	3	0.115
61	1	0.038	4	0.154
62	6	0.231	10	0.385
63	4	0.154	14	0.538
64	2	0.077	16	0.615
65	0	0.000	16	0.615
66	0	0.000	16	0.615
67	3	0.115	19	0.731
68	2	0.077	21	0.808
69	1	0.038	22	0.846
70	1	0.038	23	0.885
71	0	0.000	23	0.885
72	1	0.038	24	0.923
73	1	0.038	25	0.962
74	0	0.000	25	0.962
75	0	0.000	25	0.962
76	1	0.038	26	1.000
Total	26	1.000	26	1.000

b.

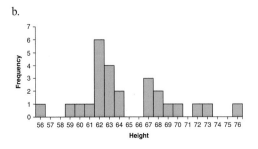

c.

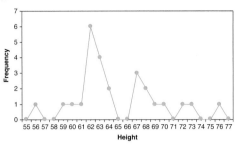

d.

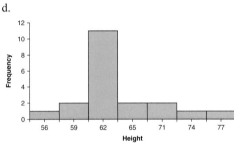

e.

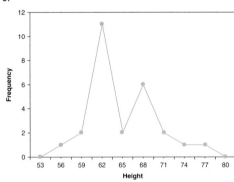

f.

   5 69
   6 01222222333344777889
   7 0236

16.

a.

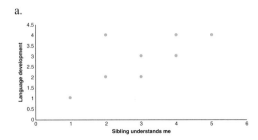

b. There is only one group of subjects in the dataset. And generally, people with high scores on one variable tend to have high scores on the other variable.

17.a.

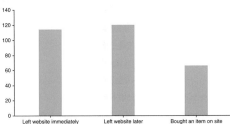

b.

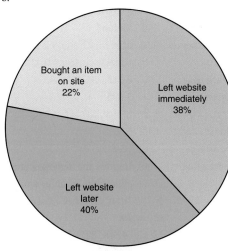

c. Because the data are nominal or discrete.

18.Distorting the axis and creating the incorrect graph type.

19.a.

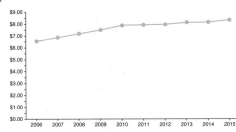

b. Ticket prices have been rising year after year. They rose more quickly from 2006 until 2010 and more slowly after that.

20.Unskewed and slightly platykurtic.

Chapter 4

1. a. The range because it is the range of 100% of the scores, while the interquartile range is the range of the middle 50% of scores.

b. The range because it is dependent solely on the minimum and maximum scores, while scores in the middle of a distribution can affect the standard deviation.

c. $\hat{\sigma}_x$ because it has a denominator of $n - 1$, instead of n. The smaller denominator will make the overall value of the number higher.

2. Because the mean is the "balance" point where all deviation scores cancel out.

3. a. The use of $n - 1$ instead of n in the denominator of a standard deviation or variance calculation.

b. Standard deviation and variance.

c. When using sample data to estimate the population standard deviation or variance.

4. Mode and trimmed mean.

5. Mean and median.

6. Because models of central tendency and variability produce different information, and neither one presents a complete understanding of the distribution.

7. a. 18

b. 19

c. 22.384

d. 22.309

e. The median and mode are lower than the mean. Because the mean and the trimmed mean are close together, they are probably a more accurate model for this dataset. Data are likely positively skewed because the mean > median.

f. 28.

g. 9.887.

h. 97.756.

i. The sibling ages were slightly younger on average, but also more variable.

8. a. 85.

b. 85.

c. 81.4.

d. 84.375.

e. The mean is lowest because the score 45 is an outlier and is skewing the mean to the left.

f. 49.

g. 7.

h. 13.458.

i. 181.114.

9. a. 18.

b. 21.5.

c. 22.417.

d. 23.4.

e. 17.

f. 11.

g. 5.838.

h. 34.083.

10. a. Answers will vary.

b. The average of all deviation scores will be zero because all deviation scores must sum to zero. Summing them and then dividing by n (to obtain an average) will always produce a result of zero.

11. a. These people will drag down the mean time individuals view the company website. If they are not customers, including them in a calculation of the mean will produce a mean that is an underestimate of the actual mean time that customers do visit the website.

b. The trimmed mean would eliminate most or all of the people from the calculation, ensuring that the trimmed mean will better reflect actual customer behavior.

Chapter 5

1. By adding, subtracting, multiplying, and dividing every score by a constant.

2. To convert scores into a different unit or to force a distribution to have a predetermined mean and/or standard deviation.

3. $M = 0$, $SD = 1$.

4. The score is below the original mean.

5. $M = 0$, $SD = 1$.

6. a. 9.3 weeks.

b. 1.8 weeks.

c. Positively skewed and mesokurtic.

d. Subtract 65.1 and then divide by 12.6.

7. a. 0.2609 seconds.

b. 0.0353 seconds.

c. Positively skewed and leptokurtic.

8. a. $M = 14.6$, $SD = 2.797$.

b. −1.645, −0.930, −0.572, −0.572, −0.215, 0.143, 0.143, 0.858, 1.216, 1.573.

c. No.

d. Skewness = 0.10, kurtosis = −0.60.

9. a. 50%.

b. 50%.

c. 15.87%.

d. 2.28%.

e. 0.13%.

f. 34.13%.

g. 68.26%.

h. 81.82%.

i. 95.26%.

j. 99.87%.

k. 40.32%.

10. a. Mark's.

b. Tammy and Phillip.

c. Mark and Maren.

d. Phillip.

11. a. $M = 6.142$, $SD = 2.022$.

b. −0.812, −0.466, −0.416, −0.367, −0.317, −0.218, −0.218, −0.169, −0.119, −0.021, 0.029, 3.095.

c. $M = 0$, $SD = 1$.

d. No.

e. 12.4.

f. Because the highest score is an outlier, and it is pulling the mean to a value that is higher than 10 of the other 11 scores.

12. +0.70.

13. a. −4, 48, 82, 92, 108, 122.

b. 80 because that is the mean of the new dataset.

c. 5.8, 8.4, 10.1, 10.6, 11.4, 12.1.

d. −21, −8, 0.5, 3, 7, 10.5.

14. a. $M = 2.6$, $SD = 4.427$.

b. −1.491, −1.039, −0.813, −0.587, −0.587. 0.542, 0.768, 0.994, 0.994, 1.220.

c. No.

d. Skewness = −0.11, kurtosis = 1.40.

15. a. Mean = 7.8, no change to SD.

b. Mean = 0.68, SD = 0.12.

c. Mean = 3.8, no change to SD.

d. Mean = 16.8, no change to SD.

e. Mean = 5.3, no change to SD.

f. Mean = 27.2, SD = 4.8.

g. Mean = 21.76, SD = 3.84.

h. Mean = 0.34, SD = 0.06.

i. Mean = 5.4, SD = 0.6.

j. Mean = 11.6, SD = 2.4.

k. Mean = 32.4, SD = 4.8.

l. Mean = 7.3, no change to SD.

Chapter 6

1. Empirical probability distributions are created with real data, while theoretical probability distributions are created through probability theory.

2. a. The event has a 0% chance of happening (i.e., it is impossible).

   b. The event has a 1 in 5 chance (i.e., 20% probability) of occurring.

   c. The event has a 1 in 2 chance (i.e., 50% probability) of occurring.

   d. The event has a 3 in 4 chance (i.e., 75% probability) of occurring.

   e. The event will certainly happen (i.e., a 100% probability).

3. Generalization allows researchers to make an inference about the population based solely on sample data. It is important because collecting population data is usually difficult or impossible.

4. The standard error is the standard deviation of the sampling distribution, and it is a measure of sampling error.

5. Have a larger sample size, or collect more samples.

6. a. 1/13 (or .077).

   b. 1/13 (or .077).

   c. ¼ (or 0.25).

   d. ½ (or 0.50).

   e. 4/13 (or .308)

   f. 3/13 (or .231).

   g. 4/13 (or .308).

   h. 0/13 (or .000).

7. a. 1/16 (or .063).

   b. 1/169 (or .006).

   c. 1/169 (or .006).

   d. 1/169 (or .006).

8. a. .633.

   b. .567.

   c. .800.

   d. .208.

   e. .087.

f. .040.

g. Because the probabilities in 8a–8c are calculated by adding probabilities together, while joint probabilities in 8d–8f are joint probabilities calculated by multiplying probabilities by each other. Multiplying probabilities will always produce a smaller result than adding probabilities.

9. a. $0.75^8 = 0.100$.

   b. ¼ (or 0.250).

   c. Gambler's fallacy. The reasoning is incorrect because the events are independent, and earlier test questions have no influence on the correct answer of a later test question. I would explain the principle of independence to the student and tell them that any such "streaks" in their test answers are pure chance.

10. a. 1/10 (or .100).

    b. 1/5 (or .200).

    c. 1/100 (or .010).

    d. This is an example of the hot hand fallacy. Their reasoning is flawed because sometimes – by pure randomness – events can happen relatively frequently within a small number of trials. If there were an infinite number of trials, all families would be selected an equal number of times.

11. The hot hand fallacy.

12. Fifty trials are usually not enough for a normal distribution to form. She needs to have many more trials in order to produce a normal distribution.

13. a. 24.583.

    b. 1.106.

    c. 6.995.

    d. A normal distribution.

14. a. 4.42.

    b. 0.591.

    c. 4.380.

    d. Yes, because the mean and standard deviations of the sampling distribution of means can be used to estimate the population mean and standard deviation.

    e. No impact on the estimate of the population mean.

    f. No impact on the standard error.

15. Because as each player is chosen, the remaining number of individuals that can be selected decreases. Therefore, each remaining player's probability of being selected increases. Thinking about this sort of thing, instead of spending time improving his jump shot, is the reason Carlos isn't picked first for basketball.

16. a. 2.829.

   b. 1.960.

   c. 0.730.

   d. 1.212.

   e. 2.580.

   f. 0.097.

   g. The standard error increases.

   h. The standard error decreases.

Chapter 7

1. $H_1 : \overline{X} < \mu$, $H_1 : \overline{X} > \mu$, and $H_1 : \overline{X} \neq \mu$. The first two alternative hypotheses are appropriate for one-tailed tests. The last alternative hypothesis is only appropriate for a two-tailed test.

2. Raising the alpha value or increasing the sample size makes it easier to reject the null hypothesis. Decreasing alpha or the sample size makes it harder to reject the null hypothesis.

3. Because it would indicate that the sample would be impossible to draw from the population – which clearly could never be true.

4. Because they were two-tailed tests, which require two critical values.

5. Both formulas have two steps: (1) subtract the distribution mean from the value, and (2) divide the result by the distribution standard deviation.

6. They should follow the *Price Is Right* rule and use the row in Appendix A1 that has the value closest to the z-observed value without exceeding it.

7. Rejecting the null hypothesis does not provide proof that the therapy is effective. The null hypothesis may have been rejected solely because of a Type I error, or because of a reason other than the effectiveness of the therapy.

8. a. Sample and population.

   b. $H_0 : \overline{X} = \mu$.

   c. 0.05.

   d. Two-tailed test.

   e. $H_1 : \overline{X} \neq \mu$.

   f. –2.235.

   g. +1.96.

   h. Reject the null hypothesis.

   i. 0.0129.

   j. 0.50.

   k. Retain the null hypothesis.

9. a. Sample and population.

   b. $H_0 : \overline{X} = \mu$.

   c. 0.05.

   d. One-tailed test.

   e. $H_1 : \overline{X} > \mu$.

   f. 1.86.

   g. 1.650.

   h. Reject the null hypothesis. Teenagers send more messages (on average) than the population.

   i. 0.0314.

   j. 0.25.

   k. Retain the null hypothesis.

   l. Retain the null hypothesis.

10. a. Sample and population.

   b. $H_0 : \overline{X} = \mu$.

   c. 0.05.

   d. Two-tailed test.

   e. $H_1 : \overline{X} \neq \mu$.

   f. –0.074.

   g. +1.96.

   h. Retain the null hypothesis.

   i. 0.4721.

   j. 0.019.

   k. Retain the null hypothesis.

   l. Retain the null hypothesis.

   m. Retain the null hypothesis.

   n. Reject the null hypothesis.

11. Researcher no. 2. Because a smaller *p*-value would produce a larger effect size, and would therefore be more likely to reject the null hypothesis.

12. Stephanie is more likely to reject the null hypothesis because her sample size is larger.

13. a. 0.0217.

   b. Based on his observed value, he should reject the null hypothesis because his *p*-value is smaller than the typical alpha value of .05.

   c. It is the probability of making a Type I error if the null hypothesis were perfectly true.

14.a. Sample and population.
  b. $H_0 : \overline{X} = \mu$.
  c. 0.05.
  d. Two-tailed.
  e. $H_1 : \overline{X} \neq \mu$.
  f. −3.696.
  g. $\pm$1.96.
  h. Reject the null hypothesis.
  i. 0.0002.
  j. 0.394.
  k. Reject the null hypothesis.
  l. Reject the null hypothesis.
  m. Reject the null hypothesis.
  n. Reject the null hypothesis.
  o. Reject the null hypothesis.
15. Retain the null hypothesis.
16. 0.
17. The population mean and sample mean are .4 SD apart.
18. Austin, because the larger sample size makes it more likely that he will reject the null hypothesis.
19.a. Sample and population.
  b. $H_0 : \overline{X} = \mu$.
  c. 0.05.
  d. Two-tailed test.
  e. $H_1 : \overline{X} \neq \mu$.
  f. 1.22.
  g. $\pm$1.96.
  h. Retain the null hypothesis.
  i. 0.1112.
  j. 0.121.
  k. Reject the null hypothesis.
  l. Retain the null hypothesis.
  m. Reject the null hypothesis.
  n. Retain the null hypothesis.
  o. Retain the null hypothesis.

Chapter 8

1. Both tests are NHSTs, and a z-test is merely a simplified version of a one-sample t-test.
2. When the population standard deviation (σ) is not known.
3. To compare the t-observed value to the t-critical values for different alpha values that correspond to the correct degrees of freedom. If the null

hypothesis is rejected when $\alpha = .01$, then $p < .01$. If the null hypothesis is rejected when $\alpha = .05$, but not when $\alpha = .01$, then $.05 > p > .01$. If the null hypothesis is retained when $\alpha = .05$, then $p > \alpha$.
4. "Statistically significant" results are merely results where the null hypothesis was rejected. Importance is judged on the basis of context and whether the results matter to researchers, patients, etc.
  a. If the null hypothesis was rejected for a trivial study (e.g., the difference between two groups' ability to do a cartwheel).
  b. If the null hypothesis was retained, but the effect size is still large enough to have an impact on individuals' lives (e.g., a therapy that reduces the risk of suicide, but the sample size was too small to reject the null hypothesis).
5. The t-distribution is platykurtic, whereas the z-distribution is normal. The differences between the two are greater with fewer degrees of freedom.
6. HARKing is "hypothesizing after results are known." It is forming or changing a research hypothesis to conform with results after data collection. It is a questionable research practice because it distorts the scientific literature.
7. Statistical, clinical, and practical significance. Statistical significance merely states whether the null hypothesis was rejected. Practical significance is determined by whether the results matter or are noticeable in everyday life. Clinical significance refers to whether patients move from a group needing therapy to a group that does not need therapy.
8. a. 2.
  b. 11.
  c. 21.
  d. 99.
  e. 411.
9. a. Use the *Price Is Right* rule and select the row with the degrees of freedom that is closest to the actual degrees of freedom without exceeding it.
  b. The row for 110 df.

10. a. Sample and population.

   b. $H_0 : \overline{X} = \mu$.

   c. 0.05.

   d. Two-tailed test.

   e. $H_1 : \overline{X} \neq \mu$.

   f. 19.

   g. −2.235.

   h. ± 2.093.

   i. Reject the null hypothesis.

   j. $.01 < p < .05$.

   k. 0.5.

   l. Retain the null hypothesis.

   m. 68% CI = [13.52, 13.88].

   n. 90% CI = [13.405, 13.995].

   o. 98% CI = [13.283, 14.117].

11. a. Sample and population.

   b. $H_0 : \overline{X} = \mu$.

   c. 0.05.

   d. Two-tailed test.

   e. $H_1 : \overline{X} \neq \mu$.

   f. 23.

   g. 4.199.

   h. ± 2.069.

   i. Reject the null hypothesis. This means that anthropology students have higher grades, on average, than the population.

   j. $p < .01$.

   k. 0.857.

   l. Reject the null hypothesis.

   m. 68% CI = [3.07, 3.21].

   n. 90% CI = [3.02, 3.26].

   o. 98% CI = [2.97, 3.31].

12. Daniel, because his study has the larger sample size.

13. Becky, because her study has the larger effect size.

14. a. Reduce the z^* value.

   b. Decrease n.

   c. Increase z^* and decrease n.

15. a. 0.52.

   b. 0.68.

   c. 0.87.

   d. 1.00.

   e. 1.31.

   f. 1.81.

16. Because only an infinitely wide confidence interval could include every possible population mean that the sample could have been taken from.

17. a. Sample and population.

   b. $H_0 : \overline{X} = \mu$.

   c. 0.05.

   d. Two-tailed test.

   e. $H_1 : \overline{X} \neq \mu$.

   f. 0.794.

   g. ± 2.000.

   h. Retain the null hypothesis.

   i. $p > .05$.

   j. 0.088.

   k. Retain the null hypothesis.

   l. Reject the null hypothesis.

   m. Retain the null hypothesis.

   n. Retain the null hypothesis.

   o. 50% CI = [74.329, 75.87].

   p. 69% CI = [73.96, 76.24].

   q. 99% CI = [72.19, 78.01].

18. a. Sample and population.

   b. $H_0 : \overline{X} = \mu$.

   c. 0.05.

   d. Two-tailed test.

   e. $H_1 : \overline{X} \neq \mu$.

   f. 17.

   g. 2.12.

   h. ± 2.110.

   i. Reject the null hypothesis; this means the yoga group's anxiety scores are higher than 30.

   j. $.01 < p < .05$.

   k. 0.5.

   l. Retain the null hypothesis.

   m. 42% CI = [33.85, 36.55].

   n. 79% CI = [32.14, 38.26].

   o. 95% CI = [30.40, 40.00].

Chapter 9

1. Both procedures are members of the general linear model. A paired-samples t-test is just a one-sample t-test where the scores are difference scores and the null hypothesis is that the mean of these difference scores is equal to zero.

2. Subtract one score in the pair from the other score in the pair.

3. A natural pairing occurs when the pairs are naturally occurring outside the study (e.g., siblings, spouses, teachers, and students). An artificial pairing occurs when the researcher creates the pairing.

4. Subtract one from the number of pairs.
5. Same as in a one-sample *t*-test: compare the *t*-observed value to the *t*-critical values for different alpha values that correspond to the correct degrees of freedom. If the null hypothesis is rejected when α = .01, then $p < .01$. If the null hypothesis is rejected when α = .05, but not when α = .01, then $.05 > p > .01$. If the null hypothesis is retained when α = .05, then $p > α$.
6. The two effect sizes differ in their denominators. The denominator for Cohen's *d* is the pooled SD of both scores; the denominator for Glass's Δ is the SD of the control group.
7. a. 10.
   b. 27.
   c. 96.
   d. 122.
   e. 411.
8. a. Each score has one (and only one) matching score in the other group.
   b.

Family no.	Difference score
1	−3
2	−1
3	0
4	0
5	−2
6	−3
7	0
8	−2
9	1
10	1
11	0
12	0
13	1
14	−3
15	−3
16	−1

   c. M = −.9375, SD = 1.526.
   d. $H_0 : \overline{D} = 0$.
   e. 0.05.
   f. One-tailed test because the researcher would expect that families spend more time together after a parenting class.
   g. $H_1 : \overline{D} < 0$.
   h. 15.
   i. −1.753.
   j. −2.457.
   k. Reject the null hypothesis.

l. −0.55.
m. −0.614.
n. −0.465.
o. Because Glass's Δ uses the control group SD as the denominator. If the intervention changed the SD of the scores, then using Glass's Δ as an effect size may be appropriate.
p. $.01 < p < .05$.

9. a. Each score has one (and only one) matching score in the other group.
   b. $H_0 : \overline{D} = 0$.
   c. 0.05.
   d. One-tailed test, because it is reasonable to expect that the patients would have lower depression after therapy.
   e. $H_1 : \overline{D} > 0$.
   f. 17.
   g. 1.74.
   h. 2.871.
   i. Reject the null hypothesis.
   j. 0.677.
   k. $p < .01$.
10. a. Each score has one (and only one) matching score in the other group.
   b. $H_0 : \overline{D} = 0$.
   c. 0.05.
   d. One-tailed test, because it is reasonable to expect that the patients would have lower fantasy behavior after therapy.
   e. $H_1 : \overline{D} > 0$.
   f. 17.
   g. 1.74.
   h. 1.3.
   i. Retained the null hypothesis.
   j. 0.306.
   k. $p > .05$.
11. As the sample size increases, it becomes easier to reject the null hypothesis.
12. Setting his alpha value very low will reduce the probability that he makes a Type I error, but it increases his probability of Type II error. Additionally, there is always the possibility of making an error in a null hypothesis test, regardless of the alpha level.
13. a. $H_0 : \overline{D} = 0$.
   b. 0.05.

c. Two-tailed because there is no prior research or theory guiding Audrey's expectations for the results.

d. $H_1 : \overline{D} \neq 0$.

e. 33.

f. +2.042.

g. 3.372.

h. Reject the null hypothesis.

i. 0.578.

j. $p < .01$.

k. Because the null hypothesis is rejected, Audrey can conclude that the twins differ in their levels of extraversion.

14. a. $H_0 : \overline{D} = 0$.

b. 0.05.

c. Two-tailed because there is no prior research or theory guiding Audrey's expectations for the results.

d. $H_1 : \overline{D} \neq 0$.

e. 14.

f. +2.145.

g. 2.162.

h. Reject the null hypothesis.

i. 0.558.

j. $.01 < p < .05$.

k. Because the null hypothesis is rejected, Audrey can conclude that the twins differ in their levels of extraversion.

l. Because the effect sizes are approximately the same, both fraternal and identical twins differ in extraversion by approximately the same amount.

15. a. $H_0 : \overline{D} = 0$.

b. 0.05.

c. Two-tailed because there is no prior research or theory guiding Audrey's expectations for the results.

d. $H_1 : \overline{D} \neq 0$.

e. 80.

f. +2.000.

g. 1.739.

h. Retain the null hypothesis.

i. 0.193.

j. $p > .05$.

Chapter 10

1. There is no relationship between scores in the different groups (unlike in the paired-samples t-test).

2. The standard deviation of the combined data from the two groups.

3. The pooled standard deviation is the square root of the pooled variance.

4. Statistical power is the ability of an NHST to reject the null hypothesis.

5. Effect size, sample size, alpha, and study design.

6. In the same way as the other t-tests: compare the t-observed value to the t-critical values for different alpha values that correspond to the correct degrees of freedom. If the null hypothesis is rejected when $\alpha = .01$, then $p < .01$. If the null hypothesis is rejected when $\alpha = .05$, but not when $\alpha = .01$, then $.05 > p > .01$. If the null hypothesis is retained when $\alpha = .05$, then $p > \alpha$.

7. It is the probability of making a Type I error if the null hypothesis were perfectly true.

8. Variance ratio of 10:1 or less and a sample size ratio of 4:1 or less.

9. a. 23.

b. 1,508.

c. 68.

d. 28.

e. 159.

10. a. The sample members do not have a clear person in the other group that corresponds to them.

b. $H_0 : \overline{X}_1 = \overline{X}_2$.

c. 0.05.

d. Two-tailed test.

e. $H_1 : \overline{X}_1 \neq \overline{X}_2$.

f. 86.

g. +2.00

h. Pooled SD = 15.236, pooled variance = 232.14.

i. −2.003.

j. Reject the null hypothesis.

k. $.01 < p < .05$.

l. Type I error.

m. 0.447. This effect size means that the means for the two groups are 0.447 SD apart.

n. No.

o. Judged by the .80 standard, the power is adequate. This is important because the study could detect an effect size if one exists in the population.

11. a. The sample members do not have a clear person in the other group that corresponds to them.

b. $H_0 : \overline{X}_1 = \overline{X}_2$.

c. 0.05.

d. One-tailed test.

e. $H_1 : \overline{X}_{Young} > \overline{X}_{Older}$.

f. 1,819.

g. 1.658.

h. Pooled SD = 5.823, pooled variance = 33.912.

i. 1.504.

j. Retain the null hypothesis.

k. $p > .05$.

l. Type II error.

m. 0.156.

n. Yes, the sample size ratio is 17.6:1.

12.a. The sample members do not have a clear person in the other group that corresponds to them.

b. $H_0 : \overline{X}_1 = \overline{X}_2$.

c. 0.05.

d. One-tailed test.

e. $H_1 : \overline{X}_{Early} > \overline{X}_{Regular}$.

f. 1,557.

g. 1.658.

h. Pooled SD = 0.603, pooled variance = 0.363.

i. 5.060.

j. Reject the null hypothesis.

k. $p < .01$.

l. Type I error.

m. 0.337.

n. No.

13.a. The sample members do not have a clear person in the other group that corresponds to them.

b. $H_0 : \overline{X}_1 = \overline{X}_2$.

c. 0.05.

d. Two-tailed test.

e. $H_1 : \overline{X}_1 \neq \overline{X}_2$.

f. 155.

g. ± 1.980.

h. Pooled SD = 11.799, pooled variance = 139.211.

i. −1.764.

j. Retain the null hypothesis.

k. $p > .05$.

l. Type II error.

m. .314. These two groups' means are .314 SD apart from one another.

n. Yes. The variance ratio is 11.33:1.

14.a. The sample members do not have a clear person in the other group that corresponds to them.

b. $H_0 : \overline{X}_1 = \overline{X}_2$.

c. Two-tailed test.

d. $H_1 : \overline{X}_1 \neq \overline{X}_2$.

e. 283.

f. $+2.617$.

g. Pooled SD = 2.75, pooled variance = 7.561.

h. 3.791.

i. Reject the null hypothesis.

j. $p < .01$.

k. Type I error.

l. .582. These two groups' means are .582 SD apart from one another.

m. Yes. The sample size ratio is 4.48:1.

15.a. The results of a null hypothesis test say nothing about replication. Additionally, because of the possibility of a Type I error, Jim cannot possibly know whether his null hypothesis is false.

b. Jim's p-value indicates the probability that he would obtain his results (or more extreme results) from a population where the null hypothesis was perfectly true.

16.a. Statistical significance has nothing to do with importance.

b. Because of the possibility of Type I error, a null hypothesis test can never fully disprove a null hypothesis.

c. The best way to determine replicability is to actually conduct a replication. Because the null hypothesis statistical significance test data would be based on a single study, it can say little (if anything) about replication.

d. Because the p-value is based entirely on the assumption that the null hypothesis is true. Therefore, it cannot state anything about the probability that the null hypothesis is false.

e. Because unlikely events happen all the time. The fact that results would be unlikely if the null hypothesis were true does not indicate that the null hypothesis is actually false.

Chapter 11

1. Type I error inflation is the increase in the probability of making a Type I error as the number of statistical significance tests grows.

2. To prevent Type I error inflation by decreasing the testwise alpha level. This keeps the experimentwise alpha level low.

3. The number of groups.

4. (1) The improvement of predictions compared to the baseline model of $\hat{y} = \bar{y}$. (2) Percentage of dependent variance that is shared with the independent variable's variance.

5. By conducting a *post hoc* test.

6. An unpaired two-sample *t*-test is a special case of ANOVA; they are both members of the general linear model.

7. The group means are the predicted dependent variable values (i.e., $\hat{y}$ values) for group members.

8. Labels ignore context; a "small" effect size may be very important, while a "large" effect size may be trivial. Also, a label on an effect size is not a full interpretation because the standards of a "small" or a "large" effect size are not consistent across fields of research. Finally, these labels are entirely subjective.

9. a. Residual.

   b. η^2.

10. By finding the degrees of freedom between groups and the degrees of freedom within groups and using the *F*-table (i.e., Appendix A3) to identify the proper *F*-critical value that corresponds to the predetermined alpha value.

11. a. 6.

    b. .265.

    c. .05 / 6 = .0083.

    d. .01 / 6 = .0017.

    e. There would be fewer NHSTs to conduct, and the testwise Type I error would not be so small, reducing the probability of a Type II error.

12. a. 15.

    b. .5367.

    c. .05 / 15 = .0033.

    d. .01 / 15 = .0007.

    e. There would be fewer NHSTs to conduct, and the testwise Type I error would not be so small, reducing the probability of a Type II error.

13. a. Because her independent variable is nominal-level data, and it has three groups.

    b. Teenagers, young adults, and elderly adults.

    c. $H_0 : \bar{X}_1 = \bar{X}_2 = \bar{X}_3$ or $H_0 : \bar{X}_1 = \bar{X}_2 = \ldots = \bar{X}_k$.

    d. One-tailed test; all ANOVAs are one-tailed tests because the sampling distribution (*F*-distribution) is positively skewed.

    e. 3.68.

    f.

	Teenagers	Young adults	Elderly adults	Total
Score	2	5	4	
Score	4	5	5	
Score	4	1	4	
Score	5	2	2	
Score	3	3	1	
Score	1	4	3	
$\sum Y$	19	20	19	58
$\sum (Y^2)$	71	80	71	222
N	6	6	6	18
$\bar{Y}$	3.167	3.333	3.167	3.222

    g.

	SOS	df	MS	F_{obs}
Between	0.111	2	0.056	0.024
Within	35	15	2.333	
Total	35.111	17		

    h. Retain the null hypothesis.

    i. $p > .05$.

    j. $\eta^2 = 0.003$. Predictions of the dependent variable based on group means will only be 0.3% better than predictions based on the baseline model. Or, the dependent variable shares only 0.3% of its variance with the independent variable's variance.

    k. No, because the null hypothesis was retained.

    l. 3.014.

    m. HSD for teenagers and young adults = –0.267. HSD for teenagers and elderly adults = 0.267. HSD for young adults and elderly adults = 0. Because none of these HSD values exceed the critical *q* value, there are no statistically significant differences among any of the group means.

n.

	Teenagers	Young adults	Elderly adults
Residual	$2 - 3.167 = -1.167$	$5 - 3.333 = 1.667$	$4 - 3.167 = 0.833$
Residual	$4 - 3.167 = 0.833$	$5 - 3.333 = 1.667$	$5 - 3.167 = 1.833$
Residual	$4 - 3.167 = 0.833$	$1 - 3.333 = -2.333$	$4 - 3.167 = 0.833$
Residual	$5 - 3.167 = 1.833$	$2 - 3.333 = -1.333$	$2 - 3.167 = -1.167$
Residual	$3 - 3.167 = -0.167$	$3 - 3.333 = -0.333$	$1 - 3.167 = -2.167$
Residual	$1 - 3.167 = -2.167$	$4 - 3.333 = 0.667$	$3 - 3.167 = -0.167$

14. a. Because her independent variable is nominal-level data, and it has three groups.
  b. Groups A, B, and C.
  c. $H_0 : \overline{X}_A = \overline{X}_B = \overline{X}_C$ or
     $H_0 : \overline{X}_1 = \overline{X}_2 = \ldots = \overline{X}_k$.
  d. One-tailed test; all ANOVAs are one-tailed tests because the sampling distribution (*F*-distribution) is positively skewed.
  e. 3.63.
  f.

	Group A	Group B	Group C	Total
Score	8	13	7	
Score	12	10	15	
Score	16	9	10	
Score	7	14	15	
Score	11	16	12	
Score	19		4	
Score	14			
Score	6			
$\sum Y$	93	62	63	218
$\sum (Y^2)$	1,227	802	759	2,788
n	8	5	6	19
$\overline{Y}$	11.625	12.4	10.5	11.47

  g.

	SOS	df	MS	F_{obs}
Between	10.162	2	5.081	0.294
Within	276.575	16	17.286	
Total	286.737	18		

  h. Retain the null hypothesis.
  i. $p > .05$.
  j. $\eta^2 = 0.035$. Predictions of the dependent variable based on group means will only be 3.5% better than predictions based on the baseline model. Or, the dependent variable shares only 3.5% of its variance with the independent variable's variance.
  k. No, because the null hypothesis was retained.
  l. 2.998.

m. HSD for Groups A and B = −0.849. HSD for Groups A and C = 1.233. HSD for Groups B and C = 2.082. Because none of these HSD values exceed the critical q value, there are no statistically significant differences among any of the group means.

n.

	Group A	Group B	Group C
Score	$8 - 11.625 = -3.625$	$13 - 12.4 = 0.6$	$7 - 10.5 = -3.5$
Score	$12 - 11.625 = -1.625$	$10 - 12.4 = -2.4$	$15 - 10.5 = 4.5$
Score	$16 - 11.625 = 4.375$	$9 - 12.4 = -3.4$	$10 - 10.5 = 0.5$
Score	$7 - 11.625 = -4.625$	$14 - 12.4 = 1.6$	$15 - 10.5 = 4.5$
Score	$11 - 11.625 = -0.625$	$16 - 12.4 = 3.6$	$12 - 10.5 = 1.5$
Score	$19 - 11.625 = 7.625$		$4 - 10.5 = -6.5$
Score	$14 - 11.625 = 2.375$		
Score	$6 - 11.625 = -5.625$		

15. a. Because his independent variable is nominal-level data, and it has four groups.
  b. Plane, train, car, and bus groups.
  c. $H_0 : \overline{X}_A = \overline{X}_B = \overline{X}_C = \overline{X}_D$ or
     $H_0 : \overline{X}_1 = \overline{X}_2 = \ldots = \overline{X}_k$.
  d. One-tailed test; all ANOVAs are one-tailed tests because the sampling distribution (*F*-distribution) is positively skewed.
  e. 3.07.
  f.

	Plane	Train	Car	Bus	Total
Score	4	5	6	4	
Score	6	5	4	3	
Score	3	6	2	3	
Score	1	4	5	5	
Score	5	2	6	1	
Score	6	3			
Score	5	2			
Score		4			
$\sum Y$	30	31	23	16	100
$\sum (Y^2)$	148	135	117	60	460
N	7	8	5	5	25
$\overline{Y}$	4.286	3.875	4.6	3.2	4.0

  g.

	SOS	df	MS	F_{obs}
Between	5.696	3	1.899	0.664
Within	54.304	21	2.858	
Total	60	24		

  h. Retain the null hypothesis.
  i. $p > .05$.

j. $\eta^2 = 0.0949$. Predictions of the dependent variable based on group means will only be 9.49% better than predictions based on the baseline model. Or, the dependent variable shares only 9.49% of its variance with the independent variable's variance.

k. No, because the null hypothesis was retained.

l. 3.532.

m. HSD for plane and train groups = 0.595. HSD for plane and car groups = –0.455. HSD for plane and bus groups = 1.572. HSD for train and car groups = –1.050. HSD for train and bus groups = 0.977. HSD for car and bus groups = 2.027. Because none of these HSD values exceed the critical q value, there are no statistically significant differences among any of the group means.

n.

Plane	Train	Car	Bus
Score	4 – 4.286 = –0.286	5 – 3.875 = 1.125	6 – 4.6 = 1.4	4 – 3.2 = 0.8
Score	6 – 4.286 = 1.714	5 – 3.875 = 1.125	4 – 4.6 = –0.6	3 – 3.2 = –0.2
Score	3 – 4.286 = –1.286	6 – 3.875 = 2.125	2 – 4.6 = –2.6	3 – 3.2 = –0.2
Score	1 – 4.286 = –3.286	4 – 3.875 = 0.125	5 – 4.6 = 0.4	5 – 3.2 = 1.8
Score	5 – 4.286 = 0.714	2 – 3.875 = –1.875	6 – 4.6 = 1.4	1 – 3.2 = –2.2
Score	6 – 4.286 = 1.714	3 – 3.875 = –0.875		
Score	5 – 4.286 = 0.714	2 – 3.875 = –1.875		
Score		4 – 3.875 = 0.125		

16.a. Because her independent variable is nominal-level data, and it has three groups.

b. Groups A, B, and C.

c. $H_0 : \overline{X}_A = \overline{X}_B = \overline{X}_C$ or $H_0 : \overline{X}_1 = \overline{X}_2 = \ldots = \overline{X}_k$.

d. One-tailed test; all ANOVAs are one-tailed tests because the sampling distribution (F-distribution) is positively skewed.

e. 3.63.

f.

	Capital city	Suburbs	Rural	Total
Score	10	7	1	
Score	3	10	8	
Score	2	4	9	
Score	7	6	5	
Score	6	7	7	
Score	5	2	6	
Score	8	5	4	
Score	2	9	8	
$\sum Y$	43	50	48	141
$\sum (Y^2)$	391	360	336	987
n	8	8	8	24
$\overline{Y}$	5.375	6.25	6	5.875

g.

	SOS	df	MS	F_{obs}
Between	3.25	2	1.625	0.22
Within	155.375	21	7.399	
Total	158.625	23		

h. Retain the null hypothesis.

i. $p > .05$.

j. $\eta^2 = 0.02$. Predictions of the dependent variable based on group means will only be 2% better than predictions based on the baseline model. Or, the dependent variable shares only 2% of its variance with the independent variable's variance.

k. No, because the null hypothesis was retained.

l. 2.950.

m. HSD for capital and suburb groups = –0.910. HSD for capital and rural groups = –0.650. HSD for suburb and rural groups = 0.260. Because none of these HSD values exceed the critical q value, there are no statistically significant differences among any of the group means.

n.

	Capital city	Suburbs	Rural
Score	10 – 5.375 = 4.625	7 – 6.25 = 0.75	1 – 6 = –5
Score	3 – 5.375 = –2.375	10 – 6.25 = 3.75	8 – 6 = 2
Score	2 – 5.375 = –3.375	4 – 6.25 = –2.25	9 – 6 = 3
Score	7 – 5.375 = 1.625	6 – 6.25 = –0.25	5 – 6 = –1
Score	6 – 5.375 = 0.625	7 – 6.25 = 0.75	7 – 6 = 1
Score	5 – 5.375 = –0.375	2 – 6.25 = –4.25	6 – 6 = 0
Score	8 – 5.375 = 2.625	5 – 6.25 = –1.25	4 – 6 = –2
Score	2 – 5.375 = –3.375	9 – 6.25 = 2.25	8 – 6 = 2

17.a. Because his independent variable is nominal-level data, and it has five groups.

b. Groups A, B, C, D, and E.

c. $H_0 : \overline{X}_A = \overline{X}_B = \overline{X}_C = \overline{X}_D = \overline{X}_E$ or $H_0 : \overline{X}_1 = \overline{X}_2 = \ldots = \overline{X}_k$.

d. One-tailed test; all ANOVAs are one-tailed tests because the sampling distribution (F-distribution) is positively skewed.

e. 2.61.

f.

	Group A	Group B	Group C	Group D	Group E	Total
Score	4	3	5	8	2	
Score	6	1	6	7	6	
Score	2	4	5	8	4	
Score	7	5	4	6	8	
Score	6	5	4	1	6	

(cont.)

	Group A	Group B	Group C	Group D	Group E	Total
Score	7	9	8	3	7	
Score	8	2	7	4	9	
Score		4	9	6	9	
Score		7	3	8	8	
Score			4	8	7	
$\sum Y$	40	40	55	59	66	260
$\sum(Y^2)$	254	226	337	403	480	1,700
N	7	9	10	10	10	46
$\overline{Y}$	5.714	4.444	5.5	5.9	6.6	5.652

g.

	SOS	df	MS	F_{obs}
Between	22.984	4	5.746	1.136
Within	207.451	41	5.060	
Total	230.435	45		

h. Retain the null hypothesis.

i. $p > .05$.

j. $\eta^2 = 0.0997$. Predictions of the dependent variable based on group means will only be 9.97% better than predictions based on the baseline model. Or, the dependent variable shares only 9.97% of its variance with the independent variable's variance.

k. No, because the null hypothesis was retained.

l. 4.039.

m. HSD for Groups A and B = 1.696. HSD for Groups A and C = 0.286. HSD for Groups A and D = –0.248. HSD for Groups A and E = –1.183. HSD for Groups B and C = –1.410. HSD for Groups B and D = –1.945. HSD for Groups B and E = –2.879. HSD for Groups C and D = –0.534. HSD for Groups C and E = –1.469. HSD for Groups D and E = –0.935. Because none of these HSD values exceed the critical q value, there are no statistically significant differences among any of the group means.

n.

	Group A	Group B	Group C	Group D	Group E
Score	4 – 5.714 = 1.714	3 – 4.444 = 1.444	5 – 5.5 = –0.5	8 – 5.9 = 2.1	2 – 6.6 = –4.6
Score	6 – 5.714 = 0.286	1 – 4.444 = 3.444	6 – 5.5 = 0.5	7 – 5.9 = 1.1	6 – 6.6 = –0.6
Score	2 – 5.714 = 3.714	4 – 4.444 = 0.444	5 – 5.5 = –0.5	8 – 5.9 = 2.1	4 – 6.6 = –2.6

	Group A	Group B	Group C	Group D	Group E
Score	7 – 5.714 = 1.286	5 – 4.444 = 0.556	4 – 5.5 = –1.5	6 – 5.9 = 0.1	8 – 6.6 = 1.4
Score	6 – 5.714 = 0.286	5 – 4.444 = 0.556	4 – 5.5 = –1.5	1 – 5.9 = –4.9	6 – 6.6 = –0.6
Score	7 – 5.714 = 1.286	9 – 4.444 = 4.556	8 – 5.5 = 2.5	3 – 5.9 = –2.9	7 – 6.6 = 0.4
Score	8 – 5.714 = 2.286	2 – 4.444 = –2.444	7 – 5.5 = 1.5	4 – 5.9 = –1.9	9 – 6.6 = 2.4
Score		4 – 4.444 = 0.444	9 – 5.5 = 3.5	6 – 5.9 = 0.1	9 – 6.6 = 2.4
Score		7 – 4.444 = 2.556	3 – 5.5 = –2.5	8 – 5.9 = 2.1	8 – 6.6 = 1.4
Score			4 – 5.5 = –1.5	8 – 5.9 = 2.1	7 – 6.6 = 0.4

18.a. Because his independent variable is nominal-level data, and it has three groups.

b. Inner-city dwellers, suburban residents, and rural residents.

c. $H_0 : \overline{X}_1 = \overline{X}_2 = \overline{X}_3$ or $H_0 : \overline{X}_1 = \overline{X}_2 = \ldots = \overline{X}_k$.

d. One-tailed test; all ANOVAs are one-tailed tests because the sampling distribution (F-distribution) is positively skewed.

e. 3.88.

f.

	Group A	Group B	Group C	Total
Score	9	3	5	
Score	11	1	6	
Score	7	4	5	
Score	12	5	4	
Score	11	5	4	
$\sum Y$	50	18	24	92
$\sum(Y^2)$	516	76	118	710
N	5	5	5	15
$\overline{Y}$	10	3.6	4.8	6.133

g.

	SOS	df	MS	F_{obs}
Between	115.733	2	57.867	23.147
Within	30.000	12	2.500	
Total	145.733	14		

h. Reject the null hypothesis.

i. $p < .01$.

j. $\eta^2 = 0.7941$. Predictions of the dependent variable based on group means will only be 79.41% better than predictions based on the baseline model. Or, the dependent variable shares only 79.41% of its variance with the independent variable's variance.

k. Yes, because the null hypothesis has been rejected.

l. 3.082.

m. HSD for Groups A and B = 9.051. HSD for Groups A and C = 7.354. HSD for Groups B and C = −1.697. Because the first two HSDs are larger than the q critical value of 3.082, it is apparent that the null hypothesis for the ANOVA was rejected because there is a statistically significant difference between the means for Groups A and B and between Groups A and C. There is no statistically significant difference between the means for Groups B and C.

n.

	Group A	Group B	Group C
Score	9 − 10 = −1	3 − 3.6 = −0.6	5 − 4.8 = 0.2
Score	11 − 10 = 1	1 − 3.6 = −2.6	6 − 4.8 = 1.2
Score	7 − 10 = −3	4 − 3.6 = 0.4	5 − 4.8 = 0.2
Score	12 − 10 = 2	5 − 3.6 = 1.4	4 − 4.8 = −0.8
Score	11 − 10 = 1	5 − 3.6 = 1.4	4 − 4.8 = −0.8

Chapter 12

1. B (strongest) and D (weakest).

2. B (strongest) and C (weakest).

3. (1) The improvement of predictions compared to the baseline model of $\hat{y} = \bar{y}$. (2) Percentage of dependent variance that is shared with the independent variable's variance.

4. Both are NHST procedures that are members of the general linear model. Both are correlations, but the unpaired two-sample t-test is a correlation adapted to a dichotomous nominal variable.

5. Correlation does not imply causation. Samantha's logic would only be correct if a person's level of wealth causes them to be happy (or not). However, if a person's happiness level causes their wealth (or poverty) or if an unknown third variable causes both variables, then Samantha's reasoning would be incorrect.

6. With only a correlation between two variables, it is possible that a third variable that is not part of the model is the cause of the relationship between the original two variables.

7. a. Positive.

    b. Negative.

    c. Negative.

d. Positive.

e. Negative.

f. Negative.

g. Negative.

h. Positive.

i. Positive.

j. Positive.

8. a. A tightly packed oval of dots that goes from the top-left quadrant to the bottom-right quadrant.

    b. A moderately tight oval of dots that goes from the top-left quadrant to the bottom-right quadrant.

    c. A wide oval of dots that goes from the top-left quadrant to the bottom-right quadrant.

    d. Scatterplot filled with dots randomly spread out through the entire scatterplot.

    e. A moderately tight oval of dots that goes from the bottom-left quadrant to the top-right quadrant.

    f. A tight oval of dots that goes from the bottom-left quadrant to the top-right quadrant.

    g. A tight oval of dots that goes from the bottom-left quadrant to the top-right quadrant.

    h. A straight line of dots that goes from the bottom-left quadrant to the top-right quadrant.

9. $r = -0.782$.

10. a. $r = 0.472$.

    b. $H_0: r = 0$.

    c. 6.

    d. ± 0.707.

    e. Retain the null hypothesis.

    f. $p > .05$.

    g. $r^2 = 0.2228$.

    h.

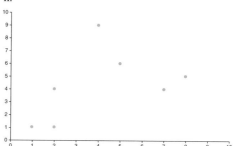

    i. Yes, because the correlation is positive. However, it is important to recognize that the evidence is weak due to the small sample size (with the correlation not being statistically significantly different from zero).

11.a. $r = +0.685$.

b. H_0: $r = 0$.

c. 10.

d. +0.498.

e. Reject the null hypothesis.

f. $p < .01$.

g. $r^2 = 0.4693$.

h.

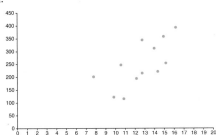

12.a. $r = 0.044$.

b. H_0: $r = 0$.

c. 10.

d. +0.576.

e. Retain the null hypothesis.

f. $p > .05$.

g. $r^2 = 0.0020$.

h.

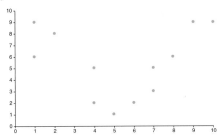

13.a. $r = -0.252$.

b. H_0: $r = 0$.

c. 10.

d. +0.576.

e. Retain the null hypothesis.

f. $p > .05$.

g. $r^2 = 0.0633$.

h.

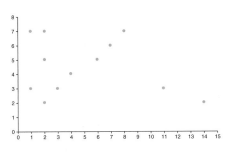

14.a. $r = 0.011$.

b. H_0: $r = 0$.

c. 13.

d. +0.514.

e. Retain the null hypothesis.

f. $p > .05$.

g. $r = 0.0001$.

h.

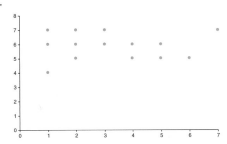

Chapter 13

1. Because the regression line always passes through $(\overline{X}, \overline{Y})$, as the mean of z-scores is always zero, when both variables are z-scores, that point will be $(0, 0)$.

2. Regression towards the mean.

3. As a result of regression towards the mean, the predicted values for a dependent variable will always be closer to the mean than are the independent variable values. But rare events are outliers and very different from the mean, so unlikely events are difficult to predict with regression equations.

4. Homogeneity of residuals.

5. Restriction of range.

6. Instead of an oval or circle of dots, the dots in the scatterplot form a different shape, such as a trumpet or a fan.

7. Calculate the correlation coefficient with and without the outlier; if the two are similar, the outlier is not distorting the correlation. If the two correlations are different, the outlier is distorting the coefficient.

8. Because only outliers that are far from the regression line will influence it, as the regression line attempts to minimize the squared residuals of every sample member. This will cause the individuals furthest from the data to have the most influence because the regression line will need to be closer to the outlier(s) to reduce those squared residuals as much as possible.

9. a. +2.88.
   b. +2.09.
   c. +0.86.
   d. +0.29.
   e. 0.
   f. −0.43.
   g. −1.37.
   h. −1.80.
   i. −2.30.
   j. Regression towards the mean.

10. a. $b = .49$, $a = .942$.
    b.

x_i	y_i
0	0.942
1.8	1.824
3.0	2.412
4.2	3.000
5.8	3.784
5.9	3.833
10.0	5.842

11. a. −0.35.
    b. −0.28.
    c. −0.25.
    d. −0.08.
    e. 0.
    f. +0.04.
    g. +0.12.
    h. +0.28.
    i. +0.35.
    j. Regression towards the mean.

12. a. $b = -.788$, $a = 16.034$.
    b.

x_i	y_i
0	16.034
1.8	14.616
3.0	13.671
4.2	12.726
5.8	11.466
5.9	11.388
10.0	8.159

13. Restriction of range.

14. a. $r = -.421$.
    b. $\hat{z}_y = -.421 z_x$.
    c. $b = -0.720$, $a = 8.389$.
    d. $\hat{y}_i = -0.720 x_i + 8.389$.

e.

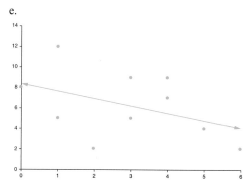

f. No

g.

z_x	z_y
−3	1.26
−2.5	1.05
−1	0.42
0	0.00
1.8	−0.76
2.0	−0.84
3.5	−1.48

h.

x	y
0	8.39
1	7.67
2	6.95
3	6.23
4	5.51
5	4.79
6	4.07

i.

ID	x	y	Residual
1	3	9	9 − 6.23 = 2.77
2	5	4	4 − 4.79 = −0.79
3	3	5	5 − 6.23 = −1.23
4	4	9	9 − 5.51 = 3.49
5	2	2	2 − 6.95 = −4.95
6	1	5	5 − 7.67 = −2.67
7	0	8	8 − 8.39 = −0.39
8	4	7	7 − 5.51 = 1.49
9	6	2	2 − 4.07 = −2.07
10	1	12	12 − 7.67 = 4.33

j. Individual no. 7 has the smallest residual.
   Individual no. 10 has the largest residual.

15. a. $r = .219$
    b. $\hat{z}_y = .219 z_x$
    c. $b = 0.213$, $a = 4.161$
    d. $\hat{y}_i = 0.213 x_i + 4.161$

e.

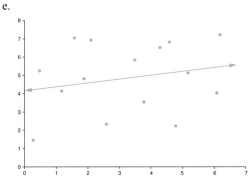

f. No.

g. A.

z_x	z_y
−3	−0.656
−2	−0.437
−0.8	−0.175
0	0.000
0.6	0.131
1.2	0.262
2.4	0.525

h.

x	y
0	4.16
1	4.37
2	4.59
3	4.80
4	5.01
5	5.23
6	5.44

i.

ID	x	y	Residual
1	3.5	4.971	$3.5 - 4.971 = -1.471$
2	4.8	4.566	$4.8 - 4.566 = 0.234$
3	5.2	4.267	$5.2 - 4.267 = 0.933$
4	7.0	4.502	$7.0 - 4.502 = 2.498$
5	2.2	5.185	$2.2 - 5.185 = -2.985$
6	5.1	5.270	$5.1 - 5.270 = -0.170$
7	4.0	5.462	$4.0 - 5.462 = -1.462$
8	6.5	5.078	$6.5 - 5.078 = 1.422$
9	2.3	4.715	$2.3 - 4.715 = -2.415$
10	4.1	4.417	$4.1 - 4.417 = -0.317$
11	5.8	4.907	$5.8 - 4.907 = 0.893$
12	6.8	5.142	$6.8 - 5.142 = 1.658$
13	7.2	5.483	$7.2 - 5.483 = 1.717$
14	6.9	4.609	$6.9 - 4.609 = 2.291$
15	1.4	4.225	$1.4 - 4.225 = -2.825$

j. Individual no. 5 has the largest residual. Individual no. 6 has the smallest residual.

16. Converting data to z-scores makes the two variables have an SD of 1. When both SDs are equal to one another, the formula $b = r\frac{s_y}{s_x}$ simplifies to $b = r\frac{1}{1} = r(1) = r$. Because b is the slope of the regression line, r must be the slope of the regression line when both variables have been converted to z-scores.

17. When the variables are converted to z-scores, both will have a mean of 0. When $\overline{X} = 0$ and $\overline{Y} = 0$, the formula $a = \overline{Y} - b\overline{X}$ simplifies to $a = 0 - b(0) = 0 - 0 = 0$, meaning that the y-intercept will always be zero when the variables are converted to z-scores. This is why the standardized regression line always passes through $(0, 0)$.

18. $r_{\text{pb}} = 0.447$.

Chapter 14

1. B.

2. Both compare a sample statistic with a theorized parameter. In a one-sample t-test, the null hypothesis would be that the sample mean is equal to a theorized score (see Chapter 8), while a one-variable chi-squared test's null hypothesis is that the sample proportions are equal to the theorized proportions. Therefore, a one-variable chi-squared test is the same procedure as a one-sample t-test, except adapted to nominal-level data.

3. Both procedures are members of the general linear model. A two-variable chi-squared test is a correlation that has been adapted for nominal-level data.

4. Relative risk is the ratio between the proportions of individuals in two groups experiencing the outcome of interest. Therefore, the relative risk describes how much more likely members of one group are to experience the outcome of interest compared to the baseline group.

5. The "file drawer problem" is the tendency for studies that retain the null hypothesis to go unpublished. This distorts the research literature and makes correlations and effect sizes look stronger in a meta-analysis than they really are.

6. (1) Meta-analyses are better than traditional literature reviews at synthesizing literature. (2) Combining many studies increases the overall sample size; this increases power and produces results that have greater precision. (3) A meta-analysis can resolve the contradictions of the scientific literature. (4) Meta-analyses can help researchers determine whether study characteristics can affect results that make effect sizes systematically larger or smaller.

7. a. The null hypothesis is that the proportions in the sample are equal to the proportions in the population (.59 for females and .41 for males).
   b. One-tailed test. All chi-squared tests are one-tailed tests because the sampling distribution is positively skewed.
   c. 1.
   d. 3.841.
   e. 0.065.
   f. Retain the null hypothesis.
   g. Female OR = 0.975, male OR = 1.036. Females were .975 times as likely to be selected for Dante's survey, whereas males were 1.036 times as likely to be selected for the survey. Both of these values are close to 1.0, so Dante's sample is representative of the population of students in his program.

8. a. The null hypothesis is that the proportions in the sample are equal to the proportions in the clinic population.
   b. One-tailed test. All chi-squared tests are one-tailed tests because the sampling distribution is positively skewed.
   c. 4.
   d. 9.488.
   e. 10.395.
   f. Reject the null hypothesis.
   g. Depression OR = 1.058, anxiety disorders OR = 0.962, eating disorders OR = 0.974, intellectual disabilities OR = 0.385, other diagnosis OR = 1.758. The first three groups all have odds ratios close to 1, indicating that they are proportionally represented in the sample. However, people with intellectual disabilities are very underrepresented, while

individuals in the last group are 1.758 times as likely to be in the sample, and are therefore overrepresented.

9. a. 1 / 1.5 = 0.667.
   b. 1.5 / (1 + 1.5) = 0.60.

10. a. The relative risk of 0.31 indicates that vaccinated individuals are 31% as likely to have the disease as those non-vaccinated. The relative risk of 1.0 indicates that side effects are equally likely for both vaccinated and non-vaccinated groups.
    b. The vaccine is effective, and it is safe for patients.

11. a. 11.
    b. 19.675.
    c. 54.594.
    d. Reject the null hypothesis.
    e.

Jan	Feb	Mar	Apr	May	Jun	Jul	Aug	Sep	Oct	Nov	Dec
1.359	1.158	1.326	1.208	1.309	1.057	0.772	0.755	1.108	0.638	0.755	0.554

    f. There were more athletes born in the first 6 months of the year and in September than what would be expected if the athletes were born equally frequently across the months. This is indicated by the fact that those are the odds ratios greater than 1.0. With the exception of September, this supports Barnsley et al.'s (1985) hypothesis that older hockey players on youth teams had an advantage in their athletics training.

12. Because the two odds ratios are reciprocals of one another: 1 / 2.5 = 0.4, and 1 / 0.4 = 2.5. These two studies are equivalent to each other because the baseline group has been switched. When the baseline group and the group of interest are switched, the odds ratio becomes the reciprocal of the original odds ratio.

13. .80 = 4 / 1 = 4.0. Plugging this odds ratio into Formula 14.7 produces 4 / (1 + 4) = 4 / 5 = .80.

14. a. The independent and dependent variables are unrelated.
    b. One-tailed test. All chi-squared tests are one-tailed tests because the sampling distribution is positively skewed.

c. 1.

d. 3.841.

e.

Contingency table of observed counts

	Graduated	Did not graduate	Total
Male	28	8	36
Female	42	12	54
Total	70	20	90

Contingency table of expected values

	Graduated	Did not graduate	Total
Male	28	8	36
Female	42	12	54
Total	70	20	90

f. 0.

g. Retain the null hypothesis.

h. 1.0.

i. The null hypothesis perfectly fits the data, as indicated by the chi-squared value of 0 and the odds ratio of 1. This indicates that both outcomes are equally likely for males and females.

15. a. The independent and dependent variables are unrelated.

b. One-tailed test. All chi-squared tests are one-tailed tests because the sampling distribution is positively skewed.

c. 6.

d. 12.592.

e.

Company	Repeat customers	Non-repeat satisfied customers	Non-repeat/ dissatisfied customers	Total
A	39.92	25.21	8.87	74
B	21.58	13.63	4.79	40
C	65.27	41.22	14.50	121
D	44.23	27.94	9.83	82
Total	171	108	38	317

f. 3.049.

g. Retain the null hypothesis.

h. 0.673.

i. The odds ratio indicates that other companies (B, C, and D combined) are 0.673 times as

likely to have repeat customers. Because the odds ratio value is less than 1, this means that company A is better than other companies at attracting repeat customers.

16. a. The independent and dependent variables are unrelated.

b. One-tailed test. All chi-squared tests are one-tailed tests because the sampling distribution is positively skewed.

c. 2.

d. 5.991.

e.

Student groups	Donated	Did not donate	Total
Athletics	12.76	16.24	29
Academic	22	28	50
Citizenship	9.24	11.76	21
Total	44	57	100

f. 0.019.

g. Retain the null hypothesis.

h. 0.338.

i. Athletics alumni are 0.967 times as likely to donate to their scholarship fund compared to academics alumni. Because this odds ratio is close to 1.0, it indicates that the two groups are approximately equally likely to donate.

Chapter 15

1. There are two independent variables; one has four categories, and the other has two categories.

2. Pearson's r is a special case of multiple regression with one independent variable.

3. Both multiple regression and ANOVA are members of the general linear model. ANOVA is just a special case of multiple regression, so both procedures will produce the same results.

4. Confirmatory factor analysis starts with a model, and attempts to determine whether the data fit the model. Exploratory factor analysis has no pre-determined model and is atheoretical.

5. Do not put total trust and confidence in a single study. Consider findings (including your own) in context. Report all statistics needed to fully interpret your data and to later include it in a meta-analysis. Report all procedures in a detailed manner, and engage in replication studies.

6. Often, detecting Simpson's paradox requires including an additional independent variable in the statistical model, and it may be difficult to know that it is important to include that variable in the model.

7. a. Multicollinearity occurs when independent variables in a statistical model are correlated.

   b. It can make it more difficult to reject the null hypothesis of $\beta = 0$ for an independent variable. This increases the probability of making a Type II error and may make independent variables seem less important than they really are.

   c. Check for multicollinearity by examining the variance inflation factor (VIF) or the tolerance value. Also, researchers can avoid including unnecessary or superfluous independent variables.

8. When the independent or dependent variables are ordinal-level data.

9. Conducting a 2×2 ANOVA would reduce the Type I error that occurs with multiple null hypothesis tests. A 2×2 ANOVA would also permit the examination of an interaction in the data.

10. a. Multivariate analysis of variance (MANOVA).

    b. Conducting three ANOVAs

11. ANOVA.

12. a. 2.

    b. Variable 1: sociology = 1, social work = 0, anthropology = 0. Variable 2: sociology = 0, social work = 1, anthropology = 0. In this coding scheme, anthropology is the baseline group. Other coding schemes are possible, as long as the baseline group has a value of 0 for both groups, and each of the other groups is labeled "1" in one variable and "0" in the other (with only one group labeled "1" for any variable).

13. Multiple regression.

14. a. (1) Predictions made with the statistical model are 74.4% better than predictions made with the baseline model. (2) 74.4% of the dependent variable's variance is shared with the variance of the independent variables.

   b. (1) Predictions made with the statistical model are 31.2% better than predictions made with the baseline model. (2) 31.2% of the dependent variable's variance is shared with the variance of the independent variables.

   c. (1) Predictions made with the statistical model are 0.4% better than predictions made with the baseline model. (2) 0.4% of the dependent variable's variance is shared with the variance of the independent variables.

15. a. The new variable raised the accuracy of predictions by 4.5%; therefore, it makes a unique contribution to the fit of the statistical model.

    b. This new variable's inclusion in the model does not improve predictions of the dependent variable. The variable is not a useful addition to the statistical model.

16. The AUC means that if a person is selected at random from each of the groups, the college student will have a higher level of political activity than the non-college student 62% of the time.

17. a. A randomly selected member of the higher scoring group will out-score a randomly selected member of the other group 92.2% of the time.

    b. A randomly selected member of the higher scoring group will out-score a randomly selected member of the other group 71.3% of the time.

    c. A randomly selected member of one group will out-score a randomly selected member of the other group 50% of the time.

    d. A randomly selected member of the lower scoring group will out-score a randomly selected member of the other group 41.2% of the time.

    e. A randomly selected member of the lower scoring group will out-score a randomly selected member of the other group 33.1% of the time.

    f. A randomly selected member of the lower scoring group will out-score a randomly selected member of the other group 1.2% of the time.

18. a. An interaction would indicate that the impact of one of the independent variables may change, depending on a person's score on the other independent variable.

b. Like the visual model of an interaction in the chapter, the graph would have one of the independent variables on the horizontal access and the dependent variable on the vertical axis. The second independent variable would be represented as multiple lines on the graph (one line for each category in the second independent variable). If there is an interaction present, the lines will be nonparallel.

References

Abelson, R. P. (1985). A variance explanation paradox: When a little is a lot. *Psychological Bulletin*, *97*, 129–133. doi:10.1037/0033-2909.97.1.129

Abelson, R. P. (1997a). On the surprising longevity of flogged horses: Why there is a case for the significance test. *Psychological Science*, *8*, 12–15. doi:10.1111/j.1467-9280.1997.tb00536.x

Abelson, R. P. (1997b). A retrospective on the significance test ban of 1999 (if there were no significance tests, they would be invented). In L. L. Harlow, S. A. Mulaik, & J. H. Steiger (Eds.), *What if there were no significance tests?* (pp. 117–141). York, NY: Psychology Press.

Acar, S., Sen, S., & Cayirdag, N. (2016). Consistency of the performance and nonperformance methods in gifted identification: A multilevel meta-analytic review. *Gifted Child Quarterly*, *60*, 81–101. doi:10.1177/0016986216634438

Ackerman, P. L. (2014). Nonsense, common sense, and science of expert performance: Talent and individual differences. *Intelligence*, *45*, 6–17. doi:10.1016/j.intell.2013.04.009

Agresti, A. (2007). *An introduction to categorical data analysis*. Hoboken, NJ: John Wiley & Sons.

Allen, P. J., & Baughman, F. D. (2016). Active learning in research methods classes is associated with higher knowledge and confidence, though not evaluations or satisfaction. *Frontiers in Psychology*, *7*(279), 1–7. doi:10.3389/fpsyg.2016.00279

Alpert, M., Kotsaftis, A., & Pouget, E. R. (1997). At issue: Speech fluency and schizophrenic negative signs. *Schizophrenia Bulletin*, *23*, 171–177.

American Educational Research Association (2006). Standards for reporting on empirical social science research in AERA publications. *Educational Researcher*, *35*, 33–40. doi:10.3102/0013189x035006033

American Psychological Association (2010). *Publication manual of the American Psychological Association* (6th ed.). Washington, DC: American Psychological Association.

American Psychological Association Publications and Communications Board Working Group on Journal Article Reporting Standards (2008). Reporting standards for research in psychology: Why do we need them? What might they be? *American Psychologist*, *63*, 839–851. doi:10.1037/0003-066x.63.9.839

Anderson, N. H. (1961). Scales and statistics: Parametric and nonparametric. *Psychological Bulletin*, *58*, 305–316. doi:10.1037/h0042576

Andrews, D. A., & Bonta, J. (2010). *The psychology of criminal conduct* (5th ed.). New Providence, NJ: Anderson Publishing.

Andrews, D. A., Bonta, J., & Wormith, J. S. (2011). The Risk-Need-Responsivity (RNR) Model: Does adding the Good Lives Model contribute to effective crime prevention? *Criminal Justice and Behavior*, *38*, 735–755. doi:10.1177/0093854811406356

Ángeles Quiroga, M., Escorial, S., Román, F. J., Morillo, D., Jarabo, A., Privado, J., et al. (2015). Can we reliably measure the general factor of intelligence (*g*) through commercial video games? Yes, we can! *Intelligence*, *53*, 1–7. doi:10.1016/j.intell.2015.08.004

Asparouhov, T., & Muthén, B. (2009). Exploratory structural equation modeling. *Structural Equation Modeling: A Multidisciplinary Journal*, *16*, 397–438. doi:10.1080/10705510903008204

Baddeley, A. (2003). Working memory: Looking back and looking forward. *Nature Reviews Neuroscience*, *4*, 829–839. doi:10.1038/nrn1201

Bangert, A. W., & Baumberger, J. P. (2005). Research and statistical techniques used in the *Journal of Counseling & Development*: 1990–2001. *Journal of Counseling & Development, 83*, 480–487. doi:10.1002/j.1556-6678.2005.tb00369.x

Barnett, V. (1978). The study of outliers: Purpose and model. *Journal of the Royal Statistical Society. Series C (Applied Statistics), 27*, 242–250. doi:10.2307/2347159

Barnsley, R. H., & Thompson, A. H. (1988). Birthdate and success in minor hockey: The key to the NHL. *Canadian Journal of Behavioural Science/Revue canadienne des sciences du comportement, 20*, 167–176. doi:10.1037/h0079927

Barnsley, R. H., Thompson, A. H., & Barnsley, P. E. (1985). Hockey success and birthdate: The relative age effect. *Journal of the Canadian Association for Health, Physical Education, and Recreation, 51*, 23–28.

Barrick, M. R., Stewart, G. L., & Piotrowski, M. (2002). Personality and job performance: Test of the mediating effects of motivation among sales representatives. *Journal of Applied Psychology, 87*, 43–51. doi:10.1037/0021-9010.87.1.43

Baskett, T. F., & Nagele, F. (2000). Naegele's rule: A reappraisal. *BJOG: An International Journal of Obstetrics & Gynaecology, 107*, 1433–1435. doi:10.1111/j.1471-0528.2000.tb11661.x

Baumberger, J. P., & Bangert, A. W. (1996). Research designs and statistical techniques used in the *Journal of Learning Disabilities*, 1989–1993. *Journal of Learning Disabilities, 29*, 313–316. doi:10.1177/002221949602900310

Bavelier, D., Achtman, R. L., Mani, M., & Föcker, J. (2012). Neural bases of selective attention in action video game players. *Vision Research, 61*, 132–143. doi:10.1016/j.visres.2011.08.007

Bem, S. L. (1974). The measurement of psychological androgyny. *Journal of Consulting and Clinical Psychology, 42*, 155–162. doi:10.1037/h0036215

Berkson, J. (1944). Application of the logistic function to bio-assay. *Journal of the American Statistical Association, 39*, 357–365. doi:10.2307/2280041

Bickel, P. J. (1965). On some robust estimates of location. *Annals of Mathematical Statistics, 36*, 847–858. doi:10.1214/aoms/1177700058

"Bird 'explodes' after flying in path of fastball." (March 26, 2001). *ESPN*. Retrieved from http://static.espn.go.com/mlb/news/2001/0325/1161522.html

Blackstone, W. (1765/1892). *Commentaries on the laws of England*. Retrieved from https://books.google.com/books?id=xic0AAAAIAAJ

Blanca, M. J., Arnau, J., López-Montiel, D., Bono, R., & Bendayan, R. (2013). Skewness and kurtosis in real data samples. *Methodology: European Journal of Research Methods for the Behavioral and Social Sciences, 9*, 78–84. doi:10.1027/1614-2241/a000057

Bland, J. M., & Altman, D. G. (1994a). Statistic notes: Regression towards the mean. *British Medical Journal, 308*(6942), 1499. doi:10.1136/bmj.308.6942.1499

Bland, J. M., & Altman, D. G. (1994b). Statistics notes: Some examples of regression towards the mean. *British Medical Journal, 309*(6957), 780. doi:10.1136/bmj.309.6957.780

Borgatta, E. F., & Bohrnstedt, G. W. (1980). Level of measurement: Once over again. *Sociological Methods & Research, 9*, 147–160. doi:10.1177/004912418000900202

Bouchard, T., Jr. (2014). Genes, evolution and intelligence. *Behavior Genetics, 44*, 549–577. doi:10.1007/s10519-014-9646-x

Bouter, L. M., Tijdink, J., Axelsen, N., Martinson, B. C., & ter Riet, G. (2016). Ranking major and minor research misbehaviors: Results from a survey among participants of four World Conferences on Research Integrity. *Research Integrity and Peer Review, 1*(1), 17. doi: 10.1186/s41073-016-0024-5

Bransford, J., Vye, N., & Bateman, H. (2002). Creating high-quality learning environments: Guidelines from research on how people learn. In P. A. Graham & N. G. Stacey (Eds.), *The knowledge economy and postsecondary education: Report of a workshop* (pp. 159–198). Washington, DC: National Academy Press.

Browne, K. D., & Hamilton-Giachritsis, C. (2005). The influence of violent media on children and adolescents: a public-health approach. *Lancet*,

365(9460), 702–710. doi:10.1016/S0140-6736 (05)17952-5

Brydges, C. R., Reid, C. L., Fox, A. M., & Anderson, M. (2012). A unitary executive function predicts intelligence in children. *Intelligence, 40*, 458–469. doi:10.1016/j.intell.2012.05.006

Buckner, J. C., Mezzacappa, E., & Beardslee, W. R. (2003). Characteristics of resilient youths living in poverty: The role of self-regulatory processes. *Development and Psychopathology, 15*, 139–162. doi:10.1017/S0954579403000087

Burt, S. M. (2015, September 29). 7 male athletes that have proved the "Sports Illustrated cover jinx" to be a myth, *New York Daily News*. Retrieved from www.nydailynews.com/sports/athletes-covered-sports-illustruated-10-times-article-1.2379001

Butcher, J. N., Dahlstrom, W. G., Graham, J. R., Telleen, A., & Kaemmer, B. (1989). *MMPI-2 manual*. Minneapolis, MN: University of Minnesota Press.

Calvin, C. M., Fernandes, C., Smith, P., Visscher, P. M., & Deary, I. J. (2010). Sex, intelligence and educational achievement in a national cohort of over 175,000 11-year-old schoolchildren in England. *Intelligence, 38*, 424–432. doi:10.1016/j.intell.2010.04.005

Capraro, R. M., & Thompson, B. (2008). The educational researcher defined: What will future researchers be trained to do? *Journal of Educational Research, 101*, 247–253. doi:10.3200/JOER.101.4.247-253

Caspi, A., Williams, B., Kim-Cohen, J., Craig, I. W., Milne, B. J., Poulton, R., Schalkwyk, L. C., et al. (2007). Moderation of breastfeeding effects on the IQ by genetic variation in fatty acid metabolism. *Proceedings of the National Academy of Sciences of the United States of America, 104*, 18860–18865. doi:10.1073/pnas.0704292104

Centers for Disease Control (2012). *Anthropometric reference data for children and adults: United States, 2007–2010*. Retrieved from www.cdc.gov/nchs/data/series/sr_11/sr11_252.pdf

Centers for Disease Control (2016). *Results for general population influenza vaccination coverage*. Retrieved from www.cdc.gov/flu/fluvaxview/interactive-general-population.htm

Cioffi, F. (1998). *Freud and the question of pseudoscience*. Peru, IL: Open Court.

Clark, C. L., Shaver, P. R., & Abrahams, M. F. (1999). Strategic behaviors in romantic relationship initiation. *Personality and Social Psychology Bulletin, 25*, 709–722. doi:10.1177/0146167299025006006

Cleary, T. A. (1968). Test bias: Prediction of grades of Negro and White students in integrated colleges. *Journal of Educational Measurement, 5*, 115–124. doi:10.1111/j.1745-3984.1968.tb00613.x

Clotfelter, C. T., & Cook, P. J. (1993). Notes: The "gambler's fallacy" in lottery play. *Management Science, 39*, 1521–1525. doi:10.1287/mnsc.39.12.1521

Cohen, J. (1962). The statistical power of abnormal-social psychological research: A review. *Journal of Abnormal and Social Psychology, 65*, 145–153. doi:10.1037/h0045186

Cohen, J. (1968). Multiple regression as a general data-analytic system. *Psychological Bulletin, 70*, 426–443. doi:10.1037/h0026714

Cohen, J. (1988). *Statistical power analysis for the behavioral sciences*. Hillsdale, NJ: Lawrence Erlbaum Associates.

Cohen, J. (1992). A power primer. *Psychological Bulletin, 112*, 155–159. doi:10.1037/0033-2909.112.1.155

Cohen, J. (1994). The earth is round ($p < .05$). *American Psychologist, 49*, 997–1003. doi:10.1037/0003-066x.49.12.997

Cole, T. J., Freeman, J. V., & Preece, M. A. (1998). British 1990 growth reference centiles for weight, height, body mass index and head circumference fitted by maximum penalized likelihood. *Statistics in Medicine, 17*, 407–429. doi:10.1002/(sici)1097-0258(19980228)17:4<407::aid-sim742>3.0.co;2-l

Conroy, R. M. (2012). What hypotheses do "nonparametric" two-group tests actually test? *Stata Journal, 12*, 182–190.

Copeland, R. (2014, February 6). Vegas gamblers keep vigil on aging slot machine they expect to pay off millions. *Wall Street Journal*. Retrieved

from www.wsj.com/articles/SB1000142405
2702303973704579354830486470944

Cortina, J. M. (2002). Big things have small
beginnings: An assortment of "minor"
methodological misunderstandings. *Journal of
Management, 28,* 339–362. doi:10.1016/s0149-
2063(02)00131-9

Costa, P. T., Jr., & McCrae, R. R. (2008). The revised
NEO Personality Inventory (NEO-PI-R) *The Sage
handbook of personality theory and assessment*
(Vol. II, pp. 179–198). Thousand Oaks, CA: Sage.

Crocker, L., & Algina, J. (2008). *Introduction to
classical and modern test theory.* Mason, OH:
Cengage Learning.

Cronbach, L. J. (1957). The two disciplines of
scientific psychology. *American Psychologist, 12,*
671–684. doi:10.1037/h0043943

Cumming, G. (2007). Inference by eye: Pictures of
confidence intervals and thinking about levels of
confidence. *Teaching Statistics, 29,* 89–93.
doi:10.1111/j.1467-9639.2007.00267.x

Cumming, G. (2008). Replication and *p* intervals: *p*
values predict the future only vaguely, but
confidence intervals do much better. *Perspectives
on Psychological Science, 3,* 286–300.
doi:10.1111/j.1745-6924.2008.00079.x

Cumming, G. (2010). *p* values versus confidence
intervals as warrants for conclusions that results
will replicate. In B. Thompson & R. F. Subotnik
(Eds.), *Methodologies for conducting research on
giftedness* (pp. 53–69). Washington, DC:
American Psychological Association.

Cumming, G. (2014). The new statistics: Why and
how. *Psychological Science, 25,* 7–29.
doi:10.1177/0956797613504966

Cumming, G., Fidler, F., Leonard, M., Kalinowski,
P., Christiansen, A., Kleinig, A., et al. (2007).
Statistical reform in psychology: Is anything
changing? *Psychological Science,* 18, 230–232.
doi:10.1111/j.1467-9280.2007.01881.x

Cumming, G., & Finch, S. (2005). Inference by eye:
Confidence intervals and how to read pictures of
data. *American Psychologist, 60,* 170–180.
doi:10.1037/0003-066X.60.2.170

Cumming, G., & Maillardet, R. (2006). Confidence
intervals and replication: Where will the next

mean fall? *Psychological Methods, 11,* 217–227.
doi:10.1037/1082-989x.11.3.217

Deary, I. J., Strand, S., Smith, P., & Fernandes, C.
(2007). Intelligence and educational achievement.
Intelligence, 35, 13–21. doi:10.1016/j.
intell.2006.02.001

Deary, I. J., Whalley, L. J., Lemmon, H., Crawford,
J. R., & Starr, J. M. (2000). The stability of
individual differences in mental ability from
childhood to old age: Follow-up of the
1932 Scottish Mental Survey. *Intelligence,
28,* 49–55. doi:10.1016/S0160-2898(99)00031-8

Deary, I. J., Whiteman, M. C., Starr, J. M., Whalley,
L. J., & Fox, H. C. (2004). The impact of
childhood intelligence on later life:
Following up the Scottish Mental Surveys of
1932 and 1947. *Journal of Personality and Social
Psychology, 86,* 130–147. doi:10.1037/0022-
3514.86.1.130

DeCarlo, L. T. (1997). On the meaning and use of
kurtosis. *Psychological Methods, 2,* 292–307.
doi:10.1037/1082-989x.2.3.292

Dellinger, A. B., & Leech, N. L. (2007). Toward a
unified validation framework in mixed methods
research. *Journal of Mixed Methods Research, 1,*
309–332. doi:10.1177/1558689807306147

Department for Work and Pensions (2015).
Percentages of individuals with incomes below the
UK mean, by ethnicity: Tax years 1994/1995 to
2012/2013. Retrieved from www.gov.uk/
government/publications/percentages-of-
individuals-with-incomes-below-the-uk-mean-by-
ethnicity-tax-years-19941995-to-20122013

Der, G., & Deary, I. J. (2006). Age and sex differences
in reaction time in adulthood: Results from the
United Kingdom Health and Lifestyle Survey.
Psychology and Aging, 21, 62–73. doi:10.1037/
0882-7974.21.1.62

DiCicco-Bloom, B., & Crabtree, B. F. (2006). The
qualitative research interview. *Medical Education,
40,* 314–321. doi:10.1111/j.1365-
2929.2006.02418.x

Diefenbach, G. J., Abramowitz, J. S., Norberg,
M. M., & Tolin, D. F. (2007). Changes in quality
of life following cognitive-behavioral therapy for
obsessive-compulsive disorder. *Behaviour*

Research and Therapy, 45, 3060–3068. doi:10.1016/j.brat.2007.04.014

Dunn, O. J. (1961). Multiple comparisons among means. *Journal of the American Statistical Association, 56*, 52–64. doi:10.1080/01621459.1961.10482090

Durlak, J. A. (2009). How to select, calculate and interpret effect sizes. *Journal of Pediatric Psychology, 34*, 917–928. doi:10.1093/jpepsy/jsp004

Faragher, E. B., Cass, M., & Cooper, C. L. (2005). The relationship between job satisfaction and health: A meta-analysis. *Occupational and Environmental Medicine, 62*, 105–112. doi:10.1136/oem.2002.006734

Feig, S. (2010). Cost-effectiveness of mammography, MRI, and ultrasonography for breast cancer screening. *Radiologic Clinics of North America, 48*, 879–891. doi:10.1016/j.rcl.2010.06.002

Feingold, A. (1988). Matching for attractiveness in romantic partners and same-sex friends: A meta-analysis and theoretical critique. *Psychological Bulletin, 104*, 226–235. doi:10.1037/0033-2909.104.2.226

Ferguson, C. J. (2009). An effect size primer: A guide for clinicians and researchers. *Professional Psychology: Research and Practice, 40*, 532–538. doi:10.1037/a0015808

Fidell, L. S., & Tabachnick, B. G. (2003). Preparatory data analysis. In J. A. Schinka & W. F. Velicer (Eds.), *Handbook of psychology, Vol. II: Research methods in psychology* (pp. 115–141). Hoboken, NJ: John Wiley & Sons.

Fidler, F. (2010). Statistical significance, result worthiness and evidence: What lessons are there for giftedness education in other disciplines? In B. Thompson & R. F. Subotnik (Eds.), *Methodologies for conducting research on giftedness* (pp. 71–88). Washington, DC: American Psychological Association.

Fidler, F., & Cumming, G. (2007). Lessons learned from statistical reform efforts in other disciplines. *Psychology in the Schools, 44*, 441–449. doi:10.1002/pits.20236

Fidler, F., Cumming, G., Thomason, N., Pannuzzo, D., Smith, J., Fyffe, P., et al. (2005). Toward improved statistical reporting in the *Journal of Consulting and Clinical Psychology*. *Journal of Consulting and Clinical Psychology, 73*, 136–143. doi:10.1037/0022-006x.73.1.136

Finch, S., Cumming, G., & Thomason, N. (2001). Reporting of statistical inference in the *Journal of Applied Psychology*: Little evidence of reform. *Educational and Psychological Measurement, 61*, 181–210. doi:10.1177/0013164401612001

Flynn, J. R. (1984). The mean IQ of Americans: Massive gains 1932 to 1978. *Psychological Bulletin, 95*, 29–51. doi:10.1037/0033-2909.95.1.29

Flynn, J. R. (1987). Massive IQ gains in 14 nations: What IQ tests really measure. *Psychological Bulletin, 101*, 171–191. doi:10.1037/h0090408

Foroughi, C. K., Serraino, C., Parasuraman, R., & Boehm-Davis, D. A. (2016). Can we create a measure of fluid intelligence using Puzzle Creator within Portal 2? *Intelligence, 56*, 58–64. doi:10.1016/j.intell.2016.02.011

Fox, J., & Anderegg, C. (2014). Romantic relationship stages and social networking sites: Uncertainty reduction strategies and perceived relational norms on Facebook. *CyberPsychology, Behavior & Social Networking, 17*, 685–691. doi:10.1089/cyber.2014.0232

Frey, B. S., Savage, D. A., & Torgler, B. (2011). Who perished on the *Titanic*? The importance of social norms. *Rationality and Society, 23*, 35–49. doi:10.1177/1043463110396059

Friendly, M., & Denis, D. (2005). The early origins and development of the scatterplot. *Journal of the History of the Behavioral Sciences, 41*, 103–130. doi:10.1002/jhbs.20078

Gagné, F., & Gagnier, N. (2004). The socio-affective and academic impact of early entrance to school. *Roeper Review, 26*, 128–138. doi:10.1080/02783190409554258

Galton, F. (1886). Regression towards mediocrity in hereditary stature. *Journal of the Anthropological Institute of Great Britain and Ireland, 15*, 246–263. doi:10.2307/2841583

García-Pérez, M. A. (2017). Thou shalt not bear false witness against null hypothesis significance testing. *Educational and Psychological Measurement, 77*, 631–666. doi:10.1177/0013164416668232

Gasper, J., DeLuca, S., & Estacion, A. (2012). Switching schools: Revisiting the relationship between school mobility and high school dropout *American Educational Research Journal, 49*, 487–519. doi:10.3102/0002831211415250

Gelman, A., & Stern, H. (2006). The difference between "significant" and "not significant" is not itself statistically significant. *American Statistician, 60*, 328–331. doi:10.1198/000313006x152649

Glass, G. V. (1976). Primary, secondary, and meta-analysis of research. *Educational Researcher, 5* (10), 3–8. doi:10.3102/0013189X005010003

Glass, G. V. (1977). Integrating findings: The meta-analysis of research. *Review of Research in Education, 5*, 351–379. doi:10.3102/0091732X005001351

Golden, C. J. (1976). Identification of brain disorders by the Stroop Color and Word Test. *Journal of Clinical Psychology, 32*, 654–658. doi:10.1002/1097-4679(197607)32:3<654::aid-jclp2270320336>3.0.co;2-z

Goltz, H. H., & Smith, M. L. (2010). Yule-Simpson's paradox in research. *Practical Assessment, Research & Evaluation, 15*(15), 1–9. Retrieved from http://pareonline.net/getvn.asp?v=15&n=15

Gorard, S. (2005). Revisiting a 90-year-old debate: The advantages of the mean deviation. *British Journal of Educational Studies, 53*, 417–430. doi:10.1111/j.1467-8527.2005.00304.x

Gorsuch, R. L. (1983). *Factor analysis.* Hillsdale, NJ: Lawrence Erlbaum Associates.

Gottfredson, L. S. (1997). Why g matters: The complexity of everyday life. *Intelligence, 24*, 79–132. doi:10.1016/S0160-2896(97)90014-3

Granic, I., Lobel, A., & Engels, R. C. M. E. (2014). The benefits of playing video games. *American Psychologist, 69*, 66–78. doi:10.1037/a0034857

Greenwald, A. G. (1975). Consequences of prejudice against the null hypothesis. *Psychological Bulletin, 82*, 1–20. doi:10.1037/h0076157

Grover, S., Biswas, P., & Avashthi, A. (2007). Delusional disorder: Study from North India. *Psychiatry and Clinical Neurosciences, 61*, 462–470. doi:10.1111/j.1440-1819.2007.01694.x

Haller, H., & Krauss, S. (2002). Misinterpretations of significance: A problem students share with their teachers? *Methods of Psychological Research Online, 7*(1), 1–20. Retrieved from www.dgps.de/fachgruppen/methoden/mpr-online/issue16/art1/haller.pdf

Hart, B., & Risley, T. R. (2003). The early catastrophe: The 30 million word gap by age 3. *American Educator, 27*(1), 4–9.

Harter, H. L. (1960). Tables of range and studentized range. *Annals of Mathematical Statistics, 31*, 1122–1147. doi:10.1214/aoms/1177705684

Hidalgo, B., & Goodman, M. (2013). Multivariate or multivariable regression? *American Journal of Public Health, 103*, 39–40. doi:10.2105/AJPH.2012.300897

Ho, H.-K., Nelson, E. A. S., Li, A. M., Wong, E. M. C., Lau, J. T. F., Mak, K. H., et al. (2008). Secular changes in height, weight and body mass index in Hong Kong children. *BMC Public Health, 8*, 320–329. doi:10.1186/1471-2458-8-320

Hoenig, J. M., & Heisey, D. M. (2001). The abuse of power. *American Statistician, 55*, 19–24. doi:10.1198/000313001300339897

Hollingworth, L. S. (1919). Comparison of the sexes in mental traits. *Psychological Bulletin, 16*, 371–373. doi:10.1037/h0075023

Holzinger, K. J., & Swineford, F. (1939). A study in factor analysis: The stability of a bi-factor solution. *Supplementary Educational Monographs, 48*, 1–91.

Huberty, C. J. (2002). A history of effect size indices. *Educational and Psychological Measurement, 62*, 227–240. doi:10.1177/0013164402062002002

Hummel, T. J., & Sligo, J. R. (1971). Empirical comparison of univariate and multivariate analysis of variance procedures. *Psychological Bulletin, 76*, 49–57. doi:10.1037/h0031323

Ioannidis, J. P. A. (2005). Why most published research findings are false. *PLoS Medicine, 2*(8), e124. doi:10.1371/journal.pmed.0020124

Jacobson, N. S., & Truax, P. (1991). Clinical significance: A statistical approach to defining meaningful change in psychotherapy research. *Journal of Consulting and Clinical Psychology, 59*, 12–19. doi:10.1037/0022-006x.59.1.12

Jamieson, A. (2015). Couple wins $1.5 million in Britain's lottery twice in two years. *NBC News*. Retrieved from www.nbcnews.com/news/world/couple-wins-1–5-million-britains-lottery-twice-two-years-n334466

Jamieson, S. (2004). Likert scales: How to (ab)use them. *Medical Education, 38*, 1217–1218. doi:10.1111/j.1365-2929.2004.02012.x

Jensen, A. R. (1969). How much can we boost IQ and scholastic achievement? *Harvard Educational Review, 39*, 1–123. doi:10.17763/haer.39.1.l3u15956627424k7

Jensen, A. R. (1991). Spearman's *g* and the problem of educational equality. *Oxford Review of Education, 17*(2), 169–187.

Jensen, A. R. (1998). *The g factor: The science of mental ability*. Westport, CT: Praeger.

Jeynes, W. H. (2003). A meta-analysis: The effects of parental involvement on minority children's academic achievement. *Education & Urban Society, 35*, 202–218. doi:10.1177/0013124502239392

John, L. K., Loewenstein, G., & Prelec, D. (2012). Measuring the prevalence of questionable research practices with incentives for truth telling. *Psychological Science, 23*, 524–532. doi:10.1177/0956797611430953

Johnson, D. E. (1986). Demonstrating the central limit theorem. *Teaching of Psychology, 13*, 155–156. doi:10.1207/s15328023top1303_18

Johnson, W., Brett, C. E., Calvin, C., & Deary, I. J. (2016). Childhood characteristics and participation in Scottish Mental Survey 1947 6-day sample follow-ups: Implications for participation in aging studies. *Intelligence, 54*, 70–79. doi:10.1016/j.intell.2015.11.006

Jones, T. A. (1969). Skewness and kurtosis as criteria of normality in observed frequency distributions. *Journal of Sedimentary Research, 39*, 1622–1627.

Karlberg, J., & Luo, Z. C. (2000). Foetal size to final height. *Acta Paediatrica, 89*, 632–636. doi:10.1080/080352500750043909

Kenaszchuk, C. (2011). Ideas and approaches towards strengthening the quantitative science for the interprofessional field. *Journal of Interprofessional Care, 25*, 239–240. doi:10.3109/13561820.2011.564458

Kerr, N. L. (1998). HARKing: Hypothesizing after the results are known. *Personality and Social Psychology Review, 2*, 196–217. doi:10.1207/s15327957pspr0203_4

Kieffer, K. M., Reese, R. J., & Thompson, B. (2001). Statistical techniques employed in *AERJ* and *JCP* articles from 1988 to 1997: A methodological review. *Journal of Experimental Education, 69*, 280–309. doi:10.1080/00220970109599489

Kim, H., & Stoner, M. (2008). Burnout and turnover intention among social workers: Effects of role stress, job autonomy and social support. *Administration in Social Work, 32*(3), 5–25. doi:10.1080/03643100801922357

Kintsch, W. (1998). The representation of knowledge in minds and machines. *International Journal of Psychology, 33*, 411–420. doi:10.1080/002075998400169

Kirk, R. E. (1996). Practical significance: A concept whose time has come. *Educational and Psychological Measurement, 56*, 746–759. doi:10.1177/0013164496056005002

Kline, R. B. (2005). *Principles and practice of structural equation modeling* (2nd ed.). New York, NY: Guilford Press.

Kline, R. B. (2013). *Beyond significance testing: Statistics reform in the behavioral sciences* (2nd ed.). Washington, DC: American Psychological Association.

Klomp, J., & De Haan, J. (2008). Effects of governance on health: A cross-national analysis of 101 countries. *Kyklos, 61*, 599–614. doi:10.1111/j.1467-6435.2008.00415.x

Kobrin, J. L., Patterson, B. F., Shaw, E. J., Mattern, K. D., & Barbuti, S. M. (2008). *Validity of the SAT for predicting first-year college grade point average*. New York, NY: College Board.

Komlos, J., Hau, M., & Bourguinat, N. (2003). An anthropometric history of early-modern France. *European Review of Economic History, 7*, 159–189. doi:10.1017/S1361491603000066

Komlos, J., & Lauderdale, B. E. (2007). The mysterious trend in American heights in the 20th century. *Annals of Human Biology, 34*, 206–215. doi:10.1080/03014460601116803

Konstantopoulos, S., Modi, M., & Hedges, L. V. (2001). Who are America's gifted? *American Journal of Education, 109*, 344–382. doi:10.1086/444275

Kornrich, S. (2016). Inequalities in parental spending on young children, 1972 to 2010. *AERA Open, 2*(2), 1–12. doi:10.1177/2332858416644180

Kryst, Ł., Kowal, M., Woroncowicz, A., Sobiecki, J., & Cichocka, B. A. (2012). Secular changes in height, body weight, body mass index and pubertal development in male children and adolescents in Krakow, Poland. *Journal of Biosocial Science, 44*, 495–507. doi:10.1017/S0021932011000721

Kuhn, T. S. (1996). *The structure of scientific revolutions* (3rd ed.). University of Chicago Press.

Kulik, C.-L. C., & Kulik, J. A. (1982). Effects of ability grouping on secondary school students: A meta-analysis of evaluation findings. *American Educational Research Journal, 19*, 415–428. doi:10.3102/00028312019003415

Kupka, R. W., Altshuler, L. L., Nolen, W. A., Suppes, T., Luckenbaugh, D. A., Leverich, G. S., et al. (2007). Three times more days depressed than manic or hypomanic in both bipolar I and bipolar II disorder. *Bipolar Disorders, 9*, 531–535. doi:10.1111/j.1399-5618.2007.00467.x

Lacritz, L. H., Barnard, H. D., Van Ness, P., Agostini, M., Diaz-Arrastia, R., & Cullum, C. M. (2004). Qualitative analysis of WMS-III logical memory and visual reproduction in temporal lobe epilepsy. *Journal of Clinical & Experimental Neuropsychology, 26*, 521–530. doi:10.1080/13803390490496650

Lane, D. M., & Dunlap, W. P. (1978). Estimating effect size: Bias resulting from the significance criterion in editorial decisions. *British Journal of Mathematical and Statistical Psychology, 31*, 107–112. doi:10.1111/j.2044-8317.1978.tb00578.x

Larsen, R., & Warne, R. T. (2010). Estimating confidence intervals for eigenvalues in exploratory factor analysis. *Behavior Research Methods, 42*, 871–876. doi:10.3758/BRM.42.3.871

Lewis, J. D., DeCamp-Fritson, S. S., Ramage, J. C., McFarland, M. A., & Archwamety, T. (2007). Selecting for ethnically diverse children who may be gifted using Raven's Standard Progressive Matrices and Naglieri Nonverbal Abilities Test. *Multicultural Education, 15*(1), 38–42.

Leys, C., Ley, C., Klein, O., Bernard, P., & Licata, L. (2013). Detecting outliers: Do not use standard deviation around the mean, use absolute deviation around the median. *Journal of Experimental Social Psychology, 49*, 764–766. doi:10.1016/j.jesp.2013.03.013

Li, L. M. W., Masuda, T., & Jiang, F. (2016). Influence of cultural meaning system and socioeconomic change on indecisiveness in three cultures. *Journal of Cross-Cultural Psychology, 47*, 508–524. doi:10.1177/0022022116631824

Lieberson, S., & Mikelson, K. S. (1995). Distinctive African American names: An experimental, historical, and linguistic analysis of innovation. *American Sociological Review, 60*, 928–946. doi:10.2307/2096433

Lilienfeld, S. O., Sauvigné, K., Lynn, S. J., Latzman, R. D., Cautin, R., & Waldman, I. D. (2015). Fifty psychological and psychiatric terms to avoid: A list of inaccurate, misleading, misused, ambiguous, and logically confused words and phrases. *Frontiers in Psychology, 6*. doi:10.3389/fpsyg.2015.01100

Lindley, D. V., & Scott, W. F. (1995). *New Cambridge statistical tables* (2nd ed.). New York, NY: Cambridge University Press.

Linn, R. L., Graue, M. E., & Sanders, N. M. (1990). Comparing state and district test results to national norms: The validity of claims that "everyone is above average." *Educational Measurement: Issues and Practice, 9*(3), 5–14. doi:10.1111/j.1745-3992.1990.tb00372.x

Lovie, A. D. (1995). Who discovered Spearman's rank correlation? *British Journal of Mathematical and Statistical Psychology, 48*, 255–269. doi:10.1111/j.2044-8317.1995.tb01063.x

Lubinski, D., & Benbow, C. P. (2006). Study of Mathematically Precocious Youth after 35 years:

Uncovering antecedents for the development of math-science expertise. *Perspectives on Psychological Science, 1,* 316–345. doi:10.1111/j.1745-6916.2006.00019.x

Lubinski, D., Webb, R. M., Morelock, M. J., & Benbow, C. P. (2001). Top 1 in 10,000: A 10-year follow-up of the profoundly gifted. *Journal of Applied Psychology, 86,* 718–729. doi:10.1037/0021-9010.86.4.718

Makel, M. C. (2014). The empirical march: Making science better at self-correction. *Psychology of Aesthetics, Creativity, and the Arts, 8,* 2–7. doi:10.1037/a0035803

Makel, M. C., & Plucker, J. A. (2014). Facts are more important than novelty: Replication in the education sciences. *Educational Researcher, 43,* 304–316. doi:10.3102/0013189x14545513

Marcus-Roberts, H. M., & Roberts, F. S. (1987). Meaningless statistics. *Journal of Educational and Behavioral Statistics, 12,* 383–394. doi:10.3102/10769986012004383

Matz, D. C., & Hause, E. L. (2008). "Dealing" with the central limit theorem. *Teaching of Psychology, 35,* 198–200. doi:10.1080/00986280802186201

Maxwell, S. E. (2004). The persistence of underpowered studies in psychological research: Causes, consequences, and remedies. *Psychological Methods, 9,* 147–163. doi:10.1037/1082-989x.9.2.147

McBee, M. T., & Matthews, M. S. (2014). Welcoming quality in non-significance and replication work, but moving beyond the *p*-value: Announcing new editorial policies for quantitative research in *JOAA*. *Journal of Advanced Academics, 25,* 73–87. doi:10.1177/1932202x14532177

McBee, M. T., Peters, S. J., & Waterman, C. (2014). Combining scores in multiple-criteria assessment systems: The impact of combination rule. *Gifted Child Quarterly, 58,* 69–89. doi:10.1177/0016986213513794

McCloskey, D. N., & Ziliak, S. T. (2015). The unreasonable ineffectiveness of Fisherian "tests" in biology, and especially in medicine. *Biological Theory, 4,* 44–53. doi:10.1162/biot.2009.4.1.44

McCoach, D. B., & Siegle, D. (2009). The first word: A letter from the co-editors: Effect sizes – an explanation of *JAA* editorial policy. *Journal of Advanced Academics, 20,* 209–212. doi:10.1177/1932202X0902000201

McDaniel, M. A., Pesta, B. J., & Gabriel, A. S. (2015). Big data and the well-being nexus: Tracking Google search activity by state IQ. *Intelligence, 50,* 21–29. doi:10.1016/j.intell.2015.01.001

McGrath, R. E., & Meyer, G. J. (2006). When effect sizes disagree: The case of *r* and *d*. *Psychological Methods, 11,* 386–401. doi:10.1037/1082-989x.11.4.386

Meehl, P. E. (1990). Why summaries of research on psychological theories are often uninterpretable. *Psychological Reports, 66,* 195–244. doi:10.2466/pr0.1990.66.1.195

Meyer, G. J., Finn, S. E., Eyde, L. D., Kay, G. G., Moreland, K. L., Dies, R. R., et al. (2001). Psychological testing and psychological assessment: A review of evidence and issues. *American Psychologist, 56,* 128–165. doi:10.1037/0003-066x.56.2.128

Micceri, T. (1989). The unicorn, the normal curve, and other improbable creatures. *Psychological Bulletin, 105,* 156–166. doi:10.1037/0033-2909.105.1.156

Miller, G. A. (1956). The magical number seven, plus or minus two: Some limits on our capacity for processing information. *Psychological Review, 63,* 81–97. doi:10.1037/h0043158

Miller, G. A. (1975). Stanley Smith Stevens. In *Biographical Memoirs* (Vol. 47, pp. 423–459). Washington, DC: National Academy of Sciences.

Moffitt, T. E., Caspi, A., Harkness, A. R., & Silva, P. A. (1993). The natural history of change in intellectual performance: Who changes? How much? Is it meaningful? *Journal of Child Psychology & Psychiatry & Allied Disciplines, 34,* 455–506. doi:10.1111/j.1469-7610.1993.tb01031.x

Moore, D. A. (2016). Preregister if you want to. *American Psychologist, 71,* 238–239. doi:10.1037/a0040195

Morris, J. D., & Lieberman, M. G. (2015). Prediction, explanation, multicollinearity, and validity concentration in multiple regression. *General Linear Model Journal, 41*(1), 29–35.

Morris, P. E., & Fritz, C. O. (2013). Methods: Why are effect sizes still neglected? *The Psychologist, 26*, 580–583.

Mueller, C. M., & Dweck, C. S. (1998). Praise for intelligence can undermine children's motivation and performance. *Journal of Personality and Social Psychology, 75*, 33–52. doi:10.1037/0022-3514.75.1.33

Murray, L. W., & Dosser, D. A. (1987). How significant is a significant difference? Problems with the measurement of magnitude of effect. *Journal of Counseling Psychology, 34*, 68–72. doi:10.1037/0022-0167.34.1.68

Norcross, J. C., Hailstorks, R., Aiken, L. S., Pfund, R. A., Stamm, K. E., & Christidis, P. (2016). Undergraduate study in psychology: Curriculum and assessment. *American Psychologist, 71*, 89–101. doi:10.1037/a0040095

Norman, G. (2010). Likert scales, levels of measurement and the "laws" of statistics. *Advances in Health Sciences Education, 15*, 625–632. doi:10.1007/s10459-010–9222-y

Nuijten, M. B., van Assen, M. A. L. M., Veldkamp, C. L. S., & Wicherts, J. M. (2015). The replication paradox: Combining studies can decrease accuracy of effect size estimates. *Review of General Psychology, 19*, 172–182. doi:10.1037/gpr0000034

Okbay, A., Baselmans, B. M. L., De Neve, J.-E., Turley, P., Nivard, M. G., Fontana, M. A., et al. (2016). Genetic variants associated with subjective well-being, depressive symptoms, and neuroticism identified through genome-wide analyses. *Nature Genetics, 48*, 624–633. doi:10.1038/ng.3552

Open Science Collaboration (2015). Estimating the reproducibility of psychological science. *Science, 349*(6251), aac4716-1-aac4716-9. doi:10.1126/science.aac4716

"Orleans man wins Hoosier lottery – twice" (2015, June 25). *WBIW*. Retrieved from www.wbiw.com/local/archive/2015/06/orleans-man-wins-hoosier-lottery–twice.php

Osborne, J. W. (2008). Sweating the small stuff in educational psychology: How effect size and power reporting failed to change from 1969 to 1999, and what that means for the future of changing practices. *Educational Psychology, 28*, 151–160. doi:10.1080/01443410701491718

Paas, F., Renkl, A., & Sweller, J. (2003). Cognitive load theory and instructional design: Recent developments. *Educational Psychologist, 38*, 1–4. doi:10.1207/S15326985EP3801_1

Paek, S. H., Abdulla, A. M., & Cramond, B. (2016). A meta-analysis of the relationship between three common psychopathologies – ADHD, anxiety, and depression – and indicators of little-c creativity. *Gifted Child Quarterly, 60*, 117–133. doi:10.1177/0016986216630600

Patel, J. K., & Read, C. B. (1996). *Handbook of the normal distribution* (2nd ed.). New York, NY: Marcel Dekker.

Pearson, E. S. (1936). Karl Pearson: An appreciation of some aspects of his life and work: Part I: 1857–1906. *Biometrika, 28*, 193–257. doi:10.1093/biomet/28.3-4.193

Pearson, E. S. (1938). Karl Pearson: An appreciation of some aspects of his life and work: Part II: 1906–1936. *Biometrika, 29*, 161–248. doi:10.1093/biomet/29.3-4.161

Pearson, E. S. (1939). William Sealy Gosset, 1876–1937: (2) "Student" as statistician. *Biometrika, 30*, 210–250. doi:10.1093/biomet/30.3-4.210

Pearson, K. (1896). Mathematical contributions to the theory of evolution. III. Regression, heredity, and panmixia. *Philosophical Transactions of the Royal Society of London. Series A, Containing Papers of a Mathematical or Physical Character, 187*, 253–318. doi:10.2307/90707

Pearson, K. (1900). On the criterion that a given system of deviations from the probable in the case of a correlated system of variables is such that it can be reasonably supposed to have arisen from random sampling. *Philosophical Magazine Series 5*, 157–175. doi:10.1080/14786440009463897

Pearson, K. (1910). On a new method of determining correlation, when one variable is given by alternative and the other by multiple categories. *Biometrika, 7*, 248–257. doi:10.2307/2345385

Plackett, R. L. (1983). Karl Pearson and the chi-squared test. *International Statistical Review, 51*, 59–72. doi:10.2307/1402731

Popper, K. R. (1935/2002). *The logic of scientific discovery.* New York, NY: Routledge.

Poropat, A. E. (2009). A meta-analysis of the five-factor model of personality and academic performance. *Psychological Bulletin, 135*, 322–338. doi:10.1037/a0014996

Poston, J. M., & Hanson, W. E. (2010). Meta-analysis of psychological assessment as a therapeutic intervention. *Psychological Assessment, 22*, 203–212. doi:10.1037/a0018679

Rajecki, D. W., Appleby, D., Williams, C. C., Johnson, K., & Jeschke, M. P. (2005). Statistics can wait: Career plans activity and course preferences of American psychology undergraduates. *Psychology Learning & Teaching, 4*, 83–89. doi:10.2304/plat.2004.4.2.83

Rambo-Hernandez, K. E., & Warne, R. T. (2015). Measuring the outliers: An introduction to out-of-level testing with high-achieving students. *Teaching Exceptional Children, 47*, 199–207. doi:10.1177/0040059915569359

Reed, T. E., Vernon, P. A., & Johnson, A. M. (2004). Sex difference in brain nerve conduction velocity in normal humans. *Neuropsychologia, 42*, 1709–1714. doi:10.1016/j.neuropsychologia.2004.02.016

Remschmidt, H. E., Schulz, E., Martin, M., Warnke, A., & Trott, G. E. (1994). Childhood-onset schizophrenia: History of the concept and recent studies. *Schizophrenia Bulletin, 20*, 727–745.

Reyes, C. J., & Asbrand, J. P. (2005). A longitudinal study assessing trauma symptoms in sexually abused children engaged in play therapy. *International Journal of Play Therapy, 14*(2), 25–47. doi:10.1037/h0088901

Reynolds, C. R. (2010). Measurement and assessment: An editorial view. *Psychological Assessment, 22*, 1–4. doi:10.1037/a0018811

Robinson, D. H., & Kiewra, K. A. (1995). Visual argument: Graphic organizers are superior to outlines in improving learning from text. *Journal of Educational Psychology, 87*, 455–467. doi:10.1037/0022-0663.87.3.455

Rodgers, J. L. (2010). The epistemology of mathematical and statistical modeling: A quiet methodological revolution. *American Psychologist, 65*, 1–12. doi:10.1037/a0018326

Rogers, K. B. (2007). Lessons learned about educating the gifted and talented: A synthesis of the research on educational practice. *Gifted Child Quarterly, 51*, 382–396. doi:10.1177/0016986207306324

Rosenthal, R. (1979). The file drawer problem and tolerance for null results. *Psychological Bulletin, 86*, 638–641. doi:10.1037//0033-2909.86.3.638

Rosnow, R. L., & Rosenthal, R. (1989). Statistical procedures and the justification of knowledge in psychological science. *American Psychologist, 44*, 1276–1284. doi:10.1037/0003-066x.44.10.1276

"Russian scientists seeking Lake Vostok lost in frozen 'Land of the Lost'?" (2012, February 2). *Fox News.* Retrieved from www.foxnews.com/scitech/2012/02/02/russian-scientists-lost-in-frozen-land-lost/

Ruxton, G. D., & Beauchamp, G. (2008). Some suggestions about appropriate use of the Kruskal–Wallis test. *Animal Behaviour, 76*, 1083–1087. doi:10.1016/j.anbehav.2008.04.011

Ryan, T. A. (1959). Multiple comparison in psychological research. *Psychological Bulletin, 56*, 26–47. doi:10.1037/h0042478

Savalei, V., & Dunn, E. (2015). Is the call to abandon *p*-values the red herring of the replicability crisis? *Frontiers in Psychology, 6*(245), 1–4. doi:10.3389/fpsyg.2015.00245

Schimmack, U. (2012). The ironic effect of significant results on the credibility of multiple-study articles. *Psychological Methods, 17*, 551–566. doi:10.1037/a0029487

Schmidt, F. L. (1996). Statistical significance testing and cumulative knowledge in psychology: Implications for training of researchers. *Psychological Methods, 1*, 115–129. doi:10.1037/1082-989x.1.2.115

Schmidt, F. L., & Hunter, J. E. (1977). Development of a general solution to the problem of validity generalization. *Journal of Applied Psychology, 62*, 529–540. doi:10.1037/0021-9010.62.5.529

Schmitt, D. P. (2015). Statistical abracadabra: Making sex differences disappear. *Psychology Today.* Retrieved from www.psychologytoday.com/blog/sexual-personalities/201512/statistical-abracadabra-making-sex-differences-disappear

Schönbrodt, F. D., & Perugini, M. (2013). At what sample size do correlations stabilize? *Journal of Research in Personality, 47,* 609–612. doi:10.1016/j.jrp.2013.05.009

Sedlmeier, P., & Gigerenzer, G. (1989). Do studies of statistical power have an effect on the power of studies? *Psychological Bulletin, 105,* 309–316. doi:10.1037/0033-2909.105.2.309

Senn, S. (2011). Francis Galton and regression to the mean. *Significance, 8,* 124–126. doi:10.1111/j.1740-9713.2011.00509.x

Shaw Taylor, L., Fiore, A. T., Mendelsohn, G. A., & Cheshire, C. (2011). "Out of my league": A real-world test of the matching hypothesis. *Personality and Social Psychology Bulletin, 37,* 942–954. doi:10.1177/0146167211409947

Simmons, J. P., Nelson, L. D., & Simonsohn, U. (2011). False-positive psychology: Undisclosed flexibility in data collection and analysis allows presenting anything as significant. *Psychological Science, 22,* 1359–1366. doi:10.1177/0956797611417632

Simpson, E. H. (1951). The interpretation of interaction in contingency tables. *Journal of the Royal Statistical Society. Series B (Methodological), 13,* 238–241.

Sireci, S. G., & Hambleton, R. K. (2009). Mission – protect the public: Licensure and certification testing in the 21st century. In R. P. Phelps (Ed.), *Correcting fallacies about educational and psychological testing* (pp. 199–217). Washington, DC: American Psychological Association.

Skidmore, S. T., & Thompson, B. (2010). Statistical techniques used in published articles: A historical review of reviews. *Educational and Psychological Measurement, 70,* 777–795. doi:10.1177/0013164410379320

Skidmore, S. T., & Thompson, B. (2011). Choosing the best correction formula for the Pearson r^2 effect size. *Journal of Experimental Education, 79,* 257–278. doi:10.1080/00220973.2010.484437

Slade, M. K., & Warne, R. T. (2016). A meta-analysis of the effectiveness of trauma-focused cognitive-behavioral therapy and play therapy for child victims of abuse. *Journal of Young Investigators, 30*(6), 36–43.

Smith, G. (2016). A fallacy that will not die. *Journal of Investing, 25*(1), 7–15. doi:10.3905/joi.2016.25.1.007

Smith, M. L., & Glass, G. V. (1977). Meta-analysis of psychotherapy outcome studies. *American Psychologist, 32,* 752–760. doi:10.1037/0003-066x.32.9.752

Smith, R. L., Ager, J. W., Jr., & Williams, D. L. (1992). Suppressor variables in multiple regression/correlation. *Educational and Psychological Measurement, 52,* 17–29. doi:10.1177/001316449205200102

Sommer, M., & Arendasy, M. E. (2014). Comparing different explanations of the effect of test anxiety on respondents' test scores. *Intelligence, 42,* 115–127. doi:10.1016/j.intell.2013.11.003

Spearman, C. (1904a). The proof and measurement of association between two things. *American Journal of Psychology, 15,* 72–101. doi:10.2307/1412159

Spearman, C. (1904b). "General intelligence," objectively determined and measured. *American Journal of Psychology, 15,* 201–293. doi:10.2307/1412107

Spearman, C. (1906). Footrule for measuring correlation. *British Journal of Psychology, 2,* 89–108. doi:10.1111/j.2044-8295.1906.tb00174.x

Spinath, B., Freudenthaler, H. H., & Neubauer, A. C. (2010). Domain-specific school achievement in boys and girls as predicted by intelligence, personality and motivation. *Personality and Individual Differences, 48,* 481–486. doi:10.1016/j.paid.2009.11.028

Steering Committee of the Physicians' Health Study Research Group (1988). Preliminary report: Findings from the aspirin component of the ongoing Physicians' Health Study. *New England Journal of Medicine, 318,* 262–264. doi:10.1056/NEJM198801283180431

Steinemann, J. H. (1963). Note on "correction for restriction of range." *Psychological Reports, 13,* 538. doi:10.2466/pr0.1963.13.2.538

Sterling, T. D. (1959). Publication decisions and their possible effects on inferences drawn from tests of significance – or vice versa. *Journal of the American Statistical Association, 54*, 30–34. doi:10.1080/01621459.1959.10501497

Stevens, J. P. (2002). *Applied multivariate statistics for the social sciences*. Mahwah, NJ: Lawrence Erlbaum Associates.

Stevens, S. S. (1936). A scale for the measurement of a psychological magnitude: Loudness. *Psychological Review, 43*, 405–416. doi:10.1037/h0058773

Stevens, S. S. (1946). On the theory of scales of measurement. *Science, 103*, 677–680. doi:10.1126/science.103.2684.677

Stigler, S. M. (1986). *The history of statistics: The measurement of uncertainty before 1900*. Cambridge, MA: Harvard University Press.

Stigler, S. M. (1997). Regression towards the mean, historically considered. *Statistical Methods in Medical Research, 6*, 103–114. doi:10.1177/096228029700600202

Stigler, S. M. (1999). *Statistics on the table: The history of statistical concepts and methods*. Cambridge, MA: Harvard University Press.

Stoloff, M., McCarthy, M., Keller, L., Varfolomeeva, V., Lynch, J., Makara, K., et al. (2010). The undergraduate psychology major: An examination of structure and sequence. *Teaching of Psychology, 37*, 4–15. doi:10.1080/00986280903426274

Strenze, T. (2007). Intelligence and socioeconomic success: A meta-analytic review of longitudinal research. *Intelligence, 35*, 401–426. doi:10.1016/j.intell.2006.09.004

Stroop, J. R. (1935). Studies of interference in serial verbal reactions. *Journal of Experimental Psychology, 18*, 643–662. doi:10.1037/h0054651

Sundali, J., & Croson, R. (2006). Biases in casino betting: The hot hand and the gambler's fallacy. *Judgment and Decision Making, 1*, 1–12.

Taylor, H. C., & Russell, J. T. (1939). The relationship of validity coefficients to the practical effectiveness of tests in selection: Discussion and tables. *Journal of Applied Psychology, 23*, 565–578. doi:10.1037/h0057079

Terman, L. M., Lyman, G., Ordahl, G., Ordahl, L., Galbreath, N., & Talbert, W. (1915). The Stanford revision of the Binet–Simon scale and some results from its application to 1000 non-selected children. *Journal of Educational Psychology, 6*, 551–562. doi:10.1037/h0075455

Thompson, B. (1992). Two and one-half decades of leadership in measurement and evaluation. *Journal of Counseling & Development, 70*, 434–438. doi:10.1002/j.1556-6676.1992.tb01631.x

Thompson, B. (1996). AERA editorial policies regarding statistical significance testing: Three suggested reforms. *Educational Researcher, 25*(2), 26–30. doi:10.2307/1176337

Thompson, B. (2001). Significance, effect sizes, stepwise methods, and other issues: Strong arguments move the field. *Journal of Experimental Education, 70*, 80–93. doi:10.1080/00220970109599499

Thompson, B. (2002a). "Statistical," "practical," and "clinical": How many kinds of significance do counselors need to consider? *Journal of Counseling & Development, 80*, 64–71. doi:10.1002/j.1556-6678.2002.tb00167.x

Thompson, B. (2002b). What future quantitative social science research could look like: Confidence intervals for effect sizes. *Educational Researcher, 31*(3), 25–32. doi:10.3102/0013189x031003025

Thompson, B. (2004). *Exploratory and confirmatory factor analysis: Understanding concepts and applications*. Washington, DC: American Psychological Association.

Thompson, B. (2007). Effect sizes, confidence intervals, and confidence intervals for effect sizes. *Psychology in the Schools, 44*, 423–432. doi:10.1002/pits.20234

Thompson, B., Diamond, K. E., McWilliam, R., Snyder, P., & Snyder, S. W. (2005). Evaluating the quality of evidence from correlational research for evidence-based practice. *Exceptional Children, 71*, 181–194. doi:10.1177/001440290507100204

Thorndike, R. L. (1942). Regression fallacies in the matched groups experiment. *Psychometrika, 7*, 85–102. doi:10.1007/bf02288069

Townsend, M. (March 13, 2015). "Tigers rookie James McCann hits bird with foul ball." *Yahoo! Sports*. Retrieved from sports.yahoo.com/blogs/mlb-big-league-stew/tigers–james-mccann-hits-bird-with-foul-ball-012602154.html

Trafimow, D. (2014). Editorial. *Basic and Applied Social Psychology*, *36*, 1–2. doi:10.1080/01973533.2014.865505

Trafimow, D., & Marks, M. (2015). Editorial. *Basic and Applied Social Psychology*, *37*, 1–2. doi:10.1080/01973533.2015.1012991

Tufte, E. R. (2001). *The visual display of quantitative information* (2nd ed.). Cheshire, CT: Graphics Press.

Tukey, J. W. (1962). The future of data analysis. *Annals of Mathematical Statistics*, *33*, 1–67. doi:10.2307/2237638

Tukey, J. W. (1991). The philosophy of multiple comparisons. *Statistical Science*, *6*, 100–116. doi:10.1214/ss/1177011945

U.S. Census Bureau (2013). *America's families and living arrangements: 2012*. Retrieved from www.census.gov/prod/2013pubs/p20-570.pdf

Urbina, S. (2014). *Essentials of psychological testing* (2nd ed.). Hoboken, NJ: John Wiley & Sons.

Vacha-Haase, T., & Thompson, B. (2004). How to estimate and interpret various effect sizes. *Journal of Counseling Psychology*, *51*, 473–481. doi:10.1037/0022-0167.51.4.473

Vadillo, M. A., Hardwicke, T. E., & Shanks, D. R. (2016). Selection bias, vote counting, and money-priming effects: A comment on Rohrer, Pashler, and Harris (2015) and Vohs (2015). *Journal of Experimental Psychology: General*, *145*, 655–663. doi:10.1037/xge0000157

van der Eijk, C., & Rose, J. (2015). Risky business: Factor analysis of survey data – assessing the probability of incorrect dimensionalisation. *PLoS ONE*, *10*(3), e0118900. doi:10.1371/journal.pone.0118900

Vargha, A., & Delaney, H. D. (1998). The Kruskal–Wallis test and stochastic homogeneity. *Journal of Educational and Behavioral Statistics*, *23*, 170–192. doi:10.2307/1165320

Vernon, P. E. (1947). Research on personnel selection in the Royal Navy and the British Army.

American Psychologist, *2*, 35–51. doi:10.1037/h0056920

Vinten, J., Adab, N., Kini, U., Gorry, J., Gregg, J., & Baker, G. A. (2005). Neuropsychological effects of exposure to anticonvulsant medication *in utero*. *Neurology*, *64*, 949–954. doi:10.1212/01.wnl.0000154514.82948.69

Vinten, J., Bromley, R. L., Taylor, J., Adab, N., Kini, U., & Baker, G. A. (2009). The behavioral consequences of exposure to antiepileptic drugs *in utero*. *Epilepsy & Behavior*, *14*, 197–201. doi:10.1016/j.yebeh.2008.10.011

Viswesvaran, C., & Ones, D. S. (2000). Measurement error in "Big Five Factors" personality assessment: Reliability generalization across studies and measures. *Educational and Psychological Measurement*, *60*, 224–235. doi:10.1177/00131640021970475

Volker, M. A. (2006). Reporting effect size estimates in school psychology research. *Psychology in the Schools*, *43*, 653–672. doi:10.1002/pits.20176

Voracek, M., Mohr, E., & Hagmann, M. (2013). On the importance of tail ratios for psychological science. *Psychological Reports*, *112*, 872–886. doi:10.2466/03.pr0.112.3.872–886

Waite, K., Cardon, T., & Warne, R. T. (2015). Survey of siblings: Perceptions of individuals with siblings with and without autism spectrum disorder. *Journal of Psychology and the Behavioral Sciences*, *24*(1), 12–21.

Warne, R. T. (2009). Comparing tests used to identify ethnically diverse gifted children: A critical response to Lewis, DeCamp-Fritson, Ramage, McFarland, & Archwamety. *Multicultural Education*, *17*(1), 48–53.

Warne, R. T. (2011a). Psychometric impacts of above-level testing. (Unpublished doctoral dissertation, Texas A&M University, College Station, TX).

Warne, R. T. (2011b). Beyond multiple regression: Using commonality analysis to better understand R^2 results. *Gifted Child Quarterly*, *55*, 313–318. doi:10.1177/0016986211422217

Warne, R. T. (2014a). A primer on multivariate analysis of variance (MANOVA) for behavioral scientists. *Practical Assessment, Research & Evaluation, 19*(17), 1–10.

Warne, R. T. (2014b). Using above-level testing to track growth in academic achievement in gifted students. *Gifted Child Quarterly, 58,* 3–23. doi:10.1177/0016986213513793

Warne, R. T. (2014c). Two additional suggested reforms to encourage replication studies in educational research. *Educational Researcher, 43,* 465. doi:10.3102/0013189x14562294

Warne, R. T. (2016). Testing Spearman's hypothesis with advanced placement data. *Intelligence, 57,* 87–95. doi:10.1016/j.intel.2016.05.002

Warne, R. T., Anderson, B., & Johnson, A. O. (2013). The impact of race and ethnicity on the identification process for giftedness in Utah. *Journal for the Education of the Gifted, 36,* 487–508. doi:10.1177/0162353213506065

Warne, R. T., Doty, K. J., Malbica, A. M., Angeles, V. R., Innes, S., Hall, J., et al. (2016). Above-level test item functioning across examinee age groups. *Journal of Psychoeducational Assessment, 34,* 54–72. doi:10.1177/0734282915584851

Warne, R. T., Godwin, L. R., & Smith, K. V. (2013). Are there more gifted people than would be expected in a normal distribution? An investigation of the overabundance hypothesis. *Journal of Advanced Academics, 24,* 224–241. doi:10.1177/1932202x13507969

Warne, R. T., Lazo, M., Ramos, T., & Ritter, N. (2012). Statistical methods used in gifted education journals, 2006–2010. *Gifted Child Quarterly, 56,* 134–149. doi:10.1177/0016986212444122

Warne, R. T., & Liu, J. K. (2017). Income differences among grade skippers and non-grade skippers across genders in the Terman sample, 1936–1976. *Learning and Instruction, 47,* 1–12. doi:10.1016/j.learninstruc.2016.10.004

Warne, R. T., Nagaishi, C., Slade, M. K., Hermesmeyer, P., & Peck, E. K. (2014). Comparing weighted and unweighted grade point averages in predicting college success of diverse and low-income college students. *NASSP Bulletin, 98,* 261–279. doi:10.1177/0192636514565171

Warne, R. T., & Price, C. J. (2016). A single case study of the impact of policy changes on identification for gifted programs. *Journal for the Education of the Gifted, 39,* 49–61. doi:10.1177/0162353215624159

Warne, R. T., Yoon, M., & Price, C. J. (2014). Exploring the various interpretations of "test bias." *Cultural Diversity and Ethnic Minority Psychology, 20,* 570–582. doi:10.1037/a0036503

Wasserstein, R. L., & Lazar, N. A. (2016). The ASA's statement on *p*-values: Context, process, and purpose. *American Statistician, 70,* 129–133. doi:10.1080/00031305.2016.1154108

Watson, D., Klohnen, E. C., Casillas, A., Nus Simms, E., Haig, J., & Berry, D. S. (2004). Match makers and deal breakers: Analyses of assortative mating in newlywed couples. *Journal of Personality, 72,* 1029–1068. doi:10.1111/j.0022-3506.2004.00289.x

Werblow, J., & Duesbery, L. (2009). The impact of high school size on math achievement and dropout rate. *High School Journal, 92,* 14–23.

Wiberg, M., & Sundström, A. (2009). A comparison of two approaches to correction of restriction of range in correlation analsis. *Practical Asessment, Research & Evaluation, 14*(5), 1–9.

Wilcox, R. R. (1998). How many discoveries have been lost by ignoring modern statistical methods? *American Psychologist, 53,* 300–314. doi:10.1037/0003-066X.53.3.300

Wilkinson, L., & Task Force on Statistical Inference (1999). Statistical methods in psychology journals: Guidelines and explanations. *American Psychologist, 54,* 594–604. doi:10.1037/0003-066X.54.8.594

Winch, R. F., & Campbell, D. T. (1969). Proof? No. Evidence? Yes. The significance of tests of significance. *American Sociologist, 4,* 140–143. doi:10.2307/27701483

Wolraich, M. L., Wilson, D. B., & White, J. (1995). The effect of sugar on behavior or cognition in children: A meta-analysis. *Journal of the American Medical Association, 274*(20), 1617–1621. doi:10.1001/jama.1995.03530200053037

Woodberry, K. A., Giuliano, A. J., & Seidman, L. J. (2008). Premorbid IQ in schizophrenia: A meta-analytic review. *American Journal of Psychiatry*, *165*, 579–587. doi:10.1176/appi.ajp.2008.07081242

Yettick, H. (2015). One small droplet: News media coverage of peer-reviewed and university-based education research and academic expertise. *Educational Researcher*, *44*, 173–184. doi:10.3102/0013189x15574903

Yule, G. U. (1903). Notes on the theory of association of attributes in statistics. *Biometrika*, *2*, 121–134. doi:10.2307/2331677

Zar, J. H. (2005). Spearman rank correlation. In P. Armitage & T. Colton (Eds.), *Encyclopedia of biostatistics* (2nd ed., Vol. VII, pp. 5095–5101). Hoboken, NJ: Wiley.

Zientek, L. R., Capraro, M. M., & Capraro, R. M. (2008). Reporting practices in quantitative teacher education research: One look at the evidence cited in the AERA panel report. *Educational Researcher*, *37*, 208–216. doi:10.3102/0013189X08319762

Zientek, L. R., & Thompson, B. (2009). Matrix summaries improve research reports: Secondary analyses using published literature. *Educational Researcher*, *38*, 343–352. doi:10.3102/0013189X09339056

Zientek, L. R., Yetkiner, Z. E., & Thompson, B. (2010). Characterizing the mathematics anxiety literature using confidence intervals as a literature review mechanism. *Journal of Educational Research*, *103*, 424–438. doi:10.1080/00220670903383093

Zimmerman, D. W. (1997). Teacher's corner: A note on interpretation of the paired-samples *t*-test. *Journal of Educational and Behavioral Statistics*, *22*, 349–360. doi:10.3102/10769986022003349

Zwick, R. (2006). Higher education admissions testing. In R. L. Brennan (Ed.), *Educational measurement* (4th ed., pp. 647–679). Westport, CT: Praeger Publishers.

Name Index

Figures and tables are noted in bold typeface.

Yetkiner, Z.E., 295
Yettick, H., 2
Yoon, M., 12, 390
Yule, G.U., 465

Zar, J.H., 471
Zientek, L.R., 92, 171, 279, 295, 479
Zimmerman, D.W., 215, 252
Zwick, R., 387

Subject Index

Entries in bold type denote figures or tables.

outlier, 78–79, 82, 387–390, **388**
outliers in math ability example, 78

p. See p-value
paired samples *t*-tests
  alpha (α) setting, 219, 230
  critical value determination, 222, 230
  effect size calculation, 225–226, 232
  form data groups, 217, 230
  GLM, 218–219
  null hypothesis definition, 217–218, 230
  observed value calculation, 222–224, **223**, 231
  one-tailed or two-tailed test, 219–222, **220**, 230
  p-value, 227, 232
  sample size sensitivity, 229
  statistical significance, 229
  subjective decisions, 229
  Type I and II errors, 216–229
  uses for, 215–216
  value comparison, 217–225, **225**, **231**, 231
parameter model, 86
parametric statistics, 470
parental spending on children example, 9
peak (kurtosis), 52–53, **52–53**
Pearson's *r*
  defined, 330–333
  interpreting, 336–338, **337**
  in the NHST context, 343–349, **344**, **347**
  obtaining stable, 349
  predictions using, 369–371, **371**
percentages, 38, **38**
personality and job performance example, 5
personality-sex interaction in school grades example, 457
physical activity in gym classes example, 455
pie charts, **62–65**
planned contrasts tests, 303
platykurtic distribution, 52, 54
point estimates, 196
point-biserial correlation, 390
pooled standard deviation, 226
pooled variance, 249
population
  applying a sample to, 127
  and inferential statistics, 140–146, **141**
  problems with estimating parameters of, 195–197
  in the quantitative research process, 4
population standard deviation, 86–88

population variance, 89
positive correlation, 336
positive skewness, **50**
power. *See* statistical power
practical significance, 194
prediction. *See* regression line
Price Is Right rule, 158, 186, 247
probability distribution. *See also* statistics
  comparing empirical and theoretical, 135–139, **137**, **139**
  conditional, 465
  defined, 127, 129, 132–135, **132**, **134–136**
  empirical, 128
  guided practice, 130–131
  independent outcomes, 131–132
  and inferential statistics, 140–146, **141**
  joint, 129
  marginal, 465
  multiple outcomes, 129
  theoretical, 129
  trial, 128
proportions, 38, **38**
p-value
  ANOVA procedure, 310
  continuous nature of, 407–409
  defined, 166
  one-sample *t*-test, 193–195
  one-sample *t*-test for any number, 201–202
  paired two-sample *t*-tests, 227, 232
  unpaired two-sample *t*-tests, 252–255
  variance in, **296**

Q-table, 500
qualitative research, 6–13
quality of life improvements after therapy example, 229–232
quantitative research
  classifications of, 6
  domination in the behavioral sciences, 1–2
  process of, 3–6
quartile, 85
quasi-experimental research, 6
questionable research practice, 185
Quetelet's data example, 48

r^2, 346–347
R^2, 448–449
random assignment, 351

range
  normal distribution, 85, 89, **107**
  restriction absence, 385–387, **387–388**
ratio data, **24**, 25–26
reductionism, 22
reference group. *See* baseline group
regression line
  defined, 376
  guided practice, 380
  standardized regression equation, 372–374,
    373–375, 385
  unstandardized regression equation, 371–372,
    372
regression to the mean in patients with high blood
    pressure example, 369, 382
regression towards the mean, 380–383, **381**
rejection region, 152–153, **153**, 159
related-samples *t*-test. *See* paired samples *t*-test
relative risk, 428–429
reporting impossible *p*-values example, 166–170
research
  exploratory, 281
  HARKing as a questionable practice, 185–186
  mixed methods methodology, 22
  planning ahead before conducting, 445
  separating good from bad, 2
  statistical power in design of, 252
research hypothesis (quantitative research), 3–4
research question (quantitative research), 3–4
residual
  linear regression, 375–378, **376–378**
  Stroop Test, 291–293, **292**
resilient children in poverty example, 79
restriction of range, 385–387, **387–388**
right skewed. *See* positive skewness
risk-need-responsivity model (RNR), 9

sample (selection)
  ANOVA procedure, 297
  application to a population, 127
  and the central limit theorem, 146
  error in point estimates, 195–197
  and inferential statistics for a population, 140–146,
    141
  NHST procedures' sensitivity to size of, 166–168,
    195
  paired two-sample *t*-tests, 215–216
  in the quantitative research process, 4
  and statistical power, 251–252

sample size selection
  odds ratios, 426
  paired two-sample *t*-tests, 229
sample standard deviation, 86–88
sampling distribution, 141
sampling error, 141
scale
  and linear transformations, 115
  and *z*-scores, 115
scattergram. *See* scatterplot
scatterplot
  correlation coefficient, 339–343, **339–343**
  defined, 64–66, **65**
Scheffé's *post hoc* test, 304
schizophrenia in children example, 243–244
scientific theory
  defined, 12
  falsifiability in, 4
  and scientific laws, 14
  versus a theoretical model, 11–13, **13**
shoulders (kurtosis), 52–53, **52–53**
sibling relationships and autism example, **8**, 35–38,
    35–38, **65**, 217–218
Simpson's paradox, 464–466
Simpson's paradox in gifted education example, 464
skewed data example, 51
social sciences (statistics in), 2–3
social workers' job satisfaction example, 163
Spearman's *r* (rho), 470
special case (statistical), 171
Sports Illustrated curse example, 382
SPSS. *See* Statistical Package for the Social Sciences
stability of extraversion example, **337**
standard deviation
  defined, 86
  estimating population, 143
  guided practice, 90
  and linear transformations, 105–107, **107**
  and mean deviation, 88
standard error (SE), 143
standardized regression equation
  formula, 369–370
  guided practice, 379
  regression line, 372–374, **373, 375, 385**
standardized scores. *See* *z*-scores
statistical assumptions, 84
statistical models, 10, 86
Statistical Package for the Social Sciences (software)
  ANOVA procedure, 322–327, **324–326**